The 50 STATES ☆☆☆☆☆☆☆☆☆
and Their
Local Governments

The 50 STATES ☆☆☆☆☆ and Their ☆☆☆☆ Local Governments

Karl A. Bosworth

James W. Fesler

Dayton D. McKean

Harvey C. Mansfield

Robert L. Morlan

Allan R. Richards

Victor G. Rosenblum

York Willbern

Under the editorship of **James W. Fesler**

YALE UNIVERSITY

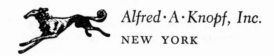

Alfred·A·Knopf, Inc.

NEW YORK

This is a Borzoi Book,
Published by Alfred A. Knopf, Inc.

First Printing

Library of Congress Catalog Card Number: 66–12816
Manufactured in the United States of America

Preface

The American Assembly, headquartered at Columbia University, has held over thirty conferences, each bringing together several score leaders from the fields of business, labor, agriculture, the professions, the political parties, and government to consider issues of public moment. The eighth of these conferences, held in October, 1955, focused on the problems of the nation's state governments. A volume of background papers, *The Forty-Eight States: Their Tasks As Policy Makers and Administrators*, was prepared for the participants. The present textbook has been prepared by the editor and the five contributors to *The Forty-Eight States*, supplemented by two authors on topics not embraced by the original volume. Although revision and expansion have been substantial, the authors have drawn freely on their 1955 essays.

Our decision to undertake preparation of this book was stimulated by the gratifying reception given *The Forty-Eight States* by state legislators, administrators, opinion leaders, and teachers. As a matter of fact, this reception indicated so widespread a concern with the vitality of state governments that, with the encouragement of the American Assembly, regional assemblies were called in the South and in the Pacific Northwest, and state assemblies were held in Arkansas, California, Georgia, Illinois, Massachusetts, New Mexico, Oklahoma, Vermont, and Wyoming.

Our obligations are many, including as they do our debt to the great number of scholars on whose research we have drawn. Henry M.

Wriston and Clifford C. Nelson, the successive presidents of the American Assembly, generously granted permission to revise *The Forty-Eight States* and to publish the revision in textbook form. The late V. O. Key, Jr., initially encouraged our proceeding with the project. Hugh Douglas Price read the entire manuscript with critical acumen. Wives are the unsung heroines of most books that get written. Ours will be glad that this one is done.

It is customary to divorce all those acknowledged from responsibility for errors in the finished product, but this may be taken for granted. A greater difficulty is to assign responsibility for a work to which several authors have contributed. In this instance, the chapter authors have patiently indulged the editor in his inclination to add a paragraph here, rearrange a sequence of topics there, and otherwise endeavor to weld the parts into a whole. Errors in individual chapters, therefore, cannot justly be attributed to the chapter authors, nor necessarily to the editor. Let us say, then, that responsibility is mixed, save that each author is free of all responsibility for chapters other than his own.

James W. Fesler

New Haven, Connecticut
October 1966

Contents

Figures

Tables

The 50 STATES ☆☆☆☆☆☆☆☆☆
and Their
Local Governments

chapter *1*
☆☆☆☆☆☆☆☆

Introduction

S tate and local governments invite study for several reasons. First,
the substance of their activities is intrinsically important for American society. What they do *does* matter. Second, they are intricately inter-
woven into the fabric of the American political system. Neither that
system nor its national government segment can be understood without
analysis of the roles of state and local governments. Third, the future scope
of their activities and their roles in the American political system depend
upon how effective they are in making policy and in translating that policy
into action.

Yet the problems are complex. Consider one example—urban redevelopment. Should a particular city government adopt a redevelopment
program at all? That is, should it buy private real estate in blighted and
deteriorating areas, demolish the buildings acquired, sell the cleared land
to private buyers free of the cost of the demolished buildings, and refuse to
sell to prospective buyers whose proposed uses or building designs do not
conform to standards set by the city's redevelopment plans? In a preponderantly urban civilization such as that of the United States today, the
revitalization of central cities will strike many as an essential activity for
city governments; others, however, will view the displacement of residents
and of established business firms as the extreme of governmental interference with private rights and the free market.

But urban redevelopment is not a purely local government concern; its progress has depended heavily on the whole American political system. Note how the question of a city's decision to adopt a redevelopment program may be affected by the fact that the federal government offers to pay two-thirds of the city's redevelopment costs (which are mostly the value of the buildings bought and demolished by the city). Suppose, too, as is true in some states, that the state government has offered to pay one-sixth of the redevelopment costs. This leaves the city government responsible for covering only the remaining one-sixth; but the federal government will count toward this (that is, credit the city with the dollar amount of) the city's capital investments in new schools, libraries, parks, sewers, etc., in the redeveloped area. These financial provisions, which substantially relieve the city taxpayers of the cost of their city's redevelopment, naturally have strings attached. The federal and state governments will make their grants only after they review the city's redevelopment plans to see that they conform to federal and state policies and standards. Furthermore, the local financial accounts for the program must follow prescribed forms and the program's staff members must abstain from political activity.

Yet the cities are not merely passive recipients of higher governments' largesse. United States senators and congressmen have voted the program because enough of them come from urban areas, because the President's election depends heavily on the large urbanized states, because national organizations of cities and of mayors have lobbied in Washington. A state legislature, even though it may be disproportionately representative of rural and small-town constituencies, will have voted to help the program along because enough urban-based legislators demanded a quid pro quo for continuance of generous state aid to the less urbanized areas of the state and because the urban vote weighs heavily in the statewide elections for the governorship. Nor can it be said that the federal and state agencies administering the redevelopment grants operate in a vacuum and are free to impose vexatious requirements on the city redevelopment agencies. Much interplay among the three levels of agencies goes on. The city agencies' complaints of excessive procedural requirements will be sympathetically considered at higher levels. Not least important is the fact that the agency staffs at all three levels share a desire to see the redevelopment program achieve its objectives, which depends in turn on effective and "clean" administration that will win and maintain popular support.

Whether a blight-threatened city adopts a redevelopment program and whether it carries it through to a successful conclusion depend ultimately on the city's own political system. Not many cities have taken

advantage of what appears a relatively cost-free opportunity to make themselves more economically viable and more socially attractive as places to
live. Why not? The crucial factor appears to be the kind of men the city's
voters elect to the mayoralty and the city council. The mayor or other
leader or leadership group must deliberately decide to invest energy to
arrest deterioration of the business district and to clear out the slum areas.
To overcome inertia and the opposition of established interests, the political leadership must win sufficient support from the general public and the
community's economic and politically significant interests. And, lest the
program fail even after adoption, the city government must be able to
recruit and keep a competent technical staff of engineers, city planners,
lawyers, housing experts, and property appraisers. Somehow, too, it must
build into this staff the attitudes and behavior patterns that will result in
humane and sympathetic administration, one that is sensitive to the problems of rehousing displaced families, relocating displaced business firms,
and constructively dealing with the delicate problems of racial discrimination.

In sum, city redevelopment programs, designed to remake the base of
urban civilization, indicate how important the substance of state and local
activities can be and how interlocked the national, state, and local segments of American government are. Further, they suggest how much a state
or local government's own capacity to make and execute policy determines
its degree of responsiveness to its people's needs. This, in turn, foretells
that government's future significance in the American political system.

1. *The Scope of Responsibilities*

One might suppose that the intrinsic importance of what state and local
governments do was so apparent that no demonstration would be necessary. This, however, is not the case. Many of us have an imperfect appreciation of the significance of the state and local governments because we have
never stepped outside the American system to compare these governments
against a world scale. More important, we are commonly victims of a
political rhetoric that regularly bewails the supposed decline of state and
local governments and darkly implies a conspiracy to transfer their functions to power-hungry Washington bureaucrats.

Facts may be poor matches for rhetoric, but we can at least try to
discover what the relevant facts are and whether they indicate that the
scope of state and local responsibilities is or is not significant. Though a

judgment of whether something is significant is itself often very much a personal matter, the personal element can be substantially reduced when, as here, we can so relate facts as to make the principal judgments comparative ones. We shall compare American states and major cities with foreign nations, using the simple measures of population and area. Then, using data for governmental expenditures and employment, we shall examine the place of state and local governments' aggregate of activities in the total of American governmental activities and in the American economy. Finally, we shall look more closely at the kinds of functions that are performed primarily by state and local governments.

POPULATION AND AREA. Suppose that the American union were dissolved and each of the states had to take its place among the nations of the world. Would they appear significant or insignificant in such company? We can get one perspective by using population as a measure of significance—that is, by fitting the 50 states into a ranked list of 132 countries so as to have 182 governments in order of population served in the year 1961 (see Table 1.1). In the top half of this list are the governments with populations of over 4 million, and we find that 14 American states would fit in here. For example, New York and California, if independent, would rank 28th and 30th, between Canada and South Africa, and with North Vietnam in between. Pennsylvania has almost as many people as the Netherlands and more than Peru or Australia. Illinois, Texas, and Ohio outrank such countries as Belgium and Portugal. And Michigan has almost as many people as Greece, and more than Sweden or Austria.

While population is probably the most appropriate rough guide to the relative significance of governments' responsibilities, we can get another valuable perspective by comparing the size of the areas they govern. By this measure, Alaska would rank 16th and Texas, 38th. In all, 10 American states would fall in the top half of the list, outranking 67 countries (among them the United Kingdom, Greece, Czechoslovakia, Hungary, Portugal, Austria, the Netherlands, and Belgium).[1]

EXPENDITURES. Probably the most frequently used broad measures of what the American governments do at each level are their direct general expenditures[2] and the share of the national economy's total output

---

[1] *Computed from data in Bruce M. Russett, et al.*, World Handbook of Political and Social Indicators (*New Haven, Conn.: Yale University Press, 1964*), pp. 139–41, *and U.S. Bureau of the Census*, Statistical Abstract of the United States: 1964 (*Washington, D.C., 1964*), pp. 169 and 906–08.

[2] "*General*" *expenditures are all expenditures except* (a) *benefit and refund payments of public-employee retirement and other social insurance systems, and* (b) *spending for state and local liquor stores and for local water, electric, transit, and gas*

Table 1.1. *Distribution of American States in a Population Ranking of Foreign Countries and American States, 1961*

Decile (=18 or 19 countries/states)	Population Range of Decile			Number of American States in Decile	Cumulative Number of American States
I	694.2 to	27.2	million	0	0
II	26.6 to	14.2	million	2	2
III	13.8 to	8.9	million	4	6
IV	8.6 to	6.2	million	2	8
V	5.6 to	4.11	million	6	14
VI	4.1 to	2.9	million	10	24
VII	2.8 to	2.1	million	6	30
VIII	2.0 to	1.3	million	5	35
IX	1.2 to	656.0	thousand	8	43
X	642.0 to	179.0	thousand	7	50

SOURCES: For country rankings and populations, Bruce M. Russett, et al., *World Handbook of Political and Social Indicators* (New Haven, Conn.: Yale University Press, 1964), pp. 18–21; "countries" include "colonies for which data are generally available," *ibid.*, p. 11. For American states' populations in 1961, U.S. Bureau of the Census, *Statistical Abstract of the United States: 1964* (Washington, D.C., 1964), p. 11.

of goods and services that they purchase.[3] By these measures we can derive the following summary picture of the relative significance of state and local governments:

1. *In 1964–65 state and local governments spent 43 percent of the country's total outlays for general governmental purposes* ($75 billion out of $174 billion).

2. *In terms of domestic activities, state and local government expendi-*

---

utilities. "Direct" expenditures are those made directly by a particular governmental level for its own purposes regardless of the source of money; these more nearly indicate where functions are actually performed than the alternative of including in a governmental level's expenditures the amounts that that level passes on as grants-in-aid to the levels where the work is done. Data expressing the total of all governments' general expenditures need not be qualified as "direct," since the governmental levels are not treated separately; similarly, combined state-local totals need not be so qualified.

[3] Sources of the data presented or summarized in the text are: U.S. Bureau of the Census, Governmental Finances in 1964–65 (Washington, D.C., 1966); same, Census of Governments: 1962, Vol. VI, No. 4, Historical Statistics on Governmental Finances and Employment (Washington, D.C., 1964); and, for relation to total and sector outputs of goods and services, the Economic Report of the President . . . January 1966 (Washington, D.C., 1966), pp. 209, 217, 220. Concepts, use of fiscal and calendar years, and methods of calculation for the Census Bureau reports and the Economic Report are not identical; none of the individually numbered statements in the text mixes data from both sources.

tures are much more significant; in 1964–65 they accounted for 69 percent of the total outlay. Of the federal government's direct general expenditures of $99 billion in 1964–65, national defense and international relations drew $56 billion, and another $9 billion was interest on the national debt (mostly incurred for national defense).[4] But if we eliminate these items and focus on domestic functions, the federal government's direct general expenditures are reduced to about $34 billion, compared to the state and local governments' $75 billion; the total for all governments thus comes to $109 billion.

3. *State and local governments account for 10 percent of the total output of goods and services by the American economy (the gross national product).* This makes them an "industry" of greater economic importance than, for example, all of private construction, or all producers' durable equipment, or the country's total exports *and* imports.[5] In fact, in 1965, state and local purchases of goods and services were about the same as the federal government's.

4. *State and local general expenditures in 1964–65 were more than twice those of 1955.* This 122 percent growth was a greater increase than that for direct general expenditures of the federal government (55 percent) and slightly greater than the federal government's increase for primarily domestic activities (117 percent). Some of this growth simply reflected the extension of the same services to a growing population.[6] But state and local general expenditures *per capita* grew from $189 to $387 during the decade, a 105 percent increase.

5. *The state and local governments' share of the economy's total output of goods and services grew from 7.6 percent in 1955 to 10 percent in*

---

[4] *This choice of "nondomestic" categories for subtraction is conservative. Space research and technology costing $5.1 billion in 1964–65 is not counted here as nondomestic (the Council of Economic Advisers includes it in the national defense category, but the Census Bureau does not); nor are veterans' services ($6.4 billion in 1964–65) so counted.*

[5] *We cite the export-import total for its interest, though only the net difference enters into the gross national product.*

[6] *Growth of dollar expenditures also reflects rise in prices of goods and services. If one were to apply to federal direct general expenditures the 34 percent price increase from 1955 to 1965 for federal purchases, the apparent expenditures increase (55 percent) would be in fact only 16 percent. The federal government's primarily domestic expenditures would show an increase of about 34 percent (rather than the apparent 117 percent increase). Similarly, the 40 percent price increase for state and local purchases over the period would change the apparent 122 percent increase in state and local activity to something nearer 60 percent. These are rough calculations, as not all direct general expenditures are for purchases of goods and services; some, for instance, are welfare payments and other subsidies to individuals and business concerns whose own purchases follow a different pattern and so a different average of price increases.*

1965. This upward trend (a 32 percent increase) is less striking than other measures because the private sectors of the economy also registered vigorous growth.

EMPLOYMENT. Another, but less comprehensive, measure of state and local governments' importance is the number of their employees.[7] On this point, the facts show:

1. *In 1965, state and local governments employed 8 million of the 10.6 million civilian employees of all American governments, a tidy 75 percent.*[8]

2. *State and local governments accounted for about 84 percent of all governmental employees engaged in domestic activities in 1965.* Of the federal government's 2.6 million employees, 1.1 million were working on defense and international relations, leaving only 1.5 million performing domestic functions—the sole occupation of all 8 million state and local employees.

3. *State and local governments employed 12 percent of all nonagricultural wage and salary workers in the American economy in 1965.*

4. *State and local employment increased 58 percent between 1955 and 1965.* This contrasts markedly with the federal government's increase of only about 9 percent. In effect, the state and local governments, in expanding by almost 3 million employees in a decade, took on the equivalent of more than the whole federal government's civilian employment of 1965.

5. *State and local employment's share of the country's nonagricultural wage and salary workers increased from about 9 percent in 1955 to 12 percent in 1965.*

FUNCTIONS. Overall statistical measures of activity carry us only a limited distance in gauging the importance of what state and local governments do. But the kinds of social and economic problems that they tackle directly bear on such an appraisal. These are fully considered in a later chapter. Here it suffices to recall a theme developed by Coleman Woodbury: "Of the traditional three levels of government in the United States," he says, "local government contributes most to the quality of our

---

[7] *Sources of the data presented are: U.S. Bureau of the Census,* Public Employment in 1965 (*Washington, D.C., 1966*); *same,* Census of Governments: 1962, *Vol. VI, No. 4,* Historical Statistics on Governmental Finances and Employment; Economic Report of the President . . . January 1966, *p. 238. Because of different methods of calculation, the public employment figures used in the* Economic Report *differ from those in reports of the Bureau of the Census.*

[8] *The figures presented above include both full-time and part-time employees. Conversion to "full-time equivalence" would reduce total governmental employment, and state and local employment, by 1 million, but with slight effect on the percentage shown.*

civilization and its day-to-day life." The national government's responsibilities for national defense, international relations, and economic growth and stability protect and undergird the nation, but this "does not make a civilization—certainly not a high one."

> *. . . local public agencies, in educating our children and many adults, protecting the public health and safety, maintaining peace and order, providing most of our facilities for noncommercial recreation, making more tolerable the frictions and costs of urban civilization, influencing markedly the amenities and satisfactions of our residential areas, guiding the processes by which newcomers to urban areas (many of them poor, ignorant, and inexperienced in urban ways of living) learn to adjust to new conditions and responsibilities, and providing opportunities for direct participation in public affairs, play a more significant role [than the national government] in determining the quality of our increasingly urban civilization.*[9]

It is revealing to look down a list of general governmental functions and to compare the direct expenditures of the federal government and the state and local governments. The picture that results is this (functions are listed in descending order of total general expenditures by all governments): [10]

Federal Government Spends Directly ⅔rds or More of Total	State and Local Governments Spend Directly ⅔rds or More of Total
National defense and international relations	
	Education
	Highways
Interest on general debt	
Natural resources	
	Health and hospitals
	Public welfare

---

[9] Coleman Woodbury, Urban Studies: Some Questions of Outlook and Selection (Pittsburgh: Institute of Local Government, Graduate School of Public and International Affairs, University of Pittsburgh, 1960), p. 13.

[10] Any list of functional categories is bound to be somewhat arbitrary (e.g., should "health and hospitals" be one category or two? should "natural resources" include costs of the farm price stabilization programs?). This list includes all general expenditure categories accounting for at least $1 billion (and 0.6 percent) of all governments' general expenditures, as shown in U.S. Bureau of the Census, Governmental Finances in 1964–65 at pp. 7 and 11, except for "financial administration," "general control," and "housing and urban renewal" (the last because the state-local share, 57 percent, does not qualify under the ⅔rds criterion). Amounts of direct expenditures by levels of governments are shown on pp. 22f of the Census report (which pages also illustrate the variety of ways of classifying functions).

Federal Government Spends Directly ⅔rds or More of Total	State and Local Governments Spend Directly ⅔rds or More of Total
Postal service	
Space research and technology	
Veterans' services	
(not elsewhere classified)	
	Police protection
	Sanitation
Water transport and	
terminals	
	Local fire protection
Air transportation	
	Parks and recreation
	Correction

More precise comparisons will be found elsewhere in this book, and due account will be taken of federal financial assistance for state and local units' performance of their functions. This rough comparison, however, suffices to reenforce Woodbury's observations and extend them to state as well as local governments.

Quantitative statements such as we have made undoubtedly lack romance, but they are useful counters to florid statements lamenting the "insignificance" of state and local governments and their supposed "decline" since the good old days. The facts seem to establish pretty firmly that (a) the populations and areas of many states would entitle them to significant rank among the nations of the world; (b) the aggregate of state and local activities accounts for a large part of the total range and volume of governmental services in the United States; (c) the state and local governments' role has in recent years been increasing both absolutely and relatively; and (d) the functions directly performed by state and local governments are vital to a high level of civilization.

2. Roles in the American Political System

What has been said to this point shows how difficult it is to talk about state and local governments in isolation. Urban redevelopment, the illustration used earlier, seems as local a responsibility as one can think of. Yet the stimulus and aid of the federal government, and sometimes of state governments, account for much of the progress to date in remaking the downtown areas of our big cities. The attempt to assess the significance of the responsibilities carried by state and local governments led us inevitably to comparisons with the federal government or, putting it slightly differently, to ascertaining the state and local share of total governmental activity in the United States. But such comparisons tend to exaggerate the separateness of the several levels of American government.

If state and local governments are difficult to understand by themselves—that is, with the federal government left out—the reverse is equally true. Neither the American political system as a whole nor the federal government can be understood apart from the state and local political systems and the governments that are both the creatures and the regulators of those systems. There are two reasons for this. One is that what the federal government decides to do, and how it chooses to do it, depends on what the state and local governments are able or willing to do, and on how competent their performance is likely to be. The federal government, in taking on certain jobs and in deciding whether to do them alone or in partnership with the state and local governments, is often merely moving in to fill a vacuum. What is thought to need doing by some government is more likely to become a federal responsibility if it is not being done at all or if it is being poorly done by the other governments in the American system. The second reason is that decision making in the federal government can be understood only when it is viewed as a process that elaborately interrelates the national, state, and local political systems. So much is this true that, if its very complexity did not get in the way of analysis, "the American political system" would be the appropriate focus of study, rather than any one "level" of government.

The two elements interact: the distribution of functions both reflects and affects the political patterns of the American system. It will be convenient, however, to look separately at each in this preliminary effort to see where the state and local governments fit in.

DISTRIBUTION OF FUNCTIONS. American history reveals marked shifts in ways of characterizing the respective roles of the federal, state, and local governments. When adoption of the American Constitution was under consideration, James Madison wrote in *The Federalist*,

> The powers delegated by the proposed Constitution to the federal government are few and defined. . . . [They] will be exercised principally on external objects, as war, peace, negotiation, and foreign commerce; with which last the power of taxation will for the most part be connected. The powers reserved to the several States will extend to all the objects, which, in the ordinary course of affairs, concern the lives, liberties and properties of the people; and the internal order, improvement, and prosperity of the State.[11]

---

[11] *Essay No. 45*, The Federalist, *edited by Jacob E. Cooke (Meridian paperback edition. Cleveland: World Publishing Co., 1961), pp. 308–14, at p. 313.*

he likelihood or unlikelihood that a lower level will deal with it effectively; he intensity of pressures for and against meeting the problem; and the political responsiveness of policy makers at each level. Two traditional elements continue to be influential: the legal power of each level to apply sanctions, and the allegiance popularly accorded such values as decentralization, local self-government, and grass-roots democracy. To put it a bit differently, "states' rights," with its emphasis on the reserved powers of the states, has lapsed as an acknowledged constitutional barrier to federal action (partly because so many problems, having become regional or national in their dimensions, have worked themselves into the scope of the constitutional provisions that grant specific powers to the federal government). Even where the federal government constitutionally may not, or does not choose to, exercise direct power over citizens, it can indirectly (and constitutionally) achieve its objectives by influencing the states to carry out national policies. What the state governments themselves may do in relation to previously local affairs has seldom turned on provisions of the federal Constitution, nor has it been narrowly circumscribed by the state constitutions.

3. Although formal, legal barriers can now be surmounted by higher levels of government, common sense wars against the quick conclusion that the days of state and local government are numbered. No country as large as the United States, and rarely any larger than, say, New York State, attempts to operate a governmental system by having all legislative decisions made at the center and all administrative actions taken through national administrative agents. We can therefore confidently assume a continuing need for three levels of government in the United States. And we can also assume that tradition has a firm enough grip so that, however inappropriate their boundaries may appear, the states as we know them will continue to be the intermediate level in the system.

4. Though it therefore remains convenient to talk about levels of government, the essential reality today is the complex pattern of interpenetration among the three traditional levels of government. The pattern of American government has altered so much that one needs to find terms that distort reality less than the word "levels." One of the most thoughtful students of intergovernmental relations, Morton Grodzins, has suggested that our habit is to think of "layer cake" government, when what we have in fact is "marble cake" government. Earlier writers have spoken of "cooperative federalism" and of the role of "the states as agents of the nation."

Part of the interpenetration of levels is political, to which we shall give attention shortly. But the other part concerns the distribution of responsi-

Some forty years later, a discerning French observer, Alexi
found that reality conformed to Madison's prediction. "
Government scarcely ever interferes in any but foreign
governments of the states really direct society in Ameri
"America is therefore pre-eminently the country of state
government." [12]

Even when the federal government became more activ
directing society in America, constitutional doctrines of fede
mutually exclusive spheres of state and federal power. And
governments generally enjoyed no legal autonomy vis-à-vis th
ments, they were regarded as a "level" of government tha
responsibility for "local affairs."

Dynamic developments in the country's social and e
altered all this. They strained, almost beyond recognition, th
and rigid patterns inherited from constitutional doctrine an
practice. One was the vertical pattern of a series of *levels* of
each supposed to correspond to a neat parcel of distinct fun
other was the horizontal pattern of state boundaries and
horizontal pattern of local government boundaries marking off
areas, each distinct from its neighbors at the same level and ea
separate government.

The story is usually told in terms of centralization, and
though this were a peculiarly American phenomenon instead of
leled in most modern nations. Rather than repeat the familiar
story of the movement of power to the national level of governme
dimensions of social and economic problems made local and state
ries increasingly irrelevant, let us attempt to summarize the basic
in the present distribution of functions.

1. The functions of government in general in the United St
substantially greater than they were in the past. Here we refer le
expansion in the list of governmental functions, though this is par
reckoning, than to the expansion, elaboration, and intensification d
governments do under long-familiar functional categories. An expan
federal government activities is therefore not necessarily a subtraction
state and local activities, for state and local governments have al
panded their own work.

2. For better or worse, the question of what a higher level of g
ment can do or should do turns less nowadays on constitutional issues
on pragmatic considerations—the nature of the problem to be dealt

---

[12] *Alexis de Tocqueville,* Democracy in America, *Henry Reeve (trans.), Ph
Bradley (ed.) (New York: Vintage Books, 1954), Vol. I, pp. 264 and 435.*

bilities for governmental functions. Today scarcely any governmental function belongs entirely to a single level, though the concept of allocating bundles of whole functions to particular levels was basic to earlier practice and analysis. In a preceding section we listed functions for which the federal government accounts for two-thirds or more of the country's direct governmental expenditure and those for which the state and local governments account for two-thirds or more. What we excluded were the federal government's grants-in-aid to state and local government (ranging from one-third to one-half of state and local direct spending for such functions as public welfare, highways, and housing and urban renewal) and the technical assistance provided by the federal government (for example, the Federal Bureau of Investigation's fingerprint identification laboratory, training schools for local police, and compilation and publication of crime statistics). Through grants and technical assistance, the federal government implements national policy and influences state and local policy and administration. In addition, direct performance of clearly federal functions affects state and local performance of "their own" functions; one among many possible examples is the Defense Department's award and termination of defense contracts to industrial companies, on whose earnings and employment of workers state and local communities are dependent for economic health, for tax revenues, and for minimization of demands on state unemployment insurance funds and state and local public welfare budgets.

Reversing our field, the federal government depends on state and local governments for effective performance in shared functional fields and in peculiarly national functional fields as well. A good example of the first is stream pollution, which kills fish, impairs recreational use of streams, and contaminates the water supply of downstream cities, towns, and industrial plants. The federal government has clear constitutional authority over navigable waterways, and court decisions have given this authority a broad interpretation. Local governments, on the other hand, have clear authority to build and operate sewage disposal systems for their communities. And they and the state governments have clear authority to regulate private industrial plants' waste disposal arrangements. Whether the federal government uses its powers to require that cities and industries avoid stream pollution depends on whether it finds that state and local governments are unwilling to use their powers and their tax revenues. In a case like this, the federal government must decide not only whether to use its powers, but also which powers to use and how to use them. Again, this decision would depend on how state and local governments respond to mild national measures, such as technical advice, persuasion, grants, and loans, and to the danger that a poor response may invite more stringent legislation by Congress. In this instance, state and local response has been poor, and a succession of national laws, each bringing to bear more direct exertion of national authority, has been necessary.

In its distinctively national functions, the federal government is also dependent on state and local governments. For one thing, the major state universities provide the professional training of many who become the federal government's career civil servants. The faculties of these universities also conduct much of the basic and applied research underlying federal programs in atomic energy, space exploration, communications satellites, and national and international economic policy. When the head of a major foreign state comes to address the United Nations General Assembly, the New York City and New York State police may carry much of the burden of protecting his safety, and if he tours the country, the police of many other cities and states may find themselves involved in international relations. The bodily safety and peace of mind of the federal government's postmen as they make their rounds depend on whether local ordinances require confinement of dogs and on whether local dogcatchers do their jobs well. The National Guard of Arkansas, which one day is obeying the governor's command to keep Negro children out of a high school, may the next day be obeying the President's command to protect the same children's right to go in. The families of those stationed at national defense installations depend on the school systems of nearby communities, and all at the installations turn to these communities for recreational facilities. Constitutional interpretation has accorded the federal government an overriding control of rail transportation; yet even here, the survival of an interstate rail commuter service of a deficit-plagued railroad may turn on the willingness of the affected state governments to subsidize the company and on the ability of the several governments to come to agreement on the share each will contribute.

In sum, then, we can see a great hodgepodge of shared and interdependent functions, rather than a neat allocation of whole functions among three distinct levels of government. And as constitutional doctrines have been adjusted to social and economic developments it is pragmatic rather than legalistic tests that have come to determine which governments shall do what. Because higher levels of government embrace the larger geographic areas into which many problems have spilled, because they usually have superior financial resources, and because legal restrictions on their powers have eroded, this determination of which governments shall do what is generally the responsibility of the higher levels—of the states vis-à-vis local governments and of the federal government vis-à-vis both state and local governments. How this kind of policy determination is made is therefore dependent upon the political institutions and processes of the higher levels of government. We have suggested that an important factor in this determination is the judgment of those at the higher level of the willingness and ability of the lower level to grapple with the problems that (in the higher level's judgment) cannot be left untended to. To an important degree, therefore, we cannot understand what the national government does without understanding what state and local governments are willing and able to do. There is, however, another factor. This is the way in which the higher level's policy-making institutions and processes are constructed and operate.

POLITICAL INTERPENETRATION. The American political system is a complicated jigsaw puzzle interlocking the three levels of government. This necessarily means that neither the whole system, nor that of the national government alone, can be understood without appreciating the ways in which state and local governments and their political communities fit into the pattern. Many of the essentials of the pattern are deliberate and will be found in the Constitution itself and in its contemporary gloss, *The Federalist*. Some of the essentials are outside the formal structure and need to be extracted from the operations of our political parties, the workings of the administrative process, and the way that interest groups operate in trying to influence policy.

Consider the making of a decision by Congress that poses the question of whether the national government should or should not take over or actively influence a policy area previously occupied primarily by the state governments. In much popular discourse we are accustomed to hearing that "the national government" has decided to adopt a policy or that it has seized functions that might better be left with the states. Such phrasing tends to personalize "the national government" and give it a will of its own. The fact is, however, that under our political system, the national government's policy machinery is heavily infiltrated with people who represent, and are highly responsive to, constituencies much smaller than the nation. The arithmetic of votes in Congress is related (though not in a 1 to 1 ratio) to each legislator's calculation of his constituents' probable behavior when he seeks reelection. A United States senator with a normal instinct for political survival will be attentive to opinion and political forces in the state that elects him, and a United States representative to those of an even smaller constituency, one sometimes smaller even than the constituency that elects the mayor of his city. As Madison put it, almost two centuries ago, ". . . members of the Fœderal Legislature will be likely to attach themselves too much to local objects. . . . Measures will too often be decided according to their probable effect, not on the national prosperity and happiness, but on the prejudices, interests and pursuits of the governments and people of the individual States." [13]

What the formal provisions for make-up of the Congress mean for the perspective of those who make national policy decisions is reinforced by both formal and informal features of the American system. Election administration and determination of qualifications of voters for national officials are constitutionally left to the individual states, although constitutional amendments and implementing laws have forbidden discrimination by sex or race. Our national parties are highly decentralized structures usually described as weak confederations of state and local political organizations. National political conventions that choose presidential candidates are, again, assemblages of state delegations.

Federalism itself, reinforced by the degree of autonomy enjoyed by state and local party organizations, substantially assures that one party's winning of national power will not leave the minority party powerless. When one party manages to capture the Presidency and both houses of Congress, the other one will still have control of a number of state governments or of governorships or individual houses of the state legislatures. This means that the minority party is not suddenly stripped of all political power. Instead, from the political bases it has established in certain states, it is in a position to mount a hopeful effort to displace the majority party at subsequent national elections and to extend its control of other state governments. This situation enhances the prospects for the long-range survival of the two-party system and affects the current behavior of the majority party in Congress as well. The majority party must practice restraint and accommodation in dealing with the minority members of Congress, for only thus can it hope for such treatment when it becomes the minority—a prospect made the more probable by the minority party's control of a number of state and local governments. This behavioral pattern of the majority party is further induced by its own members' responsiveness to local constituencies and by the relative autonomy of the majority's state and local political organizations. Moreover, it may need to attract some minority members' votes as substitutes for the votes of those majority members who desert their party's national position to avoid alienating constituents on whom their reelection depends.

---

[13] *Essay No. 46*, The Federalist, *pp. 315–23, at p. 318.*

The point should be clear without abundance of detail: Policy making by the national "level" of government is so much a product of what state and local governments, their party organizations, and the constituencies do or might do that one must understand these in order to understand national politics and decisions.

National administration, as well as policy making, has substantial decentralist elements. If national grant-in-aid programs influence state and local governments, it is also true that the execution of these national programs depends on state and local administrative agencies (some of them in governments controlled by the national minority party). This dependence leads to a considerable toleration of diversity, a great hesitancy to take disciplinary action (such as withholding grants from particular states), and a deliberate effort to obtain advice from state officials in working out details of a national program. Some strictly national programs operate through, or with the counsel of, state and local citizen committees, and the choice of members is often based on the advice of state and local officials and congressmen or on elections by local constituencies. Illustrative are the thousands of farmer committees associated with national agricultural programs, the local draft boards, the grazing-control boards in the West, and in wartime, the price and rationing boards.

Much of what we have said about national-state and national-local relations can, with slight changes, be applied to state-local relations. Here again, Madison is remarkably pertinent: "Every one knows that a great proportion of the errors committed by the State Legislatures proceeds from the disposition of the members to sacrifice the comprehensive and permanent interests of the State, to the particular and separate views of the counties or districts in which they reside." [14]

We need one other element to appreciate the degree of interpenetration of the three levels. An interest group desiring to get a policy adopted or a proposed policy defeated prefers that the decision be made by that level of government whose political make-up preconditions it to act as the interest group wishes. The play of these private forces, therefore, has a good deal to do with which governments do what. It is not surprising, then, that labor organizations and urban interests, despairing of support at the state level, have often sought national legislation, while some business interests have decried the federal government's "embarking on a radical new philosophy, a philosophy which calls for the Federal Government to take over responsibilities which heretofore have been state and local." The distinguished banker who spoke in this vein in the early 1960's cited as

---

[14] Ibid.

examples the housing law, the urban renewal program, the aid given for local highway projects, the proposed aid to education, and "huge Federal outlays for local welfare purposes." The theme struck is rarely that the needs will be better and more fully met if the federal government stays out, but rather that

> If Americans are to have a sense of pride, of strength, of well-being that comes with accomplishment, the individual, the family, the local community must bear ultimate responsibility for their own welfare even though personal sacrifices are required. Only in this way can we have a strong, self-reliant and a more vigorous America. . . . Involved is our own future way of life: whether we are to become increasingly soft and dependent on government, or stand as families and individuals on our own two feet.[15]

The passage inadvertently reveals an unconscious association of ideas, but one that is consciously made by some interest groups, namely, that leaving matters to local governments will often mean leaving them to no government at all. That is to say, local governments will not legislate on the problems, and so they will be left to private individuals without any governmental "interference." Much the same kind of play of forces and expectations accounts for the support accorded by certain interest groups to the states' resistance to "federal encroachment."

This review of the role of state and local communities both in the performance of governmental functions and in the political process makes apparent the need to understand the state and local levels if we are to understand the American political system and even its national level. It also shows us how much what the national government chooses to do depends upon how satisfactorily the state and local governments perform as political systems in their own right.

3. Political Systems

If we can speak of "the American political system," we can also speak of tens of thousands of state and local political systems, each uniquely condi-

---

15 George Champion, "Taxes and the Government Debt: A Plan for the 1960's," Tax Review, 23 (March 1962), 9–12. Mr. Champion, Chairman of the Board of Directors of the Chase Manhattan Bank, resumed the theme before the Illinois Bankers Association in 1965, advocating the business community's support of "the free consensus of the marketplace, . . . the independent judgment of the millions rather than the controlled judgment of the faceless few in Washington." The New York Times, May 26, 1965, p. 65.

tioned by its particular environment. An understanding of how they, singly or collectively, attempt to fulfill the requirements of a healthy political system has value for two quite different purposes. The first we have already noted. State and local governments' roles in the larger system of American government are in great part a consequence of their degree of success as political systems. Concerned citizens, therefore, have reason to seek to know how well state and local governments do perform, what their particular strengths and weaknesses are, and whether and how changes might be made to improve their performance. As in the medical world, diagnosis should precede prescription, and both diagnosis and prescription should draw on laboratory studies and the accumulation of clinical findings from comparable cases. The state and local governments' health is a matter of practical concern and of applied science, but behind the application must be the basic knowledge.

Here, indeed, is the second purpose of developing an understanding of this multitude of political systems. For a political science to exist and advance, much of the basic research must derive, refine, and test hypotheses by observation of real political systems. Because in logic, at least, this basic research should precede the practical business of the recognition and diagnosis of symptoms of malfunctioning and the prescription of remedies, we shall consider first the way in which the study of state and local political systems may contribute to the larger objective of a deeper understanding of political systems in general.

UNDERSTANDING POLITICAL SYSTEMS IN GENERAL. American local and state governments offer to the inquiring mind virtually limitless scope for asking basic questions about how a political system does work, how it ought to work, and how the gap between the actual and the ideal can be narrowed. In fact, they open up two very different opportunities for the understanding of political systems. On the one hand, any local or state community can profitably be studied by itself. On the other, the 90,000 local governments (or the 50 states) present a stunning opportunity for comparing, classifying, and appraising alternative kinds of political systems.

Any local political community can be taken as a living illustration of men's efforts to govern themselves by institutionally relating power and responsibility, individual ambition and common purpose, expert competence and popular rule. Observations of such a community can be highly suggestive for theoretical speculation about such great issues as justice, truth, authority, and liberty. The perceived realities of local political life may remind the philosophically inclined that theory and prescription ultimately rest on a premise about the nature of man; but perhaps the realities will be unsettling enough to induce recognition of variety by rephrasing the premise so that it speaks of the natures of men. Whether philosopher or empiricist, a student's close observation of the sequence of events leading to a particular local decision can help to develop a more sensitive understanding of the realities of the political process, a "feel" for how and why things happen, and don't happen, in a political system. Compared to a national government covering a wide territory, employing an army of administrative agents, and buffeted by a multitude of well-organized pressure groups, many a local community must seem simplicity itself. A small town, for example, offers a relatively simplified political system, easy to analyze, yet it can suggest many critical questions to apply to larger and more intricate political communities.

But, for all that, a science advances only a limited way if it depends upon what a single case can teach us about a whole class of phenomena. Study of a single community misses the variety of political systems represented by the multitude of local communities, fails to alert the student to critical factors that may be hidden rather than overt in the particular community examined, and above all, leaves unused the powerful analytical tool of comparison and contrast.

Here, quite obviously, state and local governments provide an unequaled assemblage of cases for comparative study. Take the 50 state governments as an illustrative category. They have the advantage of certain basic similarities, similarities that qualify them for membership in a particular set of cases, that exclude all other governments from the set, and that simplify analysis by holding some important variables constant. Thus as the Constitution ordains, they are all at the intermediate level of governments, they all have a "republican form of government," they all have the same formal range of powers, and they all are bound by the same national constitutional restrictions on interference with private rights. And because they have lacked originality in using their power to devise their own machinery, all have much the same formal institutional arrangements—governor, two-house legislature (with one exception), supreme and inferior courts, and administrative departments. Yet for all these largely formal similarities, the state governments have important institutional differences, operate in and on different environments, and perform at different levels of public satisfaction. For purposes of basic research, as well as applied research designed to stimulate improvement, the identification and interrelation of the environmental, institutional, procedural, and human behavior patterns that distinguish the states with better performance records from the states with less satisfactory records would clearly advance political science. That is, it would enrich our understanding of political systems in general, and particularly of that large category of political systems that purport to be democratic.

At the local level, there are even more opportunities for comparative analysis. Furthermore, at this level we can deal more frequently with organic communities. And, in terms of sheer numbers, local communities lend themselves particularly well to comparative analysis. For one thing, though they have a great variety of institutional arrangements, we can find a large number of communities using the same institutional arrangement. For example, we can compare and contrast all cities of a certain population class and try to find out why some choose a city-manager form of government, some a strong-mayor form, some a weak-mayor form, some a commission form. Or we can take just those cities with a city-manager form, appraise the varying results, and develop a generalized statement of conditions under which such a form leads to one result rather than another.

Several things need to be said about how this kind of study bears upon the development of political science. First, though our examples seem closely related to applied rather than basic research and seem to lead to restricted rather than broad generalizations, neither need be true. A deep understanding of American state governments can strengthen understanding of all intermediate-level governments in the world, particularly of those in the more developed countries and those purportedly democratic in principle. An even more universal problem is the government of local communities. At both intermediate and local levels the basic institutional patterns are quite few, and the task therefore is to specify the conditions under which one rather than another seems from experience to be the more appropriate to achieve specified goals.

Second, what we have described as opportunities largely remain just that. Though Aristotle set the example of collecting, classifying, and comparing data from many communities, and derived from such data generalizations about the tendency of each type of political system to develop into another type, his example has not been widely followed in the study of American state and local governments. Factual information of a quantitative character (thanks largely to the Bureau of the Census) has been gathered and classified, and in the last decade or so, some probing comparative studies have been made, but with a very limited number of cases. To these must be added a few case studies of single communities that, because they were made with sensitivity to the larger theoretical issues of the working of *any* political system, have strengthened the base for a truly comparative analysis. These contributions, however, leave still in the future the full exploitation of the rich experience of state and local governments.

Third, this state of affairs means that the logical sequence of basic research first, then applied research on the foundation thus established, cannot very well be followed. Not that there has not been basic research, even before the recent studies to which we have alluded. But it has been scattered. Bits and pieces are available, and can be drawn on by those seeking to meet practical problems of governance. On the other hand, gaping holes in our knowledge exist, the completed bits and pieces are difficult to fit together, and the design of the whole is likely to be elusive. Problems clamor for "solutions," and those responsible for dealing with them must prescribe without being fully confident of the correctness of the diagnosis or the appropriateness of the remedy. Those who write books like this one share in these disabilities. Judgment of what a healthy political system is, recognition of symptoms of ill health, diagnosis of the specific malfunctioning, and prescription of remedy are, in these circumstances, bound to rest on research findings on some matters, on sensitivity developed by personal experience and observation, and on individual concern for particular values.

APPRAISING STATE AND LOCAL POLITICAL SYSTEMS. Whether one is a liberal or a conservative, a centralist or a decentralist, the critical questions for the future roles of state and local governments are the same: Can the state and local governments perform their current responsibilities or their newly emerging responsibilities? Even if they can, will they? If they cannot, or will not, should the responsibilities be left unperformed? If they will need to be done somehow, should the federal government perform them directly, or should the federal government go at the task indirectly, making it both possible and attractive for the state and local governments to do them? The answers will depend substantially upon one's evaluation of the state and local governments as political systems. In other words, the key to whether these governments can and will fulfill the responsibilities and opportunities that now face them is the set of institutions and processes through which these governments decide what to do and proceed to get it done. It does no good for state and local governments to complain of being robbed of powers by the national government if they do not make good use of the powers they now have. For if they fail the test of competence, of capacity for the use of power, they weaken their claims to repossess powers lost to the national government, to retain powers now in hand, and to expand powers over the problems of a complex, technologically advanced, urban-metropolitan civilization.

The quality of performance of a political system—in this case, a state or local government—can be approached in either of two ways. One method is to consider each function separately—education, highways, welfare, health and hospitals, crime control, utilities regulation, and each of the many other activities where what a state or local government does is of moment to a large proportion of its citizens. The other is to consider such a government as a whole, with the focus on its ability to make sound and acceptable decisions and to implement them.

In considering the first method, we find that each function has its distinct standards of measurement, its special controversies over goals and methods, its separate group of knowledgeable people, both lay and professional. Furthermore, as noted earlier, a state or local government is autonomous in few, if any, of these functions. Accomplishing goals important to the public depends on the joint effort of national, state, and local governments, for all three are partners in joint attacks on each of the evils and hazards that are of public concern. And, in many instances, even at a single level, the adjoining and overlapping governments have to combine their efforts lest a problem facing them all yield to none.

To gauge total governmental achievement in each function and to separate out the share of a state or a local government in that achievement appears, then, an exceedingly complex undertaking. It might also be frustratingly inconclusive. For we would inevitably be led back from the functional parts to the whole that is a state or local political system. To be sure, no mechanical nicety in governmental processes would be admirable if it yielded no gains against ignorance, disease, poverty, automobile congestion, industrial accidents, or abuse of resources or of economic power. Yet every program a state or local government undertakes depends for its content and its execution on the general capacity of the political system to make and administer policies.

Although one chapter is wholly concerned with *what* state and local governments do and the others retain it as a background theme, we shall mainly focus upon *how* these governments perform as political systems and as wholes, not as mere assemblages of a miscellany of substantive functional activities.

This is an appropriate focus for both basic and applied political science, but it by no means disposes of some of the most difficult problems to which the student should be alert. First, what shall be the standard for judging the performance of a political system? "Systems theory" suggests one such standard—sheer survival of the system. The assumption of systems theory is that a system's survival demonstrates both its satisfactory adjustment to its external environment and its satisfactory resolution of threatening tensions within itself. Those who so wish may take comfort in the fact that all state governments and most general-purpose local governments have survived. But many will demand a stricter standard. Without arguing the universality of the standard, we think it appropriate in the America of the latter half of the twentieth century to orient our inquiry to the state and local governments' capacity to exercise power responsibly, democratically, intelligently, and efficiently. The heart of the matter is the making and administration of policy, for there rests the capacity to govern.

We can apply to this standard no nicely graduated scale of measurement. Nor, indeed, does the evidence available lend itself to refined measurement. But gross comparisons are possible, whether among different governments or between governmental levels, in terms of the elementary standards of responsible behavior, democratic representation, informed policy making, and efficient decisional and administrative processes.

Second, how can one appraise a political system without analytically sorting out its separate elements for study? The answer is that one cannot and that we have not. We must, for example, talk for a time about political parties, and then about the legislature, and then about the governor. The problem is not that of analysis into elements, but of resynthesizing these elements into the whole. More especially, it is that of treating each element with a constant awareness that it is not really separate but a part of the whole. This is the approach we follow in the chapters that deal with the various elements. The merit system of civil service recruitment, for instance, may be admirably attuned to the value of administrative efficiency, but its bearing on the health of political parties, with their important role in responsible and democratic government, needs, and receives, appraisal.

Third, how can one make generalizations about state government or municipal government when there are 50 of the one and 18,000 of the other? The answer here is that one must. But clearly there are ways of bringing discriminating judgment to bear. The beginning of wisdom in these circumstances is to have constantly in mind the variety that exists in fact, without lapsing into the conviction that nothing useful can be said because every case is unique. The variety at first seems overwhelming. Eight of the 50 states contain about half of the national population. Rhode Island and New Jersey have over 800 persons per square mile; Alaska has half a person (statistically speaking) and Nevada fewer than three persons per square mile. In four states the federal government owns between 64 and 94 percent of the land. The states of Alaska and Wyoming each receive federal grants-in-aid that, on a per capita basis, are about six times what New Jersey or Florida receives. Much that is true about the governor of North Dakota, with a salary of $13,000, is not likely to be true about the governor of New York, with a salary of $50,000, and this disparity in salaries is probably the least important difference between them. The Mississippi and Illinois legislatures have little in common other than the Mississippi River. Even neighbors like Washington and Oregon have very different politics. About a fifth of our states are one-party states. The principal industry of several states is the care and feeding of tourists.

One escape from the appearance of limitless variety is by recognizing that states (or local governments) lend themselves to grouping by particular items of similarity. Useful generalizations may then be made for each group. So far, regrettably, little grouping of this kind has been done in political science. The tendency until recently has been either to group states geographically so that one may talk generally about the South, New England, or the Middle West or to dichotomize too easily by setting up the simple categories of one-party and two-party states.

For purposes of political analysis, more sophisticated groupings are needed. We know, for example, that state politics and the state-local division of powers and labor are profoundly affected by the balance of urban, suburban, and rural interests within their borders. Three or four characteristic patterns occur frequently enough to be classified. In over a dozen states, one metropolitan city—a Chicago, a Baltimore, a New Orleans—stands politically arrayed against the rest of the state. Such a city often decides the governorship and other statewide election results. But it is usually underrepresented in the state legislature, though faster suburban growth and legislative redistricting have lately repaired some of this relative disadvantage. Sometimes the big city—Boston, Atlanta, Honolulu—is the state capital; more often, as in New York and Michigan, it is not. Outside the South, the big city usually has a party majority opposite to that of the rest of the state, although its business leaders are frequently allied on economic issues with the rural legislative leaders. In another half dozen or more states a bipolar rivalry between two major cities, dividing both parties, is the key to the state's politics. In Pennsylvania, Missouri, and California, for example, the two United States Senate seats are generally allotted to the two leading cities or to the areas they dominate; the governor must beware of too close identification with either; and the rural legislators play each against the other in a state capital that is a small neutral city. Again, in states as different as Connecticut and Texas, a number of cities, each with its local machine but no one or two of them predominant, find common interests in some general urban issues, yet fail to form any durable alliance against the rural areas. Finally, there are states —Connecticut, New Jersey, Maryland, Virginia, Wisconsin—which adjoin a huge metropolis in another state. In each of these, an important section of the state consists of well-to-do "dormitory" or "playground" suburbs whose commuter inhabitants are absorbed in the life of the "foreign" metropolis. They are interested in the politics of their "home" state chiefly for its bearing on the outcome of presidential elections, though school facilities and tax rates may periodically engage their attention.

If the grouping of governments into categories meaningful for generalizing purposes has as yet advanced little, there remains the recourse of prudent, tentative, and qualified generalization. This should be understood as the orientation which this chapter and all that follow are meant to express. Generalize we must, but what is set forth should be regarded as tentative hypotheses that state our current and imperfect understanding of state and local governments as political systems. It is a happy circumstance that within recent years a significant number of talented scholars have come to direct their energies to basic research on the ways in which state and local governments perform as political systems. As this research progresses and attracts still other scholars, prevailing hypotheses will be tested and rejected or refined, to the end that general propositions may have firmer foundations than mere plausibility.

4. A Preliminary Stock-taking

It will be useful for introductory purposes to survey rapidly the kinds of questions that receive detailed treatment in the chapters that follow. Such a survey may also sharpen the reader's awareness of how much such questions need attention both by political scientists and by those who will shape the political institutions and processes of the future—public officials, politicians, journalists, businessmen, labor leaders, and the honorable, if less numerous, part-time civic reformers.

THE HERITAGE. No one who studies state and local governments can fail to be impressed by the extent to which they are creatures of their past. This is true both of formal arrangements and of standards of behavior —rectitude, responsibility, responsiveness, and the rest. Nearly all the state constitutions antedate the twentieth century. This is not necessarily bad; a good old constitution may be preferable to a bad new one. Unfortunately, most of them reflect the nineteenth-century distrust of state governments generally and of each branch particularly. The result was an excess of democracy, expressed in withholding of powers from the legislature, fragmentation of executive authority, and politicalization of the judiciary.

Hog-tied, drawn, and quartered, many a state government was no government at all. The kingdom was but the sum of its numerous petty and often unpretty principalities. With such a heritage, state governments today find it hard to do the kind of job that will attract and hold public confidence. Even where there's a will, there may be no way.

In the course of two centuries, few observers have pointed with pride to American state governments. They were not thought good models by the framers of the United States Constitution. We have already noted Madison's criticism of the parochial outlook of state legislators, which was the more serious because "the legislative department is everywhere extending the sphere of its activity, and drawing all power into its impetuous vortex." [16] A century later, Theodore Roosevelt, who had sat in three sessions of the New York legislature, reported "much viciousness and political dishonesty, much moral cowardice, and a good deal of actual bribe-taking at Albany." [17] When Lord Bryce published his *Modern Democracies* in 1921, he judged that "State Legislatures do not enjoy the confidence of the people," that "the State Judiciary is, in the large majority of the States, inferior in quality to the better part of the Bar that Practises before it," that "the administration of criminal justice is . . . in many States so ineffective that offenders constantly escape punishment," and that "the power of wealth, and particularly of great incorporated companies, to influence both legislatures, and the choice of persons to sit in legislatures and on the judicial Bench, has been formidable." [18] In the 1950's, the temporary Commission on Intergovernmental Relations and, in the 1960's, the Advisory Commission on Intergovernmental Relations found their principal focus of concern to be not any striking disposition of the federal government to seek power but the striking incapacity of many state and local governments to make a good case for retaining or expanding their powers. Thus, the first of these commissions, despite its having started with a strong bias against the growth of national power, submitted to President Eisenhower in 1955 a final report that sharply questioned "the readiness of the States to discharge greater responsibilities." The softness of its impeachment was more a matter of language than of meaning:

> . . . *the more effectively our State and local governmental structures, procedures, and policies can be adapted to present-day govern-*

---

[16] *Essay No. 48*, The Federalist, *pp.* 332–38, *at p.* 333.

[17] *Quoted in* James Bryce, The American Commonwealth, *new edition* (New York: Macmillan, 1921), Vol. I, *p.* 546.

[18] James Bryce, Modern Democracies (New York: Macmillan, 1921), Vol. II, *pp.* 154f.

mental objectives, the less occasion there will be for bypassing State action in the future. . . .

The success of our federal system . . . depends in large measure upon the performance of the States. . . .

The Commission finds a very real and pressing need for the States to improve their constitutions . . . to make sure that they provide for vigorous and responsible government, not forbid it.

Citizens who fail to understand the essential conditions of effective government in their home States may unintentionally promote the centralization they deplore.[19]

Although both commissions gave considerable attention to ways of improving federal grant-in-aid programs, the commission of the 1960's, like that of the 1950's, has devoted most of its reports to ways of strengthening the structures, procedures, and policies of state and local governments so that inherited patterns may no longer obstruct effective performance.

Because the dead hand of the past has so tenacious a hold on the state and local governments, our current understanding requires appreciation of how these governments became what they are. Two of the following chapters trace this process of "becoming."

THE AMERICAN SYSTEM. Placing state and local governments in time is one way of getting perspective. Another is to place them contemporaneously in what may be called the American system, that is, in the full context of the American government, society, and economy. We have already signaled the importance of this perspective. Two later chapters explore the matter much more thoroughly, first by examining individually and collectively the more important substantive functional programs that draw on the policy-making and administrative resources of state and local governments, and second by untangling the web of intergovernmental relations.

POLITICS. We have set our focus on the capacity to govern, and identified the making and the administration of policy as the processes that are crucial for effective governing. Politics is basic to policy making and by no means irrelevant to administration. It sets the moral tone of state governments. It conditions relations between governor and legislature, between upper and lower legislative houses, between the governor and other executive officials and agencies, between the national government and the state government, between the state government and local govern-

---

[19] *U.S. Commission on Intergovernmental Relations,* Final Report (*Washington, D.C.,* 1955), *pp. 4, 36, 38, 56, 58.*

ments. Private interest groups are a part of the picture, for their influence on the formal holders of governmental power depends very much on the range of public and private interests to which officeholders in the political system must be responsive. Unless politics broadens the base of responsiveness, officials will respond too readily to the few interests whose agents lease hotel rooms at the capital for the duration of each legislative session.

The politics of state government is something we do not know enough about. Official commissions studying governmental reorganization and like problems write reports that pay their respects to "good government" and are studiedly quiet about the political process that contributes to or detracts from the opportunities for good government. Yet no responsible student could write an analysis of the United States government or the British government without attention to the two-party system, nor could he write about the French or Italian government without attention to the multiparty system.

A number of states, not all of them in the South, do not have a two-party system in state politics. For such states, factional and largely personal warfare at primaries and conventions is more significant than two-party warfare at the final elections. Perhaps those who would improve state government should concern themselves more with how decisions are made within a party than with the final election.

If the two-party system promotes responsibility, one might devote thought to what conditions would foster development of such a system where it does not exist and to how such conditions might be established. Many states have what is widely accepted as a two-party system, but in fact "anything goes." Neither party has a consistent orientation on policy, neither has a satisfactory way of deciding what that orientation should be if one is desired, and neither demands that candidates and officeholders operating under the party label pay attention to and act in accord with the party's policy.

The visibility of state government is low. People are not interested. This may be because state functions are not important (though this proposition cannot stand up under scrutiny), or because state functions are so diverse as not to make up a policy package, or because newspaper reporting is inadequate for maintenance of an informed public, or because some state officials prefer the security of obscurity.

But an even more basic reason may be that the parties do not present the people with a choice of policies. Even though the functions of state government do affect most citizens, if the election of one or the other party is irrelevant to the direction or pace of state activity, indifference by those eligible to vote should occasion no surprise. We may need greater focusing of two-party contests on the power to determine state policies. Otherwise, the parties may simply vie for vividness of candidates. Personal politics is not the avenue to responsible government.

The politics of many local governments has been disinfected, and sterility is often the consequence. Nonpartisan elections are prescribed in many communities, either because local affairs are thought to concern administrative efficiency rather than choice among policies or because well-intentioned civic reformers have obtained legislation reflecting their disdain for politics, parties, and politicians as divisive, self-seeking, and corrupt. If the history of local government provides ample documentation to account for such disdain, there is also persuasive contemporary evidence that nonpartisan elections attract less interest and participation by the citizenry. In other local communities, where the opportunity for two-party rivalry is formally available, the voters are often confronted by a no-choice situation, with a single candidate standing uncontested for an office.

Before "party government" and two-party competition are chosen as a basis for improving the visibility of state and local governments and thus democratizing them by arousing citizen interest and activity, several implications will need to be examined. Does such a choice not mean abandonment of the direct primary and reliance instead on party conventions for the choosing of candidates? This will reduce the chance for ambitious adventurers to vault to leadership of a party. But to what degree will it bring back the boss, whose wings the direct primary and nonpartisan elections were designed to clip? To what extent are conditions sufficiently different from those of the late nineteenth and early twentieth centuries so that party organizations can be expected to behave responsibly?

POLICY MAKING. Lawmaking is central to policy making. Not that there are not other ways of making policy. In some states a considerable amount of policy has been put into the constitution itself, and changes are made by constitutional amendment at every election. In some states particular interest groups, lacking sufficient leverage in the legislature, may get laws adopted directly by the people or may get the people to veto laws passed by the legislature. Some decision making that used to be thought appropriate for the legislature has now been shifted to regulatory commissions and other administrative agencies.

Nonetheless, under the principles of representative government, it is the state legislature that is expected to settle most policy questions. If it is to perform its important role satisfactorily, it needs to be reasonably representative of the public in whose name it acts, responsive to the interests of the community that is the state, and rational in assembling and considering the appropriate facts, opinions, and policy alternatives. As a legislature is a group of men, someone inside or outside the group must take a leadership role. Furthermore, arrangements need to exist for moving the work along at a reasonable pace and for reducing the confusion that many men and many bills can create.

Three questions are especially important to the lawmaking process: (1) Are state legislatures representative? (2) Should the emergence of the governor as legislative leader be welcomed and further encouraged? (3) Can the capacity of the legislature for informed, orderly deliberation be increased? Chapters 8 and 9 examine each of these in detail.

Of the three questions, the first is by all odds the most urgent. Nothing in state government has so justly been condemned as the discrepancy between the pretense to representative government and the fact of deliberate rejection of representative principles. Though urbanization has accentuated the problem, the discrepancy is nothing new. In his *Notes on Virginia*, Thomas Jefferson cited it as one of the "very capital defects" in Virginia's constitution:

> *Among those who share the representation, the shares are very unequal. Thus the county of Warwick, with only one hundred fighting men, has an equal representation with the county of Loudon, which has 1,746. So that every man in Warwick has as much influence in the government as 17 men in Loudon.*[20]

Criticizing the system on the level of principle as Jefferson did is fully justified. But underrepresentation of the majority of the statewide electorate has a practical side as well. The statewide majority is likely to restrict the legislature's power by constitutional amendment, to place greater trust in the governor elected by the statewide majority, to resort frequently to the initiative and referendum and constitutional amendment processes to enact measures unwelcome to the legislative majority. If urban and suburban interests are underrepresented in the state legislature, they are likely to turn to Washington for sympathetic consideration and legislation. These same interests may also be in constant conflict with the state government, which will predictably neglect the welfare of the cities.

If it be agreed that misrepresentative legislatures can be a principal block to the establishment of confidence in state governments, the practi-

---

[20] *Thomas Jefferson*, Notes on Virginia, *William Peden (ed.) (Chapel Hill, N.C.: University of North Carolina Press, 1955), pp. 118f. It should be noted, however, that Jefferson also criticized the degree of homogeneity of membership between the senate and the house of delegates. Pp. 119f.*

cal problems are what to do about it and who can, should, and will do it. As is noted in Chapter 8, it is unreasonable to expect the overthrow of a system by the very beneficiaries of the system—incumbent legislators, the rural and small-town interests, and their few powerful urban and suburban allies. If the legislature should, but cannot, do the job, other instruments of change may be sought. In some states this might be the people, acting through their powers of initiative and referendum, but the record is not an encouraging one. Should the judiciary then move into this "political thicket," as Justice Frankfurter characterized it? The United States Supreme Court has held that, under the Constitution, the judiciary can and must do so in cases appropriately raising representation issues, and the Court has laid down guiding principles for the apportionment of legislative seats. The consequence is that the conditions determining state policy making are undergoing revolutionary change.

The emergence of the governor as leader, where it has occurred, is one of the most important historical developments in state government. His leadership, however, is often exercised principally in setting the agenda for legislative and public discussion and in conducting intricate negotiations with political enemies, for he often lacks majority party support in the legislature. Even if his party is in control of the legislature, it may lack sufficient internal discipline to assure him of support. The strength of the Presidency has resulted in part from the accretion of power exercised in crisis situations, but it also rests on the President's greater attention-getting power with the public and on the clarity of his leadership of his party. Does the infrequency of crisis in state government preclude development of a strong governorship in relation to policy? Are governors doing enough to attract public attention to policy problems? (One governor, it is reported, found the newspapers so resistant to publishing his statements that he had to spend much time "on the road" talking to the people in their towns and villages simply in order to communicate with them.) Why are so few governors the real heads of their parties in the states? Are we electing the kind of governors who care about policy and have zest for leadership?

Legislatures are called "deliberative bodies." Sometimes they seem deliberate beyond their calling. Not infrequently, however, they take so many stitches in time, especially in the rush just before adjournment, that they precipitate sharp public criticism. How can the legislatures be better equipped to do a responsible job, tapping expert knowledge on the subjects before them and drawing fully on the views of interested groups?

ADMINISTRATION. Policy not only must be made. It must be executed. And, completing the circle, both the professionalism and the practical experience of the executing agencies feed back into the policy-making process itself.

The ascendancy of the legislature in state governments, together with the subjection of many administrative officials to popular election, has led to an executive branch without a real head. In 1835, referring to a different phenomenon, Alexis de Tocqueville used words apt for the present purpose: "The executive power of the state is represented by the governor . . . although he enjoys but a portion of its rights." [21]

Administrative organization and management have been given much attention during the past fifty years. This has been true in private business and in each of the levels of government as well. As Chapter 10 makes plain, the problem is not as simple for the state governments as it might at first appear. Nonetheless, the multitude of official and unofficial studies of state administration have hit upon much the same affirmative recommendations. Why, then, has there been such little success in getting their proposals adopted? Why is there such resistance to making the governor a real chief executive? Do we so much distrust the kind of man who sometimes reaches the governorship that we fear, to use Leslie Lipson's phrase, that the renaissance of the governor may not be accompanied by his reformation? [22]

We can easily err if we create a strong chief executive on paper but a weak one in fact. He must not merely sit at the peak of an organizational pyramid; he must have the managerial tools and the personal assistants that will enable him to be effective. If we want this to result in more efficient administration, reorganization must be more than the reshuffling and consolidation of departments at the top; there must be continuing attention to the problem at all levels so that there can be "reorganization in depth."

The man proposed in Chapter 10 as a strong chief executive on the administrative side is the same man who might provide the legislative leadership proposed in Chapter 9 and the political party leadership proposed in Chapter 6. The governor could be all three. How compatible are these roles? Will the governor have the time? and the capacity?

Administration is done by people. The need therefore seems acute for increased effort to attract able people into state service. The need for professionals in many state functions—engineers, social workers, public health doctors, teachers—has already raised the qualitative level of some state services. So too has the national government's requirement that state

---

[21] *Tocqueville,* op. cit., Vol. I, *p.* 88.
[22] *Leslie Lipson,* The American Governor: From Figurehead to Leader (*Chicago: University of Chicago Press, 1939*), *p.* 268.

employees engaged in important nationally aided activities work under a merit system and abstain from political activity. But these more or less externally imposed requirements do not get at the need for state governments themselves to show initiative and concern for getting their fair share of the cream of the classes graduating from educational institutions—many of them state-supported. Nor do they get at the need for the states to make service to the state a rewarding experience. Salaries are but part of the reward. More important to administrative and professional people may be the conviction that they are sharing in important and creative work on behalf of the public interest.

How can the states attract and motivate the best available persons, especially for the key administrative and professional posts that set the tone of state administration?

Administration, finally, is the management of money, other people's money. On the one side, dollars are the common-denominator currency of policy making. Potentially, the annual or biennial budgetary process invites a fresh look at the whole range of a government's policies and activities and a fresh determination of how to allocate the government's resources among these competing demands. Yet in few states is this opportunity really available for more than a fraction of the state's affairs, and where it is, the opportunity may be let go. Why this is so, and its consequences, are part of the analysis presented in Chapter 11. On the other side, dollars are gathered into the state and local treasuries by a variety of taxes. Their just assessment and efficient collection are among the most ancient of governmental responsibilities. Yet so much are these tasks delegated to amateur local assessors and collectors that who you are and where you live may count more than objective standards in determining how much you pay. Some whose pocketbooks are adversely affected may understandably conclude that decentralization carries too high a price.

JUDGING. Few citizens appreciated how substantially the administration of criminal and civil justice is entrusted to state and local courts and police until the assassination of President Kennedy in Dallas—a violation of no federal law and so a matter for the local police and the courts of Texas. Probably, too, few citizens have been disposed to take a hard look at this important sphere of state and local responsibility to find out whether the responsibility is being satisfactorily discharged and to search for ways of improving its institutions and processes. This is no doubt in part because of the mantle of respectability with which we clothe our judges and in part because citizens expect the professional bar to use its specialized knowledge and experience and its heavy representation in state legislatures to institute any needed reforms.

This area of citizen neglect is reviewed in Chapters 12 and 13; the material presented there makes clear that it is imprudent to treat this as a field presenting no serious problems or as one to be left to the professionals. Should some local judges receive no salaries but the fines and fees they collect? Citizens who have been caught in local speed traps may well doubt it, as may inheritors of property that has been greatly reduced in value by the time probate judges and their appointees have performed their "services." Should the probity of judges be assumed, rather than concretely assured, even though in 1965 several justices of a state supreme court were shown to have accepted bribes for a favorable decision? [23] Should each court and each judge be autonomous in scheduling the length of vacations and the load of work—although statistics reveal gross discrepancies in the disposal of cases by different courts and judges in the same state, city, or judicial district? Again, is autonomy the necessary guarantee of "judicial independence," or is there something wrong when the same facts provoke highly discrepant punishments or awards of damages depending upon which judge hears a case?

As these chapters indicate, it is our conviction that political scientists and other concerned citizens need to subject state and local judicial institutions and processes (along with prosecuting arrangements and police activities) to the same kind of scrutiny they have accorded policy-making and administrative spheres of responsibility. In doing so, they will fortunately discover that legal scholars and leaders of the bar have shown increasing concern about these problems and that they are prepared to welcome new "partners in crime."

THE LOCAL LEVEL. The same kinds of processes can be identified in state and in local government, and each process intertwines the two governmental levels. Up to a point it is therefore appropriate and feasible to discuss a process in general terms without regard to particular levels. But this mode of analysis can become cumbersome, and the analysis can lose its sharpness if the different conditioning factors of state government and local government are lightly dismissed. Both a state legislature and a village council are institutions central to "the legislative process," but homogenizing them so as to talk about legislative bodies in general can mislead as much as can the treatment of every policy-making body as a unique case. In each chapter devoted to the various governmental processes we have tried to consider both the process per se and the state-local continuities that create a flow between the levels. When a single focus was

---

[23] *The case involved one sitting justice and two retired justices of the Supreme Court of Oklahoma. Details are given in Chapter 12.*

required, however, that focus has usually been on state government.

There are things that need saying about local governments as such. Not the least important is that local government itself is a rather artificial category, including as it does both counties and municipalities, New York City and the tiniest village, local governments with general powers and a multitude of single-function special districts. General-purpose city governments are organized according to a few basic designs; the consequences of each alternative design are identified in Chapter 14, in which we have also taken a close look at the operation of city councils and related their behavior to different electoral systems.

With the spill-over of urban population from central cities into suburban cities and towns and even villages and rural areas, the governments of counties and small communities acquire a new relevance for the many who work in the city but live outside it. At the same time, this spill-over has posed acute problems of transportation from home to work, whether by commuting train or by highway, and problems of extending "urban services," such as water and electricity supply, sewage systems, fire and police protection, and air-pollution control. If "community" has any meaning in a great metropolitan aggregation, even if its meaning rests merely on the common need for urban services, should it lead to the establishment of a government that embraces the whole metropolitan area? Some students of metropolitan problems think it should, and they have proposed a new level of government that would fit in between a metropolitan area's multitude of local governments and the state government. Yet winning consent for such a dramatic innovation seems even more difficult than constructing a United States of Europe. A fascinating problem of analysis for the student of politics is the development of the strategy and tactics that might persuade, or by-pass, the many little De Gaulles who cherish the autonomy, if not the grandeur, of their local governments so much that they bridle at proposals of metropolitan union. Chapter 15 offers an orientation basic to the pursuit of such an analysis.

THE FUTURE. State and local governments, we have said, are creatures of their past. They are also creators of the future. How ably they will perform in this role depends upon their readiness to make policies responsive to the problems that will emerge and to administer those policies effectively. In the final chapter, we have made an effort to identify some of those problems, many of them simply intensifications of problems already in view, and to appraise the future role of the state and local governments.

chapter 2

☆☆☆☆☆☆☆☆☆

The Heritage of the Eighteenth and Nineteenth Centuries

G overnments, even revolutionary ones, do not spring full-grown from the air like rabbits from a magician's hat. On the contrary, every government has a past that goes far to explain its present and to set bounds of probability to its future development. This, of course, is not to say that governments never change. They do. Sometimes the change is a drastic one —from tyranny to constitutional government, from aristocracy to democracy, from colony to independent nation, from kingdom to empire. But the drama of such great shifts in ideology or systems of government attracts such attention that we are likely to neglect the way in which a long-established political system, like that of the United States, gradually adds and subtracts features that, cumulatively considered, may amount to a redefinition of the system itself.

This historical dimension of a political system eludes us if we attempt a merely contemporaneous description of the institutions and functions of government. Indeed, such a description itself suffers from its inability to distinguish between the merely current phenomena and those that are deeply imbedded in our traditions. Further, a static, still-life photograph of the present loses the explanatory power implicit in the dynamic process by which institutions become different from what they were. There is a danger that well-intentioned advocates of better government who lack the perspective of history will advance neatly rational reform proposals but reveal astonishing naïveté about the strategy and tactics required to displace long-cherished belief systems and long-entrenched holders of political power.

To understand American state and local government then, we need to view it as the product of almost two hundred years of history. The difficulty in taking this long view lies in the fact that history deals with two apparently contradictory tendencies. One tendency is toward stability: some states are still operating under their original eighteenth-century constitutions. The other tendency is toward change: universal suffrage, expansion of the federal government's powers under the Constitution, urbanization of the bulk of the population, and other developments have transformed the dimensions of our political system. These opposite tendencies must nonetheless be accommodated. This can readily be done if we recognize their complementarity, for in fact they express two of the basic requirements for a truly stable system of government. A stable system is not static; it must adapt to new conditions. Its resilience, and so its survival, depends on its capacity to absorb change without losing its fundamental character. Stability, then, is a problem in dynamics. How well American state and local governments have met this problem is a necessary part of our present inquiry.

1. *The Early State Governments* (*1776–1800*)

The Declaration of Independence resulted in the transformation of colonies into self-governing commonwealths. These early state governments expressed the dominant sentiments of the ruling class, reflected colonial experience, and set patterns to be followed or reacted against in the still-to-come Articles of Confederation and the United States Constitution.

Acting upon the advice of the Second Continental Congress, most of the states framed new constitutions. Popular participation in the process was minimal. Framed by the existing legislative assemblies or by revolutionary conventions, these constitutions were not ratified by the people. Massachusetts and New Hampshire were exceptions, and their experience inaugurated the practice of special elections to choose constitutional convention delegates and to ratify proposed constitutions.

The first constitutions embodied great principles that have continued as the foundations of modern American government. Yet for each principle there seemed a contrary one, or at least a qualification in applying it to the real stuff of political life. For the idea of popular government, there was a bill of rights that set limits to what government might do. For the idea of separation of powers, there was the countering commitment to legislative supremacy. For democracy, there were still the restriction of suffrage and the narrowing of eligibility to public office. For freedom of religion, there was the imposition of religious qualifications for voting or office.

POPULAR GOVERNMENT AND INDIVIDUAL RIGHTS. With revolutionary fever engulfing them, eight of the new states adopted bills of rights at the same time that popular government was firmly endorsed. Men were declared "free and equal." The people were named the source of power. The Massachusetts constitution stated clearly, "All power residing originally in the people, and being derived from them, the . . . officers of government . . . are their substitutes and agents, and are at all times accountable to them." What the people had given they might take back. The moral right of revolution argued by the Declaration of Independence became a legal right. Thus the Massachusetts constitution provided, "The people alone have an incontestable, unalienable, and indefeasible right to reform, alter, or totally change" their government.

The bills of rights endorsed the idea of liberty both generally and specifically, and so set bounds to what even the people's governments might do. Trial by jury was held "sacred." Ex post facto laws and bills of attainder were forbidden.[1] Excessive bail, exorbitant fines, and cruel and unusual punishments were prohibited. Freedom of the press was guaranteed. The right to keep a militia was assured. Within fifteen years these and similar provisions were included in the national Constitution's Bill of Rights. At the state, as later at the national, level the principle was established that popular government was also to be limited government.

SEPARATION OF POWERS AND LEGISLATIVE SUPREMACY. Just as the bills of rights either reflected the English heritage or were reactions against abuses recently inflicted upon the colonies, so the structure of the new governments grew out of past experience. The focus of colonial government had been the governor who, in most of the colonies, was appointed by the English king, served at his pleasure, and represented him in the colony. He was commander-in-chief of the armed forces and head of the highest colonial court. He could at least nominate, if not select, the members of his own council, which in some cases served as the upper chamber of the legislature. He could dissolve the assembly and veto its laws.

Having thrown off the yoke of concentrated executive power, a free people were not likely to reinstitute it. Instead, each new state constitution

---

[1] *An ex post facto law retroactively declares a past action, unforbidden at the time of its commission, to be a crime. A bill of attainder is a legislative act punishing a person without a judicial trial.*

either expressly affirmed separation of powers or implicitly provided for it. The Maryland constitution unequivocally proclaimed: "The legislative, executive and judicial powers of government ought to be forever separate and distinct from each other." Five other states were equally precise. In the rest, separation of powers was achieved by the descriptions of legislative, executive, and judicial duties.

In the seven most typical state governments, however, the structure revealed less a practice of separation of powers than a mere profession of it. For the legislature gained the power and prestige that the governor lost. Of such great influence was this departure from the separation of powers theory that as late as 1889 Lord Bryce could observe, "The legislature . . . is so much the strongest force in the several States that we may almost call it the Government and ignore all other authorities." [2] The people had such faith in the legislature that they allowed it to choose the other state officials, including the governor, who was limited to a one-year term and was ineligible for reelection. In only one of these seven states could he veto legislative acts. His appointing and pardoning powers were limited by an executive council also selected by the legislature. Furthermore, the legislature appointed the judges.

Though less typical, New York better serves to illustrate separation of powers and the domestic governmental experience upon which the framers of the United States Constitution could draw. The governor and the lieutenant governor were elected by the people. The governor appointed the other executive officers and the judges, whose service was dependent upon good behavior. The governor and the supreme court judges constituted a council of revision that could examine, revise, and veto legislative acts; but the legislature could overrule the council by a two-thirds vote. The governor commanded the militia, executed the laws, and convened and prorogued the legislature. Most legislators were popularly elected; the lower house, however, chose four members of the upper house. The assembly could impeach, and the senate—sitting with the supreme court—could convict, any executive or judicial officer.

LIMITED DEMOCRACY. While some state governments had the trappings of modern democracies, to call them democracies is to err. In pre-Revolutionary days, suffrage and officeholding were restricted by both property and religious qualifications. During the Revolution, the constitutions of several states liberalized the suffrage. Some reduced the landholdings required, others substituted a tax-paying requirement for the property

---

[2] James Bryce, The American Commonwealth, *new edition* (New York: Macmillan, 1921), *Vol. I, p.* 534.

one, and Vermont gave the vote to "all adult males who would take the Freeman's Oath." Meanwhile, suffrage was broadened in the cities, as some were converted from "close corporations," in whose governance only members could participate, to public municipal corporations. One leading authority holds that the Revolutionary era was the most important in the history of American suffrage, because it "committed the country to a democratic suffrage" in the future.[3] Nevertheless, universal manhood suffrage took almost two centuries to develop.

To implement the prevailing theory that both the commonalty and the aristocracy of wealth should be represented in a legislature, all states except one adopted the bicameral system before 1800. Members of the upper house usually had to meet higher property qualifications than members of the lower house. To keep the system intact, most states provided that a man must own more property to vote for candidates for the upper house than he need own to vote for members of the lower house. In North Carolina, for example, all taxpayers might vote for members of the "house of commons," but only the owners of 50 acres or more were eligible to vote for the senate members.

Although the philosophical concept of liberty espoused by the revolutionaries was broad enough to include liberty of conscience, a majority of states fixed religious qualifications for voting and officeholding that were not relaxed completely until 1810. Thus, Pennsylvania and Rhode Island allowed only members of Christian sects to vote, Massachusetts required that all popularly elected state officials profess their belief in Christianity, and New Hampshire permitted only Protestants to hold office.

CITIES, TOWNS, AND COUNTIES. In 1790, when the first national census was taken, 95 percent of the people lived in rural areas, rather than in urban centers. It was the patterns of rural government, therefore, that had greatest significance. For our purposes they have a further significance: perhaps more than any other level of present-day government, our counties and towns continue to bear the weight of the dead hand of the past. Indeed, with the clustering of population in tighter knots that usually is called urbanization, forms of government designed for a rural, scattered population are forced to deal with kinds of problems never contemplated by their designers.

The patterns of early rural governance were three, each differing from the others because of the character of the original settlers and the conditions under which they lived. In New England, the town predominated.

---

[3] *Chilton Williamson*, American Suffrage from Property to Democracy, 1760–1860 (*Princeton, N.J.: Princeton University Press*, 1960), *p.* 116.

The settlers, bound together by church, by common pasture, and by the need for protection against hostile Indians, fixed the size of a town according to the time and ease of reaching the common center. A town, in the New England sense, was not then and is not now simply a closely settled community (as is the usage of the term elsewhere); it includes rural areas and typically abuts similar neighboring towns with the result that the whole of a state's area may be accounted for by the towns. Nonetheless, the size of the town was small enough to enable all its inhabitants to get to the town meetings in good weather—but the meetings were sometimes "sparsely attended." This popular assembly legislated town policy, elected its own moderator, and chose its own selectmen to administer affairs between town meetings. In Massachusetts during the 1770's and 1780's, at least, town meetings "were usually time-consuming, sometimes corrupt, and from time to time controlled by small groups of men." [4]

In the South, the county predominated. Here, in a subtropical climate where the Indians were peaceful, the pattern of large landed estates manned by slaves resulted in a dispersion of population, rather than a concentration. To include several estates, counties had to be larger than towns. Government was in the hands of former English gentry, or their immediate descendants, who had the time, recognized the obligation, and knew well the English system of county or "shire" government, itself rooted deep in Anglo-Saxon times. The power of the county was vested in the Court of Justices, formerly appointed by the governor, but now elected at-large. The court appointed all other officers.

The third pattern, prevalent in the Middle States, was a combination of the first two and less clear-cut than either. The county and the township shared responsibility in varying degrees. In New York, for example, an elective county board of town supervisors directed county activities, but each supervisor had administrative responsibilities in his own town as well. Town boards had some fiscal and regulatory powers and controlled roads and poor relief. In contrast, Pennsylvania elected county boards, but the townships were merely administrative units without local functions of their own and were not represented at the county level. [5]

Not only did these three patterns of local government persist on the eastern seaboard, but in the nineteenth century, pioneers moving westward carried forms of local government in their baggage. Even today the varying emphases among the states on county, township, and mixed systems of

---

[4] David Syrett, "Town Meeting Politics in Massachusetts, 1776–1786," William and Mary Quarterly, 3rd series, XXI (July 1964), 365.

[5] Paul W. Wager (ed.), County Government Across the Nation (Chapel Hill, N.C.: University of North Carolina Press, 1950), pp. 5ff.

government are a historical deposit substantially accounted for by the differing origins of the early settlers.

City government in the late eighteenth century was of concern to only a small part of the American population. Though about two dozen munici-palities were incorporated, only six cities had populations of more than 8,000 persons. As the colonies became states, they acquired the power to grant and to change municipal charters. City governments were replicas in miniature of state governments, whose own practice of separation of powers, we have seen, was distant from the theory. Typically an elected, all-powerful municipal council appointed a mayor and a recorder (a type of legal adviser) for one-year terms. In contrast to the state legislature, the city council was unicameral.

To sum up, between 1776 and 1800 the states adopted new constitu-tions without great popular participation. These new constitutions ex-pressed commitment to popular government and to protection of individ-ual political rights; to separation of powers and to legislative supremacy; to democracy and to property and religious limitations on the franchise and officeholding. At the local level the varying colonial patterns of rural government persisted, and the few cities centered power in elected coun-cils.

Perhaps the most significant heritage from this period was that of the powerful legislature and weak executive. The combination typified most of the state and local governments and was repeated at the national level during the period of the Revolution and the Articles of Confederation. The delegates to the national Constitutional Convention in 1787 reacted against these precedents and followed more closely the example of the three states characterized by the most completely developed separation of powers. In turn, the national Constitution, with its provision for a strong President, greatly influenced the three states admitted to the Union in the 1790's. In the long run, however, the tradition of a weak governor, some-times coupled with a weak rather than a strong legislature, was to persist for well over a century. How much this contrasted with the national pattern is suggested by worldwide use of the phrase "presidential system of government" to refer to our kind of national government and foreign imitations of it.

2. The Democratic Reorientation (1800–1860)

The pattern of social change is so complex and historians' tastes so diverse that the explanation of historical trends is a hazardous business at best. It is convenient to speak of Jeffersonian and Jacksonian democracy. But to do so is to attribute perhaps inordinate weight to the contemporary influence of two individuals, whose own views and actions as well as those of their supporters may be wanting in perfect consistency. What one historian calls "The Age of Jackson" another may call "The Age of Egalitarianism" and offer persuasive evidence that the two are not at all the same thing.[6]

Whatever the terms we choose, the fact is that the first half of the nineteenth century witnessed a significant democratization of American government. The reader will know, however, that apart from widening the suffrage, the specific measures that express democratization are likely to vary considerably. Is the people's power greater with a strong national government or with strong state governments? with a strong legislature or with a balancing of powers? with a strong chief executive or with popular election of many executive officials? Then, as now, opinions differed.

In 1800 the Federalists, so instrumental in framing the Constitution and in creating a strong central government, were defeated at the polls. Thomas Jefferson, the successful leader of the Democrat-Republicans, carried his supporters to victory in most states. The democratic thrust thereby initiated was to be given new vigor by Andrew Jackson's election to the Presidency in 1828, the intervening and continuing extension of the western frontier, and the growth of the urban laboring classes.

DECLINE OF THE LEGISLATURE. Jefferson feared concentration of power, wherever it might be found. In commenting upon the first constitution of Virginia, he noted:

> All the powers of government, legislative, executive, and judiciary, result to the legislative body. The concentrating these in the same hands is precisely the definition of despotic government. It will be no alleviation that these powers will be exercised by a plurality of hands, and not by a single one. 173 despots [i.e., legislators] would surely be as oppressive as one.[7]

Yet, as late as 1831, when he visited the United States, Alexis de Tocqueville concluded, "In America the legislature of each state is supreme; nothing can impede its authority. . . . In juxtaposition with it, and under its immediate control, is the representative of the executive power. . . ."[8]

---

[6] Arthur M. Schlesinger, Jr., The Age of Jackson (New York: Mentor Books, 1949); and Lee Benson, The Concept of Jacksonian Democracy; New York as a Test Case (Princeton, N.J.: Princeton University Press, 1961).

[7] Thomas Jefferson, Notes on the State of Virginia, William Peden (ed.) (Chapel Hill, N.C.: University of North Carolina Press, 1955), p. 120.

[8] Alexis de Tocqueville, Democracy in America, Henry Reeve (trans.), Phillips Bradley (ed.) (New York: Vintage Books, 1954), Vol. I, p. 91.

One obvious way to reduce the evil that legislatures can do is to reduce the occasions and duration of their meetings. So, at the same time when legislators' terms of office came to be extended from the original one year to two or four years (often varying between the upper and lower houses), the states that drafted or revised their constitutions took the prudent step of limiting regular legislative sessions to one every two years. Minnesota, entering the Union in 1858, inaugurated the practice of limiting the length of this biennial regular session to 60 days. The then prevailing belief that the less often a legislature meets the less harm it can do is one that tenaciously preserves itself. Unanswered during the Jacksonian heyday—and unanswered now—is how a legislature can efficiently solve urgent and complicated problems when it meets for only 60 days every two years.

In a democracy it would seem more natural to seek cure of legislative evils by guaranteeing the people a determining role in the making and revising of constitutions; broadening the franchise if it is narrow so that the term "the people" means what it says; and assuring that the legislature claiming to speak for the people in lawmaking is truly their representative. Such efforts to democratize control of the state legislature were indeed undertaken. The practice of submitting a revised constitution to the people for ratification became widespread, and the constitutions of seven of the nine states achieving statehood between 1828 and 1860 provided for it. A second step to popularize constitutional amendment and revision was taken by a number of states: They made it mandatory for the legislature to submit to the people the question of whether to call a constitutional convention. In a few states the legislature had to submit the question to the people at periodic intervals; in others the choice of appropriate time was left to legislative discretion.

The suffrage was slowly broadened as inflation and thus rising values diminished the effects of property qualifications for voting and as the states began abandoning them. Pennsylvania had entered statehood without such a requirement, and four other states were rid of theirs by 1800. But it was 1856 before the other eight of the original thirteen states had taken like action (see Figure 2.1). In the meantime, the broad franchise principle was fully accepted by all but one of the states that entered the Union after 1790. In some states, however, abandonment of the property restriction left standing, or occasioned the introduction of, a requirement that only taxpayers could vote.

When direct democracy is not feasible, the representativeness of the legislature is a critical factor in maintenance of the democratic principle. Though perfect legislative representativeness is probably not practical, the departure from even a reasonable standard is likely to be greatest when people are on the move. For in such periods the disparity between old apportionment patterns and current facts becomes most obvious. In the first half of the nineteenth century changing settlement patterns resulted in legislative underrepresentation of the hinterland of the older states. The problem was more acute in the southern states, since the slave-holding aristocracy was concentrated in the coastal areas and the non-slave-holding common people were spread about the interior. Accordingly, the new state

Figure 2.1. *Duration of Property and Taxpaying Qualifications for Voting, 1776 to 1863*

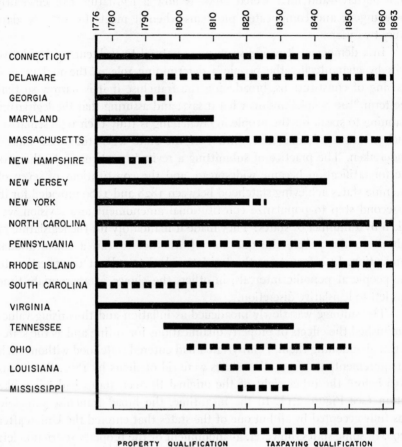

Note: After Mississippi in 1817, no state entered the Union with a property or taxpaying qualification. Vermont, Kentucky, and Indiana, which had entered earlier, had neither qualification.

SOURCE: Kirk H. Porter, *A History of Suffrage in the United States* (Chicago: University of Chicago Press, 1918), p. 110.

constitutions provided more equitable representation in the legislature or directed the legislature to reapportion itself at periodic intervals. Even so, the results of these reapportionments were never quite satisfactory to the frontier.

Strengthening the people's role did not satisfy those who distrusted the legislature. The more direct expression of distrust was the actual limitation of the legislature's power. The newer states, particularly, adopted the practice of incorporating in the constitution specific prohibitions that went beyond the traditional bills of rights—a practice whose appeal is testified to by many a state constitution still in use. In the early nineteenth century the new constitutional prohibitions were mainly in three groups: The legislatures were prohibited from chartering any bank except a state bank; their power over divorce was limited to general, as distinguished from special, acts; and they were prohibited from raising the salaries of the major state officials.

This limiting device came into more extensive use as the century moved to the halfway mark. Some states had failed in their attempts to provide adequate internal improvements; some had repudiated their debts; the panic of 1837 wreaked havoc. Financial restrictions on legislative discretion were consequently written into state constitutions. These limited state indebtedness (e.g., Maine to $300,000, Maryland to $100,000), prescribed the purposes for which debt might be incurred, set limits on the tax rate, and earmarked revenue from a specific tax for a special purpose. Most state constitutions now forbade the establishment of lotteries and specified how corporations might be chartered. Some legislatures were confined to the passage of general corporation laws rather than special legislation accommodating particular applicants. Others could grant individual charters only under stated conditions; Delaware, for example, limited the duration of a charter to twenty years and made the grant in each case dependent on a two-thirds vote in each house of the legislature.

STRENGTHENING AND WEAKENING THE CHIEF EXECUTIVE. On no other issue of state government have the American people equivocated so much as on that of the role to be played by the governor. If the legislature is too powerful or performs its functions poorly, one remedy is to strengthen the governor. But we have always feared placing great power in the hands of one man lest his character be unworthy of such trust and lest his very possession of such power enable him to subvert the formal controls established to restrain the executive. It is not surprising, then, that we may in the same historical period both increase and reduce his powers, seek both to assure his independence and to institute new controls on that independence. Because the problem is a basic one, the same ambivalence is to be found in concepts of the proper role of the mayor or other local chief executive.

The governor's role was strengthened in a number of ways in the first half of the nineteenth century. Abandoning the original constitutions' provision for his election by the legislature, the states converted his mandate to a popular one deriving from direct election by the people. His term of office was changed from one year to two, three, or (rarely) four years. Where at first only two states had given him a veto power over acts of the legislature, many others now gave him this power—though the legislature in many states could override it by a majority, rather than a two-thirds, vote. Constitutional restrictions on reelection were relaxed. Finally, a governor's independence was slightly reenforced by the requirement of an extraordinary majority to convict him on impeachment charges.

Yet the governor was the chief executive in a formal rather than a real sense. While he came to be directly elected by the people and thereby grew to be an important political leader, he was not really head of the executive branch. Initially the legislature retained the power to choose other executive officers, such as the treasurer, secretary of state, and attorney general. Then these officers, too, became popularly elected, and various states went even further, asking the people to choose the state printer, surveyor-general, auditor, superintendent of public instruction, or board of public works. In New York, despite its having been something of a model for the framers of the national Constitution, executive power became probably the most diffused of that in any state; by 1846 twelve minor offices were filled by election.[9]

The passion for electing executive officers reigned in local government as well. In 1834, for example, Tennessee counties elected their clerks, sheriffs, trustees, and registrars. Counties in other states copied the pattern. Newly admitted states followed suit. California, upon entering the Union in 1850, immediately established counties with a plethora of officers: "sheriff, district attorney, treasurer, assessor, clerk, surveyor, and constables —all elective."[10] In New England, the town meeting chose not only the selectmen, but also the assessor, collector, constable, town clerk, treasurer, overseers of the poor, school committeemen, road surveyors, and a number of other officers.[11]

---

[9] *Leslie Lipson*, The American Governor: From Figurehead to Leader (*Chicago: University of Chicago Press, 1939*), *p. 21.*

[10] *John A. Fairlie and Charles M. Kneier*, County Government and Administration (*New York: The Century Co., 1930*), *p. 31.*

[11] *Tocqueville, op. cit., pp. 63f.*

The cities in this era not only conformed to the trend of popularly electing their officials, but also drove further along the path of administrative disintegration, which later broadened into the road toward bossism. The mayoralty had been converted from election by councilmen to popular election. Furthermore, it had begun to acquire veto and appointive powers. Possibly the tendency for city councils to become bicameral, in thoughtless aping of their state and national counterparts, also enhanced the role of the mayor. But in cities, as elsewhere, the spread of popular elections to other offices counteracted these negative gestures. In San Francisco, for example, the citizens in 1852 elected the mayor, collector, treasurer, comptroller, recorder, street commissioner, attorney, marshal, and three assessors.[12] Not satisfied with simply electing the municipal department heads, cities by 1860 were further diffusing executive authority by replacing these department heads with multimember boards.[13]

In the decade prior to the Civil War, state legislators also acted to reduce the mayor's ability to govern effectively. Utilizing their authority to pass special legislation, they withdrew from the city the authority to perform, for example, health or police activities. Then they created special commissions, under the legislature's or the governor's supervision, to carry out these functions within the municipality. Municipal government was hydra-headed.

It is anomalous that the same forces stimulated both the growth of the governor's political power and the decline of the governor's and the mayor's administrative power. For the minor executive officers, converted into direct representatives of the people, were in a position to ignore the instructions of the chief executive—if, indeed, he ventured to give any.

DEMOCRATIZATION OF THE JUDICIARY. Legislative omnipotence at the state, as at the national, level was further curtailed as the courts asserted and used the power to declare legislative acts unconstitutional, and so invalid. Even before the United States Supreme Court's famous decision in *Marbury* v. *Madison* (1803),[14] some state courts had declared that certain state laws were in violation of the applicable state constitutions. But John Marshall's notable opinion served to bolster the authority of state judges. In most states at that time the judges needed any bolstering they could get, for they were elected by the legislature and in some states had fixed terms, sometimes of only a year. Where the term was

---

[12] *Thomas H. Reed and Paul Webbink* (eds.), Documents Illustrative of American Municipal Government (*New York: The Century Co.*, 1926), *pp.* 103–10.
[13] *Frank J. Goodnow*, Municipal Government (*New York: The Century Co.*, 1910), *p. 168.*
[14] 1 *Cranch* 137.

"during good behavior" and conviction on charges of impeachment was the only way to remove a judge, the judiciary was viewed dubiously by those supporting the wave of democratization of state government. The compromise struck was widespread adoption of popular election of judges coupled with the fixing of longer terms of office than those for legislators and executive officials; seven- and eight-year terms were common in a range from five to fifteen years. At the local level the justices of the peace and judges heading probate, magistrate's, and police courts also tended to become elective, but their terms were considerably shorter than those of district and supreme court justices.

DEVELOPMENT OF POLITICAL ORGANIZATIONS AND PARTIES. The fading away of the Federalist party after the Jeffersonian victories of 1800 led to a disarray in which factions and groups are more appropriate terms of reference than parties. Jefferson and his Democratic-Republican party, however, did not become so dominant without conscious use of methods that fit the standard repertoire of American political behavior. Jefferson himself, and his leaders in state governments, retained much of the inherited Hamiltonian system, sought to win over Federalist party supporters by moderate policies, and tried to convert others by judicious distribution of patronage.[15] Jefferson wrote Dupont de Nemours, ". . . we can never get rid of [Hamilton's] financial system. . . . What is practicable must often control what is pure theory." A principal form of patronage was the granting of charters to local banks by state legislatures, and Republican legislatures proceeded to capitalize on bankers' self-interest. As Jefferson wrote his Secretary of the Treasury, Albert Gallatin,

> It is certainly for the public good to keep all the banks competitors for our favors by a judicious distribution of them and thus to engage the individuals who belong to them in support of the reformed order of things or at least in an acquiescence under it.

Another form of patronage, still today an often well-hidden phase of state government, is the depositing of public funds in selected banks sometimes without requirement that interest be paid the government. Jefferson wrote that he was "decidedly in favor of making all the banks Republican by sharing deposits among them in proportion to the disposition they show."

As the Federalists lost the power of effective opposition, factions

---

[15] *The interpretation and the quotations from Jefferson's letters are from Richard Hofstadter*, The American Political Tradition and the Men Who Made It (*New York: Knopf*, 1948), *pp. 34–36.*

developed within Jefferson's Republican party, and the one obtaining control of a state government proceeded realistically to punish the other's adherents and build up a political organization. In New York in the first decade of the century, for example, De Witt Clinton, as a member of the council of appointment, was able to use patronage to control the caucuses that made local and state nominations. By the time of the 1821 Constitutional Convention, however, the faction headed by Martin Van Buren was in the ascendant. Van Buren believed that control of locally influential posts, such as the office of justice of the peace, was most important to a tight organization and that an order from his governing council in Albany "should be obeyed right down to the last officeholder in the smallest hamlet of New York." [16] In control of the state government after the election of 1822, the Van Buren group dismissed De Witt Clinton from the Canal Board, maintained close control of New York's role in national politics by preventing restoration of the people's right to choose presidential electors, and generally used state power to strengthen the "Albany Regency"—but not enough, for Clinton's People's party triumphed in 1824.[17]

The People's party, holding its first state convention in Utica in 1824, inaugurated the American practice of nominating candidates by conventions for which delegates are chosen in formally prescribed ways. Earlier, most nominations for state and local, as well as national, office had been made by legislative caucus, an informal group of party legislators. This widespread practice partially yielded to a convention system, particularly at the county level in the Middle States. There, because of the pattern of rural government, each township could serve as a unit for the choice of delegates to a county convention, a method seemingly unlikely to mature in the South, where the township was almost unknown and aristocratic control customary, or in New England, where the county had no electoral function. The first statewide nominating conventions were held in New Jersey and Delaware, probably as early as 1804. Those states not only had appropriate rural governmental organization but also were geographically small enough to make meeting on common ground relatively easy.[18] More generally, the displacement of caucus by convention at the state level was consequent on the extension of suffrage and direct election of the gover-

[16] Robert V. Remini, Martin Van Buren and the Making of the Democratic Party (*New York: Columbia University Press*, 1959), *p. 8.*

[17] *Our references to the New York experience are mostly drawn from Lee Benson,* op. cit.

[18] M. Ostrogorski, Democracy and the Organization of Political Parties (*New York: Macmillan*, 1902), *Vol. II, pp. 50ff.*

nor. At first the delegates were self-appointed, but the 1824 New York People's party convention regularized the choice of delegates, and by the 1830's the delegate convention prevailed everywhere except in the South. Finally, in 1831, the Anti-Masonic party held the first of America's national party conventions.

Proliferation of state and local elective offices and growth of the national spoils system strengthened political organization and made possible its abuse. It was New York's political careerist, William Marcy, who first said, "To the victor belong the spoils," and it was Andrew Jackson who made "rotation in office" in the civil service a democratic dogma as well as a political convenience. United States senators, chosen at the time by state legislatures themselves, were often under the control of the political organization and on its behalf could influence senatorial confirmation of presidential appointments to federal positions within the states.

With the growth of strong political organizations, candidates became dependent on them not only for nomination, but also for the effective conduct of election campaigns. Loyalty to the organization by those in public office thus became a requisite for renomination, reelection, and the holding of remunerative appointments. The "political machine" was well on its way to maturity. In New York, Thurlow Weed, who as early as the 1820's was a campaign manager opposing Van Buren's Albany Regency, had become by 1839 the "dictator" of the Whig party (the antecedent of the Republican party that emerged nationally in 1856).

ECONOMIC AND SOCIAL ACTIVITIES. Democratization and egalitarianism overlap, but are open to different interpretations. Both democracy and equality may be treated simply as legal principles, applicable to the formal electoral and judicial processes. Their meanings for the substance of what government does, what policies of regulation and service it adopts, are therefore extended. The equality of men can be taken to mean that each is entitled to an equal opportunity to get as much of the world's goods and purchasable privileges as his industry, talents, and ingenuity permit—even if others must therefore get less. Democracy, by strengthening the many against the few, has often been understood to imply not only equality of opportunity at the start but moderation of inequalities at the finish. Between the Revolution and the Civil War, Americans disputed over these substantive meanings, and the dispute has yet to be resolved.

Intensive state regulation of economic affairs had been characteristic of England's mercantile system. The American colonists had not attacked the system but only its use to colonial disadvantage. Once independent, the American states continued the familiar system—fixing prices for transportation services, regulating innkeepers and peddlers, building and operating turnpikes, and licensing businesses through the issuance of charters. After 1800 the Virginia Dynasty in Washington argued that states' rights justified federal refusal of much-needed assistance to the states for internal improvements. But the state governments proceeded to invest in transportation improvements and other enterprises. The Missouri constitution of 1820 accurately expressed the temper of the times. It read: "Internal improvement shall forever be encouraged by the government of this State, and it shall be the duty of the general assembly, as soon as may be, to make provision by law for ascertaining the most proper objects of improvement. . . ." Meantime, the older states had acted. New York constructed the greatest internal improvement of the times: 400 miles of the Erie Canal. Pennsylvania, primarily through the device of "mixed corporations" jointly owned by the state and private interests, invested heavily in banks and transportation companies. In the 1820's, bank dividends were its principal source of revenue. In 1825, the state held approximately $4½ million in the stocks of mixed corporations—mainly in banks and turnpike companies, but also in bridge and canal ventures. Apart from the financial profit to the state government, the mixed-corporation device enabled the state to guide private funds into enterprises that the economy and the people needed, and it permitted the state, as co-owner, to regulate corporate activity. By the time of the Civil War, however, most states had sold both their investments in mixed corporations and their public works. Massachusetts, financially unable to invest so freely in new enterprises, used its charter-granting power as a means to encourage those banks, factories, and bridge, canal, and insurance companies that appeared of greatest public usefulness.

As time passed, corporate charters granted by state governments conferred fewer prerogatives and contained more restrictions. The boards of directors were limited in size, powers, term, and method of selection. Issuance of stock and bank notes was regulated in detail. Insurance companies faced rules limiting their risks and determining their modes of investment. Transportation charters either specified maximum rates or provided formulas for their determination. If the regulatory provisions were stricter, their enforcement was often ineffective; they were not self-executing, and the legislative investigating committees then customarily charged with their administration neither met often enough nor were expert enough. Effective or not, the state enactments of the first half of the nineteenth century contradict any impressions that America's early tradition was one

of laissez-faire economics and a public policy of governmental noninter-
vention.[19]

In the field of social, as distinguished from economic, affairs no area of
state and local activity has been more basic than education for the effectiveness of American democracy. Nonetheless, the growth of free public
education lagged considerably behind recognition of the need by Thomas
Jefferson and others well before 1800. In 1782, for example, Governor
Clinton of New York urged, "It is the peculiar duty of the government of a
free state, where the highest employments are open to citizens of every
rank, to endeavor by the establishment of schools and seminaries to diffuse
that degree of literature which is necessary to the due discharge of public
trusts." Congress, in the Northwest Ordinance of 1787, declared, "Religion
and morality and knowledge being necessary to *good government* and the
happiness of mankind, schools and means of education shall forever be
encouraged." [20]

In fact, the national government proved at first to be more dedicated
to the cause of education than the state and local governments. Not only
did Congress press its views in the Northwest Ordinance, but beginning
with Ohio's statehood, Congress made it a condition of admission to the
Union that the sixteenth section of every township should be set aside as a
source of support for common schools. And in 1836–38, when the federal
government was embarrassed by a surplus of revenues (!) and transferred
it to the several states, most of the money was spent on education.

The states in their turn proved more concerned with education than
local electorates. As one writer nicely puts it, "With numerous exceptions,
local public opinion at the beginning of the century needed a large amount
of rousing to the support of the schools." This rousing was undertaken by
leaders of the states, but rousing was not merely exhortation: state subsi-

---

[19] *Much of this account of the states' economic role draws on Oscar Handlin and
Mary F. Handlin,* Commonwealth, A Study of the Role of Government in the American
Economy: Massachusetts, 1774–1861 (New York: New York University Press, 1947);
and Louis Hartz, Economic Policy and Democratic Thought: Pennsylvania, 1776–1860
(Cambridge, Mass.: Harvard University Press, 1948). *Doubters may also wish to review*
Milton Sydney Heath, Constructive Liberalism: The Role of the State in Economic
Development in Georgia to 1860 (Cambridge, Mass.: Harvard University Press, 1954);
James Neal Primm, Economic Policy in the Development of a Western State, Missouri,
1820–1860 (Cambridge, Mass.: Harvard University Press, 1954); Carter Goodrich,
Government Promotion of American Canals and Railroads, 1800–1890 (New York:
Columbia University Press, 1960); *and Carter Goodrich (ed.),* Canals and American
Economic Development (New York: Columbia University Press, 1961).

[20] *Quoted in Ernest S. Griffith,* The Modern Development of City Government in
the United Kingdom and the United States (London: Oxford University Press, 1927),
Vol. I, pp. 13f.

dies were used to induce a majority of voters in a local community to put up money of their own for free public schools. Except in the South, such school systems were widespread by 1850, and the cities were well advanced toward autonomous support of their schools from municipal revenues. State grants-in-aid, therefore, were focused more and more on encouraging rural districts to provide public schooling and on equalizing financial support among communities with varying economic resources.[21]

State and local governments acknowledged in other ways the obligation of government to serve its people both as a community and as individuals. Public sewers and public street lighting were common early in the century. In 1823, Boston built an almshouse and shortly thereafter a municipal hospital. Special schools for the deaf and dumb were provided by state governments. In 1847, Massachusetts became the first state to have a state institution for delinquent boys. Insane asylums were founded in 20 states. Imprisonment for debt had been made illegal. These examples illustrate a situation that led one commentator to speak of "the first half-century after the Revolution [as] the dawn of a more scientific and more humane age," in which prevention as well as after-the-fact relief, social responsibility as well as individual guilt, began to be accepted.[22] But it was only the dawn. The meridian still lay ahead.

SUMMARY, 1800–1860. Whatever name we choose for the first half of the nineteenth century, the consistent theme is democratization. The fact that increasing the people's share in government also weakened the people's representative body, the legislature, is one of those anomalies that enriches the theme by counterpoint harmony. It is explicable not so much in logical terms as in the historical circumstance that the powerful early legislatures had lost public confidence. Given this circumstance, it was indeed "logical" for the people to reduce the frequency and length of legislative sessions; to insist on popular participation in the revising and amending of constitutions; to extend the franchise and urge fair apportionment of legislative seats; to use the constitution to tell the legislature what it could no longer do; to make the governor a more powerful rival of the legislature by making him the people's choice, by extending his term, and by arming him with the veto power.

Democratization had impulses other than disciplining the legislature. It was natural, though not necessarily prudent, for the people to carry their

---

[21] Ibid., *pp.* 14–16.

[22] *Arthur N. Holcombe,* State Government in the United States, *3rd edition (New York: Macmillan, 1935), pp. 382f.*

Figure 2.2. Dates of Admission of States to the Union

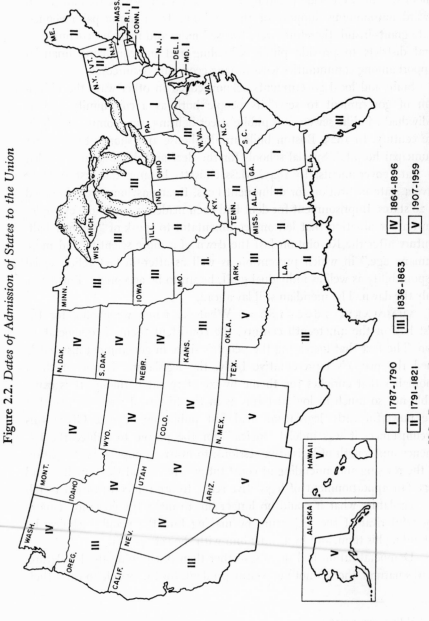

| | 1787-1790 | | III | 1836-1863 | IV | 1864-1896 |
| | 1791-1821 | | | | V | 1907-1959 |

SOURCE: U.S. Bureau of the Census, *Statistical Abstract of the United States: 1965* (Washington, D.C., 1965), p. 168.

enthusiasm for democratization over to direct popular election to every office in sight. So, a number of state executive officials became popularly elective and, as a perhaps unintended consequence, independent of the governor's direction; at both state and local levels the elective system spread to relatively minor and specialized positions. Election of judges for fixed terms also followed naturally, though its implications for judges' behavior on the bench may not have been fully weighed. A large electorate calls for a different kind of politics than an electorate restricted to the gentry and other propertyholders. By the time of Jackson's Presidency, no political faction in such a state as New York could doubt that a broadened electorate had to be appealed to in populist terms of the common man's interest or that victory required a political organization nurtured by judicious distribution of favors.

Democratization of ends was a consequence of democratization of means. Adam Smith's *Wealth of Nations*, published in the year of American independence, failed to persuade the American states to adopt a hands-off attitude toward economic affairs or to neglect collective ways of ameliorating the distress and illiteracy of the less well-to-do.

3. *Plunder and Governmental Response* (1860–1900)

The Civil War is the great watershed of American history. It made clear the direction in which American federalism was to move. It led to adoption of the first constitutional amendments of major import since the Bill of Rights, and two of them, primarily aimed at the states, remain in the 1960's at the center of legal and political disputation. The organization of the modern Republican party, which initiated the present two-party system, took place only four years before Lincoln's election. Lincoln's own administration set strong lines for national action in such economic and social affairs as the building of the transcontinental railroad, homesteading in the West, and the development of state colleges—all three subsidized by federal land grants. In the states and in the local communities, as in the nation generally, the post-Civil War period was marked by excesses of freebooting entrepreneurs and political spoilsmen that led to constitutional, statutory, and judicial restraints designed to protect the victims of what seemed an age of greed, grab, and gain.

The Fourteenth and Fifteenth Amendments bear on such different developments of the period to follow that their provisions need consideration before we proceed further. Along with the Thirteenth Amendment, which forbade slavery and involuntary servitude, these provisions were the only additions to the Constitution in the hundred years or so between 1804 and 1913. The Radical Republicans, dominant in Congress, required the southern states to ratify the Fourteenth and Fifteenth Amendments as a prerequisite to resuming participation in national affairs. Though both amendments were designed primarily to secure the rights of the Negroes freed by the Thirteenth Amendment, they eventually acquired much broader significance as limitations on state and local governments.

The Fourteenth Amendment defines United States citizenship so as to cover all persons born or naturalized in this country and subject to its jurisdiction, requires that state citizenship automatically apply to all United States citizens in their states, and prohibits the states from abridging the privileges and immunities of United States citizens. The clause, "No State shall . . . deny to any person within its jurisdiction the equal protection of the laws," is the provision most frequently used since to strike down racial discrimination by state and local governments. The clause that judicial interpretation converted into the broadest control over state and local power to determine economic and social policies reads, "Nor shall any State deprive any person of life, liberty, or property, without due process of law." The principal clause of the Fifteenth Amendment reads, "The right of citizens of the United States to vote shall not be denied or abridged by the United States or by any State on account of race, color, or previous condition of servitude."

The Fourteenth and Fifteenth Amendments each concluded with a provision that the Congress shall have power to enforce the amendment by appropriate legislation. Both amendments, of course, are enforceable against the states through the federal and state courts, under the courts' power to review state actions challenged on grounds of constitutionality. But, in addition, the national Congress is specifically empowered to legislate so as to bring to bear the force of the federal government in support of the amendments' policies on citizenship, equal protection of the laws, due process of law, and the right to vote.

SOUTHERN STATES AND THE NEGROES. Constitutionally assured of the right to vote, an assurance given substance for some years by the Freedmen's Bureau and the Union army, the freed Negroes voted. They voted mostly for carpetbaggers from the North or for other freedmen. In the seven states that had been restored to the Union by 1868, four governors and ten United States senators were men who had never seen "their" states before the war.

The southern state legislatures were models of contemporary impropriety. Uneducated, irresponsible ex-slaves and carpetbaggers transferred the taxpayers' money to their own pockets. The North Carolina legislature is said to have spent about $40,000 in two years on stationery—partly for the use of men who could not write. Newspapers favoring the incumbents were given state printing contracts at exorbitant rates and then were paid two to three times what their contracts called for. In Louisiana the average cost of a legislative session prior to Reconstruction was about $100,000, but the 1871 session cost nearly $1,000,000. Greed, incompetence, and sheer ignorance led to wild financial speculation by the legislatures. In 1872, eleven southern states had a combined debt of $130,000,000, most of which had been spent for loans and guaranties to wildcat railroad companies. Individual gain was a prime objective. Claude Bowers records that a party boss in Georgia used state money to buy himself a partnership in a railroad car company.[23] He then had the state buy cars from his company—cars that he never bothered to deliver.

With the withdrawal of the national troops, the influence of the Ku Klux Klan grew, and the southern whites gained control. The Fifteenth Amendment became more myth than reality. No longer could the southern Negro vote. Until the last decade of the nineteenth century, the southern states deprived the Negro of his vote either by threat of physical violence or by chicanery. A Ku Klux Klan warning sign at the polls was often sufficient. Only polling places a great distance from Negro residential areas were used. Or, in slightly more sophisticated fashion, the polling places would be moved without notice on election eve. The whites also negated the effect of the Negro vote by the simple device of stuffing the ballot boxes. The more refined techniques came later.

FARMERS, CORPORATIONS, LEGISLATURES, AND COURTS. A great economic revolution in the last half of the nineteenth century sharpened antagonisms between farmers and entrepreneurs and between the East and the West. Enterprising financiers and manufacturers found powerful forms of organization, and the farmers and their allies organized against them. State legislatures and state and federal courts were inevitably drawn into the battle.

The partnership form of business enterprise was unable to mobilize the quantities of capital required for building large steel mills and great railroads—a task for which the corporate form was ideally designed. Under the states' general incorporation acts the number of corporations multi-

---

[23] *Claude Bowers*, The Tragic Era: The Revolution after Lincoln (*Boston: Hough-ton-Mifflin*, 1929), *p.* 301.

plied, and when opportunity offered, corporations merged. Railroad corporations, partially financed by state governments as well as by brokerage houses and unsuspecting farmers, sold watered stock with ease. But the process of assembling money for enterprise was not without cost. When Jay Cooke and Company failed, the foundations of an overexpanded credit began to crumble. In 1873, five thousand firms failed, sustaining a total loss of about $225 million.

When the system worked, it benefited those with money to invest. But those on farms found themselves at the mercy of the marketplace, of processing firms, of the railroads that carried farm products, and of the manufacturers whose goods were sold to farmers. While between 1860 and 1890 the value of American manufactures and railroad mileage in operation quintupled, the value of all farm property only doubled. In a crisis such as the collapse of 1873, the Iowa farmer was burning his corn because it was cheaper than fuel; he could sell it for only 15 cents a bushel, though in the East corn was retailing for a dollar a bushel. There is little wonder that the farmer could talk of the "railroad robbers" and demand cheaper transportation for his products and reduced charges by the middlemen.

The Granger laws, which fixed rates and otherwise regulated railroads, were the result of this discontent. Illinois led the way, and Minnesota, Iowa, and Wisconsin quickly followed suit. Soon 25 states had adopted laws partially patterned after those of the Midwest pioneers. Typically the laws established state railroad commissions. Some, like that of Massachusetts, were weakly empowered to investigate the physical and financial condition of railroads and recommend, but not compel, maximum rates. Others, like that of Illinois, had strong statutes and strong commissions. The statute in such a state described in detail the bans on rate discrimination between different persons or between different routes of the same length. The commission was also authorized to determine maximum rates. The existence of discriminatory rates and the charging of higher rates than those fixed by the commission were statutorily declared to be prima-facie evidence of violation of the law. The commission could sue in the name of the state to enforce its regulations.

The railroads and other regulated middlemen resorted to a variety of ways to make the laws ineffective. One of the ways that did not work—at first—was to challenge the constitutionality of these significant incursions of the state governments into "private" economic affairs. In 1877, at the height of the farmers' Granger movement, the United States Supreme Court decided the case of *Munn v. Illinois*,[24] which turned on the constitu-

---

[24] 94 U.S. 113.

tionality of an Illinois Granger law establishing maximum charges for the storage of grain. The granary companies argued that the law violated the Fourteenth Amendment's guarantee against their being deprived by a state of "life, liberty, or property without due process of law." The Supreme Court disagreed. It pointed out that, historically, businesses "clothed with a public interest" had been regulated. A granary was such a business, and the state could regulate its rates. Further, "people must resort to the polls, not to the courts" to correct legislative action of which they disapprove.

The pattern had been established by the case of *Munn* v. *Illinois*. As the railroad regulatory laws reached the Supreme Court, they too were declared constitutional. If granaries and railroads were clothed with a public interest, what was not? The path ahead seemed clear: States might continue to regulate the business activities that affected their citizens. What seemed a clear path in the 1870's and 1880's, however, proved a dead end before 1900.

The principal clauses of the Fourteenth Amendment are designed to protect any *person* against the kinds of state actions listed. In 1886 the Supreme Court ruled that a corporation is a "person," even though an artificial one.[25] The consequence ever since has been that the great number of business enterprises organized as corporations have had standing to sue in courts and ask for the invalidation of state laws alleged to deny them "equal protection of the laws" or to deprive them "of life, liberty, or property without due process of law." What remained was to get the courts to find that state regulatory laws or state commission actions setting rates were indeed denying or depriving the corporations of these rights. First the "property" and then the "liberty" of these artificial persons were found to be imperiled.

In 1890 the Supreme Court ruled that the states could not permit a state commission finally to determine the reasonableness of railroad rates without appeal to the courts.[26] It was but a step for the Court in *Smyth* v. *Ames* to hold that such rates must be reasonable,[27] not arbitrary. If the rates were arbitrary, the states were taking "property" without due process of law. And what was "reasonable" rather than "arbitrary" was for the courts to decide, because it was now a constitutional question.

This doctrine was extended to the word "liberty" of the Fourteenth Amendment in the case of *Allgeyer* v. *Louisiana*.[28] Here the Supreme

---

[25] Santa Clara County v. Southern Pacific Railway Co., 118 *U.S.* 394.
[26] Chicago, Minneapolis and St. Paul Railroad Co. v. Minnesota, 134 *U.S.* 418 (1890).
[27] 169 *U.S.* 466 (1898).
[28] 165 *U.S.* 578 (1897).

Court overthrew a state law providing that Louisiana firms could purchase insurance contracts only from insurance companies regulated under Louisiana laws. Such a restriction, held the Court, interfered with a firm's liberty to contract with whomsoever it pleased.

In these momentous decisions, the Supreme Court overthrew centuries of law. The phrase "due process of law" is directly derived from the phrase "law of the land" in the Magna Carta. Since 1791, the Fifth Amendment of the Bill of Rights had provided that the national government might not deprive any person of life, liberty, or property without due process of law. Until these cases of the late nineteenth century, however, corporations had not been considered persons. And the phrase "due process of law" had meant only procedure; it had had nothing to do with the substance of the law.

By these decisions, however, the Supreme Court had given substantive content to due process of law. It placed itself in the position of being arbiter of the economic and social wisdom of state laws, for to apply a test of "reasonableness" to a policy opens a range of discretion that pits legislators and judges against each other in deciding "what's best." Since the state legislatures and the Supreme Court often made different value judgments, the due process clause greatly restricted the permissible area of state activity, which was also diminished by the Court's broadening interpretation of the interstate commerce clause. In 1887 the first national regulatory commission, the Interstate Commerce Commission, had been established to regulate rail and water transport, and state regulatory orders had to yield when they conflicted with ICC orders.

The rise of the corporation and of adventurous users of this instrument for the amassing of fortunes had provoked farmers and other "little men" of the country to form the Granger movement and then the Populist party, through which state legislatures were persuaded to enact a notable series of regulatory laws. In the end, though, the corporations found their protectors in the judiciary. Christened by the courts as "persons" and assured that any state regulatory law or order could be challenged in the courts as "unreasonable," the corporations ended the century in a confident mood, despite a continued barrage against them in legislative halls and on electoral stumps. (The Sherman Anti-Trust Act had passed Congress in 1890; William Jennings Bryan had been nominated for the Presidency in 1896 by a Democratic convention aroused by his impassioned attack on the gold standard; even the Republican Vice President elected in 1900, Theodore Roosevelt, was to emerge as a "trust-buster" President.)

THE WELFARE STATE. Though the fiction of legal personality protected corporations, it was their impersonality in pursuit of profits that often had intolerable consequences for real persons—whether customers or adult workers or children. At the same time that state and local governments faced the human problems of industrialization and economic interdependence, they found that the growth of cities and towns, fed by the inflow of aliens and native factory workers, presented problems of congested living that only governments could solve.

Part of the impetus for governmental concern with factory conditions was provided by the trade union movement, which sometimes obtained support from the powerful farmers' movement. The American Federation of Labor, organized in 1886, supplanted the earlier Knights of Labor. State labor legislation of the period had a strong orientation toward health and safety, rather than toward the economic problems of working people. Thus, factory owners were required to protect workers against fire, explosion, hazardous machinery, and insanitary conditions—an addition to costs for the factory owner and a benefit to its workers. Most of the manufacturing states limited the daily working hours in factories to ten for women and children.

The line between regulation and service by the state is a thin one. Agriculture, for example, was aided by state governments by such means as licensing of weighers of grain, regulation of the use of fences, collection of agricultural statistics, and distribution of seeds. In 1862 the federal government had established its own Department of Agriculture, primarily for the distribution of seeds and the conduct of research.

The art of medicine had become the science of medicine, and preventive health measures became more common. In 1869, Massachusetts established the first state board of health with general authority. Encouraged by the American Public Health Association, formed in 1872, other states rapidly followed the Massachusetts lead. These first state boards collected health statistics and either supervised or "encouraged" the activities of local boards of health. However, in such a state as Illinois, the state board had authority to inspect sanitary facilities in tenements and lodging houses; in cities of 50,000 or more, it could reject all building plans not having adequate provisions for sanitation. In Pennsylvania, the board of health could "afford inducements and facilities for general and gratuitous vaccination." In the cities, however, public health facilities were not brought to a reasonable level until the 1890's. Purity of water supply and disposition of wastes, for example, were both poorly provided for.

Public education grew apace. Total educational expenditures rose from about $70 million in 1870 to about $250 million in 1901–2, representing a 70 percent per capita and a 50 percent per pupil increase. The 160 public high schools of 1870 multiplied to 6,000 at the turn of the century.

Night schools, municipal normal schools, and kindergartens were begun. Libraries grew in number.

Welfare activities expanded, and the general character of this state service became recognized as the various separate state institutions were brought under state boards of welfare. Massachusetts established a board of state charities in 1863. Within twenty years, 11 other states, mostly eastern states with immigration problems, had adopted the plan which, by 1900, had become common. Collecting statistics, investigating the causes of welfare problems, and usually supervising the state institutions, such boards symbolized a developing social conscience about society's unfortunates and misfits.[29]

DIFFUSION OF GOVERNMENTAL POWER. In both state and local governments the executive power continued to be widely distributed. At the state level the awakening social conscience and the pressures of interested groups led to the establishment of many commissions and boards that were substantially independent of the governor's control. Boards for railroad regulation, agriculture, health, welfare, and a variety of more particularized concerns—plumbing, forests, fisheries, livestock—were set up by legislatures indisposed to increase the powers of the governor. So some members of some boards were elected by the legislature, others were elected by the people, and still others were appointed by the governor subject to legislative concurrence. Such supervision as was attempted was generally through the unsatisfactory medium of legislative committees. The total effect, as Lord Bryce observed it, was that "Little remains to the Governor except his veto, which is not so much an executive as a legislative function. . . . [He] has little to do, and comparatively small sums to handle." [30]

The veto, however, did strengthen the governor's legislative role. In the 1870's, many states in the North and West authorized the governor to veto any single item in an appropriation bill without having to veto the entire bill. The item veto gave the governor greater control over the budgetary process, greater indeed than the President is accorded under the Constitution.

The mayor, it is true, began to gain executive power during the 1880's and 1890's. He benefited from a decline in public confidence in the city

---

[29] *Details given on movement toward the welfare state in this period are drawn principally from Griffith, op. cit., pp. 75–107; and Schuyler C. Wallace, State Administrative Supervision over Cities in the United States (New York: Columbia University Press, 1928), passim.*

[30] *James Bryce, op. cit., pp. 531f.*

council, from the discovery that a multiplicity of independent administrative boards responded inadequately to the problems besetting the city,
and from a tendency to look to the national government as a guiding
model (there was even a brief resurgence of bicameral city councils). The
mayor now generally acquired the veto power over acts of the council
(subject to being overridden by a two-thirds vote), was allowed a larger
role in the choice of administrative officials, and was given more direct
administrative authority over police, health, and street departments, especially.[31]

Nevertheless, the cities, however well they might be organized, found
their power over municipal affairs was far from comprehensive. State
legislatures interfered with what in retrospect seems gay abandon: The
Pennsylvania legislature appointed a state commission to build Philadelphia's city hall; a Florida state commission governed Key West for two
years; the Alabama legislature abolished Mobile, and the Tennessee legislature, not to be outdone, abolished Memphis.[32] While these individual
interventions by states are not exceptional, the period also saw the beginnings of constitutional restrictions on special legislation by the states; of
legislative classification of cities into groups according to population, with
each group being given a type of city government appropriate to its
category; and even of home rule provisions according to which each city
could choose among several forms of city government or, in the case of
four states as of 1900, write their own municipal charters.

POLITICS AS BUSINESS. In an era when so much was for sale,
it is perhaps not surprising that government itself was often purchasable.
And in an era when the advantage of corporate monopoly over small
farmers, businessmen, and consumers was so apparent, the rise of the
"machine" and "boss" to consolidate political control is also not unexpected. The rise, though, is to be credited partly to peculiarities of American government. Our government as a whole was divided among three
levels; it was distributed at the lower levels among some two-score states
and hundreds of counties, cities, and towns; it was separated within each
government into legislative, executive, and judicial branches; within the
respective branches it was divided between two legislative chambers and a
series of legislative committees, distributed among a multitude of elected
executives and boards coordinate with the chief executive, and allocated to
a variety of courts that, in the politically sensitive criminal case area, could

---

[31] *Griffith*, op. cit., *pp. 107–22.*
[32] Ibid., *p. 107; and Charles R. Adrian,* Governing Urban America: Structure,
Politics, and Administration *(New York: McGraw-Hill, 1955), p. 53.*

be activated only by locally based police departments and prosecuting attorneys. Fragmentation of the official machinery of government seemed to beg for someone who could put Humpty Dumpty together again. It was the political machine and the boss that put the pieces together and, in the process, attached the strings that made Humpty Dumpty a puppet.

The first requirement, of course, was that the political organization should have the kind of unity that was so obviously lacking in government itself. Such unity was the consequence of Jacksonian democracy, with its abandonment of nominations by legislative caucus or formless assemblage in favor of the convention system with apportioned and formally designated delegates. The result was an integrated organization capable of "governing"—a system that cities, counties, and states lacked, either singly or collectively. In the party, precinct conventions chose delegates to county conventions. County conventions then chose delegates to state conventions. And the state conventions chose delegates to national conventions. Alongside each of these temporary organizations and in direct hierarchical order grew the party's permanent organization of committees and officers at each level. The machinery thus lay ready for capture and exploitation by the entrepreneurs of politics.

Other elements were at hand for completion of the picture. On the one side was a moneyed clientele seeking favors from government and especially concerned lest the developing regulatory and service state be too active in putting public interest above private gain. Here, then, was a market for the private sale of assurances of governmental action and inaction. To make these assurances marketable, however, legislators, judges, governors, mayors, police officers, and licensing officials would need to be made responsive to the boss's instructions. Obviously, the key to such responsiveness was control of appointments, elections, and of course the nominating conventions themselves. In the larger cities, especially, the great influx of immigrants and the growth of the poor in the tenements gave the boss and his precinct workers the manageable electorate they needed. Their votes could be won with kindness—getting a son out of trouble with the police, giving a basket of food at Christmas, providing minor jobs in the civil service or in cooperating sweatshops, interpreting for foreigners in an English-speaking environment, and above all, personal interest.

The base of political power was therefore local, and the rewards built on that base were substantial. Illustrative of the scale of local looting was the building and furnishing of the New York County Court House, completed in 1871 at a cost of $8 million as against the estimate of

$350,000 when it was designed. William Marcy Tweed, the boss of Tammany Hall, Mayor A. Oakey ("O.K.") Hall, Controller Richard ("Slippery Dick") Connolly, and Peter ("Brains") Sweeney are said to have devised a system of padded bills that helps to explain the disparity in estimated and actual cost. At least transcripts of payments that *The New York Times* discovered and published that year showed a carpenter "earning" $360,000 for one month's work and a plasterer, $2.9 million for nine months' work; forty chairs and three tables had cost $180,000, *repairs* for fixtures of the unfinished building cost $1.2 million, and the cost of carpets, shades, and curtains came to $675,000.[33]

Local political power interlocked with state government as local machines formed alliances or as one city machine gained dominance at the state level as well. Tammany's "Boss" Tweed fought for control of the state Democratic organization at the same time that he was vigorously milking the city's treasury. At the century's end, the "Gas Ring" of Philadelphia and Matthew Quay, boss of the Republican state machine in Pennsylvania, were not strangers. Men like Senator Platt of New York, controlling various state offices through domination of the state nominating conventions, managed to control the state legislatures both through election of sufficient members and through manipulation of the selection of presiding officers and committee chairmen. Such men controlled national as well as state patronage. With so much to offer the corporations, they also controlled the party campaign funds, which were largely fed by contributions from those corporations. If the vested interests did not volunteer gifts to legislators and political bosses, it was simply good sense for the neglected politicians to introduce legislation unfavorable to those interests, not with the intent of passing it, but with the intent of collecting a reward for not passing it. Such bald blackmail, however, declined as bosses developed more "responsible" ways of profiting from their powerful positions.

Somehow, despite the growth of this travesty of democracy, popular revulsion was able to get modestly corrective measures adopted in some of the states. Laws were adopted to regulate the nominating process, for example, by prescribing the time for choosing convention delegates, the size of the polling place, the nature of the ballot boxes, and the counting of the returns. Some states provided an available alternative for the nomin-

---

[33] *The courthouse, however, was not shoddily built. With its four-foot-thick walls, glass dome, and stained-glass windows, it was still in use in the 1960's. Details of the scandal are from* The New York Times, *March 26, 1961, Section I, p. 59.*

ating convention—the direct primary—but it was not often used. Kentucky in 1888, then Massachusetts, adopted the Australian ballot—a public ballot containing the names of all candidates that can be obtained only at the polls and that is marked in secrecy. Within ten years the other states had followed Kentucky's lead. The suffrage was extended to women for school elections in fourteen states and for all elections in four states. These, however, were scarcely adequate answers to the challenge of bossism.

SUMMARY, 1860–1900. The last half of the nineteenth century is probably the least attractive and at the same time the most modern period between American independence and 1900. The machinery of government was, for the most part, that of the original state constitutions, whether of the original 13 states or of the states admitted to the Union in the nineteenth century. Such modifications as had occurred reflected a broadening of the electorate and a distrust of both legislatures and chief executives. As the great business corporations rose alongside government, their respective powers, and particularly their respective capacities to mobilize power for a given objective, proved disproportionate. The very expansion of government's role in economic regulation and social service brought an interlocking of the two power structures that accentuated the difficulties of making the public interest and a high standard of public morality prevail. No government lives uninfluenced by its environment. But local and state governments in this period seemed more the victims than the masters of their environment. Only when popular protest movements became organized and found leaders and zealous followings—as with the Granger and Populist movements and some indignant reformist movements for the Australian ballot, civil service, and the like—was it possible to restore government, briefly or in certain segments, to the people.

chapter 3

Half of Our Century

To the man or woman who was about 20 years old in the 1960's, the period before the First World War seems ancient history; the interwar period seems an odd pair of decades, 1920–30 one of indifferent idling, and 1930–40 of vigorous tackling of depression-born problems whose sinewy resistance to being bested may surprise those born "too late"; even the 1940–50 period seems more distant than it is—a period with such curiosities as our counting Russia a staunch ally and Germany and Japan hateful enemies, American monopoly of the atomic bomb, a remarkable military mobilization and the greatest governmental regulation of the economy in our history, followed by drastic reconversion of both to peacetime levels (only in the early 1950's were the Korean conflict and the Cold War to reverse the military budget trend). Nonetheless, the first half of the present century necessarily has helped to set the course of the second half. In the area of our immediate concern here—that of state and local affairs —it preserved, altered, or rejected tendencies carried over from the nineteenth century, and it introduced innovative ideas and practices that we in our turn may preserve, alter, or reject.

1. *Mistrust and Reform* (*1900–1920*)

Prior to 1900, a few people knew that some state and local governments were corrupt. Ten years later, every man on the street knew the full extent of this depravity. Chiefly credited for this public knowledge were "the muckrakers," like Lincoln Steffens,[1] who wrote for the popular magazines. They exposed the practices of commercial government and made invisible government visible.

The main thrust of attack was directed toward the power accumulated by those who financed and controlled great corporations and toward their abuse of this power by corruption of governments as well as by individual and collective actions deemed unfair to suppliers, competitors, and customers. The Progressive movement sought to bring governmental power into the service of the people against excessive accumulation of private power and against specific abuses by those who had private power. This meant a double attack. First, American governments had to be rescued from corrupt control by private interests. Second, as the people regained control of their governments, laws needed to be passed—to conserve natural resources against predatory exploiters, to protect consumers against impure food and drugs, to prohibit child labor, to limit hours of work (in 1900 the manufacturing industries' workers averaged 62 hours per week!),[2] to break up monopolies and combinations in restraint of trade, to ban unfair methods of competition, and to strengthen regulation of railroad rates and of discriminatory practices.

POLITICAL REFORM. To the reformers of the Progressive era, governments could not serve the people well until the people had thrown out the political bosses, razed the political party structure that fostered local and state political corruption, and restricted business interests' ability to buy elections, policies, and contracts from governments. The cure for the ills of democracy was a mixture of more democracy, more efficiency, and above all, less politics. Elections without politics, politics without politicians, and a kind of antiseptic, impartial administration were the goals. Today the do-gooders of that era are patronized as overly simple in their diagnoses and prescriptions for the body politic. To view it in perspective, however, we must recall that they were reacting against scandalous excesses that brought the American democratic experiment to its lowest level. It was not unnatural for them to look around for a devil (much as "Wall Street" or J. P. Morgan served to symbolize "the interests" to be attacked by new regulatory laws) and to choose the politician and the political party as the most visible satans to be exorcised from

---

[1] See his The Shame of the Cities (New York: McClure, Phillips & Co., 1904), and Autobiography of Lincoln Steffens (New York: Harcourt, 1931).

[2] U.S. Bureau of the Census, Historical Statistics of the United States, Colonial Times to 1957 (Washington, D.C., 1960), Series D 593, p. 91.

American democracy. Furthermore, we must also acknowledge the degree to which many of their reform proposals were accepted and continue to this day as well-institutionalized parts of our governmental structure and practice. Others of their proposals remain articles of faith for present-day citizen groups that seek to improve American state and local government.[3]

The direct primary—a nominating election in which registered voters cast official ballots at the polls to determine party nominees for public office—was one of the first results of the attempt to crush boss rule and one-party politics. Convention nominations, which by now were regulated by state laws, were criticized for excluding all but professional politicians from participation in party nominations, for creating in party candidates a sense of responsibility to the boss that they carried over into public office when elected, and for enabling special interests to dominate government by buying the bosses' favor.

First used in Crawford County, Pennsylvania, the direct primary was authorized by local party rules as early as 1868. Gradually, mostly in the southern states, the idea grew, and by the turn of the century a number of states had laws permitting the optional use of direct primary elections for state as well as local officials.

In 1903 Wisconsin, under the leadership of Robert M. La Follette, became the first state to adopt a statewide, mandatory direct primary law, and the movement soon became widespread. Now the voters instead of the bosses, it was argued, would decide their parties' candidates.

The nonpartisan primary—wherein no party affiliation appears on the ballot and the two candidates with the greatest number of votes run against each other in the general election—also, it was argued, tended to restrict the all-encompassing control of the boss. California since 1913 has required the nonpartisan primary to be used for judicial, school, township, county, and municipal offices. The system was first used to make municipal nominations, but by 1920, fourteen states adopted it to nominate state judges.

Further to permit the voter a meaningful selection of public officials without either "boss" or political influence, systems of preferential voting were introduced to elect members of city councils. The Hare system of proportional representation, which has received most attention, was first adopted in the United States by Ashtabula, Ohio, in 1915; within five years, four other cities had adopted it. Under this system, the ballot contains no

---

[3] *A useful outline of some of the reform proposals and the reform movement is provided by one of its most prominent leaders, Richard S. Childs, in his* Civic Victories: The Story of an Unfinished Revolution (*New York: Harper, 1952*).

party labels and all council members are elected at-large, rather than by wards or districts; the need for a primary election is eliminated. Entitled to a single transferable vote, the voter may indicate his first, second, and as many other choices as there are candidates. An electoral quota, based on the number of valid ballots cast and the number of positions to be filled, is determined. Candidates whose first-choice votes supply them with the quota are declared elected. The winning candidates' surplus votes—those above the quota—are then transferred to other candidates in accordance with the second choice indicated on the surplus ballots, and so on, until all seats on the council have been filled.

Still other methods were devised during this era to diminish boss influence and to prevent elections from being bought. Corrupt practices acts set maximum expenditures for candidates, limited the objects for which they might legally spend money, and required reporting of expenses. Corporations were forbidden to contribute to political campaigns. So strong was this movement to restrict the influence of money on elections that in 1907 Theodore Roosevelt recommended to Congress in a presidential message that it provide money "for the proper and legitimate expenses"[4] of the national parties. Initially the idea took hold, and in 1909 Colorado appropriated public funds for the campaign use of candidates, though this law was later declared unconstitutional. Oregon and Wisconsin partially financed the publication of official campaign bulletins.

Part of the boss's ability to manage his state had been due to his control of national as well as state patronage. The boss had controlled the state legislature, and the state legislature had chosen the United States senators. Senators of the President's party had exercised their privilege of senatorial courtesy—obtaining or threatening Senate rejection of appointments to federal jobs in their states—and thus the boss had had his way.

But, typical of our traditions, a countervailing trend that was finally to cut this web of power had begun. United States senatorial candidates had begun to canvass the public in their own behalf and in behalf of those state legislative candidates favoring their senatorial candidacies.[5] This system was most widely used after the turn of the century and threatened this one aspect of boss rule. In 1904, Oregon allowed the voter to indicate his preference directly for United States senator at the same election at which state legislators were chosen. By 1911, three-fourths of the states used this system, and the state legislatures usually selected the people's choice. In

[4] Congressional Record, *December 3, 1907, p. 78.*
[5] *William H. Riker, "The Senate and American Federalism,"* American Political Science Review, XLIX (June 1955), 452ff.

1913, the Seventeenth Amendment to the national Constitution was adopted, and popular election of senators was made universal.

Still another amendment broadened popular control of government. The Nineteenth Amendment, adopted in 1920, forbade the states to deny women equal suffrage with men, and hopes were aroused that this in itself would have a purifying effect on political life. Universal suffrage had now become the legal rule, but it was not necessarily followed, for the southern states had erected barriers to the effective political participation of the Negro. After all, the Southern Bourbon argued, politics had to become the lily-white monopoly it was in ante-bellum days. Thus, by manipulation of party rules, he excluded the Negro from participation in party primary elections. Upon the assumption that the Negro was more migratory than the white, residence requirements for voting were lengthened. Presentation of a poll-tax receipt before entrance to the voting booth was required. Before a person might vote in Alabama, he had to own either 40 acres of land or other real estate with an assessed value of $300. Literacy tests required a voter to read and write an article of the Constitution.

The Fifteenth Amendment did not prevent most of these practices, since they applied to all persons, regardless of color. They disenfranchised the poor, uneducated white, however, as well as the Negro. To discriminate in favor of the poor white, "grandfather clauses" were introduced; they permitted a person to vote if his grandfather had voted, even if he could not meet the other tests. And, of course, most grandfathers had been either free, voting whites or nonvoting Negro slaves.

The turn of the century brought even further developments in the people's fight for self-government. Within 20 years, initiative, referendum, and recall were adopted in some form by 21 states. Recall—a special election held at the request of a stated number or percentage of voters to decide whether a public official shall be removed from office—was first adopted by Los Angeles in 1903. It found ready favor, and by 1926 it was available to voters of about 1,500 cities.[6] Oregon applied it to state officials in 1908, and by 1920 nine other states—mostly western ones—had followed suit. In these days, recall was not simply adopted. It was used. Popular government was here, and the people were taking advantage of it. In California alone, 76 efforts to remove public officials were made before 1920.[7]

---

[6] Leonard D. White, Trends in Public Administration (New York: McGraw-Hill, 1933), p. 225.

[7] Ibid., p. 227, drawing from Frederick L. Bird and Frances M. Ryan, The Recall of Public Officers (New York: Macmillan, 1930), p. 346.

At first used only for the removal of elected executive officers, recall was later applied by some states to appointive officers. As a result of unfavorable judicial decisions on economic and social questions, eight states extended recall to judges. Historically, the terms of state judges had now passed through several stages: life tenure, long term, short term, and —finally because of recall—uncertain term.

The initiative and the referendum grew together. The referendum— the process of referring a proposition to the people for their acceptance or rejection—took many forms. For the purpose of adopting constitutional amendments, it had a long history. Furthermore, constitutions had previously required the submission of specific issues—such as an increase in state debt or the issuance of a public utility franchise—to the voters for approval. The referendum had also been used by some cities to approve their charters and to test informally the people's wishes on current controversial issues.

The noncompulsory or optional referendum, whereby a legislative body not legally compelled to do so may submit a measure to popular vote or whereby the people by public petition may require that an existing measure be submitted to a popular vote, now grew in favor. Both it and the initiative were provided for in San Francisco's charter of 1898. By 1920 the optional referendum was available in 22 states. In these, the process could be used for the approval of ordinary, as well as constitutional, measures. The people themselves now had the means to negate laws adopted by their representatives.

While the referendum provided the people with a negative voice, the initiative enabled them to draft their own constitutional amendments and laws. Once drafted and tentatively approved by a percentage of voters on a petition, the measure introduced had to be approved by the appropriate legislative body or be submitted for approval to the vote of the electorate.

The popularization of local government went even further. Home rule —the authority of a local government to frame, adopt, and amend a charter providing for both its structure and functions, but subject to the constitution and general laws of the state—grew in favor. By 1920, constitutional home rule was available to some municipalities (usually the most populated ones) in 13 states, and home rule by legislative grant was available in 6 other states. Collectively, home rule, initiative, referendum, and recall provided the people with power, but these provisions for popular government at the same time took responsibility from elected officials— thus producing a not always happy mixture of direct democracy and representative government.

This objection applies with less force to the people's role in the amendment and revision of state constitutions. During the two decades between 1900 and 1920, approximately 1,500 constitutional amendments were proposed and 900 adopted.[8] In addition, about one-fourth of the states held constitutional conventions, but only 8 adopted new constitutions. As a result, most constitutions remained antiquated. In 1920, for example, 18 of the states had not held constitutional conventions for the previous 40 years.

EXPERTNESS AND ADMINISTRATIVE EFFICIENCY. Three developments of the period illustrate the confusion among those who sought good government. These are the growth of the merit system for state and local employees, the multiplication of independent boards and commissions in state governments, and the strengthening of the local chief executive. Mixed objectives explain part of the confusion. A negative objective was to keep politics out of administration; a positive objective was to increase administrative efficiency. The two combined to suggest the neutralization of administration, but this suggestion had to rest on an assumption that government can really be divided into two distinct compartments—policy and administration. While politics was appropriate for policy making (preferably, to be sure, a nonpartisan and unbossed politics), efficient organization and procedures were thought to be the whole of good administration.

The difficulty of so neat a dichotomy was unwittingly underlined by another source of confusion—the choice of models upon which to base reform proposals. Some reformers were strong admirers of the British government, with its strong cabinet both exercising legislative leadership and heading the executive branch. The British civil service, based upon recruitment by merit and having a top administrative class recruited from Oxford and Cambridge elite, was particularly admired (though America lacked the class structure of England and, in fact, developed a substantially different civil service system). Some reformers, despite the anti-corporation spirit of the Progressive movement, were much impressed by the way American business concerns organized themselves and developed staffs and procedures geared to the objective of cost-saving efficiency; this partly reflected the contemporaneous development in industry of the scientific management movement oriented to discovering and applying "the one best way" of performing any operation. One thing seemed clear from the

---

[8] *Albert L. Sturm*, Methods of State Constitutional Reform (*Ann Arbor, Mich.: University of Michigan Press, 1954*) *provides the best account of the amendment and revision of state constitutions.*

business analogy: the board of directors made policy, but administration was put in the hands of a responsible chief executive. So, whether the British government or the American business concern was chosen as the model, the reformers were likely to think of a strong chief executive, responsible to, but also providing leadership for, the policy-making body; an executive who directed the administrative agencies but operated through top-level administrators chosen for their capacity to ensure efficiency in operations. This attitude fitted the reform movement's broad goal of depoliticizing government's administrative work; destroying the patronage on which political parties, machines, and bosses depended; and assuring citizens an impartial, objective treatment when they had dealings with the government. How to reconcile this broad goal with the fact that governors and mayors were politicians as well was a bedeviling problem for the reformers.

Garfield's assassination by a disappointed office seeker in 1881 had spurred the intellectual drive for civil service reform and had led to the establishment of a civil service system in the national government, in New York, and in Massachusetts. While the movement among state governments stopped and was not to be revived again for 20 years, its use grew among municipal governments.

Partially as a result of the anti-boss sentiment and partially as a result of the recognition that government jobs were becoming more complicated and more specialized, 11 states, 10 counties, and some 200 municipalities had civil service commissions by 1920.[9] The notable feature of civil service reform was the independent status accorded these civil service commissions. Though appointed by the governor, the commissioners were given overlapping terms, so that no one governor could appoint a majority of the members. The very choice of the commission form of organization was intended to ensure that the several members would be checks on one another. Department heads were required to make appointments to positions covered by the civil service law only from a group of candidates certified by the commission as having the highest grades on tests administered by it.[10] The function of the commission was even more to keep out patronage appointments than to put in the most competent people for administrative tasks.

A more positive approach to efficiency, although implicit in the merit

---

[9] White, op. cit., p. 246.

[10] This, of course, is not to say that the system always worked as intended. Civil service commissions could be politicized, legislatures could restrict the number of positions under the merit system, and department heads could devise evasive tactics.

system for public employees, was wide acknowledgment that the age of specialization had arrived and that specialists' facts and judgments needed to be brought into the mainstream of policy and administration. Governments had for half a century and more been leaders in research in the natural and physical sciences. Now they saw that a rational approach to their own problems required the aid of the social sciences. In Wisconsin, the state university became virtually a fourth department of government. Robert La Follette sat in the university seminars and learned the latest economic facts and theories from Wisconsin's specialists. Professors drew upon their expert knowledge to draft legislation. And to execute these laws Governor La Follette appointed many of the same professor-specialists as state officials.[11]

Effective research in government had begun. The New York Bureau of Municipal Research was founded in 1906, and fourteen years later some 25 cities, counties, and states had followed the pattern.[12] Such research bureaus studied governmental systems, pointed out their defects, and pressed for improvement. State universities also began to create special units to provide government with research facilities and to train public servants. Governmental units and public officers formed organizations to help themselves. Thus by 1920, 17 states had leagues of municipalities, and the Governors' Conference and the International City Managers Association were established.

If the executives required scientific help, the legislators needed it no less. While the legislatures were no longer attempting to determine all details of regulation, they still needed technical knowledge to set the standards that the new administrative agencies were to apply. By 1920, three-fourths of the states had followed the "Wisconsin idea" and established some type of legislative reference bureau to provide systematized and analyzed information as an effective basis for legislation.

For all the talk of administrative efficiency, the reformers were torn among three contrary ideas. Distrust of the governor—inescapably a politician—led to the multiplication of little administrative kingdoms in the executive branch, typically commissions and boards insulated against direct gubernatorial influence by plurality of members, bipartisan membership, and overlapping terms. The goal of extending direct popular control of the people's agents led to the long ballot, which had been extended by the

---

[11] *Robert M. La Follette*, Autobiography (*Madison, Wis.: Robert M. La Follette Co., 1913*), passim.

[12] *The movement is traced in Lorin Peterson,* The Day of the Mugwump (*New York: Random House, 1961*), passim.

initiative, referendum, and recall and perpetuated by the continuance of direct election of a number of officials. Directly elected department heads, of course, need not be subservient to the chief executive. But the reformers' models of efficient administration, particularly the model of the American business corporation, led in the opposite direction: it called for a single chief executive who would direct, and be held responsible for, all administrative activities.

Independent commissions and popularly elected department heads, as we have seen earlier, were not inventions of the Progressive period. They fitted all too well with the legislature's long-standing inclination, as the rival of the governor, to keep his power minimized by excluding as much administration from his control as possible. As a result of this confluence of forces, a new independent board seemed to be created every time a new law was passed. In 1919, New York had 116 independent authorities; Minnesota, 75; Illinois, 100; Massachusetts, 61; and Idaho, 42—all exclusive of constitutionally created elective offices. Thus, a state's organization chart looked more like a Chinese puzzle than like the business concept of hierarchical organization. The governor was impotent.[13]

Although the newly created agencies were customarily not elective, they were independent of the governor's formal control. And even though some integrating tendencies had appeared, the governor was still a chief executive without power to supervise, control, hire, or fire. In the public eye he was the manager of state affairs, but in fact he was without the powers of management.

Some of the new agencies were boards composed entirely of ex officio members, of which the governor was usually one. In Illinois, he was a member of eight such boards. His time, as a result, was often spent on minutiae, rather than devoted to management of the larger affairs within his domain. Thus in New York, the governor, the president of the board of charities, and the fiscal supervisor constituted a building improvement commission, which considered the wisdom of hen houses, piggeries, and plaster bathrooms! Theoretically, this membership in a number of ex officio boards could add to the governor's influence. At least it was better than his total exclusion from participation in the more important decisions entrusted to such boards.

The most significant expansion of the governor's influence, however, was consequent on the move to modernize state budgetary processes. In

---

[13] *Leslie Lipson*, The American Governor: From Figurehead to Leader (*Chicago:* University of Chicago Press, 1939), passim.

the nineteenth century the general practice had been for each state agency to send its estimates of needed appropriations directly to the legislature, whose members also introduced their own special and local "pork barrel" appropriation measures to benefit their constituencies.[14] The twentieth century reformers' goals of economy and efficiency naturally set high priority on bringing order into financial planning, preferably incorporating a kind of discipline that would serve the interests of taxpayers. By the 1920's the executive budget—which gives the governor full responsibility for formulating expenditure estimates, anticipating revenues, and presenting them to the legislature—had been adopted by half the states. Similarly, the mayor and the city manager began to acquire the same type of budgetary authority. While the legislature still had substantial discretion in making actual appropriations, the chief executive had been given a key role in preparing a budget for the executive branch for consideration by the legislature, and this (coupled at the state level with the governor's item veto over appropriation acts) armed him for battle in one of the most crucial arenas where policy and administration meet.

Paradoxically, mayors, city managers, and comprehensive local commissions were acquiring authority at the same time that the state governors in all but the budgetary field continued to lose it. This countertrend may be partially attributed to three reasons. First, perhaps bad government in city hall is more readily discernible than bad government in dark capitol corridors. Second, the new municipal research bureaus led the citizenry to believe that municipal affairs were "nonpolitical" in nature and thus capable of being determined scientifically. Third, the trend toward local self-determination made change—and innovation—possible.

Generally, the three forms of municipal government that acquired status during this period had three things in common. The "strong mayor" plan, the commission plan, and the council-manager plan each sought further to concentrate responsibility; each utilized a unicameral council; and each employed the short ballot. Here their similarity ends.

The "strong mayor" plan, earlier adopted by some larger cities, acquired followers when it was recommended by the newly formed National Municipal League in 1899. The plan reinforced separation of powers and checks and balances. It made an elected mayor both chief political leader and general manager of the city. Independent boards lost their hydra-headed character and became single-headed departments responsible di-

---

[14] *Arthur N. Holcombe*, State Government in the United States, *3rd edition, rev.* (New York: Macmillan, 1935), pp. 358–60.

rectly to the mayor, who appointed and removed the department heads without council confirmation. The mayor prepared the annual budget, subject to council approval, and could veto council actions.

The development of the commission plan seems, historically speaking, as much a matter of chance as of change. Though the charter of Sacramento, California, embodied the basic idea of the plan as early as 1863, its popularity did not increase until later. In 1900, a West Indian hurricane struck Galveston, took 6,000 lives, and destroyed property worth $17 million.[15] As a result of the city's impending bankruptcy, the Deepwater Committee, a group of propertied businessmen, undertook to improve conditions by proposing the commission plan. A year later the Texas legislature granted the necessary charter.

Des Moines, Iowa, adopted the system in 1907, but modified it by providing for nonpartisan elections and for initiative, referendum, and recall. The commission plan discarded completely the concept of separation of powers and checks and balances. In this sense, it stands as an example of municipal innovation. Under it, the people elected five commissioners. Sitting collectively, they were the city council. Sitting individually, each was responsible for the administration of one or more municipal departments without interference from the other commissioners. One commissioner—equal to the others—was chosen mayor, although his only special prerogatives were ceremonial. The commission plan intentionally combined legislative and executive duties in the same individuals. It reached the zenith of its popularity around 1914, when it was operative in about 400 cities.[16]

The demise of commission government's popularity was at least partially due to the advent of the council-manager plan. The first city manager was used by Staunton, Virginia, in 1908; however, the city also had a mayor and a bicameral council. Richard S. Childs, in explaining how he conceived the idea of the plan, notes that Sumter, South Carolina, was the first city to adopt a genuine council-manager government.[17] However, major impetus was given to this new scheme in 1913 when it was advocated by the National Municipal League and was adopted by Dayton, Ohio. By 1920, the plan was used in about 150 cities.

The council-manager plan apes the organizational structure of a busi-

[15] *Oswald Ryan*, Municipal Freedom: A Study of the Commission Government (*New York: Doubleday*, 1915), *p.* 11.
[16] *Ernest S. Griffith*, The Modern Development of City Government in the United Kingdom and the United States (*London: Oxford University Press*, 1927), *Vol. I, p.* 276. *The number of 465 for 1915 is cited, with reservations, by Richard S. Childs in* Civic Victories, *p.* 138.
[17] Ibid., *pp.* 144ff.

ness corporation. Voters choose council members (usually five) at-large. The council theoretically determines policy and hires a manager to administer it. All city departments are responsible to the manager, who has authority to hire and fire all appointed municipal employees. The city's ceremonial functions are usually performed by the chairman of the council, the "mayor." Since the real chief executive is the city manager, the plan attempts to take politics out of government!

The goal of all three forms of municipal government advocated during this period was to strengthen responsibility. To make democracy really work, people had to have widespread power to elect officers and hold them responsible. The "strong mayor" plan sought to achieve this end by bolstering separation of powers through making the mayor a true chief executive. The commission plan and the council-manager plan both attack the problem by giving up the conventional separation of powers into legislative, executive, and judicial branches. Commission government fused legislative and executive functions into the hands of the same men. The council-manager plan completely abandoned the elective executive and, in essence, approved a new division of power that cut across legislative and executive functions in a different plane. This new division of power implicitly assumed the possibility of separating policy making and policy execution. The council was to determine what things should be done, and the specialized, professional manager (chosen by the council) was to determine how to do them—scientifically.

REGULATION AND SERVICE. The Progressives' determination to make government an instrument of the people in an increasingly populous and complex society is reflected in Table 3.1. A comparison of the 1902 and 1922 figures shows that the general expenditures by state and local governments multiplied five times and even on a per capita basis (which reveals increased services apart from those required by the 40 percent increase in population to be served) multiplied almost four times. Ideally, one would want these figures deflated to take account of the changes in the purchasing power of the dollar. As a rough estimate, this would mean cutting the apparent increase in total and per capita expenditures by half.[18] Even with this adjustment, it is clear that state and local governments in 1922 were performing services averaging about twice the intensity per person as the services performed in 1902.

The increase in population is not to be brushed aside as irrelevant to

---

[18] *The implicit price index for the gross national product, using 1929 to represent 100, averaged 47 in 1897–1901 and 52 in 1902–1906, compared to 98 in 1922. U.S. Bureau of the Census,* Historical Statistics of the United States, Colonial Times to 1957 *(Washington, D.C., 1960), Series F-5, p. 139.*

Table 3.1. *Finances of State and Local Governments, 1902–1950*

	Millions of Dollars				Dollars per Capita			
	1902	1922	1940	1950	1902	1922	1940	1950
Revenue, total	$1,048	$5,169	$11,749	$25,639				
General revenue	986	4,781	9,609	20,911	$12.46	$43.44	$72.73	$137.85
From federal government	7	108	945	2,486	.09	.98	7.15	16.39
Other (utility, liquor stores, insurance trust revenues)	62	388	2,140	4,728				
Expenditures, total	1,095	5,652	11,240	27,905				
General expenditure	1,013	5,218	9,229	22,787	12.80	47.41	69.85	150.22
Education	255	1,705	2,638	7,177	3.22	15.49	19.97	47.31
Highways	175	1,294	1,573	3,803	2.21	11.76	11.91	25.07
Public welfare	37	119	1,156	2,940	.47	1.08	8.75	19.38
Hospitals	43	200	450	1,384	.54	1.82	3.41	9.12
Health	17	58	159	364	.21	.53	1.20	2.40
Police	50	190	365	776	.63	1.73	2.76	5.12

Local fire protection	40	158	235	488	.51	1.44	1.78	3.22
Sanitation	51	189	207	834	.64	1.72	1.57	5.50
Natural resources	9	61	218	670	.11	.55	1.65	4.42
Local parks and recreation	29	85	162	304	.37	.77	1.23	2.00
Housing and community development	—	—	230	452	—	—	1.74	2.98
General control	141	313	561	1,041	1.78	2.84	4.25	6.86
Interest on general debt	68	382	653	458	.86	3.47	4.94	3.02
Other and unallocable general expenditure	98	464	622	2,096	1.24	4.22	4.71	13.82
Utility and liquor stores expenditure	82	359	1,324	2,739				
Insurance trust expenditure	—	75	687	2,379				
Indebtedness, at end of fiscal year	2,107	10,109	20,283	24,115	26.62	91.85	153.51	158.98

SOURCE: U.S. Bureau of the Census, *Census of Governments: 1962*, Vol. VI, No. 4, *Historical Statistics on Governmental Finances and Employment* (Washington, D.C., 1964), pp. 28–31, 39f.

the burdens carried by state and local governments. Much of the burden fell on municipalities, which gained about 24 million people while rural areas and small towns (under 2,500 population) gained only about 6 million. By 1920 more Americans were living in cities than in rural areas and small towns. For the first time the United States was predominantly a nation of city-dwellers.[19]

Improved modes of transportation and the expansion of mass production were both the cause and the result of this concentration of population. The concentration brought with it not only the advantages making economic growth possible, but also the problems of adequately governing and providing services for the metropolises. The problem was, among other things, one of the jurisdiction of various governmental units. Thus in 1920, the 30 extant metropolitan areas included parts of 91 counties in 39 states; within these areas were 921 governmental divisions.[20] The difficulties of the core city with its adjacent suburbs were even less well solved then than now by the techniques of annexation, special districts, and city-county consolidation.

The increasing financial demands made upon municipalities within and without metropolitan areas were great, for more services were needed and the cities sought to provide them. But their attempts led—at the local level—to further centralization of local authority in the state capitals, even though at the same time the states had begun to relinquish some authority through home rule. States began further to control local government indebtedness, tax assessment, accounting procedures, and budgeting practices,[21] and further to supervise municipal activities in such functional fields as public welfare.[22] For the localities, a compensating feature of this trend in state-local relations was the sextupling of state grants-in-aid to local governments, the bulk of it for education and highways.

A closer examination of Table 3.1 is rewarding. While state and local expenditures increased about five times, this average of all items was exceeded most notably for education and highways; in 1902 they accounted for a little over 40 percent of the general expenditures, but twenty years later they were approaching 60 percent. All along the line, though, the role of government increased; the only exceptions are local parks and recrea-

---

[19] Ibid., *Series A-195 and A-206, p. 14.*
[20] *Committee on Metropolitan Government, National Municipal League,* The Government of Metropolitan Areas in the United States (*New York: National Municipal League,* 1930), *p. 8.*
[21] *White, op. cit., pp. 49–74.*
[22] *Schuyler C. Wallace,* State Administrative Supervision over Cities in the United States (*New York: Columbia University Press,* 1928), passim.

tion, and "general control," which increased too little to counter the declining purchasing power of the dollar.

Meantime, the federal government had multiplied by more than 15 its grants to state and local governments. As we have seen earlier, this was consistent with a long tradition of federal aid, but now the aid appeared as cash gifts, in addition to grants of land and proffer of expert services. The federal government now provided a fiftieth of the general revenue of state governments. However, the grant programs did not greatly affect state activity; as yet, the amount of earmarked aid to achieve federal objectives was too small, and the conditions attached to the offer of aid did not seriously constrict state governments' discretion in administering their aided programs. The congressional acts dealt with agriculture (agricultural colleges, experiment stations, and extension services), the militia, forest preservation, vocational education, venereal disease, and highways. Until passage of the Weeks Act of 1911, extending federal aid for highway construction, Congress did not require the states to match each national dollar with a state dollar.

The state governments' changing role in the twenty-year period is apparent in the following figures for the principal identifiable purposes of states' direct general expenditures (in millions of dollars): [23]

	1902	1922
Total direct general expenditures	134	1,031
Hospitals	28	105
Education (mostly higher education)	17	164
Public welfare	10	38
Natural resources	9	61
Highways	4	303
Other	66	369

Statistics of this kind are particularly useful in indicating changes in emphasis for activities that cost money—for public employees' salaries; for purchases of land, supplies, and equipment; for construction of roads and buildings; for cash gifts. But much of what governments do that matters costs relatively little, and among such low-cost activities the order of significance is not determined by a rank-order based on expenditures. A glance at the above list of activities most prominent in terms of expenditures should be immediately revealing. These are "services." They are not

[23] *U.S. Bureau of the Census,* Historical Statistics . . . Colonial Times to 1957, *Series Y 623–642, pp. 728f.*

"regulation." Yet promotion of the public interest by regulation of private enterprise was obviously a major theme of the Progressive period. A good deal of the thrust was toward federal legislation, sometimes because state regulation had proved ineffective. But significant steps were taken at the state level to intensify regulation of public utilities (and, in a number of cities, to supplant private monopolies with public ownership and operation of water, gas, and electric utilities), and to extend governmental protection to workers in industry.

Legislatures and courts once again found themselves locked in combat. Sometimes the legislature was deliberately rejecting the common law as administered by the courts—as in the fixing of responsibility for injury to workmen. While factory inspection laws, also an important product of this period, set minimum safety and health standards to be enforced by state inspectors, workmen's compensation laws attempted to fix liability on employers for accidents suffered by their employees in the course of their work. Under the common law an injured or killed worker—or his family— had found it difficult to obtain damages in the courts if the employer could establish that the employee knew the risks when he took the job or that the employee's or a fellow employee's negligence had contributed to the occurrence of the accident. These coldly logical legal doctrines fitted ill with the growing sense that entrepreneurs should bear the real costs of producing their commodities, and not shift them to those least able to bear them. The tragedy of death or maiming would fall on workers and their families in any event, but the economic cost of lost or diminished earning power should be borne by the employer. At the same time, if owners of factories and mines became responsible for the costs of accidents, they would have a greater incentive to invest in safety and health protection measures than would be likely through the mere goading of factory inspectors. The earliest remedial legislation altered the common law defense and gave a worker's survivors the right to sue. Employment contracts that relieved the employer of liability for accidents were declared illegal. Later legislation established the public principle that the employer was liable for industrial accidents, regardless of fault, though state courts struck down much of this legislation until 1915-17, when the U.S. Supreme Court held it valid. These workmen's compensation laws were usually administered by a state industrial commission—the hope being that it would be less wedded to the common law doctrines and less employer-oriented than the courts, and that its procedures would be less costly and formidable for the injured workman.

Minimum wage laws for women and children showed a further concern for workers. Approximately one-fourth of the states either set minimum wages by statute or authorized a wage board to determine them. This movement was halted by a Supreme Court decision invalidating a District of Columbia women's minimum wage law on the grounds that it violated the due process clause.[24]

A New York law limiting the daily hours of workers in bakeries to ten was declared unconstitutional,[25] although the Court had previously upheld a Utah law fixing an eight-hour day in mines and smelters.[26] The New York law led the eminent Mr. Justice Holmes to point out in his dissenting opinion that "The Fourteenth Amendment does not enact Mr. Herbert Spencer's Social Statics."

Kansas outlawed the "yellow dog" contract, whereby a worker as a condition of his employment agrees not to join a union. The Supreme Court declared the Kansas law unconstitutional on the grounds that the liberty of an employer to contract with his employees was a property right that might not be denied without due process of law.[27]

The extent to which restrictive Supreme Court decisions affected the willingness of the states to experiment with other social and economic problems is impossible to determine precisely. However, these decisions certainly did not encourage the states to be bold.

SUMMARY, 1900–1920. Many of the Populists' ideas had by now been accepted. Direct primary elections, popular election of senators, woman suffrage, initiative, referendum, and recall had all been adopted. Education and welfare facilities had been expanded, public utilities regulated. The workingman was better provided for. Boss rule appeared to be on the way out.

The mistrust to which the muckrakers gave voice had led to reform, and the reformation had been spearheaded by the states and their municipalities.

2. Modern Times (1920–1950)

The three decades from the end of World War I to the reconversion to peaceful pursuits after World War II appear to have moved in jerks and starts—first, the prosperous twenties with their real estate booms, install-

---

[24] Adkins *v.* Children's Hospital, *261 U.S. 525 (1923).*
[25] Lochner *v.* New York, *198 U.S. 45 (1905).*
[26] Holden *v.* Hardy, *169 U.S. 366 (1898).*
[27] Coppage *v.* Kansas, *236 U.S. 1 (1915).*

ment selling, and soaring stock values; then, with the 1929 stock market crash, the bleak depression years with almost one of every four workers unemployed, near-rebellion in rural areas as farm mortgages were foreclosed, and in the cities breadlines by day and sleeping on park benches by night; next, a war whose requirements filled the empty and slack industrial plants and drew the still numerous unemployed into uniform or workclothes; finally, emergence from the war into a new scientific age and a new kind of world atmosphere—a "hot peace" or "cold war" that made grimly inappropriate the campaign slogan of 1920, "a return to normalcy."

REGULATION AND SERVICE. The scope and emphases of state and local governments' activities reflected the shifts in the national economic, social, and defense setting. Governments had more people to serve, but the number of people added in the thirty years between 1920 and 1950 was scarcely different from the number added in the thirty years preceding 1920 (45 and 43 million, respectively). The rate of increase, in other words, had declined: it was not just that the 15 percent growth rate already established for the decade 1910–20 (in contrast to the 21 percent for 1900–10) was stabilized for 1920–30 and was repeated for 1940–50, but the depression halved even that rate so that the population increased only about 7 percent between 1930 and 1940.[28] Consider just two aspects of stability and variation within the make-up of the population:[29]

Year	Aged 5 to 14 Years (Millions of persons)	Aged 65 and Over (Millions of persons)
1920	22.0	4.9
1930	24.6	6.6
1940	22.4	9.0
1950	24.3	12.3

It takes no great perception to see (a) that school expenditures by state and local governments would be likely to remain relatively stable or, if they in fact increased, that the additional money would presumably be buying a better quality of education for the individual student, and (b) that expenditures for care of the aged, with the burden falling on health and welfare programs, would probably rise—and, if they did not rise fast enough, that the "senior citizens" would collectively apply political pres-

[28] U.S. Bureau of the Census, Statistical Abstract of the United States: 1962 (Washington, D.C., 1962), Table 1, p. 5.
[29] U.S. Bureau of the Census, Historical Statistics . . . Colonial Times to 1957, Series A-72, 73, 84, p. 10.

sure to speed the rise. (The aged doubled their *proportion* of the population between 1920 and 1950.)

Where people live also affects what governments do and which governments do it. Depression, war, and the changing geography and technology of industry reshaped the face of America. Although the frontier was supposed to have disappeared about 1890 and the forty-eighth state was admitted in 1912, the mold was not yet set. People still followed where opportunity led, and fled where opportunity collapsed. This took them from state to state, and from country to city.

By 1950, half of the people were in about a fifth of the states: New York, California, Pennsylvania, Illinois, Ohio, Texas, Michigan, New Jersey, and Massachusetts. What the governments of those 9 states were to do with the traditions they had inherited was destined, therefore, to be of as much moment to the common man as the efforts at self-improvement of the other 39 state governments combined.

As early as 1920, census figures had described half the population as urban. By 1950, the proportion was up to about 60 percent. Over a quarter of the total population lived in the major cities having 100,000 people or more, and about three-fifths lived in 189 metropolitan areas. Increasingly, it could be predicted, the governmental traditions inherited from a rural society would have to be adapted to the needs of an urban majority.

Table 3.1 (see p. 84) presents the details of state and local finances for 1922, 1940, and 1950. In the eighteen years between 1922 and 1940, general expenditures had not quite doubled (from $5.2 billion to $9.2 billion), but in just the ten following years they more than doubled (from $9.2 billion to $22.8 billion). Figures for per capita expenditures sharpen the contrast: the eighteen-year increase was less than 50 percent (from $47.41 to $69.85), while for the 1940's it was a 100 percent increase (from $69.85 to $150.22). Changes in the dollar's purchasing power over the almost thirty years make the 1922–40 increase a little more significant and considerably reduce the contrast between 1940 and 1950 in actual services rendered.[30] The state and local activities that show the largest gains (at least doubling in either or both of the two periods) can be put in order of rate of increase of expenditures, as follows:

---

[30] *The implicit price index, using 1929 as 100, was 98 for 1922, 83 in 1940, and 152 in 1950. U.S. Bureau of the Census,* Historical Statistics . . . Colonial Times to 1957, *Series F-5, p. 139. The rise of 83 percent between 1940 and 1950 applies to the nation's whole gross national product. An index confined to state and local governmental purchases of goods and services shows a 90 percent rise during the same period (from 43.9 in 1940 to 83.7 in 1950, using 1954 as 100); this specialized index does not extend back to 1922.* Economic Report of the President *(Washington, D.C., January 1963), p. 179.*

1922–1940	1940–1950
	1. *Sanitation*
1. *Housing and community development*	2. *Hospitals*
2. *Public welfare*	3. *Natural resources*
3. *Natural resources*	4. *Education*
4. *Health*	5. *Public welfare*
5. *Hospitals*	6. *Health*
	7. *Highways*

Inclusion of outlays from insurance trust funds—almost wholly for unemployment compensation and public employees' retirement—would raise public welfare to second place in the 1940–50 list.[31]

Two obstacles confronted those who wished to expand the roles of state and local governments—even assuming, as was not always the case, that adequate popular support could be mustered for such expansion. One was the courts' interposing of constitutional obstacles to the states' use of their police power—the power to adopt regulatory measures for the health, safety, morals, and well-being of their citizens. The other was the need for revenue to finance expansion of services.

The Supreme Court's restrictive interpretation of state police power limited the possibility of some corrective measures. The states did not have the authority to set the prices of many commodities and services. A state law fixing the price of gasoline was invalidated;[32] so was a law limiting the fees of employment agencies.[33] An Oklahoma statute requiring a license for the manufacture, sale, and distribution of ice was overthrown.[34]

Labor laws shared the same fate. A Kansas law providing for compulsory arbitration of wage and hour disputes by a court of industrial relations[35] and a New York law setting minimum wages for women were declared beyond the states' police power.[36] Even a law that sought to protect consumers from being short-weighted when buying bread was beyond the states' powers.[37]

Some few states were, however, able to provide at least temporizing relief from depression problems. New York foreshadowed several New

---

[31] *Housing and community development had no money spent on it in 1922, so it automatically registers the greatest 1922–1940 gain, and even in actual 1940 expenditures it exceeds those for natural resources and health.*

[32] Williams v. Standard Oil Co., 278 U.S. 235 (1928).

[33] Ribnik v. McBride, 277 U.S. 350 (1928).

[34] New State Ice Co. v. Liebmann, 285 U.S. 262 (1932).

[35] Wolff Packing Co. v. Industrial Court, 262 U.S. 522 (1923).

[36] Morehead v. Tipaldo, 298 U.S. 587 (1936).

[37] Burns Baking Co. v. Bryan, 264 U.S. 504 (1924).

Deal measures. It began to develop hydroelectric facilities and provided for reforestation, farm improvement, and unemployment relief.

Generally, however, the states were unable, unwilling, or incapable of solving by themselves either the immediate plight of their citizens or the fundamental problems of the depression. Financial inability was certainly an important factor as first private charity, then local governments' relief efforts broke down, and the consequent shift of responsibility to the states failed to solve the problem of how to extract increased revenues from a depression-ridden economy. Thus after 1932 the national government began more actively both to support the needs of the hungry and homeless and to attack our sick economy directly.

The national government used its own funds to provide direct material relief, and it expanded grant-in-aid assistance to state and local governments. The direct relief system indirectly forced the taxpayers of the richer states to help support the needy of the poorer states. Between 1933 and 1937, 75 percent of the relief funds spent by all governments in the United States were supplied by the national government. Only three state treasuries supplied even as much as 50 percent of relief expenditures in their states. By contrast, 13 states' treasuries provided only 10 percent of the total monies spent in their states on relief.

The depression did not pass over the cities; they were in trouble too. As early as 1932, the federal government undertook to proffer direct financial assistance to municipalities. In that year, Congress authorized the Reconstruction Finance Corporation to lend money to cities for projects that would pay for themselves. Municipalities approaching insolvency received indirect assistance from various federal relief and public works programs. And in 1936 Congress passed a municipal bankruptcy act.

The helping hand from Washington was even further extended. To encourage the states to set up employment offices, the Congress created the United States Employment Service. The Service made direct grants to those states that established statewide employment office systems.

In these early depression days, national grants were not made contingent upon any financial contribution of the states. However, beginning in about 1935, the national government's financial assistance to each state was customarily conditioned upon the state's matching the national dollar with some percentage of the grant or some stated amount from its own funds.

Grants-in-aid enabled the states to maintain their older functions more adequately, to expand them by offering additional services, and to engage in new undertakings. In these programs, distribution of funds among the states varied with such factors as area, population, and per capita income. The intention was to distribute the funds where the greatest amount of service was needed.

These grant-in-aid programs grew extensively in the thirties and forties. The national government in 1950 contributed ten times the amount to the state and local governments that it did in 1932. In 1950, national contributions to the states accounted for one-seventh of total state expenditures; whereas in 1932, national contributions had amounted to only one-thirteenth. The impact of the grant-in-aid system on policy making is discussed in detail in Chapter 5. It suffices to note here that, by mid-century and despite its relatively recent development, the grant system had been maturely developed and had become one of the traditions embedded in state and local government.

At about the same time that the grant-in-aid program was accelerated, a rejuvenated Supreme Court was permitting greater freedom for regulation and service by both nation and state. Until 1937, the state's police power had played an intermediate role in a three-step constitutional doctrine. On the one hand, the Court's acceptance of "dual federalism" set up the states' police power as a barrier to congressional lawmaking: Congress could not "invade" the realm reserved for state action under the police power. On the other hand, the Court's interpretation of the Fourteenth Amendment's due process clause meant that the states could not use their police power for regulatory purposes in ways that might strike the Court as "unreasonable" invasions of the liberty or property of private corporations and individual workers. And, of course, the states could not use their police power (or their taxing power) in ways that would "burden" interstate commerce. The result, many observers thought, was to create a no-man's land, an area where there was a vacuum of governmental power despite the obvious existence of problems crying for governmental action.

As criticism mounted, the Supreme Court effected what many regard as a constitutional revolution. From 1937 on, a majority of the Court came to uphold congressional acts despite challenges that they regulated local business, farmers' plantings and marketings, and workers' freedom to bargain individually rather than collectively. The constitutionality of federal grant-in-aid programs—or, at least, the impossibility of successfully maintaining a suit in the courts against such programs—had been established in the 1920's, and Congress's general freedom to use its spending power to achieve goals it thought desirable was also well established. Whether and how national power was to be exercised thus became a matter for legislative, rather than judicial, judgment. If some thought that this meant that the Constitution was gone, it did not itself mean that national policy would be centralist. The Congress that was to make the decisions remained an assemblage of senators and representatives highly attentive to opinion in their states and congressional districts, the constituencies on which they depended for election.

The new Court also proved itself less willing than its predecessor to invalidate state regulatory laws. The states' police power thus expanded without constitutional amendment. This came about very simply through the Court's development of a doctrine of self-restraint. The "reasonableness" of economic and social policies, which had been opened for judicial decision by the interpretation of the due process clause, now was recognized as a matter of wisdom and judgment—and judges have no exclusive patent on such qualities. While the courts might still strike down state laws as unconstitutional, either because they trespassed on national powers or because they were indeed irresponsible and arbitrary uses of the police power against private persons and corporations, the courts generally abstained from substituting their judgments for those of state legislatures on the wisdom of social and economic legislation.

Paradoxically, while the states thus gained greater legal freedom to experiment, to attempt bold new ventures, to regulate economic evils, they seemed more reluctant to do so. The increased activities of the states up to mid-century were more an extension in depth than in breadth.

CONSTITUTIONAL INADEQUACY. While the states were expanding their functions and to a limited degree undertaking new ones, the structure of their governments was in some ways becoming less competent to carry out the new duties but in other ways was becoming more able to do so.

The oldest, if not the heaviest, burden that the average state had to bear was its constitution. Three states operate under eighteenth-century constitutions. They could be fortunate; after all, the national Constitution is also an eighteenth-century document. Most of the states, however, are using constitutions adopted in the nineteenth century (see Table 3.2)—a period not notable for legislative genius. Only 12 of the present constitutions were adopted during the twentieth century.

While most state constitutions have not been recently revised, they have been amended in some respects. Indeed, excessive amendment is one reason why the constitutions need revision today. The amendments have added a mass of legislative detail that restricts the operation of government —much to the delight of some special interests. The average state constitution is four times as long as the United States Constitution. Louisiana holds the record: its constitution is 27 times as long as the national one.

Length alone is not the only reason our constitutions have burdened state government in modern times. Generally, they preserve a structural framework of government that is more reminiscent of the nineteenth

Table 3.2. *Effective Dates of Present State Constitutions*

(As of 1965)

1780–1820	1867–1897	1901–1921
1780 Massachusetts	1867 Maryland	1901 Alabama
1784 New Hampshire	1868 North Carolina	1902 Virginia
1793 Vermont	1870 Illinois	1907 Oklahoma
1820 Maine	Tennessee	1912 Arizona
	1872 West Virginia	New Mexico
	1873 Pennsylvania	1921 Louisiana
	1874 Arkansas	
	1875 Nebraska	
1843–1864	1876 Colorado	
1843 Rhode Island	Texas	
1848 Wisconsin	1879 California	1945–1947
1851 Indiana	1887 Florida	1945 Georgia
Ohio	1889 Montana	Missouri
1857 Iowa	North Dakota	1947 New Jersey
1858 Minnesota	South Dakota	
1859 Oregon	Washington	1959–1965
1861 Kansas	1890 Idaho	1959 Alaska
1864 Nevada	Mississippi	Hawaii
	Wyoming	1964 Michigan
	1891 Kentucky	1965 Connecticut
	1894 New York	
	1895 South Carolina	
	1896 Utah	
	1897 Delaware	

SOURCE: *The Book of the States: 1966–67* (Chicago, Ill.: Council of State Governments, 1966), p. 10, corrected to reflect late 1965 adoption.

century than of the twentieth. Executive power is diffused among several elected officials. Legislative power is severely curtailed and, until the 1960's, was often exercised by men chosen from districts containing disproportionate numbers of voters. The voter is faced with a ballot containing so many names and so many issues that intelligent selection is a virtual impossibility.

ELECTIONS AND REPRESENTATION. The adoption of the Nineteenth Amendment, in effect constitutionally conferring the franchise upon women, meant that now for the first time the suffrage was indeed universal—at least, according to the intent of the Constitution. But in the South, intent and practice did not necessarily coincide. Arbitrarily administered literacy, educational, residence, and poll tax laws limited the Negro's participation in general elections.

Some southern states sought further to limit the Negro's electoral influence. By various legislative and political devices, they strove to prevent his membership in the Democratic party and thus his participation in primary elections. Since nomination by the Democratic party in the southern states was tantamount to victory in the general election, the Negro was in effect disenfranchised. Because of the delay in getting Supreme Court rulings, these states were successful in their purposes. Indeed, from 1935 to 1944 their efforts were not only successful, but also constitutional.[38] Even after 1944 the southern states continued to try to find devices to limit the Negro's right to vote, especially in primary elections.

The pure direct primary began to fall somewhat from favor. Historically, it had been a nominating election in which the candidates' names were placed on the ballot as a result of a given number or percentage of voters' having signed a petition and in which the candidate having the greatest number of votes was declared nominated. Now, however, this pattern tended to be altered.

Some states, dissatisfied with the direct primary, returned to the older convention method of nomination. A number of southern states provided for a run-off primary between the two candidates compiling the greatest number of votes in the free-for-all primary election, provided that no candidate had received a majority of votes in the free-for-all. In essence, this system assures nomination by majority, rather than plurality.

In the first half of the century, about eight states experimented with a pre-primary designating convention, an attempt to combine party organizational influence with popular participation. The pre-primary designating convention endorsed a slate of candidates whose names usually appeared first on the primary election ballot, which also carried the names of candidates not so endorsed.

In 1934, California modified the system of selecting judges, and Missouri followed suit in 1940. Heretofore, judicial power had often been granted to men chosen for their popularity rather than for their judicial ability. The Missouri plan, however, restricted the governor's authority to appoint judges of the highest courts to those persons recommended to him

---

[38] *See* Grovey *v.* Townsend, 295 *U.S.* 45 (1935); *and* Smith *v.* Allwright, 321 *U.S.* 649 (1944).

by a commission composed of judges, lawyers, and laymen. After serving a year, the appointed judge runs against himself in a popular election. Essentially, the people vote on the question: "Shall the judge be retained in office?" Other states have considered, but rejected, this innovation.

The states' innovation and experimentation with nominations and elections did not carry over to the state legislature. The one exception was Nebraska's state legislature. Partially as a result of the National Municipal League's recommendation in its Model State Constitution of 1920 and partially because of the state-stumping activities of the late Senator George W. Norris, Nebraska adopted a one-house legislature in 1934. The constitutional amendment provided for 30 to 50 legislators elected on a nonpartisan ballot. No other state has taken up the idea, although some have considered it.

Clearly the dead hand of the past has rested on our state legislatures into modern times. In Connecticut, towns that existed before the adoption of the state constitution in 1818 were guaranteed no reduction of their membership in the state house of representatives. And despite substantial shifts in population, in 1950, 9 states elected legislatures that had not been reapportioned for thirty-four or more years, while 15 states elected on the basis of apportionments over twenty years old.

Two separate problems have been involved. The traditional strength of particular types of areas may be such that no constitutional amendment or legislative act designed as a reapportionment may get at the root difficulty—the need to represent *people* and thus establish the political equality of men. The New Mexico legislature, for example, was reapportioned by constitutional amendment in 1949. Yet each legislator chosen by Harding County represented 1,500 people, while each Bernalillo County legislator represented 21,000 people. The point to be noted is that reapportionment is not per se equitable reapportionment. In California, the 2,750,000 people of Los Angeles County elected one senator; the 10,000 people of two rural counties also elected one senator. The second problem has been simply the reluctance of legislatures to pay attention to the last, or even the next-to-last, census, if doing so would have unhappy results for party majorities in the legislatures and for the local and economic interests to which they are responsive. The combination of the two problems often resulted in underrepresentation of the larger municipalities and their consequent inability to get the legislature to pass laws permitting them to solve their special urban problems. Although from 1940 to 1950 the legislatures of about half the states were reapportioned, the average legislature was still based on an apportionment more than fifteen years old.

THE REORGANIZATION MOVEMENT. The laws of unrepresentative legislatures and the provisions of old constitutions together had historically placed the governor in a position from which he could not govern. He had little to govern. State law was administered by other elective executives and by boards responsible to the legislature. The Progressive demands to return government to the people meant that people must understand the government and be offered meaningful choices. Despite some reformers' early emphasis upon subjecting more offices to popular election, the democratic logic of fixing responsibility upon a visible chief executive whom the people could discipline at the polls coincided substantially with the conclusion of those who wanted to increase efficiency and economy in government. The governor was the beneficiary of these two lines of thought.

Though there had been some earlier rumblings, in 1910 President Taft appointed an Economy and Efficiency Commission, which provided the impetus for state interest. New York and Illinois took action first, and spurred by the demand that the increasing state services be matched by improved administration, the reorganization movement was in full swing by the twenties.

The reorganization movement assumed that there was no danger in increasing the authority of the governor if his responsibility were commensurately increased. To this end, its proponents argued for a consolidation of all state agencies into a limited number of departments directly responsible to the governor. The departments were to be headed by responsible directors, rather than by boards. The governor was to have help from a number of staff agencies in charge of budgeting, purchasing, and personnel. In essence, these goals combined, at the state level, the organizational structure of the "strong mayor" plan with the expert staff assistance recognized as appropriate by the council-manager plan. In part at least, the states were learning from their municipalities.

Though not all the states reorganized in the period 1920–50, they were all affected by the movement, some making constitutional changes and others making only statutory changes. The degree of integration of agencies under the governor varied among the states. Special interests were able to prevent the integration of some boards that regulated them, since they had found the independent units easier to control. Generally, the organizational changes seem to have been guided more by the traditions of the states than by abstract management principles. While the immediate effect of reorganization is to decrease the number of independent agencies, the effect is not lasting; legislatures tend to create new agencies to implement each new policy.

The national Commission on Organization of the Executive Branch of Government (the first Hoover Commission), which was established in 1947, initiated among the states the last reorganization surge prior to mid-century. Approximately three-fourths of the states reinvestigated the executive branch under that impetus.

The results were not heartening. The legislatures and the people were, for the most part, either opposed or indifferent to the various proposals. For example, approximately fifty constitutional amendments providing for reorganization were defeated to every one adopted. Where statutory changes resulted, greater attention seems to have been paid to top-level management and administrative procedure than to major structural reforms.

Meanwhile a few counties began to be affected by the reorganization virus. Durham County, North Carolina, adopted the county manager plan in 1930. Twenty years later the counties in 21 states were empowered to adopt it, but only 11 counties had done so.[39]

From 1920 to 1950, the number of municipalities using the council-manager plan increased more than sixfold. At the same time, the role of the city manager changed from that of business manager-engineer to community leader partly because municipal affairs no longer (if they ever did) conformed to the reformers' model of mere "housekeeping" and partly because neither the ceremonial mayor nor the plural council provided the leadership needed.

Reorganization *qua* reorganization at any level of government accomplishes little. The creation of a personnel division under the governor's aegis can be the centralized office for political jobbery. Governors inclined toward political skullduggery are not hampered by streamlined organizations, paper merit systems, or centralized purchasing units. Municipal councils so inclined need not be hampered in making administrative, as opposed to policy, decisions even under the council-manager plan. While reorganization does not guarantee efficient government, it can make available to executives—other circumstances permitting—the machinery through which administration can be efficient.

3. *Our Traditions*

No tradition in state and local government is so strong as tradition itself. In government, as in all institutions, the present and the future are rooted

---

[39] *Childs*, op. cit., *pp. 209–11.*

in the past. No fundamental changes, not even those we call revolutionary, arise from a vacuum.

The influence of tradition upon state governments has not all been a product of unconscious development. Indeed, when a state considers statutory or administrative innovation, the first thing a state official is likely to ask is, "Why should we change what we're used to?" His second question may well be, "What have the other states done about it?" A history of government in the United States might, with rare exceptions, be a tribute to the persistence of old ideas and a description of new ideas traded among municipalities and among the states, as well as among municipal, state, and national governments. Yet tradition has been stronger than innovation, even when the innovation was only mimicry of some other government.

The strength of tradition is not all sentiment and inertia. Separation of powers and checks and balances are regarded by some people as rational parts of the American creed. Yet at the same time and without public objection, the executive function is fused with the legislative function in the commission form of government and subordinated to it in the council-manager form. Even bicameralism in legislative organization takes its place as part of the checks and balances system, and in spite of the Nebraska experience, is thus resistant to reconsideration. Yet only a handful of city councils are now bicameral. The weak governorship, so much in contrast to the strong Presidency in the same country, has roots in eighteenth-century dislike of the British colonial governor, but draws too on deep fears of tyrants, fears that are reenforced by the world's providing fresh examples for each generation. This tradition is followed by counties, most of which cannot even be said to have a chief executive. Yet, throughout the twentieth century, municipal executives—mayors, managers, and commissioners —have gained in power.

The contrast between the state and the modern municipality at mid-century is probably attributable to at least two factors: First, people tend to believe—rightly or wrongly—that government close to home is not only the best government (in itself a traditional belief), but also the one most easily controlled. Thus, the types of safeguards required of state governments are not needed locally. Second, large numbers of people have come to believe that municipal government activities are beyond the pale of politics. With the existing structural safeguards and with the people's awareness of what goes on, tyranny would be impossible. Perhaps the people's memory is short, and they forget the city bosses of the turn of the century. Perhaps they have not learned that the reformers who turned the rascals out can in time be themselves turned out or even become the latter-day rascals. But consistent thinking is not essential to the maintenance of traditions. The most tyrannical of governors, men who lack capacity for the responsibilities of high office, constantly reenforce the tradition that the office of state governor, at least, should be kept weak in power.

Perhaps most important, tradition is kept green by those who profit from the arrangements that have become traditional. A constitutional provision apportioning legislative seats, a statute creating a regulatory commission independent of the governor, development of a custom of gubernatorial deference to an organized group when appointments are made to a particular agency—all these vest interests.

Interests that have become vested are not readily bested, at least not on the battlefield that they themselves have chosen and even shaped. The effort required to dislodge them is often so great that all but zealots will prefer to accept the landscape as an environment more suitable for scattered sniping than for pitched battle.

Writing to John Taylor of Carolina in 1816, Thomas Jefferson put it all succinctly: ". . . an unorganized call for timely amendment is not likely to prevail against an organized opposition to it. We are always told that things are going on well; why change them?" [40]

Yet change does occur, and often it is at the expense of vested interests. The suffrage has broadened as religion, property, race, and sex have lost their restrictive power. Choice of nominees for state office has shifted from legislative caucus to convention to direct primary. The breadth of state activities has increased, as has the depth of penetration of most of the older activities. The burden of state taxation has shifted from property to individual and corporate income and to consumers' expenditures. New ways of participating in legislation have been opened to the people by the initiative and referendum. The governor has become more of a legislative leader.

Cities are less boss-ridden than they have been in the past. Home rule has become possible. Municipal governments have charters permitting them to operate more efficiently and to perform broader services. Even counties—long the "dark continent of American politics"—have shown some improvement. And the availability of special districts at least permits one method of providing people with services.

But somehow tradition still thwarts the development of responsible, representative governments in the states. Distrust mingled with contempt,

---

[40] *Adrienne Koch and William Peden* (eds.), The Life and Selected Writings of Thomas Jefferson (*New York: Modern Library*, 1944), p. 672.

indifference, and mistaken ideas about democracy block the development of a representative, responsible, powerful legislature; of a chief executive and policy leader in the person of the governor; and of the emergence of a healthy two-party system through which the people may make their choices on major policy issues. United States Supreme Court Justice Brandeis once wrote:

> . . . *It is one of the happy incidents of the federal system that a single courageous state may, if its citizens choose, serve as a laboratory; and try novel social and economic experiments without risk to the rest of the country.*[41]

Yet the states have rarely taken advantage of their opportunity. Unfortunately, when they were most inclined to innovation, the Supreme Court's interpretation of the Constitution was narrow and perhaps thwarted further attempts at social and economic experimentation.

Nor have the states served as laboratories to experiment with structural changes in their governments. Though they are bound only by the constitutional requirement that the form of their government be a "republican" one, the three basic organs of state government—the legislature, the chief executive, and the judiciary—have remained fundamentally unchanged, despite some alterations in the power relationships among the three. The states seem to have followed the practice "Monkey see; monkey do." Inventiveness has not been characteristic of their efforts. No state, for example, has experimented with a cabinet form of government in which the governor would be chosen by the legislature. No state has seriously considered hiring a manager and investing him with the authority to administer the affairs of state—either under gubernatorial or legislative supervision. Indeed, the states seem to have followed Justice Sutherland's philosophy and "put a great deal of faith in experience and very little in mere experiment." [42]

About one hundred eighty years ago James Madison prophesied, "If . . . the people should in [the] future become more partial to the fœderal than to the State governments, the change can only result, from such manifest and irresistible proofs of a better administration, as will overcome all their antecedent propensities." [43] Let traditionalists ponder that.

---

[41] New State Ice Co. *v.* Liebmann, 285 *U.S.* 262 (1932).

[42] *Quoted in Charles Fairman,* American Constitutional Decisions, *rev. edition* (New York: Holt, 1950), p. 340.

[43] *Essay No. 46,* The Federalist, *Jacob Cooke (ed.) (Middletown, Conn.: Wesleyan University Press, 1961) at p.* 317.

☆ ☆ ☆ ☆ ☆ ☆ ☆ ☆

chapter 4

Functions of State and Local Governments

State and local governments comprise all but one of the some 90,000 units of government the Census Bureau counted in the United States in 1962. Yet they cannot be well understood in isolation; they are parts of the total American system of government. The national government looms large in that system both in direct policy making and administration and in its power to affect other American governments. But in the total system, state and local governments have important and distinguishable powers; they interact with each other, and they affect the national government's scope and manner of operation. To understand state and local governments, therefore, we need both to know the functions they perform for the people within their jurisdictions and to understand the intricate pattern of intergovernmental relations.

In any ultimate sense, neither the federal system, nor the states, nor even local governments are ends in themselves. The final objects of government were never better and more succinctly expressed than in the preamble to the American Constitution: to "establish justice, insure domestic tranquility, provide for the common defense, promote the general welfare, and secure the blessings of liberty. . . ." How well state and local governments meet these larger goals is the measure of their continuing justification. Our present concern, therefore, is not simply to catalog the *formal* powers of these governments. Nor is it only to clarify what these governments actually do—an exercise that is nonetheless essential in view of the crocodile tears periodically shed to dramatize a supposed danger of atrophy of state and local governments. Beyond this, we need to match their activities against human purposes, in the light of the processes by which policies are adopted.

Whether the problems confronting society are reasonably well identified and responsibly dealt with is a critical test for determining whether particular governments will retain, expand, or contract their roles in the total system. The main premise of federalism, as also of local self-government, is that division and distribution of governmental power in the United States are not only unavoidable but desirable. That premise fails if state and local governments do not satisfactorily contribute to the final goals of organized society. The stakes in their performance of their missions are therefore the vitality and viability of the American system as it has thus far evolved.

Two secular trends, to be elaborated as we proceed, need summary statement at the outset. The first is well known: the apparently irreversible overall expansion of governmental functions taken all together—a trend related to the growth of population, gross national product, urban life, and the rising tide of social expectations. The second, not quite so obvious, is the simultaneous shift in the composition, or mix, of functions as among the levels of government—whereby, increasingly, planning is undertaken, broad policies are determined, and funds are raised at successively higher levels, while operations are expanded at lower levels and funds flow outward and downward to support them. This is the often decried trend toward "centralization." In the upshot, states and municipalities have found more and more to do, notwithstanding the great growth in national functions.

In this chapter we shall give more attention to state than to local governmental activities. The latter are more familiar and, if not less controversial in particular cases, are more likely to involve questions of capability, of degree, and of ways and means. Questions of principle—what functions are proper to local governments—are less in dispute than questions of feasibility.

1. *The Jobs of the States*

It does not take much reading of constitutions and charters to learn that these documents—which speak largely in terms of enabling and limiting—

supply only a partial answer to the question: What do governments do? For state government functions are inherently relative. They are relative to the place of the states as middlemen in the system; to the differences among the states in resources, policy concerns, and influence of organized interest groups; to the shifting trends in these respects over the years; and to changes in the underlying sense of community among their citizens.

THE STATES AS MIDDLEMEN. The United States Constitution is the source of the *powers* of the national government, but the states look to it chiefly for *limitations* on their powers. Yet some part of the states' independence is traceable to the Constitution because, so far as the Union is concerned, they are free to do anything not forbidden by that document. Explicitly, they are all forbidden to make treaties with foreign countries, to coin money, to impair the obligation of contracts, to tax imports or exports, or to deny "due process" or "equal protection" in their treatment of individuals or corporations. Implicitly, by interpretation, they are forbidden, for example, to burden interstate commerce unduly, either by regulation or taxation, or to interfere with the exercise of other national powers. But these prohibitions still leave much leeway.

It would be tedious, however, to canvass the state constitutions for a compilation of all their powers. The states, to begin with, can make and change their own constitutions, within the federal limitations just noted; indeed, these constitutions are the source of most of the legal limits on their powers. They can raise and spend their own funds, though they are no longer self-sufficient financially. Subject to the Fourteenth Amendment, the federal Voting Rights Act of 1965 and similar restraints, they conduct both federal and state elections and provide most of the legal controls over parties and elections. They enact and enforce the main bodies of civil and criminal law. Subject to desegregation requirements, they control the public education systems. They license occupations, charter corporations, and regulate utilities, insurance, and other businesses. They establish, help support, and regulate the counties, municipalities, and other political subdivisions.

The practical importance of these powers to the states is reenforced by their substantial opportunities to influence what the national government does. Their constitutional equality of status and their equal representation in the Senate—a compromise with the principle of majority rule that is one of the prices of our federal system—are basic. Therefore, New Jersey can stand up to New York, and Arizona to California.

The influence of the states is also greatly enhanced by the ability of state officials and political leaders to infiltrate, sometimes to enfeeble, and more often to bend to their interests or inclinations, the powers and agencies of the national government. This will be taken up later, but it should be pointed out here that infiltration through the party system shows up in a variety of ways. For instance, very early in our history senators came to realize the advantages of collective bargaining with the President over appointments. Using the rule of senatorial courtesy, individual senators of the President's party have commonly taken it as a matter of right that they should name the key national field officials in their states, as well as a share of the officials in Washington. In this way and with the added leverage of major committee chairmanships, Reed Smoot (R., Utah), Kenneth McKellar (D., Tenn.), and Pat McCarran (D., Nev.)— to name a few prominent examples from the past generation—built up private empires in the executive branch at public expense. And, presumably, these empires were responsive to the senators' bidding and to the interests of their constituencies. More often, perhaps, senators in suggesting names to the President are only conveyor belts for the wishes of state and county political leaders. These leaders also control the electoral fortunes of a large proportion of the House membership and thereby introduce another decentralizing influence into national councils. The Presidency too, since each state's electoral votes are cast by the unit rule, must ordinarily be sensitive to local political reactions, especially in the larger, doubtful states.

Political forces operating through the party system, in sum, commonly keep national actions vis-à-vis the states far inside the boundaries judicially conceded to the national government under the Constitution. The Supreme Court has been most insulated from these forces and has therefore been—except in the historic slavery controversy—quite consistently nationalist in doctrine. But the characteristic deference of Congress to state wishes has shown up again and again: in recent years, for example, in connection with state "fair trade" laws and in the long delay and controversy over national subsidies for schools, until the breakthrough came in the School Aid Act of 1965.

The states' other face looks downward to the local governments. Here the powers reserved to them under the national Constitution become apparently plenary, save for federal limitations and any home-rule limitations of the states' own constitutions: in theory, state-local relations are not federal. Every local unit traces its legal existence and powers to state enactments. State constitutions, laws, and regulations not only establish local governments, but also place limits, furnish aid, and provide supervision in a great variety of forms. Municipal charters and local taxing and borrowing powers tend to be even more specific and limited. Many local administrative actions are subject to state approval or audit. State legislatures intervene in county and municipal affairs by means of special enabling or restraining acts. When local officials complain of overcentralization, as they have for the past half century, they have their state capitals in mind.

But just as the influence of the states reaches upward into the national government, so they themselves—and for the same reasons—are infiltrated, sometimes spurred, sometimes paralyzed, by the interests of their supposedly subordinate legal creatures. The U.S. State Department and the Governor of Maryland, for example, tried for years to get the Maryland legislature to pass an antidiscrimination law applicable to restaurants along Route 40, the usual highway for African diplomats traveling between Washington and United Nations headquarters in New York. But the eastern shore people, whose counties were overrepresented in the legislature, wanted no such law. By the time a watered-down law was finally forced through, the problem was out of state hands; it was merged in the larger controversy resolved in the public accommodations provisions of the Civil Rights Act of 1964. The multiplicity of elected local officials, their statewide organizations, the county and city political machines, and the locally oriented legislators make state-local relations usually in fact federal, whatever the theoretical plenitude of state powers. Local governments, like the states when they look upward, want help without controls—all sugar and no medicine. The states themselves are in the middle, competing with national and local governments for power and politically interlocked with both.

VARIATIONS AMONG STATES. No two states are alike, not even the Dakotas. Nor is any state in the 1960's the same as it was a decade or two earlier, though the degree of stability and variation is itself one of the characteristic variables in comparing the states. We noted some of these variations in Chapter 1, so that here we need merely underline their relevance to the shaping of what the states do. Though state boundaries are apparently immutable—and logically indefensible—the populations within them have altered greatly. While between 1910 and 1960 the populations of a few states—Vermont and Nebraska, among others—have remained stable, those of others—Florida, Arizona, Nevada, California— have multiplied several times over. The composition of some individual state populations has changed as much as their numbers—in proportions of whites and nonwhites, in proportions of children and "senior citizens" to the working-age population, in rural-urban-suburban balance, in types of occupations.

State governments and their localities respond not only to the changing shape of the problems facing their changing people, but also to the relative weight and effectiveness of the demands that are pressed upon their policy makers. Within living memory, it was practical politics to think of many states and sections in terms of common commodity interests —the cotton states, the silver states, the wheat states. While more than traces of these identifications persist, the list of states with any single prevailing interest of that sort is steadily dwindling. The Southwest has supplanted the Southeast in cotton production. The resort industries have changed the complexions of Florida, Arizona, and Nevada and are making headway in New Hampshire. Oil has made Texas something more than one big cattle ranch, and has begun to dissolve the homogeneous wheat economy of North Dakota. One discernible and significant consequence of this general trend toward economic diversification in the postwar years has been a marked leveling of the previously sharp differences in per capita income among the states. Substantial differences remain, as Table 4.1 shows, but the range from Delaware to Mississippi is now less than 3 to 1. Far greater disparities can be found among the counties of most states.

Not long ago, too, the governments of a number of states could be considered, for many purposes, as subsidiary instruments of one or another of the great industrial and transportation corporations that dominated the business world at the turn of the century. A classic example was California, where for many years what was good for the Southern Pacific Railroad was good enough for the state. Here again, diversification has helped to emancipate state governments from monopolistic control. The eastern railroads, so long accustomed to having their way with the legislatures of their states, are no longer a match for the trucking lobbies. Thus, state and local governments have greater freedom of action and a greater choice of policies in a more diversified society.

Despite the pace of change, historical factors may tend to set the general level of public expectations and so influence the scope and scale of governmental effort in a particular field. This influence may limit, rather than expand, what a government does. Take education, for example. In the Northeast, private colleges were well established long before the nineteenth-century fight for free public education was won. From Maryland to Maine, accordingly, schooling at public expense, furnished by local governments, generally stopped with the high school, though New York City and a few other municipalities maintained city colleges. The better-off and the particularly apt pupils who wanted to go on to college could look to private resources; but the rest, on whom further education was thought to be wasted, were expected to go immediately to work. So these state govern-

Table 4.1. *State and Local General Expenditures, Per Capita and Per $1,000 of Personal Income, 1964–1965*

| States | Population July 1, 1965 (000) | Personal Income Per Capita 1964 | | General Expenditures | | | | State and Local Shares of Direct General Expenditures * (%) | |
| | | | | Per capita | | Per $1,000 of personal income | | | |
		DOLLARS	RANK	DOLLARS	RANK	DOLLARS	RANK	STATE	LOCAL
United States average †	—	$2,566	—	$387	—	$153	—	34.9%	65.1%
Alabama	3,463	1,749	47	307	45	178	20	47.2	52.8
Alaska	253	3,116	5	928	1	302	1	74.0	26.0
Arizona	1,609	2,233	31	415	18	189	14	41.5	58.5
Arkansas	1,960	1,655	48	264	49	162	27	50.2	49.8
California	18,608	3,103	6	534	4	177	21	27.3	72.7
Colorado	1,969	2,566	18	481	6	188	15	35.2	64.8
Connecticut	2,833	3,281	2	402	21	126	48	43.1	56.9
Delaware	505	3,460	1	479	8	142	39	50.1	49.9
Florida	5,805	2,251	29	359	31	162	26	35.8	64.2
Georgia	4,358	1,943	41	310	42	162	28	38.6	61.4
Hawaii	711	2,622	14	494	5	195	11	65.9	34.1
Idaho	692	2,020	39	393	24	194	12	45.8	54.2
Illinois	10,646	3,041	7	366	29	122	49	36.1	63.9
Indiana	4,886	2,544	19	345	33	137	43	35.8	64.2

State									
Iowa	2,760	2,376	24	393	23	166	24	39.6	60.4
Kansas	2,234	2,346	27	385	27	165	25	35.8	64.2
Kentucky	3,179	1,830	46	308	43	169	23	52.6	47.4
Louisiana	3,534	1,877	44	392	25	213	6	52.8	47.2
Maine	993	2,132	35	313	40	147	34	51.6	48.4
Maryland	3,521	2,867	10	363	30	130	44	32.6	67.4
Massachusetts	5,349	2,965	9	409	20	138	42	32.0	68.0
Michigan	8,220	2,755	11	399	22	147	35	32.1	67.9
Minnesota	3,555	2,375	25	433	15	184	16	32.0	68.0
Mississippi	2,322	1,438	50	297	46	207	9	44.0	56.0
Missouri	4,498	2,600	17	324	39	127	45	41.0	59.0
Montana	706	2,252	28	464	11	206	10	48.8	51.2
Nebraska	1,477	2,349	26	342	34	145	37	34.5	65.5
Nevada	440	3,248	3	636	2	211	7	40.2	59.8
New Hampshire	669	2,377	23	340	35	146	36	47.6	52.4
New Jersey	6,775	3,005	8	354	32	119	50	23.9	76.1
New Mexico	1,029	2,041	38	437	14	218	3	51.4	49.6
New York	18,075	3,162	4	480	7	153	31	22.3	77.7
North Carolina	4,914	1,913	42	265	48	140	41	38.9	61.1
North Dakota	652	2,133	34	460	12	218	5	52.8	47.2
Ohio	10,247	2,646	12	331	36	127	46	27.7	72.3
Oklahoma	2,483	2,083	37	379	28	183	18	54.1	45.9
Oregon	1,900	2,606	15	471	10	184	17	45.4	54.6
Pennsylvania	11,522	2,601	16	327	37	127	47	38.9	61.1
Rhode Island	891	2,514	20	391	26	152	32	48.3	51.7

(Table 4.1 continued)

States	Population July 1, 1965 (000)	Personal Income Per Capita, 1964		General Expenditures				State and Local Shares of Direct General Expenditures * (%)	
				Per capita		Per $1,000 of personal income			
		DOLLARS	RANK	DOLLARS	RANK	DOLLARS	RANK	STATE	LOCAL
South Carolina	2,543	$1,655	49	$238	50	$143	38	47.3%	52.7%
South Dakota	703	1,879	43	417	16	218	4	52.5	47.5
Tennessee	3,846	1,859	45	283	47	154	30	42.2	57.8
Texas	10,552	2,188	32	326	38	151	33	34.2	65.8
Utah	990	2,156	33	455	13	210	8	48.4	51.6
Vermont	397	2,119	36	414	19	189	13	59.7	40.3
Virginia	4,456	2,239	30	311	41	141	40	42.0	58.0
Washington	2,990	2,635	13	475	9	181	19	42.2	57.8
West Virginia	1,812	1,965	40	307	44	157	29	57.7	42.3
Wisconsin	4,145	2,490	21	416	17	169	22	27.5	72.5
Wyoming	340	2,441	22	612	3	249	2	52.1	47.9

* "Direct general expenditures" attribute grants-in-aid money to the final spending level of government, rather than to the grant-giving level.

† United States averages include the District of Columbia.

SOURCE: U.S. Bureau of the Census, Governmental Finances in 1964–65 (Washington, D.C., 1966), pp. 45, 50–52.

ments spent relatively little even on elementary and secondary education until well after World War I and into the depression years, when increasing needs and diminishing local resources led to grudging state grant-in-aid systems adapted from other parts of the country. They spent still less on higher education. Even after federal WPA and PWA funds during the depression enabled them to build up the physical plants of their neglected land-grant colleges and normal schools, operating budgets were miserly.[1] Efforts to improve them encountered resistance from friends of the church-connected colleges heavily concentrated in that area and of the hard-pressed smaller nonsectarian colleges, who did not welcome the prospect of increased competition from better state-supported institutions. So, to this day, the northeastern state universities get treated as country cousins.

West of the Appalachians, by contrast, it was taken for granted that schooling should be furnished at public expense. This attitude dates from the school allotments in the old Western Reserve, and, consequently, private colleges play a lesser role. Shared revenues and state grants-in-aid for the school system and state support for higher education have accordingly been forthcoming over a longer period and on a more substantial scale, though local resources have contributed importantly too. In the South local poverty and limited horizons severely handicapped the growth of all public education at least through the first third of the twentieth century. When the southern states set about in earnest to improve matters, local resources were altogether inadequate. Consequently, the highest percentages of state aid in the total outlays for school systems are characteristically to be found in these states.

THE DECLINING SENSE OF COMMUNITY. While the states are units of political organization, few of them are any longer communities in the social or sociological sense. Aside from Texans, a special breed, their citizens do not share many common interests as such, or acquire a distinctive common outlook. There are, however, offsetting influences. For example, the Chamber of Commerce, the American Federation of Labor, the Farm Bureau, the American Legion, the political parties are organized in federal structures and thus have state-based units. Many professions and licensed occupations—law, medicine, teaching, undertaking, and the like—also have statewide associations. Where these are strong and active, they may contribute to a psychological sense of identification with the state as more than an artificially bounded area. Nevertheless, the basic fact stands

---

[1] *New York was an exception to this slur. Though it did comparatively little for higher education generally, its State College of Agriculture at Cornell was the best in the East and one of the best in the nation.*

out. Sentiments of patriotism and community in this country are reserved for the Union rather than the states. But it was not always so.

One consequence is that decisions about what the state governments are to do are often made by "insiders" who operate in comparative obscurity and are often out of phase with the problems and wishes of a protean and highly interactive, but inattentive, public. State officials have a hard time drawing public attention to their problems and activities; indeed, because of this, state government and politics may attract a disproportionate number of people who prefer to operate outside the spotlight. No verbatim records preserve state legislative debates. Committee hearings are seldom recorded and are sketchily reported in the press. Few agencies have regular press offices, and statehouse and courthouse reporters write for the inside pages of their papers. Governors from time to time can highlight an issue—that is one of their main functions—but state business generally is conducted in an atmosphere of low visibility.

It is a paradox that part of the discrepancy between what state and local politicians do and what the people need results from the close identification that a politician must maintain with his state and with the community where he votes. This tends to limit his range of interests. Yet continued local residence is a legal and practical *sine qua non* for those who would make careers of state and local politics—so much so, that Robert Kennedy's successful entry into the New York senatorial campaign in 1964 seemed like a defiance of the law of gravity, even though he moved into a political vacuum.

To the optimistic, local residence may appear ideally appropriate since local candidates should have a deep understanding of the people's needs. But the reasons for the tradition are otherwise. Most of those who reach, or reach for, positions of political power benefit from a highly stabilized set of state-made rules of the game that they can master and that make their overthrow by "upstarts" and newcomers difficult. These rules—on residence and registration of voters, methods of nomination, qualifications of candidates, constituency boundaries, forms of ballots, terms and emoluments of offices, counting and contesting of election returns—generally discriminate against people who move about. Complementary rules require state or local residence for appointment to administrative and civil service positions.

The formal rules are reenforced by practical circumstances. Long residence in a constituency helps the politician to develop the personal ties and build the political "organization" he needs to be elected to office. Even if he is appointed, rather than elected, he must usually be firmly identified with the state and with a particular locality whose political strength he can help to mobilize for elective officials. Compare these formal and informal conditions for the emergence of policy makers and administrators for state and local governments with the conditions for careers in large private corporations or in the permanent career service of the federal government. There, continued local residence is a matter of indifference if not an impossibility. The loyalties of the one are attached to a local area, and of the other to a national institution.

State and local politics, accordingly, are mainly the province of the stay-at-homes in an increasingly mobile society. This not only tends to give a parochial cast to the officials' perceptions of the problems that face the people but also means that their education, formative occupations, and experience of the world may put blinders on them that distinctively affect their capacity to devise solutions even to the problems they discern.[2] The functions of state and local governments reflect these partial views of reality.

GENERAL CHARACTERISTICS. Three broad characteristics stand out in a survey of state functions and their development since 1955—for that matter, from the turn of the century: (1) their overall expansion, (2) their relativity to the environment in particulars, and (3) their movement from indirect to direct methods of administration.

Overall expansion can be easily, if roughly, measured in terms of money and employees. Aggregate state expenditures increased from $20.4 billion in 1955 to $45.5 billion in 1965. After allowing for the increase in population and rising price levels, this *rate* of growth scarcely maintained the expansive pace in state activities during previous decades of this century—when, except for the depression decade, growth more than doubled. But in *absolute* terms of billions of dollars, it is unprecedented. Or consider the growth in the states' civilian employees in the decade, a 69 percent increase that contrasts significantly with the mere 9 percent increase in federal civilian employment. There was horizontal expansion as the range of state activities widened and expansion in depth as previously existing functions were developed. In part this came about through national stimulants to higher nationwide levels of performance, as in the case of improved unemployment benefits; in part also through state responses to the shortcomings in local government resulting from want of interest,

---

[2] *Sociological aspects and political implications of different career paths are explored in a comparison of the careers of 100 U.S. senators and the heads of the 100 largest corporations by Andrew Hacker, "The Elected and the Anointed," American Political Science Review, 55 (September 1961), 539–49.*

jurisdiction, money, or technical competence. At the same time, though, local government expenditures and employment increased in pace with those of the state governments.

Second, the states everywhere appear to do some part of almost everything, and the whole of very little. What will be done in any particular state and field of activity is relative to what is being done by other governments, to what is being done privately, and to other factors. This shows up in any functional comparison between state governments. Public welfare is a good example. In 1965, the 50-state average per capita outlay under that heading was about $28. But Oklahoma and Louisiana spent more than twice that average, most of it for old-age assistance. And at the other end of the scale, New Jersey spent about half, and Indiana and Virginia, at the bottom, a third or less of the national average. The Old Dominion lets fortune and misfortune rest where they fall; in Oklahoma, the state is every brother's keeper.

Or take California and New York, the two most populous states and among the best governed. In 1965, they were roughly equal in population, each with almost a tenth of the national total, and each spent over a tenth of aggregate state expenditures. Each state government raised about 45 percent of the combined total of its area's state and local taxes. It is no surprise, in view of the geography, to learn that California paid more than New York for highways and state police and spent three times as much on natural resources. Nor, in view of the trek of "senior citizens" to California —and the past history of the Townsend movement and similar agitations there—that the state spent over half again as much as New York for public welfare. On the other hand, New York spent about two-thirds more for health and hospitals and thirty times as much for airports. For housing and urban renewal, California spent 2 percent of the all-states total, but New York spent 45 percent. In judging contrasts like these, it is necessary to take into account the total situations of the two states.[3]

The third characteristic of the growth of state functions—increasing use of direct administrative methods of securing social objectives in place of indirect encouragements and deterrents—is not peculiar to the states nor to the present time; it has been a notable feature, too, of the federal government's growth since the Civil War and of state, municipal, and some county governments for the past half century. The figures already

---

[3] *Statistics given, or relied on for other statements in this and the preceding two paragraphs, are drawn from U.S. Bureau of the Census, Compendium of State Government Finances in 1965 (Washington, D.C., 1966); and same, Public Employment in 1965 (Washington, D.C., 1965), and comparable reports for earlier years.*

Table 4.2. State and Local General Expenditures, by Functions, Per Capita, 1964–1965
(Dollars per capita)

State	Total	Education	Highways	Public Welfare	Health and Hospitals	Sanitation	Police Protection	Fire Protection	Local Parks and Recreation	General Control and Financial Administration	Interest on General Debt	All Others
United States average*	$387	$149	$ 63	$33	$28	$12	$13	$ 7	$ 6	$14	$13	$ 49
Alabama	307	108	67	36	20	8	7	3	3	9	9	37
Alaska	928	247	327	26	30	7	16	6	2	37	26	205
Arizona	415	185	72	22	15	15	16	5	5	16	7	56
Arkansas	264	99	53	34	19	6	6	3	1	9	6	29
California	534	203	61	56	33	11	19	10	10	21	14	92
Colorado	481	221	71	52	31	8	12	7	5	19	10	45
Connecticut	402	140	72	32	23	15	14	11	5	15	21	55
Delaware	479	199	112	23	24	7	11	3	5	17	30	46
Florida	359	128	62	22	33	13	14	5	8	16	13	45
Georgia	310	114	50	27	34	8	8	4	5	11	10	41
Hawaii	494	158	51	21	32	26	15	10	12	24	21	124
Idaho	393	147	103	26	26	5	10	5	3	14	5	50
Illinois	366	138	57	35	30	13	15	6	7	13	13	37
Indiana	345	176	54	15	24	11	9	6	3	12	9	27
Iowa	393	175	88	31	24	8	9	4	4	14	6	31

(Table 4.2 continued)

State	Total	Education	Highways	Public Welfare	Health and Hospitals	Sanitation	Police Protection	Fire Protection	Local Parks and Recreation	General Control and Financial Administration	Interest on General Debt	All Others
Kansas	$385	$167	$ 83	$27	$25	$ 9	$ 8	$ 4	$ 3	$14	$11	$33
Kentucky	308	110	66	32	20	13	7	3	1	10	14	31
Louisiana	392	123	76	58	22	18	11	4	4	11	16	47
Maine	313	108	79	30	16	4	8	7	2	13	9	37
Maryland	363	146	54	19	33	16	16	7	5	13	17	37
Massachusetts	409	122	60	46	37	12	15	14	6	17	17	63
Michigan	399	178	48	25	34	18	13	7	6	13	14	43
Minnesota	433	179	83	37	31	12	9	5	8	14	13	41
Mississippi	297	105	72	29	25	4	7	2	1	8	9	34
Missouri	324	121	64	33	25	11	12	5	5	11	8	28
Montana	464	182	140	25	17	6	10	4	3	17	9	50
Nebraska	342	144	80	20	21	8	8	4	4	12	6	35
Nevada	636	200	167	20	44	17	23	12	19	28	15	92
New Hampshire	340	119	85	24	21	8	9	8	3	13	10	40
New Jersey	354	136	48	19	24	15	18	9	7	15	15	48

New Mexico	437	197	91	20	33	13	9	4	3	18	7	42
New York	480	165	49	49	40	16	23	12	9	19	22	76
North Carolina	265	117	40	19	22	9	8	3	2	10	5	30
North Dakota	460	174	115	14	30	5	7	3	8	15	7	83
Ohio	331	126	60	20	26	13	10	6	4	12	10	44
Oklahoma	379	143	70	21	66	6	8	4	3	11	11	35
Oregon	471	204	101	21	29	10	13	6	5	21	11	50
Pennsylvania	327	126	54	20	27	10	12	4	4	13	15	42
Rhode Island	391	128	70	25	40	18	14	11	3	16	12	54
South Carolina	238	103	42	21	16	4	7	2	1	8	4	29
South Dakota	417	161	139	13	25	5	8	2	3	14	3	43
Tennessee	283	98	68	25	20	9	8	4	4	9	9	29
Texas	326	146	61	17	24	10	10	5	5	10	11	28
Utah	455	219	96	21	28	10	9	4	5	14	7	42
Vermont	414	157	121	20	33	6	7	4	1	16	7	41
Virginia	311	126	73	19	13	10	9	4	3	11	11	32
Washington	475	189	81	21	41	18	12	7	6	19	13	68
West Virginia	307	113	76	17	36	8	6	3	2	11	7	26
Wisconsin	416	175	66	27	29	19	13	9	10	15	9	44
Wyoming	612	205	225	43	22	7	12	5	2	18	7	64

* United States averages include the District of Columbia.

Note: Table 4.2 shows combined state and local expenditures. See Chapter 5, where the emphasis is on the separate levels, for state-only and local-only figures.

SOURCE: U.S. Bureau of the Census, *Governmental Finances in 1964–65* (Washington, D.C., 1966), pp. 45–48.

given on state employment, and the comparable tendencies in local employment, show how clearly it marked the trend of the 1950's and 1960's.

The growing reliance on administration is hardly a deliberate policy—a good deal of political mileage can still be got from denunciations of fattening bureaucracy. It is, for the most part, an accumulation of separate responses to feelings of popular impatience with the results of self-help (or helplessness) in meeting conditions beyond satisfactory individual or family control. More and more conditions are falling under that description. The states have moved to supplant or supplement the uncertain remedies of lawsuits with administrative regulatory systems; they have moved to supplement private and local government financial resources; they have moved to supply previously nonexistent services and facilities calculated to afford minimum standards of health, shelter, institutional care, recreational opportunities, occupational training, mobility.

TRADITIONAL FUNCTIONS. The traditional occupations of state government were centered in the state capitols and county courthouses. They concerned the business of lawmaking, law enforcement, revenue, an embryonic administrative complex, and the politics of parties, personalities, and interests. These all survive in an active and enlarged form today and are discussed in later chapters of this book. Only one needs notice here: the provision and modification of the general legal fabric of rights and duties within which individuals, families, associations, and business firms go about their affairs, whether or not they ever consult a lawyer or appear in court. A growing network of federal laws and regulations is superimposed on this fabric, taking precedence in cases of conflict, and a subordinate mesh of municipal regulations fills many of the interstices. But the basic general coverage is supplied mostly by the states, acting through their legislatures, courts, and administrative arms.

Among these matters of homely concern are the conditions of marriage and divorce, custody, inheritance, and commitment to mental institutions; the registration and validity of wills, deeds, and mortgages; the permissible terms and enforceability of business contracts; liability for damages in accident and negligence cases; and the main range of criminal law—murder, rape, arson, robbery, theft. Within some federal limitations, each state makes and changes its own law on all these matters, and few citizens fail to encounter one or another of them at some time. Maintaining and modifying this body of law is a major responsibility of the states. Unspectacular as most of these topics are, and unedifying as the states' processes often are, it is nevertheless a major public service to handle them as sensibly and acceptably as circumstances permit. This is the workaday governmental contribution to the business of social adjustment to changes in conditions and concepts of justice. Local governments have neither the jurisdiction nor the resources to handle more than a part of it, and the national government would be clogged, and justice denied by delay, if it all went to Washington.

2. *The Jobs of Local Governments*

Local governments, as the next chapter explains more fully, are of several sorts—counties, townships, incorporated municipalities, and special districts—with boundaries overlapping so that any one person or locality is usually within the jurisdiction of several. The functions of any particular local government accordingly depend a good deal on what else is being done by the others in the same neighborhood. Special districts, the most numerous category, are created to perform (and usually stick to) a single function and activities closely related to it. Their names are self-explanatory—for example, school district, irrigation district, sanitary (sewage) district. Commonly, they have their own tax levies. Townships, another numerous but relatively unimportant category, are subdivisions of counties. For historical reasons they are found in only 16 states, mostly in the Midwest, and ordinarily only in rural or unincorporated suburban areas. Their functions are correspondingly quite limited, usually having to do with rural schools and local road maintenance, and they subsist on small earmarked portions of the local property tax, often supplemented by state grants or rebates of portions of state-collected taxes.

County and municipal (city or town) governments, by contrast, are general-purpose units and consequently of greater significance. At the turn of this century they raised and spent, in the aggregate, a little more public money than the states and the national government combined. Today they are still the units with the most direct and frequent contact with the largest number of people. Their functions, therefore, depend chiefly on the immediate needs and characteristics—the geography, history, climate, demography, and economy—of the particular areas and populations in their jurisdictions.

Some such needs are old and more or less common to all, and so regularly fall to the counties: the machinery of justice—sheriffs, coroners, prosecutors, judges, juries, and jails—and the registry of legal documents such as deeds, mortgages and wills; records of births and deaths; the qualification of voters and conduct of elections; public health officers and

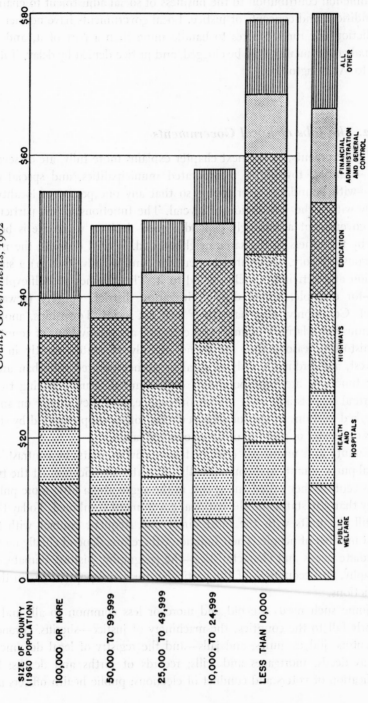

Figure 4.1. Per Capita Expenditure by Function for Population-Size Groups of County Governments, 1962

SOURCE: U.S. Bureau of the Census, Census of Governments: 1962, Vol. IV, No. 2, Finances of County Governments (Washington, D.C., 1964), p. 7.

hospitals; the maintenance and improvement of county roads; the provision or supervision of schools; and the relief of the poor. However, since all but a few of the 3,000 counties in the United States are rural or near-rural in character, and depend chiefly on the property tax, supplemented by some state grants or rebates, the common level of county performance in meeting these minimum needs of civilized society is quite low in both quality and quantity. (See Figure 4.1.) Those that contain large cities have potential tax bases for doing better, but in these cases the cities have usually undertaken most of the increased responsibilities and developed most of the additional sources of revenue. On the whole, counties in well-to-do surburban areas have been the most successful in raising their sights and improving their capabilities.

Among traditional county functions, the registration of voters was dramatically lifted from local obscurity into national prominence in the 1960's by the widespread demonstrations that culminated in the passage of the Voting Rights Act of 1965. Led by Martin Luther King's Southern Christian Leadership Conference, the NAACP and other civil rights organizations, and enlisting college students and ministers of the Gospel from the North as well as Negroes South and North, protest marches and sitdowns and attendant incidents of violence and official repression brought one southern county seat after another into the headlines and onto the TV screens across the nation, as efforts were made to oblige recalcitrant election officials to register would-be Negro voters. The 1965 law, probably the most sweeping federal intervention in this field since Reconstruction days, outlawed literacy tests in counties where less than half the population of voting age was registered to vote, or actually voted, in November, 1964, and—bypassing the slow uncertainties of lawsuits—authorized the appointment of federal registrars to enroll those who were refused registration by officials of those counties. No transformation of county functions by the processes of technological advance in prosperous suburbs has effected more significant social change than this act presaged in some of the least prosperous counties in the land.

City and town governments (outside New England, where "towns" are more like pint-size counties) do nearly everything (and more) that county governments do, but on a more intensive, specialized, and expensive scale. That, after all, is the basic reason for their separate incorporation as municipalities—to provide for the special public needs of urban living that the county government cannot afford to meet. To take but a few examples, cities cannot get along with the jack-of-all-trades sheriff and judge who suffice for the county. They need precinct organizations for

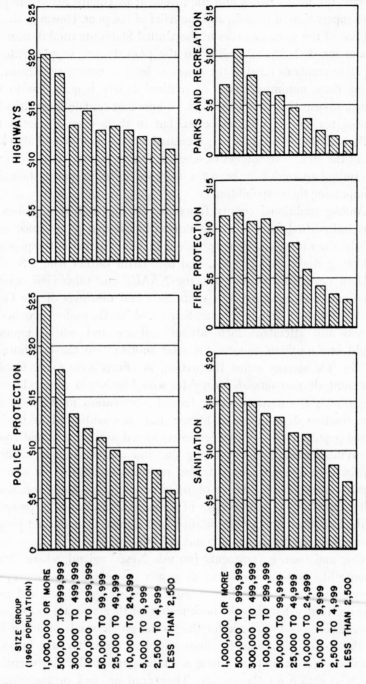

Figure 4.2. Per Capita Expenditure of Various Size Groups of Municipalities for Selected Functions, 1962

SIZE GROUP
(1960 POPULATION)

1,000,000 OR MORE
500,000 TO 999,999
300,000 TO 499,999
100,000 TO 299,999
50,000 TO 99,999
25,000 TO 49,999
10,000 TO 24,999
5,000 TO 9,999
2,500 TO 4,999
LESS THAN 2,500

POLICE PROTECTION

HIGHWAYS

SANITATION

FIRE PROTECTION

PARKS AND RECREATION

SOURCE: U.S. Bureau of the Census, *Census of Governments: 1962*, Vol. IV, No. 3, *Finances of Municipalities and Township Governments* (Washington, D.C., 1964), p. 10.

street patrols, burglary, homicide, and vice squads; they need night courts, domestic relations courts, and juvenile courts. They need elaborate fire-fighting forces. They need street paving and lighting and repair. They furnish public utilities and services on an enormous scale. Depending on size and other factors, the proportion of municipal resources committed to these services varies a good deal (see Figure 4.2).[4]

Viewed as problem-solving institutions in the larger context of a rapidly urbanizing society, city governments are on the firing line. They must cope with nearly all the most urgent contemporary social problems: the effects of automation on employment, desegregation of racial and ethnic groups, education and housing for the underprivileged, birth control and juvenile delinquency, urban renewal, mass transportation facilities, and a host of others. One of the most perplexing problems, as will be seen in the next chapter, is that of devising satisfactory ways of cooperating with impinging governmental units in the same area in order to solve metropolitan problems that none can handle alone.

3. *Education*

By any measure, public education is the largest and most important state and local government activity. Over a third of state general outlays, both direct and intergovernmental, and almost half (45 percent in 1964–65) of local expenditures are made for this purpose. Outside the federal establishment, teachers make up by far the most numerous category of public employees; they and other educational employees account for almost half of all state and local employment. In 1965, public school pupils made up over five-sixths of the population of school age (50 million between 5 and 17 years). Yet, paradoxically, the substantive problems of public education have ordinarily engaged no corresponding proportion of the time and concern of governors, legislatures, mayors, and city councils. For despite its many controversial features, public school education has become largely the province of professional educators; its politics is usually insulated from other forms of local political contest, and its revenues and outlays are separated from regular budgetary channels. Only recently has the issue of racial desegregation brought the schools into the general political arena.

---

[4] *For comparisons of the effects of size, and other data on county and municipal functions, see U.S. Bureau of the Census, Census of Governments: 1962, Vol. IV, No. 2, Finances of County Governments; and No. 3, Finances of Municipalities and Township Governments (Washington, D.C., 1964).*

PUBLIC SCHOOLS. For the age brackets where school attendance is compulsory, schools must be located conveniently close to the homes of the pupils. Accordingly, the establishment and administration of the schools have historically been, and for the most part remain, a local concern and responsibility. The main lines of organizational cleavage within the system are geographical boundaries and age levels.

In the open spaces of the Plains States from Missouri and Kansas to the Dakotas, we can still find a large number of small, all-purpose educational units suited to sparse populations and scant resources. In 1965, over a third of the 27,000 local school districts in the United States were located in seven states in this region—many of them with less than 15 pupils each, mostly taught in one-teacher schools spread over a number of grades.

However, paved roads, school buses, and snow plows, together with state aid, have helped to transform most school systems, especially during the past decade. They have helped them to realize, among other objectives, the financial economies of large-scale operations and the qualitative advantages of greater specialization. The large-scale operations have been the combined result of the consolidation of districts and of the rapid growth of new population concentrations, particularly in metropolitan suburbs and in newly developed areas.

Specialization has proceeded along several broad program lines, which have been adapted to local conditions. For example, there is a sharper differentiation according to age in order to segregate pupils at the puberty stage—in junior high schools—from the younger children on the one hand and the older adolescents on the other. The range of grades has also been extended by introducing kindergartens—and even pre-kindergarten classes —at the bottom and adding "community" or junior colleges at the top. The latter have usually been launched with two-year curricula (sometimes later extended to four) and are the only institutions of "higher" education that have generally remained under the jurisdiction of the public school authorities. In another form of specialization, pupils are taught in separate groups based on capacities, handicaps, career objectives, and other characteristics. The School Aid Act of 1965—a major breakthrough after years of controversy—authorized federal grants for libraries, laboratories, and other facilities that strengthen these trends toward specialization.

The evolution of educational programs has gone hand in hand, through the decade of the 1950's and beyond, with a sharp increase in enrollment (Table 4.3) and a massive growth in investment in plant and equipment. In 1965, over a quarter of the total population was of school age, up from one-fifth in 1950, and 95 percent of the potential pupils were

Table 4.3. *Public School Statistics*

State	Population Aged 5–17, July 1, 1965 (000)	Public School Enrollment, Fall, 1965 (000)			Percent Enrollment of Population Aged 5–17, 1965–66	Percent Change in Elementary and Secondary Enrollment 1955–56 to 1965–66	No. of School-age Children (5–17) per 100 Adults Aged 21–64, 1964
		Total	Elementary	Secondary			
All states and D.C.	49,997	42,244	26,666	15,579	84.5%	40.0%	52
Alabama	964	830	463	367	86.1	18.4	59
Alaska	72	60	41	19	83.1	108.1	59
Arizona	440	406	296	110	92.2	101.1	57
Arkansas	513	453	252	201	88.3	8.5	56
California	4,600	4,300	804	1,496	93.5	91.1	49
Colorado	523	487	288	199	93.1	54.3	54
Connecticut	700	566	398	168	80.8	52.6	48
Delaware	137	112	64	48	81.5	74.7	55
Florida	1,405	1,221	688	533	86.9	80.2	50
Georgia	1,185	1,055	695	360	89.1	26.1	56
Hawaii	193	162	94	68	84.0	36.6	56
Idaho	197	174	92	81	88.2	26.5	61
Illinois	2,660	2,108	1,376	732	79.3	45.5	49

(Table 4.3 continued)

State	Population Aged 5–17, July 1, 1965 (000)	Public School Enrollment, Fall, 1965 (000)			Percent Enrollment of Population Aged 5–17, 1965–66	Percent Change in Elementary and Secondary Enrollment 1955–56 to 1965–66	No. of School-age Children (5–17) per 100 Adults Aged 21–64, 1964
		Total	Elementary	Secondary			
Indiana	1,295	1,140	702	438	88.0%	33.6%	54
Iowa	725	625	445	179	86.2	19.6	55
Kansas	581	517	372	145	89.0	27.2	54
Kentucky	850	677	445	232	79.6	17.6	56
Louisiana	1,012	803	505	297	79.3	38.6	62
Maine	257	223	149	74	86.6	33.0	54
Maryland	927	762	441	321	82.2	58.6	53
Massachusetts	1,296	1,030	620	410	79.5	39.1	48
Michigan	2,270	1,975	1,165	810	87.0	47.1	57
Minnesota	968	805	450	355	83.2	39.0	58
Mississippi	677	583	358	226	86.1	14.4	65
Missouri	1,115	963	609	354	86.4	31.7	51
Montana	196	167	109	58	84.9	33.2	59
Nebraska	381	320	196	124	84.0	25.4	54
Nevada	110	106	67	39	96.4	163.3	50

State							
New Hampshire	169	129	83	46	76.2	46.8	52
New Jersey	1,633	1,286	845	441	78.8	53.4	46
New Mexico	310	268	152	116	86.5	51.2	67
New York	4,206	3,190	1,838	1,352	75.8	31.9	44
North Carolina	1,334	1,182	851	331	88.6	17.8	55
North Dakota	183	149	98	51	81.4	20.9	61
Ohio	2,735	2,270	1,621	649	83.0	43.1	54
Oklahoma	620	608	356	252	98.1	23.0	50
Oregon	494	447	274	173	90.5	37.1	53
Pennsylvania	2,854	2,190	1,226	963	76.7	25.6	48
Rhode Island	219	155	89	65	70.5	36.4	46
South Carolina	743	636	387	249	85.6	17.1	61
South Dakota	195	167	111	56	85.8	31.3	59
Tennessee	1,005	872	567	305	86.8	20.5	53
Texas	2,850	2,468	1,830	638	86.6	43.0	56
Utah	296	286	166	120	96.8	48.2	65
Vermont	105	84	55	29	80.0	23.6	54
Virginia	1,158	987	636	351	85.3	38.0	52
Washington	780	724	400	325	92.9	31.7	53
West Virginia	489	429	240	189	87.6	-4.5	56
Wisconsin	1,108	859	516	343	77.5	45.9	56
Wyoming	93	86	50	36	92.8	30.7	56

SOURCES: Research Division, National Education Association, *Estimates of School Statistics, 1965–66* (Washington, D.C., December, 1965), p. 24; and *Rankings of the States, 1966* (Washington, D.C., January, 1966), pp. 11, 17.

enrolled, all but 14 percent of them in public schools. The public school enrollment was about 42 million, up 68 percent from 1950. Current expenditures for local schools were $18.9 billion, compared to $7.4 billion in 1955, and over the same period, capital outlay had gone from $2.8 to $3.5 billion.[5]

But these changes in programs, enrollments, and expenditures were by no means evenly distributed nor uniform in pace: we have nothing corresponding to the European tradition of a central ministry of education that fixes curricula, sets standards, and allocates budgets all over the country. On the contrary, practically every type of program known in the past half century—even to the use of McGuffey's *Reader*—can be found in operation today at one place or another. Three states saw their enrollments doubled between 1955 and 1966, while Arkansas had a rise of only 9 percent over the decade and West Virginia actually suffered a net loss.[6] Current expenditures per pupil in average daily attendance, the handiest overall guide to the relative quality of the educational effort of the states, averaged $532 across the nation in 1966. But these expenditures were $400 or less in ten states and almost $900 in New York; and the range was even greater among individual school districts [7] (see Figure 4.3).

The disparities of all sorts in the variegated array of public schools, however, would undoubtedly be much greater today but for two sets of developments, one financial and the other administrative, that together have had markedly equalizing effects. On the financial side, the large-scale introduction of state money has transformed the general picture, and federal funds have begun to transform it further. The proportion of school revenues derived from state sources, which had never reached 20 percent before the Depression, approached 30 percent in 1939–40 and 40 percent by 1949–50. It has stabilized at about that ratio since then, though the absolute amounts have continued to rise. New York started the trend with a "foundation" program guaranteeing each locality a fixed amount per pupil in average daily attendance to ensure minimum standards in instruction, teacher qualification and compensation, and other contributions to

---

[5] *All educational statistics, unless otherwise noted, are derived from U.S. Bureau of the Census, Statistical Abstract of the United States: 1966; Governmental Finances in 1964–65; and Census of Governments: 1962, Vol. VI, No. 4, Historical Statistics on Governmental Finances and Employment; and Research Division, National Education Association, Estimates of School Statistics, 1965–66 (Washington, D.C., 1965), and Rankings of the States, 1966 (Washington, D.C., 1966).*

[6] *Research Division, National Education Association, Rankings of the States, 1966,* p. 17.

[7] U.S. Bureau of the Census, Statistical Abstract of the United States: 1966, p. 125.

Figure 4.3. *Current Expenditure per Pupil in Average Daily Attendance—Public Elementary and Secondary Day Schools, 1965*

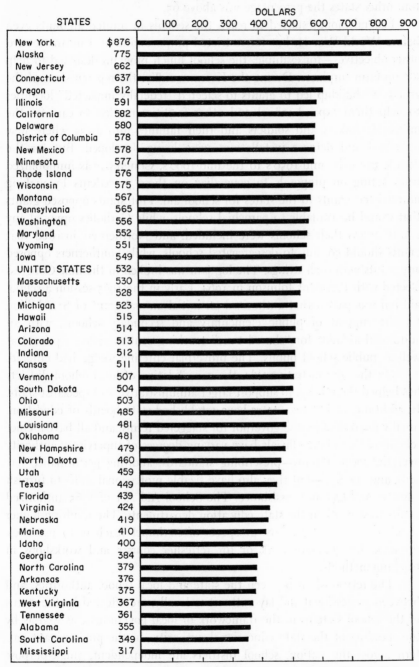

STATES		DOLLARS
New York	$876	
Alaska	775	
New Jersey	662	
Connecticut	637	
Oregon	612	
Illinois	591	
California	582	
Delaware	580	
District of Columbia	578	
New Mexico	578	
Minnesota	577	
Rhode Island	576	
Wisconsin	575	
Montana	567	
Pennsylvania	565	
Washington	556	
Maryland	552	
Wyoming	551	
Iowa	549	
UNITED STATES	532	
Massachusetts	530	
Nevada	528	
Michigan	523	
Hawaii	515	
Arizona	514	
Colorado	513	
Indiana	512	
Kansas	511	
Vermont	507	
South Dakota	504	
Ohio	503	
Missouri	485	
Louisiana	481	
Oklahoma	481	
New Hampshire	479	
North Dakota	460	
Utah	459	
Texas	449	
Florida	439	
Virginia	424	
Nebraska	419	
Maine	410	
Idaho	400	
Georgia	384	
North Carolina	379	
Arkansas	376	
Kentucky	375	
West Virginia	367	
Tennessee	361	
Alabama	355	
South Carolina	349	
Mississippi	317	

SOURCE: U.S. Bureau of the Census, *Statistical Abstract of the United States: 1966* (Washington, D.C., 1966), p. 104.

the quality of education. By 1965 only four states, resisting the trend, still contributed less than 15 percent of school revenues; on the other hand, in four other states the percentage was above 65.

Federal money started to reach the schools in limited amounts even before World War II, but for restricted purposes and as a means toward other objectives—for example, the school lunch program designed to help use up farm surpluses. During the Korean conflict the repercussions of the armament buildup led to grants to selected "federally impacted" localities to help them expand school and other facilities needed to care for the influx of workers and soldiers and their families into areas where new industrial and defense installations were being developed. But for the decade from the mid-1950's to the mid-1960's, Congress was immobilized from acting on proposals to generalize on these precedents by making unrestricted grants to the states for school aid. Protestants opposed grants that would be available to parochial schools, while Catholics opposed any grants unless their schools were included; and Northerners insisted that grants should go only to desegregated schools, while Southerners opposed any grants with such strings. The log jam was broken in the new Congress elected with President Johnson in 1964. Early in the 1965 session a school aid bill was passed that authorized an initial annual grant of $1.1 billion for the support of public elementary and secondary schools, with an additional amount for "shared time" teaching centers open to private as well as public school pupils. The proverbial entering wedge had entered.

On the administrative side, the consolidation of local school districts has helped the schools to support larger administrative and specialist staffs. In addition, all but two states have established state boards of education, usually appointed by the governor for staggered terms, and all have a chief school officer. These officials have varying degrees of supervisory authority over the local systems—prescribing standards, auditing performance records, and the like—but they also have sizable professional staffs to furnish advisory and technical assistance. The School Aid Act of 1965 authorized grants to strengthen the state education departments. The resulting higher standards and better salary prospects often impel teachers to use their summers for graduate work or for refresher courses and workshops in teaching methods.

The relationships between the state and local school authorities, and between professional and lay authorities locally, are affected by the status of the school systems in the framework of local government as well as by the standing of the state educational authority. In the predominant pattern across the nation, school districts are independent, single-purpose units of government. But in four states, all schools are administered as departments within the regular county, city, town, or state governments, and in seventeen other states the situation is mixed. The 1962 *Census of Governments* counted nearly 2,400 of these "dependent" school systems, including the largest one in the country, in New York City. In these systems, which enroll over a fifth of the country's public school pupils, the school budgets must compete directly in a political forum against other claims on municipal funds. Orthodox doctrine among school administrators condemns this arrangement; however, orthodox doctrine in public finance and public administration applauds it.

Whatever the merits of the argument over an autonomous status for the schools in the abstract, practical considerations set limits to extreme solutions in the direction either of subservience or of complete independence. For one thing, the magnitude and technology of school operations in our age and public attention to the quality of their performance inevitably put their conduct and planning mainly in the hands of professionals. Lay officials cannot cope with their complexities. So the day is past or passing when the school systems were a hunting ground for patronage, when school superintendents, board members, or state legislators connived with textbook publishers on the adoption of texts and when nepotism prevailed in the appointment of teachers. Furthermore, professional organizations— particularly the teachers' associations federated in the National Education Association—have become major influences on legislative and administrative policy, marshaling support for programs they have decided to approve and fending off unwanted developments. Within some bounds, then, professional educators and administrators run the schools whether the system is labeled dependent or independent.

On the other hand, the financial and personnel requirements of the schools have become so large that they cannot be considered and disposed of altogether independently. The day is gone when a single earmarked tax sufficed and school authorities could be told to work out their problems within the revenue it yielded. Seeking new money, whether to be furnished by direct state subsidy, or by the relaxation of local taxing, borrowing, or debt limits, or by larger federal grants, automatically brings school problems into a broader political forum. And school authorities needing more qualified teachers cannot regularly disregard the broader policy views they encounter in the teachers' colleges, which constitute their main sources of supply, and which are likely to reflect statewide or even national trends of opinion on educational affairs.

Then, too, from time to time issues arise that stir intense emotional reactions from parents and the outside public—issues that cause lay intervention and that can only be resolved in political contests and compromises. When these are localized and transient, like community flare-ups over sex or drinking or athletic scandals, they can be contained locally; when they are abstract and generalized, like an anti-communism crusade, they can sometimes be settled innocuously by a statewide law imposing a mandatory course, say, in American history. But when they involve religion or race relations, the general constitutional formulas of church-state separation and of equal protection of the laws, flexible as these have proved to be, have not sufficed to still controversies, in which school authorities inevitably become embroiled. For example, recurrent religious disputes center on such questions as whether school bus service shall be provided at public expense for parochial as well as public school pupils (this has been approved in all or parts of 13 states); whether and in what manner—on or off school premises, etc.—"released time" for religious classes may be allowed (13 states have enabling laws but usually school boards proceed without express authority); whether Bible-reading or a flag salute shall be compulsory, and so on.[8] Supreme Court decisions on these topics are confusing and apparently are widely disregarded in practice. Far more serious troubles, involving boycotts, sitdowns and mass protests, both by Negroes and by whites, have attended the efforts of school authorities to cope with the problems of desegregation, North and South. Success in these endeavors, where it has come, has been as much the product of political skills as of professional competence.

SCHOOL DESEGREGATION. When the Supreme Court in 1954 ruled unanimously in *Brown* v. *Board of Education* that the operation of segregated schools was an unconstitutional denial of the equal protection of the laws, it set in halting but forward motion a series of painful and fundamental readjustments in many systems of public education—readjustments marked in a few cases by the most serious confrontations of state and federal power since the Reconstruction era. The impact was felt first in the South, where school segregation was required by law; but during the

---

[8] *The Supreme Court, in* Engel v. Vitale, 370 *U.S.* 421 (1962), *outlawed the use in New York schools of a 22-word prayer, composed at the direction of the state Board of Regents and carefully contrived to avoid giving offense to any sect, even though any child who objected, or whose parents objected, was to be excused from attendance while the prayer was uttered. The Court's opinion reads: ". . . it is no part of the business of government to compose official prayers for any group of the American people to recite. . . ." The Court was not moved by references to official chaplains, the phrase "In God we trust" on coins and currency, or other numerous examples of religious symbols under official sponsorship. See also* School District of Abingdon Township v. Schempp, 374 *U.S.* 203 (1963), *forbidding compulsory Bible reading in schools.*

initial decade after the *Brown* decision most of the resulting action took place outside the schools. Three broad choices were available: compliance, "token" integration, and active resistance. The District of Columbia led the procession to full compliance, followed by the border states from Delaware to Oklahoma. To ease this transition, many school boards adopted step-by-step plans, integrating one grade each year. North Carolina chose the intermediate course with a "pupil placement" law authorizing local boards, on application, to assign pupils, white or Negro, to particular schools after examining their qualifications. This law, not discriminatory on its face, was sustained; in operation it allowed a limited number of selected Negro pupils to be admitted peaceably to previously all-white schools. Virginia, Louisiana, and Arkansas took the offensive in "massive resistance," with laws authorizing their governors to close the schools in any county if a federal court ordered them integrated, and providing tuition payments for pupils in private schools. These laws were declared unconstitutional.[9] Alabama and Mississippi waited to be smoked out. To break the resistance in the Deep South, litigation was not enough. In 1957 in Little Rock, and again in 1962 in Oxford, Mississippi, the National Guard was federalized and regular army troops were rushed in to enforce federal court desegregation orders, against the efforts of recalcitrant state governors to thwart them by force. These events, together with the passage of the Civil Rights Act and the outcome of the presidential election in 1964, spelled the end of overt state defiance. As the first decade came to a close, the legal barriers erected by the states were down; small but significantly growing numbers of Negro pupils were enrolled in desegregated schools; and an apparently irreversible upward trend—fostered by the School Aid Act of 1965—was under way.

By this time the focus of attention was turning to the no less intractable problems of de facto segregation in northern metropolitan areas. There, the white populations had been moving for two or three decades to the new real estate developments and new schools of the mushrooming suburbs, while emigration from the South added to the disproportionate concentration of Negroes in the central sections of the cities, with their old schools. A striking example is Washington, D.C., where some 85 percent of the enrollment in the desegregated public schools is Negro. The central cities had limited resources of their own to cope with the needed readjust-

---

[9] Bush *v.* Orleans Parish School Board, 364 *U.S.* 500 (1960); Griffin *v.* Prince Edward County School Board, 377 *U.S.* 218 (1964); and see J. W. Peltason, 58 Lonely Men: Southern Federal Judges and School Desegregation (*New York: Harcourt*, 1961); and Corinne Silverman, The Little Rock Story, *Inter-University Case Program*, No. 41, reprinted in *Edwin A. Bock and Alan K. Campbell (eds.)*, Case Studies in American Government (*Englewood Cliffs, N.J.: Prentice-Hall*, 1962).

ments. Few of them could expand their taxing jurisdictions to take in the suburbs by annexation. Between 1950 and 1960, 8 of the 10 (and 19 of the 50) largest cities in the nation—all north of the Ohio River—actually declined in population. Meanwhile their growing Negro populations became increasingly militant, and formed voting blocs potentially too strong to be disregarded in city and state elections. Under these pressures New York, Chicago, and other urban school authorities experimented with expedients to improve the quality and equality of education—expedients that in turn sometimes provoked white counter-protests. North and South, the school authorities in 1965 entered the second decade after *Brown* with a mandate but not yet an adequate program.

HIGHER EDUCATION. State and local governments are deeply involved in the quantity and quality of American higher education. A little over a third (762) of some 2,100 colleges and other institutions of higher education are publicly supported; yet in 1964 almost two-thirds of the nation's students were enrolled in them.[10]

Half of these public institutions are junior or "community" colleges that do not offer four-year programs or confer bachelor's degrees. Though they form the most numerous single category of public institutions of higher education and their number is growing rapidly, they are the midgets in enrollments and financial resources. They are usually governed by local bodies, under state supervision, and derive their funds mostly from local sources—county, municipal, or district—often supplemented by modest state grants. By contrast, only 20 public institutions that offer bachelor's or higher degrees are under such local control.

Next in number are the nearly 200 teachers' colleges (although some have dropped that designation and have broadened their programs toward a general liberal arts curriculum). They are almost entirely state supported. Even though they have their own boards of trustees, they generally maintain close ties with the state departments of education, since their programs are so largely geared to state teacher-certification requirements. Also of modest proportions in numbers, students, staff, and resources are the

---

[10] *Statistics on higher education are from Office of Education, U.S. Department of Health, Education, and Welfare,* Digest of Educational Statistics: 1964 Edition (Washington, D.C., 1964), *pp. 92f, 104; same,* Educational Directory, 1963–64, Part 3, Higher Education, *pp. 12f; U.S. Bureau of the Census,* Compendium of State Government Finances in 1966, *pp. 13, 28f; same,* Statistical Abstract of the United States: 1966, *p. 139; and, for individual institutions,* The World Almanac: 1964 (New York: New York World-Telegram and Sun, 1964), *pp. 513–32. Enrollment figures vary, both between and within cited sources, because of different treatment of degree and nondegree students, resident and extension students, etc., but general proportions are not significantly affected.*

publicly supported liberal arts colleges and the specialized technological (agricultural and engineering) and other professional institutions.

The giants in the field are to be found among the 98 state-supported universities that mount a varied educational program of liberal arts and technical and vocational studies, with three or more professional schools and graduate work leading to the doctorate of philosophy and other advanced degrees. Almost everywhere outside of New England and New York, they are the largest schools in their states, and many of them, like the state universities in California, Michigan, Minnesota, and Illinois, have huge enrollments.[11] With a few exceptions, the largest ones are among the 68 land-grant institutions, which were established and have been supported in part by original grants of public lands and continuing funds to the states from the federal government; they enroll over a third of the country's university students. To deal with many of their common problems, from athletic rules to library acquisition policies, the land-grant institutions have formed regional associations and conferences. In addition, they have established national associations, notably the Association of Land Grant Colleges and Universities, to formulate their positions and represent their interests in both congressional legislation and administrative policies affecting such lively concerns as the terms and distribution of federal grants and contracts.

As a class, the state institutions confront much the same problems as their private counterparts. But they display characteristic differences because they are accountable to a wider and more varied clientele than students, parents, alumni, and donors. Their admission policies are much less restrictive. Their tuition and fees are much lower, at least for state residents. Only 22 of them were included in a 1961 listing of 171 institutions with endowments of $5 million or more—only seven above $25 million and two (California and Texas) above $100 million. To be sure, they have behind them the potential of the taxing and borrowing powers of their states. But they must accordingly consider sentiments dominant in the state legislatures and organized interests influential in guiding those sentiments. They are governed by boards of trustees, either appointed by the governor or popularly elected for staggered terms—a means of insulating them from direct involvement in political controversies. This uncertain shield is occasionally reinforced by their accrediting associations, which can suspend an institution from good standing—a mild form of boycott that

---

[11] *Dwarfing them all is the City University of New York, with its four municipally supported colleges, enrolling over 100,000 students.*

bears most heavily on students about to graduate or transfer—in an overt case of outside political intervention. But the trustees are not ordinarily immune to prevailing attitudes among the citizenry. Unless the state institutions are engaged in important federally financed activities, like the University of California's atomic energy contracts, they are at once sustained and limited by the degree of effectively articulated support mustered on their behalf within their states.

The richest states do not make the greatest investment, proportional to their resources, in their colleges and universities. California, Michigan, New York, and Illinois rank highest in absolute amounts, but five poorer states (Alaska, Colorado, New Mexico, Oregon, and Utah) lead in relative effort, spending over $50 per capita and $20 or more per $1,000 of their residents' personal income. Altogether, the states spent $5.3 billion on higher education in 1965, which was about 13 percent of their total general expenditures and quite a leap from the $2.6 billion they spent for that purpose in 1959.

4. Transportation

HIGHWAYS. The second largest state activity, measured by money outlays, and the most visible physically, is the provision and maintenance of highways. Good roads have transformed the American way of living— and of dying. Highway accidents caused 49,000 deaths in 1965, and over four million personal injuries: casualties at these rates over the previous decade took a larger toll than all the combat losses suffered by the armed forces of the United States since the Civil War. Safety measures, as well as construction and maintenance, are therefore a leading objective of government policy.

Of the 3.6 million miles of streets and roads sufficiently marked or improved to be distinguished from paths and trails, nearly nine-tenths are classed as rural. About one-tenth are under municipal jurisdiction and are located where almost two-thirds of the population lives. Of the total, 900,000 miles are part of the federal-aid system, and these carry about half of all traffic. Slightly over 1 percent of the total mileage is included in the 41,000-mile Interstate System currently under construction; when completed, this system is expected to carry over 20 percent of the total traffic. Evidence of the impatience of users with the existing road conditions, and of the well-organized desire of highway contractors to be helpful in ameliorating them—in short, the emphasis on new construction and improvements—can be seen in the large proportion of all highway and street expenditures ($8.4 billion of $12.3 billion in 1964–65) that goes for capital outlays in comparison with maintenance.

Viewed historically, the highway system has evolved mostly by super-imposing on the earlier network of country roads and city streets—once almost entirely a local responsibility to build and maintain [12]—a succession of fewer, but much more modern and expensive, highways. These have been financed on more and more generous terms by successively higher levels of government. By the mid-1920's, as automobiles came into general use, every state had established a unified highway department, already a requisite of eligibility for federal grants. State primary and secondary road systems were recognized as state responsibilities, taken over from the county commissioners. By 1964, these accounted for over 650,000 miles. Earlier, the Federal Highway Act of 1921 had authorized matching funds for a federal-aid primary system, originally limited to 7 percent of the rural mileage then existing. In 1944, Congress approved the designation of a federal-aid secondary system to speed the improvement of feeders and connecting links. Annual federal grants for the improvement of primary, secondary, and urban roads—the so-called ABC funds—are allocated among the states by a complicated statutory formula based on area, population, and postal-route mileage.

The 1944 act also authorized the Interstate System, at first on a 50–50, then a 60–40 ratio of federal to state and local funds; but progress was too slow to satisfy users and builders. In the postwar years, over a dozen states, mostly in the East, where traffic densities were highest, followed the earlier lead of Pennsylvania in reverting to the ancient device of tolls as a means of financing the construction and operation of limited-access turnpikes. Some two dozen more states adopted the same method for new bridges or tunnels at bottleneck points. Separate authorities, distinct from the regular highway departments, were usually created to manage these ventures. This assured administrative flexibility and avoided constitutional limits on bor-rowing because only the toll revenues and not the "full faith and credit" of the states were pledged. Most of these toll roads quickly proved to be moneymakers, and some 2,000 miles of such facilities were constructed.

---

[12] *But the old National Road, a main route for the westward migration of settlers, was authorized by Congress in 1806 and built at federal expense. Begun in 1815 at Cumberland, Maryland, the first section reached to Wheeling. Under the jurisdiction of the Corps of Engineers it was extended to Columbus, Ohio, 1825–1833; to Vandalia, Illinois, by 1840; and eventually to St. Louis. Control of the road was turned over to the states through which it ran, and they charged tolls for its maintenance.*

However, federal grants were denied to toll roads, and the impetus for this method of development waned when a few of the more optimistically conceived—notably the West Virginia Turnpike—ran into financial difficulties by overestimating their markets.

A turning point in highway policy was reached when the Eisenhower administration rejected suggestions that the federal gasoline tax (and with it, federal highway grants) be abandoned, to leave the highway field to the states. Instead, the Highway Act of 1956, which was supplemented by further legislation in 1961, committed the federal government to the completion of the Interstate System by 1972, changed the matching ratio to 90–10 for the roads in that system, doubled the federal gas tax in three years, and made a permanent appropriation of all federal receipts from gasoline and other highway-related taxes into a Federal Highway Trust Fund. The Bureau of Public Roads reimburses the states from this fund for approved construction expenditures, in accordance with apportionments made three years in advance to permit orderly planning. The principle of earmarking funds had been long entrenched in state finances as a means of securing autonomy against either executive budgetary supervision or legislative raids; it has thus become a permanent feature of federal highway financing also. Federal outlays from the fund, taking ABC and Interstate grants together, were about $4 billion in 1965–66 compared with $596 million in federal aid for roads a decade earlier. These federal contributions amounted to 49 percent of all highway capital expenditures by all units of government.

This is not to say that the states have shirked their shares. State gas taxes that averaged 4.25 cents a gallon in 1947 averaged 6.41 cents in 1965, and related taxes rose at least correspondingly. In 1965, the states collected $7.0 billion from highway users (not counting federal grants and other income) and passed along nearly a quarter of that, $1.6 billion, for county and local roads and streets. More clearly symptomatic, the states have become the prime operating agencies in the field: they determine the routes, draw the detailed plans, secure federal approval if federal funds are involved, buy or condemn the rights of way, let the contracts, supervise the actual construction, and maintain the completed highways.[13]

Some of these responsibilities strain the capabilities and integrity of

---

[13] *Statistics in the preceding paragraphs are drawn from the U.S. Bureau of Public Roads,* Highway Statistics: 1963, *and* Highway Statistics: Summary to 1955 *(Washington, D.C., 1957); and U.S. Bureau of the Census, Statistical Abstract of the United States: 1966, Compendium of State Government Finances in 1965, and* Governmental Finances in 1964–65.

state agencies. In locating routes, highway departments must often arbitrate local differences and override local objections. In procuring rights of way, they open up opportunities to real estate speculators. In letting contracts, they are tempted to favoritism among contractors, who in turn may be tempted into kickback arrangements. And in the maintenance of crews and in the stockpiles of equipment and materials for roadwork, opportunities for diversion and corruption exist in every state capital and county courthouse. The complaints of disappointed bidders, the alertness of newspaper reporters, and the discipline of federal inspections and audits form secondary lines of defense against these temptations; but considering the magnitude of their operations, it is not surprising that the breath of scandal should touch highway departments probably more often than any other branch of state government.

In the field of highway safety, the states also carry the main burden of responsibility, though the range of activities directed to that end is so broad as to leave a share for everyone. The problem is unrelenting. Despite the decrease in the traffic fatality rate (from 7.6 deaths per 100 million miles traveled in 1950 to 5.6 in 1965), the increase in driving (840 billion vehicle miles in 1964) has raised the annual number of accidents, slowly but without any let-up. Statistics and exhortation on the subject come from the National Safety Council, a private organization supported by insurance companies. Highway-design research comes from the federal government and certain university centers; automobile design from the manufacturers, now prodded by federal as well as state legislation; local street markings and traffic controls from municipal authorities; and driver education from the high schools and auto clubs. But the principal operating controls—driver and vehicle testing, licensing, and registration; highway markings and maintenance; speed limits and other safety regulations; and policing and enforcement—come from the states. By 1963, twenty-five states had a state police organization with general enforcement powers, more or less in the pattern of the State Constabulary first established by Pennsylvania in 1905. Of the rest, all but Hawaii had a highway patrol—a state police with jurisdiction largely limited to highway traffic control.[14]

AIRPORTS. From the standpoint of state participation, the field of aviation presents the sharpest possible contrast to the highway picture. Military, aerospace, and civilian airline affairs are in federal hands; the

---

[14] The Book of the States, 1966–67 (*Chicago: Council of State Governments, 1966*), *pp. 322–26, and ibid., 1964–65 (1964), pp. 461–66. Traffic fatality data from U.S. Bureau of the Census, Statistical Abstract of the United States: 1966, pp. 568, 571.*

major terminals, with a few exceptions,[15] are municipal concerns aided and supervised by the federal government. The federal grants go directly to the airport authorities. As a result, the states have been helpless witnesses [16] to the wholesale industrial relocations and readjustments attendant on the technological changeover to jets, missiles, and rockets—changes with far-reaching consequences for the tax bases, employment rolls, and demands for public services within their jurisdictions.[17] These consequences have been an even livelier subject of anxiety and competition for the munici-palities most affected.

Another sharp contrast emerges in a comparison of the federal aid programs for airports and highways. The whole scale of federal aid for airports has been relatively minute. Over the 15 years 1947–63, a total of about $1.5 billion in public funds was invested in almost 1,800 federal aid airports, a little less than half of it from federal grants. The total is far less than any recent single year's federal outlay on the Interstate Highway System alone, and the annual contributions—$70 million in 1964–65—make up less than 1 percent of all federal grants. The federal investments in control towers, beacons, traffic and safety, weather, communications systems and the like have been made by the Federal Aviation Agency and other federal agencies directly.[18]

What is left for the states? Chiefly, a finger in the Air National Guard and some provision for, and control over, the facilities for private aircraft—so-called "general aviation," a rapidly growing category. In addition to the federal aid airports, about 1,800 publicly owned airports are sufficiently improved to be distinguished from cow pastures; beyond these, there are the private flying fields. In the aggregate, general aviation (company-owned and individually owned planes used for business, recreation, farm-ing, ranching, forest and wildlife conservation, etc.) accounts for more

---

[15] How the Port of New York Authority, a bi-state agency with no taxing power but a superior credit rating, came to supplant the City of New York as the airport developer for that metropolis is analyzed by Herbert Kaufman, "Gotham in the Air Age," for the Inter-University Case Program series, reprinted in Harold Stein (ed.), Public Administration and Policy Development (New York: Harcourt, 1952), pp. 143–98. The Dulles International and Washington National airports, serving the nation's capital, are operated by the Federal Aviation Agency itself.

[16] Perhaps as a symbol of futile indignation, the Maine state legislature in 1960–61 adopted an act requiring any person who intends to launch or fire a missile or rocket to obtain the prior approval of the State Aeronautics Commission. The Book of the States, 1962–63, p. 356.

[17] The end of an era was marked in 1960 when, for the first time in a generation, no U.S. aircraft manufacturer building transport planes received an order for a piston-engine aircraft. Ibid., p. 353.

[18] Figures from The Book of the States, 1964–65, p. 377, and U.S. Bureau of the Census, Governmental Finances in 1964–65, p. 22.

airport use, in stops and take-offs, than the airline carriers; and these planes must be registered in their home states. But state controls must everywhere be subordinated to federal requirements, civil and military; and the practical problems in keeping track of large numbers of vehicles and operators that can quickly escape their jurisdictions have inhibited the development of any controls or services by the states that match those administered for surface transportation by the state police and highway patrols or motor vehicle departments. For example, only 13 states operated airports in 1963.

5. *Planning, Public Business, and Private Enterprise*

In the realm of economic affairs, state and local governments confront a bewildering variety of often conflicting demands and opportunities for action. Space limits us to a sampling, with illustrations, of some of the principal ways of dealing with them.

PLANNING. In a rational world it might be supposed that the first essential step for any government, state or local, is to make a plan for the future development and well-being of its people: to draw up a comprehensive inventory of needs, to review the means available for meeting them, to determine the priorities of importance among them, and then to channel public (and induce the channeling of private) resources to these ends—with time schedules if possible. In the actual world, and in the general sense of looking ahead by trying to anticipate contingencies, warning of impending problems, and moving toward preferred objectives, no doubt every public official and agency engages in some planning. But it would be nearly as true to say that a major innovation is hardly ever brought about until some crisis or catastrophe dramatizes the need for it, after it has become far more expensive to introduce than when the experts first clearly foresaw the need. State and local budgets, and capital improvement programs (where they exist), are limited vehicles for planning, but they are seldom sufficiently comprehensive or flexible to accommodate more than marginal adjustments. Systematic planning, coupled with the stable political power and the administrative direction required to bring plans to fruition, is a rare phenomenon in the upper policy levels of governments. On the record, those who argue for muddling through and making progress by incremental steps have the better claim to realism. Nevertheless, planning as a function and as a profession has been gaining recognition gradually and probably will receive more—but within limits.

During the 1930's, under the stimulus of federal grants then available for that purpose, nearly all states established "planning" boards or commissions. These bodies typically turned their attention to long-range studies of capital improvement needs or natural resource potentialities and had little influence on current activities. Many of them came to an end, at least temporarily, during World War II. During the first postwar decade, planning efforts were renewed, but their emphasis shifted sharply. Usually called "development" rather than "planning" agencies, they concentrated less on research than on attracting tourist trade and new industry to bring more money and jobs into their states—a competitive course that relied on advertising, salesmanship, offers of tax concessions for new plants, and in some states, tax-exempt help with financing. In a growing economy it is hard to say how much net effect these efforts had apart from other factors.

In the mid-1950's a new trend in planning emerged, again stimulated by federal grants and affecting both states and cities; by the mid-1960's it was accelerating sharply. The states, for their part, were becoming hesitantly involved in such matters as watershed development, abatement of river pollution, and civil defense arrangements—matters that spilled over local jurisdictions. The cities confronted the massive and complex problems of urban renewal. The outlays in prospect called for huge sums, and prudence dictated planning and cooperation among the governmental units concerned, before the main outlays were committed. The emerging pattern, borrowing from the highway experience, accordingly provided modest federal grants first to state or local planning bodies to support the preparation of specific proposals, with expert help. Then, if hearings, negotiations, and modifications resulted in the approval of these proposals by all the participating governments, larger federal grants to the local operating authorities followed. The federal Housing and Home Finance Agency and the Department of Health, Education and Welfare were the principal federal grantors; the cities were the chief beneficiaries.

Municipal planning has centered on the control of land use, historically the province of local zoning authorities, but increasingly the business of housing and urban redevelopment agencies. In the largest cities the capital budgeting processes also enter the planning structure. Congressional approval, in 1964 and 1965, of the Appalachia and Anti-poverty bills and broadening of the Area Redevelopment programs served to strengthen the states' shares in public planning. But the creation of the newest cabinet level department in 1965, the Department of Housing and Urban Development (successor to the HHFA), gave symbolic as well as tangible recognition to the mounting priorities of urban needs.

Notwithstanding these advances, obstacles to comprehensive planning remain embedded in the political system. The states usually have any single functional field so little to themselves that the leverage they can exert on the total outcome may not seem worth the expense of supporting elaborate planning bodies with jurisdictions broader than the fields in which federal funds are offered. Municipal planners quickly run into the tangles of metropolitan areas. And the functional experts, planning within their compartments and having sympathetic access to their federal counterparts with funds to dispose of, are restive under the restraints of central reviewing bodies. Another source of uncertainty contributes to an opportunistic attitude toward planning: governors and mayors are important in securing the changes that plans are conceived to bring about. But governors and mayors come and go; their enthusiasms wax and wane. Effective planning calls for sustained work and a steady hand on the tiller.

NATURAL RESOURCES AND OUTDOOR RECREATION. The bounties and beauties and dangers of nature attract people, and thereby the attention of governments, from motives of gain, of the enjoyment of leisure, and of protection. The pioneers who won the West, it is said, felt free to help themselves to anything that was not screwed down. Ever since, under the general rule of American law that title to the land surface or a riparian ownership carries with it the right to anything underground or accessible to the shore, natural resources have lured developers and speculators, hydroelectric power companies, miners and drillers, hunters and fishermen. Some states draw revenues from "severance" taxes on extractive industries like copper mining, or from oil royalties or hunting licenses. Nearly all states have some form of safety and liability laws directed against the hazards of accidents in mining. In the case of oil, an elaborate network of state regulations, reenforced by an interstate compact, limits and prorates production in order to sustain prices. On the public lands in the western states, federal regulations govern mineral leasing, cattle grazing, and timber cutting. Everywhere, forest fire fighting enlists the cooperation of all governments in the area of an outbreak. Conservationists have waged an uphill battle on many fronts to secure state laws asserting a public interest in scenic, historic, and recreational resources. Yet they have achieved some success—for example, reforestation and strip-mining laws.

All states have departments of agriculture and experiment stations, but many of the former have historically been as much concerned with the politics of state and county fairs as with improving farm technology. Except perhaps in a handful of states with well-developed professional services (California, Wisconsin, New York and Florida, for example), agriculture has been better promoted by the cooperative extension service that links county and federal funds under the supervision of the land-grant agricultural colleges and by the newer, federally sponsored soil conservation districts. And except for California's gigantic state-financed water diversion project, the large-scale development of water and electric power resources, as well as flood control and river navigation works, have been mainly federal undertakings. When entire riversheds are treated integrally, this seems inevitable. But locally organized irrigation districts distribute to farmers the waters impounded by federally constructed dams, and state law governs the water rights.

In the postwar years, prosperity, mobility, and urban growth have contributed to a great upsurge of support for public development of parks, beaches, and other recreational facilities—along with the mushrooming private outlays on pleasure boats, ski resorts, motels, camps, and the like. The trend affects all levels of government. Publicly maintained places for family trips and outings have multiplied, but it is harder to discover where, within a reasonable distance, the Boy Scouts can go hiking any more. The National Park Service has taken the lead in the acquisition and improvement of park lands and wildlife refuges. It has relaxed its formerly aristocratic attitude; once esoteric beauties of nature are now accessible to the millions. And the states have emulated this example, pressured by crowded city-dwellers seeking temporary escape from confinement. All states—with New York, California, Michigan, Ohio, and Pennsylvania in the van, as measured by daily attendance—maintain state parks, and less than a quarter of the states fail to register at least a million park visitors annually in the facilities they provide. Municipalities, harder pressed for space and confronted with much higher real estate prices, nevertheless have an even more urgent need for neighborhood recreation centers; school playgrounds and vacant lots are no longer adequate. Private philanthropy often aids municipal efforts, but they run a Malthusian race against growing populations and rising costs.

PUBLIC OWNERSHIP. Earlier in this century the choice among the alternatives of "free" competition, publicly regulated monopoly, and government ownership was an issue that stirred fierce controversy. Rhetorical flourishes on the theme of socialism are still occasionally heard from opponents of recent innovations like medicare, water fluoridation, and urban renewal. But the post office and public schools set earlier and logically awkward precedents against ideological absolutes as the determinants of public policy in economic affairs. Today the flames of passion have cooled on this issue, and pragmatic considerations usually settle the outcome in particular cases. Publicly supported research and public subsidies from state and local governments are too common for comment. In this section we glance at some examples of public ownership and operation of business-type activities.

We noted earlier that most sizable municipalities (as well as many smaller ones), but very few states, furnish one or more utility services—water, light and power, gas, or transit—directly to their residents and charge them for it. Apart from sewage disposal and garbage and trash collection, which are almost universally municipal functions but often are not separately charged for, the most common of such services is water supply. Only Indianapolis and Omaha, among the 43 cities with over 300,000 population in 1960, depend on private water companies.[19] Municipal electric (and less often, gas) systems and consumer-owned electric cooperatives in rural areas (sponsored by the Rural Electrification Administration) are the principal alternatives to reliance on private utilities for distribution of these services. In the transit field, public and private systems alike have proved vulnerable to the competition of automobiles. Financial considerations have frequently dictated public subsidy or operation as the only way to avoid abandonment. Even for the other utilities, ideological cleavages do not suffice to explain more than a fraction of the choices between private and public enterprise. Because of the heavy capital investment required, private mismanagement, or labor disputes, the practical choice may have been municipal service or none. And in at least one instance, in rural New York, a town has done so well on its electrical system that it had no other taxes. Taken all together, cities derived some $3.8 billion of revenues from their utility operations in 1964–65 and with few exceptions ran them in the black.

The states' role in this general area has been residual. They have built or operated time-honored types of public facilities like bridges, terminals, and ferries without undue misgivings, when neither municipal nor private enterprise proved adequate to the exigencies of public demands. So, for example, the state of Washington stepped in to keep the Black Ball ferry system going on Puget Sound,[20] California has crisscrossed San Francisco

---

[19] *In four other states, Connecticut, Maine, Nevada, and West Virginia, the principal cities—none so large as the two named—rely on private suppliers. Oakland and several other San Francisco Bay area cities (except San Francisco itself) do not operate municipal systems; they are served by the Hetch-Hetchy Water Supply and Power Project. U.S. Bureau of the Census, City Government Finances in 1964–65, Tables 3, 6, and 7.*

[20] *See William J. Gore and Evelyn Shipman, Commuters v. the Black Ball Line, Inter-University Case Program, No. 42 (Indianapolis: Bobbs-Merrill, 1959), reprinted in Edwin A. Bock (ed.), State and Local Government: A Case Book (University, Ala.: University of Alabama Press, 1963).*

Bay with bridges, and half the states can point to similar operations of more than local importance. Several of the bridges are interstate or international joint ventures. Nevertheless, and despite Justice Brandeis' famous dictum about individual states serving as experimental social laboratories, the states have usually looked skeptically at unconventional proposals. The state-owned Bank of North Dakota and the North Dakota Mill and Elevator Association have survived the taint of their Nonpartisan League origins to become profitable concerns.[21] The principal exception to the states' general lack of daring is so unusual as to be *sui generis:* the California undertaking, without federal aid, to divert and channel the mountain waters of its northern rivers hundreds of miles through the Central Valley into the parched southern region.[22]

PRIVATE ENTERPRISE. The states' relation to business has more typically been one of service and regulation. The health of business within the state is not only a natural concern, but occupies the attention of state policy makers because it so directly and indirectly affects both employment and the state's tax revenues. This helps explain the caution with which governors and legislators view proposals that opponents claim will "drive business away." It helps, too, to account for the eagerness with which state development commissions seek to attract industry from sister states.

Despite the appealing simplicity of this favoring posture toward business and industry, state governments have long been regulators, and not just promoters, of business. The states' regulatory range is so broad that it can only be illustrated here. The states have passed laws designed to protect workers' health and safety, workmen's compensation laws to compensate for industrial accidents, laws protecting the workers' right to organize labor unions for collective bargaining (along with "right-to-work" laws in states that are less enthusiastic about unions), "fair trade" laws that attempt to restrict retailers' right to compete on price (there is an art to the naming of laws to make them seem other than they are), milk control laws that not only protect consumers' health but also protect producers or dairies or both against rigorous price competition, and licensing regulations for many professions and occupations.

Historically, the most important efforts by the states to regulate

---

[21] *At their inception they were attacked in the courts as uses of state funds not for a public purpose; see Green v. Frazier, 253 U.S. 233 (1920).*

[22] *California voters in a 1960 referendum adopted the water plan, to be financed by borrowing $1.75 billion—by far the largest bonding authorization ever approved by popular vote in the United States.*

business have been addressed to public utilities, banking, and insurance. State commissions to regulate public utilities in transportation (especially railroads, trucks, and buses), electricity, gas, water, telephones and the like were instituted to protect the consuming public against private monopolies that were not disciplined by competition. The state commissions, in other words, provided the substitute for competition. Their typical concern was ensuring quality of service and reasonable rates. Banking and insurance departments of state governments are further designed in part to protect the public against misrepresentation and loss of funds.

In these traditional areas of state regulation, two problems have hampered the states' effectiveness. In virtually all states, the business involved has become national or regional, rather than local, so that the federal government has substantially taken over the principal regulatory responsibility. Even in banking and insurance, although the federal government does not monopolize their regulation, the industry itself is basically national either because the principal individual companies are national in operation (in insurance) or because the interdependence among enterprises (in the banking system) is an established fact. The second problem has been the tendency of most state regulatory agencies to become too closely identified with the industries they are supposed to regulate. The reasons for this are complex and vary by state and by field of regulation.[23]

LIQUOR CONTROL. The states have had to choose between "public enterprise" and regulated "private enterprise" in the sale of alcoholic beverages. Despite peculiar features of the industry and of public opinion toward it, the abrupt constitutional necessity of making this choice might be expected to furnish some generalizations on when states "socialize" and when they merely regulate. For the Twenty-First Amendment, repealing the Eighteenth and dissolving the implied restraints of the commerce clause that apply to state regulation of other commodities, put it squarely up to the states to decide on the policies to govern the sale and use of liquor within their borders—an issue that had divided sentiments and inflamed passions for a half century before and defied a national solution. After 1933, the states were free to continue prohibition; reopen the field to private enterprise and tax it and regulate it, loosely or closely; or enter the business themselves. They could also redelegate their newly gained discretion and let their subdivisions exercise the choice by local option. Against this last course lay the same practical objection that the prohibition states

---

[23] *An examination of the varied pattern can be found in James W. Fesler*, The Independence of State Regulatory Agencies (*Chicago: Public Administration Service*, 1942).

themselves had encountered earlier—the difficulty of preventing a too ready (and profitable) seepage from wet areas into dry.

A generation after 1933 the passion had gone out of the issue, the last dry state—except Mississippi, until 1966—had plumped for repeal, and the other states were seemingly content with the choice each had made between the remaining two broad alternatives. Thirty-four states chose private retailing, subject to state regulation, and allowed their subdivisions more or less leeway in local option toward strictness or laxity. These states (along with Mississippi—then legally dry, revenue-wet) collected $836 million in sales and license taxes from the private liquor traffic in 1965. The other 16 states chose to establish state monopolies, presumably in order to gain a fuller control of the traffic and minimize prior abuses.[24] None of these states went into the manufacturing end of the business, and none of them encouraged sales by advertising. Nevertheless, despite the austerity of their facilities and their usually inconspicuous locations, these 16 state-store systems had net sales of $1.3 billion in 1965. On these sales they realized a net profit of $258 million, a 20 percent margin most of which went into their general revenue funds.[25]

6. Health and Welfare

Life expectancy at birth, which stood just short of 50 years for the general population of the United States at the beginning of the twentieth century, by 1960 had reached the biblical goal of three score years and ten. (This *average* increase of 20 years included a near-doubling in the life expectancy of nonwhites during the same 60-year period, from 34 to 64 years.) The comparison gives a rough index to the magnitude of the improvements in the public health of the nation, as well as one clue to the growing welfare problems that attend such longevity. The scale and scope of public activities in these two broad fields have been altered almost beyond recognition during the past quarter-century and especially since World War II.

HEALTH. The American people spent over $38 billion in 1964 (up from $12.2 billion in 1950) on health and medical care; and about a quarter of the sum, in both years, was in the public sector. The national

---

[24] *A few municipalities in other states also operated city-owned liquor stores; they had sales of $92 million in 1964–65. U.S. Bureau of the Census,* City Government Finances in 1964–65, *p. 6.*

[25] *Statistics from the U.S. Bureau of the Census,* Compendium of State Government Finances in 1965, *p. 45.*

government looks after the health of members of the armed forces and inmates of veterans' hospitals. The other federal contributions to the total effort before the arrival of medicare were chiefly the conduct and support of research, for which large grants are made; grants for hospital construction under the Hill-Burton Act of 1946; policing the marketing of drugs; gathering and publishing statistics; and furnishing program leadership—for example, breaking the taboo on the public mention of venereal disease a quarter-century ago.

State and local governments, as might be expected, are heavily engaged in the direct operation of health programs and facilities, but they have some supporting and regulatory roles as well—for instance, the education and licensing of doctors, dentists, and professional nurses.

Physicians come somewhat oftener than once a thousand among the general population—66 per 100,000 in Alaska (the lowest ratio), 211 in New York (the highest), and 151 on the national average. Even before medicare, a third of them were "socialized"—i.e., did not engage in private practice. The national average and the corresponding average for dentists —56 per 100,000 people—have remained little changed for the past 15 years; only the number of nurses has increased relatively as well as absolutely. The states license practitioners, but in doing so rely almost entirely on the professional societies that dominate the examining boards. The county medical societies or the hospital medical staffs control the access of individual physicians and surgeons to particular hospitals and so enforce the major distinction between general practitioners and specialists. The resulting stability in the supply perhaps partly explains, and certainly contrasts with, the sharp increase in medical care costs over the same period: Between 1950 and 1965 the medical care component of the Consumer Price Index rose nearly twice as rapidly as the whole index. But if it has become expensive to call a doctor, it is also expensive for a doctor to prepare for his calling. Here again the states, with the help of federal grants, are heavy subsidizers; about 40 percent of the 90 or so medical schools in the country are state-controlled.[26]

The range of state and local health programs is too wide and varied to list. Earlier, the combating of communicable diseases was a prime object;

---

[26] *Statistics in this section from U.S. Department of Health, Education and Welfare, Health, Education and Welfare Trends, 1965, esp. Part I, p. S-26; U.S. Bureau of the Census, Statistical Abstract of the United States: 1966, pp. 65–68. See also the annual education number of the Journal of the American Medical Association, e.g., November, 1964. The ratios given in the text are indicative rather than exact, depending on the bases of computation; official sources vary.*

but as the deadly killers of that time—smallpox, malaria, tuberculosis, typhoid, pneumonia—and now polio—have successively been brought under control, the emphases have shifted to longer-range if less spectacular concerns, and the channels of effort have broadened. Hospitals—their operation, expansion, and modernization—remain a principal part of the public health domain: over half the hospital beds in the country are provided by state and local governments. These are supplemented by outpatient services and maternity health clinics. The schools have become the vehicles for immunization programs and school-lunch buildups. The main supply lines of drinking water and of food—from the packing plants, dairy farms, and canneries through the markets to the restaurants and food stores—have become the objects of sanitary codes and inspection systems. The aim is prevention rather than remedy, though health authorities commonly have summary powers to seize and destroy items that will not pass inspection. Problems of stream pollution, air pollution in cities, and sewage treatment have moved onto the agenda of state as well as municipal health authorities. The official dissemination of birth control information and contraceptives is still a troublesome problem.

Most of these matters are problems for professionals to work out, and the funds at their disposal for these purposes have been steadily expanding. In health programs as in other governmental activities, however, administrators from time to time encounter barriers of popular feelings that do not yield to scientific arguments, and in these cases political judgment determines what professionals are allowed to do. So three-quarters of the population are exposed to unnecessary dental troubles because their water supply is not fluoridated; planned parenthood clinics are not generally available where they are most needed; syphilis is not yet eradicated because so many people prefer privacy to help.

MENTAL HEALTH. Perhaps nowhere in the health field have new concepts of treatment challenged traditional methods and institutions with the call for such radical departures as in mental health care. A generation ago state authorities generally supposed they had fulfilled their obligations by providing untrained custodial care in insane asylums; the local police and the lockups sufficed for alcoholics and drug addicts; retarded children were problems for their families to cope with. The current governmental attack on mental health problems has not yet gone very far in relation to the need, but rehabilitation has come to replace the hopeless goal of mere custody. Inmates have no votes and few friends. Nevertheless, the combined efforts of federal, state, and local authorities are enlisted in innovations in treatment that cut across older procedures in mental health, welfare, and law enforcement. A new profession has arisen, dedicated to the new goals and methods. State expenditures alone for the current operation of their mental institutions are now more than a billion dollars a year and account for over half of all state expenditures for health and hospitals. Some results of the campaign to return mental patients to the living world can be seen by comparing 1945 and 1965. In 1965, more people were admitted to state and local government mental hospitals than in 1945, both absolutely and proportionally (164 per 100,000 population, as against 93), but many more patients, absolutely and proportionally, were discharged or placed on "extramural care" (593 per 1,000 average resident patients, as against 158 in 1945). One consequence was that the actual number of resident patients in such state and local mental hospitals at a given time steadily declined each year from the 1955 peak of 559,000 to the 1965 figure of 491,000, and the average ratio of patients per 100,000 of the total population fell from 363 in 1945 to 259 in 1964.[27]

WELFARE. Perhaps the most significant, and certainly one of the largest, examples of the recent assumption and reallocation of governmental responsibilities is in the welfare field. Public welfare (without counting social insurance programs financed from trust funds) now ranks third, after schools and highways, among the objects of state and local expenditures. The states, except for some workmen's conspensation laws, scarcely entered the welfare field until after 1920. And the national government, with minor exceptions, stayed out of it until after 1930, when the dimensions of the problem during the Depression overwhelmed the states. The historic landmark was the passage of the Social Security Act in 1935 and its validation two years later by the Supreme Court as a proper exercise of the taxing power of Congress. After over a quarter-century of operation and numerous liberalizing amendments, this act outlines broadly the division of effort among levels of government in meeting welfare needs and the chief types of programs to be offered. A generation later another great leap was taken when Congress, in 1964 and 1965, enacted the Anti-Poverty Program (Equal Opportunity Act) and medicare, which expanded both the range and scale of welfare undertakings.

If we view the system and its complicated parts as a whole, a principal welfare objective is the maintenance of income for families or individuals when their earnings otherwise fail—permanently or temporarily—to meet minimum needs of civilized living. Without that, all their other difficulties

---

[27] *U.S. Department of Health, Education, and Welfare*, Health, Education, and Welfare Trends, 1965, *Part I, pp. S-29f.*

are compounded. To this end the federal government provides the main vehicles: first, by civil service and military pensions and veterans' benefits to care for the superannuated and permanently disabled for whom it is most immediately responsible—and so to set an example; and second, and more importantly, by the old-age, survivors and disability insurance system (OASDI) for workers (and their dependents) who have retired from private employment, including self-employment. This system is financed by payroll taxes paid into the federal social security trust fund. As of the end of 1964, OASDI protected about 90 percent of the 72 million people gainfully employed and in 1965 was sending monthly benefit checks to almost 21 million people; among these beneficiaries were some three-fourths of the population aged 65 and over. This proportion is growing.

OASDI, basic as it is, leaves untouched many needs that fall to the states and localities to meet—in administration if not necessarily in financing. Among the earliest of these to be recognized was compensation for industrial accidents. Even before World War I, some states had moved to supplant the meager and uncertain remedies of the common law with workmen's compensation laws which are now nearly universal. Either through private insurance carriers or state systems, employers, as a part of their cost of doing business, must pay premiums for automatic payments for injuries incurred in the course of employment. The Social Security Act attacked another and more extensive hazard of industrial society, unemployment. By means of a federal tax-offset device, the states were at once prodded and enabled to pass laws establishing unemployment compensation systems for workers laid off in private industry. These laws are closely linked in administration with the state employment services and provide payments more or less related to previous earnings. Collective bargaining contracts often call for supplements to these payments.

The Social Security Act also authorized federal grants to the states for "categorical assistance" payments to many of the needy who could not qualify for, or had exhausted, unemployment benefits: those who were too old to be reemployed or who had retired before OASDI payments were available; those who were too young to have held a covered job for the qualifying period; dependent children in fatherless households; the blind or otherwise physically handicapped. The federal grants require matching state funds, and the states on their own raise additional revenues for welfare purposes. The states may make their payments directly to the beneficiaries or pass the money along to county and municipal authorities for local administration. At the end of the line, residual "general relief"— for needy people not cared for by private charity and not fitting the categories recognized by federal or state programs—remains the province of local authorities.

In the aggregate, in 1965, social insurance and welfare expenditures from federal funds totaled $32 billion, and from state and local funds, about $9 billion. Public assistance payments alone, in 1965, gave recipients nearly $2.9 billion from federal funds, and $2 billion from state sources and local sources.[28]

Maintenance of income is fundamental, but in many circumstances not enough. A few examples will suggest the range of further needs, human as well as financial, and the governmental tasks they entail. Modest monthly checks do not cover major medical expenses; hence medicare, started in 1966, provides the costs of hospital care under social security for people over 65 and a voluntary insurance program to cover doctors' bills. Modest monthly checks will go further if some basic nutritional needs are supplied; so the depression-born food stamp plan was made permanent in 1964, to give people on relief an allowance in stamps that they can redeem for food, but not cash, in grocery stores. Modest monthly checks do not ensure prudent spending, so social case-workers are assigned to help relief recipients work out their domestic problems. Modest monthly checks, finally, do not fill the needs of orphans and neglected children for whom institutional care and adoption agencies must be provided; or solve the problems of juvenile delinquents, of unwed expectant mothers, of newly released prisoners, alcoholics and narcotics addicts, and other social outcasts; or supply the training or retraining that may rehabilitate those who are presently without employable skills or incentives to cultivate them. In these hard-core social problem areas, the objectives of health, education, and welfare converge to make work for state and local governments.

Because public welfare expenditures, unlike highway programs, do not leave physical structures for all to see, and unlike education, take the form usually of money payments to the beneficiaries, a far more detailed system of audit and supervision is applied by the granting governments. This entails a growing professional bureaucracy and raises outcries against "centralization," which the states must listen to, as well as utter themselves. Since the states and localities are incapable of controlling population movements or anticipating economic cycles as they can control school systems and anticipate from birth statistics the number of kindergarten entrants five years in advance, their role in public welfare is inevitably more

---

[28] *Figures from U.S. Department of Health, Education and Welfare*, Health, Education and Welfare Trends, 1965, *Part I, p. 40.*

of administration than policy. But they have policy choices in going beyond the minimum national standards; or contrariwise, in discriminating against voteless newcomers within their borders, by setting long residence periods for eligibility.

7. Conclusion

No single or static job description for the states and the local governments will do. The picture is changing as old programs are reshaped to fit new needs and new thinking about continuing needs. Illustrative is the impact of urbanization on state governments. When city people have cars but cannot picnic in their own backyards and find city parks drab and over-crowded, state parks are called for; and if the streams within reach of the urban fisherman are fished out, state hatcheries must restock them. When upstream cities pollute their rivers, downstream cities demand state abatement measures; New York in 1965 voted a $1 billion bond issue for this alone. When central cities pollute the drifting air with noxious gases, suburban cities complain. When many families choose to live amid suburban trees and lawns while the breadwinner of each spends his days working in the city, the state is under pressure to ensure that commuting by train and car is unimpeded by railroads' profit-loss statements or by highway congestion. When national rent controls were lifted after World War II, a few states stepped into the breach to restrain the inevitable excesses when demand for urban housing so far exceeded supply. When Negroes migrate to crowded quarters in northern cities, pressures build up for state anti-discrimination measures. And the spotlight on street crime, today focused on local governments, forecasts more work for the states tomorrow.

The state governments, we have seen, have the inherent problems of middlemen in attracting attention to their work. The scope and intensity of that work depends not only on recognizing the need for public intervention, but also on the states' place in the American system of government. Federal or local governments, or all three levels of government, may combine resources to cope with a given situation, rather than leave it to the state governments alone. What seems clear, however, is that the jobs of the states are at present critically important to our society. The states cannot be written off. Their capacity for exercising policy-making power, for administering programs, and for financing the work to be done is therefore of vital concern. No one ever suggests writing off the local governments; yet their capacity too is a critical determination of what functions they in fact perform. It is a paradox that the rapid growth of the economy in the 1960's has poured the bulk of unprecedented revenues into federal pockets, while the domestic burdens of our society fall so largely in the laps of the states and localities.

chapter 5

Intergovernmental Relations

In the totality of American society, many of the social structures that link individuals and groups—families, churches, business firms, trade associations, and unions—pay scant attention to the geographical boundaries of political jurisdictions. In this chapter we are concerned with some structures that must mind their territorial limits: with the relations between formal units of government, national, state, and local. But we need to bear in mind that the animating motives of official action commonly spring from less formal types of association. The complex of intermediate and lower-level governments in a federal system performs an important political service in articulating, aggregating, and urging the interests and demands of the overlapping functional groups located wholly or partly within their several jurisdictions. Since there are three levels of government, we can on that basis distinguish four broad categories of relationships: (1) national-state; (2) state-to-state and local-to-local, that is, between governments on the same level; (3) state-local; and (4) national-local.

1. *The States and the Nation*

In some ways the states are constitutionally indispensable to the national government. For example, through the Electoral College they elect the

President and Vice President. They are also needed to ratify constitutional amendments—thus any thirteen of them have a veto on any proposed change in the national Constitution. Among their most important functions, they conduct national elections; determine voting qualifications (subject to the sharp restrictions of the Voting Rights Act of 1965); and set the boundaries of congressional districts, within the limits of the one man-one vote principle. This is a short list, and no doubt national substitutes could be devised. (Through the Seventeenth Amendment, state legislatures have already lost the right to appoint United States senators.) But these functions are important to this discussion because they enable state interests, especially through the party system, to influence the behavior of national officials; and this influence of the states tends to offset the expanding powers of the national government. For instance, it was not politically feasible to submit the Seventeenth, Eighteenth, and Twenty-fourth Amendments to the Constitution to the states until after more than three-fourths of them had already aligned their own policies to the proposed national rules on woman suffrage, liquor prohibition, and poll tax requirements for voting, respectively.

ADMISSION OF NEW STATES.   The national government can admit new states by annexation (Texas, for example) or create them from territories (most recently, Alaska, 1958, and Hawaii, 1959). But it cannot carve one out of an existing state without the latter's consent—though the spirit of this prohibition was strained when forty western counties of Virginia voted against secession in 1861 and got federal help in setting up housekeeping as the state of West Virginia (admitted to the Union in 1863). Nor can any state (unless it is engaged in insurrection or occupied by a foreign power) be deprived of its two seats in the Senate without its consent. Congress can confer or impose whatever form of government it thinks fit on the territories—full self-government for the Commonwealth of Puerto Rico (the only one allowed to adopt its own constitution) and something approaching self-government for the Virgin Islands; the status of a regiment of engineers for the Canal Zone and of a battleship for Wake and Midway Islands; and a unique and wholly anomalous arrangement for the District of Columbia.[1] But a new state, once admitted, is guaranteed

---

[1] *The present form of the District's government dates in its main outlines from 1878, when it replaced a scandal-marred mayor-and-council arrangement. It provides for a weak three-man executive—two Commissioners named by the President subject to senatorial confirmation and one designated by him from the Corps of Engineers. The Congress itself is the District's only legislature. In practice, this has meant rule by the District Committees of the House and Senate and more specifically by their chairmen. These, by the operation of the seniority rule, have for the years of Democratic control of*

equality of status with those already in; it cannot be put on some second-class footing as a condition of entry.[2]

EXPANDING NATIONAL POWERS. The powers of the national government are broad, and their limits are conjectural. Those limits are ultimately determined—if the need to do so arises—by some national authority. In each of the three branches of the government, we find that these national powers are expanding. Presidential powers gained their greatest formal enlargement at the hands of Lincoln. But in the past two or three decades, the informal influence of Presidents has especially benefited from the growth of staff assistance in the Executive Office of the President and from the President's ability to use the facilities of mass communications media so as to reach a widening popular audience directly—over the heads of other elected representatives, congressional, state, and local. Congressional influence has also increased with the growth of office and committee staffs, investigations, and public hearings. And the scope of the formal powers of Congress has broadened too. For one thing, judicial decisions have freed its spending and borrowing powers from any constitutional restraint. And, especially since 1937, the Supreme Court has found a sufficient warrant in the doctrine of implied powers for all recent congressional enactments in the fields of economic and social policy. So, for instance, the federal controls over traffic in narcotics and firearms, over gambling, and over the domestic wine industry rest chiefly on the taxing power. The commerce power supports alike the settlement of labor disputes and the activities of the FBI in apprehending robbers and kidnappers. The war power has sustained far-reaching price and rent controls, and it validates the regulation of peaceful uses of atomic energy.

The national judicial power has also expanded, both by assertion and interpretation, and in ways that deeply affect the federal balance as well as the scope of discretion remaining to the states. Three examples are espe-

---

Congress invariably been Southerners—in a city whose population is more than half Negro. The District's judiciary, culminating in a Court of Appeals coordinate with those in the ten federal circuits, is also the creation of Congress. The Twenty-third Amendment, adopted in 1961, gave the District three electoral votes in presidential elections but no representation in Congress. In recent years the President has had a Special Assistant on the White House staff to look after Administration interests in District affairs.

[2] Alaska is a special case. Because of its vast area, sparse population, difficult climate and topography, Indian and Eskimo problems, and past history of federal subsidies, the Alaska Statehood Act and the accompanying Alaska Omnibus Act made unique and detailed provision for continuing federal rights and responsibilities in this state, unparalleled in the other 49. See 73 Stat. 151 (June 25, 1959); and W. A. Egan, "The Constitution of the New State of Alaska," State Government, 31 (Autumn, 1958), 213.

cially noteworthy.[3] In the public school desegregation cases [4] in 1954, the Supreme Court climaxed a decade-long trend of decisions by holding flatly, unanimously, and briefly that the "equal protection" clause of the Fourteenth Amendment makes unconstitutional any segregation of pupils by race or color in any publicly provided educational facilities. In another series of cases, still unfolding, of which *Mapp v. Ohio* [5] is an example, the Court has been extending the reach of the "due process" clause of the Fourteenth Amendment. Increasingly, it is requiring the states and their localities to provide not only the same substantive protections of civil liberties (free speech, picketing, etc.) that the Bill of Rights affords against the federal government, but also many of the same procedural safeguards in criminal prosecutions (right to counsel, freedom from unreasonable searches and seizures, etc.). In more technical terms, it is reading the limitations of the first eight amendments into the Fourteenth Amendment as restraints on the states. Finally, in the Tennessee reapportionment case in 1962,[6] the Court opened a new field of litigation, since actively cultivated, by holding that federal courts will hear complaints from voters that discriminatory malapportionments of seats in their state legislatures deny them the equal protection of the laws. The first two of these developments extend added protections to individuals or minority groups against abuses that result from the oppression or indifference of parochial majorities, while the third comes to the rescue of beleaguered majorities held in check by legislators from overrepresented rural minorities. All three add to the grounds on which a citizen may summon the national judicial power to redress a grievance he holds against his own state government.

STATE REACTIONS. It is not surprising that these trends should provoke strong criticism. Some state officials, private citizens, enterprises, and groups have reason to prefer the policies of their present state governments to those of the national government or those that redesigned state

---

[3] *A significant addition to this list is the unprecedented case of Governor Ross Barnett of Mississippi, who was enjoined to comply with the federal court orders regarding the admission of a Negro, James Meredith, to the University of Mississippi in the fall of 1962 and who was later adjudged in contempt by the U.S. Court of Appeals, sitting in New Orleans, for his handling of the situation when Meredith arrived on the Oxford campus accompanied by federal marshals. This case, still pending in 1963, undoubtedly helped restrain the resistance then offered by Governor George C. Wallace to the admission of Negroes to the University of Alabama; its final outcome sustained a qualified power in federal courts to punish even a governor for contempt, without a jury trial.* United States v. Barnett, 376 U.S. 681 (1964).

[4] Brown v. Board of Education of Topeka, 347 U.S. 483. *See the discussion in Chapter 4, pp. 134–36.*

[5] 367 U.S. 643 (1961).

[6] Baker v. Carr, 369 U.S. 186. *This case and the 1964 reapportionment cases,* Reynolds v. Sims, 377 U.S. 533, *are discussed in Chapter 9.*

governments are likely to pursue. Such critics of nationalizing trends usually invoke states' rights and commonly point to the Tenth Amendment for their constitutional argument—now as on many past occasions of historic controversy. That amendment itself reads simply: "The powers not delegated to the United States by the Constitution, nor prohibited by it to the States, are reserved to the States respectively, or to the people." The words are clear, though they do not add substance to the Constitution, for the Tenth Amendment is a constitutional tautology. The controlling question in any situation is whether a national power to act exists; and no answer to that question can be found in the amendment itself, which does not purport to answer it. When the answer has been duly determined from other sources to be "yes," the amendment is inapplicable, by its very terms; if it is "no," it only confirms what has already been decided.

In recent years state judges and legislators, as well as predictably conservative private groups, have engaged in concerted protests against this nationalizing trend. In 1959, after President Eisenhower had sent troops to Little Rock to enforce federal court orders, the annual Conference of Chief Justices of state supreme courts adopted a resolution condemning recent United States Supreme Court decisions. And the annual convention of the Daughters of the American Revolution regularly does the same.

In 1962, under the aegis of the Council of State Governments, the National Legislative Conference (composed of a number of state legislators and legislative aides) recommended, and the General Assembly of the States (with over three hundred delegates from 47 states) endorsed, three proposed amendments to the national Constitution. The first, which the General Assembly adopted by 37 states to 4, would have changed the constitutional amendment procedures specified in Article V so as to enable state legislatures to bypass altogether any congressional participation in—and hence, control over—the proposal or ratification of amendments.

The second of the proposed amendments, endorsed by a 26 to 10 vote of the General Assembly, was aimed directly at *Baker* v. *Carr:* It would have nullified that decision and have forbidden federal courts to hear any other reapportionment cases. The third proposed amendment is perhaps the most astonishing, and the General Assembly barely endorsed it—by a 21 to 20 vote. It provided for a court higher than the Supreme Court, to be called the Court of the Union, whose members would be the chief justices of the fifty state supreme courts. On the demand of the legislatures of five noncontiguous states, this court would review any decision of the Supreme Court "relating to the rights reserved to the states or to the people" by the national Constitution (that is, the Tenth Amendment again).

Working without publicity, the sponsors of these proposals within the space of a little over a year quietly secured from the legislatures of about a dozen and a half states (half the number needed) resolutions memorializing Congress to call a constitutional convention to consider one or more of these amendments. But they could not stand the light of day. Chief Justice Warren drew public attention to them in a speech, and the ensuing debate halted their progress in other state legislatures. Seen as an aspect of the movement that was also by then pushing the nomination of Senator Barry Goldwater for the Presidency, they were effectively buried in the avalanche of votes that elected Lyndon Johnson instead in 1964.

FEDERAL–STATE SUITS. Suits between the United States and a state—uncommon but not unknown—reveal the Supreme Court in another aspect of its delicate role as arbiter in our federal system. Here judicial restraint and the trend of decisions tend not to enlarge the Court's jurisdiction but rather to encourage legislative instead of judicial solutions to disputes. When Congress has firmly asserted a national power against the states, the Court has backed it up; but when the Court has asserted congressional supremacy in a disputed realm, Congress has sometimes nevertheless relinquished it to the states. A few examples will illustrate. On the one side, when Massachusetts years ago sought to enjoin the Treasury from disbursing federal funds to the states for the support of maternity hygiene clinics, the Court held that the state had no standing to be heard on the constitutional merits of a congressional appropriation.[7] When California claimed a sovereign prerogative to violate the Federal Safety Appliance Act in operating its state-owned Belt Railroad, the Court decided that the state was a "person" subject to the statute, and hence to the jurisdiction of the Interstate Commerce Commission's safety inspectors.[8] When Arizona followed up her long, lone, and unsuccessful Senate filibuster against the Boulder Canyon Project Act with a suit to enjoin the Colorado River development without her consent, the Court overrode her objections.[9] And when Congress in 1939 cut through a tangle of conflicting precedents by enacting the Public Salary Tax Act—subjecting the pay of state and municipal employees to federal income tax—the Court sustained it.[10]

On the other side, although the interest on state and municipal bonds

---

[7] Massachusetts v. Mellon, 262 U.S. 447 (1923). *Mellon was the Secretary of the Treasury.*

[8] United States v. California, 297 U.S. 175 (1936).

[9] Arizona v. California, 283 U.S. 423 (1931).

[10] Graves v. O'Keefe, 306 U.S. 466 (1939).

might be thought to have no greater constitutional immunity from federal taxes than the salaries of public officials, the Court has refrained from saying so and Congress has refrained from taxing it. When, however, the Court upset long-standing rate-fixing arrangements, blessed or counter-nanced by state insurance commissioners, by holding that the business of insurance is subject to congressional regulation as interstate commerce,[11] Congress hastily ceded the jurisdiction back to the states. In the McCarran Act of 1945,[12] Congress exempted the business from federal control in any state that has its own scheme of insurance regulation—as all states do— and put the states again in full charge. And when the Court decided against California and the Gulf states in the protracted tidelands oil controversy and held instead that the United States had the paramount interest (and so could collect the royalties from offshore drilling opera-tions), Congress again handed most of the prize back to the states.[13] On the record, an ounce of legislation has been worth a pound of litigation of this sort.

CRITERIA FOR NATIONAL ACTION. A broad array of na-tional-state relationships, then, emerges from the practical decisions of national policy makers on the division of labor between the nation and the states. Ordinarily, whole functions are not allocated to one level of government or the other; instead, specific phases or parts of them fall to each. Some generalizations about the criteria for sharing are discernible in the variety of prevailing patterns.

In matters of national defense and foreign affairs, the national govern-ment usually acts alone, not only because of its primary constitutional responsibility for these matters, but also because of the disruptive effects that could result if states intruded into these fields. Even so, it is worth noting, on the one hand, that Congress drew the states into the operation of the selective service system; and on the other, that the State Depart-ment shies away from using the treaty power to impose national regulation (on the model of the Migratory Game Bird Treaty with Canada) of topics otherwise covered by state law, such as property rights and domestic relations.

The rule of federal preemption, that the states must keep out of the

---

[11] United States v. South-Eastern Underwriters Assn., 322 U.S. 533 (1944). *The appellees in this case were insurance companies, not states, but numerous state authori-ties intervened in the appeal on their behalf as* amici curiae.

[12] 59 Stat. 33.

[13] United States v. California, 332 U.S. 19 (1947); United States v. Louisiana, *same v.* Texas, 339 U.S. 699 *and* 707 (1950). *The Submerged Lands Act of 1953 was sustained in* Alabama v. Texas, 347 U.S. 272 (1954).

field of national power lest their actions be disruptive—regardless of whether national action has occupied all the available ground—is also applied, but only spasmodically, in the areas of state taxation and regulation of interstate commerce. For example, the Interstate Commerce Commission long ago divided the country into standard time zones, to bring order into an earlier chaos; but local option about daylight-saving time then reintroduced a good deal of confusion, cleared up anew in 1966 by federal law.

The national government may not ordinarily impose mandatory duties on the states, because it would be rash or impossible to coerce them into obedience unless in the most extreme circumstances. The National Guard is one exception, however, and the conduct of national elections is another. A third is sparingly used—compelling state courts to try cases arising under national laws, as was done in the federal Employers' Liability Act, the National Prohibition Act, and the wartime Emergency Price Control Act. But these are special cases, the last category buttressed by the "supremacy" clause of the Constitution and the Supreme Court's power to reverse state court decisions.[14] No such combination of constitutional obligation and supervisory control exists in the legislative and administrative relations between the nation and the states—no counterpart here to the situation familiar in imperial-colonial relationships, where governors could be removed and colonial legislation be reserved for imperial approval before it could take effect. Congress may, however, attach conditions to federal grants and direct federal officials to withhold payments, on a finding that the conditions have been violated, as a means of inducing recalcitrant states to comply. This is not compulsion in the legal sense but it may have much the same practical effect.

When the national government exercises a constitutionally valid coercive power in domestic affairs, it confronts a triple question: (1) How far to go itself in using these national powers; (2) what to do about the area left beyond the scope of the national law—the intrastate aspects of matters nationally regulated under the commerce power; and (3) whether and how far to seek state aid in enforcing the national law. These questions have administrative as well as legal implications, for their answers in any particular case determine whether federal field offices must be established or

---

[14] *The important "supremacy" clause, appearing in Article VI of the national Constitution, reads: "This Constitution, and the Laws of the United States which shall be made in Pursuance thereof; and all Treaties made, or which shall be made, under the Authority of the United States, shall be the Law of the Land; and the Judges of every State shall be bound thereby, any Thing in the Constitution or Laws of any State to the Contrary notwithstanding."*

expanded to perform the appointed duties (and if so, how extensive the network must be), whether state governments will be used to carry them out, or whether some (and if so, what kind of) sharing of the tasks must be devised.

The first question—how far national action should go—depends, of course, on the subject matter and the extent and intensity of the national interest. National action is justified in the following situations: when the national government alone can marshal the necessary resources; when the task overruns the geographical and jurisdictional limits of the states; when nationwide uniformity is needed; when a state's action (or inaction) is injurious to the people of other states; or when states fail to respect basic political and civil rights guaranteed to everyone. But these are always matters of degree, leaving room for differing judgments as to how far the remedial national action should try to go.

On the second question the (Kestnbaum) Commission on Intergovernmental Relations [15] in 1955 proposed some sensible guides: National inaction in a field should not ordinarily bar state action; national laws should not be framed or construed to preempt the field against state action unless this intent is clearly stated; national action should not bar state action unless the two are positively inconsistent; national minimum standards should not bar the states from setting more rigorous standards; and national laws should let state authorities have administrative jurisdiction when state laws on the subject are in substantial accord.

On the third question of whether to seek state aid in enforcing national law, the record is full of disappointments, particularly in the field of national economic regulation. But friends of federalism urge that efforts to enlist state cooperation be continued, especially in relatively noncontroversial matters, such as food and quarantine inspections. The record is not much better for efforts to secure cooperation under parallel state and federal laws, except when it is limited to interchanges of information.

National aid to state and local criminal law enforcement, by contrast, has developed rapidly in recent years. Building on the precedent of the Mann Act, which made it a federal crime to transport women across state lines for immoral purposes, Congress has passed the Lindbergh kidnapping act and others designed to backstop local authorities hampered by jurisdictional boundaries and the mobility of criminals. The FBI, with its fingerprint file and the facilities of its crime laboratory, furnishes an immediate identification service to any police department on request. The national

---

[15] Report to the President (Washington, D.C., 1955), chap. 3, especially p. 70.

institutions for narcotics addicts also serve some imperative state needs. Cooperation has a brighter future in these fields than in economic regulation.

When the national government turns from regulation and law enforcement to service—that is, spending for the general welfare—it again confronts the questions of how far to go and whether to go it alone or in partnership. These questions are open to a wide range of possible answers, for the Constitution does not restrict Congress's spending power to the limits of its enumerated coercive powers. The most common justifications for national action are the inadequacy of the resources of the states, or their inequality, or the indifference of many state governments. The national contribution may consist of services or cash grants (or credit pledges) or both. The most common service is information, much of which would be simply unavailable or unusable unless it was gathered, compiled, analyzed, and published centrally. Another is research and other technical resources, human and scientific, which it would be wasteful or impossible for the states to duplicate. Similarly, new ideas arising from the operations of governments, businesses, labor unions, and farmers may be lost unless they can be fed into and distributed by a central clearing house. Thus creative thinking and planning may be more fruitful when they emanate from a central vantage point where comparisons are practicable and wider relationships are visible.

Cash outlays, the other main form of noncoercive national action, raise the question of state participation more acutely. It may be settled by the size of the outlay and its relation to the states' revenues. As we have seen, the states were in no position during the 1930's to contribute much to the huge relief programs that were required then. They were in no position in the 1920's to build the Boulder Dam, and could not now tackle the large-scale development of peaceful uses of atomic energy. Direct and exclusive national operation of public services may also be dictated by history, convenience, or efficiency, as in the cases of the post office, the old age, survivors', and disability insurance program, or the service aspects of the Coast Guard. It may be justified, too, by local indifference or hostility, as in the case of the national reservations for Indians. National grants-in-aid, however, are often effective stimulants to overcoming the states' indifference. And they can also help to equalize uneven burdens where a national minimum service level is desired, as a glance at the meager revenue sources of Alaska or Wyoming, for instance, will show.

Despite the nineteenth-century tradition, reaching down to World War I, according to which the national and state governments conducted their separate functions separately,[16] the advantages of joint action are persuasive. It improves the chances of getting auxiliary help from coercive state laws that may be needed even though the federal program is voluntary. It may gain more by allowing for individual state modifications than the loss in uniformity costs; uniformity is not always a blessing. It encourages the states to extend the benefits of a program beyond the national support level. And it saves them from the effects of being bypassed, probably a greater danger than the risk of undue deference to Washington.

FEDERAL AID. National-state cooperation is by no means wholly a matter of money, especially in a field like law enforcement, but its financial aspects are seldom far from the consciousness of the officials involved. Table 5.1 shows the general trend in federal aid since the eve of World War II in relation to other revenues of state and local governments. Since 1953, federal aid has risen relatively as well as absolutely—as a percentage of total federal budget expenditures, as a percentage of total federal cash payments to the public, and as a percentage of state-local revenues. Table 5.2 shows the distribution of federal aid by major functions. As noted in the previous chapter, highways and public assistance dwarf the other categories.

Nearly all federal aid (96 percent in 1965) takes the form of outright grants, in many cases with a requirement that the state match at least part of the federal funds. But occasionally the aid consists of federal revenues that are shared with other governments (for example, public land grazing permit fees and mineral royalties) or of repayable loans or advances (irrigation projects, state college dormitories).

Probably more important than the matching requirements in the long run are other sorts of strings often attached to grants. A universal requirement is a federal audit of payments made from grants: in the case of public assistance this is a large-scale operation to ensure that eligibility stipulations are observed. Other conditions focus on minimum technical and safety standards. Highway and community development grants, for in-

---

[16] *The reality of this tradition has been challenged in recent research.* Morton Grodzins, "The Federal System," in the *President's Commission on National Goals, Goals for Americans* (*New York, 1960*), *pp. 265ff., and Daniel J. Elazar,* The American Partnership: Intergovernmental Cooperation in the Nineteenth-century United States (*Chicago: University of Chicago Press, 1962*), *argue that the tradition is a myth obscuring the dominant fact of cooperation from the beginning. There is evidence and rhetoric on both sides. The argument seems to turn on subjective judgments as to whose view of what is "dominant."*

The most incisive and systematic recent analysis of federalism, American and comparative, in brief compass, is William H. Riker, Federalism: Origin, Operation, Significance (*Boston: Little, Brown, 1964*); *but it defines the term mechanically.*

Table 5.1. *Federal Grants in Relation to State-Local General Revenue and Federal General Expenditure, 1940–1965*

Fiscal Year	Total State-Local General Revenue (millions)	Revenue from Federal Government		Total Federal General Expenditure (millions)	Total Federal Intergovernmental Expenditure	
		Amount (millions)	Percent of state-local revenues		Amount (millions)	Percent of federal general expenditure
1940	$ 9,609	$ 945	9.8%	$ 9,780	$ 884	9.0%
1950	20,911	2,486	11.4	40,285	2,371	5.9
1955	31,073	3,131	10.1	67,203	3,099	4.6
1960	50,505	6,974	13.8	83,719	6,994	8.4
1964–65	74,341	11,029	14.8	110,129	11,062	10.0

SOURCE: U. S. Bureau of the Census, *Census of Governments: 1962*, Vol. VI, No. 4, *Historical Statistics on Governmental Finances and Employment* (Washington, D.C., 1964), pp. 35–40; and same, *Governmental Finances in 1964–65* (Washington, D.C., 1966), pp. 20, 22.

Table 5.2. *Federal Aid to State and Local Governments, by Functions,*
1956 and 1965

Function	Amount (millions)		Percent	
	1956	1965	1956	1965
Agriculture and agricultural resources	$ 389	$ 526	10.4%	4.7%
Highways	729	4,018	19.4	36.1
Housing and community development	118	683	3.1	6.1
Public assistance	1,455	3,059	38.8	27.5
Other health, labor, welfare	669	1,418	17.8	12.7
Education	225	679	6.0	6.1
All other	168	744	4.5	6.7
Total	$3,753	$11,127	100.0%	100.0%

SOURCE: U.S. Bureau of the Census, *Statistical Abstract of the United States: 1962*
(Washington, D.C., 1962), p. 417, and 1966, p. 419. The figures (prepared by the
Bureau of the Budget) are not directly comparable to those in Table 5.1 (based on
Bureau of the Census tables) because of differences in sources, definitions, etc. "Federal
aid" includes grants-in-aid, shared revenues, and net loans and advances.

stance, require the preparation of elaborately detailed plans and their
approval by a national authority before the funds are released. Preparing
adequate plans entails competent professional staff work on the part of the
recipient government. Still other conditions aim at safeguards against
partisan abuses. For example, state and local employees administering the
social security programs must be recruited and dealt with according to civil
service principles. All state and local employees paid in whole or in part
from federal funds (unless exempted by the U.S. Civil Service Commission) must avoid active participation in partisan campaigns.

In addition to its financial and technical aspects, federal aid has
broadly political implications. Federal agencies with grant funds to administer almost inevitably seek out and cultivate clients who see benefits for
themselves or their localities in prospective grants. This charts new paths
to local progress. And it also generates local pressures on state and local
authorities to espouse project proposals—and to find the matching money
for them—lest opportunities be missed and the federal funds go to rival
localities. This tendency is partly offset and partly intensified by congres-

sional concern over the geographical distribution of grants, which leads in turn to statutory formulas and provisos designed to ensure a distribution that takes as much account of the strength of state delegations in Congress as of the relative needs of their constituents. It is no accident, for example, that California leads in the amount of federal aid received, with almost 13 percent of the 1964–65 total, followed by New York, Texas, Illinois, Pennsylvania, and Michigan in that order. Thus not all the taxes of the rich go to improve the condition of the poor.

Related to this is the characteristic demand from the recipient governments and their allies in Congress that federal aid be committed over periods beyond the current fiscal year to which congressional appropriations are traditionally limited. The most spectacular example, noted in the previous chapter, is the Highway Trust Fund, into which federal gasoline tax receipts are automatically appropriated and from which firm allocations to each state are made for three years ahead. The arrangement is defended as necessary for orderly planning and efficient scheduling of construction work. But it insulates a sizable part of the federal budget from countercyclical or other economic policy adjustments that might be needed if the national economy changes.

The growth of cooperative federalism testifies to the potency of its appeals. But it also raises two broad questions for the future of federalism, one quite practical and the other more speculative. The first concerns the possibility and desirability of greater lateral integration within each state government and each local government. This has been recommended in state, county, and municipal reorganization proposals for over a generation, and meets a standard complaint of governors and mayors. Instead, cooperative federalism brings closer links between the professionals in the agencies at all three levels—national, state, and local health officials, highway engineers, welfare workers, and the like. Each of these groups has its own professional associations, its organized clienteles, its technical standards and goals. The effect of these vertical ties is to promote specialization and insularity among state and local agencies, along with demands for autonomy in policy, for earmarked revenues, and so on. If these tendencies continue to grow, how can a governor or mayor pull the strings together to maintain a balance among the activities supposedly under his jurisdiction and to exercise some general managerial oversight?

The second question concerns the historic role of the states and their subdivisions as bases of power and shelters of refuge for opposition to the policies, parties, and personalities temporarily in the ascendant in Washington. The freedom to cooperate is also the freedom to resist. There is little factual evidence to indicate that national grants have prevented the major opposition party from winning or holding state and local elective offices or that nationally aided state agencies are more supine or indifferent than those financed wholly by the states. But in the light of general human experience, it is questionable whether financial dependence and political independence can be permanent bedfellows.

2. The States as Neighbors

It was an interstate commission, the Annapolis convention, that led to the calling of the Constitutional Convention in 1787. The framers of the Constitution, however, made abundantly clear their intent that future relations among the states should not jeopardize the primacy of the Union, nor deteriorate beyond the limits of bad manners. National supremacy and interstate comity were the twin principles that were to govern the behavior of states toward each other. To restrain some temptations that would surely lead to discrimination, hard feelings, and reprisals, the framers lifted certain powers—such as regulating interstate commerce and enacting bankruptcy laws—out of the states' hands and conferred them on Congress instead. To forestall other predictable occasions for dispute, they invoked the canons of comity. Article IV requires each state to give "full faith and credit" to the public acts and records of other states; to hand over any person apprehended within its borders and accused of a crime, on demand of the governor of the accusing state; and to accord the citizens of other states the same "privileges and immunities" it allows to its own. Finally, if controversies susceptible of judicial settlement arise notwithstanding these precautions, an orderly forum is provided: the states can sue each other before the Supreme Court.

INTERSTATE COMITY. The "privileges and immunities" clause of Article IV has fallen into desuetude; as interpreted, it protects very little that is not better protected by other constitutional provisions, notably the Fourteenth Amendment, which extends to "persons"—citizens, corporations, and aliens alike. The provision for interstate rendition of criminals works slowly (because of the paperwork involved) but surely in most instances. Unneighborly irritations occasionally arise, however, when the governor of a state where a fugitive is found refuses to surrender him because he believes the accused will not get an unprejudiced trial or will be too harshly punished at home. There is no machinery to enforce rendition. The "full faith and credit" clause, on the contrary, is judicially enforceable.

It finds its severest test in divorce cases, when the courts of a state like South Carolina or New York—where divorce is allowed not at all or only very grudgingly—are asked to give effect to degrees granted in wide-open jurisdictions like Nevada.

The rules of national supremacy and interstate comity notwithstanding, there has been a zone of tolerance for state protective or retaliatory actions. Under color of a plant-quarantine inspection, for example, California forbids tourists to bring out-of-state fruits or vegetables with them when they cross its border. Dairy interests in metropolitan milksheds have used health and sanitary inspection requirements to prevent out-of-state producers from entering their protected markets. Discriminatory license requirements are a more common form of trade barrier; another hardy perennial is multiple or retaliatory taxation. Many of these ill-mannered measures were depression-born, however, and some of their hardships have been abated in recent years by reciprocity agreements.

INTERSTATE COOPERATION. The framers of the Constitution evidently viewed agreements among states with some suspicion, as likely to jeopardize national supremacy or unity. They flatly forbade any state to "enter into any treaty, alliance, or confederation," or, without the consent of Congress, to "enter into any agreement or compact with another state, or with a foreign power. . . ." So nothing could have been more literally unconstitutional than the formation of the Confederate States of America.

Apart from that episode, the remarkable fact about the first 130 years or so of interstate relations is the paucity of formal arrangements among the states. Broadly speaking, each state went its own way, and whatever it could not or would not settle went to Washington. It was not until well into the twentieth century that the increase in population and the mobility of people began to reopen in a variety of practical forms the general question: What room is there in the federal system for subnational, interstate arrangements?

The compact procedure is decidedly cumbersome. First of all, interstate negotiations must be pursued to the stage of an agreed text; then the document must be approved by the legislatures and the governors of the states involved and by Congress. This can be a delicate and hazardous task. It usually takes a long time to get the consent of Congress to any document laid before it, even in the absence of controversy. Then, too, the infrequency of legislative sessions, the shortness of gubernatorial terms, and the likelihood of party antagonisms between houses are added obstacles to what at best must be arm's-length bargaining.

In the past, compacts were used to sanction the building of private toll bridges over boundary rivers. But these were one-shot transactions: when the bridge was built, the purpose was accomplished and no continuing relations were envisioned. When the occasions for sustained interstate dealings began to multiply and diversify, there was already a premium on more convenient and reliable instrumentalities than this type of ad hoc bargaining. Congress found a permanent administrative solution to the bridge problem by delegating authority to the Corps of Engineers, under the commerce power, to hear and dispose of applications to build bridges without resort to compacts. And in some cases Congress may expedite the adoption of a compact by giving consent to it in advance.

But why use a compact at all? Why should not recourse to the national government be the general and only answer to problems beyond the competence of a single state? At least four considerations suggest that other solutions might be better in some circumstances. One is inherent in the nature of congressional politics when a regional resource—typically an interstate river development—is at issue. There is no doubt that Congress has the power to act in these cases. Furthermore, the states affected look to their congressional delegations to protect and advance their interests. But many members from states outside the area involved do not care much whether or how the issue is resolved, and some of them will trade votes on it regardless of the merits. Something is to be said, therefore, for a procedure that will confine the arena of decision chiefly to the parties with direct stakes in the controversy.

Another situation arises when the states alone possess the coercive power required—for example, to deal with people committed to mental institutions. In such a case, Congress could not itself do all that is needed. The states concerned with the ramifications of this problem beyond their borders might, of course, simply pass parallel legislation. Often, though, the necessary interstate negotiations looking toward concerted state action might better lead to a single formal compact, agreed to by the states and consented to by Congress. So the Interstate Compact on Mental Health provides for hospitalization and treatment of patients regardless of state residence requirements that would otherwise apply. Such a compact may encourage federal participation by way of grants-in-aid.

Mention of parallel legislation suggests a third situation, which is a variant of the foregoing. If parallel laws or administrative action are all that is required to solve a given problem—say, reciprocity arrangements about motor vehicle taxes or licenses—an agreement among the states may be sufficient, without congressional approval.

A fourth consideration is the occasional utility of some organized expression of the viewpoints of some or all of the states as such, and the availability of facilities for determining what consensus exists. The national government might maintain such a clearinghouse. Indeed, the Kestnbaum Commission recommended, and the Congress in 1959 established, an Advisory Commission on Intergovernmental Relations;[17] the Senate Government Operations Committee in 1962 created a Subcommittee on Intergovernmental Relations also. Helpful as these may be, the states may well prefer to use consultative mechanisms set up under their own direct auspices. Viewpoints so expressed may be special pleading, but they cannot be called illegitimate for that.

In practice, a considerable amount of such consultation has evolved outside the national government—though the Governors' Conference, now an annual event, was first assembled at the call of President Theodore Roosevelt to spark his campaign for natural resource conservation. The Council of State Governments, building on some earlier associations, was established in the 1930's; it is supported by parallel state legislation, rather than an interstate compact requiring congressional consent. The Council maintains a secretariat with headquarters in Chicago and comprises nine affiliated organizations of state officials, including the Governors' Conference. It sponsors a wide variety of cooperative activities outside the realm of partisan controversy, lobbies in Washington for state viewpoints, and publishes the biennial *Book of the States*, a storehouse of reference information and periodic reviews of state developments. As we have seen, the Council can also be propelled into the political thicket of states' rights controversy. But one of its affiliates, the older National Conference of Commissioners on Uniform State Laws, has been a leader in promoting uniform state legislation. In addition, the country has many private organizations that seek to clarify, codify, modernize, or unify the formidable mass of state law by securing parallel state action. A prominent example of these is the American Law Institute, which was launched in the 1920's by a committee of the American Bar Association headed by Elihu Root and is known for its *Restatements* of various branches of law.

Along with these developments, the compact clause has been rediscovered.[18] In 1921, the New York–New Jersey compact established the Port of New York Authority, and a few years later the Colorado River compact

---

[17] *See Deil S. Wright, "The Advisory Commission on Intergovernmental Relations: Unique Features and Policy Orientation," Public Administration Review, 25 (September 1965), 193–202.*

[18] *See Frederick L. Zimmerman and Mitchell Wendell,* The Interstate Compact Since 1925 (Chicago: Council of State Governments, 1951).

paved the way for the Boulder Dam. Although there were few additional compacts during the 1930's, they grew by leaps and bounds after World War II. Most of the recent ones establish some permanent administrative agency to carry out a continuing function. Their subject matter ranges from bridges and watershed and harbor development to control of petroleum production, crime control, forest-fire fighting, marine fisheries, the advancement of higher education in the southern and western regions, and civil defense.[19] Their reliability has been fortified by a Supreme Court ruling that valid compacts bind succeeding legislatures. And their flexibility has been revealed in a number of ways: Congress, as already noted, can give consent in advance. Compacts can be open-ended, available to any states that adopt them. Canadian provinces or Mexican states can be admitted to membership in them. Coercive powers can be given to agencies created by them. The New York–New Jersey waterfront compact for regulating longshoremen was novel not only for the drastic changes it made in the domestic law of the two states, but also for delegating to an interstate agency a limited taxing power.

Despite these recent developments, it would nevertheless be rash to conclude that compact arrangements without national participation (other than formal congressional consent) will widely supplant either direct and exclusive national action or joint national-state projects. For one thing, national agencies have often been active sponsors, lobbying in state capitals for uniform state laws and for compact proposals designed to secure state aid in furthering agency objectives—notably the civil defense and health and welfare agencies. These proposals usually contemplate joint national-state cooperation. The Delaware River Basin Compact of 1961 set a precedent in making the national government (represented by the Secretary of the Interior) a full-fledged voting member along with representatives of each of the four states concerned.

Again, it is prudent to look at compact failures, and these abound in the watershed development field. Here the TVA, a wholly national agency with a regional jurisdiction and headquarters, remains the conspicuously successful example of unified basin development and the one with the most cordial relations with the states in its area. The installations in the Colorado, Columbia, Missouri, and many smaller rivers were constructed by national agencies, except for the diversion canal and the power lines within California running to Los Angeles, which were built by a municipal

---

[19] A score of representative interstate commissions established by compacts are briefly identified in The Book of the States, 1966–67 (Chicago: Council of State Governments, 1966), pp. 278–87.

authority. The immense Central Valley water project approved by California voters in a 1960 referendum is unique in lying wholly within that state. Meanwhile, compact proposals for interstate development of the Missouri, Arkansas, Connecticut, Potomac, and other rivers have foundered in talk and disagreement on the sharing of costs and benefits. Compacts share the weaknesses of the Articles of Confederation and the UN Security Council, in which each member has a free veto. For basin development projects and other such controversial matters, the record indicates that a "more perfect union" than a compact alone is needed. And where there is national participation, the record also suggests that federal agencies will want a supervisory role, not merely that of one among equals: they are reluctant to tie their hands for the future by accepting the degree of intergovernmental commitment customary when states enter a compact.[20]

Two other bits of evidence support the conclusion that the national government will keep at least a fitful eye on interstate and national-state relationships. Following the 1955 *Report* of the (Kestnbaum) Commission on Intergovernmental Relations, President Eisenhower moved to carry out one of its recommendations by appointing a special assistant in the Executive Office of the President to advise him in working out problems of state and local relations with federal agencies; Congress adopted another of the recommendations, noted above, when it established a permanent Advisory Commission on Intergovernmental Relations with a small budget for research and conferences in this field. These steps survived the transitions from the Eisenhower to the Kennedy and Johnson administrations.

The second and equally significant episode followed the demand by Chairman Celler of the House Committee on the Judiciary in 1960 for general access, on the part of his committee, to the files of the Port of New York Authority. Upon being refused, he secured an amendment of House Rule 27, defining his committee's jurisdiction to include explicitly the function of investigating (with the aid of subpoenas if necessary) the workings of interstate compacts. When the Port Authority, backed by the two state governors, stood on its refusal to produce internal working papers —though offering masses of less sensitive documents—its executive director was convicted of contempt. On appeal the Port Authority argued that

---

[20] *Compare the words of Mr. Justice Holmes in deciding a suit brought by the U.S. Attorney General to enjoin Chicago from diverting Lake Michigan waters in excess of a specified rate: "This is not a controversy between equals. . . . The United States is asserting its sovereign power to regulate commerce and to control the navigable waters. . . . There is no question that this power is superior to that of the States . . . . "* Sanitary District of Chicago v. United States, 266 U.S. 405, 425 (1925).

it was a state agency subject to investigation only by the legislatures of the states that were party to its compact; the Department of Justice, on the other hand, argued the right of a congressional committee to investigate what the consent of Congress had called into being. The appeals court in June, 1962, set aside the contempt conviction, and the Supreme Court refused to disturb that result.[21] But the decision rested on narrow grounds and avoided the constitutional issues. It does not seem likely, therefore, that state sovereignty will entirely immunize a compact agency from a congressional investigation that is properly invoked.

3. The States and Their Localities

Constitutionally speaking, local governments are the legislative creatures of their parent states and subject to their plenary control, except as constitutional home rule provisions, legislative apportionments, prohibitions against special legislation, and the like limit state powers. The relations between the states and their subdivisions, however, depend more upon the political influence that each can muster than upon these constitutional dispositions.

The bewildering number and the variety of types of local units are described later in Chapter 15. The states have reacted to this proliferation with mixed emotions and a variety of policies. Their problem with education, for example, is chiefly financial. The school districts, wearing the badge of virtue and pointing to the inadequacies of local school levies, have established the principal claim on state aid, getting almost half of it, as Figure 5.1 shows. And school systems integrated into city and town governments, rather than operated by autonomous school districts, bring the total of educational aid to three-fifths of all state aid.

STATE AND COUNTY. The counties, wearing the badge of poverty and neglected by the citizenry, have learned nevertheless to act in concert on financial matters through their state legislators. They get over a quarter of all state aid. But they are beset by other difficulties because they are weak. The cities they surround complain of their shortcomings. Their powers have always been limited, yet because county officials have often tended to resolve conflicts of interest in favor of private interests, the states have passed many laws restricting them further. This keeps them often in the courts litigating their powers. Litigation in turn sends the county

[21] The New York Times, June 18, 1962, p. 1; November 14, 1962, p. 1.

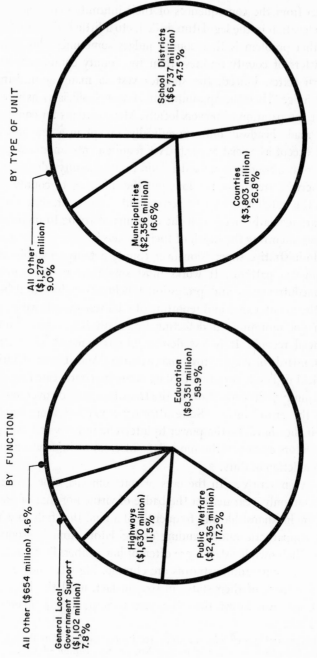

Figure 5.1. *State Aid to Localities, by Function and Type of Unit, 1965*

BY FUNCTION

BY TYPE OF UNIT

All Other ($654 million) 4.6%

General Local
Government Support
($1,102 million)
7.8%

Education
($8,351 million)
58.9%

Highways
($1,630 million)
11.5%

Public Welfare
($2,436 million)
17.2%

All Other
($1,278 million)
9.0%

School Districts
($6,737 million)
47.5%

Municipalities
($2,356 million)
16.6%

Counties
($3,803 million)
26.8%

TOTAL = $14.2 BILLION

SOURCE: U.S. Bureau of the Census, *Compendium of State Government Finances in 1965* (Washington, D.C., 1966), pp. 38f. Because of rounding, individual dollar totals and percentages do not add up to overall total.

representatives to the state legislatures to press for special and local bills to extricate them from the consequences of their infirmities. In some states the county delegation in the legislature is de facto a little legislature for the county. Another problem is that county judges sometimes appear to be more the masters of county business than the county commissioners. In some southern states, indeed, the statutes vest so many administrative duties in the judges (like the appointment of school officials) as virtually to obliterate the separation of powers locally. Merit systems for county employees have made headway only sporadically, except in a few advanced counties and except as Social Security Act requirements impose them on welfare workers as a condition for federal aid funds. County administrative standards otherwise are frequently low, but the influence of county political leaders in the statehouses may be very potent. As a result, state agencies and officials are regularly faced with the dilemma of trying to prod county officials without incurring the wrath of their backers.[22]

State administrative supervision over county activities exhibits correspondingly uneven patterns. It works most smoothly, perhaps, in such relatively noncontroversial and professional fields as public health—for example, in the maintenance and reporting of vital statistics. It works tolerably, though not promptly, in detecting irregularities by state audits of county financial records. It is less dependable as a means of obtaining acceptable standards of county road maintenance. And it is least satisfactory in the field of law enforcement. State supreme courts can reverse the decisions of county judges for errors in the trials they preside over, but they cannot oust the erring judges. State attorney generals seldom have—or relish using, if they have it—the power to intervene in trials or to supplant county prosecutors except in the most flagrant cases of injustice, abuse of process, or dereliction of duty.

STATE AND CITY. In the eyes of state officials, cities, especially large ones, commonly wear neither the badge of virtue nor that of poverty. Their needs are inexhaustible and frequently of a kind that fails to win the instant and sympathetic understanding of legislators from less populous localities; and their own legislators are often of low caliber. Partisan clashes between city and state administrators are chronic. Big city budgets sometimes approach those of their states in size; in fact, until the late 1950's, New York City's was larger than the state's. Some city problems—for

---

[22] For an illuminating, well-told case study, see Paul Ylvisaker, "The Battle of Blue Earth County," Inter-University Case Program No. 25, rev. edition (University, Ala.: University of Alabama Press, 1955); an earlier version is in Harold Stein (ed.), Public Administration and Policy Development (New York: Harcourt, 1952), pp. 89–105.

example, water supply, recreation facilities, and access highways—cannot be solved within city boundaries. Furthermore, state constitutions or laws limit municipal taxing and borrowing powers. So cities, too, are continually in need of enabling or dispensing legislation, and they demand that fund distribution formulas be revised on terms more favorable to them. But the states, in turn, accuse them of mismanagement. Thus, although their citizens cast big, often decisive, votes in statewide elections, the cities, large and small together, got less than one-sixth of all state aid in 1965.

HOME RULE. State aid to all local governments accounted for 35 percent of total state expenditures in 1965. But it was about 50 percent in Wisconsin, and over 40 percent in New York, North Carolina, and Maryland. On the other hand, state aid was under 20 percent in 15 states.

In the light of this review, the time appears ripe for reconsidering the most general issue in state-local relations, the issue of home rule. We have earlier noted that home rule was one of the principal goals of the municipal reform movement early in this century and that somewhat over half the states, by law or constitutional amendment, have adopted it or optional charter plans that go some distance toward meeting this goal. A few of these are available also to counties.

Yet it is now fairly evident that it is not enough for the states to leave their localities alone and free. The line between state and local affairs is no more capable of being sharply drawn than the line between national and state affairs. Cities and suburbs are the growing parts of the states. By the Census Bureau count in 1960, there were 212 standard metropolitan areas in the United States with a total population of 112.9 million, up from 168 such areas with 84.5 million inhabitants in 1950. This is an increase during the decade from 56 to 63 percent of the total population of the country. City problems spill out over surrounding areas, and local tyrannies and abuses may require controls from above. The states have innately superior legal powers and wider jurisdictions, and they have developed superior revenue resources. The contemporary challenge to the states is not merely to liberate their subdivisions by permissive enabling legislation that will broaden the discretionary powers of localities to cope with their problems; it is also to devise ways of bringing state leadership, technical assistance, financial and other resources more effectively to bear in joint approaches and cooperative solutions to difficulties that are beyond unaided municipal competence. Metropolitan readjustments such as urban renewal and mass transport arrangements abound with such difficulties. Concrete evidence of the challenge is to be found in recent developments in inter-local relations and direct national-local relations.

4. Dealings among Local Units

In the past, local governments, like sovereign nations, tended to go their own way. But nowadays, they are becoming increasingly aware of their dependence, not only on their parent states, but also on their neighboring and overlapping local units. This interdependence is a product of crowding and mobility; it is both the cause and the product of specialization and communication; and it teaches cooperation as a price of getting things done. Accordingly, when two or more adjoining local governments find their needs mismatched to their individual capabilities—their powers, resources, and geographic areas—a wide variety of adjustments is available in principle, if not in fact, to achieve what is desired.

The simplest form is a reciprocity agreement or a well-timed campaign of persuasion that induces parallel actions or policies: Westfield will send its firefighters to Southfield on call, if Southfield will reciprocate; two school districts will exchange pupils living near their boundaries. Such arrangements depend on an obvious mutuality of interests and have the advantage of posing no threat to the continuing power of each party to determine its future course. But reciprocity, like other forms of barter, is a clumsy medium when differing kinds of service are to be exchanged; and persuasion may founder on stubbornness or indifference.

The next alternative is to negotiate a price and enter into a contract, although an enabling statute from the state may be needed for this. On a contractual basis many and more complicated arrangements can be agreed to than simple reciprocity would sustain. For example, central cities often furnish outlying suburbs with water, sewers, and other utilities in this way; or an outlying county may lease the city a tract for waste disposal. These contracts are usually the most convenient means of settling the relationships between units with overlapping boundaries—city and county, city and school district, New York City and the Port Authority, and so on.

A third alternative is for the parties to join in creating a new special district, its boundaries suited and its powers limited to the purpose that has brought them together. In this way counties may cooperate to form a watershed conservancy district for flood control and water supply, or city and suburbs may cooperate to establish a park district. Like contracts and agreements, this method leaves the constituent units and their powers intact, and so—in the short run, at least—raises no fundamental question of the surrender or reallocation of governing powers.

A fourth alternative, quite different in this latter respect, is annexation, whereby the strongest party extends its boundaries to take in the additional territory within which it will then furnish the needed services. This may be an attractive solution if a city moves to absorb an adjoining area that is still underdeveloped or unorganized and offers services that will increase real estate values. It may also be acceptable if—as happened in the vicinity of Los Angeles—the city brings in an indispensable new water supply without which suburban real estate values would decline and makes annexation the price of water. But annexation laws, though they vary a good deal from state to state, usually require the consent not only of the annexing municipality but also of either the local government or the inhabitants in the area to be annexed. And this may be impossible to obtain. Annexation is an especially unpalatable alternative for well-settled suburban communities jealous of their self-governing powers; it reminds them of the fate of the lady who went out to ride on a tiger. A metropolitan city like Boston or Cleveland, surrounded by incorporated towns and villages, will find no solution to its cramped jurisdiction by the annexation route.

The most thoroughgoing structural solution is merger, by consolidation or federation, to form a new metropolitan government with boundaries and powers sufficiently enlarged to cope with the range of problems that frustrated its predecessor units. This is the standard recommendation of survey teams that have studied many metropolitan complexes, though occasional dissenters have protested.[23] It is the voice of sweet reason; it looks good on paper; the British Parliament has enacted it for London; and it has been adopted by voters in this country in a few instances—notably in Dade County (Miami), Florida—after lengthy educational and hard-fought political campaigns. But it has usually been rejected because it raises, inevitably, all the issues and uncertainties of a constitutional convention: who is to govern whom, and on what terms? More is involved here than structure. On the record, it seems plain that far-reaching proposals of this sort must wait until some means of organizing widespread consent to such fundamental changes has been developed. Short of that, the more limited remedies of interjurisdictional contracts and the use of special districts are about the only choices available to policy makers who are trying to surmount the limitations of local government boundaries and powers.

In these circumstances, and since the realistic alternatives in particular cases depend so much on state law, it seems plain, too, that there is a wide-

---

[23] *For example*, Vincent Ostrom, Charles M. Tiebout, and Robert Warren, "The *Organization of Government in Metropolitan Areas: A Theoretical Inquiry,*" American Political Science Review, 55 (*December 1961*), 831–43; *cf.* Robert C. Wood, "The *New Metropolis: Green Belts, Grass Roots or Gargantua,*" American Political Science Review, 52 (*March 1958*), 108–22.

open opportunity for the states to exert their leadership and lend their resources in the task of facilitating accommodations of their local communities' joint needs. This is one lesson to be drawn from California's spectacular initiative in 1960 toward solving the water-supply needs of its southern counties and cities.

5. Direct National–Local Relations

Working contacts between the political leaders of major cities and the White House or the national party headquarters are time-honored phenomena, and so are ad hoc official federal interventions in municipal affairs on occasions of disaster or crisis. Continuing and systematic direct dealings between national and city governments on a significant scale, however, are more recent.[24] They became established in the 1930's in connection with temporary work relief programs—programs undertaken after it was apparent that the relief load, centered in the cities, was far beyond the capacity of the states to support. National-local relations quickly became the mainstay of airport development, as noted in a previous chapter. Similarly, the Department of Agriculture became involved in the school lunch program, a depression remedy that has become a permanent fixture. From these beginnings, national-local relations spread during the postwar years into the fields of housing and urban renewal, hospital construction and community health activities, civil defense, school subventions—at first in "federally impacted" districts (areas with populations swollen by defense installations)—and into other aspects of urban life.

The financial outlays in these initial undertakings were relatively modest. In 1964–65, the 43 largest cities (over 300,000 population) received $303 million directly from the federal government, as against $1.6 billion from the states, though much of the latter, of course, was a funneling of federal grants. But the trend is up, and irreversible for the foreseeable future, as urbanization advances and urban representation in Congress increases. It is no accident that the main channels for national-local dealings run from the large cities.

A new era in recognition of these trends opened in 1966 with the establishment of a federal cabinet-level Department of Housing and Urban Development, authorized by Congress the previous year. An earlier proposal by President Kennedy to the same effect had failed in 1961. The new department took over the Housing and Home Finance Agency and a

---

[24] For an informed and perceptive treatment of this general topic, see Roscoe C. Martin, The Cities and the Federal System (New York: Atherton Press, 1965).

number of activities formerly lodged in the Department of Health, Education and Welfare, and elsewhere. Its creation coincided with the adoption of the Elementary and Secondary Education Act of 1965, and followed a year's experience with the Anti-Poverty Program, both of which dealt principally with urban problems. It also anticipated federal grants for costly investments in mass transit and interurban commuting facilities.

In thus giving a visible token of the higher priority now assigned to urban affairs in the councils of the nation, the decision to establish this department immediately raised difficult questions of jurisdiction within the federal government: what will be left for the functionally organized departments to do, if everything that concerns the cities is swallowed up in the new agency? But in the longer run it raises even more serious questions for the states. What will become of them as the national government increasingly deals with the cities? Except as reapportionment may alter attitudes by altering the composition of state legislatures, there is little indication that the states are willing to replace the benefits these dealings bring to the cities. Until that happens, the cities will resist state efforts to cut their direct pipelines to Washington. But the states need look no further than the fate of county governments to see the consequences of being passed by because of their own inaction.

6. State and Local Finances

The capacity of state and local governments to raise revenue and to guide that revenue into the various expenditure channels with a prudent understanding of where additional amounts will bring the greatest returns for the people is critically important to the maintenance, expansion, or diminution of the roles of those governments in the American system. Chapter 3 has shown the growth of state and local budgets and the shifts in emphasis for the 1900–50 period, and Chapter 4 has set forth the current pattern of functional activities. Here we examine the current overall pattern of revenues and expenditures and develop some generalizations that should help in appraising how the roles of state and local governments are shaped by fiscal considerations.

RELATION TO NATIONAL FINANCES. In 1950 all American governments—federal, state, and local—spent $70.3 billion. By 1960 the figure had more than doubled, to $151.3 billion, and by 1964–65 it had almost trebled, to $206 billion. Per capita general expenditures rose from $400 to $714 and, in 1964–65, to $898. The differences between 1950 and 1964–65 were by no means due to the contribution (if that is the apt term) of the federal government. On the contrary, state and local general expenditures increased by 229 percent, while federal direct general expenditures increased by 161 percent.[25] Anyone who was heard orating in this period about the stagnation of state and local governments and the growing octopus of the federal government had simply not done his homework.[26]

It is true that the federal government spends more than state and local governments combined, as indeed has been the case since the early 1940's. Of the $206 billion spent by all governments in 1964–65, the federal government's *direct* expenditures were $119 billion, while the state and local governments' were $87 billion. This roughly 60:40 percentile division between national and subnational direct governmental expenditures is, however, only one of the several ways of stating the fiscal relations between the levels of government. Much depends on the question uppermost in one's mind—or on the already-formulated answer for which one wants supporting data.

Table 5.3 can be used as a foundation for clarifying a rather complex picture. From it we draw the following summary for 1964–65:

	Expenditures*			Revenues*		
	Total = expendi- ture	Direct + expendi- ture	Grants to other gov- ernments	Receipts + from other govern- ments	Revenue = from own sources	Total reve- nue
	(a)	(b)	(c)	(d)	(e)	(f)
All	$206.0	$206.0			$202.9	$202.9
Federal	130.1	119.0	$11.1		125.8	125.8
State	45.5	31.3	14.2	$10.3	38.5	48.8
Local	56.0	55.7	0.3	15.2	38.6	53.8

* Billions of dollars.

[25] U.S. *Bureau of the Census, Governmental Finances in 1964–65* (*Washington, D.C., 1966*), *Tables 1, 2, and 3; same, Census of Governments: 1962, Vol. VI, No. 4, Historical Statistics on Governmental Finances and Employment* (*Washington, D.C., 1964*), *Tables 1, 2, 3, and 4. The percentage for federal "direct general expenditures" excludes federal grants since the same dollars are counted as state and local general expenditures. "General expenditures" exclude utility, liquor stores, and insurance trust expenditures, whereas all these are included in the grand totals reported in the first two sentences and in the "direct expenditures" of the following paragraphs.*

[26] *For a good start on that homework, see Frederick C. Mosher and Orville F. Poland, The Costs of American Governments: Facts, Trends, Myths (New York: Dodd, Mead, 1964).*

Table 5.3. *Summary of Governmental Finances, 1964–1965*

Item	Amount (billions)				
	All governments	Federal government	State and local		
			TOTAL	STATE	LOCAL
Total revenue	$202.9	$125.8	$88.1	$48.8	$53.8
Intergovernmental revenue	—	—	11.0	10.3	15.2
From federal government	—	—	11.0	9.9	1.1
From state governments	—	—	—	—	14.1
From local governments	—	—	—	0.4	—
Revenue from own sources	202.9	125.8	77.1	38.5	38.6
General revenue	170.0	106.7	63.3	30.6	32.7
Taxes	145.3	93.7	51.6	26.1	25.5
Charges & miscellaneous	24.7	13.0	11.7	4.5	7.3
Utility revenue	4.9	—	4.9	—	4.9
Liquor stores revenue	1.4	—	1.4	1.3	0.2
Insurance trust revenue	26.5	19.1	7.4	6.6	0.8
Total expenditure	206.0	130.1	87.0	45.5	56.0
Intergovernmental expenditure	—	11.1	—	14.2	0.3
To states	—	9.7	—	—	0.3
To local governments	—	1.4	—	14.2	—
Direct expenditure	206.0	119.0	87.0	31.3	55.7
General	174.0	99.1	75.0	26.1	48.8
National defense and international relations	55.8	55.8	—	—	—
Interest on general debt	11.4	8.9	2.5	0.8	1.7
All other functions	106.8	34.4	72.5	25.3	47.1
Utility expenditure	5.9	—	5.9	—	5.9
Liquor stores expenditure	1.2	—	1.2	1.0	0.2
Insurance trust expenditure	24.9	19.9	5.0	4.2	0.8
Total debt outstanding	416.8	317.3	99.5	27.0	72.5
Long-term debt	—	—	94.2	26.2	68.0
Short-term debt	—	—	5.3	0.8	4.5
Cash and security holdings	—	—	85.3	51.3	33.9
Insurance trust	—	—	41.2	31.4	9.8
Other	—	—	44.0	20.0	24.1

SOURCE: U.S. Bureau of the Census, *Governmental Finances in 1964–65* (Washington, D.C., 1966), pp. 15–23, 28.

We may start by noting that column *a* shows total expenditures for all governments as $206 billion, but the other figures in the column actually add up to $231.6 billion. The $25.6 billion difference is accounted for by column *c*, "Grants to Other Governments"; it is excluded from the overall total because the same dollars should not be counted twice—once, say, when the federal government hands them over to the states, and again when the states either use them for their own direct expenditures or pass them along to their local governments. Roughly the same discrepancy in totaling recurs in column *f* for total revenue, and for the same reason. If we ask, what are the proportions of revenue raised by American governments by their own taxes and other charges (rather than their proportions of direct expenditures), then column *e* figures tell us that the federal government raises 62 percent, compared to state and local direct revenues of 38 percent. This is not much of a departure from the 60:40 ratio for direct expenditures noted earlier, because the only change is in the way about $11 billion of federal grants are counted.

More significant are the shifts in the relation of state to local finance as one uses different measures. Notice, in column *e*, that state governments and local governments raised about the same amount ($38.5 billion) of revenue from their own sources. But, as column *b* shows, their direct expenditures are in quite different proportions, with the states spending only $31.3 billion and the local governments $55.7 billion. What was a 50:50 ratio now becomes a 36:64 ratio. One could argue from the direct revenue figures that state and local governments are about equally important in the American system of government. On the other hand, one could argue from the direct expenditure figures that the local governments perform almost two-thirds of the subnational work of American government while the states perform little more than a third of it.

Varying conclusions about the federal role in comparison with that of state and local governments can best be shown by summarizing figures for 1964–65 direct general expenditures (in billions of dollars) from Table 5.3:

	Total	National Defense and International Relations	Interest on General Debt	All Other Functions
All	$174.0	$55.8	$11.4	$106.8
Federal	99.1	55.8	8.9	34.4
State and local	75.0	—	2.5	72.5

The totals approximately reproduce the 60:40 ratio we earlier encountered for all direct expenditures (including, as this table does not, utility, liquor stores, and insurance trust expenditures). But those who argue over whether the federal government has too great a role in the American system are usually talking about the distribution of regulatory and service activities in the domestic sphere. No one argues that the federal government should yield national defense or the conduct of international relations to state and local governments; nor does anyone propose to transfer the payment of the national debt or the interest on it—both largely attributable to the costs of World War II [27]—to the state and local governments. If we eliminate these noncontroversial expenditure categories, we find that, for all other functions taken together, the federal government does less than the state and local governments. In fact, the ratio for these other functions is 32:68. This ratio, impressive enough as it stands, would be even more striking if the $6.4 billion of direct federal expenditures for veterans were classified as an obligation arising from national defense, rather than classified with "all other functions"; it would then read 27:73. [28]

SOME GENERAL TRENDS. State and local expenditures have grown faster than the population. In a significant study of trends in governmental activity, Solomon Fabricant argued persuasively that the extraordinary expansion of domestic public outlays is associated primarily with rising levels of income, and secondarily with population increases. [29] According to another study, they have also grown faster than the gross national product (GNP), which is the country's total output of goods and services. State and local expenditures together accounted for about 6 percent of GNP before and after World War I; doubled to 12 or 13 percent during the Depression (when they stayed relatively stable while GNP was cut in half); dropped to 8 or 9 percent during and immediately after World War II; but rose again to 11.6 in 1949–50 and 12 percent in 1960 despite the tremendous growth in GNP during the 1950's. [30]

---

[27] *The figures for "all other functions" also exclude the $2.5 billion paid by state and local governments as interest on general debt. The rationale for this, which is also an appropriate alternative rationale for excluding the corresponding federal figure for interest, is that though of fiscal importance, interest payments do not properly count as measures of the "activities" of governments, i.e., the services and regulatory work done.*

[28] *The narrowing of consideration to "domestic" activities of governments, especially by eliminating national defense expenditures, does not foreclose other ways of viewing the question. National defense expenditures do, of course, affect the domestic economy and society, through procurement contracts placed with American industry and through the support of a large segment of the labor force as uniformed personnel, civil servants in the Department of Defense, and workers in factories with defense contracts.*

[29] *Solomon Fabricant,* The Trend of Governmental Activity in the United States since 1900 *(New York: National Bureau of Economic Research, 1952).*

[30] *Morris A. Copeland,* Trends in Government Financing *(Princeton, N.J.: Princeton University Press, 1961), p. 47. Copeland's figures differ somewhat from those calculable from Tables C-1 and C-2 in the* Economic Report of the President . . . *Jan-*

Community and regional patterns are also discernible, though the differentials are smaller and less clearly marked than they once were. In 1902, per capita expenditures in cities of over 100,000 inhabitants averaged nearly two and one-half times the per capita outlays by the rest of the local governments. By 1950, the ratio was only 5 to 4, as the smaller places improved their standards of service. Nevertheless, per capita municipal debt in the 1950's still showed some tendency to decrease with city size. Another recent trend, however, has blurred this older characteristic graduation by size. The states and the larger city governments—which once lived hand-to-mouth—have become the holders of very large amounts of cash and securities investments, chiefly in their pension and other insurance trust funds. By 1947, state holdings of this sort equaled the total of state debt outstanding; and although the debt has grown since then, the investment holdings have grown faster. The picture is not quite so rosy for local governments, but in 1964–65 their cash and securities amounted to half their net long-term debt (see Table 5.4). This growth in investments does not, of course, diminish the current expenditures of large cities, but it helps their credit ratings and reduces their need to borrow in the public market. So it seems reasonable to suppose that the trend toward greater uniformity in per capita debt is the product not only of a leveling-up process for smaller communities but also of a leveling-down for the larger ones.[31]

The spread of urbanization and suburban development appears to have had a similar equalizing effect on regional differences in the propensity to borrow and spend for public purposes; but differences remain. The Pacific, Middle Atlantic, and New England regions, in that order, had the

uary 1966. *There the state and local governmental purchases of goods and services show the following percentages of the gross national product; the first column is based on "current dollars"—that is, without adjustment for changing purchasing power of the dollar—and the second column is based on purchasing power as expressed in 1958 dollars (and taking into account prices of goods and services purchased by governments):*

State and Local Purchases of Goods and Services
as a Percentage of the Gross National Product

Year	Based on current dollars	Based on 1958 dollars
1929	7.0%	9.1%
1932	11.0	13.6
1940	8.0	9.4
1950	7.0	7.7
1955	7.6	7.9
1960	9.2	8.9
1965	10.1	9.1

[31] *Copeland, op. cit., pp. 59, 64–69.*

Table 5.4. *Selected Items of Local Government Finances, by Type of Government, 1964–1965*
(Billions of dollars)

Item	All Local Governments	Counties	Municipalities	Townships	School Districts	Special Districts
All general revenue from own sources	$32.7	$ 6.2	$12.4	$1.5	$10.9	$ 1.8
Property tax	22.2	4.5	6.5	1.2	9.4	0.5
Other taxes and charges	10.6	1.7	5.8	0.2	1.6	1.3
Direct general expenditure	48.8	10.0	15.8	1.9	18.8	2.4
Debt outstanding, total	72.5	6.6	31.9	1.9	16.7	15.4
Cash and security holdings	33.9	—	—	—	—	—

SOURCE: U.S. Bureau of the Census, *Governmental Finances in 1964–65* (Washington, D.C., 1966), pp. 29f.

highest median personal incomes in 1960; they comprised the three highest areas also in per capita state and local taxes and debt. This tends to confirm Fabricant's conclusion. Apparently, the higher levels of living that go with higher incomes include more extensive and costly government services; and higher government costs lead to both higher taxes and more debt.[32]

Quite another sort of trend has also profoundly affected local government finances: the emergence of counties, school districts, and other special districts to prominence as spenders, taxers, and borrowers. Although a number of reasons explain the growth of special districts, most pertinent here is the fact that they are usually the easiest way of avoiding or evading the nineteenth-century legacy of constitutional and statutory limits on the taxing and borrowing powers of municipalities—limits that have proved politically difficult or impossible to repeal. Whatever the combination of motives in individual cases, the broad consequences of the dispersion of functions among special units are shown in Table 5.4. School and special districts now match municipalities, in the aggregate, in raising revenue from their own sources (grants excluded) and in borrowing, and are substantially ahead in direct general expenditures.

---

[32] Ibid., *pp. 69–71. Regional personal income rankings from U.S. Bureau of the Census, Statistical Abstract of the United States: 1965, p. 334.*

REVENUE PROBLEMS. Some further generalizations about state and local finances are significant:

1. The states and their localities have nothing resembling the monetary and credit powers of the national government. Grants-in-aid apart, their revenues and expenditures must therefore keep within amortizing distance of each other. Aggregate state and local debt, though it has more than trebled since 1950 and reached a peak of $99.5 billion in 1964–65, nevertheless amounted to less than a third of the national government's debt in 1964–65. Indeed, if allowances are made for the rises in population, price levels, and gross national product, the $99.5 billion figure for 1964–65 was less of a burden than the corresponding figure of $20 billion for 1932.

2. State governments now draw their revenues almost entirely from sources they did not use a half century ago. They have relinquished the traditional property taxes almost entirely to localities, and depend instead on general and selective sales taxes (especially on gasoline, liquor, and tobacco), license taxes of all sorts, individual and corporation income taxes, and federal grants (see Figure 5.2).

3. Local governments continue to rely heavily on property taxes, which yielded $22.2 billion in 1964–65, about half the $47.9 billion of total general revenue of local governments. But property taxes had been over 60 percent of general revenue in 1942, and 90 percent a half-century ago. So local governments, too, have been cultivating other sources—sales taxes, license taxes, charges for services, state grants, and so on. The rapid recent rise in property tax yields—the 1964–65 figure about a threefold increase over 1950 and a fivefold increase over 1942—has caused public finance experts to reconsider the traditional view of property taxes as highly inelastic. A factor in this growth has been the impact of urban renewal, stimulated by federal grants that increase downtown property values. But the main reason has been the postwar suburban real estate boom.

4. The revenue gains from the multiplication of state and local tax sources have been accompanied by a vast increase in the reporting and filing requirements imposed on taxpayers and in the administrative establishments of tax collectors. Tax lawyers and accountants have reaped a rich incidental harvest.

5. The nineteenth-century doctrine (often more doctrine than reality) that each level of government looked to its own tax and borrowing resources to support its own expenditures—or, in other words, that the federal division of powers also established the division of governmental labors—has been drastically modified by the practice and general acceptance of cooperative federalism. On the record, the national government

Figure 5.2. *Types of State Government General Revenues, 1965* *

TOTAL = $40.9 BILLION

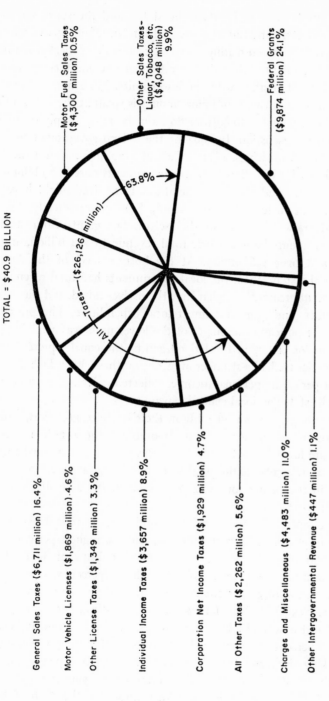

General Sales Taxes ($6,711 million) 16.4%

Motor Vehicle Licenses ($1,869 million) 4.6%

Other License Taxes ($1,349 million) 3.3%

Individual Income Taxes ($3,657 million) 8.9%

Corporation Net Income Taxes ($1,929 million) 4.7%

All Other Taxes ($2,262 million) 5.6%

Charges and Miscellaneous ($4,483 million) 11.0%

Other Intergovernmental Revenue ($447 million) 1.1%

Motor Fuel Sales Taxes ($4,300 million) 10.5%

Other Sales Taxes— Liquor, Tobacco, etc. ($4,048 million) 9.9%

Federal Grants ($9,874 million) 24.1%

63.8%

All Taxes—($26,126 million)

* "General revenues" exclude revenues of liquor stores and insurance trust funds.
SOURCE: U.S. Bureau of the Census, *Compendium of State Government Finances in 1965* (Washington, D.C., 1966), p. 6.

raises new funds more easily than the states, and the states more easily than local governments. But, defense and foreign affairs apart (where the national government can readily spend vast sums domestically by military-contract procurement), the administration of the most costly domestic programs still rests mainly with the lower units. More money is raised at the top than is spent there, and more money is spent at the bottom than is collected there. This top-to-bottom flow can be fairly simply summarized from our earlier discussion. In 1964–65 the federal government spent, out of revenues and borrowings, a total of about $130 billion, but it spent only $119 billion of this directly; the state governments raised $39 billion from their own sources and with the federal grants received might have spent $49 billion, but instead they spent only $31 billion directly; the local governments raised $39 billion themselves, but grants from state and federal governments brought their total revenue to $54 billion, and they actually spent over $56 billion. At the bottom level of the American governmental system, then, the local governments had total revenues that were 39 percent greater than what they themselves raised, and they used all these revenues, and more, for direct local expenditure. The principle of equalizing the per capita resources of the lower units was a talking point, but not a major factor, in the federal grants; the equal representation of states in the Senate had a stronger influence on these. Even Delaware, with the highest per capita personal income, collected federal grants to cover 13 percent of its state and local general expenditures.

6. The states vary considerably in their relative "tax effort," and the comparisons are by no means wholly favorable to the wealthier ones. The disparities are less when state and local expenditures are lumped together, for local governments in the wealthier states raise a larger share of the total, and in the poorer southern states consistently a smaller share; but disparities remain.

For example, it is no surprise to find that in 1965 Delaware, the wealthiest in per capita personal income, had the highest per capita state tax, $240—far above the 50-state average of $135. But that state's share of state and local taxes combined was very high (79 percent) compared with a national average of 51 percent, so the combined per capita tax there was about $302. Next door, New Jersey—ranking eighth in per capita personal income—had the second lowest per capita state tax, $80; but her localities made up 70 percent of a combined per capita total of $269. California and Ohio, ranking sixth and twelfth, respectively, in per capita personal income, each raised 45 percent of their totals at the state level, but these totals were far apart: $379 per capita for California and $225 for Ohio. At the bottom of the list were Arkansas and South Carolina with a per capita total tax of about $160, Alabama ($168), and Mississippi ($170). In each of these states, the state government raised 68 to 76 percent of the state-local total, but all of them were drawing on per capita personal incomes that were not much more than half those in the other states mentioned.

A more discriminating measure of tax effort, therefore, is to compute state-local tax totals per $1,000 of personal income. When the states are arrayed on this basis, a very different pattern emerges. The national average tax effort (so measured) among the states in 1964–65 was $105. At the head of the list were Vermont and Minnesota ($127), South Dakota, California, and Wisconsin ($126), New Mexico ($122), and Arizona, Idaho, and Louisiana ($121). At the bottom of the list were Alaska ($81), Virginia ($85), Ohio and Missouri ($87), Illinois ($89), and Delaware ($90). New Jersey, Connecticut, and Pennsylvania ($91 to $95)—all of them, like Ohio and Illinois without a state individual income tax—were down near the laggards.

According to Fabricant's generalization, one would expect the wealthier states to tax themselves much more—proportionately and not just absolutely—than the poorer. Evidently, the figures do not bear this out, though they may help explain the overall favorable ranking of California and New York. Perhaps the weight of national income taxes blinds the well-to-do in the other industrial states to their local responsibilities. And perhaps some spirit of emulation gives the poorer and more sparsely settled states incentives to lift their service levels by their own bootstraps.[33]

7. Despite the activities of state tax-equalization boards on the one hand and the effects of state aid on the other, the disparities in tax resources and efforts among counties and municipalities within states are apparently much greater than those between states. Correspondingly, the pressures for equalizing grants are heavier on the states than on the national government.

8. It is a myth that state and local governments cannot raise more taxes, however traditional their reluctance. In fact, state governments increased their total tax collections from $8 billion in 1950 to $26 billion in 1965, and local governments did almost exactly the same; though in both cases the results came more from improvements in the tax bases than from higher rates. Stronger evidence lies in the variations among states in the types of taxes they rely on. A look at the record here will show that

---

[33] *The topic of relative tax effort can profitably be pursued further in U.S. Advisory Commission on Intergovernmental Relations,* Measures of State and Local Fiscal Capacity and Tax Effort *(Washington, D.C., 1962).*

every state could substantially increase its revenues by adopting or cultivating some tax already in extensive use in other states. It will also dispel the argument that alternative forms of taxation are merely substitutes for each other and do not add to the total potential.

Every state has a gasoline tax, usually 6 or 7 cents a gallon (roughly, 20 percent of the retail selling price); this has been a virtual necessity to qualify for federal aid or to borrow for highway improvements. But only a few states—New York, Ohio, and Oregon, principally—have overcome the truckers' lobbying efforts against weight-distance taxes on heavy vehicles. Every state except Nevada has an inheritance tax, but it produces important revenue only in California, in the Northeast tier from Massachusetts to Wisconsin, and in two or three other states. Louisiana and Texas derive a third and a sixth, respectively, of their state taxes from severance taxes (taxes levied on the removal of natural products from land or water—for example, oil, gas, other minerals, timber, fish); New Mexico, Oklahoma, Minnesota, and Mississippi also rely on these taxes, but to a lesser extent. In the other oil and mining states, the producers' arguments of competitive disadvantage appear to have been more cogently put. And despite perennial proposals, no other state has followed Nevada's lead in legalizing and taxing gambling and other amusements to such a degree: the tax on amusement receipts yielded about as much revenue as the gasoline tax there in 1965. New Hampshire, however, has established a state-operated lottery, and New York collected $136 million from taxes on parimutuel betting at racetracks—an amount only $10 million less than *all* of Nevada's general revenue (even including federal grants).

The more puzzling behavior concerns sales and income taxes. As of 1965, 23 states, scattered mostly through the South and West, had a general sales tax *and also* a broad-based individual *and* a corporation net income tax. Thirteen states had no general sales tax, and seventeen, half of them in a northern tier from Maine, Rhode Island, Connecticut, and Pennsylvania west through Illinois, had no general personal income tax—though, paradoxically, these are precisely the states that make a good deal of the inheritance tax, which is also presumably based on ability to pay. Thirteen states, ten overlapping the last group, had no corporation net income tax. Four states with a general sales tax had a net income tax on corporations but not on individuals, and another four had the latter without the former. Nebraska was unique in forgoing all three types of revenue—general sales tax, personal income tax, and corporate income tax. In all, 37 states had a general sales tax, 38 taxed corporate net income, and 33 had a broad-based personal income tax. A few that forgo one or another of these nevertheless allow their municipalities to enter the field. So New York City had a sales tax long before the state adopted one, and many Ohio cities tax personal income though the state does not.

Among these revenue options, only the personal income tax appears to arouse frequent ideological and partisan controversy; the sales tax, regressive though it is, has the virtue of stability, and is widely accepted. Washington State voters, for example, have regularly rejected an income tax in successive referendums, so the state relied on the general sales tax for over half of its tax money in 1965. Yet across the Columbia River, Oregon, traditionally more conservative, got almost half its taxes from individual incomes and had no general sales tax. Further east, in Michigan, Ohio, Pennsylvania, and Connecticut, state legislators have made it an article of Republican faith to reject state income tax proposals. On the other hand, once on the books, a tax is rarely reduced because its productivity increases or repealed because of a change in party control. Seemingly, the political will to tax in a particular manner is a more restrictive factor than the economic capacity of taxpayers to absorb it.

9. There is no panacea for the states in the nostalgic proposal often heard that tax sources should be clearly segregated by a no-poaching agreement between the national government and the states. The most common targets of the proposals have been the gasoline and inheritance taxes. The Federal Aid Highway Act of 1956 removed one of these from controversy by earmarking the federal receipts for the Highway Trust Fund, to be spent by the states on a generous matching basis. State inheritance taxes are partly accommodated by a complex federal tax-credit formula that has been tightened rather than loosened since it was first introduced in 1926. When the national government relinquished most of its admissions tax (on theater, sports, etc., events) in 1954, the states— notwithstanding earlier predictions—did not move in on the abandoned territory. Nor did the 1965 repeal of the bulk of the remaining federal excise taxes enacted during World War II (that is, excluding those on liquor, tobacco and gasoline) stimulate any rush on the part of the states to lay special taxes on the items so benefited, such as jewelry, furs, cosmetics and leather goods. About half the burden of property and other state and local taxes on business is effectively shifted to the national Treasury because they are deductible business expenses for federal corporate income tax purposes. Individual taxpayers who itemize deductions also shift varying portions of their state and local taxes to the federal government. But years of talk about broad reciprocal tax immunities have brought little action beyond a firm rejection of the idea from the Treasury and a series of

Supreme Court decisions drawing uncertain lines in particular cases. The (Kestnbaum) Commission on Intergovernmental Relations canvassed the subject in 1955 and found no sweeping proposals worthy of its endorsement. So long as the power to tax is concurrent and all levels of government need more money, minor and ad hoc adjustments of particular grievances may be worked out, but comprehensive solutions encounter insurmountable obstacles.[34]

10. With national grants flowing in, state grants to localities flowing out, and some of their own taxes often permanently earmarked for roads, schools, and other specifically designated uses, state legislatures have no such comprehensive and unified controls over state spending as Congress has over the national budget. Their treasuries are in effect a bundle of conduits, only a few of which have valves within reach. In Ohio, for example, the governor's budget and the biennial general appropriation bill passed by the legislature cover only about a third of the payments the state actually makes. Outside the South, this condition is not uncommon. It is welcomed by the recipient agencies, and often by the legislators themselves, who would otherwise have more hard decisions to make. Fragmentation is thus endemic in the fiscal affairs of most states.

Fiscal fragmentation, in turn, is symptomatic of deeper political problems now emerging and not yet systematically faced. Federal grants to improve human resources—broadly, research planning and development programs in health, education and welfare—frequently bypass not only the states but also any other general-purpose government, city or county. Flexible federal contracting procedures work in the same direction by encouraging the use of negotiated awards for particular projects rather than statutory formulas for geographic distribution of appropriations. By grant or contract the funds then flow increasingly to organizations such as medical centers, universities, and voluntary agencies or even to private firms or individuals, for activities—perhaps on a neighborhood, community, or regional scale—that do not match the boundaries of any elected government short of the whole United States. This process may suit professional specialists, insofar as it concentrates funds and helps assemble the best talents for attacking intractable problems wherever they occur, regardless of political jurisdictions. But what does it do to democratic accountability? Where does it leave the local electorate?

---

[34] For a comprehensive review, see I. M. Labovitz and L. L. Ecker-Racz, "Practical Solutions to Financial Problems Created by the Multilevel Political Structure," in Public Finances: Needs, Sources and Utilization, . . . A Report of the National Bureau of Economic Research (Princeton, N.J.: Princeton University Press, 1961), pp. 135–277.

11. The success of the federal government in raising its revenue yields by lowering its tax rates broadly in 1962 and again in 1965, even in the face of budgetary deficits, held important short- and long-range implications for state and local government finances. Economists, and notably the Council of Economic Advisers, in advocating the tax cuts (notwithstanding orthodox public finance teaching to the contrary), argued that the stimulation of a more rapid rise in the gross national product—and hence in the tax base—would more than offset the losses occasioned by the drop in rates. The event bore out their predictions. In the short run, state and local governments benefited too, since their taxes tap basically the same revenue sources. For the longer run, projections of an expanding GNP, and of even greater increases in demands for domestic governmental services, opened up another possibility. Instead of reducing its tax rates further as its revenues grow, the federal government might give the economy a comparable stimulus by introducing on a large scale a new system of block grants to the states—that is, grants for general purposes to be spent as the states decided, in contrast with the present grants earmarked for specified programs.[35] This alternative in fiscal policy would tend to divert a larger proportion of the total output of goods and services into the public sector; its ramifications need investigation. It is attractive to economists who think in terms of aggregate transfers of funds and resources. But it might be harder to sell to northern congressmen, say, if they saw it as a "guaranteed annual income" likely to entrench a Governor Wallace in Alabama; or to Democratic congressmen if it would rescue Republican governors from financial pressures at home. Larger federal domestic expenditures along existing lines, as revenues increase, and without tax cuts, would have a similar effect on the economy in eliminating the "fiscal drag" on full employment inherent in a progressive tax system and in enlarging the public sector; but they encounter more resistance than do tax cuts from conservative congressmen and business spokesmen. The rising military costs of the Vietnam war, by postponing any prospect of a federal surplus, made discussion of the block-grant proposal untimely in 1965–66. But the possibilities just mentioned have the merit of seeking a solution for a longstanding paradox: In the domestic field, the federal government gets the bulk of the money while the states and localities get the bulk of the problems.

---

[35] *For elaboration and argument of this proposal, see Walter W. Heller,* New Dimensions of Political Economy (*Cambridge, Mass.: Harvard University Press, 1966*). *For a compendium of the recommendations of the Advisory Commission on Intergovernmental Relations, see its report,* Metropolitan America: Challenge to Federalism, *House Government Operations Subcommittee on Intergovernmental Relations, 89th Cong., 2nd Sess. (Committee print, October 1966).*

chapter 6

Elections and Political Parties

It is much more difficult to understand politics than atomic physics, Albert Einstein once said, because politics is more complicated than physics. Politics is, indeed, infinitely complex; two atoms of hydrogen will under given conditions behave in identical and predictable ways, but no two voters have the same personalities or life experiences, and consequently their political attitudes and behavior are not likely to be the same. Little of importance, therefore, can be said of American politics without adding qualifications and exceptions. People who blandly assert that all farmers, or all union members, or all politicians behave, believe, or vote some way or other are usually making only unsupportable assertions.

In the past decade we have had more studies in state and local politics than ever before. Incomplete as they are, we now know more than we did; but we need more of them, and they need to be repeated at intervals, for the fifty states and their local governments are in a process of constant change. Great population shifts, to cite only one source of political change, will alter the politics of a state as people move in or out of it; or as they move within it, from farms and small towns to cities and suburbs.

Any discussion specifically addressed to the politics of state and local governments presents two difficulties at the outset. One is the diffusion of politics throughout governmental institutions and processes. Even a narrow definition of "politics" (as partisan politics, for example, rather than as "Who gets what, when, how?") will not avoid the fact that it enters into federal-state and state-local relations, into the legislative process, into legislative-executive relations, into the choice of judges, into administration, and into local government. The only way to convey an appreciation of this pervasiveness of politics is to reflect it in discussions focused on each of these governmental institutions and processes. But this is the province of the other chapters in this book. Consequently, in this chapter and the one that follows, we shall devote attention to elections, parties, and interest groups.

The second difficulty is in getting politics to "stand still" long enough for individual bits of it to be brought into focus. As fluid and elusive as mercury, politics is only partly explicable by noting the formally prescribed channels designed to confine and guide it. Practitioners of the lively art of politics are ingenious in turning formal rules to their own advantage and, indeed, in getting themselves in a position to prescribe what the formal rules shall be. This is part of the fascination that attracts us to the study of politics at the same time that it impedes our efforts to isolate, describe, and analyze distinct parts of the political life of a state or community. We must, then, speak almost simultaneously of the flavor of politics, of the varying ecological settings from state to state, of the interplay of form and substance, of election day and what has preceded it and what consequences follow upon it, of political parties and interest groups and of the behavior of individual voters.

American politics, like American life, is constantly changing. A generalization that was valid in 1900 may not be true today, and vice versa. Some of the changes that occur are so great as to represent a complete reversal of party position. The states' rights issue, for example, had seemed for more than a century to be under a sort of copyright held by the Democratic party, but on March 4, 1933, this copyright passed into the public domain, and the Republican party, long the advocate of national supremacy, took up the issue.

Some channels of party policy, like the Constitution, remain little changed from generation to generation, but among the important observable developments discussed in this and other chapters are the increasing urbanization of the states; the continued growth of metropolitan areas, some of which pay no attention to state lines; the rise of militant new interests, such as racial minorities; the decline of all minor parties and the disappearance of some; the absence of any important third-party movement; the rise of new means of political communication, such as radio and television, accompanied by public relations experts; and the development of a system of interest groups so potent as to challenge the parties as the originators and advocates of public policies.

Most serious students of American politics would probably be in substantial agreement upon the trends just mentioned. Others, but not all, assert that we are also in the midst of further developments, such as the nationalization of political issues (the acceptance of positions by national parties, which the state and local parties must accept); the rise of class politics; the development of a new sectionalism; the passing, or at least the changing, of the boss system; and a new nonpartisan politics growing up as a result of nonpartisan elections in hundreds of cities and in two states. Before much of anything can be said with certainty about these developments, however, we need the information that more research will provide.

1. *The Importance of State Politics*

State politics, like state government itself, benefits and suffers from having to operate at an intermediate level. It must compete with national and local political affairs for public attention. It gains some of its importance by serving as an avenue to national office, and some by affording a stage to men of talent who are ready to move beyond local politics. State politics is a base of strength for influencing the affairs of the loose confederation we call a major national party. Yet, if the national party is but a confederation of state organizations, the latter are often weak vis-à-vis the urban "machines" and county courthouse "gangs"—and so many a state party is itself but a confederation of local organizations. To speak of the "importance" of state politics is therefore to raise questions about the inherent and distinctive significance of the issues presented for decision by the state government, about the degree to which public attentiveness confers reputational importance on these issues and the politics surrounding their disposition, and about the importance state politics may acquire less in its own right than in recognition of its contribution to national and local politics. That is to say, state politics may be thought of as having "true" importance, attributed importance (whatever the "true" case may be), and derived importance.

LOW VISIBILITY. Much of what goes on in state politics is largely unknown to most citizens, not because there is any conspiracy of silence, but because several characteristics of state politics produce conditions of low visibility.

First, the multiplicity and distinctness of the various activities in which the states engage mean that there is no easily perceived big picture, while the increasingly technical character of these activities means that even miniature pictures of each segment of the state's work are too difficult for the layman's understanding even if he had the time to look at each and even if each were in fact static instead of constantly changing. Any student can quickly and easily confirm the changes in range, kinds, and intelligibility of state activities by comparing volume one of the session laws of his state and the latest volume. But the complexities of state affairs are so great that not even a person such as the governor, who devotes his entire time to following the government and politics of one state, can keep up with more than what seem to be the most pressing problems and trends. Some governors and some legislators become very well informed after several terms, but the best of them cannot keep up with the flow of reports, studies, surveys, and investigations that a populous state can produce. When not even a governor can keep fully informed, a citizen has even less chance, for he has other matters on his mind besides governing— such pressing matters, for example, as making a living.

Second, the visibility of one arena, such as state politics, is impaired by the competition from other arenas, as anyone who has tried to watch a three-ring circus knows. The most civic-minded citizen finds that national and world events call for their share of what time he can devote to public affairs; and his county, city, and school district call for another share. Perhaps state politics is a poor third: National and international affairs seem to involve the very future of civilization, and they have spectacular features, even interplanetary ones; on the other hand, local matters, like schools, zoning, or water fluoridation, may have the interest of immediacy and close association. With some occasional exceptions, state politics are not as spectacular as national, nor as close as local; they are merely important.

Third, in this blooming, buzzing confusion of issues and personalities, the voter is likely to give some attention only to those matters that the communications media put before him and to ignore the rest. He gets very little information about his state, for except in the capital city, the newspapers tend to ignore the state government. At the most, some of them might carry a weekly column that often emphasizes the sensational, the illegal, or the trivial. Probably not 1 percent of the voters in any state have read their state constitution or could name any state official except the governor. This low level of interest becomes immediately apparent to anybody who seeks to get a campaign under way to revise a state constitution.

We cannot hope to reverse the major trends of American society to make life simple once again, so that the citizen might follow politics easily. We cannot expect that he will abandon his job to get behind what the papers and the radio present to him or to fill the gaps in their coverage. But we may wish that the politics of the states could be presented to the busy voter as a series of broad and meaningful choices between parties, so that without having to know the names and records of scores of candidates, he could make an intelligent choice between parties and then hold answerable the party that did or did not do what he wanted. It is impossible for a voter to hold responsible an appointed official, or one elected from another county or district, though it may be possible to hold their parties responsible for their behavior. One of the sentiments most dangerous to democracy may therefore be the attitude commonly expressed in such words as "I never vote for the party; I vote for the man."

THE ROAD TO NATIONAL OFFICE. The uncertainty of our politics is such that Woodrow Wilson once said that no man of middle age should despair of becoming President. While there is no single clear avenue to preferment for the would-be statesman as there is, for instance, in England, nevertheless service in local and state politics is perhaps the commonest avenue to national office.[1] A term or two in the legislature, election as district attorney, then governor, then perhaps on to the Senate or the President's Cabinet is, with variations, a path frequently followed. There is a kind of pyramid of offices, and to go from a lower level to a higher one involves not only factors of personality and leadership, but many elements of chance as well, for a man needs to be of the right age at the right time and in the right spot. There are also more legislators than governors, and few can be rewarded. The pyramid or hierarchy is not impervious, moreover, to outsiders; the aspirant who has worked his way

---

[1] Of the members of the United States House of Representatives down through the years, "perhaps one-third served in the State legislatures before coming to the Congress. At least 17 were former governors of their States." Of the House members in March, 1953, 40 percent had served in state legislatures, 70 percent had been locally elected officers (some, of course, had had both experiences), and only one member had been a governor. George B. Galloway, History of the United States House of Representatives (House Document No. 246, 87th Cong., 1st Sess., 1962), p. 31; and computed from W. J. M. Mackenzie's 1953 table in John C. Wahlke and Heinz Eulau (eds.), Legislative Behavior (New York: Free Press, 1959), p. 279.

The 189 persons who served in the United States Senate between January, 1947, and January, 1957, had held 495 public offices before entering the Senate. Of these offices, 17 percent represented experience as state legislators, 9 percent as governors, 3 percent as holders of other state elective offices, and 9 percent as holders of local elective office; to this 38 percent total would need to be added a large portion of the almost 50 percent of offices that were classified as law enforcement or administrative without identification of their national, state, or local level. Donald R. Matthews, U.S. Senators and Their World (New York: Vintage Books, 1960), p. 283. For the Senate of March, 1953, see Mackenzie, loc. cit.

up to be available for governor may be defeated in his own party by a successful businessman, general, or other public figure who never ran for office before.

Many of our national officials come to their new responsibilities, not from such an apprenticeship in dealing with national issues as might be gained by service in the diplomatic corps or in the federal bureaucracy, but rather with experience in state politics only. This use of the states as training grounds for national politicians has, no doubt, its desirable features, for most men so trained never forget the importance of the attitudes held by the folks back home; but it also fixes upon Congress a parochialism that not all national legislatures seem to display. A partial explanation for the kind of stuff that fills the pages of the *Congressional Record* is that some of the speakers learned to talk that way when, years before, while running for the legislature, they harangued the people at the forks of the creek.

The effect on state politics of the lure of national office is even harder to assess. While the state government benefits from the services of young, talented men on the way up, it also loses them in their mature years to the national Congress, national judiciary, and national regulatory commissions.[2] To be a state legislator is not much of a career, which may explain why so few seek reelection even once and fewer still more than once. This is true even though a state is often larger than many a foreign nation, and its legislature therefore is in some ways comparable to a foreign parliament, where membership carries prestige.

THE AUTONOMY OF STATE POLITICS. State politics derives much of its importance from its relatively autonomous character. A number of factors contribute toward this autonomy, and they will be noted in due course. At this point it suffices to reflect on the curiosity that agreement on issues provides little of the cement needed to unite the politically active in either major national party. To accommodate such diversity, each state party organization enjoys considerable autonomy in relation to the national party organization. This independence, however, is not transferred to local party organizations.

Our major national parties are commonly described as loose confederations of state parties. The absence from this definition of any reference to

---

[2] *Donald R. Matthews reported that 94 percent of those United States senators whose first public office was state legislator achieved this office before they were forty years of age. The average senator was in his late forties or early fifties when elected or appointed to the Senate, and had held about three public offices that had taken about ten years of his adult life. Op. cit., p. 13f. First service at under forty was true also of about 90 percent of senators who began as law enforcement officers or statewide elective officers. Ibid., p. 52.*

issues has confused some foreign observers and appalled others. Lord Bryce, for example, quoted with approval an unnamed newspaper reporter of his day who said that the two parties were like bottles bearing different labels, but both were empty. They were not quite empty in 1888 when Bryce wrote, and they are not today. Yet not principle but the hope of office has usually been the chief binding force of our major party organizations; issues come and go, while the parties continue from one century to another. In most states the candidates wear their party labels lightly, if at all, and they pick up and put down issues largely as they please.

The two major parties wear the labels lightly, too, though some tendency may be observed for Democrats, in general, to be more sympathetic than Republicans to labor, small business, and ethnic minorities, while Republicans are more concerned with the well-being of real estate owners, large farmers, manufacturers, and taxpayers. But the observer will be disappointed if he expects too much consistency; Democrats may favor a generous welfare program in one state and oppose it in another, while Republicans may favor home rule for cities in one state and oppose it across the line.

An American voter may cast a ballot for Republican candidates for his legislature, with but the vaguest notion of how they will behave if they win. The same uncertainty confronts his Democratic neighbor next door. And when they vote for governor—usually the chief legislator and party leader—the Republican may get a Nelson Rockefeller, a Wesley Powell, or a George Romney; the Democrat an Orval Faubus, a Mike DiSalle, or a David Lawrence. When the American voter selects one or the other of the bottles Lord Bryce referred to, he may well have a general notion of what Republicans or Democrats are supposed to be like; but he cannot predict for any particular drink what taste will follow. Perhaps this often blind choice adds a sporting element to the great game of politics—at any rate, it adds to the confusion.

When the leaders of a state party draft the party platform—which in some states attracts so little public interest that it is never printed—they are not bound by any national platform. The state platform, in fact, may be adopted weeks before the national one, and in any event it may take positions on issues like civil rights that are exactly the opposite of those taken by the same party in its national platform. These heresies do not and cannot lead to excommunication by the national committee, for each state party is as independent of Washington as it is of every other state party.[3]

---

[3] *State platforms are nowhere collected, so that it is not possible to compare the positions of the state parties on any given issue for a particular campaign year. Indeed, it is not usually possible to find a collection of state platforms for a single party in any*

Probably each state has certain issues that are peculiar to itself, such as the dispute over water for Denver between the eastern and western slopes of Colorado; but the existence of such strictly state issues does not guarantee that the parties will divide along lines of the principal alternatives so that the voter may make a clear choice. On the contrary, in a two-party situation both parties may be on the same side, may equivocate, or may ignore such issues.

Few issues of importance are, moreover, without their national aspects. Problems of financing highways, schools, or urban renewal are necessarily related to what the national government does. Some state issues —for example, what level of income taxes states may impose—grow out of federal statutes or activities. The great majority of issues in American politics are not limited by state lines, and for a single state to attempt the solution of a broad problem, such as farm price supports, might impose an intolerable burden upon its economy or produce an impossible competitive situation for its industries. In such circumstances state parties and candidates cannot be blamed if they treat issues with a certain cautious vagueness. The loose character of American parties may, in fact, be their greatest virtue, for it makes possible their adjustment to a federal system, without violence. It also helps to avoid stalemate and to promote necessary compromises.

The independent character of state parties is further encouraged by the differences in their sources of financial support. Probably no state party obtains funds from national headquarters to assist in the election of candidates for state offices; instead, it has to collect its money wherever it can, and it may accept help from sources that are hostile to the policies of its national organization. On the other hand, each national organization obtains some funds from state parties in the wealthy states, and its national committee sends some of these funds into close or doubtful states to help candidates for Congress. In general, however, because the financing of parties is done at each level, money cannot be used as a means of discipline.

Whether state politics is truly important, is widely recognized as such, and is a distinct arena for exciting, significant battles over state policies are complex and perplexing questions for which there are no clear-cut clues to solutions. When description itself is thus beset with contradictory signs, prescription is bound to be hazardous. Enough has been said, however, to

---

given state unless some newspaper has printed them, because the archives of state parties vary from haphazard to nonexistent. At the local level, a city or other local unit of a party that even goes through the motions of adopting a platform or a set of resolutions is uncommon.

warrant a conclusion that exhorting the ordinary citizen to be interested, informed, and participative is *not* likely to contribute to either the real or the apparent importance of state politics. Rather, the situation is the reverse. It is greater visibility and prestige and a distinctive identity for state politics that would increase the interest of citizens, induce them to become informed, and stimulate them to participate actively in the political process.

2. *The Rules of the Game*

State and local politics have their own rules, and one of the criteria for distinguishing a professional from an amateur politician is the professional's mastery of these rules. Because the rules will be advantageous to some and disadvantageous to others, much effort is invested in keeping the old rules and, alternatively, in trying to get them changed. Some of these rules are national, but a large number are adopted by individual states, and the uniformity of some of them throughout the nation is the result of imitation or a correspondence of influential forces within the several states. Some rules are local. To play or understand the game of state and local politics, one needs to know the rules and know how to go about getting them changed. What is distinctive in this game is that playing under the rules and trying to get them enforced, maintained, or changed are *both* parts of the same game.

Our politics are largely what the United States Constitution and the state constitutions have made them. Under a different type of constitution —one establishing unicameral, parliamentary governments, for example— American parties would undoubtedly have developed in a different way. Whenever constitutional changes are proposed, therefore, politicians always consider carefully the political results they expect would follow. The reader may speculate for himself: Suppose that state and local elections, instead of coming on a Tuesday, were held over a period of two days, Saturday and Sunday. What would be the effects upon the parties, and how would these effects differ between the parties? Or suppose that a state committee could bar any candidate in the state from running under the party label. What effect would that have on party discipline?

The starting point of our exploration of formal rules is the fact that the Constitution leaves to the states great powers over politics. For much of our history they have set most of the regulations on the suffrage, party membership and organization, nominations, elections, legislative representation, and direct legislation, although the federal Constitution has been amended or interpreted to limit the states' range of discretion in setting some of these rules.

THE SUFFRAGE. The Constitution leaves to the states much of the authority to determine who shall have the right to vote. It merely forbids them to deny any citizen over 21 the right to vote because of race, color, previous condition of servitude, sex, or failure to pay a poll tax. The states have adopted many other qualifications and disqualifications, which they change from time to time.[4] The right to vote has slowly broadened in the United States. Some states, of course, have moved more rapidly than others, until today adult suffrage is almost universal.

The extent and administration of suffrage requirements are basic to the nature and functioning of parties. Membership in a party, as defined by the state laws, is confined to voters. And the candidates, too, must usually be voters. The size and nature of the electorate to which a party must appeal conditions much of what it does—the amount of money it must raise, the type of publicity it uses, the degree and extent of its organization.

The most important requirements are age, citizenship, residence, registration, and literacy. Less frequently required are an understanding of the Constitution or of the state constitution, good character, and tax paying.

Four states permit citizens of 18, 19, or 20 to vote; the remainder insist upon a minimum age of 21. All require citizenship and a period of residence. The commonest residence requirement is one year in the state, including 30 days to six months in the county and precinct; but one southern state requires two years' residence. Inability to meet residence requirements deprives more citizens of the right to vote than any other suffrage provision, for Americans are highly mobile. The Census Bureau estimates that 20 percent of the population moves in an ordinary year. This means that up to 22 million citizens of voting age imperil their votes by moving; how many of these actually lose their votes depends on whether they move out of their precinct, county, or state; what the new residence requirements are; and how soon before an election their move takes place. We do not know how many movers shift precincts or towns, but we do know that annually over 3 percent of the population moves to a different state and another 3 percent to a different county within the same state; each of these categories includes about 3.5 million people of voting

---

[4] *For a table listing the principal requirements by states see* The Book of the States: 1966–67 (*Chicago: Council of State Governments,* 1966), *pp.* 22–23.

age. One estimate is that 8 million citizens were disfranchised by residence requirements in 1960.[5]

The usual defense for the residence requirement is that the voter cannot become acquainted with local issues and candidates until he has spent some time in a place. There is something in the argument, even though it ignores many of the facts of contemporary American life; for example, a man might live in New Jersey but work in New York City, where he would read New York newspapers morning and evening and learn more about New York's government and politics than about New Jersey's, but if he should move his residence to the city, he would have to live there a year before he could vote. In some states, moreover, moving across a street into another county or election district may deprive a citizen of his vote for at least one election.

While our principal concern is with the effect of residence requirements on state and local politics, we should note that there is also an effect on the election of national officials. Clearly, a person's choice of the President and Vice President of the United States is not better informed because he has resided in a particular precinct, county, or state for a given length of time. Yet because qualifications for voting are set by state governments, millions of American citizens who move at the wrong time or the wrong distance lose their right to share in the national election. Over a third of the states have special provisions permitting new residents to vote in presidential elections, and a few allow former residents to vote in them if they cannot meet their new states' residence requirements.[6]

Registration is required in 49 states. The process is easy in some states, difficult in others.[7] It is at the time he registers that the voter demonstrates to the election officials—who have different titles in different states—his citizenship, literacy (in 16 states), length of residence, and understanding of the United States Constitution and the constitution of his state (in three states), and attests that he has never been convicted of certain disqualifying offenses (usually felonies). Although information on the administration of registration is sparse, it is commonly asserted that in many areas of the North the process is largely pro forma: the officials take the applicant's word on all or most points, unless somebody appears to challenge him, an occurrence so rare that most officials would not know

---

[5] *President's Commission on Registration and Voting Participation*, Report (Washington, D.C., 1963), p. 13. For mobility data, see U.S. Bureau of the Census, Statistical Abstract of the United States: 1966 (Washington, D.C., 1966), pp. 32f.

[6] *President's Commission on Registration and Voting Participation*, Report, p. 12.

[7] *There has not been a complete study of registration requirements since Joseph P. Harris*, Registration of Voters in the United States (Washington, D.C.: Brookings Institution, 1929).

how to deal with it. At the other extreme, there is ample evidence to indicate that for Negroes in some states in the Deep South, the process has been made time-consuming, humiliating, and technical.[8] Even Negroes with Ph.D.'s in political science, when they appeared before white registrars, have had difficulty with the "understanding" clauses.

Once registered, the voter in most states remains on the rolls as long as he lives in the election area, continues to vote, does not commit a felony or otherwise become ineligible. This system, known as "permanent registration," is used for all areas in over two-thirds of the states and in some (usually urban) areas in an additional nine. Three states, however, require reregistration for all areas and four for some areas, at statutory intervals of one to ten years—a system known as "periodic registration." This plan, though inconvenient to voters, automatically purges the lists of the names of the dead and of persons no longer eligible, whereas permanent registration, it is often alleged, invites the kind of election fraud in which votes are cast in the name of deceased or ineligible persons.

We do not have even good estimates of the number of persons who are kept from voting by registration laws and procedures. Since absentee registration is commonly not permitted except for persons in the armed forces and since registration periods are often not much publicized, sometimes short, and come at inconvenient times (for example, during summer vacation periods, or with a cutoff date as much as nine months before election day) or places (such as at the county seat), we could safely hazard a guess that there must be millions who are barred for failure or inability to register.

The total effect of the suffrage requirements and their administration is to predetermine some important characteristics of the electorate; for example, persons in the professions and upper income levels tend to move less often than others, and having more education, they take their civic duties more seriously and get themselves through the registration process. These requirements and their administration also reduce the size of the electorate, although here again, only estimates are available. In the presidential election years perhaps as many as 75 percent of those legally eligible do vote.[9] Americans often have to work hard to get to vote, but

---

[8] *See, for example, U.S. Commission on Civil Rights, 1961 Report, Book 1,* Voting (*Washington, D.C., 1961), and the Commission's* Voting in Mississippi (*Washington, D.C., 1965).*

[9] *Angus Campbell, et al.,* The American Voter (*New York: Wiley, 1960*), *pp. 94–96. In a statement published in* The New York Times, *November 28, 1956, the American Heritage Foundation estimated that 17 million voters of a potential 103 million were barred by legal devices of all sorts in 1956.*

every four years they will do it; in off-year state, municipal, and special elections, however, they will not always make the effort.

The President's Commission on Registration and Voting Participation, reporting in 1963, observed that "in some states it is easier to get a hunting or fishing license or a pistol permit than to register and vote." Among its recommended standards for the states were the following: [10]

1. State residence requirements should not exceed 6 months.

2. Local residence requirements should not exceed 30 days.

3. New state residents should be allowed to vote for President.

4. Voter registration should extend as close to election day as possible and should not end more than 3 or 4 weeks before election day.

5. Voter registration lists should be kept current.

6. No citizen's registration should be canceled for failure to vote in any period of less than 4 years.

7. Literacy tests should not be a requisite for voting.

ELECTION ADMINISTRATION. In its election law, each state is free to adopt provisions for the times, places, and conditions of elections. Federal laws set the first Tuesday after the first Monday in November as the day to choose presidential electors, senators, and members of Congress.[11] But local elections now come at any time in the year.

The election law also determines whether voters use paper ballots or voting machines in some or all areas or in some or all elections. The states differ greatly, but they appear to be moving slowly toward the use of voting machines in almost all their elections. Voting behavior is clearly affected by the form of the ballot and by the use of voting machines, but the extent and degrees of the differences are still largely unknown because of the immense difficulties in the way of research in ballot behavior.[12]

There are two principal paper ballot forms in use: First, the *party-column* ballot, in which all candidates for all offices are arranged in vertical columns by party. In some states a vote for all candidates of one party may

---

[10] *Commission on Registration and Voting*, op. cit., *pp.* 34–39.

[11] *The Constitution (Article I, Section 4) provides: "The times, places and manner of holding elections for Senators and Representatives shall be prescribed in each State by the Legislature thereof, but the Congress may at any time by law make or alter such regulations, except as to the places of choosing Senators," and (Article II, Section 1), with regard to members of the electoral college, "The Congress may determine the time of choosing the electors, and the day on which they shall give their votes; which day shall be the same throughout the United States."*

[12] *For example, most state laws require that ballots shall be destroyed after the date for permissible recounts has passed; even where they may be obtained for use by scholars, the costs of studying a trainload of paper ballots are appalling. Most voting machines give only candidate or proposition totals and so conceal the patterns of voting by individual voters.*

be cast by making one mark (X or +) in a circle above the column. This form tends to produce almost as many votes for one candidate in a party as for another, and the spoilage of such ballots is minimal. The second leading type is the *office-block* (or office-column) form, in which the names of candidates are grouped under the offices they seek. This type of ballot produces a phenomenon sometimes called voter's fatigue, for some voters will tend to vote for the highest offices (President, governor, senator) and to skip some or all of the others. The total vote cast in states using this form will usually diminish with the decreasing importance of the offices, but these totals conceal the behavior of some voters who reverse the process and, say, vote for sheriff only. The number of spoiled ballots is higher, because in spite of all instructions, such as "vote for one," some voters will mark two or more squares under the same office.[13] When a voter, holding an office-block ballot, sees unfamiliar names under some offices, he is likely to vote for the top names.[14]

The introduction of voting machines eliminates some of the frauds that are known to have occurred with paper ballots (filling in squares the voter left blank, identifying ballots, erasing votes, and an endless variety of other malpractices), but voting machines produce new problems. It is apparent, again in spite of all instructions, that some voters will go behind the curtain, turn down the little levers, check them, turn them back up, and then pull the large handle; as a result, a zero vote is cast. It is also apparent that even in this age of machinery, some voters in low-income districts fear the machines—believe that they take the voter's photograph, transmit his vote to the police, and other such absurdities. The total vote cast in these districts commonly falls with the introduction of machines and recovers, if at all, only over many years. On most types of voting machines, the names of candidates are arranged in horizontal rows, but if a party's list (or the list of candidates in a direct primary) runs over to a second or third line, such persons are at a distinct disadvantage. "The tremendous advantage enjoyed by candidates on the top line of the voting machines was illustrated in Denver [in the 1960 primary election] where not a single candidate for legislative, judicial, or other office on the bottom

---

[13] *There are various other ballot forms in use, notably the "scratch" ballot in some southern states. On this, the voter scratches out or marks through the names of candidates or propositions he does not wish to vote for. See Spencer D. Albright, The American Ballot (Washington, D.C.: American Council on Public Affairs, 1942); and Carl O. Smith, A Book of Ballots (Detroit: Detroit Bureau of Municipal Research, Report No. 148, 1938).*

[14] *Howard White, "Voters Plump for First on List,"* National Municipal Review, 39 *(February 1950), 110, and Henry M. Bain and Donald S. Hecock,* Ballot Position and Voter's Choice *(Detroit: Wayne State University Press, 1957).*

line was nominated." [15] Comparable results have been observed elsewhere. "The use of voting machines may tend to discourage voter opinion on issues," said the Toledo Municipal League when in 1960, 95.6 percent of Toledo voters who used paper ballots voted on a city school levy, but only 79.9 percent of those who used voting machines.[16] A similar result was observed in the defeat of the 1958 proposal for constitutional revision in Michigan.[17]

Voting machines do not completely eliminate all abuses. Machines have been tampered with: chewing gum has been put under the little levers; votes have been rung up on the machines before the polls opened, and so on. When he was mayor of Boston, the late James M. Curley simply assigned only three voting machines to each of the strongly Republican precincts, so that long lines of Republicans formed, and many were unable to vote before the closing hour, whereas he had eight machines available in each Democratic precinct, where the full vote was cast with no delay.[18]

Regardless of whether paper ballots or voting machines are used, state laws determine what candidates will appear on the ballot. In some southern states extensive powers are left to party officers, as was shown in 1948 when President Truman, nominated by a national convention, was nevertheless kept off the ballot in Alabama and denied the Democratic designation in Louisiana, Mississippi, and South Carolina. The common belief that a qualified American voter may vote for whomever he pleases is in need of some amendment; he may vote for the man the state election law lets him vote for.

The laws are also making it more and more difficult to vote for minor party, new party, and independent candidates, because they tend to set up for them—but not for the major parties—extremely onerous requirements to get on the ballot. In New York State, for example, the petitions must contain at least 12,000 signatures with no fewer than 50 collected from each of the 62 counties. The states learn from each other, and these and other varieties of nails and tacks are being strewn on the roads on which any but a major party candidate must run.

---

[15] Denver Post, Sept. 14, 1960.
[16] Toledo Municipal League, "Voting Machines and Voter Participation" (mimeographed), January 26, 1961.
[17] John P. White, Voting Machines and the 1958 Defeat of Constitutional Revision in Michigan (Ann Arbor, Mich.: Institute of Public Administration, University of Michigan, 1960). The use of voting machines in Michigan has also been associated with a sharp decline in voter participation.
[18] Boston Herald, December 5, 1948.

THE NOMINATING PROCESS. Federalism enables each state through its election law to regulate the process of nomination, from naming the party candidates for coroner to naming those for United States senator—or what may be even more crucial to America, the delegates to national conventions. The importance of this nominating process cannot be overemphasized. Nomination is the gateway to political power. In fact, in the one-party states, nomination is the real election, and in most of the others it sets the choice for the voters at the general election. "This year," one disgruntled voter once said to me, "we have for Congress the choice between a crook and a fool." That sort of choice, or worse, can happen, but the low turnout at primaries in the northern states indicates either that the voters do not understand or that they are not much concerned.

The principal devices for nominating candidates are: (1) the *caucus* or mass meeting—a face-to-face assembly of party members, obviously not practicable much beyond a precinct level; (2) the delegate convention, commonly shortened to the word *convention*, by which persons selected in a variety of ways choose the nominees, usually by oral voting or roll calls; (3) the direct primary, commonly shortened to *primary*, by which in a kind of preliminary election using ballots or voting machines the members of the party if the primary is "closed," or any voters if it is "open," select the candidates; and (4) *petition*, a formal demand in legal form, signed by a designated number or percentage of voters as required by law, that a nominee appear on a ballot. Specific requirements vary greatly.

No state now uses a complete convention system. All of them use either primaries alone or some combination of primaries and conventions. New York, for example, selects candidates for statewide election by conventions, other candidates by primaries. Six states have systems of pre-primary conventions in which the party organizations may designate candidates for the primaries, but anti-organization candidates may still get on the primary ballots by petition. The pre-primary convention system is favored by many political scientists and incorporated in the Model Primary Law of the National Municipal League. It enables a party to have some influence in the selection of the nominees whom it will presumably try to elect in November; yet the scheme still does not freeze out (as a straight convention system may) candidates for nomination who may not be favored by the organization but may be desired by the rank and file of party members.

Whether important or not, state party platforms could at least be presented to a convention for debate, amendment, adoption. But no one has ever invented a reasonable scheme for presenting a platform directly to the party voters in the voting booths. The best device thought up so far is to hold a post-primary convention where the nominees and other delegates, if any appear, may adopt a platform. But this post-primary convention, everywhere a sad institution, is most ridiculous in one-party areas where the real election, the primary, has already been held.

A national party cannot determine the sort of candidate who may run for office in the states under its party label. No matter what his attitudes, if he wins nomination, he is their candidate. "Any man who can carry a Republican primary is a Republican," said Senator Borah. "He might . . . believe in the communistic state, in the dictatorship of the proletariat, in the abolition of private property, and in the extermination of the bourgeoisie; yet, if he carried his Republican primary, he would be a Republican."

NONPARTISAN NOMINATIONS AND ELECTIONS. Two states (Minnesota and Nebraska) elect their legislators, almost all areas select local school boards, and about 60 percent of the cities elect their officials without any party designation on the ballots. Thus they avoid conventions and primaries for these offices. "A nonpartisan election is one in which no party label appears on the ballot, and candidates are normally nominated by a simple petition process." [19] In places where the parties are well organized and potent, taking the labels off the ballot does not take the parties out of the election process; it only puts them to the trouble of educating their followers on which candidates are the Democrats, which the Republicans. When he ran for mayor of Boston, James M. Curley never left any doubt that he was a Democrat; in Denver, Mayor Richard Batterton was often mentioned as a possible Republican candidate for governor, senator, or some other office. The aldermen in Chicago are elected on a nonpartisan ballot. In some cities, such as Detroit, a façade of nonpartisanship appears to be required by local tradition; so major parties back certain candidates covertly, giving them financial assistance and providing advertising for them by way of dummy committees, and even paying for their precinct workers. In California and in many cities and counties in the country, however, there is a strong public opinion that parties have no place in local affairs. If the party organizations in these jurisdictions back any candidates, they must do so secretly, or their efforts will do their friends more injury than good.

---

[19] Eugene C. Lee, The Politics of Nonpartisanship: A Study of California City Elections (Berkeley, Calif.: University of California Press, 1960), p. 3. This book contains an extensive bibliography on nonpartisan elections (pp. 216–224). This bibliography cites the studies by Charles R. Adrian, a leading student of nonpartisan elections.

Eugene C. Lee and a few others offer some tentative generalizations about nonpartisan elections. First, as shown by turnout, voter interest in local elections falls 20 to 60 percent, and stays down. Second, nonpartisan civic groups, though numerous, do not usually take the place of parties in the important tasks of organizing for elections, advancing candidates, or providing criticism of official conduct. Instead, such organizations as chambers of commerce, luncheon clubs, veterans' associations, women's organizations, and churches become active and influential in local politics. And these groups tend to overrepresent upper and upper-middle class occupations and interests. Third, many candidates recruit themselves, knowing what group support they can expect. Sometimes the city council members select candidates for vacancies, a sort of cooptation process. "The most frequently reported single body of political influentials is 'Main Street.' . . . Sharing this important position is the local press. . . ." [20] We may conclude that for such areas, nonpartisan politics does not usually mean no politics; it means, rather, a special kind of group politics of particularly low visibility.

DIRECT LEGISLATION. In many states, the people not only vote to nominate and elect candidates for state and local office, they also vote on constitutional and legislative measures—a form of popular participation that has no counterpart in the affairs of the federal government. The political penicillin of the Progressive period was direct legislation: the initiative, by which citizens by petition place a proposed measure on the ballot (unless the legislature enacts it in the meantime); and the referendum, by which the legislature itself or citizens by petition place an already enacted law on the ballot for popular approval or rejection.

Whether this way of legislating has proved good or bad is one of the concerns of Chapter 9 in this volume; we are concerned here with the place of direct legislation in the politics of the states. Such studies of direct legislation as we have had seem to indicate that parties rarely take sides, or even an interest, in proposals, but that interest groups do. The champion lobbyist of them all, Arthur H. Samish of California, who got into difficulties with the federal Internal Revenue Service, earned a large part of the questioned income in conducting direct legislation campaigns.

It also seems clear that voters take less interest in measures than in men. At any rate, the total vote cast, both for and against a proposal, never equals that cast for President or governor and often falls as low as 10 percent. Some of this effect, however, may be because referred measures

---

[20] Ibid., *p. 96*.

usually appear at the bottom of the ballot or in some obscure place on a voting machine. And even with the best of intentions, it is extremely difficult to describe a complicated proposed statute in the few words that can be allowed on a ballot. The reader might ask himself how he would vote on the following real proposal: "Shall an act to amend an act entitled An Act Concerning Municipal Corporations be further amended to permit said corporations to exercise the right of excess condemnation?" Yes or no? When they read this, most of the voters either voted "No" or did not vote.

MONEY. Most states have statutes, usually called corrupt practices laws,[21] regulating the use of money in elections. Such statutes commonly restrict or prohibit contributions from certain sources (for example, banks, corporations, labor unions); some seek to limit the totals to be collected either for specific offices or for campaigns; some also limit or forbid certain types of expenditures (such as "treating," or buying drinks for voters). Some of the laws apply only to general elections, others to both primaries and elections. Some have elaborate requirements for reporting contributions and expenditures at certain dates before and after elections. None has solved the important problems of loans and campaign deficits.[22] And none has provided adequate means for enforcement of the statutes.

So confused and confusing is the pattern of party finance, with money (some reported and some unreported) passing up and down and in and out among hundreds of committees, that we can only estimate the amounts and the purposes for which they are spent. Alexander Heard, whose The Costs of Democracy (1960) is the most recent complete study of money in elections, estimated that in 1952 a total of $140 million was spent, about $19 million at the national level, $67 million in state campaigns, and $53 million in district and local level activities. It has increased since 1952, reaching about $175 million in 1960 and $200 million in 1964.[23]

---

[21] The term is unfortunate, for except that they prohibit a few actions long regarded as corrupt, such as the bribery of voters, they purport to regulate behavior not in itself corrupt, such as the making of contributions by certain types of persons or groups. See Louise Overacker, Money in Elections (New York: Macmillan, 1932), pp. 1–17. The states that have such acts commonly print them as pamphlets, usually combined with the state election law, that may be obtained gratis from the secretary of state. There is no national compendium of these statutes. For tables listing their principal features, see The Book of the States: 1966–1967, pp. 28–31.

[22] Important because if financial support influences candidates, parties, and officials, the campaign contributor is usually taking a chance—his party or candidate may lose; whereas the person who makes a loan or helps to meet a deficit need not take a chance; he is in a position to demand an official or party action lest he call the loan or refuse to help with the deficit.

[23] Alexander Heard, The Costs of Democracy (Chapel Hill, N.C.: University of North Carolina Press, 1960), p. 7. His estimate excludes contributed services, such as rent-free quarters, the use of billboards without charge, the provision of automobiles to

But the total sum does not alarm students of party finance so much as its uneven distribution: a new or minor party has a desperately hard time competing in the multi-million-dollar league. The Republican party is commonly better financed than the Democratic, but the fact that Democrats often win seems to indicate that money is not everything, at least not in politics.[24] The uses to which the money is put are today generally honorable: the immense costs of television use up millions, and most of the remainder goes for headquarters expense, advertising, and travel. Only a few state party chairmen receive salaries; only full-time headquarters workers are usually paid.

3. *The Politics of Institutions*

The people's interest in and knowledge of state and local politics are significantly affected by governmental institutional arrangements, that is, by the formal organization of these governments. Depending upon what one thinks most important, these arrangements can be designed to set the scene for lively attention-getting drama or, on the other hand, to provide dim lighting and a multitude of characters who wander on and off the stage, their roles so ill-defined that the audience rapidly loses interest. But the first of these alternatives is often unsatisfactory; government is perhaps too complex to warrant a simplistic design that guarantees a hero, a villain, and a comic-relief character. Therefore, it may be more important to fragment power to avoid the abuses that Lord Acton assumed would tend to accompany power,[25] or to provide many points of access for citizens and groups to the decision-making process, or to give minorities an effective

---

transport voters to the polls, and the value of the time of the army of party workers. Possibly the money value of these and similar gifts and services would equal or exceed the cash contributions. The President's Commission on Campaign Costs followed Heard's system of exclusions and estimated that "Expenditures on behalf of all candidates for all public offices in the United States probably reached $165 to $175 million in 1960." Report (Washington, D.C., 1962), p. 9. Data for 1964 are given in Herbert E. Alexander, Financing the 1964 Election (Princeton, N.J.: Citizens' Research Foundation, 1966), p. 13.

[24] Heard believes that "money probably has its greatest impact on the choice of public officials in the shadow land of our politics where it is decided who will be a candidate for a party's nomination and who will not. . . . This influence of important fund raisers and of large contributors is more persuasive with newcomers than with demonstrated vote-getters, more controlling with challengers than with champions." Op. cit., p. 35.

[25] For a critique of Acton's dictum that "power tends to corrupt and absolute power corrupts absolutely," see Arnold A. Rogow and Harold D. Lasswell, Power, Corruption, and Rectitude (Englewood Cliffs, N.J.: Prentice-Hall, 1963).

veto over simple majorities. Yet fragmentation is not an absolute good justifying a position of "the more fragmentation, the better." The attendant obfuscation of the political scene may carry a high cost, not only in terms of public attentiveness, but also in terms of the electorate's ability to fix responsibility for the direction and pace in which public policy moves at the state and local levels and to vote accordingly on parties and candidates.

SEPARATION OF POWERS. All state constitutions, like the national one, distribute the powers of government among three branches, the legislative, the executive, and the judicial. The state constitutions are in this respect much alike, although a given power (appointment, for instance) is not always given to the same branch in all states. In spite of some constitutional phrases to the effect that no branch shall exercise a power belonging to another, the separation can never be absolute; the administration of justice, for example, involves all three.

The classic, or perhaps the literary, theory of democracy is that a majority of the voters choose a set of policies offered to them by one of the parties and elect that party's candidates, who proceed to do what the voters want done. But under a system of separated powers the voters must elect not only a majority of the legislature but the governor and a majority of the state supreme court as well. Failure to elect them all from the same party may produce stalemate. In practice, a single party cannot commonly attain this degree of control, so that deadlock can be broken only by compromise, logrolling, or the purchase of enough votes in the legislature to get a program through. Even when a governor and a majority in each house belong to the same party, the separation of powers may produce a standstill because the governor and the legislators represent different constituencies. To get his program accepted, the late Governor Harold Hoffman of New Jersey appointed so many state senators to jobs in one session that the senate lost its constitutional quorum. The separation of powers often presents, therefore, the choice between no action and unethical action. In the words of V. O. Key, Jr., "The blunt conclusion emerges that the constitutional systems [of the states] really shut the door against a popular choice between political parties." [26]

Judicial review, the right to review the constitutionality of actions of the governor and legislature, puts all the state supreme courts right into the political process. This right turns a part of our politics from discussion of policy to arguments on constitutional exegesis; the main question may be not "Would a severance tax [on the extraction of natural resources or

---

[26] V. O. Key, Jr., American State Politics: An Introduction (New York: Knopf, 1956), p. 59. Key has an entire chapter, entitled "The Frustration of Party," on the separation of powers.

the cutting of timber] be a good policy for this state?" but "Would a severance tax be constitutional?" Some state campaigns are thus fought not on questions of policy, but on questions of constitutionality. And when a majority of a state supreme court overrules a governor and a majority of the legislature, another campaign is necessary—to change the state constitution. The complexity of an already complex politics is compounded.

LEGISLATIVE REPRESENTATION. In addition to the constitutional features already mentioned, there are a number of other factors, not uniform among the states, that influence the pattern of state politics in important ways.

"The hard and simple fact," wrote the late Senator Richard Neuberger, "is that America has moved to town, but its state legislatures have not." Almost all of them have been dominated by rural areas, whose people have been, by one device or another, overrepresented. The most spectacular trick is gerrymandering—the deliberate arrangement of the boundaries of the districts from which legislators are elected so that a minority of the voters may elect a majority of the legislators, or so that a bare majority of the voters may fill almost all the legislative seats. Although the name for this stratagem is of American origin, its use is widespread. Wherever legislators are elected by areas, there is always a temptation, which statesmen have shown a remarkable inability to resist, to construct the areas so as to give one party an advantage out of proportion to its strength in the electorate. A glance at a map of the districts set up in almost any state will show the results of partisan ingenuity: the horseshoe, dumbbell, shoestring, and other curiously shaped areas. The niceties of the art of gerrymandering are many, but the two principal means are either to scatter opposition strength into a number of districts, each of which can be carried by the party doing the gerrymandering, or to concentrate this strength in one or more districts that the opposition carries overwhelmingly, thus wasting so many of their votes on a few seats that the other party wins a large majority of the total number of seats. Combinations of these methods may be utilized in the same state, depending upon the distribution of the votes. And gerrymandering may be used not only to underrepresent a party, but also to disadvantage some interest, such as labor, or some minority, such as the Negro.[27]

A state that was fairly districted at some time long ago may become, with the passage of the years and a shift in population, just as unfairly apportioned as one that has been deliberately gerrymandered. This phe-

---

[27] *The United States Supreme Court upset one particularly gross gerrymander of Negro voters in* Gomillion v. Lightfoot, *364 U.S. 339 (1960).*

nomenon is sometimes called the "silent gerrymander." The British term is "rotten borough." Since the shifts in American population have mostly been toward the cities and since in the North the farm areas have tended to vote Republican, the silent gerrymander has usually worked to the advantage of the Republican party. The state legislatures may insist that citizens must obey the state constitution and that the teachers must take oaths to support it, but for half a century or more they often violated its plain mandate that legislative districts shall be reapportioned after every census.

Some state constitutions have provided for one or both houses a sort of built-in gerrymander of one kind or another. Such provisions as that in the New Jersey constitution whereby each county, regardless of population, shall elect only one state senator, or that in the New Hampshire constitution by which each town, no matter how small, is entitled to a member of the house once in every ten years are examples. Not one overrepresented city people; all gave some sort of advantage to the people who live in rural and small town areas.

When the United States Supreme Court in 1962 upset more than a century of precedents and held that the fairness of state legislative apportionment was a constitutional question appropriate for action by the federal courts, there followed a series of decisions by state courts, and a number of legislatures that happened to be in session hurriedly reapportioned. In some of the states in which the initiative is permitted, petitions to reapportion by popular vote began to circulate. And through the door opened by the Supreme Court's decision, underrepresented citizens moved into federal district courts seeking relief of their grievances. From state and federal courts, appeals were carried to the Supreme Court, a development that could have been anticipated from the Court's failure in 1962 to provide any specifications that would need to be met for an apportionment to conform to the Fourteenth Amendment's injunction that "No State shall . . . deny to any person within its jurisdiction the equal protection of the laws." In 1964 the Supreme Court, considering a number of appealed cases, interpreted the Constitution to mean that apportionment schemes should be strictly according to population, that the rule was "one man, one vote," with that vote equal in legislative representation to any other man's vote. The interpretation was held applicable to both chambers of a state legislature; no longer could one be based on representation of population and the other on representation of counties or towns or square mileage.[28]

---

[28] Baker v. Carr, 369 U.S. 186 (1962); and Reynolds v. Sims 377 U.S. 533 (1964).

This revolutionary development in the courts may make it of only historical interest that in 1960 New Hampshire had one town with three people living in it, one of whom could, under the state constitution, be elected to the legislature. But the consequences of the system of legislative representation that has prevailed in most of our states into the 1960's are significant for anyone concerned with state politics. By the middle of the decade, a few northeastern cities were overrepresented, though some suburbs were still underrepresented.

In the northern states a Democratic governor facing a legislature that is Republican in one or both houses is a common political event. V. O. Key, Jr., studied 32 states over the 30-year period 1920 to 1950 and found that the Republicans controlled one or both houses in two-thirds of the elections in which Democratic governors won by 50 to 55 percent of the two-party vote, and "even when Democratic governors won by 60 percent or more, the chances were about one out of three that Republicans would control one or both houses of the legislature." [29] Party responsibility is, of course, impossible under such conditions.

No full study has ever been made to explore how rural rule affected the pattern of state law, but that it affected it cannot be doubted.[30] In some states the gasoline tax and motor vehicle license-fee money—even that collected from merchants' delivery trucks that never cross a city line— goes only for highways and rural roads, with nothing for city streets. Nobody ever asserts that real property in cities is commonly underassessed in relation to farm property; the situation is the other way around. Rural elections are often not subject to the same stringent regulation that is applied to elections in cities. Legislatures that deny or limit municipal home rule, that pass special legislation to limit the powers of particular cities, that distribute education and welfare funds to the disadvantage of the cities have also often shown a general neglect or misunderstanding of urban problems such as slum clearance, traffic congestion, and race relations. There has been a widespread feeling among mayors and city managers that the rural-dominated legislatures have neither coped with the cities' problems nor permitted the cities to do it.

THE GOVERNOR'S ROLE. Many people, especially those who have not read their state constitutions, think of the typical governor as a little President. Some governors, notably those in New York and New Jersey, do have powers over their state governments comparable to those the President has over the national government. And the newer state

---

[29] *Key*, op. cit., *p. 59.*
[30] *A beginning was made by Gordon E. Baker in* Rural Versus Urban Political Power (*New York: Random House, 1955*).

constitutions have tended in the direction of making the governor a little President with a cabinet responsible to him and with considerable control over the state administration. Most governors, however, do not have such powers. In about a third of the states, the governor serves a two-year term, and in some states he cannot succeed himself after one or two terms, so that he is in authority too short a time to develop much strength. Furthermore, some state constitutions admonish the governor to "take care that the laws are faithfully executed" but then proceed to stipulate that the attorney general, the treasurer, the secretary of state, and various other officials through whom he must work shall either be popularly elected or appointed for fixed terms, terms sometimes longer than the governor's. So the election of a Democratic governor with a Republican attorney general or the reverse can occur, and the next campaign can be full of charges and countercharges as to who tried to enforce the law and who tried to frustrate him in his best efforts.

The state constitutions do, however, give the typical governor some legislative powers, such as the right to address the legislature and to recommend legislation, the power to call special sessions, and the veto. Although he has no veto in North Carolina, in 39 states the governor has an item veto (the power to approve most of an appropriation act, while vetoing one or more sections of it), a power that not even the President possesses.

No governor has a seat in the legislature, but most state campaigns, like the presidential ones, have centered largely on legislative policy, proposals, and programs. A majority of all the voters of the state pass upon the candidates for governor although, as we have seen, a minority may elect the legislature; so the broader constituency that selected the governor may (and does) estimate his success and decide his reelection in terms of how well his program—more legislative than executive—was carried out. In the shorthand that historians use, they refer to the calendar periods between our elections by the names of the executives—"the administrations of Al Smith"—disregarding party control of the legislature, and they indicate by this usage how much we have come to think of the governor as chief legislator.

Through his superior access to public opinion, the governor may seek to lead the legislature to carry out the program on which he was elected, for many newspapers will carry his statements, and radio stations his speeches, when they will not carry those of a legislator. Most governors have some patronage—though the amount is shrinking with the extension of civil service—with which they can persuade some legislators. But patronage is most useful in the first year of a governor's term; as the jobs are filled, he has less and less to offer.

Most governors exercise some leadership in their parties, but the amounts and types vary widely. At one extreme, no one doubted that Governor Thomas E. Dewey was the leader of the Republican party in New York State. At the other, for years no one thought for a moment that the governor of Virginia, whoever he may have been, was the real leader of the Democratic party in that state: United States Senator Harry Byrd was. Among the identifiable patterns between these extremes are those in which the governor shares party leadership with a group of local bosses; with leaders of business, labor, or other powerful groups; with a faction in his party; with a legislative bloc; or with the senators, congressmen, state chairman, and national committeeman of his party in the state. Whatever the pattern, it has rarely remained stable over many years, with the exception of Virginia, where the Byrd machine may be traced back to colonial times. Changes occur in the structure of leadership with the varying fortunes of parties, business, and other organized groups; with changes in the characteristics of the population; with changes in the state constitution; because of the different personalities of different men at different points in the hierarchy, and in other ways.

PARTY STRUCTURE. Those parties that qualify as such under the state law find that the statute sets up for them the form of party organization and structure required or permitted. These laws differ greatly in the degree of detail they contain; in the large two-party states such as New York or California where elections are hotly contested, the statutes name almost every title for every official and describe every kind of committee that a party may or must have. The powers, duties, and liabilities of officials are specified. The size, financing, selection, authority, even the meeting dates for committees are prescribed. But the states where one party always, or almost always, wins, typically leave greater discretion to the parties to organize, within broad limits, as they wish.

Even though structures differ somewhat with the forms of local government (three states do not have counties, for example), each major party is shaped like a rough pyramid, with the organization at each level typically independent of the organization at every other level (see Figure 6.1). The arrangements would seem to provide for the rule of party units by committee, but in fact the committees may be active or not, depending upon their officers. Every committee has a chairman and one or more vice chairmen, plus a secretary and some other officers. They need not be members of the committee at the time they are elected by it, because the chairman may in fact be designated by the principal candidate who won in the primary: the nominee for governor, senator, congressman, mayor, or other office, depending on the committee's level and area of jurisdiction. Such a candidate commonly picks the man who served as his campaign manager in the primary campaign. If the candidate wins, the chairman may continue year after year, and he may receive some public job in addition. If the candidate loses, the chairman may or may not remain until

Figure 6.1. *Typical Organization of a Major Political Party*

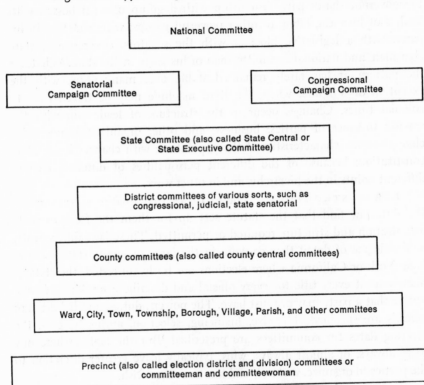

the next election. This arrangement obviously produces a continual turnover among party officers with the accompanying results of inefficiency, inadequate records, lack of experience and political acquaintance, and so forth. The chairmen, it should be added, do not know one another, even at the same level, and they do not generally have any meeting or convention to discuss their problems or campaigns.

Two exceptions should be noted. The American county, with its characteristically commission or collegiate type of government, has no executive, so county chairmen do not rotate in office as rapidly as state, district, and some other chairmen, and they are not usually responsible to the state chairman in any way. A second exception is in what have been the one-party states in the South, where the real election has been the Democratic primary. The situation there is changing, but the formal organization, set up to win general elections, has been substantially useless. It has been generally ignored in the Democratic party, and in the Republican party it has functioned in the selection of delegates to national conventions and in dealing with Republican Presidents on patronage.[31]

Several causes appear to be operating to build up alongside the formal, legal party structures in some states one or more informal structures. Examples are such organizations as the Young Democrats and the Young Republicans, the Republican Assemblies, and the Democratic Clubs of California.[32] Because the formal organization is usually dominated by persons who have worked in the party for years, the enthusiastic young newcomer feels that his capacities are not recognized, or are not utilized enough, so he and his friends may decide to start a club or other association. Then, too, persons who are greatly attracted to some candidate, such as Adlai Stevenson, or who are devoted to some ideology, such as liberalism or conservatism, which they want the party to espouse, may become impatient with older party officers who may tend to take the professionals' casual attitude toward candidates and issues. The election laws that establish the formal organizations also limit what they may do, but the informal associations are not bound by these legal limitations, and they may as a consequence perform useful services for a party, especially raising money. But there appears in most states to be a certain amount of friction and jealousy, sometimes denied or concealed, between the regulars and the amateurs.

Another sort of informal organization is that set up for campaign purposes only, such as the Willkie Clubs, the Citizens for Eisenhower, the Volunteers for Nixon-Lodge, or the Goldwater clubs. Some of these campaign groups are intended to appeal to religious, ethnic, professional, regional, or other interests. The motivation behind their establishment

---

[31] *See* V. O. Key, Jr., Southern Politics (*New York: Knopf, 1949*); *and Alexander Heard, A Two-party South?* (*Chapel Hill, N.C.: University of North Carolina Press, 1952*).

[32] *Hugh A. Bone, "New Party Associations in the West,"* American Political Science Review, 45 (*December 1951*), 1115–25; *Francis Carney, The Rise of the Democratic Clubs in California* (*New York: Holt, 1958*), *also in Paul Tillett* (*ed.*), Cases on Party Organizations (*New York: McGraw-Hill, 1963*), *pp. 32–63; and James Q. Wilson, The Amateur Democrat: Club Politics in Three Cities* (*Chicago: University of Chicago Press, 1962*).

differs sharply from that behind the informal party organizations earlier described. They are bipartisan in order to attract persons away from the other party, if only for one election; and they enable a party to evade the financial limitations imposed by state and federal corrupt practices acts.

THE ELECTORAL COLLEGE. It is commonly said that any American mother's son may grow up to be President, but if any expectant mother, conscious of American history since the Civil War, has this ambition for her son, she had best be in New York, New Jersey, Ohio, Indiana, Illinois, California, or some other large and "doubtful" state. For the curious operations of the electoral college so dominate certain aspects of our politics that her son has only a remote chance to be nominated for President unless he comes from one of the half dozen states mentioned.

As is well known, the framers of the Constitution thought that by setting up the electoral college they had, as Hamilton argued in the *Federalist*, taken the selection of the President away "from the general mass" and had placed it in the hands of a select number of persons who would search the country and come up with the best possible man. As is also well known, the plan worked as intended only in the election of Washington.

The constitutional provision that each state shall have as many presidential electors as it has senators and representatives has inclined each party to pick its candidates from the states that may go either way in an election *and* carry with them a considerable number of electoral votes. Thus any race for governor of New York, which has 43 electoral votes, is a sort of trial heat for the Presidency. One recent writer on that state said, "New York politics is locally affected (one might say is sometimes afflicted) by the national ambitions of its party leaders." Much the same sentiment could be expressed about any of the other five states, notably California.

During presidential and congressional campaigns the large and doubtful states have the national money poured into them; the others get little or nothing. The speakers from national headquarters tour Illinois, but who goes to Arkansas? The politics of the small and sure states thus tend to be left out of the national stream.

The sparsely populated states such as Nevada, Vermont, and Wyoming are overrepresented in the electoral college; an elector in California represents about four times as many people as one in Nevada. But in the small states the consciousness of privilege tends to preserve and harden sentiments of state pride, a kind of subnationalism. Economic interests that happen to have their bases in the sparsely populated states, such as those represented in the farm bloc and the silver bloc, are given a political weight by the electoral college that is out of proportion to the number of people they represent. The electoral college, finally, has a depressing effect upon minor parties, for a party must get a plurality of the votes in a whole state to get a single electoral vote.

4. Conclusion

State and local politics is given much of its character by formal rules and formal institutional arrangements. Constitutions, statute books, and judicial doctrines prescribe who can vote, how elections shall be conducted, how candidates are to be chosen, whether the passage of laws is the business only of elected legislators or also a function of the voters, and what role money may play in appeals to the electorate. Similarly, constitutions, statute books, and judicial doctrines prescribe institutional arrangements that distribute the powers of government among the men chosen for public office; fix the degree to which these men must be actually representative of the citizenry for which they act; cast the chief "executive" and the courts as participants, along with the legislature, in the making of public policy; structure party organization; and interlock national and state politics.

Several broad characteristics of this formal shaping of state and local politics warrant reemphasis. Most striking—and most likely to be forgotten—is that the formal rules and institutions are themselves created by the political process. While at any given moment one may visualize a formally prescribed system within which political behavior is confined, any element of the system is subject to change by mobilization of political support for the change. The game of politics operates within rules, but it also operates on the rules. If payment of a poll tax is required in five southern states as a qualification for voting, the Constitution may be amended to forbid such a qualification for national elections, as was done in 1964 by adoption of the Twenty-fourth Amendment. If the Fourteenth Amendment is judicially interpreted to require state legislatures to be apportioned according to population, an attempt may be made to amend the national Constitution so as to permit representation in one chamber of counties, towns, or other areas without regard to population; such an attempt was initiated in Congress immediately following the Supreme Court's 1964 decision on apportionment.

Second, each state has great freedom in setting the rules for the political game to be played within its boundaries at both state and local levels. National prescriptions are few, though often basic, and the rules therefore can and do vary among the states. The governmental institutions, too, may be what the state constitutions make them, subject to only a few national constitutional restrictions, but here the states have chosen to be highly imitative of the federal government and of the other states; consequently, separation of powers, a two-chamber legislature, a gubernatorial veto power, a several-tiered judicial system, and other institutional patterns will be found in most states.

Third, despite their substantial degree of autonomy, the states are parts of a federal system of government, and this fact does make a difference. The national Constitution, national statutes, and national courts affect what states can do and how they may go about doing it. Political ambitions may lead state officials to orient their careers toward eventual candidacy for national legislative office, administrative office, or the Presidency itself. The significance and liveliness of the politics of the individual states vary partly according to the particular weight each state carries in national politics.

Finally, the very multiplicity and complexity of the formal rules and institutions and the variety of places one must look to find out about them (constitutions, statutes, court decisions—all of them at both federal and state levels, and some at local levels) make the game of state and local politics difficult to comprehend. One effect is to give an advantage to the political professionals, professional lobbyists, and lawyers who make a point of knowing their way around in government; the amateur politician, the civic-affairs hobbyist, the sudden convert to political activism are likely to find themselves outsmarted at critical moments. A professional team and an amateur team are not usually a fair match.

chapter 7

Patterns of Politics

E ach person is an individual, and as such, unique. Neither political leaders nor political scientists can calculate or analyze the political behavior of each of the some sixty million persons in this country who vote in national elections. Consequently, they direct their efforts toward discovering patterns of political behavior, principally by grouping people according to one or a few common characteristics and by trying to relate these shared characteristics to the political behavior of the members of each group. The same individual, of course, may appear in a number of these groups, and his political behavior cannot readily be anticipated under all circumstances. He may be under such cross-pressures that he may not act at all. Indeed, the political analyst is seldom concerned with exactly how a single individual in a group will act politically, nor does grouping individuals for generalizing purposes lead him to say that all members of the group will act a certain way. Rather, he deals in probabilities: An individual with certain identified characteristics is more likely than not to act politically in a stated way, but not every such person will do so; a group of people with a certain characteristic in common will divide about 40 percent and 60 percent (or any other set of percentages) between two alternative modes of political behavior. Such analyses, when supported by empirical data, advance our understanding but, of course, do not suggest that any human being is a mere automaton.

Concerned as we are with state and local politics, a critical characteristic affecting political behavior is the particular state and locality in which people live. Political geography is so salient a consideration that we may also take account of whole regions or sections of the country that seem to have shown discernibly distinct patterns of politics. We need also to distinguish two-party from one-party states and to explore as well the question of whether that dichotomy is too simple. Bossed and unbossed political systems behave differently, as do urban and rural areas, central cities and their suburbs. Economic and social class, sex, education, age, race, religion are attributes of individuals that affect their voting and nonvoting, their partisanship and independence, and their choice of party. Organized groups with common interests try to influence governmental decision makers; the behavior of such groups is therefore part of our concern.

Whole books are devoted to the patterns of politics associated with these and other characteristics of individuals and groups; here we can only suggest some of the more significant patterns among the states and localities.

1. *Sectionalism*

Notable similarities of behavior described in terms of large geographical areas are called sectionalism or regionalism. Sometimes we can find an identity of interest among the people in an area—dairy farming or silver mining, for example—that presumably explains why they mostly vote the same way. Again, they may tend to vote alike because of social pressure—it has not been considered good form, for example, to be a Democrat in Vermont or a Republican in Georgia. And sometimes attachment to one party or the other goes back to some ancient party battle, some struggle long ago, such as those in the aftermath of the Civil War. But, for the most part, people tend to think and act politically the way their families, their friends, and their neighbors think and act. Probably the strongest of these influences is the family. Various students of the matter have estimated that somewhere between 65 and 85 percent of the voters get their politics in the same place they get their religion—at home.[1] To the extent that this generalization can be demonstrated from election statistics and survey materials, it forms the strongest rebuttal to the Marxian hypothesis that economic interest determines behavior.

---

[1] *See Herbert McClosky and Harold E. Dahlgren, "Primary Group Influence on Party Loyalty,"* American Political Science Review, *53 (September 1959), 757–76.*

In American life the existence of sections is so well known that the common names for certain of them have passed into our ordinary speech: New England, the South, the West, and so on. Sectional consciousness is somewhat intensified by differences of dialect or accent, by problems of long standing such as race relations, and by variations in religion and country of origin. But although we know what we mean by the New England states, the description of no other section is exact, not even of the South, for some writers will include Oklahoma and the so-called Border states, others will not. Out where the West begins is a poetic and not a political place.

In attempts to improve our descriptions of sections, various interesting efforts have been made to classify the states in terms of their party adherence.[2] Using 1914–54 and national elections as their base, Austin Ranney and Willmore Kendall classified the states as (1) two-party, (2) modified one-party Democratic, (3) modified one-party Republican, (4) one-party Democratic, and (5) one-party Republican (only Vermont was put in this category). Using elections for governor in the period 1870–1950, and the number of alternations of party victories as his bases of calculation, Joseph A. Schlesinger found a somewhat different arrangement of the states.[3] All such classifications must be regarded as general and tentative: Vermont, long regarded as solidly one-party Republican, elected a Democratic congressman in 1958 and a Democratic governor in 1964. Texas, which has always been counted in the Democratic Solid South, elected a Republican United States senator in 1961; and the 1964 election shattered many traditional patterns, with the Deep South providing five of the six states that voted for the Republican presidential candidate. Predictions of future voting behavior cannot therefore be based with certainty upon past behavior, for great events such as the Civil War, the free-silver controversy, or the Depression may cause a state to change its party allegiance.

THE ONE-PARTY STATES. The eleven states that formed the Confederacy were, from the end of Reconstruction to 1928, a section commonly called the Solid South. Prohibition and Al Smith's religion cracked it then, and it has broken in presidential elections since 1948,

---

[2] *The results of these schemes vary, of course, with the factors used, for instance, whether elections for President and Congress or for governor are counted, the number of alternations in winning slates, the date at which the count begins (1854, 1860, 1896, 1900, 1912, 1914, 1932) and ends, and other considerations.*

[3] *Austin Ranney and Willmore Kendall,* Democracy *and the American Party System (New York: Harcourt, 1956), pp. 160–66; Joseph A. Schlesinger, "A Two-dimensional Scheme for Classifying the States According to Degree of Inter-party Competition,"* American Political Science Review, 49 (December 1955), 1120–28.

primarily over the issue of civil rights for Negroes. Aside from the "Presidential Republicans," however, the Republican party has found recruiting voters in the South to be hard and slow, for it cannot take a civil rights position satisfactory to the South without losing the crucial big and doubtful states in the North. It has trouble persuading Republicans to run for Congress in the South; in the elections of 1956, 1958, and 1960, for example, it allowed 70, 95, and 73 districts to go to the Democrats by default. This weakness of the Republican party in the South is further shown by the facts that after the 1960 election it did not have one southern governor, and in eleven legislatures it had only 61 Republican members, of whom 42 were in North Carolina and Tennessee, while not a single Republican got elected in Alabama, Louisiana, or Texas. President Eisenhower's sending of federal troops to Little Rock wrecked new attempts to build up "lily white" Republican organizations in the South.[4] Several southern states have some persistently Republican counties, notably in North Carolina and Tennessee, but these areas have not appeared to be expanding.

There is no solid North. Only Vermont has been said to be dependably Republican, but it failed the party in 1958 and again in 1964. After the election of 1960 it had a total of 57 Democrats in its legislature; after 1964, 65. Republican governors and legislatures are usual in Iowa, Kansas, Maine, New Hampshire, and the Dakotas. Possibly Nebraska would belong in this list except that its legislature is elected on a nonpartisan ballot.

It would be a common-sense expectation that in the strongly one-party or modified one-party states a pattern of factionalism would develop within the dominant party which would be something of a counterpart to the two-party system elsewhere. There are, indeed, some examples, such as the Byrd and anti-Byrd factions in Virginia, and the Long and anti-Long factions in Louisiana; and sometimes a sort of subsectionalism—Piedmont versus Tidewater in the Carolinas, east versus west in Kansas, north versus south in Vermont—may be rather dimly seen. For most of these states, however, common sense lets us down, and the typical pattern of politics seems to be one of temporary, shifting factions following different leaders. The foremost student of the subject, V. O. Key, Jr., whose *Southern Politics* is the standard book, said that this personal factionalism might best be described as a no-party politics. In the welter of factions there is not the slightest approach to a system of party responsibility where the party stands answerable for the behavior of its nominees if they win;

---

[4] *Kenneth N. Vines*, Two Parties for Shreveport (*New York: Holt, 1959*); *also in Paul Tillett* (*ed.*), Cases on Party Organization (*New York: McGraw-Hill, 1963*), *pp.* 183–210.

instead, in the primary of the dominant party the voter must choose among the conflicting claims and extravagant promises of many candidates for office, all running on their own. The complexity of this factional politics is so great that for the South it cannot be described except in a long book.

THE BORDER STATES. John H. Fenton studied four of the states that lie between the North and the South: Maryland, West Virginia, Kentucky, and Missouri. Some writers would add Oklahoma to this group. Although the Republican party is strong and active in these states, they tend to go Democratic in most elections; they "lean Democratic," as George Gallup says. In the four states he examined, Fenton found the Democratic party divided into a Bourbon, or "gentry," faction opposing in the Democratic primary what he called a "common man" faction, made up of "urban Negroes, coal miners, urban workers, and yeoman farmers." These factions usually come together after the primary to oppose the Republicans in the general election, which "is commonly a war for patronage and contracts rather than a conflict of interests." [5]

NEW ENGLAND. The six states of the Northeast once formed a solid Republican section, but now there are two New Englands, an upper and a lower.[6] The three upper states of Maine, New Hampshire, and Vermont have tended in varying degrees to vote Republican; and Massachusetts, Rhode Island, and Connecticut have tended to vote Democratic. New England is unique among the sections in that the town is the principal unit of local government and politics; the county clique, the courthouse gang, well-known in most parts of the nation, is unknown or unimportant in New England; but this fact does not make New England politics smell sweeter—only different. New England politics exhibits a tension between Protestants and Catholics and between different ethnic groups (French-Canadians versus Irish or Italians) that has diminished or disappeared in most sections.

THE TWO-PARTY STATES. The positions of the major parties in the remaining states vary from those where either party may win any statewide office to those where one party or the other usually wins.[7] In all of the two-party states, each of the parties has a going organization and offers candidates for all or almost all of the statewide offices, whereas in

---

[5] *John H. Fenton*, Politics in the Border States (*New Orleans: The Hauser Press,* 1957), *p. 208.*
[6] *Duane Lockard*, New England State Politics (*Princeton, N.J.: Princeton University Press,* 1959), *p. 4.*
[7] *The states of the West, including newly admitted Alaska and Hawaii, are all two-party states. See Frank H. Jonas (ed.),* Western Politics (*Salt Lake City: University of Utah Press,* 1961).

some states in the Deep South the Republican party has not regularly even gone through the motions of nominating candidates for governor.

In the two-party states, however, there are one-party islands—cities or counties that always or almost always go Democratic or Republican as the case may be. The general tendency is for the cities to be Democratic, the rural counties and suburbs Republican. It has been estimated, in fact, that about half of the electoral areas in the United States are one-party. In these areas, whether they appear in two-party states or not, the voter has no real choice for the legislature unless he can exercise it in a majority party primary.

With some exceptions, party organization is strongest in the states east of the Mississippi and north of the Ohio and Potomac rivers. The Committee on American Legislatures of the American Political Science Association found in a survey that in the 1950's, "Party spirit and cohesion in terms of a reasonable degree of regularity in party voting on important measures and effective party organization within the legislature were indicated as strong in 12 of the 19 two-party states, as moderately strong in 4, and as relatively weak in 3." [8]

Some people who are familiar with a tight precinct-by-precinct, ward-by-ward organization such as Tammany had in its most successful periods leap to the conclusion that all parties in all states are so constructed. Actually, the farther West one looks, the looser the organizations appear. Don M. Muchmore vividly described the situation in California:

> In the East a man might well be the captain of his precinct for thirty years, know all the . . . voters in his area, together with their public and personal business, and be able to predict within 5 or 10 percent the probable outcome of any election in his own district. In California a precinct captain, if there is one, is fortunate if he has the same neighbors overnight. Because of this unsettled condition, an efficient and continuing precinct organization just doesn't exist. . . . In a sample Los Angeles County precinct over a 2-year period, 19 percent of the people had moved away, 3 percent had died, 3 percent had changed their party registration, and 17 percent had been removed from the rolls for failure to vote. . . . A 42 percent change in a 2-year period. . . . [9]

---

[8] Belle Zeller (ed.), American State Legislatures (New York: Crowell, 1954), p. 204.

[9] In David Farrelly and Ivan Hinderacker (eds.), The Politics of California (New York: Ronald Press, 1951), p. 87. The wrangling auxiliary groups in the California parties are described by Totton J. Anderson in Jonas, op. cit., pp. 69–91.

At the county level the Democratic party probably has a going organization in 2,500 of the nation's 3,050 counties. In some urban counties like Cook County, Illinois, or Hudson County, New Jersey, it is set up clear down to a block system. In some counties in Maine and Vermont, on the other hand, it is only a skeleton organization where it exists at all. And there are all degrees in between. Because of its weakness in the South, the Republican party probably does not have lively organizations in more than 2,000 counties.

A CONSERVATIVE–LIBERAL REALIGNMENT? In attitudes of conservatism-liberalism a certain sectional difference may be detected between the major parties, but no political terms are more slippery than these two. The Republican party tends everywhere to be conservative, although in Delaware and Pennsylvania it is more conservative than in New York or North Dakota. In the North the Democratic party tends to be the liberal party, but in the South, especially on matters of race relations, it is conservative. On certain issues, however, such as public power, the southern Democratic party is more liberal than much of its northern wing. In the two states that elect their legislatures on nonpartisan ballots, Nebraska and Minnesota, it is said that the voting in the houses tends to divide along conservative versus liberal lines, and that the conservatives are mostly Republicans; the liberals, Democrats. Any of the generalizations on this legislative behavior, however, are bound to be based upon personal judgments, particularly upon what constitutes conservatism or liberalism.

The conservative attitudes of many southern Democrats in Congress, which since around 1938 have led them to vote on many issues with northern Republicans rather than with northern Democrats, have made some people hopeful that a new sectional realignment of the parties could be brought about. Senator Karl Mundt and others set up a formal organization that tried between the elections of 1948 and 1952 to produce a new arrangement. Nothing came of it. Other people, devoted to democracy, have long urged in print and speech that our party system should be in fact more nearly a system, one that the voters could understand and in which they could record their choices.

In a lecture at Princeton, New Jersey, in 1950, Thomas E. Dewey, then governor of New York, poured scorn on such perennial proposals:

> *These impractical theorists with a "passion for neatness" demand that our parties be sharply divided, one against the other, in interest, membership, and doctrine. They want to drive all moderates and*

liberals out of the Republican party and then have the remainder join forces with the conservative groups of the South. Then they would have everything neatly arranged, indeed. The Democratic party would be the liberal-to-radical party. The Republican party would be the conservative-to-reactionary party.

The results would be neatly arranged, too. The Republicans would lose every election, and the Democrats would win every election.[10]

Our parties, like our society, are in a process of continual evolution. Little evidence is available at present to indicate the type of new alignment that Governor Dewey feared, though the Goldwater forces' capture of the national Republican party in 1964 demonstrates that the ambition to sharpen lines between the parties retains some vitality.

2. Other Components of Party Preferences

SOCIAL AND ECONOMIC CLASS. The history of American parties seems to show something of a relationship between class and party. The Federalist-Whig-Republican succession has tended, with some exceptions, to represent business, finance, industry, and large-scale farming. In other words, it has had an upper and upper-middle class orientation. The Democratic party since Jackson has tended, again with exceptions, to speak for city workers, recent immigrants, organized labor, and small farmers, particularly those producing for export. In other words, it has had a middle and lower class orientation. But any explanation of American politics based upon class breaks down before it can be carried much beyond vague generalizations, for three principal reasons:

Class, as an explanation of politics, is too simple to account for the facts. In the words of a contemporary French writer on political parties, Maurice Duverger, "The coincidence between party and class that is affirmed by the Marxists is valid only for primitive social classes that are undeveloped and undifferentiated; all progress in a class introduces into it diversities which tend to be reflected on the political plane and in the division of parties." [11] Religion is such a diversity.

Second, the whole constitutional and legal structure of the United

---

[10] *From the text of the speech, provided by Governor Dewey.*

[11] *Maurice Duverger,* Political Parties: Their Organization and Activity in the Modern State *(New York: Wiley, 1954), p. 238.*

States is hospitable to sectional or area politics, inhospitable to class politics. Candidates must run for office in wards, cities, counties, districts, or states—not in classes. These electoral areas, particularly the larger ones, rarely coincide with any kind of class, so that a representative may speak for the combination of classes that forms a majority—or that he thinks may form a majority—in his district.

Third, there is no general agreement upon what classes there are in this or in most societies. Different writers use from two to a dozen classes; some use income as the criterion of class membership, others wealth; some use social class (who associates with whom); and still others use combinations of these and other standards. Some treat American Negroes as a caste, not as a class. No scheme has proved satisfactory for the assignment to classes of important segments of the population, such as teachers, soldiers, or public employees.

Notwithstanding the unsatisfactory nature of class as an explanation of politics, we may make some general comments. The American people are not class conscious. When the matter is brought to their attention by interviewers for surveys, they recognize that some sort of class structure exists, and if they are given a set of classes on which they are asked to rate themselves, a great majority (60 to 90 percent) will select some sort of middle class. Politics in the United States is a vehicle of social mobility, as sociologists would say; that is, a person may rise in the class structure by means of a successful political career, or he may go down as a result of some political action or event with which he has been associated.

Since the beginning of public opinion polls in the 1930's, hundreds of surveys of political opinion have been conducted. When the replies of people who call themselves Democrats or Republicans were broken down by income level, there was until 1964 an invariable tendency for most of the prosperous, the well-to-do, the managerial—whatever the name of the class used—to call themselves Republicans. But in 1964 all categories showed Democratic pluralities. The lower the economic level, the greater the tendency of people to think of themselves as Democrats. Farmers, who constitute a steadily diminishing factor in national voting, may be thought of as a special economic group because of the chronic overproduction of American agriculture; they have been voting Democratic about ten to twenty percentage points more than they have been voting Republican. These surveys, of course, use national samples, and the results cannot be applied to any particular state, especially not to the one-party states.

If the major parties represented the same economic classes, it would be reasonable to expect that they would be at least roughly equal in their attempts to raise money for campaigns. But, in fact, the Republican party in the northern states can as a rule collect many dollars for every dollar the Democratic party can. Scores of investigations, the financial reports of parties, the common judgment of politicians and newspapermen all bear out the fact that the parties have been considerably unequal in ability to attract funds. It seems logical to conclude, therefore, that a substantial proportion of the groups economically favored in our society have been more attached to the Republican than to the Democratic party.

OTHER PERSONAL CHARACTERISTICS. With the development of polls and surveys, perhaps no branch of political science has advanced so rapidly in the last fifteen years as the study of voting behavior. A score of books and hundreds of articles have been written on the subject, and no more than an attempt to note the principal findings can be made here.[12]

More than half (53 percent, 1964) of Americans of voting age think of themselves as Democrats, according to George Gallup; 25 percent call themselves Republicans; and the remainder are independents, persons not affiliated with either major party. These independents have been shown in many studies to be those who know and care least about politics; in fact, the highest proportion of nonvoters appears among them. The party differences between men and women are so slight as to be negligible.

A tendency to vote Republican increases with the number of years of education, but the rate is so close to income or occupation scales that it is hard to separate causes. In 1964, persons over 50 years of age were about 10 percent more Republican than people under 30, and the proportion of independent voters was found to diminish with age. Families in which the head is a member of a labor union are strongly Democratic: 61 percent, 1952; 59 percent, 1956; 65 percent, 1960. Negroes, long Republican, changed in large numbers in 1934 and have not returned; in the three presidential elections (1952, 1956, and 1960) they voted Democratic by 79 percent, 61 percent, and 68 percent; their opposition to Goldwater in 1964 brought the total to 94 percent. Religion also makes a difference: Jews were Democratic in 1964 about 62 percent to 13, with the remainder independent. Catholics, long generally Democratic, were slowly moving Republican until 1960, when apparently about 6 million of them returned

---

[12] *In addition to the works already cited, see Bernard Berelson, et al.,* Voting *(Chicago: The University of Chicago Press, 1954); Angus Campbell, et al.,* The Voter Decides *(Evanston, Ill.: Row, Peterson, 1954); Angus Campbell, et al.,* The American Voter *(New York: Wiley, 1960); V. O. Key, Jr.,* Public Opinion and American Democracy *(New York: Knopf, 1961); Paul Lazarsfeld, et al.,* The People's Choice *(New York: Duell, Sloan and Pearce, 1944); and the files of the* Public Opinion Quarterly *and the* International Journal of Opinion and Attitude Research.

to vote for Kennedy. Protestants are preponderantly Democrats (about 43 percent as against 36 percent Republican, the remainder unattached).

CITIES AND SUBURBS. It has already been noted that city people tend to vote Democratic; it may be added that, in general, the bigger the city, the higher the percentage of the Democratic vote. The Republican national chairman attributed Kennedy's victory to the big city vote. In a survey of the results of 1960, the Republican National Committee reported: "A substantial loss was suffered by the Republican presidential ticket in the big cities. Of the 40 cities over 300,000, Vice President Nixon carried 14 to President Kennedy's 26." In seven important states, moreover, the big city vote carried the states: [13]

	Outstate Plurality	Big City Plurality
New York	498,523 R	882,189 D
Pennsylvania	306,698 R	423,024 D
New Jersey	36,978 R	59,069 D
Maryland	11,777 R	88,047 D
Michigan	244,880 R	311,721 D
Minnesota	17,682 R	39,700 D
Illinois	447,454 R	456,312 D
Total	1,563,992 R	2,260,062 D

The suburban vote in the North has, with some exceptions, tended to be Republican. In 1960, however, the suburban voters did not stand by the Republican party:

> The decline in the Republican vote in the big cities was coupled with a decline in their suburbs. In the nineteen areas studied the magnitude of the decline in the Republican percentage of the vote was about the same as in the city adjoining each area. There was a gain in only one suburban area, Kansas City. In ten areas the decline in Republican per cent was greater than the national average decline.[14]

3. Bosses and Machines

The term *boss* is one that Americans have added to the English language. Although the word is sometimes used as an epithet for any political leader

---

[13] *Republican National Committee*, The 1960 Elections: A Summary Report with Supporting Tables (*Washington, D.C.,* 1961), *p.* 16.

[14] Ibid., *p.* 20. Because of the peculiarities of the Goldwater campaign, the 1960 election may prove to be more representative of basic tendencies than 1964. The decline of 9 percentage points of the Republican vote in major cities (1960–1964) was greater than might reasonably have been expected.

the speaker dislikes, its difference from *leader* lies in the fact that a real boss governs through his control of the machinery of his party, and that he governs beyond the office, if any, that he holds. It was this irresponsibility of ruler to ruled that Elihu Root denounced as the "invisible government" of New York: "Then Mr. Platt ruled the state; for nigh upon twenty years he ruled it. It was not the governor; it was not the legislature; it was not any elected officers; it was Mr. Platt. And the capitol was not here; it was at 49 Broadway with Mr. Platt and his lieutenants." [15]

URBAN, STATE, AND RURAL BOSSES. In spite of the fact that we have had scores of bosses, we are at the moment short of conspicuous examples. Tammany Hall lies in ruins since the overthrow of Carmine De Sapio—though Tammany has been shattered before and recovered. The best-known of the contemporary state machines is the Byrd machine in Virginia, which *The New York Times* once called "the most urbane and genteel dictatorship in America." No doubt bosses take on the coloration of the age in which they live, and perhaps the successful ones are not anxious for publicity these days.

Among the state bosses of recent years, other than those already mentioned, have been Edward H. Crump of Tennessee, Huey Long of Louisiana, David C. Stephenson of Indiana, Boies Penrose of Pennsylvania, and J. H. Roraback of Connecticut. Others whose power over their states was never fully consolidated were Frank Hague of New Jersey, Joseph Pew of Pennsylvania, Eugene Talmadge of Georgia, "Alfalfa Bill" Murray of Oklahoma, Tom Pendergast of Missouri, and Theodore Bilbo of Mississippi.

Bosses come in all sizes. Mayor Richard J. Daley has often been referred to as the boss of Chicago, but each of the 50 aldermen is boss in his own ward.[16] The boroughs of New York City have and have had their bosses; a famous one was Edward J. Flynn of the Bronx, who in 1947 published a book about the boss business with the paradoxical title, *You're The Boss*. There have been unknown numbers of bosses of counties, such as E. Brooke Lee of Montgomery County, Maryland. A contemporary is Leander Perez, boss of two parishes (counties) in Louisiana, who made himself nationally famous by defying the Catholic bishop of New Orleans on desegregation of Catholic schools. Occasionally there are families of

---

[15] *Elihu Root*, Addresses on Government and Citizenship (*Cambridge, Mass.: Harvard University Press*, 1916), *p.* 202.

[16] *There have been many books on Chicago bosses. For one such account, see Martin Meyerson and Edward C. Banfield*, Politics, Planning and the Public Interest (*New York: Free Press*, 1955), *pp.* 64–75.

bosses, such as the McFeeleys of Hoboken, the O'Connells of Albany, or the Parrs, who ruled eighteen Texas counties along the Mexican border.

Just as there are state machines and big city machines—though not as many as there were—so there are rural and local machines. How many, no one knows; there is no census of them. The late Lane Lancaster made the following comments:

> It is safe to say that, in nine-tenths of the counties in the United States, public affairs are in the hands of what the irreverent call the "courthouse gang." This "gang" may be described as a more or less permanent group of elective and appointive officeholders together with private individuals whose business normally brings them into contact with public officials. . . . Whatever the geographical location may be, the courthouse is certainly the political center of the county. To it and from it run the tangled threads of influence and power, favoritism and discipline, by which the somewhat furtive gentlemen in power keep the "organization" intact. The doings of the gang are perhaps not so dramatic as the gorgeous pillaging of a Tweed or a "Doc" Ames, and they certainly have not had so good a press, but no veteran need feel diffident in the presence of his urban brethren. The mere fact that the stakes are smaller in the average rural county does not mean that the game need not be played with acumen.[17]

Every time some big boss dies, retires, or goes to jail, the newspaper headlines refer to him as "the last of the bosses," "the last of the great bosses," or "the last of the old-fashioned bosses." We may, of course, hope that the statements are right, for the existence of these domestic dictators contradicts what American democracy stands for. But in view of the long history of bossism and in view of the fact that the causes of the system are still with us, we might better hesitate before joining in obsequies that may prove to be premature.

CAUSES OF BOSSISM. Observers differ on the causes of bossism, but there is a rough measure of agreement. First, there is an observable tendency in all human associations for one or a few ambitious individuals to rise to the top, the "iron law of oligarchy" as Robert Michels called it. This centralizing tendency is particularly notable when a group like a political machine must make binding but secret decisions, or when it engages in some illegal or extra-legal undertakings. Second, all the constitu-

---

[17] Lane Lancaster, Government in Rural America, 2nd edition (New York: Van Nostrand, 1952), pp. 57–58. See also Lloyd Warner, et al., Democracy in Jonesville (New York: Harper, 1949), pp. 214–35.

tional and legal forms that make real party responsibility difficult or impossible make boss government easier. If real leadership cannot be exercised by and within the legal government, an extra-legal government may grow up outside. A boss may arise who can bring the separated powers together—who can within limits control governor, legislature, and courts. So Jim Curley was not disliked by all the well-to-do in Massachusetts; he was expensive, but "He gets things done." Third, the vast multiplication of the units of local government—there are some 90,000 in the United States —with the resulting conflict and overlapping of authority is so bewildering to the half-interested citizen that he makes no attempt to understand the labyrinth. The boss, however, needs to understand it, because he must utilize its possibilities for patronage; so for a brokerage fee he may produce a kind of administrative unity in what would otherwise be an administrative wilderness.

Other reasons are long ballots; short terms of office; the ineligibility of officials, no matter how successful, to succeed themselves; frequent elections; the complexities of the primary system; and the large amounts of money available to any machine that can offer protection compared with the inadequate amounts available to anti-organization or reform groups or candidates. Probably no single cause produces the boss and the machine. Rather, the natural tendency of some persons to rise to the top of any association may produce a boss in the right set of political and social circumstances.[18]

4. Interest Groups

The most complete knowledge about the operations of the parties and factions in a state is only part, and perhaps the smaller part, of understanding its politics. Limited as they are by constitutional and statutory requirements, our parties mainly pursue a politics of place and position and leave the politics of public policy to organized interest groups. It is policy rather than place, however, that touches the voter: it will not much matter to him who is auditor, secretary of state, mayor, assessor, or county counsel; but when the American Legion gets through a bonus that he has to pay

---

[18] *This analysis agrees with that of a leading American sociologist, Robert K. Merton, in his* Social Theory and Social Structure *(New York: Free Press, 1949), pp. 70–80. His examination of the functioning of the boss and the machine led him to state on page 79 what he called "a basic theorem," that "any attempt to eliminate an existing social structure without providing alternative structures for fulfilling the functions previously fulfilled by the abolished organization is doomed to failure."*

for, or when the Dairymen's League gets through a law or ordinance that increases his milk bill by 30 percent, it does matter. The weakness of party has been the strength of organized groups. William Allen White, one of the most astute of American political observers, saw this clearly and expressed his view of it vividly:

> *The fiction of one vote for one person is still maintained politely in high-school classes in civil government; but men and women who touch practical politics, if only obliquely, know that they now may have as many votes in government as they have interests. . . . [The ruling classes]* are those who use their craft societies, medical associations, farm bureaus, labor unions, bankers' associations, women's leagues, and the like to influence government. Of course, it takes time and intelligence, and a little money, but not much. For fifty dollars a year [in membership dues] the average family ought to be able to buy half a dozen powerful votes in government, each vote ten times as powerful as the vote guaranteed by the Constitution.[19]

THE NUMBER AND VARIETY OF GROUPS. In the capital city of most states, more than two hundred organizations with some interest or an exclusive interest in what the state government does will have their headquarters. Scores, even hundreds, of other organizations will send an officer or a delegation to town when something comes up that affects them. The process in local government is discontinuous: a county board or city council may go on for years without contact with any groups, and then suddenly some ordinance or other action will arouse the bird watchers, the religious groups, or the taxpayers to banner waving, picketing, petition signing, or whatever is appropriate. Alphabetically, the associations may range from the American Automobile Association to the YWCA, and the policies in which they are interested will range from alcohol to zoning.

Studies in northern cities indicate that there is approximately one formal organized group for each seven persons. Americans are obviously joiners. In spite of our vaunted individualism, our typical behavior when we want government to do or not to do something is to form an association, club, committee, council, league, society, or union—or to become members of an existing group. As individuals, most of us cannot leave our families and our occupations to go to the statehouse, the courthouse, or city hall to watch legislative matters affecting us, to urge the executive to

---

[19] *William Allen White,* Politics: The Citizen's Business (*New York: Macmillan,* 1924), *p. 15.*

sign or veto, to see that administrative agencies carry out laws as we wish, or to defend or oppose legislation or administrative rules in the courts. Instead, our combined membership dues and contributions go to hire specialists—lobbyists and lawyers—to do the work for us.

FEDERALISM AND INTEREST GROUPS. The federal structure has led most large interest groups to set up their organizations along state lines. Labor, business, veterans', and religious associations are examples. Under optimum conditions it is then possible for the groups to control on their chosen issues whatever party is in power, or on occasion, both parties. This, plus the discouraging effect of state election laws and the electoral college on minor parties, may well account for the vast proliferation of associations in the United States (there are some 300,000 of them). Almost every conceivable interest seems to seek separate representation, and if it could afford to do so would have a headquarters and a corps of lobbyists in the capital city of every state.

THE LOBBY. The terms *lobbyist* and *lobby* carry no odor of sanctity, but actually a lobby is good or bad, or neither good nor bad, depending upon one's interests and attitudes toward the group and its methods. Thus the Women's Christian Temperance Union and all the other organizations that go to make up what is often called the "dry lobby" regard the Distilled Spirits Institute, the liquor dealers' associations, and the rest of the "wet lobby" as being engaged largely in the work of the devil. The wets, for their part, believe that the drys are aiming to bring back Prohibition with all the evils of the speakeasy and the gangster. Whether an organization is good or bad, therefore, depends upon one's point of view. Whether its methods are reprehensible depends upon one's standards, which among individuals will vary from "any port in a storm" to "no good end can be reached in a bad way." And because certain lobbyists will never knowingly let any legislator hunger or thirst, we must not conclude that all lobbyists are ready to trample each other to pick up the check.

A more fundamental difficulty with the term *lobbyist* is that it ignores what is an increasingly important part of the work of the representatives of groups: following the administration and the courts. The Legion, say, obtains a statute to give veterans various preferences in civil service examinations, appointments, and tenure in jobs. But the law is far from being self-executing; in fact, civil service commissions will tend to make rulings inconsistent with it, and appointing officers will avoid it by a seemingly endless variety of devices. Instead of spending his days in the legislative lobby, therefore, the man for the Legion must spend his days arguing with civil service commissions, appealing for and staging hearings, registering complaints with personnel officers, and if these fail, fighting their rulings or decisions in the courts. Much the same sort of life is led by the representatives of the chambers of commerce, the teachers' associations, and many others. Although the word *lobbyist* does not cover these important activities, we lack one that does.

THE INVISIBLE GOVERNMENT. Difficult as it is for the voters, busy with their own affairs, to follow the activities of political parties, their factions, and their public men, it is impossible for them to follow the doings of two hundred or more interest groups. Not even the newspaper reporters can keep up with them.

Many of these organizations, however, are seeking objectives that are as clearly and exclusively political as are the objectives of the parties. Many of them seek (and obtain) laws or administrative determinations that touch every person in a state. But in spite of this public character of their objectives, few will reveal their membership lists, their sources of income, their expenditures, their internal politics and factionalism, or their methods. For these reasons William Allen White and others gave to the array of group politics the term Elihu Root coined for the boss system, "the invisible government." The term is appropriate, for a great part of their activities is unknown to the public.

PATTERNS OF INTEREST GROUP POLITICS. No two governments have identical sets of groups or identical group politics; some, in fact, are unique. The Mormon Church, for example, holds a position in Utah politics that no religious organization holds in any other state. Colorado alone has an old-age pension group called the National Annuity League that appears to be stronger on pension matters than either or both political parties. But in spite of differences, a few identifiable clusters of interests are influential in most state and local politics. Volumes have been written about these interests; all that we shall attempt here is to identify them and give a few specific examples.

Farmers and farm organizations have been active in politics since colonial times. The Proclamation of 1763, which shut off westward expansion, attracted farmers to the Revolution. From that date to this, farm groups have sought cheap land, low taxes on land, easy laws for debtors, good rural roads, and regulation of grain elevators, stockyards, and freight rates. There are about 30,000 farm organizations, some confined to a single state or to a specialized kind of agriculture, but the Big Four are the Grange, the Farmers' Union, the Farm Bureau, and the National Council of Farmer Co-operatives.

Labor too has been a force in politics since the organization of the first union in 1790. Although there are hundreds of unions, the great bulk of the 18 million members belong either to the C.I.O. or to the A.F.L., which have been joined since 1955 in an uneasy merger known as the A.F.L.-C.I.O. Union labor is reputed to be strongest in the politics of Michigan and strong elsewhere in the North, but weak in the South and West. Its concentration in the underrepresented cities strengthens its position in some of them but weakens its influence in the legislatures, even though it can tip the balance to elect governors in many industrial states.

Business and industry are everywhere active in interest group politics, although obviously the kind of business that is influential varies widely: insurance in Connecticut, finance in New York, oil and gas in Texas, and so on. No one organization speaks with authority for all businesses, although the broadest associations are the chambers of commerce. Some cities have business groups interested in the economic welfare of some particular part of the city; the Fifth Avenue Association in New York is an example. The rise of shopping centers and discount houses that are open on Sundays has produced in many cities a curious alliance between the Downtown Merchants Association and the Council of Churches to obtain or enforce ordinances that limit Sunday selling. Every state has some trade associations, such as the retail merchants' associations, that are necessarily active at the capitol, and every state also has businesses whose very existence depends upon licenses or franchises—utilities, liquor, horse-racing, for example—enterprises that are commonly supposed to be immersed in politics of every kind, at every level.

There are a dozen or more veterans' organizations, but the American Legion, with its two and a half million members and a post in almost every town and village, overshadows them all. It is the only one that is influential in the politics of every state. Its list of legislative and adminstrative victories—state bonuses, teachers' oath laws, veterans' tax preferences and exemptions, and many others—is more impressive than that of any other group.

Scores, perhaps hundreds, of the actions of governments affect religious bodies, from health regulations (such as vaccination and the fluoridation of water supplies) to the food served on certain days of the week to the inmates of institutions. Even more important, they are concerned with broad questions of public policy such as education. The principal religious groups therefore have representatives—sometimes a whole staff—in capital cities to make their wishes known to state officials. City councils and county boards are peculiarly susceptible to pressure from local religious organizations; to offend "the church people" is in many places a quick way to political oblivion.

Some two hundred professions, from architects to undertakers, are licensed in some or all states, commonly by separate licensing boards for each, and more professions seek licensing laws every year. The politics involved in getting the bills passed, obtaining satisfactory appointees on the boards, issuing rules, policing the professions, opposing other professions (lawyers versus realtors, M.D.'s versus osteopaths and chiropractors) is infinitely complex and never-ending.

Public employees, whether or not they are politically appointed, are an important interest in politics. They commonly have a large number of associations that work together, with the possible exception of the teachers' groups, which usually go their own way.

Even the governments within the states have their associations, such as the leagues of municipalities, to present their views to appropriate state agencies. It seems odd that the constitutional representative system appears to the local governments so inadequate that they must hire their own staffs and have an office near the statehouse. But the states, too, have their own organizations, such as the Council of State Governments, and some cities and states have full-time paid lobbyists in Washington. Thus the process operates in all directions.

In the politics of certain states, various racial or nationality groups are important, such as Negroes, French-Canadians, Spanish-Americans. And some other interests, like the League of Women Voters or a taxpayers' association, will be influential in still other states. But only the most intimate acquaintance with the politics of a particular state will enable anyone to describe with confidence its interest groups and their objectives. The situation, moreover, is extremely flexible: new groups form, old ones disappear, coalitions form and dissolve, and groups change objectives.

SOME UNSOLVED PROBLEMS. Essentially the groups are not responsible to the voters whose affairs they influence: the voters, for instance, do not select the officers of the state bar association, yet in more than half the states the association determines who may practice law. In fact, nonresidents, who cannot be reached by state process but contribute to or work in groups in various states, may influence public policy in most important ways.

Another problem lies in the inequalities among the groups: Some have millions to spend, others little; some, notably the bar, have many members in public positions, others do not; and still others, like the associations of newspapers, have special access to the channels of communication. And not all interests are represented; for example, children, the very poor, the chronically ill. Each state has a medical society, often very potent, but try to find a patients' association. There is always a state bar association, and often there are city, county, and district bar associations; but where is there a clients' association?

The secretaries and other officers of associations commonly assert that they speak "for all," or "for 90 percent" of the apple growers, veterans, mayors, or whatever the interest is. Actually they may not; perhaps fewer than 10 percent of the apple growers even know the organization exists. But as long as groups may keep their lists of members secret, no one can challenge their claims.

When any group influences government, however, then its own private government—its constitution, the conduct of its elections, who decides its positions on public policies, who pays its bills, and so on—properly becomes a matter of public concern. When a state turns over to a private group the administration of some law, as it does to the professional associations, for example, then the internal politics of the group are doubly affected with a public interest. The iron law of oligarchy works in groups as much as in parties, and there is every reason to believe that some associations are not little democracies but little dictatorships.

No state has even walked up to these problems, much less tried to solve them. About all they have done is to forbid bribery; 43 states also have some sort of statute, generally unenforced and often unenforceable, purporting to regulate legislative lobbying.[20]

BENEFITS OF GROUP POLITICS. Group politics has come to be as much a part of the political scene as party politics, and the groups do many good things that the parties cannot. They superimpose upon geographical representation a rough kind of functional representation; the parties, resting upon areas, are insufficiently refined instruments to represent the multitude of interests in society. Second, some of the groups initiate public policies and point out the need for legislation or administrative or judicial action. Third, they perform a critical function in examining bills, rules, judicial decisions, and administrative actions. Fourth, they seek to get candidates for office to express themselves on the issues in which the groups are interested, when often the candidates would much prefer to say nothing as eloquently as possible. If a candidate wins, some groups will try to hold him to his promises. Fifth, they may have an educational function, bringing information on the issues both to their own members and to the public. Finally, they help to overcome to some extent the difficulties inherent in the system of separated powers. Essentially

---

[20] Belle Zeller, "State Regulation of Lobbying," in The Book of the States: 1962–63 (Chicago: Council of State Governments, 1962), pp. 80–86.

nonpartisan and working on all branches, they may get a government to move that is constitutionally inclined to deadlock and stalemate. All these services, some people would say, are only part of the good that bad men do. But they are done, nevertheless.

5. *Conclusion*

Those interests that presently have things pretty much their own way are certain that our politics is the best of all politics in the best of all possible worlds. For them, any change would be undesirable. People who are not much affected, or who are unaware of being much affected, are also likely to resist change. The ancestor worshippers see something sacred in old state constitutions and laws, and no complaint about their operations impresses them; there was a member of the 1947 New Hampshire constitutional convention who got himself elected, he said, because he did not want one word in the ancient constitution changed—not even *shillings and pence to dollars and cents*. These and other conservatives will assert that even if things are perhaps not perfect, human fallibility is such that if we change anything we might do worse.

Most serious students of our politics, however, believe that it suffers from a basic and dangerous weakness: the inability of the majority of the people, through parties, to govern. In the words of the Committee on Political Parties of the American Political Science Association:

> *Either major party, when in power, is ill-equipped to organize its members in the legislative and executive branches into a government held together and guided by a party program. Party responsibility at the polls thus tends to vanish. This is a very serious matter, for it affects the very heartbeat of American democracy.*[21]

Today there is a high degree of agreement among specialists that improvement needs to be made in state politics, with two objectives: simplicity and responsibility. That is, statutory and constitutional changes should aim to simplify governments so that the voter can understand them and follow what they do; he should also be able to make an intelligent choice between broad alternatives of policy presented to him by different parties. The necessary corollary is that he must be able to hold answerable

---

[21] *"Toward a More Responsible Two-party System, A Report of the Committee on Political Parties of the American Political Science Association,"* American Political Science Review, 44 (*September* 1960), *supplement*, V.

the party that wins. Such a system is likely never to be fully attained, but some steps may be taken toward it; we may assume that no single political device will bring perfection and that no amount of sermonizing to voters on a more active citizenship will do it, either.

Many of the statutory changes needed have already been discussed in these pages, such as laws to give parties control of their own membership and nominating processes. Some statutes, such as those in the South that make a two-party system difficult, ought to be repealed. Any district system of representation is bound to produce some inequalities, but if the legislatures were half as devoted to democracy as they profess to be, they would of their own volition repeal the gerrymandering districting laws and attempt fair and honest apportionment. Most of the legislatures, however, have had to be prodded by the courts, and the federal courts at that, before reshaping themselves to ensure true representation of the people whose agents they purport to be.

A responsible two-party system in the states will not, however, be attained by statutory changes only. Constitutional amendments will be needed if we are to have representative legislatures, a less wide separation of powers, unrestricted reelection of satisfactory governors, a short ballot, and other basic changes.

☆☆☆☆☆☆☆☆☆

chapter 8

Legislators and Governors

In the making of state policy there are many participants, but the critically important ones are the legislators and the governor. The greater part of a state's policy is contained in its statutes and in its constitution. And it is the legislators and governors who enact statutes, propose and often even ratify constitutional amendments, and call conventions for substantial constitutional revision. Finally, the governor, in addition to his power to approve or veto legislation, can often exert considerable influence on policy through the administrative departments in the executive branch.

As policy makers, then, the governor and the legislators decide what *ought* to be. To be sure, they often reach the conclusion that what already is ought to continue to be. A single legislative session, therefore, never opens the whole range of state policies for reconsideration. However, moderate or small changes are regularly made in the prevailing policies, and there is always the possibility of major changes. This possibility gives hope to those who want the policies changed, arouses fear in those who want existing policies to stand, and provides a dramatic setting for those who work in the political processes.

In this setting, the legislators and governors play many roles. The legislators are counters for a continued recording of election results. They are actors in the rituals of civic conflict and deliberation who debate issues, initiate motions, raise points, ask questions. They are instructed delegates, directed to perform a hundred chores for their parties and their constituencies. They are men with notions, ambitions, and reputations to build, sustain, or repair. They are leaders or would-be leaders who anticipate the desires of others, or they are followers taking guidance from others—or, at times, they exchange these roles. They are members of parties, factions, and blocs. And, perhaps most critically, they are the ones who give or withhold consent to policy proposals.

A governor, too, performs roles that compete for his time and sometimes conflict, though a talented man can artfully blend these roles and alternate them for mutual reenforcement. If he wants the role, the governor can be the chief legislator, who proposes major policy measures and induces legislators to support them. He is formally, and sometimes truly, the state's chief executive, overseeing the administration of state programs. Often he is the leader of his party, though here he must counter bids from other powerful men. To help him assert his leadership, he may be able to control patronage appointments, influence the award of contracts for state printing, supplies, equipment, and construction, and reward or punish local political organizations by indicating which localities he wishes to have benefit from state construction projects. In addition, he can influence public opinion: more than any other state official, he has the opportunity to get his views before the public through the press, radio, television, and personal appearances. Much of the time he has no serious competition for public attention on state affairs, because the legislature meets infrequently and briefly. Furthermore, the governor is the official spokesman for the state in its relations with the federal government and with other states. His office is the magnet for mayors, heads of major interest groups, and others seeking support for legislative or administrative measures. It is also a port of call for groups of school children, whose teachers want them to meet the governor and hear him speak on civic virtue.

How well legislators and governors play their roles as policy makers is in part an accident of personal qualities, in part a product of institutional and procedural arrangements for policy making, and in part the fruit of the electoral and political party system. We shall in this chapter consider the legislators and the governor separately, though a state's policy-making mechanism (the subject of the following chapter) is so like a bicycle built for two that the potential for collaboration and for conflict can never be far from mind.

1. Representation in the Legislature

Precisionists in terminology distinguish between democratic and republican forms of government. The purely "democratic" form calls for all policy decisions to be made directly by the people—an arrangement now found principally in a few Swiss cantons and the surviving town meetings of New England. The purely "republican" form is representative government—an arrangement where the people periodically elect legislators who make the policy decisions. The American Constitution (Article IV, Section 4) reads, "The United States shall guarantee to every State in this Union a Republican form of government. . . ." and, in a phrase that has recently proved even more significant for legislative representation (Amendment XIV, Section 1), "No State . . . shall deny to any person within its jurisdiction the equal protection of the laws."

In practice the refinements of exact language are not observed—we freely speak of American government as one that is intended to be democratic—and the terms "democratic," "republican," "representative," "the people," and "equal protection of the laws" gain their meaning less from etymologists and political theorists than from the operation of institutions and from judicial interpretation.

Legislative institutions and electoral systems illustrate this most sharply. If proposed policy changes must pass not one house of a legislature, but two or (to be fanciful) three or four houses, does this depart too far from the essential idea of democracy or of a republican form of government to exceed our tolerance for inexact use of language? Must the representation system ensure that the legislature be a small mirror image of the electorate of the state, or, if not, how much distortion is permissible before the government ceases to be democratic, republican, and representative, as these terms are commonly understood? That such terms are inexact need not mean that they are infinitely elastic. A word, as Justice Holmes remarked, is but the skin of a living thought. "Democracy," "republic," "representativeness," express ideals to which most Americans say they are committed. Our inquiry therefore is not just a pursuit of terminological exactitude; rather, it is an examination of how far state legislative arrangements correspond to these important elements of the American belief system.

THE BICAMERAL TRADITION, THE UNICAMERAL ALTERNATIVE. American state legislatures have traditionally been bicameral. The only present exception is Nebraska, which has had a single-house legislature since 1937. Yet the only unique characteristics of state senators compared to members of the lower house are that there are fewer of them and that they speak for larger areas. And usually they have four-year terms, while the more populous house serves for two years (as does Nebraska's single chamber).

Why do we have two houses in all but one of our states? Imitation of the national government is probably the most significant reason, although colonial practice and early imitation of the English Parliament also had something to do with it. Soon after the formation of the Union some state senates had a class aspect, with property or higher property requirements being specified for members of the senate or for persons voting for senators, but these differences were wiped out with the spread of suffrage.

The fact that the Nebraska legislature consists of only one house is largely due to the efforts of the late United States Senator George Norris. In a well-organized campaign, he simply told the voters there that they would be better off with a unicameral legislature. That the plan was voted on in the Depression year of 1934 may help explain why the Nebraska voters were willing to challenge the uniform pattern.[1] A persuasive case, however, can be made for the unicameral state legislature on its own merit. With fewer total members, the prestige of each position in the legislature is enhanced, making these positions more attractive. And, with only one ring in the circus, public attention can be more easily focused on the legislative process. Shenanigans are more open to view, and responsibility —individual and collective—more readily determined. There is no need for a conference committee to settle disagreements between the houses in anonymity and without much recourse. The task of the executive and others having business with the legislature is simplified because there is only one house and the number of committees is perhaps half or less than half that in two-house legislatures. Finally, the single house should cost less; but legislative costs are so small a portion of the state total as to make this at best a flimsy argument.

The Nebraska unicameral legislature established rules and practices for itself that were designed to prevent hasty or ill-considered action and, in general, is reported to have conducted itself with decorum. One particularly noticeable result is that final decisions to pass or defeat bills are spread more evenly over the session rather than being heavily concentrated in its last weeks or days, as is common in most state legislatures.[2] A. C. Breckenridge's study of the Nebraska legislature after twenty years of unicameral operation reports much useful information about its organization and practices. However, on all critical points he found it impossible to distinguish the results of unicameralism from the results of the nonpartisan

---

[1] A description of the adoption of unicameralism in Nebraska and a statement of then current expectations by a participant in the reform movement may be found in John P. Senning, The One-house Legislature (New York: McGraw-Hill, 1937).

[2] Belle Zeller (ed.), American State Legislatures (New York: Crowell, 1954), chap. 4; and Richard C. Spencer, "Nebraska 'Unicam' Operates Smoothly," National Civic Review, 50 (September 1961), 424ff.

election system that was initiated at the same time.[3] But he did find that the unicameral legislature had left Nebraska's conservative fiscal traditions unmodified, and he seems to suggest that organized interests find this legislative body as easy to manipulate as does the governor, perhaps easier.[4]

A bicameral legislature offers more hope than the unicameral to those who see a need for state policy changes. The mental processes of legislators facilitate this result. If a bill can be got out of committee in one house, it may be possible to round up enough members for passage with perhaps the mental notation that if it is a "bad bill," the other house will stop it. And if attempts to persuade one house seem to fail, efforts to get the other house to move an identical bill may succeed. Once one house has passed the bill, its chances are enhanced in the second house. For example, if the senate passes it, some members of the house may hesitate to oppose it lest bills in which they are interested be stopped in the senate.

Thus it may sometimes be easier to get a bill through a two-house legislature than through a unicameral one. Where authority for decisions is more widely shared, it may be easier, in case of doubt, to say yes. And with many legislatures seeming to be unduly cautious or conservative, it may be unwise to make changes in organization which, by increasing the members' sense of responsibility, could harden their conservative bent. Although this line of interpretation is speculative, and would require substantial research for confirmation, it may serve as consolation to those who realistically recognize the probability that most states will retain bicameralism even though both houses must be apportioned by population.

REPRESENTATION AND MISREPRESENTATION: THE STATES' RECORDS. Legislatures, however composed, may give some attention to statewide issues, but this is less likely when the systems of apportioning seats, districting, and electing legislators greatly overrepresent some elements of a state's population in the legislature and underrepresent others.

It is perhaps symptomatic of the illness of democratic political institutions in the states that most constitutions have not provided for their

---

[3] A. C. Breckenridge, *One House for Two, Nebraska's Unicameral Legislature* (Washington, D.C.: *Public Affairs Press*, 1957).

[4] *Breckenridge reported the body unwilling to call a constitutional convention or to redistrict in accord with constitutional directions and changes in population. Subsequent to his study, however, the legislature and the people approved a constitutional amendment allowing area as well as population to be considered in determining legislative districts. The passage of this amendment freed the legislature from its earlier obligation to conform with a straight population requirement. Although it had not reapportioned seats since 1935, it did so in 1963 using the new formula. This, however, has run afoul of the Supreme Court's 1964 standard of substantial population equivalence.*

legislators to represent equal numbers of people. In early 1964 only 17 of the state senates and 20 of the lower houses were directed by state constitutions to be constructed basically in accord with population or number of voters. Thus for over half the legislative bodies, the state constitutions specified other standards, such as at least one seat for each county or town, or they fixed legislative district boundaries without relation to population.[5] Mixtures of population and other criteria have been common, and these usually operate to give population a minor weight in determining seats. In addition, the legislatures themselves have often neglected their constitutional obligation to reapportion seats, with the effect that shifts in population have not been followed by changes in representation.

The results of these vagaries are widespread, but some of the statistical consequences have become well known. One approach to measuring the representativeness of state legislative bodies is to compute the percentage of a state's population, cumulating from the smallest population district upward, that could elect a majority of a state legislative body.[6] If nearly 50 percent of the population is needed to provide such a legislative majority, the body is substantially representative in relation to population. The smaller the population percentage figure, the less representative the legislative body is in terms of population. Columns (1) and (2) of Table 8.1 show the percentages for every state as of mid-1964. The state legislative bodies falling in the top and bottom fifths in terms of representativeness by this measure are ranked in Table 8.2. We find there that Oregon is the only state whose two houses both fall in the top fifth, while Florida has the dubious distinction of having extreme unrepresentativeness in both its houses.

Another way to measure representativeness is to compare the largest and smallest numbers of people represented by members of the same

---

[5] The Book of the States: 1964–65 (*Chicago: Council of State Governments*, 1964), *pp. 62–66. The data are for January, 1964. Gordon E. Baker*, State Constitutions: Reapportionment (*New York: National Municipal League, 1960*) *analyzes the terms and operation of the provisions in force at the time of his study. Tables conveniently classifying state senates and houses by bases of representation in January, 1962, appear in Glendon Schubert* (ed.), Reapportionment (*New York: Scribner's, 1965*), *pp. 67–76.*

[6] *Manning J. Dauer and Robert G. Kelsay, "Unrepresentative States," National Municipal Review, 24 (December 1955), 571–87. For mid-1966 state-by-state data on the percentage of the population that can elect a majority of each legislative house, see Congressional Quarterly Weekly Report, 24 (June 17, 1966), pp. 1288f. These data reflect the flurry of reapportionment actions since 1962 and especially 1964 Supreme Court decisions. Many of these actions are temporary or are being challenged in the courts, and a number of states will need to reapportion again.*

legislative body. In the early 1960's, one California senator, for example, represented over 6 million people, while at the other extreme, another one represented only about 14,000. In the Vermont house of representatives, one member represented 25,531 people, while another spoke perhaps as loudly and certainly voted with equivalent effect though he represented only 38. In other words, in California each of the voters in the least populous senatorial district had a weight in the legislature that was 420 times as great as that of each voter in the least populous district; for Vermont the corresponding ratio was 935 to 1. A related measure involves comparing the largest and smallest constituencies not to each other but to the average population per legislative seat (i.e., by dividing the state's population by the number of members of the legislative body). This approach can be elaborated by working out the actual deviations from the average by the two extremes or by the population of every legislator's constituency, and then computing the average deviation for the whole house or senate.

None of the measures is wholly satisfactory.[7] The minimum percentage of the state's population that could elect a majority of the members of a legislative body is a useful index of representativeness, but it is theoretical in character, as the constituencies of all the least populous districts do not necessarily choose legislators of the same party nor do they choose legislators who, crossing party lines, will regularly, or even on major questions, vote together. Much less satisfactory, except for shock value in dramatizing the issue of representativeness, is the contrast of the two legislators from the largest and smallest constituencies. This particular disparity in representation could be insignificant if all or most of the other members came from constituencies with populations close to the average number indicated by dividing total state population by number of legislative seats. Furthermore, if a state corrected merely the two extreme cases, it would improve the apparent representativeness of its legislature by this measure, without in fact materially altering it. The method of measuring deviations from the average for every legislative seat is revealing within the individual state, but state-to-state comparisons become complicated because the significance of different distribution patterns has to be weighted. (For example, which is less representative: a state legislative body most of whose seats deviate slightly from the average, but some of which are extreme

---

[7] A *variety of alternative statistical techniques are reviewed and appraised in* Hayward R. Alker, Jr., *and Bruce M. Russett, "On Measuring Inequality,"* Behavioral Science, 9 (July 1964), 207–18. *See also Glendon Schubert and Charles Press,* "Measuring Malapportionment," American Political Science Review, 58 (June 1964), 302–27, *and as corrected in December 1964, at 966–70.*

Table 8.1. *Representativeness of State Legislative Bodies*

State	Minimum % of State Population That Can Elect Majority of Senate or House (June 1964)		Relative Equality of Representational Unit Populations (March 1962)		Fair Apportion-ment Score (March 1962)
	Senate (1)	*House* (2)	*Senate* (3)	*House* (4)	*State legislature* (5)
Alabama	27.6%	37.9%	.47	.55	12.3
Alaska	41.9	47.3	.52	.67	50.4
Arizona	12.8	46.0	.35	.65	39.6
Arkansas	43.8	33.3	.81	.70	69.2
California	10.7	44.7	.29	.71	20.2
Colorado	33.0	45.1	.63	.65	54.7
Connecticut	32.0	12.0	.63	.39	27.4
Delaware	22.4	18.5	.55	.48	50.6
Florida	15.2	26.9	.42	.44	17.3
Georgia	48.3	22.2	.45	.43	−4.9
Hawaii	18.1	38.4	.53	.71	62.6
Idaho	16.6	44.0	.45	.63	45.1
Illinois	28.7	39.9	.61	.75	47.2
Indiana	40.5	47.6	.73	.69	69.8
Iowa	38.9	44.8	.58	.55	15.0
Kansas	47.8	19.4	.48	.51	11.5
Kentucky	46.6	44.8	.67	.58	13.9
Louisiana	33.0	33.1	.62	.58	40.4
Maine	46.9	39.7	.74	.75	73.2
Maryland	14.2	42.3	.47	.55	30.5
Massachusetts	44.6	45.3	.86	.75	80.4
Michigan	29.0	44.0	.60	.69	44.1
Minnesota	40.1	34.5	.53	.50	1.8
Mississippi	37.2	41.2	.66	.56	42.4
Missouri	47.8	20.3	.73	.54	46.2
Montana	16.1	40.8	.43	.71	46.8
Nebraska*	43.9	—	.68	—	80.9
Nevada	8.0	29.1	.33	.53	25.3

(*Table 8.1. continued*)

State	Minimum % of State Population That Can Elect Majority of Senate or House (June 1964)		Relative Equality of Representational Unit Populations (March 1962)		Fair Apportionment Score (March 1962)
	Senate (1)	*House* (2)	*Senate* (3)	*House* (4)	*State legislature* (5)
New Hampshire	45.3%	43.9%	.76	.70	88.0
New Jersey	19.0	46.5	.54	.74	60.2
New Mexico	14.0	42.0	.39	.63	23.7
New York	41.8	34.7	.76	.68	69.2
North Carolina	47.6	27.1	.67	.64	58.3
North Dakota	31.9	40.2	.61	.65	39.3
Ohio	44.8	29.4	.79	.67	90.3
Oklahoma	44.5	32.5	.45	.56	11.9
Oregon	47.8	48.1	.77	.81	89.0
Pennsylvania	43.4	42.7	.65	.73	70.8
Rhode Island	18.1	46.5	.51	.63	42.3
South Carolina	23.3	46.0	.51	.84	56.4
South Dakota	38.4	38.6	.66	.76	62.7
Tennessee	44.5	39.7	.62	.61	71.8
Texas	30.3	38.7	.56	.65	40.0
Utah	21.3	33.3	.60	.67	73.4
Vermont	47.0	11.9	.79	.33	46.9
Virginia	41.1	40.5	.68	.65	43.8
Washington	33.9	35.3	.68	.73	62.6
West Virginia	46.7	40.6	.74	.75	67.2
Wisconsin	48.4	45.4	.80	.75	58.5
Wyoming	24.1	46.5	.59	.71	62.3

* Unicameral legislature.

SOURCE: Columns 1 and 2, National Municipal League, "Comparative Data on the Composition of State Legislative Districts of 1964 or To Go into Effect in 1965 Sessions" (mimeographed, New York, June 16, 1964); columns 3, 4, and 5, Glendon Schubert and Charles Press, "Measuring Malapportionment," *American Political Science Review*, 58 (June 1964), 302–27, at 320–22, 325ff, as corrected in December 1964, at 966–70.

Table 8.2. *State Legislative Bodies, Ranked by Minimum Percent of*
Population That Can Elect Majority of Members, June 1964

Most Representative

Senate	House
(Range: 50.1–45.3%)	(Range: 48.1–44.8%)

1. Kansas	1. Oregon
2. Georgia	2. Hawaii
3, 4. Missouri, Oregon	3. Alaska
5. Vermont	4, 5, 6. New Jersey, Rhode Island, Wyoming
6. Maine	7, 8. Arizona, South Carolina
7. West Virginia	9. Massachusetts
8. Kentucky	10. Kentucky
9. Ohio	
10. New Hampshire	

Least Representative

Senate	House
(Range: 21.3–8.0%)	(Range: 27.6–11.9%)

41. South Carolina	40. Delaware
42. New Jersey	41. North Carolina
43. Rhode Island	42. New Mexico
44. Idaho	43, 44. Iowa, Florida
45. Montana	45. Georgia
46. Florida	46. Missouri
47. Maryland	47. Kansas
48. Arizona	48. Connecticut
49. California	49. Vermont
50. Nevada	

SOURCE: National Municipal League, "Comparative Data on the Composition of State Legislative Districts of 1964 or To Go into Effect in 1965 Sessions" (mimeographed, New York, June 16, 1964).

deviations, or one with no extreme deviations but a number of seats that are considerably over or under the average?)

The fact that legislation must pass both houses of a bicameral legislature tends to be ignored by statistical approaches that make separate comparisons of state senates and state houses of representatives. A poorly representative senate can block the wishes of an admirably representative house. Yet, because the senate also depends on the house for legislation wanted by senators (and depends, too, on the governor who is elected by the whole state), there is room for bargaining in which spokesmen for the majority of the state's population can achieve some modest victories. Entirely different is the legislative situation where neither house is so apportioned as to respond to majority wishes.

An important effort by Glendon Schubert and Charles Press [8] to meet a number of the difficulties apparent in simple statistical comparison among legislative bodies has yielded a classification of the house and senate of each state by the degree to which it approaches perfect representativeness. This is based on calculating the variation from such representativeness for every legislative seat of each chamber. These data are then averaged to provide a measure of each chamber's relative equality of representative unit populations. The figures for each legislative body in March, 1962, are shown in Table 8.1, columns 3 and 4. For convenience, Table 8.3 ranks the most and least representative bodies in accordance with this index.[9]

The same authors have rated the states on a more complex basis. They introduce such considerations as the greater weight to be given underrepresentation of large numbers of people as compared with overrepresentation of a few; the greater representativeness where most districts fall close to the ideal (that is, the average population found by dividing the state population by the number of legislative seats) compared with a situation in which many districts tend toward the extremes of overrepresentation and underrepresentation; and the inappropriateness of treating both chambers of a bicameral legislature as equal in weight (they regard the senate as the weightier of the two, because it shares in the governor's appointment power and because the senators' longer terms and larger constituencies tend to give them greater political influence). Taking such factors into

---

[8] *Schubert and Press, op. cit.*

[9] *Tables 8.2 and 8.3 are both confined to the top and bottom fifths of the 50 senates and 49 houses. Differences between the two tables are accounted for largely by the two different measures applied. However, it should be noted (a) that some differences may stem from the two different dates of the data (March, 1962 and June, 1964, during a period of considerable reapportionment activity) and (b) that some differences are nominal (not only may variation in the order of a particular body within the top or bottom fifth be less significant than the fact that it falls within the same fifth in both tables, but some bodies included in one table may barely miss inclusion in the other (e.g., Massachusetts' senate and house both appear in the top fifth in Table 8.3, but only the house appears in the top fifth in Table 8.2, the senate barely failing to do so because it ranks twelfth instead of among the top ten).*

Table 8.3. *State Legislative Bodies, Ranked According to Extent to Which Equal Populations Are Actually Represented by Legislators, March 1962*

Most Representative	
Senate (Range: .86–.74)	*House* (Range: .84–.74)
1. Massachusetts	1. South Carolina
2. Arkansas	2. Oregon
3. Wisconsin	3. South Dakota
4. Ohio	4. Massachusetts
5. Vermont	5. Illinois
6. Oregon	6. Wisconsin
7. New York	7. Maine
8. New Hampshire	8. West Virginia
9. West Virginia	9. Pennsylvania
10. Maine	10. New Jersey

Least Representative	
Senate (Range: .46–.29)	*House* (Range: .55–.33)
41. Alabama	40. Iowa
42. Georgia	41. Missouri
43. Idaho	42. Nevada
44. Oklahoma	43. Kansas
45. Montana	44. Minnesota
46. Florida	45. Delaware
47. New Mexico	46. Georgia
48. Arizona	47. Florida
49. Nevada	48. Connecticut
50. California	49. Vermont

SOURCE: Glendon Schubert and Charles Press, "Measuring Malapportionment," *American Political Science Review*, 58 (June 1964), 302–27, at 320–22, as corrected in December 1964, at 966–70.

account, a "fair apportionment score" was developed for each of the states: it is shown in column 5 of Table 8.1. By this measure, the most and least fairly apportioned state legislatures as of March, 1962, were as follows:

Most Representative (Range: 90.3–69.8)	**Least Representative** (Range: 23.7– –4.9)
1. *Ohio*	41. *New Mexico*
2. *Oregon*	42. *California*

3. *New Hampshire*
4. *Nebraska*
5. *Massachusetts*
6. *Utah*
7. *Maine*
8. *Tennessee*
9. *Pennsylvania*
10. *Indiana*

43. *Florida*
44. *Iowa*
45. *Kentucky*
46. *Alabama*
47. *Oklahoma*
48. *Kansas*
49. *Minnesota*
50. *Georgia*

REPRESENTATION AND THE UNITED STATES CONSTITU-
TION. Until 1962, the question of how well a state legislature represented
the population of that state depended for its answer almost wholly on the
initiative of the legislature and its capacity to resist the initiatives of others.
That is, legislatures had reapportionment powers under those state constitutions that prescribed the population principle in whole or in part; and in
those states where constitutional apportionment principles seriously neglected population, the legislatures were assigned central roles in initiating
amendments or calling constitutional conventions. There were also, of
course, a minority of states where the people might use the initiative or
referendum to amend the constitution or enact a statute if the legislature
proved obstreperous. And in nearly half the states, the state supreme court
had reviewed statutes reapportioning legislative seats, but in most of these
states this was only a negative control on legislative initiatives. The court
could not force the legislature to take appropriate action, nor did it usually
venture beyond holding an apportionment act unconstitutional. For the
most part, then, legislators' consciences were their guide.

A major revolution in representation was initiated by the United States
Supreme Court's decision in *Baker* v. *Carr*,[10] on March 26, 1962. By a 6 to
2 vote, the Court held that a federal court can take jurisdiction of a
complaint that a state's apportionment of legislative seats violates the
"equal protection of the laws" clause of the Fourteenth Amendment. The
case before it had been appealed from a three-judge United States District
Court for Tennessee, which had said,

> *With the plaintiffs' argument that the legislature of Tennessee
> is guilty of a clear violation of the state constitution and of the rights
> of the plaintiffs the Court entirely agrees. It also agrees that the evil is
> a serious one which should be corrected without further delay. But
> even so the remedy in this situation clearly does not lie with the courts.
> It has long been recognized and is accepted doctrine that there are*

---

[10] 369 U.S. 186 (1962).

indeed some rights guaranteed by the [Federal] Constitution for the violation of which the courts cannot give redress.[11]

The Tennessee constitution provided that representation in both houses should be based on numbers of qualified voters and required the state legislature to reapportion every ten years. In fact, though, there had been no reapportionment for sixty years—since a statute of 1901, which, the plaintiffs charged, was even at the time it was enacted a violation of the state constitution's apportionment formula. Moreover, Tennessee was one of the states that did not provide for direct popular action via the initiative or referendum.

The United States Supreme Court reversed the district court's conclusion that the evil complained of (and which the district court had already said did exist) could not be tried in the federal courts. It held, instead, that a federal court can hear and provide a remedy where a constitutional claim is successfully made that an apportionment is so discriminatory that it "reflects no policy, but simply arbitrary and capricious action," and is thus offensive to the Fourteenth Amendment's requirement of equal protection of the laws. A concurring opinion by Justice Clark used more vivid language about Tennessee's apportionment: "a topsy-turvical of gigantic proportions," "a crazy quilt without rational basis," but he and Justice Stewart (also concurring) made clear their view that only extreme inequalities without rational basis warranted court intervention. Neither believed that the Constitution requires numerical equality of representation throughout a state or that it forbids the weighting of votes. The Supreme Court sent the case back to the district court "for further proceedings consistent with this opinion."

The Court's opinion, while holding apportionment controversies justiciable, gave little guidance to the district court or to other courts as to what characteristics warrant a finding that a particular state's apportionment denies equal protection of the laws, or as to how a court should proceed to remedy an unconstitutional apportionment. Furthermore, it said nothing about whether one house of a bicameral legislature could be substantially less reflective of population distribution if the other one did reflect it, a question much in doubt because of "the Federal analogy"—the bicameral Congress with equal representation of states in the Senate and popular representation in the House of Representatives. Other decisions about representation and equivalence of voting power followed, but while they could be viewed as straws in the wind, none was directly addressed to

---

[11] *Quoted in* Baker v. Carr, *at p.* 197.

representation in state legislatures [12] or clarified the standards of fair apportionment.

On June 15, 1964, however, the Supreme Court announced a group of six landmark decisions on state apportionment.[13] In the leading case of the group, *Reynolds* v. *Sims*, Chief Justice Warren spoke for the Court on the major principle: "We hold that, as a basic constitutional standard, the Equal Protection Clause requires that the seats in both houses of a bicameral state legislature must be apportioned on a population basis." Though acknowledging that "mathematical nicety is not a constitutional requisite," he wrote that "the basic principle of representative government remains, and must remain, unchanged—the weight of a citizen's vote cannot be made to depend on where he lives." What is required, as a result of these decisions, is "that a State make an honest and good faith effort to construct districts, in both houses of its legislature, as nearly of equal population as is practicable." The "Federal analogy" of the Congress was held inapplicable to state legislatures. Also irrelevant, it was held in the Colorado case, is the fact that in some states the voters have, by initiative or referendum, approved an apportionment scheme based on a principle other than population; "a citizen's Constitutional rights can hardly be infringed upon because a majority of the people choose to do so." Similarly, it made no difference whether an apportionment was embodied in a statute or in the state constitution; state constitutions as much as statutes must respect rights guaranteed by the federal Constitution.

Not all the members of the Court agreed with the decisions or with the Chief Justice's general principles. Justice Harlan dissented at length. Of the seven justices remaining, two, Justices Clark and Stewart, would apply less stringent tests of constitutionality, ones that would hold unconstitutional only those legislative apportionments that are completely lack-

---

[12] In *Gray* v. *Sanders*, 372 *U.S.* 368 (*March* 18, 1963), *the Court held that Georgia's county-unit system of weighting votes in statewide primary elections according to county of voters' residence denied equal protection of the laws. In* Wesberry v. Sanders, 376 *U.S.* 1 (*February* 17, 1964), *the Court held that attacks on state legislatures' districting plans for elections to the United States House of Representatives are justiciable and that there must be substantial equality of population among a state's congressional districts; in this case the Court relied on constitutional provisions for election of the House of Representatives "by the People" and for apportionment of the House's seats among the states according to their population, provisions which, of course, do not have relevance for state legislatures' own systems of representation.*

[13] Reynolds v. Sims, 377 *U.S.* 533 (*Alabama*); WMCA, Inc., v. Lomenzo, 377 *U.S.* 633 (*New York*); Maryland Committee for Fair Representation v. Tawes, 377 *U.S.* 656; Davis v. Mann, 377 *U.S.* 678 (*Virginia*); Roman v. Sincock, 377 *U.S.* 695 (*Delaware*); *and* Lucas v. Colorado General Assembly, 377 *U.S.* 713. *A week later the Court announced similar decisions, without opinions, affecting nine other states.*

ing in rationality or that are mere "crazy quilts" clearly revealing invidious discrimination against certain voters; they would permit some departure from the population principle, certainly in one house if not in both.

Two practical questions arising from these cases are: (a) What measures shall be applied in testing the states' conformity with the standard that the members of a legislative chamber should represent equal populations "as nearly . . . as is practicable"; and (b) how far can a state depart from exact equality of population without risking judicial scrutiny. In the cases before it, the Court relied primarily on two measures: the minimum percentage of state population that is theoretically capable of electing a majority of the legislative body and the population ratio between the most populous legislative district and the least populous one.[14] The Court had insisted that both senate and house must represent population. Many of the apportionment schemes were so far from this standard of representativeness that few would doubt their unconstitutionality. Virginia appears to have been close to the borderline, as a combination of districts with over 40 percent of the state's population would be needed to elect a majority of legislators in each chamber, and the extremes of large and small districts showed ratios (2.65 to 1 and 4.36 to 1 for senate and house, respectively) nearer to fairness than any of the six states except possibly Colorado.[15] Yet eight of the justices agreed that the Virginia apportionment was unconstitutional.[16] Subsequent court decisions will outline the bounds of tolerance for departures from the admittedly unattainable perfect representation of population.

The dramatic significance of the Court's decisions of June, 1964, was demonstrated by the reaction in Congress.[17] In August the House of Representatives voted in favor of a bill denying federal district courts

---

[14] *In some of the cases the Court cited other specific disparities between particular districts and counties and gave figures to illustrate the debasement or enhancement of the weight of a citizen's vote depending on where he lived.*

[15] *In the Colorado case, only the senate's apportionment was under attack; its population-variance ratio was 3.6 to 1 (cf. the house's 1.7 to 1), and about 33 percent of the population could elect a majority of its members (cf. the 45 percent to elect a house majority).*

[16] *Justices Clark and Stewart relied not on the strict equal-population standard, which they disapproved of, but on the standard that an apportionment must be shown to have a rational basis and must involve no invidious discrimination. In this particular case, Arlington and Fairfax counties and the City of Norfolk appeared to have been discriminated against even in comparison with other urban areas such as Richmond.*

[17] *The account of Congressional reaction to* Reynolds v. Sims, *and the roll call vote data, are drawn principally from the* Fall 1964 CQ Guide to Current American Government *(Washington, D.C.: Congressional Quarterly Service, 1964), pp. 53–57, and* Representation and Reapportionment *(Washington, D.C.: Congressional Quarterly Service, 1966), pp. 27–37.*

jurisdiction over state legislative apportionment questions and denying the Supreme Court the right to review any federal or state court action on apportionment.[18] The bill, however, having failed to get consideration in the Senate, did not become law.

In the Senate, the focus from the start was on initiation of a constitutional amendment that would permit states to apportion one legislative house on a basis other than population alone. Clearly, however, such a proposed amendment would have better chance of ratification from state legislatures still apportioned on the old bases. Delay of reapportionment by population was therefore an immediate strategic goal. Senators critical of the Court's decisions, led by Senator Everett Dirksen, attempted in 1964 to pass legislation that would forbid federal courts' entry or enforcement of reapportionment orders for a period of from one-and-a-half to four years. A successful filibuster by northern liberals forced abandonment of this mandatory-delay proposal and substitution of a mild measure that urged, but did not require, federal district courts to give state legislatures up to six months to comply with a reapportionment order. Even this measure did not become law, for the House failed to pass it. In 1965 and 1966, attention shifted from delay of court orders to the proposed constitutional amendment itself. In August, 1965, the Senate defeated Senator Dirksen's amendment.[19] Although after that defeat the amendment was redrafted extensively to attract support from some of its critics,[20] this milder measure

---

[18] *The vote was as follows:*

	Yeas	Nays
Total	218	175
Republicans	122	35
Democrats	96	140
Northern Democrats	12	124
Southern Democrats	84	16

The Republican platform, adopted July 14, 1964, included a plank urging a constitutional amendment and legislation "enabling states having bicameral legislatures to apportion one house on bases of their choosing including factors other than population." The Democratic platform, adopted on August 25th, made no reference to reapportionment.

[19] *A majority of votes favored the amendment, but a two-thirds vote is required for proposal of constitutional amendments. The vote was as follows:*

	Yeas	Nays
Total	57	39
Republicans	29	3
Democrats	28	36
Northern Democrats	10	33
Southern Democrats	18	3

[20] *The redrafted proposal, Senate Joint Resolution 103, was introduced by Senator Dirksen on August 11, 1965, and reported without recommendation by the Senate*

failed in April, 1966, to win the necessary two-thirds support of the Senate.

One reaction to the Court's *Baker* v. *Carr* decision of 1962 was a series of resolutions by state legislatures asking for the calling of a national constitutional convention to propose an amendment freeing the states from federal courts' prescription of apportionment standards.[21] Despite the goad of *Reynolds* v. *Sims* in 1964, this movement lost steam in 1965. If proposal by the states was not likely, ratification was even less so. More and more state legislatures had been reapportioned on a population basis. By one estimate, as many as 46 states would enter the 1966–67 state elections with their legislative districts based substantially on population. Few such legislatures could be expected to favor going back to the abandoned system, and ratification of such a move by three-fourths of the 50 legislatures had lost credibility as a political goal.

ISSUES IN THE REPRESENTATION DEBATE. Unless the Constitution is amended to undo the Supreme Court's rulings on apportionment principles, there can be no doubt that state legislative apportionments must henceforth satisfy the standards traditionally attached to the "equal protection of the laws" clause. On this point, eight of the nine

---

Judiciary Committee on March 4, 1966; the Committee split 8 to 8 on the merits (but 9 to 7 on reporting the bill), with 4 Republicans and 4 southern Democrats favoring the resolution, and 7 northern Democrats and 1 Republican disapproving it.

The resolution requires that each legislature ratifying the proposed amendment include one house apportioned on the basis of substantial equality of population. Section 1 of the amendment itself requires that each state legislature be apportioned by the people of the state at the general election for U.S. Representatives following the year of a decennial census. "In the case of a bicameral legislature, the members of one house shall be apportioned among the people on the basis of their numbers and the members of the other house may be apportioned among the people on the basis of population, geography, and political subdivisions in order to insure effective representation in the State's legislature of the various groups and interests making up the electorate. In the case of a unicameral legislature, the house may be apportioned among the people on the basis of substantial equality of population with such weight given to geography and political subdivisions as will insure effective representation in the State's legislature of the various groups and interests making up the electorate."

Section 2 requires that an apportionment plan go into effect only after being approved by a majority of those voting at a statewide election. "If submitted by a bicameral legislature the plan of apportionment shall have been approved prior to such election by both houses, one of which shall be apportioned on the basis of substantial equality of population; if otherwise submitted [i.e., by a unicameral legislature] it shall have been found by the courts prior to such election to be consistent with the provisions of this Constitution, including this article. In addition to any other plans of apportionment which may be submitted at such election, there shall be submitted to a vote of the people an alternative plan of apportionment based solely on substantial equality of population. The plan of apportionment approved by a majority of those voting on that issue shall be promptly placed in effect."

[21] *Under Article V of the Constitution, "The Congress . . . on the application of the legislatures of two thirds of the several States, shall call a convention for proposing amendments."*

justices of the Court fully agreed in 1964. Six of these eight agreed that the standards are more rigorous than those that would disqualify only those apportionments that are completely lacking in rationality, create a crazy quilt, "reflect no policy, but simply arbitrary and capricious action or inaction," or "prevent ultimate effective majority rule." [22] Instead, the standard is equal representation for equal numbers of people, without regard to place of residence, and this standard is applicable to both the upper and the lower house of a state legislature.

On the appropriateness of this standard and the consequences of its application, however, there remains ground for debate even among those without a special axe to grind. The "one-man–one-vote" advocates stand on a principle of democracy and representative government that to many seems incontrovertible. Without equal voting weights for individual citizens, a minority of the electorate may choose a majority of the legislature or even the extraordinary legislative majority necessary to overcome gubernatorial vetoes. This can hardly be said to be the "majority rule" that is the premise of democracy. This is clear when a majority of both legislative houses is normally elected by a minority of the electorate. But is it also true when a popular majority controls one house and a popular minority the other? "One-man–one-vote" advocates can see little or no distinction: minority control of either house is a denial of the democratic principle, and, in practical terms, the minority-controlled house can block action by the population-based house. That the reverse is also true—the majority-controlled house can block action desired by the minority-controlled house—does not really balance the scales, for the house of the minority is usually the more conservative body; its interest lies more often in inaction rather than in action.

The arguments the other way have a pragmatic rationality that is appealing. It can be easily demonstrated that virtually all governments, including those that purport to be democratic and representative,[23] have distorted popular representation in one or both legislative houses, and often in other parts of the government. The United States Congress, the electoral college, and the state legislatures themselves are obvious examples. Aside from this argument from political experience, it can be effectively reasoned that the fashioning of a government is a task of much

---

[22] *The phrases come from dissenting and concurring opinions of Justices Clark and Stewart (the latter contributed the phrase on systematic frustration of majority rule, citing the Tennessee circumstances as set forth in* Baker v. Carr).

[23] *Except the "pure" democracies where the people themselves adopt the legislative measures.*

intricacy; it involves not only the accommodation of majority rule, but also the assurance of political stability. Such stability is promoted by giving recognition to minorities that might otherwise become so frustrated as to resort to extra-legal threats against the regime. Furthermore, when the popular majority is concentrated in a small part of the total area and has great congruity of interests (as when the majority of a state's population is in a single major metropolitan area or a single city), turning over all state policy decisions to their representatives may mean the blatant overriding of the interests of people living elsewhere in the state.

Part of the genius of American politics, it is widely believed, lies in its pluralism—the multiplicity of avenues of access to decision makers so that no interest fails to get a fair hearing at some point in the policy-making process, which in essence is the negotiation and adjustment of conflicting points of view. This pluralistic feature can be seriously compromised, it is argued, if both houses of the legislature, as well as the governor, directly represent the same majority of the electorate. Those who hold this view also treat the statistical contrasts between popular and legislative majorities as a travesty of how decisions are made. The electorates of the least populous districts do not all vote alike. And legislators, once assembled, do not form coherent majority and minority blocs that vote together on all measures. Party memberships, urban-rural distinctions, and other favorite ways of classifying legislators do not hold firm; loose and shifting alliances are formed and dissolved as decisional questions follow one another. Perhaps this is why there is no empirical evidence that the best-apportioned legislatures give the best government. Massachusetts ranks near the top in apportionment by population, and Connecticut (or at least its house) ranks near the bottom. But the Connecticut General Assembly has the better record in considering urban interests.[24]

A major responsibility of state legislatures is to enact laws affecting local governments. There is something to be said, runs one line of argument, for letting each county or each town over a certain size have a legislator chosen by the county or town electorate. But this advantage is lost (assuming legislative bodies become unworkable over a certain size) when the population-equivalence rule forces counties and towns to be ignored when legislative districts are drawn or forces several of them to be combined into a single district.

Finally, a special case can be made for legislative apportionments that have been adopted by the statewide electorate acting by the initiative or

---

[24] Duane Lockard, The Politics of State and Local Government (New York: Macmillan, 1963), p. 319.

referendum. Surely that is democracy par excellence, even if in its wisdom a majority of the electorate chooses a scheme that precludes majority control of one or both legislative houses.

The two sets of arguments tend to pass each other by, neither engaging the other on its own ground. If the opponents of wholly population-based apportionment attempt to tackle the issue of principle, they find themselves forced to defend minority rule or at least minority veto power, and they confront the thankless task of proving that this is what democracy and representative government mean. On the other hand, if the advocates of population-based apportionment attempt to face the pragmatic case against them, they lose the advantage that the clarity of their basic principle affords. Neither they nor the pragmatists can specify standards for judging under what circumstances minority interests should be accommodated, which of the many minority interests deserve institutional recognition, or to what degree such recognition should go. And those who start from the equal-population position, even if willing to compromise, cannot accept the view that whatever any state constitution or apportionment statute provides (at least if not wholly irrational, arbitrary, or capricious) should be presumed to be a sound judgment of the appropriate way of accommodating the diverse elements in the state's particular social, economic, and political structure.[25]

WHO SHOULD REAPPORTION A STATE LEGISLATURE? Except for the House of Representatives' abortive vote to exclude federal courts from ruling on state apportionment schemes, scarcely any leading effort to undo the June, 1964, decisions aims also at undoing *Baker* v. *Carr*'s ruling that the courts can review existing apportionments and issue orders to bring them into conformity with the requirements of the "equal protection of the laws" clause. Instead, critics of the 1964 decision focus on what requirements should suffice for equal protection; in particular, they

---

[25] *A notable analysis of the reapportionment problem is in U.S. Advisory Commission on Intergovernmental Relations,* Apportionment of State Legislatures *(Washington, D.C., 1962). The commission, rather remarkably in view of its membership, voted that* " 'Equal protection of the laws' would seem to presume, and considerations of political equity demand, that the apportionment of both houses in the State legislature, be based strictly on population." *Six of the 26 members would have preferred to add the clause,* "unless the people directly determine otherwise." *Only four members (three U.S. senators and one congressman) dissented. Pp. 67–76.*

The most valuable post-1964 analysis is Gordon E. Baker, The Reapportionment Revolution: Representation, Political Power, and the Supreme Court *(New York: Random House, 1966), which is a major revision of his well-regarded earlier study,* Rural Versus Urban Political Power *(1955). Highly useful anthologies are Glendon Schubert, op. cit.; and Howard D. Hamilton (ed.),* Legislative Apportionment *(New York: Harper, 1964). Both of the latter two volumes include excerpts from the relevant Supreme Court cases.*

seek to permit representation in one house to involve elements other than population. This acceptance of the courts' role is an important concession. It appears to recognize the awkward situation that faces the many states under whose constitutions the task of reapportioning the legislature lies with the legislature itself. The primary responsibility is still there, but the courts are now a spur and, if necessary, a substitute for legislatures loath to act.

Three problems, it is well to remember, are involved in apportionment. One is the apportionment formula itself, typically embedded in the state's constitution and now required to conform to the Supreme Court's formula of substantially equal representation of population. The second is the periodic readjustment of existing apportionments among already established districts to take account of shifts in the distribution of the state's population. The third is the actual redrawing of the boundaries of legislative districts. The second and third problems are particularly difficult for legislatures themselves to deal with, and the nature of the difficulty needs to be understood.

Periodic readjustment of apportionments in response to population shifts involves increasing the representation from some areas and (unless the size of the legislature is increased) reducing the representation from others. It is the latter aspect that creates difficulties. Those legislators whose seats will be pulled out from under them by a decennial reapportionment are understandably unenthusiastic about seeing the reapportionment take place, and many of their colleagues dislike administering the *coup de grâce* to valued associates. Legislators from the sparsely settled districts in particular, even though they are not immediately threatened, recoil from speeding a process of which they themselves would someday be the victims. Furthermore, many from rural and small town areas feel that their kind of legislator is demonstrably superior to that elected from the crowded, polyglot, sometimes machine-controlled cities. Many feel, too, that urban legislators, if given legislative dominance, will show no understanding of the problems of the farming communities of the state. Even urban and metropolitan-area legislators may dislike the prospect of increased representation from their areas, lest their own prestige suffer from having to share their power as spokesmen for the local interests. Finally, members of the majority party are highly sensitive to the possibility that reapportionment will strengthen the rival party and perhaps even give it majority control.[26]

If such considerations move a legislature to forgo reapportionment at

---

[26] *The experience of the United States House of Representatives calls attention to a special factor influencing legislators' willingness to reapportion. If a legislative body's*

the end of one decade (even if this violates an obligation imposed by the state constitution), the fat is in the fire. For the pain of adjustment to a twenty-year movement to cities and suburbs from farms and small towns, or from one part of the state to another, will predictably be far more acute than if the adjustment had been made in two stages—one every ten years. In these circumstances a larger number of legislators are directly threatened by reapportionment, and some of them, by reason of their seniority and the legislative competence they have developed, will be among the leaders of the legislature whose cooperation is essential to passage of a reapportionment bill. When a legislature goes along this way for many decades (in Tennessee, it will be recalled, for over sixty years), the agony of suddenly facing up to reapportionment responsibilities may be too great for the legislators to bear.

It is customary to condemn legislatures that have long ignored their constitutional obligations to reapportion. But it might be fairer to condemn those that miss the first or second decennial opportunity and to concede that a legislature that has come to be a gross distortion of the state electorate cannot fairly be expected to lead the revolution against itself. Recognizing that it is politically unrealistic to expect legislators to practice hara kiri is what underlies the transfer of the periodic reapportionment responsibility to other state officials and boards, the inclusion in the state constitution of consequences (such as statewide election of all legislators) even more horrible for legislators to contemplate than the effects of reapportionment, and the intervention of the judiciary.

The actual redrawing of the boundaries of legislative districts is a task often, but not always, integrally connected with periodic reapportionment. Even with a result that provides districts of substantially equal populations, it is possible for the boundaries to be so drawn as to favor one party more than the other. Not surprisingly, this possibility for gerrymandering is eagerly embraced by the party controlling the state legislature.[27] It takes into account the geographic distribution of party preferences among the electorate and sees to it that the maximum number of seats are kept

---

size can be increased to accommodate additional members from areas of increased population, no existing member need lose his seat by voting for reapportionment (unless redrawing of district lines works to his disadvantage). But if the size of the body is constitutionally limited, or is already as large as desirable, reapportionment will deprive some existing members of their seats. The U.S. House membership reached 435 in the apportionment following the 1910 census (having increased every decade since 1790). The Congress failed to reapportion the House after the 1920 census and, to avoid such a failure after 1930, it established in 1929 a system of reapportionment that takes effect automatically if Congress fails to act.

[27] Where the two houses are controlled by different parties, either a "deal" must be negotiated or a stalemate results in failure to reapportion.

reasonably safe for the dominant party and that there is a maximum wastage of votes for the opposition. It is easy to condemn the practice, but again political realism might make one wonder more at failures to make the most of the opportunity presented. In other words, the behavior condemned can be expected as long as men are not angels, and neither exhortation to angelic behavior nor an appeal to the electorate to vote against the connivers is likely to avail.

The most readily available remedies are to provide constitutionally either for a reapportionment process that requires no redrawing of district boundaries or for some authority other than the legislature to perform the task. Two devices can eliminate the redrawing of boundaries. One is the use of already existing governmental areas such as counties, cities, and towns. Then legislative seats can simply be periodically apportioned among those areas according to their population. It is, however, more difficult to approach equality of population for each legislator using this standard, and if it is firmly applied, the more sparsely settled areas must be grouped in order to provide a constituency of sufficient population for one legislator. This scheme is also likely to mean that in a large city or other very populous area there will be several legislators to be elected at-large by the single constituency. The usual result is that they will all be of the same party, whereas if the area had been divided into electoral districts for individual legislative seats, some candidates of the area's minority party might have won election.

The second device, of a considerably more innovative character, would be to avoid both drawing boundaries and altering the number of seats assigned to an established governmental area. Instead, each governmental area would choose one legislator, and he would vote the weight of the number of people or voters he represents. For example, in the New Jersey senate, in which each county has one seat, the senator from a county with 50,000 people would have 1 vote, and the one from a county with 955,000 would have 19.1 votes. Such a scheme appeals to legislators from the less populous counties, since it would preserve their seats. The principal objection is that all 19 votes would fall to the party winning the largest county, whereas dividing the county into 19 senatorial districts would very likely result in each party winning some seats and would better reflect the electorate's views. The merits of the system, however, are unlikely to be tested, for attempts to introduce it in New Jersey and elsewhere have been blocked by judicial disapproval.[28] The problems of weighted voting in

---

[28] *The weighted voting system would be technically feasible where electric legislative machines are used, as such machines could readily add the weights of the individual*

committee action and of maintaining legislator morale in a house of un-equals also make the system unattractive to legislators.

In most of the states the constitution gives the task of reapportioning seats, at least in part, to the legislature. And in all states but Nebraska and Rhode Island, reapportionment of one or both houses is required in each ten-year period or more frequently. A few states have provided that if the legislature does not reapportion seats in a set period, it will be done by state officials—specifically designated officers, official boards, or an ap-pointed commission. In some other states the reapportioning function has been taken away from the legislators and placed in the hands of other bodies or officers—mostly ex officio. When elected state officers have this chore, the results, within the standards established, may depend on the officers' political alignments and their consciences. In many states the representation in at least one house is fixed by constitutional provision, so that the question of reapportionment responsibility does not arise, though it is now certain to under judicial prodding.[29]

The Missouri constitution of 1945 provided a novel, and perhaps seminal, method for reapportioning seats in the state senate. The state committee of each of the two major parties proposes ten names to the governor, who then appoints ten members (five from each list) to an apportionment commission to decide on districts that are within 25 per-cent of the population quota for a district. The commission is given six months to complete its chore; if it fails to do so, all state senators will be elected from the state at-large.[30] Perhaps similar evenly balanced commis-sions can best be trusted with this chore in states where the parties are competitive. And where parties are not significant, representatives of major factions may be the most suitable negotiators. But a bipartisan commission may be as subject to stalemate as are legislative houses and a governor not all controlled by the same party. Even the awful threat that in the absence of the commission's agreement all legislators will be elected from the state at-large may not avail. In Illinois a Democratic governor's veto killed the Republican legislature's 1964 reapportionment of the lower house and then a constitutionally required bipartisan commission could not reach any

---

legislators' votes. See Robert H. Engle, "Weighting Legislators' Votes to Equalize Representation," Western Political Quarterly, 12 (June 1959), 442–48, and Gordon E. Baker, State Constitutions, pp. 33f.

[29] The Book of the States: 1964–65, pp. 62–66, gives data on individual states as of January, 1964.

[30] A constitutional amendment adopted in 1966 provides a similar, but not identical, system for reapportionment of the Missouri lower house. Nominations for commission membership are made by the congressional district committees of the major parties.

decision. Consequently, in the fall of 1964 each of the 177 members of the house was elected by a statewide vote (on a 33-inch long "bedsheet ballot"!).[31]

The difficulties that political parts of state governments—legislatures, governors, and bipartisan commissions—encounter have led courts, both state and federal, to undertake actual redistricting. This goes beyond pressing the legislature to do the job and beyond approving or disapproving the plan adopted by the legislature or an appointed commission. Two kinds of judicial prescription of specific plans have emerged. One is actual court designing of a districting scheme.[32] The other is the legislature's adoption of a variety of possible schemes, among which the court is asked to choose the one it regards as satisfying constitutional standards of fairness.[33]

OTHER DIMENSIONS OF REPRESENTATION. The issue of equal representation of people wherever they reside within a state properly occupies the center of the stage.[34] Yet representation has other dimensions. There is a persistent myth that American legislators are elected almost wholly by contest between candidates of the two major parties for a single legislative seat. The facts are first, that close to half of the members of lower houses are elected from multimember districts,[35] and second, that in

---

[31] David Everson and Howard D. Hamilton, in Hamilton, op. cit., pp. 104–7. In 1965 a similar reapportionment commission in Illinois did reach agreement, by a 9 to 1 vote, on a house reapportionment plan. The New York Times, December 5, 1965, Section 1, p. 47. A Michigan bipartisan commission failed in late 1965 to redistrict the senate and house, resulting in referral of the matter to the state supreme court, which earlier had struck down the court's own 1964 plan. Ibid., January 2, 1966, Section 1, p. 52. But in March, 1966, the supreme court itself deadlocked and reinstated its 1964 plan until 1970.

[32] When the court itself takes responsibility for designing a particular scheme, it may, of course, appoint a commission, typically with a "blue ribbon" membership of prominent citizens not intimately identified with partisan activities. Illustrative is the New York Court of Appeals' promulgation in March, 1966, of a reapportionment plan drafted by a commission appointed by the court and headed by the president-elect of the American Bar Association. Ibid., March 23, 1966, pp. 1, 34.

[33] In Indiana the legislature passed eight acts, four applicable to each chamber, and asked the appropriate federal court to take its choice. The court selected the legislature's second-choice proposal for redistricting the senate and its third preference for the house. Ibid., November 21, 1965, Section 1, p. 17.

[34] Consideration of the possible major effects of the equal-population formula on state policy making is deferred to Chapter 16.

[35] Maurice Klain, "A New Look at the Constituencies: The Need for a Recount and a Reappraisal," American Political Science Review, 49 (December 1955), 1105–19; and Paul T. David and Ralph Eisenberg, State Legislative Redistricting (Chicago: Public Administration Service, 1962), p. 20. Computation of March, 1962, data in the latter study indicates that 21 percent of the house districts were multimember and 46 percent of the house members were from such districts, and that 7 percent of the senate districts were multimember and 16 percent of the state senators were elected from such districts. Overall, 19 percent of the legislative districts were multimember, and 39 percent of the state legislators came from these districts. See also Paul T. David, "1

scores of constituencies there is no contest, for the minority party fails to present a candidate.[36]

We have already noted that in a multimember district the whole legislative delegation is likely to be of one party, however large the minority vote achieved by the other party.[37] Illustrative is Cuyahoga County (Cleveland), Ohio, which until a 1965 reapportionment scheme prescribed single-member districts, elected 17 representatives at-large. People whose preference lies with the minority party may well feel that somehow representation according to numbers of people has been seriously compromised, even though such a county's allocation of seats may conform to the Supreme Court's equal-population formula.

Nonetheless, whose advantage is served by single-member districts and whose by multimember districts is not always easy to discern. Consider the interest of Negroes and whites in maximizing their respective influence on southern state legislation. In urbanized areas entitled to several representatives, a division into single-member districts would, because of residential segregation, almost certainly produce predominantly Negro and predominantly white districts. Whose advantage is thus served? At first blush it appears that the Negroes gain by their ability to send men of their own race to the legislature. This probably explains why Negroes have tended to favor single-member districts and segregationist and conservative whites to favor making the whole county or city a multimember district that, assuming white voters are a majority of the electorate, can send an all-white delegation to the legislature. But sophisticated assessment of the situation by some Negroes in Dade County (Miami), Florida, suggests an alternative calculation of advantage.[38] By this reckoning, single-member white districts would tend to elect highly conservative, segregationist white

---

Member vs. 2, 3, 4, or 5," *National Civic Review,* 55 (*February* 1966), 75–81. *See also* Representation and Reapportionment (*Washington, D.C.: Congressional Quarterly Service,* 1966), *pp.* 25, 65.

[36] *The proportion of uncontested seats varies greatly by state. In* 1948 *elections the percentage figure for the lower house was* 4.7 *percent for Connecticut,* 5.0 *percent for Indiana,* 18.5 *percent for Ohio (but* 32.1 *percent of single-member districts only),* 21.4 *percent for Missouri,* 31 *percent for Iowa, and counting only single-member districts,* 42 *percent for Massachusetts.* V. O. Key, Jr., American State Politics: An Introduction (*New York: Knopf,* 1956), *p.* 190. *In Kansas, uncontested seats rose to* 71 *percent of house seats in one election and in the senate to* 63 *percent; the Kansas average for elections during the* 1940–62 *period was* 34 *percent of house seats and* 28 *percent of senate seats.* Earl A. Nehring, "Party Competition in Kansas State Elections," *Your Government* (*Lawrence, Kan.: University of Kansas*), 18 (*Oct.* 15, 1962), 1–3. *In recent years the national party organizations have encouraged competition for these offices wherever possible, with significant effect.*

[37] *Illinois, because of a system of cumulative voting, is a conspicuous exception.*

[38] *Paul T. David, op. cit., p.* 76, *drawing on a paper by Manning J. Dauer for the Dade County analysis.*

legislators. But the county's at-large delegations of 14 house members and 2 senators (as of 1965) tend to vote as liberals in the legislature, presumably because in a competitive at-large election the Negro vote weighs heavily in determining who wins legislative seats. The gain in influence on state policy may be more to be valued in the long run than the symbolism of according a few Negroes the dignity of membership in the state legislature.

Where elections are uncontested because only one party puts up a candidate, the people are obviously deprived of a choice.[39] In particular, the members of the minority party, independents, and disgruntled members of the majority party are left without the beginning of an opportunity for legislative representation of their views. If we add to such uncontested districts those where candidates of the minority party, though formally entered in the race, never have a chance of winning, we get a picture that corrects a widespread misconception. States are usually classified as two-party competitive states on the basis of statewide elections (for example, for governor, other state executives, United States senator, and presidential electors) or on the basis of closeness of party divisions in the legislature. On closer inspection, however, some of the states so classified turn out to be in considerable part simply aggregates of one-party districts; only the fact that some districts are dominated by one party and some by another accounts for the state's overall appearance of competitive politics.

Perhaps members of the minority party in a district that offers them no candidate to vote for can take comfort in feeling that their interests are indirectly represented by some other district's legislator who belongs to their party. This, however, depends upon the similarity of the districts (for example, urban or rural) and also on the individuals' capacity for sublimating their frustrations as citizens of their own communities.[40]

-----

[39] *The fact that voters may be able to make a choice in the dominant party's primary is rarely a satisfactory answer; it is likely to exclude members of the minority party (though this varies by state election laws) and to make candidacies turn on personality and fluid factionalism, with little clear identification of candidates with policy issues.*

[40] *The significance of uncontested legislative-seat elections deserves a closer examination than can be given here. (1) Various changes (for example, in the South, in mobility of population, and in the sophistication of parties' strategy and tactics) are probably causing a decline in the proportion of no-contest elections, but its current rate and long-term potential require investigation. (2) As noted below in this chapter, an increase in party responsibility and two-party competition in the legislature seems closely associated with "a sorting out of legislative constituencies so that the districts represented by the respective parties are more homogeneous" and distinct from the kind of constituencies that choose the opposition party's legislators (Thomas A. Flinn, "Party Responsibility in the States: Some Causal Factors,"* American Political Science Review,

2. The Legislators

Almost 8,000 men and women are elected to the state legislatures of the country, roughly 6,000 to serve in the lower houses and 2,000 to serve in the senates. In other words, it takes about fifteen times as many legislators to make the laws of the states as it does to make the laws of the nation. Some may think this is too many. Others may question whether existing political processes ensure that enough able people offer themselves to the electorate, that the best legislators continue to serve, and that the legislators, even if elected from equal districts, are truly representative of the people of the state.

HOW BIG SHOULD A LEGISLATIVE BODY BE? No state senate is as large as the United States Senate, and no state has a lower house as large as the United States House of Representatives. State senates average about 40 members, with extremes of 20 and 67. Lower houses range from 35 to 400, the average being about 120.[41] Though some of the smallest legislative bodies are in states of small population, the implied converse does not always hold. New Hampshire has the largest lower house, with 400 members; the largest state senate is Minnesota's, with 67 members. There is some tendency toward decreasing the size and some argument among professional reform groups for encouraging this tendency. But most of the states have not been impressed by it. Reconstruction of the legislatures under pressure from the federal courts may, however, result in some adjustment of size; this is particularly likely among the larger ones, whose size partly reflects an effort to give every county or town at least one representative.

Many criteria have been asserted with regard to the size of legislative bodies, but they lead to no clear prescription. When the election districts

---

58 [March 1964], 71). Though the implications are startling, investigation is needed into whether such distinctive homogeneity of a party's legislative constituencies is aided by a state's having a large number of truly competitive election districts rather than by each party's having a large number of "safe" election districts. If noncompetitive district elections promote party responsibility in the legislature, the no-contest election question loses some force but the new paradox (electoral noncompetition = legislative competition) requires further examination. Two cautions need to be stated: (a) The reasoning gives no support for the same party's dominance in most districts; (b) the scholars who have found the close association between party responsibility and party constituencies' homogeneity do hold that "As the margins of one-party or non-party areas retreat, party responsibility will grow." (Ibid., p. 60).

[41] Averages and specific sizes are for the period immediately before the Supreme Court's 1964 decision on reapportionment. Under the impact of these rulings, the states' reapportionments have sometimes altered the size of one or both legislative houses, but the situation remains too fluid for a definitive appraisal.

are so small that it is difficult to find suitable candidates within the population, the legislative house may be too large. On the other hand, it may be too small if a representative has so many constituents that he can know little about them or they cannot effectively communicate with him.

If we assume that the function of legislative bodies is to express and dramatize the conflicts within the societies they represent and to resolve those conflicts by decisions that the mass of the people will accept as binding them, perhaps large numbers are desirable. There are many facets of interest in our contemporary societies and there is a greater likelihood that more of these different interests may be voiced in legislative deliberation if the number of members is large. Members of a small legislative body may become so cozy in their "club room" relationships that conflict is not well aired and personalities and feelings about fellow members become important factors in debate and in decision making. In contrast, the larger legislative bodies frequently seem more impersonal, more dedicated to the staging of debate on the issues.

In a larger body it may be more difficult for individual members to organize personal support and become "junior governors" without the responsibility of the governorship. Organization by the major division of party or on "liberal-conservative" lines is normally the only feasible method for effective action in a large body. On the other hand, tie votes, particularly frustrating in organizing for sessions, can more readily occur in the small ones. A large body also allows more room for members who are innocent or bold enough to proclaim that "the emperor has no clothes," or whatever is obvious but protected by a conspiracy of silence.

When we consider, too, that the function of committees may well be to mirror the electorate insofar as possible in forming the frequently final decisions of the body, the need for a sizable number of members becomes further evident. And the public is more likely to accept controversial policy decisions if there are too many legislators to blame individually—and by having, perhaps, a legislator available to answer as to "why this was done to us."

WHO GOES TO THE LEGISLATURE? Not nearly all who want to go to the legislature get there, and only some of those who do want to stay. Those who do stay are people to whom politics, or the prestige of being associated with it, has strong personal appeal. This is good, for the experience is a trying one and could not be borne unless it were personally satisfying.

For many the legislature is a trial step in a political career leading, they hope, to higher things like state or local governmental executive or judicial positions, or the Congress. For others who have had higher ambitions that have been unfulfilled but who still have a taste for politics, it is a consolation prize. For some it becomes something like a career, with committee chairmanships and interim commission memberships or chairmanships as possible prizes. Some of these careerists are also employed in local government or in business corporations. In such cases, the employers may expect the representative-employee to represent their interests as well as those of his constituency. In some instances union executives play a similar dual role.

As to occupation, various studies show businessmen (especially those engaged in insurance, real estate, and banking and investment), lawyers, and farmers predominating. These three groups typically comprise two-thirds or more of the total membership of a state legislature.[42] Studies probing educational background, race, sex, and religion of state legislators indicate that the legislators are overwhelmingly of middle-income groups, are mostly college graduates, and underrepresent minority (or, in the case of sex and "the labor class," majority) groups in the population. It can be argued that underrepresented interests are likely to be neglected by the legislature. But the implication that elected legislative bodies should reproduce almost perfectly the educational, class, and other distribution patterns of the population will not stand up to examination. The electorate chooses agents to be attentive to its varied interests, and it is not surprising that candidates who are willing to tackle the complexities of the job and those whom the electorate chooses to do so are better educated than many constituents and are already several rungs up the career ladders that American society offers.

State legislators, in fact, share in the set of characteristics that distinguish the people who run for public office from the many people who do not. Herbert Jacob has suggested that entry into elective politics depends on personality, occupation, and political opportunity.[43] The entrant's personality traits are likely to include needs for prestige, power, the opportunity to help others, conspicuousness in the public eye, and popularity (but not deep friendships). Many of these, it should be understood, are relative to the individual's own situation; a quite modest political office can satisfy

---

[42] *The data are conveniently summarized in* William J. Keefe *and* Morris S. Ogul, The American Legislative Process: Congress and the States (*Englewood Cliffs, N.J.:* Prentice-Hall, 1964), *p. 118.*

[43] Herbert Jacob, *"Initial Recruitment of Elected Officials in the U.S.—A Model,"* Journal of Politics, 24 (*November 1962*), 703–16.

the desire of a person of only moderate status to improve his prestige, power, and other indices of public standing in the community. Occupationally, the entrants into elective politics tend to be engaged in brokerage roles, bargaining with other people, and trying to reach mutually satisfying agreements. Lawyers, insurance salesmen, realtors, and independent merchants are among such people. To some extent such occupations naturally attract men with a "political personality"; more obviously, many young men choose the legal profession because they have political aspirations. In addition, though, the brokerage occupations allow time for seeking public office and for service in it while continuing the private occupation.[44] They teach skills a politician needs—bargaining, convincing, inspiring trust and confidence. They require the development of a wide acquaintanceship which is partly convertible into political support. The practitioner of these occupations comes into contact with governmental officials and politicians; consequently, he can know of opportunities for political candidacy and, better than followers of other occupations, can observe what makes for success or failure in political life.

Men with the appropriate personality characteristics and occupations get nominated and elected only if the community's political system provides the right opportunity. Certain barriers are obvious—race, religion, sex, youth, newness to the community, membership in the minority party in a one-party community, the organizational tightness of one's own political party. Less obvious is a community's appraisal of the standing of particular public offices. As Jacob puts it, "It seems likely that an individual must initially seek an office that commands about the same respect as his own social position. A plumber is unlikely to win a Senatorial seat; a millionaire is not much more likely to win a constableship." [45]

The fact that state legislators as a group are superior to the electorate in class, occupation, and education may therefore be cause for congratulation rather than condemnation. Other data on legislators, however, suggest caution in translating this into a conclusion that legislative service carries high prestige.

TERMS AND TENURE. Most state legislators are elected for terms of only two years. Only four states (Alabama, Louisiana, Maryland, and

---

[44] Most such occupations are among the few that meet the critical problem of the insecurity of elective office. A person who serves several terms in a substantially full-time office may be defeated for reelection and immediately need a private income in place of his public salary (unless he can get a patronage appointment to executive or judicial office). Law, real estate, and insurance, often organized as partnerships, enable a defeated public official to resume his private occupation immediately.

[45] Jacob, op. cit., p. 711.

Mississippi) permit members of the lower house the comfort of four-year terms, a period that most states do provide for state senators (but 13 states prescribe two-year terms even for senators). As most legislatures meet only once in the course of two years (unless a special session is called), and for only two months or so, a man can hardly have got his feet wet before he is waging a reelection campaign—if, that is, he liked the feel of the water.

Many go to the legislature, but few stay. In any year first-term legislators in the lower houses of half the states will probably be about 40 to 60 percent of the total house membership, and first-term senators in half the states will be between 20 and 50 percent of their senates.[46]

Though new senators may have served in the lower house, other freshmen are truly "greenhorns," needing to learn the rules, and, more important, needing to learn the folkways of the institution so that they can adapt their behavior toward effective playing of their roles. Many do not try. Some of them were induced to stand as candidates, however unenthusiastically, and they bring no genuine interest to the capitol's affairs. Others, engaged in law, insurance, or real estate, may have seen candidacy as an opportunity to advertise their names and the achievement of the status of legislator as a means of gaining a degree of local prestige.[47] One or two campaigns and terms may adequately serve these objectives. Most of the freshmen will serve only the one term, and their departure will usually be a voluntary retirement, rather than a consequence of unsuccessful candidacy for reelection. This high rate of turnover is an important index to the prestige of the legislature, to the effectiveness of party recruitment

---

[46] *Computed from data for 48 state legislatures in 1950 presented in Belle Zeller, op. cit., pp. 66ff. The distribution pattern is:*

First-term members as percentage of total membership	State senates (Number)	Lower houses (Number)
0–19	20	7
20–39	19	17
40–59	7	21
60–79	0	2
80–100	2	0

The median percentage for first-term members of state senates was 21, and of lower houses 39. Studies of turnover in particular states, for years other than 1950, indicate that the 1950 pattern is not atypical.

[47] *James D. Barber's* The Lawmakers: Recruitment and Adaptation to Legislative Life *(New Haven, Conn.: Yale University Press, 1965) includes a valuable treatment of the roles that freshmen legislators choose for themselves and the relation of these to the manner of their selection for candidacy and to their willingness to continue to serve in the legislature.*

of candidates,[48] and to the rewards and deprivations that legislative service entails.

PAY FOR LEGISLATORS. Although predominantly of the middle-income class, legislators are not gentlemen who can serve the state without compensation. All states pay legislators a per diem fee or salary, and most of them, in addition, provide allowances for travel, other expenses, or both. Those that provide more generously pay legislators a salary, but in only half of them is this as much as $2,000 for each year.[49] The maximum is $10,000 per year in Michigan and New York. In fact, most states pay legislators ridiculously small amounts, even taking into account the expense allowances sometimes provided. The legislators could themselves change this situation (save where the constitution prescribes the compensation), but they are notoriously skittish on the matter, fearing adverse public reaction at the next election.

The fact that many legislators must hold other jobs tests the economics of legislative representation, as well as the morals of the legislators and those they know. For the operation of our governmental institutions, we need a political class that can give its primary attention to state policies during the regular sessions and that stands ready to be called into special session at any time.

It is probably better to risk paying them adequately rather than risk their being bought and paid for elsewhere. What this adequate amount should be probably depends on the cost and standard of living in the various states. But it is safe to guess that no state is exceeding such an "adequate amount." The aggregate cost of bringing legislators' salaries up to an adequate level is minor not only in relation to the advantages to be gained, but also in relation to the total state budget. The states' legislative costs (which cover more than legislators' salaries) are only a fifth of 1 percent of total state expenditures.[50] Thus the cost of improving present salaries would be scarcely discernible.

---

[48] *Some part of turnover is the result of the local party organization's "passing around" the opportunity to run for the legislature among factions or geographical parts of the constituency. In addition, though, in many districts the nomination is not eagerly sought, and the party selects candidates of minimal qualifications who lack the ambition that would lead them to seek renomination so that they might eventually play influential roles in the legislative process.*

[49] The Book of the States: 1966–67, pp. 48f. *Varying allowances for travel and other expenses, which may exceed or fall far short of actual costs, make exact calculations of net compensation on a comparative basis difficult. See, however, the source cited, p. 43, for an effort to compute this; the range in "realized compensation" for a* biennium *is from New Hampshire's $200 to Michigan's $25,000. In 22 states the biennial amount is $4,000 or less—i.e., $2,000 or less per year.*

[50] *Computed from 1965 data. Legislative costs are given in U.S. Bureau of the* Census, Compendium of State Government Finances in 1965 *(Washington, D.C.,*

Retirement allowance systems have been initiated for legislators in some states. As anxieties about future security are factors in the moral shambles in which some legislators find themselves, such retirement systems might well be encouraged.

The employment policies of private employers are related to these problems. Consideration could be given to the establishment of policies allowing leave for legislative service and perhaps for campaigning as well. If legislative salaries are adequate, employers could avoid most of the moral issues by a system of leave without pay. If upper executives are granted leave to perform public service, why not any employee who can get himself elected to the legislature? The maintenance of democratic institutions in an increasingly urban and industrial economy may require the widespread development of tolerance for differences of opinion between employers and employees.

LEGISLATORS' BEHAVIOR. Legislators enter upon their tasks from such different personal backgrounds, from such different types of constituencies, and with such different degrees of aspiration for a legislative or wider political career that their behavior on the job varies greatly. An important influence is the nature of the political system in their particular state. For those serving in highly competitive two-party states, party advantage and party loyalty usually are relevant factors in their behavior; for those serving in one-party states, the absence of challenge by minority party legislators makes voting "the party line" meaningless, and shifting factional alliances, sectional and program interests, and deference to the governor's program and to his electoral or primary vote play a larger part in their voting.

It is almost impossible to generalize about their behavior on a scientific basis, even if we avoid simplistic herding of "all" or "most" legislators into one category. No substantial empirical study can embrace the nearly 8,000 current state legislators and their 99 legislative chambers, let alone capture a sufficient number of earlier-serving legislators to counteract any accidental results from the moment-in-time snapshot.[51] States differ in the extent to which they use roll-call voting, which provides essential research data on individual legislators' behavior. Valuable studies do exist on particular states and groups of states, and these permit some general

---

1966), *p. 36. The national total was $97.7 million, of which $22.1 million is accounted for by New York and California.*

[51] *Application of sampling techniques is difficult because an adequate sample of each of the 99 groups of legislators has to be fairly large and the significant differences in institutional arrangements and political systems under which each group operates need to be identified and used in interpreting the behavioral data.*

propositions to be advanced, subject to possible contradiction or modification as other states come under researchers' scrutiny.[52]

Many roles are possible for legislators (though not necessarily for each one)—spokesman for his district constituency's interests; loyal party member; advocate or agent of a single economic class, ethnic group, church, industry, business, profession, or labor union; independent follower of his own judgment and conscience; ideologist and reformer. A large number of legislators, of course, do not consciously select a certain role or set of roles and act accordingly. Some profess one kind of role, but their voting indicates another is being acted out. To many, particularly the large proportion of legislators appearing for their first term, what they feel most is uncertainty. This uncertainty is not just about so sophisticated a matter as deliberately choosing a role, but about how the legislative process works, what behavior will win them the acceptance and respect of fellow legislators and especially legislative and party leaders, how they can get information and advice about the hundreds of bills that are introduced. A number will seek to avoid the agony of cross-pressures from constituency, party, personal friends, interest groups, and conscience.

In such a situation of uncertainty and potential cross-pressure the easiest solution may be to take one's cues from the experienced and prestige-carrying leaders of one's party. This is a solution that is available in some states but not in others. Many conditions need to be met—a substantially unified party leadership (else the legislator is under uncomfortable cross-pressure from the contesting leaders), an individual constituency whose preferences are not far out of line with those of the typical constituency electing legislators of the party,[53] skillful political leadership that preserves legislators' self-respect while nonetheless inducing substantial conformity to the leaders' wishes, opportunity for occasional voting for constituency's or conscience' sake on measures not critical to the party or not requiring the member's vote for passage, and of course, some prospect of leadership-dispensed rewards for loyalty, though these prospective re-

---

[52] *The literature, much of it scattered in professional journals, is helpfully summarized in Malcolm E. Jewell, The State Legislature: Politics and Practice (New York: Random House, 1962), pp. 48–76; and Keefe and Ogul, op. cit., pp. 60–69, 283–87. A particularly discriminating examination of the findings of sophisticated research studies is found in Flinn, op. cit., pp. 60–71. These convenient reviews should be consulted, as research methodology is in an active state of development and this accounts for some differences among the reported findings; these technical problems are necessarily neglected in our treatment of the topic.*

[53] *This is a factor impressively related to legislators' voting even in states where party leaders do not exert strong direction of their party's legislators. See Flinn, op. cit., p. 70.*

wards may be as vague as the possibility of being considered for career advancement in the future and as simple as an occasional kind word from a leader and other signs that one "belongs." [54]

The following propositions appear to hold for state legislators' voting behavior in states where the legislative houses are not elected on a nonpartisan ballot or are not overwhelmingly and consistently controlled by one party.

1. The frequency of party voting in state legislative bodies (that is, the proportion of roll-call votes—except those that are unanimous or substantially so—on which the parties take opposite sides, with 60 or 80 percent of each party voting together) is higher than that of Congress in New York, Pennsylvania, Rhode Island, Connecticut, and Massachusetts; moderate (about the same as that of Congress) in Ohio, Illinois, New Hampshire, Washington, and (when the parties are closely divided) Kentucky; and lower than that of Congress in Colorado, Missouri, and California.[55]

2. "Party voting in legislatures is more evident in the larger, urban, industrial states, where party alignments are likely to follow urban-rural lines." This is because each party has a reasonably homogeneous constituency distinct from that of its rival, so that legislators have less cross-pressures from party and constituency on policy questions and readily concur with their party's leaders and other legislators of their party. Where, on the contrary, each party contains legislators from a great variety of constituencies whose interests conflict, and the two parties thus overlap substantially in make-up, it is more difficult either to formulate a party program or to induce a party's legislators to vote together.[56]

---

[54] *This and the preceding paragraph draw on, but do not exhaust, the useful observations of James D. Barber in his "Legislative Strategies for Legislative Party Cohesion," Journal of Politics, 28 (May 1966), 347–67. High responsiveness to the party organization leaders, although present in Connecticut experience, which Barber's study particularly reflects, does not explain the high party cohesion in legislative voting in some other states. See Flinn, op. cit., p. 61. Most legislators (in the four states studied by Wahlke and associates) perceive themselves as playing roles as free agents, at least as regards their constituencies' particular desires. But in another state, Pennsylvania, less than a third shared this view. John C. Wahlke, et al., The Legislative System: Explorations in Legislative Behavior (New York: Wiley, 1962), especially p. 281; cf. Frank J. Sorauf, Party and Representation (New York: Atherton Press, 1963), pp. 123ff.*

[55] *Jewell, op. cit., pp. 50–53. Only state legislatures whose party voting patterns have been studied are included: in most of those states the two houses had such similar patterns that one can speak of "the legislature" rather than classify each house separately.*

[56] *Ibid., pp. 53–58. It should be noted that "urban, industrial" can mislead when applied too readily to individual districts. There are some urban, relatively nonindustrial districts and some industrial. relatively rural districts. Flinn, op. cit., pp. 65ff.*

3. Party voting is not clearly correlated with closeness of party competition in the states.[57] At the statewide level the correlation is stronger when each party's constituencies are relatively homogeneous and distinct from the other party's. In terms of individual legislators' behavior, however, "the least secure members of the legislature, i.e., the members of the winning party with lowest [election] pluralities, are less loyal to the party than are other members."[58]

4. Party voting is most common on issues involving the special interests of the parties, which also tend to be issues of little interest to the voters. Voter registration and election laws, apportionment of legislative seats, rules of legislative procedure, the civil service, state administration, and local government are usually issues of this type. In more urban and industrialized states, as might be expected from what we have already said, party voting is common on substantive programmatic issues—health, welfare, education, business regulation, labor unions, taxation, and appropriations.[59]

5. Normally, no pattern of legislators' voting exhibits as much strength and consistency as that of party voting. Intra-party factions do not have long staying power or cohesion over a wide range of issues. Urban-rural and sectional blocs (unless coinciding with the parties' respective stances) may form on particular issues and then dissolve; they are irrelevant to many legislative issues and so contribute little to attempts to explain legislators' behavior throughout a session.[60] Strong cross-party alliances, comparable to the conservative coalition of Republicans and southern Democrats, are not found in the state legislatures.[61]

3. The Governors

The President of the United States is so visible and his formal duties parallel so well those constitutionally assigned to the governor of a state that it is tempting to think that the governor can best be understood as "a little President." If one should take that step, then most of what is known about the much-studied Presidency could be transferred wholesale to anal-

---

[57] Jewell, op. cit., p. 99.

[58] Flinn, op. cit., pp. 70ff.

[59] Jewell, op. cit., pp. 59ff. Jewell relates taxation, appropriations, and appointments (other than civil service) to the question of support or opposition to the prestige and basic program of the governor's administration.

[60] Ibid., pp. 62–67.

[61] Keefe and Ogul, op. cit., p. 287. Pages 286f. summarize research findings on party cohesion in state legislatures substantially along the lines of Jewell's treatment, on which we have particularly drawn.

ysis of the governorship. The trouble is that the governor is not a little President.

The typical governor is inferior to the President in his capacity to attract public attention and, if necessary, mobilize public support. He has less freedom to appoint, remove, and give instructions to heads of executive departments. He cannot commit the government to major policies and decisions as the President can in commanding the armed forces and conducting international negotiations. Except in one-party states, the legislative majority is less likely than the congressional majority to be of the executive's party. The governor is less conscious than the President of a place in history and his dependence on its judgment. Conversely, a governor may have his sights set on higher office, but the President's only remaining ambition is to serve well in the office he has. A governor may also have advantages that the President might envy—a legislature that meets only every other year and then quite briefly, a more effective veto power over the legislature's appropriations of funds, even the chance to look forward to further service in public office after the governorship, or to the resumption of an interrupted private occupation (instead of wondering what can possibly follow the Presidency). The differences are too substantial to ignore by generalizing about "chief executives," or by emphasizing how much the President and governor alike have come to find their most significant roles not as executives but as participants with the legislative houses in formulating and adopting public policies.

THE GOVERNORSHIP. It is significant that the governorship cannot be meaningfully discussed by itself. The governor's role is a set of relationships to other parts of the governmental and political system—to the legislature, to the heads of major departments, to the bureaucracy, to his political party and to the opposition party, to the press, to the electorate, to a variety of interest groups. His power is relative to that of other participants in the system. His success or failure depends on his skill in using the resources available to him to bring enough of these other participants into collaboration in order to move toward objectives to which he is committed.

Within his state the governor, like the President nationally, has two key advantages: his singular role and his electoral constituency. Because the governorship is held by a single person, the institution need not, like the legislature or a group executive (for example, an executive cabinet), bog down so readily in irresolution, inconsistency of successive decisions, or lack of a strategic plan that distinguishes relative priorities and carries through from proposal to decision to execution. Because the governor's electoral constituency is the whole state, he has a claim to speak for the state's "general interest" in contrast to each legislator's identification with a much smaller constituency. Both of these factors give him a prominence that no legislator can match, while the dignity of the office and its range of concerns permit him to outshine any head of an administrative department, even if, like the governor, he is elected on a statewide basis.

TERM OF OFFICE. The states have been following what is generally regarded as a wholesome tendency to lengthen the governor's term to four years.[62] Thirty-nine of them had adopted this period as of 1966; the rest have two-year terms. Where his term is four years, the governor has an opportunity to develop his policy leadership out of his experience and to formulate ideas about how the administrative machinery can be improved. However, in 13 of the states with four-year terms, the constitutions forbid governors a second successive term [63] (and two states with two-year terms limit their governors to two successive terms, thereby also limiting tenure to four years). This contrasts with the national Constitution, whose Twenty-second Amendment permits the President to serve two four-year terms.[64]

So apparently prosaic and formal a matter as a constitutional barrier to reelection has in fact both theoretical and practical import. A good deal of theoretical writing about representative government assumes that those vested with large amounts of political power will normally be subject to the people's judgment of their stewardship at a subsequent election.[65] This assumption is supposed to have two consequences on the actual behavior of officeholders: (a) An incumbent will be more responsible, and more

---

[62] *The wholesomeness of the trend from two- to four-year terms may be open to argument. Legislators are generally elected at two-year intervals. If at alternate elections there are no gubernatorial candidates to emphasize programs and to dramatize party differences, public interest may flag at these off-year elections and elected legislators may be less clearly bound to the governor's (or opposition party's) policies. Given the prevalently low degree of public interest in state government, some risk of greater discontinuity in the governorship may be a reasonable price to pay for increasing the meaningfulness of state elections.*

[63] *Most southern and border states have the one-term, four-year limit; of the total of 15 states with such a limit, only Indiana and Pennsylvania are in other regions.*

[64] *A person who acts as President or succeeds to the Presidency on the death or disability of the President may serve a maximum of six or ten years, depending upon whether he served more or less than two years of his predecessor's term. The first case under this provision of the Twenty-second Amendment was Lyndon B. Johnson, who may constitutionally serve two four-year terms in addition to his year and two months during President Kennedy's uncompleted term.*

[65] *For simplicity we state the assumption broadly. The earlier discussions of legislators' turnover and the remarks in this section about governors demonstrate that the assumption would need substantial rephrasing and qualification to be sound, even in the absence of formal obstacles to reelection.*

responsive to the people's needs and wishes, if he is constantly aware that his performance will be judged when he seeks reelection; and (*b*) his ability to win the support of other participants in policy making and politics during his term will be affected by their expectations as to whether he will or will not be likely to continue in office.

In the case of a key post such as the governorship there are further derivatives of these general consequences. A governor reasonably confident of long tenure in office is more likely to be interested in long-range development of the state; he can afford to take an interest in ten-year plans, in initiating projects whose benefits will not appear for several years (for example, highway or school construction programs), in planting seeds of policy ideas that will not grow to command popular and legislative majorities until several years of widespread discussion have passed. On the other hand, a governor whose vision is confined by a four-year limit on his period of service is likely to see his influence wane in the last year or two of his term; the ban on a second four years may thus reduce his period of practical power to two or three years. This is because he will already have dispensed most of the rewards at his disposal (patronage appointments, local projects, etc.) and so will have lost bargaining power with the men whose support he needs and who adapt their behavior to prospective rewards and deprivations.

Well before the governor's term ends, some key figures, even in his own party, will be emerging as his potential successors. Unless he has built up enough political strength to dictate who his party's nominee shall be or to make his endorsement a potentially critical factor, these prospective heirs (often in the legislature or the executive branch) will play their own game rather than his. Less prominent legislators, executive officials, and local party leaders will also tend to cultivate alliances useful in the future, rather than to follow the leadership of the "dying king." Some legislative measures may be postponed by the governor and his party if they see a likelihood that the opposition will win the next election (perhaps because the governor cannot be the party's candidate) and so can be made to bear the onus of passing unpopular but needed measures (tax increases, for example). Or the opposition party (which often controls one or both legislative houses) may postpone enactment of some measures if it antici-pates winning the governorship and so wants to get credit for popular measures or wants to make patronage appointments under new and ex-panded programs.[66]

---

[66] *So far as the argument here depends on two-party competition, it identifies less the evils in states that now forbid a second term (since most such states are one-party*

This is of course no argument for granting lifetime tenure to governors. Nor does it assume that every governor, if there are not constitutional barriers to it, should or will seek renomination and reelection. The governorship for some is a stepping stone to nomination for the Presidency, appointment to the President's cabinet, or election to the United States Senate. And some governors must retire because of demonstrated unfitness in the post, or the emergence of abler and more attractive candidates in their own parties, or the opposition party's ability to win the electorate's preference. The basic position is that the governors who wish to seek reelection and can command sufficient party support to win renomination should not be barred from doing so. Most political scientists view the Twenty-second Amendment's limitation of the President to two four-year terms as an unwise provision. But one may leave open the question of the wisdom of some similar limitation on a governor's tenure [67] without weakening the case against the one-term, four-year limitation on such tenure.

CAREER PATTERNS. The governorship of a state is a position of high distinction, considerable power, and great responsibility. Among offices within the gift of the statewide electorate, its only rivals are the two United States senatorships. Though the relative prestige of the governorship varies among the states, over time, and with the personal qualities of the incumbent, it is often sufficient for its holder to play a national role concurrently with or subsequently to his governorship. He may do this as state party leader in a major national party (whose strength, as we have seen, lies in the state and local organizations), as head of the state's delegation to the national party convention, as a possible nominee for the Presidency or Vice Presidency, as an appointee to the President's cabinet or to an ambassadorship, or as a United States senator.[68] There is little doubt that many governors keep these possibilities in mind or that their performance as governors is affected by them. Most will prudently remain aware that their records during their gubernatorial service must be able to sustain searching scrutiny if their further ambitions are to be realized.

The paths to the governorship are varied, but some patterns can be

---

southern and border states) than the evils avoided by the two-party states that lack such a ban.

[67] Seven states set two successive four-year terms as the limit.

[68] Recent illustrations in the national appointive office field are the following former governors: Chief Justice Earl Warren (California); Secretary of the Interior Douglas McKay (Oregon); Secretary of Agriculture Orville L. Freeman (Minnesota); Secretary of Commerce Luther H. Hodges (North Carolina); Secretary of Health, Education, and Welfare Abraham Ribicoff (Connecticut); Under Secretary of State Averell Harriman (New York); Under Secretary of Commerce LeRoy Collins (Florida); Assistant Secretary of State G. Mennen Williams (Michigan); and U.S. Representative to the United Nations Adlai Stevenson (Illinois).

discerned. Joseph A. Schlesinger has examined the careers of the approximately one thousand elected governors serving in the period 1870–1950.[69] Over 90 percent had held a public office at some point before reaching the governorship. Over half had served in the state legislature, a third in law enforcement offices (attorney, judge, police commissioner, sheriff, etc.), and almost as many in appointive administrative offices outside the law enforcement category. Less than a fifth had held local elective office, and the same proportion applied to statewide elective office [70] and to federal elective office.

The pattern is different and quite blurred when one inquires about immediate steppingstones to the governorship. Only 20 percent of the governors moved directly to the post from membership in the state legislature. Of the governors who had had experience in statewide or federal elective offices, over 80 percent usually moved directly from such offices to the governorship, but as already noted, such experience applied to only about two-fifths of all the governors. This does not mean that there are no patterns of direct ascent to the governorship. Rather, individual states, and sometimes regions, often have quite clear patterns even though they tend to get lost in national averages. For example, half of Montana's governors came directly from law enforcement positions, and half of Massachusetts' from statewide elective offices. If arrival by 30 percent or more of a state's governors from the same type of steppingstone can be taken as showing a state pattern, then 25 of the states qualify—10 of them showing the state legislature as the immediate source of this proportion of their governors, 6 drawing on law enforcement offices, 4 on statewide elective offices, and 3 on administrative offices.[71] In some states one can even find a sharply defined promotional ladder of several rungs. For example, six of Vermont's seven governors from 1930 to 1950 were lieutenant governors when elected to the top office; typically such men had served as legislators before reaching the lieutenant governorship and about half of these had been speaker of the house or president *pro tem* of the senate.

National patterns have changed over time. The most dramatic and consistent change has been in the legislative experience of the governors. Those with such experience have dropped steadily from 65 percent in the 1870's to 41 percent in 1940–50. And those for whom being a legislator was

---

[69] Joseph A. Schlesinger, How They Became Governor (*East Lansing, Mich.*: Governmental Research Bureau, Michigan State University, 1957).

[70] "Local elective office" and "statewide elective office," like that of "appointive administrative office," exclude local and state law enforcement offices, which Schlesinger treats as a separate category.

[71] The principal steppingstone in Ohio has been membership in Congress, while Idaho has drawn directly from local elective offices more than from other sources.

their last office before the governorship have dropped from 33 percent to 13 percent.

In general, then, American governors have had experience in government and politics, mostly in state legislatures, law enforcement, and administrative posts. However useful some experience in such settings may be, half or less of the governors with such experience have moved directly from it to the governorship, direct access to that post being more common for those who have reached a statewide elective position or a federal elective post such as congressman. Individual states have distinctive patterns of careers leading to the governorship. These patterns shift over time, the most notable being the steady drop in the proportion of the nation's governors who have had legislative experience or for whom such experience was an immediate steppingstone to the governorship.

4. Conclusion

The formal arrangements for policy makers do not of themselves disclose the substance and process of policy decisions in the states. These formal facts as treated in this chapter do, however, establish or describe those aspects of the governmental institutions that create the opportunities and prescribe the limits for the operative political systems. To a considerable degree these formal aspects are the constitutional bases for the policy-forming systems.

Consider, for example, the different possibilities for acquiring a central, guiding role in our states for modern governors with four-year terms in contrast with the one-year-term governors common in our early state governments. Consider also the possible stimuli or limitations that may act upon a governor when he cannot succeed himself in contrast to the different possible calculations of a governor who constitutionally may, and hopes to, stay in office for a longer period.

The formal arrangements for representation in the legislatures all operate within systems of popularly elected representatives. Yet the changes being wrought in the systems of representation in response to federal court pressure are commonly viewed as revolutionary in the sense that changed publics or combinations of publics may soon be decisive in their influence over state policies. Old "ruling groups" will lose their veto power over policy and will have to seek popular support for programs. And groups that have made political careers largely out of protest will be thrown into power and forced to learn responsible roles for the conduct of government.

chapter 9

Policy Making

From a simple viewpoint, state policy making is a process in which legislative bills are introduced, a budget is presented, and legislative procedures result in enacted or defeated measures. But the more sophisticated viewer is aware of the continuous conflicts and disagreements within society that may break out as state policy controversies. Once they do, demands are made on behalf of one or more of the elements in the political system, and evasive, diversive, or confronting countermeasures are advanced by others. In focusing on the ways in which policy making is structured, we should, then, bear in mind the complexities of the political environment that were detailed in previous chapters. Any political element that stands to gain or lose by state policy actions—be it the Boy Scouts in need of a camping space on state property or the Republican party looking for an election victory—should be expected to be active in the policy-making processes. And at any particular time a mayor, a corporation executive, a judge, a labor or religious leader, an administrator of a state program, or the head of a taxpayers' organization may be as significant a demander, arbiter, or definer of state policy issues as a governor, a legislative committee, or a party platform committee. The policy battles shift from one theater to another and engage changing political elements as the issues and the ways of organizing influence change.

1. *What Is Policy?*

In one sense, policy matters are those that require for decision the attention and consent of important actors on the political scene, such as
legislators, governors, or—where issues are determined by ballot—the voters. Given the possibilities of controversy, we cannot define in advance
which event will be routine and which will become a policy battle. Thus
the buying of one piece of land by a state may be a routine matter resolved
by an official and a private party, whereas the buying of another may be
accomplished only after political leaders have organized for civic combat,
shouted at each other, and perhaps met privately to "see if we can work
this problem out."

From another point of view, state policies are the uniformities of the
system, the settled courses of action generally followed by officials and
employees, and by the populace when acting in relation to state governments. One who knows a state's policies knows that the state's agencies do,
or do not do, certain things. If he knows the policies well, he may know the
circumstances under which official actions will follow one or another
pattern. A state may have a policy, for example, of employing only residents unless there is a finding that a particular skill is scarce. In the latter
case there would be a policy of considering nonresidents for that work. But
state policies are not always as clear as this example may seem to suggest.
What, for instance, does "scarce" mean, who decides, and are there other
exceptions?

HOW ARE POLICIES MANIFESTED? Policy decisions in many
cases take the form of constitutional provisions or of statutes, that is,
legislative acts adopted in a prescribed procedure. But the policy-decision
process must be viewed broadly, for decisions that a governor of one state
may have the power to make may call for a constitutional amendment in
another state or legislative action in a third. The rates of pay for certain
officials or employees are an example.

We tend in our culture to pay deference to the written word. Thus we
say we have "a government of laws and not of men," and there is a
tendency to emphasize as policy the authoritative words of constitutions,
statutes, judicial decisions, and administrative regulations. However, the
politically significant policy is operating policy. Therefore, the astute observer who wants to learn the effective policies of a state will look not only
to its constitution and the annotated statutes but to its administrative
operations as well. For example, under the same statute one institution for
young men who violate the law may be operated as a maximum-security

prison, while another may be little more than an enclosed school for basic studies and vocational training.

The wording of the statutes does, of course, have some effect on operating policy. Moreover, administrators will always be ready to point to the legal words and phrases which appear to legitimize their actions. However, the concepts of office and function that they bring to their work give much of the content to the effective public policies; this is true, at least, so long as these concepts are accepted (perhaps tacitly), rather than challenged, by other holders of political authority.

In many instances state policies may not even be set down in written words, but instead are based on understandings reached between the administrators and legislative committees or other power centers. There may, for instance, be nothing in the statutes that requires the state high-way department to provide roadside picnic grounds or "rest areas"; yet as a result of understandings reached with a legislative committee, the state may have such a policy, at least for the time being. In like manner, a state university negotiating for its appropriations may find that the way to attain this objective is to go along with those legislators who want it to retain some program of questionable educational value or to initiate some service to organized labor, local government officers, or some business group.

There are many uncertainties and inconsistencies in the policies of the states. The authoritative language of constitutions, legislative enactments, judicial decisions, or administrative regulations may not seem to apply to given circumstances. The meanings of different statutes may seem to conflict, and the correct interpretation of statutory language is frequently uncertain. As a result of citizen apathy, group demand, or the direction of political superiors, formal policies may be unevenly applied, with enforcement of particular laws or fuller provision of services more certain in some localities than others. Citizen attitudes and organization thus have a continuing relation to policy formation, nullifying enactments here and quickening or modifying official behavior there. These matters cannot much engage us here, but we should recognize them as a part of the policy-formation process. In fact, these day-to-day and month-to-month modifications in state policy tell us much about the developments in a state's political system, giving us clues to which groups are gaining or losing influence.

SUBSTANCE OF STATE POLICY. The subjects of state policy making have a fantastic variety as seen in the proposals that come to the legislatures. When one considers how state governments touch the lives of patients, students, prisoners, highway travelers, business and occupational licensees, public welfare clients, and taxpayers, to name just a few, it is not difficult to understand why a great number of citizens are ready to voice their aspirations for a more perfect state government. Furthermore, the legislature may have to consider proposals to modify the criminal law, change the laws governing public utilities, business organizations, the relations between individuals, and the workings of local governments. There hardly seems room, therefore, for the less urgent proposals—to name a new state flower or to dedicate a park to some departed nature lover. But to be realistic, we must recognize that there is obviously room for the latter kind of proposals and for any others that please a legislator or his supporters.

In any particular era the subjects of state policy often reflect developments in the nation as a whole. In recent decades, for instance, the higher birth rate and the increase in the number of older people have directed state policy decisions toward education, treatment of chronic disease, and special programs for the aged. Technological changes bring changes in state policy. For example, new approaches in the treatment of mental illness—for reasons both humane and economical—were quickly followed by policy changes regarding the treatment and care of patients. Furthermore, national associations and clearing houses for governors and department heads encourage an exchange of ideas that often results in some states imitating the policies of others.

Other outside influences can also affect state policy. For example, international tensions may raise questions about the adequacy of a state's educational system or the need for bomb shelters. Competition among regions for industrial settlement, for vacation travelers, and for business generally has become an important factor in state policy making, often converting state agencies and governors into salesmen.

The organization and management of local government are everywhere a state policy problem; in the more urban areas, they tend to become a dilemma. One illuminating example is in the area of taxes. The states' role as tax-gatherer for local governments is undergoing a revolution. In 1963–64, for example, state payments to local governments actually exceeded the total state tax collections of only ten years before. Yet these fiscal-policy victories for local governments have been occurring in a period when pressures for expanded state programs, especially in higher education, welfare, health, highways, and recreation, have tended to make state policy battles basically fiscal contests.

2. The State Constitution

These running policy controversies take place for the most part within the relatively fixed framework of the state constitution, which describes much of the formal system of government and thus determines who may make or influence various kinds of important decisions. In addition, in some states it may also include more detailed rules of government that, in effect, freeze large areas of state policy against the whims of popular government, a characteristic for which persons familiar only with the United States Constitution are likely to be unprepared.[1]

CONSTITUTIONAL ESSENTIALS AND NONESSENTIALS. In our political tradition, the essential elements of a state constitution are not extensive. They include a bill of rights, a formal distribution of legislative, judicial, and executive powers, rules on suffrage and on the electoral basis of the governorship and legislature, and provision for amendment or revision of the constitution. Anything added to a constitution beyond these essentials is, directly or in practical effect, a limitation on the powers of the legislature and the governor to make decisions on policy.

Earlier chapters in this book trace the historical development of the loci of power in state governments from the early confidence in the legislatures through the later tendencies to trust others (including the governor) more, and to trust no one very much. What makes our analysis somewhat difficult is that today we have constitutions from all the periods of our history, with some of the documents amended very little and others gloriously patched.

The length of a constitution has an important bearing on state policy. About half of the current ones have more than 15,000 words. The others range from about 5,000 to 7,000 words in Vermont, Connecticut, and Rhode Island to 70,000 in California and 227,000 (!) in Louisiana. Generally, more words mean that more matters will be determined and controlled by the constitution and fewer will be left for decision by the regular

---

[1] *Students of state constitutions are currently blessed with an edition of* Index Digest of State Constitutions (*New York: Oceana Press, 1959*) *prepared under the auspices of the Legislative Drafting Research Fund of Columbia University. For the fifty constitutions the* Digest *provides a topical analysis showing under each subject heading the provisions of each state constitution on that point. The Fund has also supervised the publication of the full texts of the constitutions as of December 31, 1960, in two volumes under the title,* Constitutions of the United States: National and State (*Dobbs Ferry, N.Y.: Oceana Publications, Inc., 1962*). *Supplements to the* Index Digest *are published to record changes in the constitutions.*

legislative processes. This tendency to take power away from the legislature has been a nineteenth- and twentieth-century phenomenon that contrasts sharply with the disposition in both the national and early state constitutions to make an uncomplicated, generous grant of power to the people's representatives in accordance with the principles of republican government. Twentieth-century constitutional English, however, is not necessarily verbose: the constitutions of the two newest states, Hawaii and Alaska, both have less than 15,000 words.[2]

States that have tended to freeze moderate to large numbers of decisions into the constitution have done this by elaborating on the essential elements of a constitution, by providing for more than the minimum constitutional organs of government, and by spelling out rules of government, grants and denials of power, and legal principles on an almost unimaginable variety of subjects.

One consequence is the difficulty of adapting the machinery of state and local governments to changing circumstances. Illustrative are constitutional provisions that diffuse power by listing a number of elective state executive offices, that detail a complete state court system, that specify much election law, that freeze county and other local government arrangements, and that enshrine an older era's civil service doctrine in a way that handicaps the introduction of modern management and staffing methods. The grants of taxing and borrowing powers to state legislatures and local governments are often so hedged about with prohibitions, exceptions, and limitations as to impede the responsible use of these powers to finance governmental programs. Over 80 percent of the constitutions have provisions affecting education and corporations. Among other subjects dealt with by some state constitutions are agriculture, banking, health, highways, insurance, labor, liquor, mines, public works, railroads, and water rights and harbors.

Two collateral problems are produced by these attempts to define, grant, and deny legislative powers on a variety of subjects. One is the large role that falls to the courts, because of the need for authoritative interpretation of the constitutional provisions. It is by no means clear that judges are better "legislators" than those the constitution drafters sought to protect us from. The other problem is the frequent need for amendment. A count has shown that the more recent, detailed constitutions have in

---

[2] *The periods of adoption of state constitutions are shown in Table 3.2 at page 96. For the constitutions' exact dates and their present length, see the tabulation that appears regularly in* The Book of the States, *published biennially by the Council of State Governments, Chicago.*

their relatively young lives been amended much more often than the five oldest ones with their uncomplicated grants of power to the legislatures. One scholar has even raised the question of whether the detailed ones did not compromise the very idea of representative government.[3]

In view of the foregoing considerations, several issues may be raised: Can the states' failure to respond to many current problems be explained in part by the narrowed scope of decision left by these constitutional restrictions? Should responsible policy makers be allowed the "out" of saying, "Yes, I know, some other states have met that problem; but our constitution so hampers us in that area that it is doubtful that we could do anything effective"?

Should groups seeking reforms in state government (or seeking privileges from the state) be permitted to write their reforms into the fundamental law where these authoritative words may live to plague citizens seeking to meet some future problems?

When constitutional revision is undertaken, should one of the major objectives be to omit unessential detail and expand the scope of the normal legislative processes? (The difficulty of achieving such an objective is shown by the fact that when students of state government consider model drafts of constitutional language, they are inclined to write in their favorite reforms.)

Is public apathy toward state government perhaps related to these constitutional restrictions on legislative power? And does this public apathy, in turn, tend to make the legislators irresponsible? If they had real power, that is, if almost *anything* could happen when the legislature meets, isn't it likely that state governments would seem more important in the lives of their people?

Now that the office of governor offers an opportunity for responsible policy leadership, should we give these powers now stored in the constitutions back to the legislatures so that the governors and the legislators may use them?

AMENDING THE CONSTITUTION. The adoption of constitutional amendments is frequently an important element in the making of state policy decisions. But if this is required often or if the amendment

---

[3] *"The only conclusion warranted by the realities of the state constitutional order is that the legislatures are hamstrung by numerous limitations on their powers. What we have, in short, is a serious compromise of the philosophy of representative government. There is little prospect of lifting the state legislative institution to the level of quality and performance that we ought to expect of it until we give it man-sized authority."* Jefferson B. Fordham, The State Legislative Institution (*Philadelphia: University of Pennsylvania Press*, 1959), *p. 29.*

process is difficult, decision making may be unduly hampered. The states with long, detailed constitutions must, of course, make frequent amendments; however, even those with short, simple ones must occasionally alter a term of office or take an obsolete pay restriction out of the constitution.

It is generally agreed that constitutions as the reflections of more fundamental political beliefs should be more difficult to amend than the ordinary statutes, and constitution drafters have tended to protect this principle. In just over one-fourth of the states, for example, an amendment must be approved in two sessions of the legislature. In other words, the legislature must remain favorable to the proposal. In most states, however, legislative action on an amendment can be completed in one session. A two-thirds or three-fifths favorable vote by both houses is necessary in over half the states—usually with the vote counted as a proportion of the total membership of each house, rather than of those present and voting. As a result, members who are absent or not voting are in effect counted as votes against the proposal.

Furthermore, in all states but Delaware a popular vote on the proposed amendment is required. In most of them a simple majority of those who vote on the issue determines it. However, a few constitutions require something larger than a simple majority or—an even more difficult hurdle —a majority of those voting at the election. As amendments are typically presented at regular general elections and many persons vote only for parties or candidates, disregarding the "issues" on the ballot, the requirement of a majority of those voting at the election may make it difficult, if not impossible, to amend a state's constitution. That is why the Illinois constitution was not amended for over forty years, although numbers of proposed amendments went to the people. Many of them received a majority of the votes cast on the issue, but none received a majority of those cast in the election. Finally, by an elaborate campaign of voter education, a "Gateway" amendment was passed, permitting a two-thirds favorable vote on an amendment to approve it.

In contrast, the amendment process seems easy in a number of states —particularly those with long, detailed constitutions—and, as a result, many amendments are put before the voters. A study by Albert L. Sturm showed that over a fifteen-year period 9 states had approved constitutional amendments at a rate of 2 or more per year.[4] Since their present constitutions were adopted, voters in California, Louisiana, and South Carolina have approved 350, 460, and 251 amendments respectively, an annual

---

[4] *Albert L. Sturm,* Methods of State Constitutional Reform *(Ann Arbor, Mich.: University of Michigan Press, 1954).*

average of 4, 13, and 4. With these proposals coming to the voters for ratification in batches of 3 or 4 to 40 or more, along with candidate elections, one may question the level of attention given these issues.

Many proposed amendments affect only local governments or areas and might be judged hardly worthy of the legislature's time, let alone the voters'. Although states with cumbersome constitutions—mostly in the South—would be in straitjackets if they could not readily amend them, one might wish they had constitutions more nearly limited to fundamental law so that they could make more appropriate demands on their voters and give their legislatures needed authority.

CONSTITUTIONAL REVISION. Amending a constitution changes it only in bits and pieces. A more thoroughgoing change can be achieved through constitutional revision, which requires a state constitutional convention or commission. However, the states seem reluctant to take such a drastic step. For although recent issues of the biennial *Book of the States* have said that "Approximately one-third of the states were more or less seriously interested in constitutional revision," [5] only 4 constitutions had been revised in more than sixty years: New Jersey in 1947, Georgia and Missouri in 1945, and Louisiana in 1921. Michigan and Connecticut joined this select group in 1964 and 1965. The need to adapt state systems of representation to the requirements of the federal courts has temporarily stimulated the calling of constitutional conventions which in some states have gone beyond the representation question to other revisions.

The constitutions of all except 11 states provide for the calling of constitutional conventions and in 7 of these 11 exceptions, the legislative authority to call such conventions has been established. Usually the legislature must vote to create a convention—in about half the cases by an extraordinary majority—and then the issue of holding the convention must be approved by popular referendum. In a few states the issue must be submitted to popular referendum periodically, at intervals of seven, ten, sixteen, or twenty years.

The delegates to the convention are elected in accord with either constitutional provisions or legislative determinations. They meet, organize, seek informational assistance, divide up the tasks among committees, and in most cases eventually report with a recommended revision. Finally, the revision is put to a popular vote to determine whether or not it will be adopted.

An alternative to the constitutional convention is gaining some adher-

---

[5] The Book of the States: 1966–67 (*Chicago: Council of State Governments, 1966*), *p. 10.*

ents. This is the device of the constitutional commission, a relatively small appointive body authorized by the legislature or the governor, which makes studies and proposes revised drafts of the whole or parts of the constitution. Three of the modern constitutional revisions have come about through this device—in Georgia, Michigan, and New Jersey—although in the last two cases a constitutional convention was eventually used before ratification was achieved. The revision proposed by a constitutional commission must normally go through the regular amendment process, that is, it is submitted to the populace by the legislature as an amendment to the existing document.

The anomaly that constitutional revision has been actively promoted in a good share of the states but little or nothing done about it until recently is not too difficult to explain. We like to have our institutions reviewed periodically and we are certainly in favor of progress. It follows, then, that assigning a group to study a constitution and look for ways of improving it seems eminently reasonable to us. However, wise observers of governmental institutions, of whom the late Lane Lancaster was more prescient than most on this point, call attention to the fact that, however bad governments appear to reformers, they operate fairly well for those who actively manipulate them.[6] Thus to talk of constitutional revision or of a convention that could make important changes in the manipulators or their habits is to threaten the established order.

Most of the proposals are probably gimmicks for gaining something else. Thus, if the state labor council or the state League of Women Voters talks of a constitutional convention or the governor pleads for constitutional revision, they are probably simply trying to soften up, or to put off balance, the professional policy makers in order to get them to accept less threatening proposals: more money for the schools, broader coverage in unemployment compensation, or some statutory administrative reorganization. If the members of the established order are currently vulnerable because of an indefensible system of representation, public scandals, or some awkwardness in the practice of governmental arts, a threat of constitutional revision may make them receptive to lesser reforms.

It is, of course, possible that pressure for general constitutional revision may bring about more modest constitutional changes by the amendment process. A series of these modest changes may then cumulate to the point of effecting some significant changes in the constitutional frame-

---

[6] *Lane Lancaster*, Government in Rural America (*New York: Van Nostrand,* 1937), *p. 404.*

work of a state. Such changes by amendment, however, are made within the tolerance of the existing political system. It is the opening up of the wide freedom for change that a constitutional convention might provide that is shocking and frightening to the established order.

Constitutional revision is a matter of obvious interest to individuals with an academic or avocational interest in state government. However, unless such individuals find power wielders as allies, the opportunities for putting those ideas into practice by revising state government are certain to be limited.[7]

3. *Special Legislation*

If because of constitutional limitation the scope of normal legislative action seems too narrow in many states, there are also complaints that the scope of action of some legislatures is too broad. It is said, for example, that legislatures spend too much time on legislation pertaining to particular persons, cities, towns, villages, special districts, townships, and counties, and not enough on the important policy issues of the states. Furthermore, according to these views, legislators tend to meddle in the affairs of particular local governments in their districts.

LOCAL LAWS. Some state constitutions leave legislatures free to pass laws affecting individual local governments as well as general laws affecting the whole state. In some of these, a referendum is required in the locality before the act goes into effect. In other states the constitution forbids the legislature to move by special act where a general act can be made effective. Such a provision usually leaves the special act to the legislature's discretion. Still other constitutions forbid special acts pertaining to a variety of subjects, including cities and other general municipal corporations. Under these last two forms of restriction, legislatures may

---

[7] A scholar's opportunities for writing about state constitutions and their revision can be more rewarding than his attempts to modify governments. The National Municipal League had a foundation grant for a State Constitutional Studies Project, the publications of which started appearing with the League as publisher in 1960. A series of five are called background studies: Robert B. Dishman, State Constitutions: The Shape of the Document (1960); Bennett M. Rich, State Constitutions: The Governor (1960); Ferrel Heady, State Constitutions: The Structure of Administration (1961); Robert S. Rankin, State Constitutions: The Bill of Rights (1960); and Gordon E. Baker, State Constitutions: Reapportionment (1960). In another series from the same source are John P. Wheeler, Jr., The Constitutional Convention: A Manual on Its Planning, Organization and Operation (1961); Salient Issues of Constitutional Revision, edited by John P. Wheeler, Jr. (1961); Charlotte Irvine and Edward M. Kresky, How to Study a State Constitution (1962); and The Model State Constitution (6th edition, 1963).

pass acts that are general in form but in fact pertain to a single municipality or solve a particular local government's problem.

A different approach is municipal home rule, whereby state law gives the cities freedom to act in many of their local affairs, including the right to alter their forms and functions of government without specific legislative authority. In legislation affecting these home-rule cities, the legislatures may then be limited to matters of state concern, including education, public safety, health, and perhaps finances and streets. Although municipal home rule has been thought an effective way of keeping local government business out of the legislative halls, it has in fact been only partially successful. The organized policemen and firemen, for example, as performers of a "state" (public safety) function may go to the state legislature to get benefits they cannot get from their city councils.

The problems of government in urban areas composed of central cities and surrounding towns are thought by some students to be crying for bold, experimental action that would require state legislation. Any form of constitutional home rule that confers these rights on existing municipalities in perpetuity, as Ohio's home rule apparently does, precludes such bold action. In other words, constitutional home rule may relieve a legislature of the power to pass some local bills, but it also limits its power to meet one of the most important problems of states suffering from "surburbanitis." If such arguments seem persuasive, the conferral of home rule on cities might be worded so as specifically to reserve the legislature's power to reconstruct local government institutions, including boundaries, either generally or particularly in metropolitan areas.

OTHER SPECIAL LEGISLATION. The Connecticut General Assembly was perhaps showing compassion in declaring by special act that one of its citizens, then in this country, was bound in civil matrimony to his Japanese girl friend, who was still in Japan, so as to beat an Army deadline for marrying and bringing home Japanese wives. However, if a legislature spends much of its time on individual matters such as this, or on claims for damages against the state, or on the granting and amending of corporation charters, it may lack the time for other matters.

Although the case against special legislation is a strong one, it can sometimes be useful. For one thing, special legislation can reinforce a state's system of party leadership by assuring support of its legislative program. The disgruntled, anarchic, and obdurate members (as well as the loyal ones) of a party's legislative majority must be kept in line by the leaders if the party's program is to be enacted. One of the ways leaders can keep legislators from "straying off the reservation" is to offer party support for the enactment of special laws that are important to these legislators but of little or no importance in terms of broad policy. Such "deals" may be a less costly way of getting support than bargaining with them over larger policy questions, such as exemptions of whole industries from general regulatory or taxation measures—in other words, the bargaining away of the public interest (as perceived by the more responsible party members) to accommodate private interest groups favored by individual legislators of doubtful party loyalty.

A second contribution of special legislation is to resolve problems that either have no other forum in the governmental structure (for example, a court or an administrative agency) or if they do have such a forum, that would get entrapped in formalities of procedure and doctrine that might fail to resolve them equitably. True enough, a legislator with the power to introduce special legislative measures on behalf of individual constituents or municipalities has a considerable opportunity for favoritism, and he may be able to demand reciprocal favors from those he is able to assist. However, governments must provide a way by which they may be petitioned for fair, compassionate, even indulgent treatment by individuals whose interests are threatened by the general rule or the formal machinery of law.

Special or local legislation may provide, not only for individuals, but also for local governments or other public or philanthropic corporations, a more positive, certain, and clear corrective device than litigation in the courts. Consider, for instance, the case where such an organization issues bonds or enters into some contract in good faith, but the transaction turns out to be legally imperfect. Where the imperfection is merely technical or is a minor incident in a complex and already completed sequence of events, validation by the legislature may be a useful alternative to litigation that could lead to a court ruling invalidating or nullifying the action that has been taken.

Perhaps prohibiting special legislation will raise the general standard of political bargaining among legislators. But if not, party leaders will either be weakened or be forced to step up the use of other inducements to legislators' party regularity; among these are patronage appointments, favoritism in award of government contracts for construction and supplies, and as we have noted, concessions on general legislative measures. Increased use of inducements such as these may seem scarcely preferable to special legislation itself.

4. Direct Legislation

The normal processes of state policy formation—either in the form of constitutional or statutory provisions—were supplemented in a number of states with the adoption of the initiative and the referendum.[8]

THE INITIATIVE. These two devices were largely a product of the period from the late 1890's until the First World War. Under the initiative, a proposed change in law may be "initiated" by securing voters' signatures on petitions. Twenty states permit this for changes in statute law, and thirteen of those twenty also permit constitutional amendments to be initiated.[9] In some of them the proposed change goes directly to the voters at an election for approval or disapproval. In others it goes to the legislature and is referred to a popular vote (if it is a simple legislative act) only if the legislature fails to adopt the proposal as submitted. In the last eventuality, the legislatures of some states may place alternative proposals before the voters along with the popularly initiated measures.

The initiative is thus intended to permit the adoption of policies on which the legislature has refused to yield. A statewide vote may be won by a popular majority significantly different from the aggregated majorities in the districts used for choice of legislators. Even the possibility of its use can sometimes stimulate the legislature to act lest its prestige suffer. The initiative can be useful to some special interest groups, and it has been used in the past by governors who were trying to overcome the inertia of unrepresentative legislatures. Another attraction to the proponents of an initiated law or amendment is the opportunity to state their measure in the terms they desire—in contrast to the ordinary legislative process in which amendments and substitute bills commonly convert a legislative idea into a compromise reflecting a variety of values.

For the most part the initiative has not lived up to either the hopes or fears that surrounded its adoption. The device has been used so much in some states that the ballots have become overlong. But generally the voters have shown discrimination. In the states allowing constitutional amendments to be initiated, they are much less likely to adopt amend-

---

[8] On the Constitutional initiative, see Albert L. Sturm, Methods of State Constitutional Reform (Ann Arbor, Mich.: University of Michigan Press, 1954), chap. IV. On the whole topic, with analysis of the terms and operation in each state, see Hugh A. Bone, The Initiative and Referendum (New York: National Municipal League, 1959).

[9] The constitutional initiative states include Arizona, Arkansas, California, Colorado, Massachusetts, Michigan, Missouri, Nebraska, Nevada, North Dakota, Ohio, Oklahoma, and Oregon. Legislative acts may be initiated in these states and in the following: Alaska, Idaho, Maine, Montana, Oklahoma, South Dakota, and Utah.

ments sponsored by popular initiative than those presented to them by the legislature. In the fifteen-year period ending with 1952, only 38 percent of the "initiated" amendments received the necessary votes, whereas 61 percent of those that were proposed by the legislature were approved.[10]

However, some strange proposals do get accepted. Initiated measures committing sizable blocks of state revenues to particular programs, such as aid to the aged or to local governments, have been adopted, thereby creating embarrassing situations for state governments. Increasingly the device seems available not to "the people" but rather to groups with the funds necessary to get the required number of signatures on the petition. An invasion of the system of representative government, the initiative finds its defense primarily in situations where the legislature refuses to correct some "fault" in its own organization or procedures.

THE REFERENDUM. In contrast to the initiative, the protest referendum is a form of popular veto of legislation. In the twenty-two states [11] that permit its use, a group of citizens opposed to some legislative enactment may, by getting a sufficient number of names on petitions, keep the act from going into effect until a popular vote has been had on the issue. The popular vote, in effect, is on the question: Shall or shall not the act complained of become law? And a simple majority of those voting on the issue normally determines it. The evidence at hand suggests that voters more frequently agree with the legislature than with those protesting. Yet there is the risk that a well-organized minority may succeed in vetoing measures as a result of light voting on the referred measure.

The protest referendum has possibly a strategic merit. When constitutional changes increasing the legislature's powers for policy decisions are being sought, it may be possible to quiet some of the doubts by making the protest referendum part of the arrangement.

In about half of the protest referendum states, an optional referendum is also available. This device allows the legislature, in passing a bill, to provide that it will go into effect only if the voters approve the measure at a subsequent election. Thus the legislators can dodge responsibility on a hotly controversial matter such as daylight saving time, the fluoridation of water, or "right to work" laws by "letting the people decide." In such circumstances those legislators who believe that in a representative government the legislature should face up squarely to its responsibility subject themselves to charges of being "against democracy."

---

[10] *Derived from information in Sturm, op. cit., pp. 76 and 153.*
[11] *All of those having the initiative plus Maryland and New Mexico.*

5. *Lawmaking: Informed, Orderly Deliberation*

In the making of a state's laws the legislature and the governor are the decisive participants, yet they operate in a field of many forces—the pressures of narrow interest groups, the demands of local governments and local party leaders, the federal government's offers of grants-in-aid for particular programs, the conflicting desires of the taxpaying public and the beneficiaries of state services, the distinct orientations of urban, suburban, small town, and rural residents. Some may say that these forces to a substantial degree determine state policies; few can deny that they set outer limits to what a governor and legislature may venture to do. Yet the play of these forces on the lawmaking process is itself shaped by the formal machinery provided by constitution, statutes, and customs, by the structuring of the state's political system, and by the qualities of men and women who serve in the legislature and the governorship.[12]

The separation of powers is the least helpful of constitutional formulas for understanding the states' lawmaking processes. To think of the governor principally as the chief executive is to ignore his development, in most states, into the chief legislator. This growth of his legislative role makes it almost impossible to discuss either the governor or the legislature without constant attention to the ways in which they interact. The interaction is itself remarkably complex and various, so that generalization, whether descriptive or prescriptive, is hazardous.

It is, then, largely a matter of convenience that our discussion of lawmaking is organized to give attention, first, to the adequacy of arrangements for informed, orderly deliberation, with emphasis on the legislature; second, to the adequacy of policy leadership for decision making, with

---

[12] *One of the more literate of the participant-observers of the conflicts encountered in our state legislative processes was the late philosopher, state senator, and poet T. V. Smith, who summarized: "To the legislator, interests of equally good citizens seem to be just the way they seem to be—in conflict through long and wearing days" from which conflicts legislators must create "out of stiff opposition a sort of bastard reasonableness." He further stated: "His compromises constitute the democratic process in its living reality. Seen from the shining cliffs of perfection (the vantage of ignorance and the source of undiscriminating criticism), it is a thing poor enough indeed; but seen in the perspective of its only living alternative—dictatorship—legislative maneuvering becomes blessed, blessing those who give and those who get—blessing, indeed, all alike with the perpetuity of a process that peaceably institutionalizes the very principle of violence itself." In "Two Functions of the American State Legislator," The Annals, 195 (January 1938), 185. A recent useful treatise is William J. Keefe and Morris S. Ogul, The American Legislative Process, Congress and the States (Englewood Cliffs, N.J.: Prentice-Hall, 1964). The American Assembly has sponsored a second publication on the American states, this one focused on state legislatures, entitled* State Legislatures in American Politics, *edited by Alexander Heard (Englewood Cliffs, N.J.: Prentice-Hall, 1966).*

emphasis on the governor's role; and finally to the opportunities for criticism and protest.

Before ideas become laws, there are many stages of decision. The idea may originate anywhere and with many different persons. In the process that follows—whether the proposal relates to gambling at bazaars, taxation, or highway drainage—the answers to many questions may be sought. How will this proposal change existing policies? What are its probable consequences? What are other solutions to the problem? What have other governments done about the matter and with what result? Will it be constitutional? How have the courts interpreted the proposed words and phrases? How will this policy be administered? How much discretion will administrators have and how will this discretion be guided by statutory words? Whom will the proposal affect? What will their reactions be if it is adopted? How many of them will be affected, and in which of several ways? Who is for this proposal, who is against it, and which groups have not declared themselves? What does John think? Is Ed satisfied? What did the head of the department say? Has the governor said anything about this?

The deliberative process may range from public discussion in which mass organized support or objections are put forth to discussion among the more influential few. The process may include tentative decisions, modifications of decisions, compromises, and final decisions—final, at least, for the time being.

THE FORMAL DELIBERATIVE PROCESS. The deliberative process is acted out—and frequently is partially carried out—in the rituals of the legislative procedure. These rituals include, with variations and much elaboration, several phases:

1. A bill is introduced. (At this stage, too, arrangements are made for printing the bills—and sometimes digests of bills—and for informing the members and the public of bills introduced.)

2. It is referred to a standing committee, which may do nothing about it and thereby possibly kill the bill. Or it may hold hearings at which nonmembers can usually appear, and, after that, the measure may be amended and by vote the bill may be killed or given a favorable recommendation to the house.

3. The bill is then considered by the house, as a forum for debate, if it has been favorably reported by the committee or removed from committee decision. If it survives one such consideration, the usual procedure provides at least a second opportunity for debate before this house takes final action on it.

4. These rituals are repeated in the other house. If the second house

amends the bill, it goes back to the first one for consideration of these amendments. In cases of disagreement a special joint committee of the two houses (a conference committee) may be formed to seek a compromise, which is then referred back to both houses.

5. After it has been passed, the bill goes to the governor. He can either approve it or veto it. In the latter case, the bill goes back to the legislature, if it is still in session, for possible revision, passage over the governor's veto, or death by inaction.[13]

Throughout this ritual records are kept. Among the more important of these are the journals, usually published daily, showing the actions of each house, and the digests (where they exist) published periodically during the session showing how far each bill has progressed, or where it died.

It is evident that these rituals emphasize deliberateness, whatever the quality of the deliberation. Though the rituals may be abbreviated at times, they are the formalized arrangements that permit the competition of ideas to enter the policy-making process.

THE PUBLIC'S INFORMATION AND PARTICIPATION. The press coverage that the state government gets, or doesn't get, affects the information that the people of a state need if they are to participate in state policy making. However, editors of daily newspapers and other news channels frequently set a low value on state government news. Not uncommonly, news of local and national government, not to mention beauty contests, seems to be valued higher.

Usually, the larger dailies keep a bureau or a reporter at the capitol only during legislative sessions, and depend on the national wire services the rest of the time. Under this policy (and it affects the wire services also), the start of legislative sessions is frequently a time for hiring additional news staff, and novices break into daily newspaper work by helping interpret state government to the people. However, even for able people who spend their full time on them, state governments are rather complex phenomena to comprehend. The novice and the pedestrian newsgatherer are therefore dependent on news sources whose reliability they are unequipped to judge.

Even when the state news reporters are veterans, the reporting is not uncommonly somewhat erroneous or incomplete, or it misses the point. Frequently, the reporters are not informed, sharp, or vigorous enough to ask the right questions of enough people. Although there are numerous

---

[13] *The governor of North Carolina has no veto power.*

newsmaking points in state governments, newsmen are inclined to concentrate on a few, except when handouts of news are announced. One reporter may concentrate on political gossip and election prospects, while another may seem to be concerned only with the highway department.

The character of state news reporting is further affected when newspapers do not pay their reporters enough to command their full services and so permit them to accept public relations retainer fees from groups who wish to suppress or color news or to favor particular news sources. When in addition editors play at king-, governor-, or senator-making, the character of the reporting is also affected. Editorial writing can be fairly significant in state policy matters. Although the readership of the editorial page may not be large, it is likely to include a large share of readers who are significant in state policy making. Yet, if the editorials use what to the knowing are false premises based on misinformation or misunderstanding, the newspaper's influence may be small.

The quality of state government news reporting and editorial writing might be helped by annual short courses or week-long institutes sponsored by universities, each for a region of several states. Newspapers would need to pay the expenses of reporters, as well as sponsor the cost of the instructional program. Another possibility might be to recruit as state government reporters persons who have combined an apprenticeship in journalism with college or graduate training in state government and politics.

The approach of the news-gathering and disseminating agencies to state government news can give emphasis and impetus to policy discussion, or it can do quite the reverse. If the bread and butter of state reporting consists of personalities or material derived from press releases like the trend in the incidence of measles or the number of roads closed for maintenance or reconstruction, little stimulation is given to the decision-making phases of state government. In contrast, when the implications of new policy proposals and the consequences of past policy decisions are explored intensively and thoughtfully, a paper can provide sound news as well as perform a public service.[14]

The files and memories of the administrative staffs of state government agencies are among the best available stores of information on state policies. These agency people know what they are doing, what they aren't

---

[14] *For an account by its managing editor of the vigorous efforts of* The Tampa Tribune *to expose corruption and mismanagement in Florida state and city government and to get policy issues before the citizenry, see* V. M. Newton, Jr., Crusade for Democracy (*Ames, Iowa: Iowa State University Press, 1961*).

doing, what they could be doing, and to some extent what their like numbers in other states are doing and thinking. These are among the sources to which reporters who write useful news stories must go for their information.

Certain problems arise, however, in considering administrative agencies as active publicizers of policy issues. For one thing, some administrators may be too engrossed in their existing routines to think about any different ones. There is also the problem of ethics. How far is it proper for governmental administrators to go in publicizing their agencies and in seeking public approval of new policies? That some administrators go well beyond any proper limits in selling their agency as they compete with others for the state's money is well known. However, one would have only blame for an educational administrator who didn't call the public's attention to the problems of facilities and instructors for an approaching increase in school population, or a state administrator of tuberculosis sanatoria who didn't report publicly the progressive depopulation of sanatorium beds since the development of new methods for controlling the disease. In most areas of government operation, administrators can do much to educate the public with regard to the present and foreseeable tasks of their agencies without raising questions of propriety.

Administrative publicity serves several useful purposes. Relations with clients can be improved. (For example, the fisherman appreciates being told how many fish of which varieties are being planted in which streams.) Employee morale can be enhanced through reports of agency accomplishment. But policy information for the general public and for the influential is fully as important as these more specialized needs.

POLICY RESEARCH. The device of forming official groups of citizens—legislators or laymen or both—with the view that these groups will employ researchers and other specialists, become informed on matters relating to a set of policy issues, decide on policies that should be adopted, and make recommendations to the legislature in an informative report has had wide use in state government. Some such groups are continuing bodies and have a relatively unlimited scope of subjects. Legislative councils are the most important examples. Other groups are formed for some particular inquiry and will usually be disbanded when a report is submitted; these will here be called study commissions.

The study commissions may be sponsored by governors alone, by governors and legislatures jointly, or by legislatures alone. The governor may sponsor one when he wishes to build public support and information for some at least moderately complex policy proposal, such as an administrative reorganization, tax reform, or a combined state and local highway, roads, and street program. It may be a matter on which the governor believes there is need for much public education before decisions can be reached. He may also have no fixed bias about the precise terms of the policy to be proposed, but know that there is a problem to be solved, and expect that any commission he helps select, and perhaps staff, will produce recommendations he can support. A governor may also use this device when he feels a need to show his concern about a matter of interest to some portion of the public and yet wants to escape personal identification with a particular solution.

Legislators who have been unsuccessful in accomplishing some legislative goal may get a study commission created to inquire further into the matter, in the hope that a report presented to a later session of the legislature will help achieve the necessary majorities. Or a study commission may also come into being so that legislators may receive expense money and perhaps a per diem fee for visiting the capital between sessions, as well as enjoy publicity, prominence, and a sense of power over the administrative agencies they are studying. In a few states, such as New York, Massachusetts, Michigan, and California, some commissions have been continued from one legislative session to another in such a manner that they are practically continuing activities of the states. Naturally they fail to give the timely and sharp focus to particular problems that is the special virtue of temporary commissions.

The abuses of the legislative study commissions may in some instances be no worse than boondoggles for the benefit of the legislators and, incidentally, the researchers. In other instances, these commissions may represent challenges by a handful of legislators to the executive authority of the state. They are then efforts to supplant the governor by supervising administrative activities for which the commission members lack both authority and responsibility. Sometimes commissions may try to build campaigns against the governor's policies. When the legislative majority is of a different party from that of the governor, such opportunities are likely to be seized upon.

In contrast to temporary study commissions, the legislative council is a committee of legislators from both houses, usually from 12 to 20 in number, who are appointed by the presiding officers of the houses and given a permanent staff of research and clerical personnel. They commonly meet quarterly, although they may meet more frequently or have committees that do so. Proposals for studies may come from the legislature in the form of resolutions requesting a study of a particular subject. More commonly, they come from individual legislators, and in some cases they are relayed from individuals outside the legislature, including the governor. In 1964, 38 states had legislative councils or similar bodies under different names.

Legislative councils differ greatly on one practice: whether they will make policy recommendations to the legislature or simply transmit to it informational research reports prepared by the staff. The first practice assumes that there are numerous areas of study on which general agreement could be reached and on which the council could present a carefully devised legislative program. Although numbers of councils follow, at least in part, practices reflecting some such assumption, the pattern has elsewhere been criticized and rejected. Members of the legislature who are not council members may rebel at having a "little legislature" prejudge issues for them. Besides, what is a noncontroversial item to some members may seem highly controversial to others. Perhaps more important, those members of the legislature who with governors, governor-nominees, party leaders, and others seek to plan and place before the legislature policy programs with high priorities see policy-proposing legislative councils as threats to their system. If one sees party and gubernatorial responsibility in policy formation as desirable, then a well-organized competing system must be recognized as a threat.

Legislative bodies must have the right to seek information that is useful in their deliberations and to seek it independently if need be. They must also develop among their members individuals who have sufficient information to qualify for legislative leadership positions, such as the committee chairmanships and majority and minority leadership roles. Service on study commissions and legislative councils may help develop such informal leadership. Standing committees of legislatures need research assistance during sessions, and this can be borrowed from legislative council research staffs. Finally, individual legislators need the informational assistance that such a permanent research staff may be able to give.

Yet there is a compromise available to meet these needs. If a legislative council that concentrates on informational research is maintained, it can serve as a professional staff of researchers for the legislature. If the legislature wants to sponsor a proposal on a particular matter, it can create a special study commission that can perhaps use the researchers of the legislative council. Furthermore, governors have their own channels and means for influencing and courting these developments; thus, they may request the legislature to establish study commissions on matters of interest to them.

One great lack in most states is year-round research bureaus for the major parties that could help develop informed deliberation on state policy. Party policy planning and platform building, as well as campaigning, are in many situations hampered by a simple lack of information. A governor running for reelection may have state employees available to work on policy plans for his campaign, but what of the opposing candidate? Platform committee members for state party conventions commonly rely on some relatively brief part-time assistance in canvassing platform material. Nominees for governor frequently need lots of assistance in learning the reasons for their party's platform and in developing their personal campaign material. Candidates for the legislature need to know what issues they are supposed to be campaigning about. Year-round party research bureaus exploring possible issues, accumulating information on them, and standing ready to sap information from the state bureaucracy, the experts on any and everything, and the libraries could help state policy making become a better battle of ideas. Interest groups that now seek to serve in this capacity (taxpayers' organizations and labor unions, among others) lack the general view that the parties, seeking statewide popular majorities, must have. Yet the parties must feel that policy issues matter, else research will not matter.

LEGISLATIVE COMMITTEES. The state legislatures could not operate without heavy reliance on their standing committees. The hundreds or thousands of bills introduced each session are normally referred by the presiding officer of each house to supposedly appropriate standing committees. But, except in those few states where committees must, under strict rules, report all bills back to their houses, most of these bills die in committee. If this were not true, our legislatures would be in more nearly continuous session.

Nearly all of the nation's legislative houses have too many standing committees. For example, Arkansas had 69 house committees until they were cut to 26 in the early 1960's. But those who doubt that legislatures are capable of self-improvement will be pleasantly shocked to find that they are slashing the number of committees, even though a large number makes many members happy by enabling more of them to be chairmen and to sit on several committees. In the nation generally, between 1946 and 1965 the median number of house standing committees dropped from 39 to 21, and of senate committees from 31 to 20. Encouraging as this trend is, it remains true that half the senates and houses have more committees than the median figure shown. Eight houses and two senates still have between 41 and 51.[15]

---

[15] The Book of the States: 1966–67, *p. 68.*

If committees are to reflect in some fashion the sentiments of their houses, it is thought that they need to be fairly large. But if they are both large and numerous, each member serves on several different ones. Scheduling committee meetings then becomes difficult, attendance goes down, and thus decisions are often made by a small portion of the committee membership. Under the usual rules any member can frequently stop committee consideration of any bill he dislikes by raising the issue of a quorum.

The answer to this melée is obviously fewer committees, with members serving on only one or two of them. Reducing the number serves to make each committee more important, and thus perhaps more satisfying to its members. Each member cannot range so widely on legislative topics then, but more of them will probably have opportunities to participate in the review of some bills of general importance.

Three states—Massachusetts, Maine, and Connecticut—have for many years used joint committees almost exclusively. That is, the senate and house members of the appropriations committee, for example, sit together in at least parts of their deliberations. This device saves a great deal of time for administrators and other citizens who attend public committee hearings. It also gives an opportunity for disagreements between committee members from the two houses to be compromised before either house gives consideration to a bill. If the house or senate members wish to deliberate and report separately on their recommendations, as is likely in many cases if the houses are of different party majorities, this is also possible.

Fortunately, most state legislatures have avoided the mechanical seniority system for selecting chairmen of standing committees, which is a major flaw in the organization of Congress. The chairmen have great responsibility in planning and conducting their meetings, in leading their committees to decisions, and in presenting those decisions to the houses. Governors, speakers, and other party leaders need to participate in the selection of these men so as to ensure their effectiveness and general political responsibility. (One of the few advantages of having numerous committees is that it permits distrusted members who are in a position to demand some committee chairmanship to be relegated to spots where they can do little harm.)

Although the chairmen of the committees are normally a part of the leadership system, with responsibilities to higher leaders, they have an obligation to observe standards of fairness. These include scheduling hearings on members' bills as far as time will permit and, when public hearings are held, giving adequate notice of the hearings. The standards of fairness also require that bills approved by committee majorities be reported, whether or not the chairman approves of them.[16]

Committees are at the heart of the deliberative process as the legislatures participate in it. It is here that notions about desirable policy changes on a subject are collected, that decisions are made on what is "important enough" to consider, that relevant knowledge and impressions are exchanged and values compared in accepting or criticizing given bills or in choosing the words, phrases, and numbers for statutory language. Here leaders may learn of relevant factual claims previously unknown or of sentiments previously unconsidered.

SESSIONS. In nine states the legislature meets annually in regular session; in the remainder regular sessions are held every two years. A shift back to annual sessions has started in recent years, with 19 states in all scheduling annual meetings; 10 of these, however, limit one session of each biennium to matters relating to budgets and finance. Although problems of foreseeing revenue returns and expenditure requirements more than two years in advance have been a principal argument for the return to annual sessions, the limitation to budgetary matters seems like an attempt to permit carpenters to nail but not saw. The frequency with which special sessions have been called in a number of biennial-session states makes the shift to annual sessions largely a formalization of existing practice.

In many of the states the business of state government is big enough and fraught with enough continuing problems to justify annual sessions. In making such changes, however, legislators need to understand that administrative programs cannot be planned and executed in precise time patterns of twelve months and that program changes must normally be cast in longer time periods.

As for the length of the regular sessions, the constitutions of over half the states limit them to a maximum number of calendar or legislative days, often as few as thirty or sixty. But these limitations are in many cases becoming unrealistic in view of the numbers of issues to be considered in committee and in the houses.

Although these limitations may seem to be the cause of the unseemly rush of business in the last days of limited sessions, the formal limits probably aggravate the situation only slightly. Some decisions get delayed

---

[16] *On this and other aspects of legislators' behavior, see John C. Wahlke, Heinz Eulau, William Buchanan, and Leroy C. Ferguson,* The Legislative System *(New York: Wiley, 1962).*

in all legislatures. In those without a formal time limit, a closing date is normally agreed upon among the leaders, thus forcing compromise and decision on the remaining bills. Nevertheless, an important advantage of the unlimited session is that the closing date can be revised when stalemates prevent the enactment of bills.

Some reformers have suggested that state legislatures, like city councils, be in practically continuous session, taking recesses between relatively short meeting periods. This could be the eventual outcome in some states. The contrary and generally prevailing view is that both the governmental administration and others likely to be affected by state policy changes need closed seasons on legislation in which they can get along with their work under existing policies. Administrators, too, need some escape from legislators' importuning on administrative details.

6. *Lawmaking: Policy Leadership and Decision Making*

Policy leadership entails finding issues, crystallizing the proposed terms of policy changes, and ensuring effective operation of the established decision-making systems. It is of necessity a joint effort in our complex political and lawmaking systems, and the quality of the leadership depends not only on mechanisms and procedures but also on the character of those who hold the leadership posts.

FINDING ISSUES. There is no lack of proposals for legislation, but not all of them deserve serious consideration. On the other hand, some proposals that deserve attention may be so mildly advocated that they risk being overlooked. Finding issues, therefore, is not the same as finding proposals for legislation. Instead, those proposals must be sorted out and most of them put aside because of low priority; attention must be given to the unorganized or unrepresented interests whose needs may not be well articulated amid the cacophony of competing organized interests; finally, legislation must be fashioned out of the bits and pieces of narrowly conceived proposals and the accompanying counterproposals of opposing interests.

Competing political parties are issue finders. In the search for ways to win elections they need broadly appealing ideas. The parties (or factions in one-party states) generally agree about the ways of conducting their government, but the competition stimulates the search for attractive policy innovations. Parties have some tendency to be cautious in espousing ideas that may antagonize voters, but if one party competes with ideas, the other is inclined to respond. However, as mentioned earlier, state party research staffs could generate even more ideas.

Some individual legislators search for broad issues and policy solutions that go beyond the needs of their localities and the interest groups that may have helped elect them. These men are, in effect, in training for positions of greater leadership, and the parties may well seek means of using their "good" ideas and recruiting such men into the legislative leadership system.

Governors and candidates for governor are frequently more courageous than their parties in espousing policy ideas. They win all or lose all in competitive elections and know, therefore, that they must risk antagonizing some voters in order to attract greater numbers. Moreover, they also know that they will likely be much better known for their policy accomplishments than for their administrative performance.

The minority party can also be influential in policy making. In fact, recent electoral experience suggests that the two parties are more competitive in more states than has generally been thought. For example, in 42 of the 50 gubernatorial elections held for terms extending at least through 1963, the winning candidate received less than 60 percent of the votes, and in 30 of those elections he had less than 55 percent.[17] Thus a minority that can poll on the order of over 40 percent of the popular vote is at least a potential threat, while a 45 percent or better share makes it a clear and present danger. If the minority party espouses well-developed policy programs and makes gains in its popular vote, it is likely to find the majority party adopting parts of its program in an effort to reduce the threat.

ORGANIZATION FOR DECISION. A large number of people take part in the making and influencing of decisions on state policies. But this very breadth of participation makes some systematic provision for policy leadership essential. One candidate for the leadership role is the legislature's own group of formally designated leaders—presiding officers of the houses, committee chairmen, majority and minority leaders. But the governor is a strong competitor for the role. In some states the real guidance is provided by an informal group, either of fixed membership and

---

[17] *U.S. Bureau of the Census*, Statistical Abstract of the United States: 1964, (*Washington, D.C.*, 1964), *p. 379. The elections used for our calculation are the latest recorded in the table—all 40 elections held in 1962 and 1963, and for states whose governorships were not at stake in those years, the elections of 1960 and 1961.*
Of the 50 gubernatorial elections held for terms extending at least through 1965 (including the 26 such elections in 1964 and so affected in part by the unique features of the Goldwater candidacy), 35 were won by less than 60 percent of the votes, and 21 of those by less than 55 percent. Statistical Abstract: 1965, p. 382.

designated as a steering committee or of shifting membership; among the likely members are the legislature's formal leaders, some influential legislators lacking formal leadership positions, party leaders outside the legislature, and the governor or his representatives. This group may be supplemented by caucuses of all legislators of a party or of legislators from a particular section of the state. Rarely, these days, does a political "boss" with no governmental office monopolize or dominate the policy-leadership function. In effect, then, the states may have several alternative, competitive, or overlapping systems for reaching decisions about state policies.

The relations among these decisional systems can be best illuminated by focusing on the governor. There are several reasons for this: in many states he is in fact the policy leader; his achievement of this role is a relatively recent and highly significant development; apparently, he has had to assume the role of policy leader in order to win both the party and the administrative leadership; [18] and, finally, the claims of legislators and others to policy leadership can be best understood as challenges to the governor's existing or potential dominance. Among the elements contributing to the governor's position of strength are his budget responsibilities, his special position (though not in all states) as chief executive vis-à-vis the administrative departments, and the fact that he is at the center of the political communication process. Other elements of his strength, such as the electorate's endorsement of his campaign platform and his possession of the veto power, will be treated as aspects of his relations with the legislature.

The executive budget, which is almost universal among the states, has given the governor an opportunity to take the initiative in the most encompassing set of policy decisions that a legislative session makes. Budget decisions are, on a more general level, decisions on tax rates and tax policy and on the general scale of state activity. How much money agencies "need" depends upon the premises entertained by the estimator, and the estimates can vary substantially.

In presenting his budget a governor can propose levels of state activities that fit his policies, but such proposals these days normally take all the revenue of existing taxes. Thus there is little leeway for the legislators. If they want to spend more, they face the prospect of deficits or additional

---

[18] *This thesis—that policy leadership came first in the growth of the governor's role —is well argued in Coleman B. Ransone, Jr., The Office of Governor in the United States (University, Ala.: University of Alabama Press, 1956), which is the principal recent work on the governorship.*

taxes. On the other hand, if they try to cut back the amounts of proposed appropriations, they will hear the complaint that the figures are being "cut below what the governor says we need."

The governor's (and the legislature's) discretion in fiscal policy is hampered by past decisions to tie up state money in special funds dedicated to particular purposes. Under such arrangements, revenue from a particular tax or fee is committed to a particular program regardless of the amount of revenue and the current usefulness of the program. At the same time, other pressing needs may go unmet. (Even without the special-fund device, large amounts of revenue may be dedicated to payment of debt service, employee retirement costs, matching costs for federal grants, or employee pay-increment systems.) As a result, a constant battle to get and keep revenues in a general fund is usually necessary to allow both the governor and the legislature to make revised decisions on spending and tax policy.

Although portions of the state budget may be "frozen" by the dedication of revenues to particular purposes, a governor is in a position to exercise much initiative in budgetary policy decisions. He must, however, have an adequate budget staff if he is to make reasonably informed decisions. Even though he may have to compromise in securing an enacted budget, if he uses his influence, the bargaining will start from his figures and completed plan rather than from those of the agencies and interest groups.

The newly elected governor faces a problem in budget planning if he must present a budget to the legislature within a few weeks of taking office. The device of allowing a governor-elect to appoint budget advisers who can start work several weeks before the inauguration appears to be a useful solution, as is his power to call budget hearings during the same period.

A governor gets an excellent education if he takes his role as executive and political head of the state seriously. As chief executive he has a special opportunity to tap the expert knowledge in the administrative departments. If he has a staff of his own to multiply his effectiveness, he has an advantage that no legislator can match. And simply because he occupies so conspicuous and influential a position, information flows to him from people who are served, regulated, and taxed by the state and, of course, from high and low participants in the political process.[19]

He is in a position to learn "what is wrong" with his state government.

---

[19] *The average governor sees 10 to 25 persons and receives over 100 letters a day.* Ibid., *pp. 125, 128.*

The dangerous, the inconsistent, and the ridiculous, along with the fruitful and promising, in state administration are impressed upon him by administrators, by complaints from the public, and by his own aides if his office is appropriately staffed. At the same time, he hears the pleas of all those who would alter the state's programs. A governor, therefore, is given remarkable opportunities to mold out of his gubernatorial experience informed, balanced policy proposals—some modest, some major—for the legislature, and he is in an advantageous position to press these proposals to the point of decision. Unless the legislature is by essential composition hostile to gubernatorial initiatives, he can serve as a corrective force for the ills of inertia, obsolescence, and neglected opportunities for improved state services.

The governor's staff is vital to his success. Its members serve as additional eyes and ears, as handlers of routine, as reviewers, analyzers, and proposers. They can bring skills to the task that the governor may lack. They can work within his stated policies and privately known values. Without them his full role as leader cannot be realized. Yet in about half the states, it appears, the governor has only one or two nonclerical assistants.[20]

THE GOVERNOR AND THE LEGISLATURE. State policy making occurs in a variety of political settings that render foolish most generalizations made on a national basis about the relations between the governor and the legislature. The governor's party may (a) overwhelmingly control both legislative houses, (b) have a slight to adequate majority in both houses, (c) have a majority in only one house, or (d) be the minority in both houses. If one were to add party names to governor and legislative majorities and minorities, the number of possible situations would double. Using the simpler scheme given above, however, we can assign the first pattern to the one-party states, and the other three to the two-party competitive states.

A more complex set of patterns could be developed by considering two other factors. One is that two-party states and those in subgroupings according to degree of party competitiveness can be identified either by looking at statewide election figures or by looking at the division of party control within the government (e.g., between the governor and the legislative houses, or between the two houses). The results differ principally

---

[20] Ibid., p. 344. The study covers 25 states, of which roughly half support the statement here. Ransone devotes a substantial chapter to "A Staff for the Governor's Office," pp. 302–62.

because one or both houses may be malapportioned so that it does not approximate the statewide party preferences of the electorate.[21] Consequently, division of party control within the state government may indicate a two-party pattern that contrasts with the electorate's preference for one of the parties.

Second, instead of looking at party division within the government at a single point in time, we could consider the patterns over a longer time period. An occasional division of party control is less serious than its persistence, and a persistent division is more serious if it significantly discriminates against one party more than the other. Figure 9.1, based on a study by V. O. Key, Jr., shows how the pattern of divided control persisted in the individual states in the period 1931–52 (except in Minnesota and Nebraska, which have nonpartisan legislatures). Of the 15 states completely free of divided control, all except South Dakota were ones in which a single party was dominant continuously, without change of its control of the governorship and both houses at any election—in other words, the southern states and Vermont and New Hampshire. Of the other 31 states, 16 had divided control for 36 to 64 percent of the period, and 15 states "enjoyed" the same phenomenon for 9 to 28 percent of the time. The Democratic party suffered more persistently than the Republican from divided control. Among the 32 states with competitive parties, when a Republican candidate for governor won 60 percent or more of the popular vote, his party always won control of both houses of the legislature, but in 37 percent of the 1930–50 elections where a Democratic governor was chosen by a large popular majority, the Republicans nonetheless managed to control one or both legislative houses. Overall in these 32 states, a successful candidate for governor had one or both houses in opposition following 51 percent of the elections if he was a Democrat, but following only 18 percent of the elections if he was a Republican.[22] New York is a notable instance of the Democrats' frustration. From 1900 to 1950, the Democrats held the governorship slightly over half the time, but only for two years did they also control both legislative houses and only for an additional four years did they control even one house in addition to the governorship. In both 1930 and 1934, their candidates, Franklin D. Roose-

---

[21] *The results may also differ, even under an equal-population apportionment of legislative seats, either because the aggregate of majorities won by successful candidates in individual districts is not necessarily the same as a pooling of all votes throughout the state or because districts, though equal, have been gerrymandered to depreciate the votes of one party and enhance the votes of the other.*

[22] V. O. Key, Jr., American State Politics: An Introduction (*New York: Knopf, 1956*), *pp. 55, 60.*

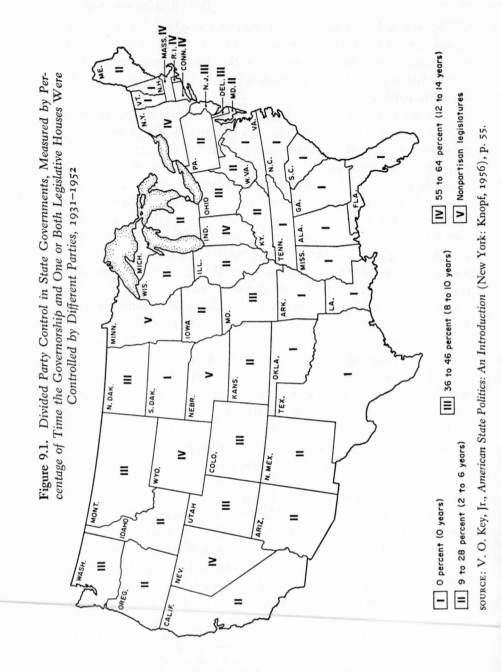

Figure 9.1. Divided Party Control in State Governments, Measured by Percentage of Time the Governorship and One or Both Legislative Houses Were Controlled by Different Parties, 1931–1952

I 0 percent (0 years)

II 9 to 28 percent (2 to 6 years)

III 36 to 46 percent (8 to 10 years)

IV 55 to 64 percent (12 to 14 years)

V Nonpartisan legislatures

SOURCE: V. O. Key, Jr., *American State Politics: An Introduction* (New York: Knopf, 1956), p. 55.

velt and Herbert Lehman, won over 60 percent of the two-party vote, but the Republicans retained control of both legislative houses.[23]

Table 9.1 gives a detailed accounting for the period 1954 to 1964. In four of the six election years shown, over a third of the states divided the control of policy centers between the parties. Outside the South, divided rule was about as common as party government. Throughout the decade only 14 states were consistently free of divided control, and 13 of them were solidly Democratic southern or border states; the other, South Dakota, was solidly Republican except for one election when it switched to fully Democratic control.[24] At the other extreme, 8 states had divided government for at least 83 percent of the period.[25]

Democratic governors appeared less doomed to frustration than in the 1931–52 period. Even outside the South they had about a 50-50 chance, as did the Republican governors, of finding favorable legislative majorities in both houses (and, too, of finding one or both houses under the opposition party's control).[26]

A governor's policy leadership must necessarily be attuned to the partisan composition of the legislature. There are therefore a number of styles of leadership. Even if the governor finds himself faced with outsize majorities of his party in both houses, he may have problems. Overwhelming party majorities may have little or no opposition to hold them together and may actually be a congeries of factions stronger than the party. In such a situation the governor has the possibility of putting together working majorities out of past alliances and the promise of future patronage. He is

---

[23] *Ransome, op. cit., pp. 187f; Key, op. cit., p. 59.*

[24] *In this period the consistently Democratic-control states were 11 of the 12 southern and border states shown on Table 9.1 (Oklahoma having meantime broken its record by electing a Republican governor in 1962), plus Kentucky and Missouri. Figure 9.1's solidly Republican-control states, New Hampshire and Vermont, fell from this category by electing Democratic governors in 1962 and 1964.*

[25] *Connecticut, Michigan, Montana, Nevada, New Jersey, Oregon, Pennsylvania, and Rhode Island. Inclusion of each of the last three in the group results from the arbitrary decision to classify as "divided control" a government in which one legislative house is evenly divided between the parties even though the other house and the governorship are controlled by one party.*

[26] *Of the 183 cases of Democratic governors shown in Table 9.1, and the 125 of these in which both legislative houses were also Democratic, 66 may be subtracted as belonging to the 11 southern states. The interparty comparison then appears as follows for the 1954–64 period:*

Democratic governor		Republican governor	
With both houses	117	With both houses	100
Democratic	59	Republican	51
With one or both		With one or both	
houses opposed	58	houses opposed	49

Table 9.1. *Party Control of Governorship and Legislative Houses, by States, 1954–1964*

State	1954	1956	1958	1960	1962	1964
Alabama	DDD	d d d	DDD	d d d	DDD	d d d
Alaska	. . .	. . .	DDD	d DD	DD½	d DD
Arizona	DDD	DDD	RDD	RDD	RDD	DDD
Arkansas	DDD	DDD	DDD	DDD	DDD	DDD
California	R R R	r ½ R	DDD	d DD	DDD	d DD
Colorado	D R R	DDD	DDD	d DD	R R R	r R D
Connecticut	DDR	d R R	DDD	d DR	DDR	d DR
Delaware	r D D	RDD	r R D	DDD	d DD	DDD
Florida	DDD	DDD	d DD	DDD	d DD	DDD
Georgia	DDD	d DD	DDD	d DD	DDD	d DD
Hawaii	. . .	. . .	. . .	r r d	DDD	d DD
Idaho	R R R	r R R	RDD	r R R	R R R	r R R
Illinois	r R R	R R R	r R D	D R R	d R R	DRD
Indiana	r R R	R R R	r R D	DDR	d R R	DDD
Iowa	R R R	DRR	DRR	R R R	DRR	DDD
Kansas	R r R	DRR	D r R	R R R	R r R	R R R
Kentucky	d d d	d d d	d d d	d d d	d d d	d d d
Louisiana	d d d	DDD	d d d	DDD	d d d	DDD
Maine	D R R	DRR	DRR	R R R	R R R	r D D
Maryland	RDD	r d d	DDD	d d d	DDD	d d d
Massachusetts	R R D	DRD	DDD	RDD	DDD	RDD
Michigan	D R R	DRR	DR½	DRR	R R R	RDD
Minnesota	D . .	D . .	D . .	R . .	D . .	d . .
Mississippi	d d d	d d d	d d d	d d d	d d d	d d d
Missouri	d DD	DDD	d DD	DDD	d DD	DDD
Montana	r R D	RDD	r DD	RDR	r DR	RDD
Nebraska	R . .	R . .	D . .	D . .	D . .	D . .
Nevada	RRD	r R D	DRD	d RD	DRD	d ½D
New Hampshire	R R R	R R R	R R R	R R R	DRR	DRR
New Jersey	d r r	d r d	d r d	d r d	d r d	d r r
New Mexico	D d D	RDD	DDD	RDD	D d D	DDD
New York	DRR	d R R	R R R	r R R	R R R	r D D
North Carolina	d DD	DDD	d DD	DDD	d DD	DDD
North Dakota	R R R	R R R	R R R	DRR	DRR	DRD
Ohio	DRR	R R R	DDD	d R R	R R R	r ½ R
Oklahoma	DDD	d DD	DDD	d DD	RDD	r DD
Oregon	R R R	D½D	RDD	r DD	RDD	r DR
Pennsylvania	DRD	d R R	DRD	d ½D	R R R	r RD

Rhode Island	D½D	DRD	RDD	DDD	RDD	RDD
South Carolina	DDD	d DD	DDD	d DD	DDD	d DD
South Dakota	RRR	RRR	DDD	RRR	RRR	RRR
Tennessee	DDD	d DD	DDD	d DD	DDD	d DD
Texas	DDD	DDD	DDD	DDD	DDD	DDD
Utah	r R R	RRR	r R D	RDD	r R R	DDD
Vermont	RRR	RRR	RRR	RRR	DRR	DRR
Virginia	d d d	d d d	d d d	d d d	d d d	d d d
Washington	r R D	DDD	d DD	DDD	d DD	RDD
West Virginia	dDD	RDD	r DD	DDD	d DD	DDD
Wisconsin	RRR	r R R	DRD	DRR	DRR	RRD
Wyoming	RRR	r R R	DRD	d RR	RRR	r R D

Summary Analysis *	1954	1956	1958	1960	1962	1964	Total Cases
States with partisan elections	46	46	47	48	48	48	283
Undivided control	31	28	28	30	32	27	176
Divided control	15	18	19	18	16	21	107
Both legislative houses opposed to governor's party	7	12	11	11	11	10	62
One legislative house opposed to governor's party	8	6	8	7	5	11	45
Democratic governor	26	28	33	33	32	31	183
With both houses Democratic	17	17	24	22	21	24	125
With one or both houses opposed	9	11	9	11	11	7	58
Republican governor	20	18	14	15	16	17	100
With both houses Republican	14	11	4	8	11	3	51
With one or both houses opposed	6	7	10	7	5	14	49

Key: D, R = Democratic or Republican control of governorship or legislative house following election held in year indicated (includes control of legislative houses in which some, but not all, seats were at stake in the election).

d, r = Democratic or Republican control of governorship or legislative house in the year indicated, but as the result of an election in an earlier year (e.g., an odd-numbered year, or for a term longer than two years).

½ = Equal division of legislative house seats between the two parties.

Sequence of symbols for each year = governorship, upper house, lower house.

* In the summary analysis a house evenly divided has been counted as opposed to the governor's party. Eight such cases occur, but with only one for each columnar year, except for two each in 1956 and 1964.

SOURCE: U.S. Bureau of the Census, *Statistical Abstract of the United States: 1959* (Washington, D.C., 1959), pp. 355f; same, 1965 (Washington, D.C., 1965), p. 382f.

probably well advised to participate in the organization of the houses, creating his working majority by sharing in the choice of the speaker and the chairmen of the more important committees. He may even need to see to it that there are enough factions so that a majority cannot be achieved for the organization of either house without his intercession. These key legislators then become his lieutenants and counselors in the policy-making processes.

When the governor has small party majorities in both houses, the opposition party can generally be depended upon to help keep the majorities together at least some of the time. It can remind the majority that they will look foolish or irresponsible by not supporting their popularly elected leader. Although the elements making up the majority groups may dictate some of the choices for the important formal leadership positions in the legislature, a governor needs to have these men on his side and to recruit natural leaders to his team of lieutenants and counselors. If he cannot hold his majorities together, he may have to court the support of some of the minority. They, too, have bills they wish to get enacted.

When a governor has a majority in only one house, he may find it easier to organize the leadership system in this house. If there are fewer claimants for patronage or other favors, they may be better satisfied. Furthermore, the members of the governor's party in this house may know that the chances for getting some of their measures through the other house may be dependent on the governor's influence there. The house with the majority opposed to the governor is likely to feel its "minority" position. The campaign of the governor and his party in the other house has convinced the electorate, and the governor may sound even better after he has the confidence of office. The opposing house may also feel the political necessity of enacting some of the governor's proposals so that he cannot continue to talk about them currently and in the next election. What is finally enacted may depend both on negotiation between top leaders on both sides and on threats that each house will not adopt the other's bills, but once the best available bargains have been reached on major policies, the bills are passed.

When both houses are controlled by the party in opposition to the governor, he may yet be able to assert some policy leadership. By organizing the minority in each house as effective spokesmen for his point of view and by expounding his policy desires in a "nonpartisan" fashion from the eminence of the gubernatorial position, he may acquire some noticeable popular support for his bills. However, to achieve this he will need to consult selected leaders from the opposition as well as his own legislative lieutenants.

In all the above situations the governor has one special weapon, the threat of veto (except in North Carolina). Most of the members have a few bills they would like to see become law, and some have lots of them. These bills usually pertain to localities, to damage claims, to the interest of some group, or are the inventions of their sponsors. They may reflect matters of political urgency in the local constituency, or simply matters of personal pride. In either case a member, regardless of his party, doesn't want his bill vetoed, should it get as far as the governor's office. Most governors, however, veto many of these bills. In fact, New York governors have vetoed as many as one-fourth of all bills passed. These member bills do, however, help to lubricate the legislative processes: members try to favor the bills of others so that, when the time comes, their bills, too, may be favored.

If, as commonly happens, most of these members' bills get through in the flood of bills enacted in the last days of a legislative session, the governor will usually have an absolute veto over them either because the legislature has adjourned before he takes up the bill or because it is too busy to consider overriding vetoes. Therefore, he will probably sign or veto the bills largely on their merits from his point of view, rather than on the basis of the legislative support of the sponsors. As his point of view is likely to be generally responsible, perhaps the processes of representative democracy, with the governor as chief legislator, can serve us well.

The veto has positive uses as well as negative ones, for it allows the governor to mold the terms of bills in the legislative process. He may do this by announcing that one bill needs additional safeguards or that another is not specific enough. Although he may not explicitly threaten to veto the bill unless the suggested change is made, legislators can usually judge the degree of his determination.

Both by his example and by direct hint or threat, a governor can affect the moral tone of the legislative process. If, for example, it becomes known that contractors and suppliers wishing to do business with the state had better see the "governor's man," if the governor appoints to high public office persons who had previously peddled their political influence to high bidders, or if he or a member of his official family participates in the parties given for legislators by lobbyists, the legislators may easily be lulled into a mood in which anything goes. Even his neutrality on these matters may be interpreted as tacit consent. On the other hand, if the governor indicates clearly that he is not for sale and does not approve of those who are and that he will not let scandal mar his administration, the moral climate of the legislative process may be noticeably heightened. One should not assume, however, that governors can avoid all contact with former boodlers or other tawdry characters thrown up by the electoral processes. A governor may need their votes or their support for his programs, but he can teach them the rules of the game that are to be enforced during his administration.

THE NONGOVERNOR AND ALTERNATIVE LEADERS. A great risk of our separation of powers system is that some individuals elected to the post of chief executive may not want to govern. Perhaps some of them do not understand the system and fail to recognize a vacuum in policy leadership that other men, likely less responsible, will try to fill. And some governors seem to know what the role calls for but are incompetent to carry it out. One such started out to assume policy leadership, received a few rebuffs, and withdrew to the easier chores of the office. When an aide later drew up a list of over twenty "accomplishments" of his administration, the governor was so pleased that he ordered a million copies printed.

Another problem is that a governor can easily be diverted from governing. Thousands of people are happy to take up his time in the office or to invite him to make ceremonial appearances at ground breakings, dedications, and fund drive "kick-offs," and on the luncheon and dinner circuit. Such deference may be completely satisfying, even if the governor has few victories on the policy front. On the other hand, if the governor is ambitious—and he probably is or he would not be there—he may want to avoid offending people in policy hassles and may be more interested in building a machine for future elections than in making a record of his capacity for governing.

What can be done about these nongoverning governors? One solution would be to avoid nominating and electing them in the first place. They can't always be spotted, but if they haven't done an apprenticeship in politics and do not enjoy manipulating people and situations, cannot bargain, or do not take temporary defeats in stride, perhaps they do not belong in the governorship. If a weak governor is already in office, what can be done to provide leadership in policy making? One possibility is that the leaders of the governor's party, the staff of his office and the central management offices, and leaders in the legislature may construct a partially effective council and power combination. There is risk, though, that such an arrangement will degenerate. Members of such a power alliance may start acting on their own rather than consulting the others; or the governor may undercut them by taking a different position on some matter than the one they have planned. For if he has not made his own decisions, he may not be able to remember what they were.

What is likely to happen is that various would-be leaders will spring up in and outside the legislature, and government policies will reflect these tendencies to go in a variety of directions. A group counseling the governor may advise him to veto measures that depart most from a generally responsive and responsible program, but the opportunities for positive program development will have been let go, and it may be necessary to take some of the "bad" to get the "good."

7. Criticism and Protest

We have emphasized the importance of leadership in the decision-making processes because of two risks: (1) that the states will not take enough vital steps to perform the roles left for them in our federal system and (2) that they will tend to become the vehicles, and their people the pawns, of those interest groups that can frequently manipulate the governments for desired privileges and advantages. Such emphasis should not, however, overshadow the place of criticism and public protest in the legislative process.

It is the essence of the democratic system that there can be a variety of viewpoints. Although it may be important to seek generally responsive and responsible policy leadership, it is also important to preserve in the legislatures the forums, organization, and practices for criticizing the programs of would-be leaders.

Maintaining or invigorating the two-party system in the legislatures is probably the readiest basis for active programs of criticism. It is the business of the opposing party group to find and proclaim limitations in the governor's program—an interest unduly favored here, a need overlooked there, or an unfair procedure proposed somewhere else. However, an opposing party group seeking to gain strength or to win the governorship will not ordinarily be carping and unselective in its criticisms if it wishes to appear attractive to voters. It is, in effect, campaigning for the next election, but the deliberative process nevertheless benefits.

As has been indicated earlier, the parties are more evenly matched in many states than are their legislative representations. In these states, greater representativeness could raise the level of legislative criticism. The pretense of one-party systems covering a wide range of view-points in the Deep South is an obstacle to the development of more searching and responsible criticism in the legislatures there.

If criticism is to be effective, the critics may need more information than is given them in the official presentations of policy proposals. A gubernatorial leadership system does not need to be so tight that legislators have no other source of information than the governor's team. It is here that the arrangement of having auditors under the jurisdiction of the legislature, a small legislative research staff, and party research bureaus may assist the deliberative process.

All leaders need critics, especially those who would wield political power. Governors may think their critics are too many and too hostile, but they need only remember that they are participants in the battles of men's aspirations. These battles, structured in systems of representative government, are our way of deciding on governmental policies.

8. Conclusion

This chapter and the preceding one have considered the principal participants in state policy making and have tried to convey a sense of the complexity of the settings, processes, and behavioral patterns through which policies are proposed, shaped, and adopted.

Two developments recently set in motion are likely to materially alter our current understanding of state policy making. One is the reapportionment of state legislatures in substantial accord with the Supreme Court's 1964 standard of equal representation. This may have striking effects on such questions as bicameralism, relations between the governor and the legislature, the responsiveness of state policy to urban and suburban needs, federal-state-local relations, and the roles and internal power structures of the Republican and Democratic parties. These possibilities are explored in the concluding chapter, as is the second development that promises to alter our understanding of policy making. This is the growing volume and sophistication of scholarly probing into how state policy is made, to the end that there can be sharpened perceptions of the actual linkages among institutional arrangements, of the recruitment and motivational drives of legislators and governors, and of the achievement of responsive and responsible decision making. In due course, a deeper understanding of how, and why, policy is made can have practical consequences. Civic leaders and groups appear eager to invest their energies in improving their state governments. But if they are not to become frustrated and discouraged, they need to concentrate on those aspects of policy making that are strategically important, and they must pursue the tactics that are likely to be most effective. Although stimulation and guidance of such activist citizens and groups is not the dominant motivation in scholarly research, these are nonetheless byproducts of no little significance.

chapter 10

☆☆☆☆☆☆☆☆☆

Administrative Organization

The administration of a state or local government can be large- or small-scale in size, or fall at any point between. As we have seen in other connections, states differ greatly; the same is true of local communities. The largest of these in population, financial resources, and complexity of social and economic life confront all the problems of "big government" and many of the problems of "big business." The personnel required for administration may be so numerous that organizing them presents difficult problems of division of labor along with its converse, coordination. Large-scale administration also risks being plagued by the less desirable features of bureaucracy—procedural red tape, delay, dampening of creativity, impersonal treatment of citizens. Allocating and administering the substantial amounts of money at a large government's disposal require sophisticated budgetary procedures. The volume of administrative work often justifies the use of automatic data-processing equipment that would be uneconomical for smaller governments.

The smallest of the state and local units of government, on the other hand, face their own special problems. Many must depend heavily on elective or appointive officials serving only part-time, or upon ill-trained clerks who have worked for years without challenge to their comfortable adherence to the old and often minimal ways of performing their functions. Such governments can have few if any workers with specialized professional abilities and certainly cannot afford the best. Therefore, though on paper their functions may be the same as those of larger states and localities, their performance in areas such as public health, education, utilities regulation, licensing, and social welfare is likely to be amateurish or to be performed by trained people not well enough qualified to obtain the better-paying posts in larger governments.

To illustrate the gap between large and small among the states, one need only consider ranges like the following: In October 1965, the state government of California had 185,000 employees; New York, 149,000; and Pennsylvania, 106,000. At the other extreme, Nevada had 5,400; Wyoming, 6,500; and Alaska, 6,700. The October monthly payrolls of the state governments were $110 million for California, $72 million for New York, and $42 million for Pennsylvania, whereas Nevada and Wyoming paid only $2.7 million each, and Vermont, about $3 million.[1] The ratio for the extremes (California and Nevada) was therefore 34 to 1 for employment and 41 to 1 for payrolls. Although the formal patterns for other parts of the state government may be similar—an elected governor, a bicameral legislature, a supreme court and lower courts—and even the overall administrative organization may appear similar, California's and Nevada's administrative operations are of astonishingly different orders of magnitude. Though neighbors geographically, they are worlds apart administratively.

The far greater disparities in scale of administration among local governments make them universes apart. New York City in October 1965 had over 320,000 employees and a monthly payroll of $184 million (note that this was over twice the employment and payroll figures for the New York State government!). At the other extreme are the towns, villages, and special districts in which a mere handful of individuals do the minimal administration needed, most of them on only a part-time basis. One might suppose that Rome, one of 15 cities in the state of New York with a population of over 50,000, would serve as a midway point. Yet Rome has a staff of only 784 and a monthly payroll of about $228,000; the ratio of New York City to Rome thus is 408 to 1 for employment and 807 to 1 for payroll. To be sure, New York City is *sui generis*. More typical of our large cities are Chicago's 40,000 and Los Angeles's 38,000 employees (these do not include schoolteachers, as New York's total does). Yet their tasks of organizing and directing such administrative "armies" against the complex challenges of great metropolises dwarf not only the administrative prob-

---

[1] *U.S. Bureau of the Census*, Public Employment in 1965 (*Washington, D.C.*, 1966), *pp. 1of.*

lems of lesser cities, towns, and villages, but those of over half the states as well.[2]

In some important ways the administrative problems of the state and local governments are even more difficult than those of the federal government, because for the last decade and more they have been experiencing acute growing pains (see Table 10.1). The increase between 1955 and

Table 10.1. *Direct General Governmental Expenditure by Level of Government, 1955–1965 ***
(Billions of dollars)

	1955	1960	1964–1965	Percent Increase, 1955–1965
Federal	$64.1	$76.7	$99.1	54.6%
Defense, international relations, and interest on the public debt	48.3	55.1	64.8	34.2
Nondefense	15.8	21.6	34.3	117.1
State	11.2	17.8	26.1	133.0
Local	22.5	34.1	48.8	116.8

* "Direct general governmental expenditure" excludes intergovernmental expenditures and insurance-trust, utility, and liquor stores expenditures.
SOURCE: U.S. Bureau of the Census, *Census of Governments: 1962*, Vol. VI, No. 4, *Historical Statistics on Governmental Finances and Employment* (Washington, D.C., 1964), pp. 35f, 41f, 44f; and same, *Governmental Finances in 1964–65* (Washington, D.C., 1966), p. 23.

1964–65 in direct general governmental expenditures by state governments has been about 133 percent and that of local governments 117 percent, while the federal government has shown only a 55 percent increase. Even though federal nondefense expenditures, as well as state and local expenditures, have grown, the administrative problems have been different. The federal government, already accustomed to large-scale administration, could easily absorb a further growth. But for the state and local governments, and particularly the cities, the change has meant that they have crossed the threshold from small-scale to large-scale administration, a development that not all have managed with grace.

State and local administration is also important in ways less measurable than money and employees. It is important to the people. Education,

---

[2] *U.S. Bureau of the Census*, City Employment in 1965 (*Washington, D.C., 1965*), *pp. 5–14.*

highway and urban transportation, public welfare, public health, industrial safety, regulation of utilities, banks, insurance, professions—these are not light responsibilities. It is important, too, in terms of complexity because its functions are so diversified. And the complexity is compounded by the need to link what the particular state or local administration does with what the other two governmental levels are doing in the same fields.

The millions of administrative employees of state and local governments are not mere errand boys, doing the bidding of political office-holders. Campaigns for election to public office, the decisions of voters at the polls, and the negotiations and enactments of the legislative assemblies are all basic and fundamental in the American system. But the process of government has only begun when these activities are concluded. Only in the most general and rudimentary way do the people really govern themselves through the ballot box, and legislatures can consider only a small fraction of the tremendous range of problems of public policy. Most of the policy decisions about mental health institutions, for example, are made by the doctors (and the nurses and attendants) who actually administer them; the colleges and universities are run by their trustees, administrators, and faculties; the highways are planned, located, constructed, and maintained by the administrative employees of the highway departments. The decisions made by the electorate at the ballot box and the legislators in the assembly are made on the advice of the administrators, and the administrators give much of the real content to electoral and legislative decisions after they are made.[3]

1. Organizing the Administration

THE INHERITED PATTERN. In the earliest days of American state government, as explained in Chapter 2, executive or administrative activities were dominated by the legislatures. The American Revolution had been a war as much against colonial governors as against British rule—the two were hardly separable in the minds of the people. Thus although the first state constitutions provided for a separation of powers, the legislatures completely dominated the government.

---

[3] *The reader will by this point be well aware that scarcely any general statements are true of all state or all local governments. In at least one state, the constitution specifies the individual highways; and within each state or local government, the degree of delegation to administrators or of reliance on them for advice varies among functional fields, the more technical and politically irrelevant fields allowing greatest scope for the autonomy of administrators.*

As the legislature gradually lost its preeminence during the nineteenth century, it was replaced largely by the electorate rather than by the executive. When the original constitutions began to be revised, the compelling motive was the extension of the suffrage and increased participation by the electorate. Not only was the governor to be independently elected, but the other executive officers and the judges were also subjected to popular choice.

This process of increasing the scope of popular election continued well into the twentieth century. It produced the "long ballot," common in many states. In recent years, in a few states, there has been a slight reduction in the number of elected officials. Yet, in 1963 the number of state executive and administrative officials elected by the people or the legislature in each state averaged between 9 and 10. The range was from 1 (the governor) in New Jersey to 42 in Nevada.[4]

It is proper to say that most American states have a plural executive, although the elected officials do not ordinarily form a collegial body as they do in a cabinet system.[5]

Despite some evidences of distrust, Americans have not hesitated to use government in a great many ways. When a social problem of any consequence appears, the reaction of the people frequently is "Let there be a law" on the subject. Soon thereafter, and sometimes at the same time, the reaction is "Let there be an agency." As new functions develop and segments of the old functions become more important, new agencies are created and old ones divided.

The extent of agency proliferation is revealed by a 1950 count in a sample of 23 states.[6] Only two of these states had fewer than 50 agencies, and nine of them had over 100, including counts of 140 and 172. Even the "major departments" ranged from 9 to 78. Although some of the states in the sample have reduced these numbers since 1950, in general more agencies have been created than have been abolished or consolidated. The development of such a great number of separate agencies has been a cause for concern by many observers of state government. The job of holding 30,

---

[4] The Book of the States: 1964–65 (Chicago: Council of State Governments, 1964), p. 151. North Carolina has 110 elective state officials, but 100 are the university system's regents; these are omitted in our calculation. Exclusion of Nevada's 9 regents would reduce that state's elective figure to 33, still the highest of all states.

[5] In a few instances, constitutions or statutes require that certain of the elected executives act in collegial fashion. The most prominent example is in Florida, where a "cabinet" of elected officials performs various crucial functions, including the preparation of the budget.

[6] Reorganizing State Government (Chicago: Council of State Governments, 1950), p. 12.

or 50, or 70, or 100 state agencies separately responsible, whether to the electorate, the legislature, or the governor, seems an impossible task. To control and coordinate them adequately appears to present very great difficulties.

DEMANDS FOR CHANGE. Along with these tendencies toward "administrative sprawl" has been a substantial contrary tendency, generally called the state reorganization movement. President Taft's Commission on Economy and Efficiency in the national government in 1910–12 led to a number of reorganization studies and proposals in the states—first of all, in Oregon, Wisconsin, Massachusetts, and New Jersey. A carefully studied and comprehensive set of proposals was made in New York in 1915, but the first sweeping administrative reorganization took place in Illinois in 1917 under the leadership of Governor Lowden. In a new civil administrative code, the state consolidated about 54 independent agencies into 14, and the heads of nearly all of these new departments were made subject to appointment by the governor.

The example of Illinois was followed by many other states, and the movement continued, at an uneven pace, through the 1920's and 1930's. By the beginning of the Second World War, nearly every state had had reorganization studies and proposals and about 30 states had been significantly reorganized, some even two or three times. Since the war, particularly in the years 1947 to 1954, the states have shown an even greater interest in reorganization proposals.

For the cities, there were also very substantial reform movements, beginning even earlier than the state reorganization movement, involving first the commission form of government and then increasingly the city-manager form. Since these reforms concerned the whole governmental system, not just administration, they are discussed in Chapter 14. The reorganization movement also had some impact on counties and other territorial units, particularly in regard to budgeting and other staff services, but reorganization of these units was of relatively much less significance.

LITTLE HOOVER COMMISSIONS. Reorganization study commissions in the states were frequently patterned after the national Commission on Organization of the Executive Branch of the Government, of which former President Herbert Hoover was chairman and which reported its conclusions in 1949. In fact, the analogous state bodies were generally known as, and sometimes formally named, Little Hoover Commissions. Between 1947 and 1954, approximately 35 states had official reorganization studies made by study commissions that varied in size from 4 to 41 members, most of them having some 7 to 13.

Altogether, these studies were quite impressive. Although they varied in the amount of financial support they received and in the intensity and quality of the study efforts, there were many instances of thorough, searching investigation and thoughtful recommendations. The results, however, have been very modest, if we reckon them in terms of legislative enactment of commission recommendations. In 1953, after 24 states had completed their studies and given state legislatures one session or more in which to consider commission recommendations, the legislative response in only 2 of the 24 states—New Hampshire and New Jersey—was definitely positive. An evaluation by Karl A. Bosworth concluded that in 9 of the 24 states the legislative reception was either completely negative or so slight as to be regarded as a "soundly negative response," while in the other 13 some 30 to 50 percent of the commission proposals were adopted.[7] Although occasional steps toward reorganization have since been taken, events since the publication of this study do not indicate that the pattern of generally negative response has changed substantially. It is still appropriate to remark on "such meager accomplishment from so much effort."

GUIDING PRINCIPLES OF THE REORGANIZATION MOVE-MENT. With rare exceptions and minor qualifications, all the state reorganization movements of the last fifty years have been dominated by the same assumptions or "principles." Many years ago, A. E. Buck, one of the most active of the reorganizers, stated them this way:

1. *Concentration of authority and responsibility*
2. *Departmentalization, or functional integration*
3. *Undesirability of boards for purely administrative work*
4. *Coordination of the staff services of administration*
5. *Provision for an independent audit*
6. *Recognition of a governor's cabinet* [8]

Support for the sixth of these principles has not been as uniform or as widespread as for the others, but the other five could be stated as the credo of most of the commissions.

In 1949, the Council of State Governments sponsored a conference of representatives of twenty state reorganization commissions that were then active. The consensus of their deliberations was summarized as follows:

In general it was felt that reorganization movements should result in strengthening the office of the governor; reducing the independent

---

[7] Karl A. Bosworth, "The Politics of Management Improvement in the States," *American Political Science Review,* 47 (1953), 84–99.

[8] A. E. Buck, The Reorganization of State Governments in the United States (*New York: Columbia University Press,* 1938), *pp.* 14–28.

agencies and administrative boards and commissions and grouping them into major departments; extending the gubernatorial power of appointment and removal of department heads; and strengthening executive controls over budgeting, accounting, purchasing, state property, etc. At the same time, it was pointed out, it is of the utmost necessity to revise legislative procedures in the direction of greater efficiency, and to provide the legislature with more effective reporting and auditing controls—in order that the executive may be held to proper accountability.[9]

The national Commission on Intergovernmental Relations, in its June, 1955 report, said that there was "substantial agreement" that these arrangements "if generally applied, would greatly strengthen state administration." [10]

Perhaps the most basic of the reorganization "principles," and the one most difficult to realize in practice, is that of unifying the executive branch under the governor. The state reorganization commissions have consistently urged the general principle of executive unity, although the recommendations of many have stopped short of complete adherence. Concentration of authority and responsibility, it was argued, is essential both to good management and to democratic control of policy.

The grouping of related agencies into a few major departments has also been considered essential. The most frequently used summaries of the effect of reorganization programs have been comparisons of the number of independent agencies existing after the reorganization with the number existing before; the most successful reorganization was supposedly the one that found the largest number of agencies and reduced it to the smallest number.

The substitution of single administrators for boards or commissions as the heads of agencies has been another goal of the reorganizers. The multiplication of boards and commissions has been one of the most significant and notable features of the growth of state administration in the last 80 or 90 years. Studies by the Little Hoover Commissions found, for example, that Nevada had 73 boards and commissions, Washington had 56, and Mississippi had 50 that were appointed by the governor and numerous others chosen in other ways. Many of these boards and commissions, of course, have comparatively unimportant responsibilities, but there remain a number of major departments that are headed by boards or

---

[9] Reorganizing State Government, *p. 1.*

[10] *U.S. Commission on Intergovernmental Relations,* Final Report (*Washington, D.C.,* 1955), *p. 45.*

commissions and that thus disregard a canon of the reorganizers' creed. It is true, of course, that boards have not been universally or completely condemned by reorganization surveys. Advisory boards without the power of decision have frequently been advocated. Furthermore, boards have been considered useful for "quasi-legislative" and "quasi-judicial" work, although an exact definition of these functions, as distinguished from other "administrative" work, has been lacking. It is when boards, instead of single individuals, are made the heads of major departments of state administration that reorganizers protest.

The most widely accepted feature of the reorganization programs has been the provision of certain central staff services and controls. In considerable measure these central staff services have been of the housekeeping variety: central purchasing of materials and supplies, including the rental of state property; operations of central warehouses; maintenance of central records on state property; maintenance and general control of buildings and grounds; supervision of public printing; operation of a central motor pool; central mailing, messenger, and telephone service. The provision of a central personnel agency has been made partly for economy in housekeeping but is intended more particularly to improve and maintain a higher quality of personnel. In some of the reorganization proposals, consideration was given to a state planning agency which would provide coordinated forethought for various state activities and programs. Probably the most important, and certainly the most widely adopted, of the central staff services and controls is that of a unified budget. Associated with the budget are various types of controls over expenditures after appropriations are made.

Last of the commonly accepted "principles of reorganization" is that of an independent audit, although there has been some confusion between the function of *approval* of expenditures and that of *examination* of expenditures. The proposals have generally suggested that approval of expenditures is an administrative control which should not be performed independently of the elected chief executive, but that examination of expenditures, with a report, usually to the legislature, should be completely independent. The standard phrases used to differentiate between the two are "an executive budget" and "a legislative audit."

2. Fragmentation of the Executive Branch

PRESSURES FOR SEPARATISM. The central tendency followed by all the reorganization surveys has been to concentrate authority and responsibility. These proposals for administrative integration have not, however, been overwhelmingly successful. There have been many pressures leading to the dispersion of administrative activity among separate and independent agencies. Some of these pressures for separatism may be suggested:

1. *"Normal" drive for agency autonomy.* It seems to be an innate characteristic of administrative agencies to desire independence. The Mississippi Legislative Fact-finding Committee on Reorganization of State Government summarized the uniform response of agency heads to the committee's proposals for integration; the typical agency head wrote:

> *I think this is one of the very best things that has ever been done in the State of Mississippi and I have long been of the opinion that this work should have been accomplished in the past. However, my department is of a type, character and kind that cannot be consolidated with any other agency, as its duties and functions are unique, and a reduction of personnel or a transfer of any duties of this department would work a hardship and prevent certain citizens from receiving benefits to which they are entitled.*[11]

2. *Historical background of separate responsibility to the electorate.* Most of our present state constitutions were written during the two or three generations when the strength of Jacksonian democracy was at its highest. During this period the standard prescription for the ills of democracy was more democracy. It was felt that the way to ensure responsiveness to popular wishes was to provide for popular elections. Some of the most important of the early state government officials, such as the attorney-general, the secretary of state, and the treasurer, were subjected to popular election. Then as some of the other functions of state government increased in importance, the heads of the agencies administering these functions were also made elected officials. Although the ballot therefore grew so incredibly long that this tendency to add elective offices has largely been stemmed, it is still very difficult, often impossible, to change an agency head from an elective to an appointive status.

In the first place, the voters have become accustomed to voting for that office and have a tendency to feel that it is appropriately elective. Second, the appeal of "direct responsibility to the people" is difficult to overcome. Third, the incumbent of an elective post has, by definition, a political following of some consequence, and his position of independence

---

[11] *Quoted by Bosworth, op. cit., p. 90.*

will not lightly be tampered with by knowledgeable legislators. Finally, there is some political advantage to a party or a faction in having a long ballot; particular sections or racial or nationality groups or individual leaders can be appeased or courted by being given one of the elective slots.

3. *"Reform" movements for special functions.* The political process is not always spotless. When there is evidence of scandal in some sensitive place, interested, indignant, and outraged citizens frequently attempt to haul an activity that seems important to them out of the political process. In Alabama, when scandals, or alleged scandals, developed in the prison system, the remedy applied by the legislature and widely endorsed by the press was to set up an independent board of corrections and institutions to replace the politically appointed head of the department. It has seemed to many thoughtful citizens who are sincerely interested in effective performance of certain functions that the only escape from the petty, particularistic, discriminatory, and sometimes even corrupt administration by low-grade politicians was complete independence for the function in order that it might be cleaned up and boosted to a higher level of operation.

4. *Clientele and interest group attitudes.* American society is largely pluralistic. Most individuals have stronger loyalties to particular groups of which they are members than to the community as a whole, or at least these special loyalties are much more clearly discernible. For example, the Farm Bureau (a private organization of farmers) wants the state's agricultural extension service subject to its control, not subject to general control by the governor and legislature. The Parent-Teachers Association feels that the education department should be sacrosanct and untouchable by "political" hands. If a reorganization commission tries to tamper with a fish and game bureau, the organized sportsmen are likely to raise enough furor to make the commission wonder what happened to it.[12]

Not only do the clientele groups want their agencies separate; they also want their money separate. The motorists' associations have been instrumental in getting constitutional amendments forbidding the "diversion" of gasoline tax revenues. The education associations insist that new taxes be earmarked for schools. Every group that has set up a governmental licensing program wants the license fees kept out of the general fund.

Each interest group, identifying the public interest with its own, feels that it can best ensure that its affairs are properly considered by keeping

---

[12] A *vivid case study of such an effort is* Thomas H. Eliot, "Reorganizing the *Massachusetts Department of Conservation,"* in Edwin A. Bock (ed.), State and Local Government: A Casebook (*University, Ala.: University of Alabama Press, 1963*), *pp.* 315–34.

the agency and funds involved "independent"—meaning independent of everyone but the particular interest concerned. For general, ballot-box politics there is substituted the politics of special influence, often with the highest of motives.

5. *Professionalism.* One of the most significant and sweeping developments in the public service, particularly in this century and this generation, has been the rise of many strong professions. Teaching, social work, highway engineering, tax assessing, purchasing, librarianship, forestry, penology, and many others, as well as the traditional professions of law and medicine, are deeply involved in the public service. These professions have organized bodies of knowledge, generally available only to members; group standards of training and performance; codes of ethical conduct; and, particularly, close group ties and associations.

The growth of professionalism has promoted respect for and recognition of technical expertness, facilitated communication and the spread of new developments, and produced a degree of group loyalty, discipline, and satisfaction that have been tremendous assets to public administrative agencies. The development has been enthusiastically welcomed by many observers and participants in the administrative process. The 1936 *Municipal Year Book* suggested that professionalization of public officials was "the key opening the door to effective democracy." If legal and political controls of administrative officials are inadequate, as they obviously are, the self-control and self-stimulation of professional organization and activity might fill the gap.

Professionalism, however, produces particularly strong tendencies toward separatism. Sometimes the special insistence on professional independence can be traced in some measure to the resistance of the traditional political structure to the development of the special training, security of tenure, and personal mobility inherent in the growth of professions. Stronger, probably, is the fact that a profession is necessarily set apart by the possession of a special lore, and its members have a strong group consciousness that leads them to insist on being distinct from the common herd. This desire for independence is one of the most powerful disintegrating forces acting upon governmental organization. In bringing a particular professional group closely together, it tends to shatter general political control. For social workers and teachers, professional ties may become stronger than ties to political superiors.

Professionalization as a disintegrating force is closely related to the pressures of special clientele groups and to functional links to other levels of government.

6. *Functional links to national government.* The various governmen-

tal functions are no longer, if they ever were, divided sharply between the different levels of government in this country. In each field of activity in which there is a state or a local governmental program, there is usually also a national program. Furthermore, there are a great many interrelationships between the national, state, and local programs. These tend to link national activities with state activities, and state activities with local ones in each specific function, but they make it difficult to associate the various programs at a particular level with each other.

The strongest link between national, state, and local governments is often the grant-in-aid. The Secretary of the Treasury tabulated 75 different programs under which federal grants were made to state and local governments in 1965.[13] A few of these are made directly from the federal government to local governments, but most are made to or through state government agencies. For the fiscal years 1962–65, national grants-in-aid made up 14 to 15 percent of total state and local general revenues. The percentage varies widely among the states—from 52 in Alaska to 9 in New York.[14]

The conditions accompanying the grants tend to destroy central political control at the state level. True, the state can refuse to accept the national grants, but this is not a practical alternative. The program area itself is specified; sometimes the specification is rather narrow, leaving no room for political choice at the state level. Through matching requirements, the grant-in-aid programs require the use, for federally specified purposes, of state funds that might otherwise be used in another way, narrowing still further the range of political control at the state level. In some instances, the terms of the grant specify particular types of administrative arrangements or agencies.

In all instances, the administration of the grant programs is subject to some degree of control from Washington. State agencies' work plans, financial accounting arrangements, and rules for disbursing funds must meet national requirements, even if these administrative arrangements do not mesh with those in use in the state. Even more important, there is built up a continuing and close relationship between the national agency and the state agency involved in the particular programs that tends to supersede or weaken any relationship of responsibility to the governor through a political department head.

---

[13] Annual Report of the Secretary of the Treasury on the State of the Finances for the Fiscal Year Ended June 30, 1965 (*Washington, D.C., 1966*), *pp. 729–39.*
[14] *Percentages computed from U.S. Bureau of the Census,* Governmental Finances in 1964–65 (*Washington, D.C., 1966*), *pp. 18, 31–33.*

There can be little doubt that the national grant-in-aid system, and most of the links to national agencies, have improved the quality of administration of these particular programs at the state level. The 1955 U.S. Commission on Intergovernmental Relations, with surprisingly little dissent among its 25 distinguished members of varying backgrounds, endorsed the continuation of grant-in-aid arrangements on essentially the same basis as that on which they have been conducted, although the commission recognized that the system had various complexities and that it tended to divide, and offer opportunity to dodge, responsibility. Not only did the commission endorse the grant-in-aid system, but it suggested that the trend had been and would continue to be "toward sharper definition of objectives, closer attention to conditions and requirements, more extensive administrative supervision. . . ." [15]

This expectation that grants-in-aid and other forms of national-state cooperation will continue to expand and will be accompanied by closer attention to conditions and more extensive administrative supervision has significant implications for state administration. Important political pressures will be put on the national government as the source of funds and initiator of policies, and the state agencies will become more and more the administrative field services of nationally developed programs. The need in these circumstances will be for increasingly professional state services, able and willing to cooperate in the national programs, rather than for increased political responsibility at the state level.

7. *Desire to insulate special types of programs.* There have been widespread and frequently very influential beliefs that special kinds of governmental programs exist that should be kept in some measure apart from the political process. One of them consists of the regulatory activities, particularly those that involve determinations upon the basis of evidence presented through a formal hearing process. The independence of the judiciary has been one of the cornerstones of the English-American tradition. In agencies like the Interstate Commerce Commission at the national level and the railroad and public service commissions at the state level, procedures resemble those of the judiciary so much that there has been great reluctance to subordinate them to the direction of a political chief executive. As a result, these agencies have most frequently been headed by boards or commissions, and they have generally had substantial protection against central political control.[16]

It is also suggested that there are certain especially "controversial"

---

[15] *U.S. Commission on Intergovernmental Relations,* op. cit., *p. 119ff.*

[16] *See James W. Fesler,* The Independence of State Regulatory Agencies *(Chicago: Public Administration Service, 1942).*

areas in which freedom from political control permits a higher degree of objectivity. The promotion of fair employment practices, the control of alcoholic beverages, the equalization of property tax assessment are examples. This argument says, in effect, that some things are just too political to be given to the politicians.

Related to this are activities considered to be experimental in character. In some states, for example, special agencies have been set up to combat juvenile delinquency, or to pioneer programs of stream pollution control. Frequently it is felt that new ground is more likely to be broken by a new and independent agency than by part of the regular bureaucracy.

Trading agencies are also often exempt from many of the central controls. The corporate device has been used at the state as well as at the national level to provide the kind of flexibility and continuity that seemed to be desirable in commercial-type enterprises. Although many of these advantages could be attained without freedom from political control, it was believed that the trading agency should be free from particular controls on finances and personnel; this plus doubts about the desirability of political domination led to an insistence on administrative independence. The liquor monopolies in some states, state insurance funds, retirement systems with many attributes of an insurance system, and similar programs have been entrusted to corporations or to boards or authorities which are separated to considerable degree from the regular administrative structure. The growth of special authorities for the administration of toll roads and other transportation facilities is contributing further to the rapid multiplication of independent agencies.

8. *Political division between legislature and governor.* In spite of what seems to be a growing amount of political leadership in the governor's office, the American system of separation of powers does not always produce the highest degree of mutual trust between the legislature and the governor. In many states, the governor has been the choice of an electoral majority largely urban in character, whereas the legislature was until very recently chosen on an apportionment basis practically guaranteeing rural control.

When it is at odds with the governor, or even restive under gubernatorial leadership, the legislature, being responsible for the basic outlines of administrative organization, will normally feel it can keep control of an activity better if the activity is administratively independent of the governor. Or it may feel that an activity is better free from any central political control rather than subject to the control of the governor. This is true not only in the initial organization of new agencies, for which the legislature is responsible, but also in any reorganization proposals that suggest the subjection of heretofore independent or partially independent agencies to gubernatorial control.

In local governments, the separation of powers between legislative bodies and the executive is less pronounced, and this particular drive for administrative separatism is less noticeable.

9. *Dissatisfaction with central political processes.* Underlying many of the various pressures for separatism outlined above is a considerable degree of distrust of the political systems of our state and local governments. Many people feel that these systems do not produce qualified and responsible leaders. For programs that they consider important, this leads them to prefer professional responsibility, clientele and interest group influences, boards of unpaid citizens, and national prescription of program and administration to the kind of central leadership actually produced by the political process.

A paragraph from a resolution passed by a group of leading citizens in Birmingham, Alabama, opposing a bill that would have increased the governor's control over the state department of public welfare is typical of this attitude:

> *The hundreds of thousands of recipients of public assistance in the State of Alabama require the most thoughtful, considerate, humane and knowledgeable service the state and counties can provide. This means that no political considerations whatsoever should be permitted to intrude in the administration of such services. Under the proposed Bill, the selection of public welfare staff, from the State Commissioner down to the subordinate employees in every county department, is wide open to political manipulations. This could result in trafficking in human misfortune.*

This objection to administrative integration, of course, goes to the heart of the matter. The basic assumption of the proponents of reorganization is that the popular will is satisfactorily expressed through the political process of electing the legislature and, in particular, the governor. Many persons, on the other hand, feel that state and local politics as presently conducted are based upon a lack of attention to issues, upon excessive attention to personality, and so are not properly organized to produce any real consensus on governmental programs. They prefer, then, to trust the narrower, special, and concealed politics of influence that is brought to play upon administrative agencies largely independent of central political control. They do not believe, in other words, that the forces which combine to produce a majority of those voting in a state or local election are the best forces to which the conduct of public programs can be entrusted. The tendency produced by this belief would be, and has been, to make election politics a sort of game with comparatively limited stakes, and to remove most of the activities actually administered at these levels from this central political game and leave them instead under the control of the diverse forces of a highly pluralistic society.

DEVICES FOR SEPARATISM. Agencies can be held out of the main administrative structure in various ways and degrees. Separate election of the agency head is the clearest type of independent status. The appointment power may be vested in persons other than the chief executive, or his discretion may be limited by narrow qualifications of office, or by prescribed terms of office, or by limitations on the power to remove. Agencies headed by boards or commissions, especially if the members have long and overlapping terms, are substantially insulated from executive control. Public corporations, which appear to be multiplying, are designed to exercise governmental functions independently. At the local level, separate local governments—school, soil conservation and many other special districts—are created, often for areas which do not coincide with those for general governments, in order to keep certain functions out of the central channels of political control and responsibility. Revenues may be earmarked for particular uses, in order that funds for an agency or program may be protected from executive and even legislative budgetary controls.

These formal arrangements for administrative separatism are not always the really determinative criteria of the degree of central political control. Sometimes elected or other apparently independent agency heads are closely tied into the central political machinery, chiefly where the party or factional organization is strong, and the elected official is part of the same "organization" as the governor. In other instances, where the agency head is subject to appointment, the strength of a particular clientele group or profession may be so great that there is, in reality, a very high degree of administrative independence. This may be true, for example, in the public health department, or in a fish and game agency, in which the professional or the interest group may be potent enough to ward off any attempt by the chief executive to influence the program or the level or manner of expenditures.

3. *Separatism versus Integration*

Should state administrations be reorganized into streamlined pyramids of hierarchical authority and responsibility? Should the "executive branch" of state government be a unity, with the office of governor at the top? Should the dozens and scores of administrative agencies be grouped into a few departments subject to gubernatorial authority and assisted and controlled by central staff agencies for budgeting, purchasing, personnel, and so on? Or should agencies dealing with specialized functions keep their close ties to their clientele, develop their own professional specialization, cultivate their connections with national and local agencies, and avoid contacts with "politics" of the type usually practiced by state governors and their cohorts?

There need be no single answer to this central question of state administrative organization. There should, however, be thoughtful consideration of the implications of the question and, perhaps, commitments to certain tendencies or directions of movement.

THE CASE FOR INTEGRATION. Two closely related basic arguments for administrative integration are apparent. The first of the arguments is the desirability of coordinating state administrative activities. The activities of the government should be consistent; the more independent agencies, the more possibilities for inconsistencies. An integrated, systematic, and rational program of activities for state government calls for an integrated, systematic, and rational arrangement of administrative agencies.

Some question arises about how real the need for coordination of state programs is. Historically, and perhaps still in many states, the activities of state governments have been confined to a number of areas having no particular relationship to each other. State government was, and may yet be, multipurpose without being comprehensive. This has been one of the reasons why governors' cabinets have been neither widely used nor effective. Between the state superintendent of education and the state highway director there was little common ground, to use as examples the biggest functions of state government. Areas in which they did impinge on each other, such as a school transportation program, could easily be "coordinated" informally by negotiation between the departments affected.

Coordination, however, involves more than reconciling occasional cases where programs seem to overlap. It can also achieve economies through joint housekeeping activities. The purchase of supplies, the use of transportation facilities, the use of state buildings and land offer obvious opportunities and should be considered from the standpoint of the entire state government, rather than from that of a single agency. It is in this type of "coordination" that the reorganization proposals have had greatest success.

Even more important is the budgetary aspect of coordination. Any state government has limited financial resources, and choices must be made as to the comparative desirability and urgency of the various programs. Informed and rational choice between alternative ways of using limited funds is only possible if there is some vantage point from which all the programs can be studied and evaluated.

This vantage point could be the legislature. But the legislature has obvious shortcomings in this regard: It meets for limited and infrequent sessions, it is composed of part-time amateurs, and it cannot adequately supervise the necessary staff. Most states have realized for a quarter to a half century that for the whole of state government, only the governor is in a position to prepare an adequate budget, subject to criticism and change by the legislature. This was thought by many to be the task of a chief administrator, but it is now recognized more clearly that, to the degree to which they can be separated, preparation of the budget is much more a political than an administrative task. The governor seems best equipped for this key administrative function because he is ordinarily the most prominent politician of the state.

The other basic argument for administrative integration is that responsibility to the people is furthered if there is a single focus for the whole governmental program. The great numbers of people doing the actual work of state government can be responsible to the citizens of the state through two chief channels: first, by control over administrative programs and actions by an elective legislature and an elective chief executive; second, by the diverse and complex kinds of influence that can be exerted upon specific administrative individuals and agencies through direct contacts, group associations, pressures of specific opinion channels, and the myriad interrelationships that connect people working at specific jobs with the people whom those jobs interest and affect. The assumption of the proponents of administrative integration is that the simpler, clearer, cleaner, and more wholesome lines of responsibility lie in the main channel of the elective process, that is, through the responsibility of the legislature and the governor to the people.

The first Hoover Commission, on the first page of its first report, stated the same proposition:

> *The President, and under him his chief lieutenants, the department heads, must be held responsible and accountable to the people and the Congress for the conduct of the executive branch.*
>
> *Responsibility and accountability are impossible without author-*

ity—the power to direct. The exercise of authority is impossible with-
out a clear line of command from the top to the bottom and a return
line of responsibility and accountability from the bottom to the top.[17]

If the word "governor" is substituted for "President," and "legislature" for
"Congress," the most important axiom of most studies of state administrative organization would be clearly stated.

Thoughtful persons will realize that it is a great oversimplification to
expect, in any arrangement of public institutions, a single line of responsibility. Administrative agents will be guided in their decisions by many
intricate lines of influence. They will be responsive to the law as they read
it; to the courts, for all American officials live in the shadow of the
courthouse; to administrative superiors of various kinds; to office and
professional associates for following and upholding socially accepted standards; to public and group opinion; to consciences formed by education
and experiences stemming from childhood.

Some of these "lines of responsibility" can be emphasized and
strengthened in relation to others, however. It seems likely that responsibility to a general public interest may be better achieved through a main
line of political responsibility focused on the legislature and the governor,
than through the limited, specific, hidden responsibilities involved in some
of these other relationships. The great body of the public is poor enough as
a competitor with the organized groups who are especially interested in the
activities of an agency, even when the agency has an overriding responsibility to the popularly elected chief executive. In a health department
controlled by doctors, for example, the doctors will protect the public
interest as they see it, even though at times they will inevitably confuse
their own interests with the public interest. If a board to regulate the price
of milk is controlled by the producers and distributors of milk, the consumers' interest may be given only lip service. Much justification exists for the
basic assumption that the dominant and overriding line of responsibility
should be to the public as a whole through the medium of the ballot box
and for the corollary that the clearest line of responsibility to the whole
public at the ballot box is through the election of the governor. Furthermore, if visibility is a desirable characteristic for the operations of government in a democratic society, it seems likely that public scrutiny and
attention will be better focused upon operations conducted in the main
political channels than upon those conducted in separate, independent,
and sometimes concealed channels of political influence and control.

---

[17] *U.S. Commission on Organization of the Executive Branch of the Government,*
General Management of the Executive Branch (*Washington, D.C., 1949*), *p. 1.*

DOUBTS ABOUT INTEGRATION. The validity of these basic arguments for administrative integration—the need for coordination of governmental programs and the likelihood that a higher degree of responsibility to the whole population can be achieved through integration—appears to depend upon two fundamental conditions: First, are the state governments actually engaged in programs of real consequence to the whole people? And second, does the central political system operating in the states provide for real responsibility to the whole people for the conduct of these programs? The two conditions are of course interrelated.

If state programs do not in actuality impinge substantially upon the lives of the majority of the people, there is no real reason why the limited clientele groups involved or the qualified professional groups should not run the programs. And if the actual operation of the political system does not present the public with significant and meaningful program alternatives, and the legislative and gubernatorial elections are determined on the basis of personality attributes unrelated to program, or upon irrational campaign appeals, or upon arrangements between political leaders more interested in petty spoils than in program goals, there will be appropriate reluctance to substitute a sham political responsibility for a real professional or clientele or intergovernmental responsibility. It follows, then, that the desirability of systematic administration depends upon the existence of systematic politics. If the major portion of the population does not use the state political process to control the selection of major governmental programs, there is no basis for the arguments for a rationally organized administration.

We are confronted with a chicken-and-egg proposition, however. A chief reason why state governments have not been entrusted with greater program responsibilities is doubt about the competence of an irrational and disorganized administrative system. Furthermore, if the governor were actually in the driver's seat of the state government, the stakes of the political game would be so increased as to make serious participation by an interested citizenry much more likely. Responsibility is the great developer of men.

We should recognize, though, that separatism and integration are not opposites without middle ground. Even in an agency that appears completely independent, the governor may have much influence simply because he has received a majority of the popular vote, has influence with the legislature, and has public prestige and constitutional responsibilities. And even in an agency over which the governor appears to have complete control, the influence of a special clientele, of the group connections and thought habits of the employees, of interested legislators and legislative committees, and of intergovernmental relationships will be of incalculable importance. Agencies can be grouped all along a spectrum from nearly complete independence to nearly complete subordination to central political control. The essential questions of public policy are the direction in which agencies and activities should be shifted and the degree of shift that should be encouraged.

It may be that some agencies need to be much further along the road to administrative integration than others. All states have, in fact, made this distinction, linking some agencies much more closely into the hierarchy than others. It is doubtful, however, that the calculations upon which the respective decisions were based were completely rational, or that the decisions should be left unquestioned. The basic and highly complex calculation required is the weighing of the actual need for coordination and for responsiveness to central political control against any valid pressures for independence. In some cases, budget and financial tools will provide enough central control; in others, as great a degree of subordination as possible may seem indicated; in still others, a high degree of autonomy may be permitted.

The continuing resolution of the conflict must be made, it seems, in each state on the basis of its own political situation, history, and program needs. It would seem not to be an accident, for example, that the governor of New York is much more the chief administrator than is the governor of New Mexico.

CRUCIAL ROLE OF THE CHIEF EXECUTIVE. It has been implicit in all these discussions of state administrative organization that the governor is the key figure in the administrative process. The governor is and will be the chief administrator of the state because he is, and to the extent that he is, the chief politician of the state.

If he is a substantial political leader himself or if he represents a real political leadership, and if he has been chosen governor by the majority of the people in order to produce a particular program or tendency in government, the pressures will be very strong to give him the tools with which to produce that program or tendency. If he is chosen on the basis of "irrelevant" personal considerations, or if he is the instrument or spokesman of a group interested primarily in the patronage and contract spoils of office, or if it is the tradition of the state that the governor not concern himself much with important public matters, the pressures for independent boards and clientele representation and similar devices for separatism will be very strong.

An interesting question may be raised as to the correlation between a man's ability to produce an electoral majority and his ability to administer a large organization. At the level of the national government, there appears to be a very high correlation, provided primarily by the nominating process and only secondarily by the actual election process. A man with the characteristics to satisfy the widely diverse elements in one of our great modern parties and with the ability to work with "the organization"—a requisite for nomination and election—will almost certainly have in large measure the high politico-administrative skills required at the top level of government. Some of the same tendencies are also apparent at the state level, but exceptions are much more likely. The political system in many of our states is so disorganized that individuals who have no organizational ties or who are not acceptable to divergent groups can be elected purely on personality. In fact, the supplanting of convention nominations by the direct primary has made this possibility much more likely. Such a "maverick" may secure and retain popularity at the polls without having any real understanding of how to lead an organization such as a political party or an executive branch.

Although the position of the governor as political leader and chief of administration is largely determined by the political pattern of a particular state, we can identify a few aids to gubernatorial responsibility. Use of a four-year rather than a two-year term and indefinite eligibility for reelection would seem to be important in providing a context for more effective and responsible gubernatorial leadership. The quality of the administrative machinery of a state can be changed comparatively little in two years. Only if a governor is in a position to concern himself about a considerable period of future time is he likely to be motivated to a real interest in improved administration, and only if administrative officials must reckon with the possibility of continuing influence from the governor will his leadership be very effective. Much of the same regard for the future will be present, of course, in a well-organized and closely knit party or political faction with a real prospect of continuing in office for considerable time. When the governor is merely a bird of passage, however, central leadership and concern about general administrative improvement are not to be expected, although specific agencies with effective functional responsibilities may have enough stability to generate within themselves a concern about improved administrative quality.

The battery of powers available to the governor is also closely related to the effectiveness with which he is likely to conduct his administrative tasks. Some obvious examples are appointment and removal powers, control over finance and personnel, and similar direct administrative controls.

Another important area is his legislative power. If the governor has the item veto, or power to reduce items in appropriation bills, his influence will be vastly increased. And the greater his legislative role, the greater his responsibility for programs, and the greater the degree to which he will be required to concern himself about the administration of the various programs.

Finally, although political and executive responsibility rests on a single individual, the office of governor must be institutionalized if it is to play a really important role. One form of institutionalization is purely political. In some states the governorship is in the hands of a group or faction for which the governor himself is merely chief spokesman. Another form of institutionalization is the development of a staff for the governor, for in many states an important reason why the governor has limited influence and control is that he has an inadequate staff. He needs staff assistance in his relationships with the legislature and with the public and also in his relationships with administrative agencies. Only if the governor has a personal staff able to discover and advise him on matters of administrative importance can he be effectively responsible for what goes on. There is considerable variety in the titles of personal staff aides ("administrative assistant," "executive secretary," "legal advisor," "press secretary," or just "assistant") and in their actual work assignment, but these staff assistants constitute an important extension of the personality and influence of the chief executive himself. It is through his staff that the office of chief executive becomes an institution rather than a single person.

The strength of central executive control over administration has been particularly enhanced by one of the most important trends in public administration in this century—the steady and universal growth of central staff agencies, a development similar to that in large business enterprises. This trend is a part of the general movement for administrative organization described earlier in this chapter. The staff services most commonly centralized are finance (including budget, accounting, purchasing and supplies, buildings and land, etc.), personnel, and planning. If money and supplies, people, and plans are subject to central supervision, many economies can probably be effected and a higher degree of consistency and responsibility promoted. Although there are complaints from time to time about the restrictions and hampering controls of central staff operations upon the freedom and initiative of operating agencies, there is little doubt as to their utility, within limits. In state and local governments, instances in which central budget, accounting, purchasing, or personnel controls have been applied in a restrictive manner seem to be greatly outweighed by the much more frequent situations in which there is completely inadequate central attention to these matters.

Finance and personnel are certainly critical and pervasive components of any governmental program. In state and large local governments, central staff agencies concerned with these operations are frequently strong and effective; their role is described in the next chapter. As Chapter 4 has indicated, central concern with planning, as a distinguishable executive staff activity, is much less developed and accepted.

A few state and local governments have established central staffs devoted to management improvement throughout their jurisdiction. Under ideal conditions, such a staff can counsel the chief executive on larger problems of administrative organization and procedure and so seek steadily to improve the overall effectiveness of administrative activities. A management improvement staff can also help the operating agencies by serving as a consultant for such agencies and by stimulating each of them to develop a vital concern for administrative organization and methods. Central management staffs need an entrée, however, if they are to be effective. A weak executive is in no position to open doors to agencies claiming independence. The management improvement staffs seem most effective when attached to the central budget division or department of finance; there the necessity of critically examining the agencies' estimates of their financial needs affords a ready excuse for inquiry into their administrative efficiency.

SEPARATISM—AN ILLUSTRATION. Because it is impossible to discuss individually the organization of many of the specific functions of state government, we shall concentrate on one of the most important —education—as a concrete example. In most states, public education is at the top of the list of state governmental expenditures. The division of responsibility between state and local government may vary, but there is strong state concern for education in every one of the states.

Many of the pressures producing administrative separatism are present in high degree with regard to the function of public education. The separate election of state school officers is embedded in many state constitutions; there is usually a strong and active clientele group; the extent and degree of professionalism is very high; and there are indications that ties with the national government will grow, especially in some areas. Two of the most widespread devices for securing administrative independence— board administration and earmarking of revenue sources—are widely practiced.

The chief state school officer, head of one of the largest and most important departments of state government, is chosen in one of four different ways: He is elected directly by the voters (22 states); he is appointed by an elected board (8 states); he is appointed by a board that is appointed by the governor (15 states); or he is directly appointed by the governor (5 states).[18] Either of the first two methods is strongly separatist in tendency and the third only slightly less so; and these are the methods used by most states.

Although both have elements of separatism, professionalization and popular election are not mutually consistent. Those who rise to the top through professional channels frequently lack the personality or skills to win election in a political campaign that, because it is overshadowed by other political campaigns, places a particular premium upon eye-catching tactics or a familiar name. In recent years, the tendency has been away from the elective state superintendent; the movement has been led not by the advocates of integration, but by the advocates of professionalism. For example, in 1949 the Texas State Teachers Association led a campaign that replaced an elective state superintendent with an appointive state commissioner of education who, according to the statute, must "be a person of broad and professional educational experience, with special and recognized abilities of the highest order, . . . [who] shall be eligible for the highest school administrator's certificate currently issued by the State Department of Education; and shall have a minimum of a Master's degree from a recognized institution of higher learning." Schoolteachers in the process of getting themselves anointed with the special oil of professional training refused to continue to serve under the supervision of a man not so qualified. Similar movements have developed in other states.

The state education associations, parent-teachers associations, citizens' committees for better schools, and similar groups are potent interest groups in most states. They would be unhappy with the notion that the schools should be considered a regular department of state or local government, subject to the political control of the governor, or even of a city council. The interest group attitude, as well as the prevailing professional one, is that schools are too distinct and important to be considered a part of "politics." In South Dakota, although the chief state school officer is elected, the constitution prescribes that he be chosen in a "nonpolitical" election.

The various arguments against board administration have had little effect on public education. At the local level school boards are almost

___

[18] The Book of the States: 1966–67, p. 288. Data inconsistent with these appear on p. 138.

universal, and they are widely used at the state level. For higher educational institutions, boards are practically always present.

Interest groups and professional groups supporting education have been successful in many instances in securing earmarked sources of revenue. In Alabama, for example, practically all the receipts from the state sales and income taxes must go into the Special Educational Trust Fund, from which they can be taken only for the support of schools.

Enough has been said to indicate that public education, perhaps the most important of the functions of state government, poses the basic problem of state administrative organization very clearly. Will education be better coordinated with public health, with public welfare programs (such as the care of dependent children), with efforts to control juvenile delinquency, with library service programs, with the conservation of natural resources (through resource-use education), with safety programs, and with other activities of state government if the state department of education is subject to the same administrative superior as are the other departments? Can more rational purchasing, control of state land and buildings, and accounting be conducted if state departments of education are subject to central financial control? Should the personnel employed by the state education agency be subject to the same classification, pay, and retirement programs as other state employees? Can the comparative evaluation of the financial needs of public education be better conducted if its financial support comes from the same fund as the financial support for other functions? An even more basic question: Will the education program be more responsive to the wishes of the majority of the people if the governor is responsible for the way in which it is conducted?

Or will the function be more competently, honestly, skillfully, and responsibly conducted if it is kept apart from central political and administrative control?

4. Prospects for Reorganization

There is more variety and more evidence of change and innovation in the patterns of local administrative organization than in those at the state level, but we shall reserve consideration of developments at the local level for the general discussion of local government and here concentrate on the state.

Most state administrations are not now organized in a very systematic or rational fashion, but an appeal to symmetry and order is far from enough to overcome the inertia of the status quo. As the preceding discussion has indicated, there are many pressures for an atomistic and particularized approach to the problems of state government. Legislative bodies are reluctant to tamper with existing arrangements unless the pressures for change are very strong. Electorates are difficult to mobilize for the calling of constitutional conventions or for the approval of amendments to constitutions, in which some of the existing organization is legitimized.

Generally speaking, significant changes in the organization of state administration have come only when the incumbent governor has placed his full political strength behind the proposals. The 1917 Illinois reorganization was brought about by Governor Lowden; the Virginia reorganization, by Governor Byrd; and the Alabama reorganization, by Governor Dixon. The various significant developments in administration in the state of New York have been associated with the strong political leadership of Governors Smith, Roosevelt, Lehman, Dewey, Harriman, and Rockefeller. In all the states in which the Little Hoover Commission proposals received even a reasonably favorable response, the governors were active in sponsoring them. In some states, gubernatorial support has not been sufficient to secure sweeping administrative changes, but on the other hand, such changes have been extremely rare when gubernatorial support was lacking.

In most states, however, there appears to be little gubernatorial impetus for leading a reorganization crusade. Most governors can look forward to only a brief tenure in office, and most of their attention is necessarily occupied with a few major items of policy controversy that seem urgent at the time. These may involve organizational arrangements, but they are seldom related to any broad reorganization program. "Administrative reorganization" and "management improvement" are probably good words, politically speaking, and most governors will indicate that they are in favor of them. But such words, however acceptable they may become, are not tangible enough to fire the popular imagination. Furthermore, governors who actively push a program that involves increasing their own legal powers leave themselves wide open to charges of self-aggrandizement and "dictatorship."

Most important, the dominant political forces in the states have frequently been uninterested in any overall rationalization of administrative structure and operations. Although there is strong opposition to substantial increases in the level of taxation required by expanded functions of state government, the total impact of state tax systems has not in the past been so drastic as to produce widespread concern for management improvement as an economy device, as has been the case at the national level and in many cities. Furthermore, a large portion of the state tax burden has been levied in such a way as to avoid pinching politically potent groups in unmistakable fashion. Gasoline taxes, sales taxes, and comparatively mild and not particularly progressive income taxes have produced a substantial amount of feathers without much notice from the goose, a situation in sharp contrast with the heavy progressive income tax of the national government and the heavy property tax of many local units.

Most of the groups who have gone to state government for positive governmental programs have been willing to settle for—indeed have eagerly sought—a separate professionalized service without much concern for overall state management. Public education, the largest state function, is an excellent example of this tendency; the licensing and control of professional groups is another. Yet some other groups of the state's clientele, such as the prisoners in penitentiaries and the patients in mental hospitals, have comparatively little influence. There has certainly been a dearth of support for sweeping proposals to improve the general quality of administration in state governments.

Probably the most important factor that may lead to administrative rationalization is the enhancement of the role of the governor as political leader of the majority. At national, state, and local levels, one of the noteworthy developments in political evolution has been the growing importance of the chief executive as the focus of political leadership and responsibility. His constituency is based on the whole rather than on any part. His actions are the most completely visible of any of the agencies of government. Insofar as the political process operates to produce a consensus on governmental programs, that consensus is most nearly represented by the program of the governor. Furthermore, it is the governor's "administration" that is held responsible—the popular (and appropriate) concept is that such-and-such was done during the Jones administration, or that the Smith administration did this and refused to do that. The strong tendencies that have made the governor a political and legislative leader must also tend to make him chief administrator, inasmuch as the administration of programs cannot be separated from their inception and enactment and modification.

If governors of sufficient political power become convinced that strengthening central control of administration is essential to the accomplishment of political programs, and if they feel strongly that the quality of administrative performance is a part of their political responsibility, the greatest available force will probably have been added to the not always imposing pressures for administrative change. It must be remembered, of course, that piecemeal change in administrative arrangements occurs much more frequently than wholesale reorganization and that its cumulative impact may be much greater. Human institutions as complex and as deeply rooted as state administration are not often changed suddenly and radically.

chapter 11

Personnel and Money

O rganization provides the structure of state and local administration, but its purposefulness and vitality depend upon the processes for staffing that structure and for obtaining, allocating, and keeping track of the money that flows through it. How these two basic processes are handled largely determines the quality of administration. Although, as in other fields, the individual state and local governments differ markedly, their general level of performance has been inferior to that of the federal government, and their claim to retain responsibility for important activities suffers from the comparison. Consequently, groups which are eager to have programs carried out effectively turn to the federal government either to perform the work directly or to prescribe administrative standards to be observed by the state and local governments.

1. Workers in the State Vineyard

The most significant single key to effective management of the public business is people—the kind of people and how well they work. If administrative tasks can be done by people who are highly competent, strongly motivated, possessed of the expertness and consistency of approach produced by continuous tenure, responsive to the public interests and desires, and effectively led, there will be few obstacles that cannot be overcome. If state and local administrations fail to attract and retain enough people with these qualities, they cannot expect to be assigned many of the really important tasks of modern society.

We have, unfortunately, comparatively little knowledge on any systematic basis of the qualities and capacities of state and local administrative personnel, or even of the arrangements by which they are actually chosen, assigned to jobs, motivated, or assisted into productive careers. Not only does each state differ in some measure from all others, but most state governments have several different systems of personnel management within their own services. Employees of some of the state agencies receiving federal grants-in-aid are frequently covered by special civil service programs; employees of state higher educational institutions (often the largest single group of state employees) are rarely covered by general state personnel programs; and often particular state agencies such as the state police or the state auditing office have separate personnel arrangements. Furthermore, each local unit of government has its own personnel system. These differ greatly in their relationships with the state—sometimes general or special state legislation substantially regulates local personnel practices, sometimes the local systems are completely autonomous. Public school employees in North Carolina, for example, are all considered to be state employees, and in many other states their qualifications, pay levels, retirement systems, and other features are closely regulated by state law; yet in still other states each local school district determines its own personnel policies subject only to minimum state control. Almost the same range of differences exists for local welfare employees or local highway employees.

Although the quantitative differences among the states can be specified more readily than the qualitative, we are poorly equipped to explain even what we can measure. Thanks to the Bureau of the Census,[1] we know that for every 10,000 people, state and local governments employ 358 people on a full-time or full-time equivalence basis (including full-time equivalence of part-time employees' service) and that 90 of these are working for state governments and 268 for local governments. We are prepared for great disparities among the states on these last two measures, for the respective roles of the state and the local governments are differ-

---

[1] *U.S. Bureau of the Census*, Public Employment in 1965 (*Washington, D.C.,* 1966), *p. 10. The data are for October, 1965. The national average and the local-governments average are slightly inflated by inclusion of the population and local employees of the District of Columbia.*

ently conceived in the several states (for example, New Jersey with 315 state and local employees per 10,000 population has 60 in the state government and 255 in local governments, whereas Hawaii with a ratio of 389 state and local employees has 274 in the state government and 115 in local governments). What is surprising is the degree of variation among states in the ratio to population when we combine state and local employees. For every 10,000 people, Wyoming state and local governments have 496 employees; Alaska, 454; Kansas and Colorado, 436. Washington and New York rank eighth and ninth with 406 employees. At the other extreme, each 10,000 people in Arkansas is served by only 296 state and local employees, and in South Carolina, Kentucky and Pennsylvania by 300, 301, and 303. Neither geographical region nor density of population can be a criterion, for states neighboring those named and with similar population densities are found on the other side of the national average. Why each 10,000 people in the one set of states should need from 103 to 200 more state and local public servants than an equivalent population needs in the second set of states is a puzzle yet to be solved.[2]

Among the local governments of the country there appears to be a clearer pattern, which was revealed in a 1962 study.[3] Though not all signs point in the same direction, the number of employees per 10,000 population does vary in relation to the population the government serves. However, the least populous and most populous areas require the greatest number of employees. Thus, counting together all the local government employees within a county, from 264 to 268 employees (on a full-time equivalence basis) were needed in 1962 to serve 10,000 people both in the average county of less than 10,000 population and in the one with 250,000 or more. From these largest and smallest county population groups, the ratio dipped symmetrically through the 230's for intermediate-size county areas down to about 225 employees per 10,000 for those with 25,000 to 100,000 people. This neat pattern, however, is the product of quite different tendencies in the functional fields of employment. Education, accounting for over half the employment, had a straightforward inverse relation to

---

[2] See, however, U.S. Bureau of the Census, Census of Governments: 1962, Vol. III, Compendium of Public Employment (Washington, D.C., 1963), pp. 5f, where explanatory weight is given to regional variations and to diversity in the volume of employment for education.

[3] Ibid., pp. 136, 319, 376. All employment data are on a full-time equivalence basis. In 1965, local governments employed 268 employees per 10,000 population, with a range by states from 115 in Hawaii to 336 in Wyoming. U.S. Bureau of the Census, Public Employment in 1965, p. 10. For the nation's and each state's local government employees per 10,000 inhabitants, by functions, see ibid., pp. 28–30.

county populations, from 122 education employees per 10,000 population in counties with 250,000 or more people steadily upward to 161 such employees for counties with less than 10,000. Contrariwise, the rest of local government functions, taken as a group, vary almost directly with population; in 1962 they required 146 employees per 10,000 people in the most populous counties, and fell steadily to 89 employees in the 10,000–25,000 population group before rising to 103 for the least populous counties.

While these figures for all local governments include such governmental units as school districts, other special districts, and townships, the most significant employment patterns are those of municipal and county governments. Among eleven size groups of municipalities (except for one curiosity),[4] the number of employees engaged in common municipal functions in 1962 almost steadily declined from 115 per 10,000 population for the largest population class (a million or more people) down to 41 per 10,000 for the smallest class (municipalities of less than 2,500 people).[5] As Figure 11.1 reveals, cities of over half a million people invest considerably more manpower in police protection than do cities of smaller populations, and although the sharp breaks occur at different population levels, almost every major category of service except streets and highways shows in general a lessening of the public employment rate, with less population.

County governments have a pattern that contrasts with that of the cities. Excluding the education function (which distorts totals because practice varies as to whether the county government, rather than school districts, performs the function), county government tasks in 1962 needed 72 employees per 10,000 people in the counties with less than 10,000 people, and the need dropped steadily to 35 employees in counties with 50,000 to 100,000 people (above 100,000, however, the figure rose slightly to 38 employees). The rate of county governments' public employment, in other words, has an inverse ratio to population (see Figure 11.2).

The pattern of employment in city governments and county governments thus differs in an interesting and perhaps significant manner. The

---

[4] *The oddity occurs in the three classes fitted between 100,000 and 500,000 population figures: in the top of this group (300,000 to 500,000), there were 91 employees for each 10,000 people; in the middle group (200,000 to 300,000), the ratio rose to about 98; and then, in the 100,000 to 200,000 group, the ratio fell back to 93 employees before continuing the downward trend in smaller municipalities. The manpower requirements in the 200,000–300,000 population class were particularly higher than those of the 300,000–500,000 class for sanitation, water supply, fire protection, and "general control" (municipal council, mayor's office, courts, legal services, personnel administration, planning and zoning, etc.).*
[5] *"Common municipal functions" accounted for about three-fourths of all full-time equivalent municipal employment in the country. This Census Bureau category facilitates intercity comparisons by excluding the distorting effect of functions that some but not all municipalities perform.*

Figure 11.1. *Municipal Government Employment for Common Municipal Functions, by Size of Municipality, October 1962*

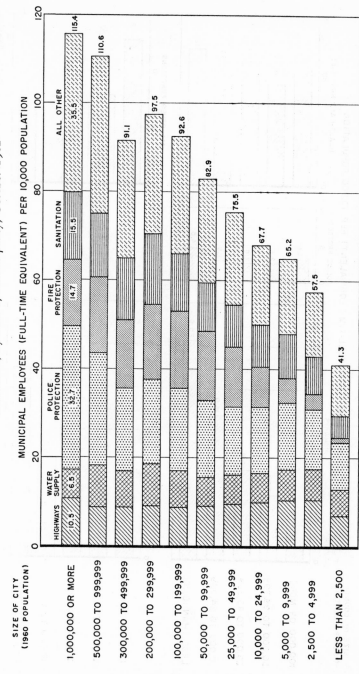

SOURCE: U.S. Bureau of the Census, *Census of Governments: 1962*, Vol. III, *Compendium of Public Employment* (Washington, D.C., 1965), p. 16.

Figure 11.2. *County Government Employment for Functions Other Than Education, by Size-Class of County, October 1962*

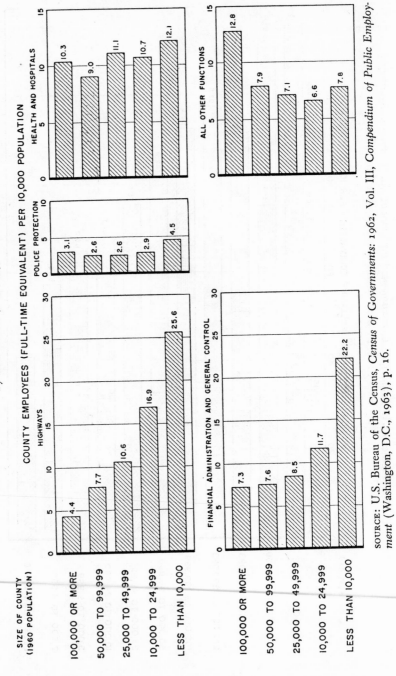

COUNTY EMPLOYEES (FULL-TIME EQUIVALENT) PER 10,000 POPULATION

SIZE OF COUNTY
(1960 POPULATION)

HEALTH AND HOSPITALS

100,000 OR MORE — 10.3
50,000 TO 99,999 — 9.0
25,000 TO 49,999 — 11.1
10,000 TO 24,999 — 10.7
LESS THAN 10,000 — 12.1

ALL OTHER FUNCTIONS

100,000 OR MORE — 12.8
50,000 TO 99,999 — 7.9
25,000 TO 49,999 — 7.1
10,000 TO 24,999 — 6.6
LESS THAN 10,000 — 7.8

POLICE PROTECTION

100,000 OR MORE — 3.1
50,000 TO 99,999 — 2.6
25,000 TO 49,999 — 2.6
10,000 TO 24,999 — 2.9
LESS THAN 10,000 — 4.5

HIGHWAYS

100,000 OR MORE — 4.4
50,000 TO 99,999 — 7.7
25,000 TO 49,999 — 10.6
10,000 TO 24,999 — 16.9
LESS THAN 10,000 — 25.6

FINANCIAL ADMINISTRATION AND GENERAL CONTROL

100,000 OR MORE — 7.3
50,000 TO 99,999 — 7.6
25,000 TO 49,999 — 8.5
10,000 TO 24,999 — 11.7
LESS THAN 10,000 — 22.2

SOURCE: U.S. Bureau of the Census, *Census of Governments: 1962*, Vol. III, *Compendium of Public Employment* (Washington, D.C., 1963), p. 16.

more populous the city, the more employees per 10,000 people; the more populous the county, up to about 100,000 inhabitants, the smaller the number of employees per 10,000 people.

Interpretation of public employment figures of the kind presented here is made difficult not only by the contrary directions in which they sometimes seem to move but also by the variety of causal factors that may or may not be operative. One interpretation of the high public employment ratios of large cities might emphasize both (a) that the problems associated with the functions regularly performed in almost all sizes of cities—police and fire protection, sanitation, water supply, and the like—present themselves with peculiar intensity in large cities; and, equally important, (b) that large cities have chosen to provide amenities for citizens—libraries, parks, and recreation, for instance—and have chosen to provide expert administration of such overall functions as planning, zoning, and personnel administration, whereas the small cities may almost wholly neglect both amenities and the employment of experts for overall functions. Large city governments, that is, govern more because there is more governing that is needed, because the citizens want more services, and because they are willing to pay public employees' salaries to get a higher quality of governmental performance. The alternative, but more dubious, interpretation is that the larger the city, the more extravagant the government is in keeping unnecessary employees on the payroll.

The latter argument presents some difficulty when the subject shifts to county governments. Here, except for the counties with populations over 100,000, the ratio of employees used in functions other than education increases inversely to the population, with counties under 10,000 in population employing twice as many persons per 10,000 population as are employed by counties with between 50,000 and 100,000 (see Figure 11.2). The county pattern might be explained on the grounds that *any* county government requires a certain minimum number of public employees, and the ratio to population is therefore naturally greatest in the less populated counties. The difficulty here is that one would suppose the same need would apply to the smaller municipalities, but as we have seen, the ratios of municipal employees to population is less as population is less. A possible escape from this otherwise unexplained contrast may lie in the hypothesis that county governments in less populated areas do proportionately more governing than the small towns in those areas, whereas in populous areas more of the governmental work is done by cities.[6] These,

---

[6] *It appears that county and municipality ratios sharply contrast even at the same low-population categories. In 1962, county governments with less than 10,000 popula-*

however, are merely speculative lines of thought; a close look at the series of ratios of county and municipality employment to population for each state would be needed before confident explanations of the nationwide data could be formulated.

2. Spoils and Merit

The dominant feature of state and local public personnel practices during the nineteenth century was the spoils system. Persons elected to office appointed their political friends and associates to governmental posts, and these posts were considered rewards for political service rather than opportunities for careful and conscientious administrative work. In a great many states and communities it is unquestionably still true that many, perhaps most, of the positions in public service are considered a part of the spoils of office, the rewards of the politicians.

Spoils patronage is probably even more prevalent in the popular mind than it is in actuality. The degree of cynicism with regard to state employment is one of the greatest deterrents to administrative improvement. The general feeling is that "know-who" is much more important than "know-how" and "know-what" in securing state employment.

EXTENT OF THE MERIT SYSTEM. We have no accurate information about the extent to which "merit systems" have replaced patronage in the state administrative services. Although there is some information on the extent of formal merit systems, appearances are sometimes deceptive. In one state the director of personnel under the "merit system" had been the governor's campaign manager, and it seems likely that his concept of "merit" might not have been unrelated to his previous activity. Politically motivated civil service commissions have devised a number of methods of circumventing the merit system's requirements. Merit system laws, for example, usually permit agency heads to make "temporary appointments" when the civil service commission is unable to supply a list of candidates

---

tion employed for noneducational functions 72 persons per 10,000; municipalities employed fewer than this for "common municipal functions" in each of the three size classes into which the under-10,000 population municipalities are grouped. A flat, unweighted averaging of these three ratios for municipalities gives the figure of 55 employees per 10,000. These calculations are unreliable, both because the functional coverage for county and municipality ratios may differ and because averaging the three municipality ratios fails to allow for the varying number of municipalities in each size class; the latter technical defect, however, serves to understate the contrast in figures given, as about 80 percent of municipalities of under 10,000 population have populations of less than 2,500 and an employment ratio of 41.

chosen by competitive examination. Some commissions fail for years to give examinations for important categories of positions, thus enabling temporary appointments to be stretched out indefinitely. Some design experience requirements or examinations themselves so that only applicants who have already served can achieve a high rating, an attractive opportunity for temporary appointees to convert their appointments to a permanent status.

In some states, though, appointment and tenure on the basis of competence have made real headway even without the trappings of a formal central civil service machinery. In yet others, gradual progress is being made in rationalizing and improving personnel practices through the development of a personnel division in a central department of finance or administration. Such a division supplies its services and exerts its controls through its influence upon financial operations plus whatever support the governor of the moment happens to give it.

In the earlier days of civil service reform, when only agencies substantially independent of the governor were considered to be "merit system" agencies, it was easier to count off the virtuous. Only nine of the present central civil service systems of the states have been in continuous operation since before 1939, although two or three short-lived systems were established before that.

The 1966–67 *Book of the States* listed 32 of the 50 states as having civil service systems with "general" coverage. The larger ones are more likely to have general civil service systems—of the 6 states with the greatest numbers of employees, only Pennsylvania is without one. The largest state civil service system, that of New York, is also the oldest, having been established in 1883, the same year that the federal civil service agency was begun.

According to the 1963 *Municipal Year Book*, approximately 83 percent of the cities of over 25,000 population that answered a survey inquiry had some degree of formal civil service system. In only 58 percent of these, however, were substantially all the municipal employees included in the system. Civil service systems are much more extensive in the larger cities than in the smaller ones—of 56 reporting cities with over 250,000 population, 54 had all or most of their employees in civil service systems, whereas only 263 of the 493 cities between 25,000 and 100,000 population had similar coverage.[7]

---

[7] The Municipal Year Book, 1963 (*Chicago: International City Managers Association,* 1963) *p. 229.*

A major factor in extension of the merit principle in state and local governments has been the federal government's insistence that the principle be observed in health and welfare programs that are financed in part with federal grants-in-aid. In addition, a ban on active "politicking" has been imposed on all state and local employees whose work is in federally aided programs. The first requirement, that of a merit system, was instituted in 1940 for agencies administering unemployment insurance and public assistance; it has since been extended to state and local programs for public health, child welfare, public employment offices, and vocational rehabilitation. Stimulated in part by this requirement, several states have extended merit systems to other agencies or provided a degree of general coverage.

The second requirement, that of restricting employees' political activities, is embodied in the following provision of the Hatch Act of 1940:

> No officer or employee of any State or local agency whose principal employment is in connection with any activity which is financed in whole or in part by loans or grants made by the United States or by any Federal agency shall (1) use his official authority or influence for the purpose of interfering with an election or a nomination for office, or affecting the result thereof, or (2) directly or indirectly coerce, attempt to coerce, command, or advise any other such officer or employee to pay, lend, or contribute any part of his salary or compensation or anything else of value to any party, committee, organization, agency, or person for political purposes. No such officer or employee shall take any active part in political management or in political campaigns. All such persons shall retain the right to vote as they may choose and to express their opinions on all political subjects and candidates.

Such a requirement of political neutrality while holding a government position is by itself no assurance that selection of appointees will be patronage-free and according to merit or that the neutrally behaving incumbents will be protected against dismissal to make room for the "politically deserving." Nonetheless, the general orientation of such a requirement is toward reducing patronage appointments, and it is specifically designed to ensure that an employee's obligation is to devote his time to government work rather than to treat the government post as a sinecure that pays him while he does the party's political work.

PATRONAGE AND POLITICAL VALUES. Patronage and civil service are old enemies. Yet the battle is not so simple as sin versus virtue.

In some jurisdictions, spoils appointments are still so iniquitous that the civic-minded citizen has no difficulty in finding a dragon to slay. But in others his energies might better be directed to freeing his government from the dead hand of the civil service system. Both patronage and civil service systems are more complex than they appear to be on the surface, and both have been undergoing important changes in recent years.

Traditionally the cases for patronage and for civil service have had no common set of criteria. Patronage was justified as necessary to a vigorous political party system; civil service was justified as necessary to efficient administration. There was no meeting ground between the two positions, for they rested on discrete values, each commanding wide respect and neither of them dispensable. What has changed is that each position can be questioned in terms of its own key value: Patronage seems to have less to contribute to vigorous partisan politics, and civil service, at least as it is widely administered, seems to have less to contribute to efficient administration.

Consider the role of patronage in the political system. One of its most thoughtful students, Frank J. Sorauf,[8] finds that the usefulness of patronage to the parties has diminished for three reasons: (a) because it is the less desirable, poorly paid positions that are open to patronage, a result of formal or informal recognition that competent specialists must fill the higher posts; (b) because better-paying, more secure employment can be obtained in private industry, at least in generally prosperous periods; and (c) because a new administration's firing of thousands of incumbents to make room for new appointees will arouse public outrage, itself a political risk for the party. Political campaign methods have changed, too, Sorauf notes, with more stress on issues and candidate exposure on television and less reliance on the votes a patronage appointee can line up by use of his family and friends, or by door-to-door canvassing. Campaign workers now include many volunteers attracted by party, issue, or candidate, and their motivations, complex though they may be, rarely include expectation of a political-job "pay-off."

The political consequences of a general decline in patronage are especially significant, and Sorauf has stated them well. First, the great stronghold of patronage is at the local level, not only because of local government's own patronage opportunities, but also because such state and

    [8] Frank J. Sorauf, "The Silent Revolution in Patronage," Public Administration Review, 20 (Winter, 1960), 28–34. See also his "State Patronage in a Rural County," American Political Science Review, 50 (December 1956), 1046–56; and his "Patronage and Party," Midwest Journal of Political Science, 3 (May 1959), 115–26.

federal patronage as may remain is often used for appointments recommended or endorsed by the local party organization or faction. Patronage therefore strengthens local as against state and national party organizations; its decline should lower one of the barriers to party discipline and responsibility, both in the legislature and elsewhere. Second, patronage is more important to the Democratic than to the Republican party because it has greater value to the economic, occupational, urban, and minority groups attracted to the Democratic party and because that party tends to rely on patronage as a counterweight to the financial contributions that the Republican party can usually obtain from the business community.

Third, because the value of patronage depends upon economic conditions, it is less likely to be abandoned in depressed areas and communities than in the country generally. And fourth, the lessening of patronage will weaken state governors in relation to state legislatures; more than in the national government, it appears, the state chief executive has had sufficient freedom of movement (despite our general remarks about local political clearance of appointments) so that he could use his patronage as an instrument to support his policy and political leadership.[9] Sorauf concludes his analysis by suggesting that "the advancing merit systems will not kill patronage before it withers and dies of its own infirmity and old age." This is not because the merit systems' advance is slow but because patronage's decline is accelerating. This is consequent on the realization that, in its own terms of party politics, patronage is decreasingly relevant.

CIVIL SERVICE AND ADMINISTRATIVE VALUES. If attitudes toward patronage have changed, so have attitudes toward the kind of civil service system that will contribute to, instead of impede, administrative efficiency. State and local merit systems that are general in coverage and administered in all good faith have developed a special character. With few exceptions, they have been largely dominated by a conviction of the need to battle against the real and supposed threats of the political environment. They have been concerned with eradicating spoils, with protecting the integrity of "merit" against the evil intentions of the politicians. They have been concerned with seeing that positions are filled upon the basis of open competition, with the jobs going to the best qualified persons who happen to present themselves for examination. They have been concerned with the development and maintenance of classification systems to provide justice and equity in pay scales, so that one group

---

[9] For an excellent description and analysis of Governor Harriman's use of patronage, see Daniel Patrick Moynihan and James Q. Wilson, "Patronage in New York State, 1955–1959," American Political Science Review, 58 (June 1964), 286–301.

of employees would not be discriminated against by preferences given to another. They have been concerned with protecting employees against discrimination and against mistreatment by seeing that disciplinary action taken was appropriately justified. They have provided a degree of consistency and uniformity with regard to such matters as vacation, sick leave, group insurance, and retirement.

These are all useful objectives, and a great deal has been done toward increasing the rationality of personnel programs by the agencies pursuing them. In many cases, however, a price has been paid for these gains. In making sure that motives of political patronage are excluded from appointment decisions, the civil service commissions have at times excluded motives of policy achievement as well, in spite of the fact that political and program loyalty is often a better motivating factor in the public service than pecuniary compensation. In attempting to make certain that decisions concerning appointment and promotion are objectively defensible, they have frequently minimized what may well be the most important pertinent factor—the personal judgment of the supervisor responsible for the conduct of the activities. In insisting upon competitive examinations taken by "applicants," the commissions have often produced the nearly disastrous result of completely missing the possibility of recruiting those people who are good enough to have to be sought out and induced to join state service. Such people simply cannot be expected to turn up as applicants for jobs; in some professional specialties, being an applicant and being a supplicant are scarcely distinguishable. In trying to secure uniformity among various agencies with regard to classification and pay levels, the attempt to find middle ground may well have promoted mediocrity.

Increasingly, civil service agencies have seen the need to abandon their passive, negative watch-dog stance and take on a positive, even aggressive, managerial role, vigorously recruiting talented people and ensuring career opportunities and a working environment that will make such people want to continue to serve in state and local governments. By no means are all the elements for an attractive public service within the jurisdiction of the civil service agencies. The state legislature and local councils bear responsibility for low salary scales, for requirements that only local residents are eligible for civil service posts, and for many discouraging features of the working environment.

ADJUSTMENT TO REALITIES. Both patronage and the traditional civil service concepts are based on the assumption that government employment is a special plum, a sort of reward to be given to the deserving who ask for it—politically deserving in one instance, and deserving through demonstrated competence in the other. In periods of prosperity and increasing private wage and salary levels, such as this country has had for the last twenty-five years, this assumption loses much of its validity. Of what significance is the existence of a competitive examination for public health physician when no one can be found who is interested in the job?

There will, of course, always be takers for most government jobs, especially those of a routine nature. Since 1940, however, the problem has not been choosing from hordes of applicants but that of discovering and persuading people of even reasonable competence to enter the state and local service. The major problems have been to devise attractive enough incentives to interest people of competence or promise and to provide ways and means of developing the competence of those who can be recruited or induced to remain in the service.

One could take a calm and unhurried attitude toward the rate of progress in state and local personnel policies and procedures if the immediate future did not present so urgent a need. One reason for urgency is the stepping up of competition for talent because so few people of the right ages and training will be available. The total labor force of the country is expected to increase by 17.3 percent between 1960 and 1970, but in the critical working years of 25 to 44, the increase will be only 4.3 percent (the subgroup of 35 to 44 years of age will actually decrease in the period, and again between 1970 and 1975). The 25–44 age group, which was 45 percent of the labor force in 1950, will have fallen to 39 percent in 1970.[10] Yet this relatively smaller age group is the one whose members have the greatest vigor and most up-to-date training and at its lower limits are making their choices of lifetime careers.[11]

By a slightly different calculation, total employment will increase 21 percent in the decade 1960–70 and 31 percent over the fifteen-year period 1960–75. Against this estimate is the greater expected increase of government employment, which is 35 percent for 1960–70 and 51 percent for the longer period of 1960–75. For all employers, public and private, the in-

---

[10] Manpower Report of the President and A Report on Manpower Requirements, Resources, Utilization, and Training by the United States Department of Labor (Washington, D.C., 1964), p. 243.

[11] Choices of careers in local government occur later than one might suppose and often follow some experience in working for other types of employers. A survey of 1,725 municipal executives (down to division heads) showed 30 as the average age of first entering local government and a range among categories (managers, functional departments, etc.) from 27 to 35. For only 25 percent of all the executives was local government their first employer; 51 percent started in private business. Municipal Manpower Commission, Governmental Manpower for Tomorrow's Cities (New York: McGraw-Hill, 1962) pp. 145–47.

crease in employment of the much-sought-after "professional, technical, and kindred workers" will be 43 percent in 1960–70 and 65 percent in the overlapping period of 1960–75.[12] State and local governments will have to move rapidly to make their services attractive if they are to recruit trained men and women of the critical working-age groups in a period of intensified competition by private industry and the federal government.

Consider, however, the following findings of the Municipal Manpower Commission, a distinguished private study group: [13]

1. This nation needs more administrators, professionals, and technicians than it now produces—not only to meet the burgeoning demands of local governments but of all public and private enterprises.

2. The prevailing philosophy of personnel administration in most local governments is not based on the need for an adequate share of this scarce and vital talent.

3. The selection, hiring, promotion and disciplining of personnel, fundamental elements of management in any enterprise, are in too many local governments, artificially separated from, and independent of, the chief executive.

4. The personnel practices—recruitment, compensation, and career development—of local governments are unequal to the tasks of getting and keeping the number and caliber of [administrative, professional, and technical] personnel required.

5. There are able, competent, and dedicated persons in key positions in local government—but not nearly enough. The quality of [administrative, technical, and professional] personnel is, by and large, inadequate to cope with present and emerging metropolitan problems.

The concept of the civil service program as a bulwark against patronage seems less realistic than in earlier years. Without minimizing the significant areas where patronage may still be a problem, the really important personnel jobs now seem to be of another character.

PROFESSIONALS REPLACING AMATEURS. Another far-reaching development tending to make the issue of patronage versus the merit system somewhat irrelevant is the rapid professionalization of the

---

[12] Manpower Report . . . , p. 244.

[13] *Municipal Manpower Commission,* op. cit., pp. 53f. *Students considering entering municipal employment will find the volume, and especially the two appendices (pp. 127–96), informative on the opportunities for them and on the job satisfactions and dissatisfactions reported by present municipal officers.*

public service. In large measure, this reflects the continuing development of specialization and the division of labor in modern society. The functions of state and local government have developed rapidly in areas where specialized knowledge and competence are essential and inevitable. In public education, public health, and public welfare—three of the great service fields that occupy large portions of budgets and staff—there have been tremendous developments of professionalism in this century and generation. In highway construction and maintenance, policies and programs are largely under the control of professionally qualified engineers. In natural resource management and conservation, foresters and geologists and soil conservation and agricultural extension specialists are, of necessity, more widely used and better trained. In law enforcement, probation and parole, and even in penology, special professional training is being required more and more. American state and local services have been profoundly affected by the formation of professional associations and other developments that tend to raise professional standards.

Similar developments have taken place in some of the staff areas. The growth of national associations of budget officers and purchasing officers and the rather substantial degree of professionalization of public personnel specialists have been significant steps. However, there has been here, as probably in some of the professionalized operating activities, some tendency toward a "triumph of technique over purpose," through the substitution of professional pride in craftsmanship for broad-gauged concern for public needs.

Although these developments, as has been indicated in the preceding chapter, have tended to produce a less integrated administrative organization, they have had a notable effect upon the quality of performance of many of the operations conducted by state and local governments.

Yet at the state level, in particular, professionalization has largely been confined to specialists. There have been very few indications of emergence of "professional generalists" or professional public administrators. The generalists have ordinarily been the politicians, and they have been professional at the business of running for office much more than at the business of running the office. Practically nothing at the state level compares with the development of the city-manager profession in the municipalities. In a few instances, those who are the products of specialized public administration programs in the universities have been employed by the states. The largest numbers of persons who could be called, in some degree, professional generalists in state administration have been in the state budget offices and in the emerging management improvement staffs. There are a few people who have shown such competence in administration and such attachment to the public service, in both state and local governments, that they serve one administration after another and are even shifted from responsible administrative positions in one department to similar posts in another. The small but growing state and local membership in the American Society for Public Administration is an indication of the concern for the development of professional public administrators.[14]

3. Personnel Management

ORGANIZATIONAL ALTERNATIVES. The primary motivation of the civil service reformers in many states and communities has been the elimination of political spoils. Since much of the spoils was closely associated with the political activities of the governor or mayor, it was inconceivable, in these jurisdictions, that the central personnel agency be a staff agency subject to complete discretionary control by the political executive. Most of the central personnel agencies, therefore, have been rather completely independent of the governor or mayor, utilizing all or many of the available devices for separatism. The functions of the central agency, established with this primary motivation, have been as much control as service.

Arrangements for state personnel administration today reveal two patterns. Of the states giving wide jurisdiction to their central personnel agency, about half have vested the responsibility in a board, usually one whose members have overlapping terms and some protections against removal. In the rest of these states, chief responsibility for the central personnel operation seems to be vested in a single director, although a board is frequently associated with him and accorded some degree of supervisory and advisory and appellate powers. In nearly all these single-director states, the focusing of responsibility for personnel activities on a single individual is of recent origin (Maryland, which has had a single civil service commissioner since 1920, is an outstanding exception).

If the concept of the central personnel agency is that of a policeman

---

[14] *An interesting study of the career patterns of bureau chiefs in New York City government suggests that, while a higher degree of political skill may be required at the upper levels of the bureaucracy, the need for specialized competence in particular agencies is so strong that specialization is a stronger factor in career advancement than "generalist" politico-administrative achievements.* William C. Thomas, Jr., "Generalist versus Specialist: Careers in a Municipal Bureaucracy," Public Administration Review, 21 (Winter 1961), 8–15.

opposing the spoils that can be expected from the politicians, a board, as independent as possible, will be preferred. If, on the other hand, the concept is that of the central personnel agency as a tool to assist the chief executive in managing the programs of the state or local unit, the single personnel director, appointed by and completely responsible to the chief executive, will be preferred. A board would then be used only for advisory or quasi-judicial functions.

In some governments (the national government is a leading example) there has been a strong movement in recent years toward the "decentralization" of personnel activity to give the agencies that have chief responsibility for program operations a greater degree of discretion in determining classification of particular jobs, in setting job qualifications, in recruiting and rating applicants for positions, and in many other personnel activities.

There are indications here of a pattern of development. After obvious examples of spoils politics and personal favoritism, the civil service function is taken, as much as possible, from the control of politicians, put into the hands of an independent board, and the "rascals" held in check as much as possible. After the dirt of the spoils of politics and patronage appointments has been largely removed, the irksome regulations associated with detailed central control of hiring and firing and promotion and salary levels (matters that are, of course, close to the very heart of program administration) begin to appear to outweigh the possible danger of patronage. Then there sets in a tendency toward decentralizing or delegating many of these functions to the operating agencies and of integrating the personnel operation more closely into the central political control of the administrative machinery. Various states and localities are at stages along this route, and some have short-cut large portions of it.

In 1962, a major study conducted by the Municipal Manpower Commission, a specially constituted group of outstanding public administrators, concluded that most American cities have reached a stage where separate and independent personnel boards are more harmful than helpful. One of the major recommendations resulting from the study was:

> *The independent civil service commission, where it exists, should be abolished or limited to an advisory function. The independent civil service commission, a foundation-stone of the movement for better government for three-quarters of a century, has outlived its usefulness as an instrument of personnel management. Today, we must look to responsible mayors, city managers, and department heads to seek out and provide the experienced administrators, and the qualified professional and technical personnel that are required.*

Hence, where an independent civil service commission now controls the recruitment, selection, compensation, training or promotion of personnel, it should be abolished or its authority and administrative functions should be limited to an advisory role.

The mature urban units of this country—those that have grown up politically and administratively—can operate perfectly well without an independent civil service commission. For those lacking maturity, or where some local situation of a compelling nature exists, a civil service commission can be used to perform important functions apart from personnel management.[15]

AGENDA OF CONCERNS. Whether responsible to an independent board or directly to the chief executive, the central personnel agencies have many responsibilities. Among the most important are position classification and compensation plans; involvement with recruitment, selection, promotion, and separation; general policies and programs on working conditions and fringe benefits; and training.

In every state and large local government there are many departments, agencies, and bureaus. In order to approach "equal pay for equal work," reduce jealousies and frictions between the departments, and increase the possibilities for cooperative recruitment and for transfers among departments and agencies, central personnel agencies must try to analyze and classify jobs and to provide for uniformity of treatment and compensation. This is a matter of constant negotiation between the operating agencies and the personnel office. Each operating agency tends to want its own positions given high classifications and pay levels, and the central personnel agency tries to keep some degree of equity among agencies.

Responsibility for pay levels requires continuing comparisons with private employment. Some public positions, of course, have no analogue in the nongovernmental community, but the pay levels of secretaries and accountants and engineers need to have some relationship to those prevalent in comparable private positions. The nature of this relationship is only incidentally a matter of "fairness"; its real significance lies in whether it enables the government to recruit and retain its appropriate proportion of the supply of qualified workers. Unless there is strong leadership or an impelling need, the salaries of public officials, fixed through political and administrative channels, tend to lag behind those fixed in the private market (see Figure 11.3).

In the process of recruitment and selection, there is a substantial role

---

[15] *Municipal Manpower Commission, op. cit., p. 108.*

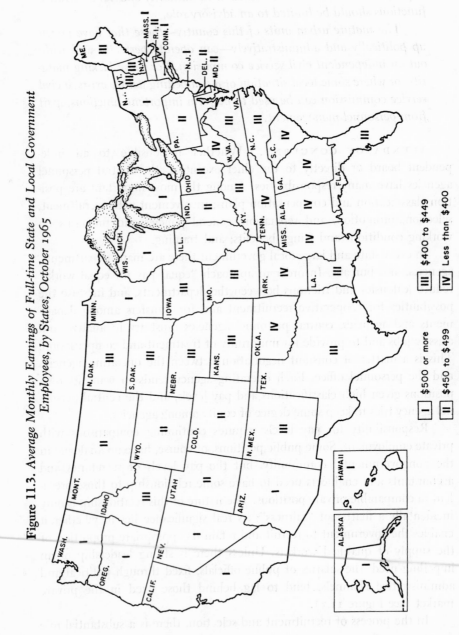

Figure 11.3. *Average Monthly Earnings of Full-time State and Local Government Employees, by States, October 1965*

I $500 or more

II $450 to $499

III $400 to $449

IV Less than $400

SOURCE: U.S. Bureau of the Census, *Public Employment in 1965* (Washington, D.C., 1965), p. 11.

for written competitive examinations, particularly for lower-level and routine positions. But with the increasing need for specialists and professionals and persons competent to make policy and provide program leadership, the "examination" process takes on a different form. The better personnel agencies assist the operating departments in trying to discover and entice qualified people to join the public service, in a world where the hunt for qualified talent becomes more and more difficult. And the "examination," though competitive, is likely to be simply a comparative evaluation of the training and experience records of the candidates.

Currently, as suggested before in this chapter, a significant recruitment problem is that of the age level of public employees. Nationally, the proportions of the population over 65 and under 20 have been increasing very rapidly, while the proportion between those ages, the normal working force, has been stable or even declining. Furthermore, in public employment, in those segments that have not been subject to recurring patronage turnover, there are great numbers of people recruited during the depression years of the 1930's, when the relative security of government employment was particularly attractive. This bulge is now approaching retirement. Many of the public services, therefore, have a special need to recruit younger people or to retain some of their better old employees beyond what has been considered normal retirement age.

Lack of strong competition for state and local governmental jobs leads them often to be filled, if filled at all, with persons from the lower socioeconomic groups in the community. Furthermore, legislation and political considerations usually minimize instances of discrimination against Negroes and other disadvantaged groups (except in the southern states) in public employment. Disproportionately large numbers of these groups may be brought into state and local public service in many jurisdictions. This development is not without precedent or social utility: urban Irish and Italian immigrants of an earlier generation have used jobs as policemen and schoolteachers as avenues for upward social mobility.

In public as well as private employment, there is increasing attention to "fringe" benefits. Every personnel agency is concerned with trying to provide equitable policies concerning such work conditions as vacations, sick leave, and work schedules. In 1965, the number of working days of paid vacation allowed state employees each year varied from 10 in several states to 24 for some employees in Mississippi, and the number of days of sick leave annually from 10 for some state employees in North Carolina to 30 for some of those in Iowa and Maryland. Group health, life insurance, and retirement programs are increasingly important. In the same year, all but 3 of the states had group hospitalization insurance programs arranged for some or all their employees, and 35 had group life insurance programs.[16] Retirement programs for state and local employees, although often still inadequate, are growing rapidly. The Census Bureau reported in 1962 that 5.4 million employees were members of state and local government retirement systems; by 1964–65, total assets of these systems were $31.8 billion, an amount nearly twice as great as it had been in 1959.[17] For some types of state employees, and even more local employees, there are still few if any programs for such fringe benefits, but the pressures for their adoption and elaboration are very strong.

Training may be a much more important public personnel responsibility in the future than it has been in the past. In view of the shortages of competent people suggested earlier, the period may be past when a government can assume that most of the task of training people for job competencies will be performed outside the public service and that recruiting can be directed to people already competent for specific tasks. Many personnel and operating agencies are beginning to face up to the needs for finding people with promise who do not have skill as accountants or social workers, for example, and for providing methods of producing those skills after employment. Even at higher executive levels, there is growing evidence that continuing opportunities for education and training produce valuable results.

EMPLOYEE ASSOCIATIONS AND UNIONS. In twentieth-century America, people who have similar interests associate in organized groupings. The professional groups mentioned earlier all have organizations. The state teachers' associations and local teachers' associations are vigorous, active, and influential. The American Public Health Association, the International Association of Chiefs of Police, the National Recreation Association, the International City Managers Association, the National Association of State Purchasing Officials are all examples of associations of public employees. By sharing ideas in meetings, publications, and study projects, these and dozens of other organizations try to advance the interests of their members and to improve the quality of their work.

They also try to raise the standards of their professions by adopting codes of ethics and setting higher qualifications for admission. Sometimes, particularly as they become large and powerful, they present the views of

---

[16] The Book of the States: 1966–67, pp. 158–161.
[17] The Book of the States: 1964–65, p. 191; U.S. Bureau of the Census, Governmental Finances in 1964–65, p. 28.

their membership before legislative bodies, usually to secure better salaries and working conditions. For example, one of the most powerful of the state lobbying organizations is the teachers' association.

Somewhat distinct from these professional organizations are the public employees' unions. Union membership is more prevalent in local government employment than at the state level, and most members belong to unions formed specifically for public employees, although some—machinists and electricians, for example—may belong to one of the traditional unions.

The attitude of responsible public officials toward these unions varies. Some strongly discourage them; others are more tolerant but will not discuss salaries or working conditions or, if they do, will reach no formal agreements. Nevertheless, in a few instances, full-fledged collective bargaining negotiations have resulted in contracts of employment. Almost always the top officials deny that the unions have any right to organize strikes, and the unions themselves are generally hesitant about using or claiming the right to use such tactics, though strikes of public employees are certainly not unknown.

The argument is frequently made that the collective bargaining procedures used in private industry are not appropriate in government since working conditions, pay levels, and other terms of employment must be determined through political and legal channels. That is why some of the most effective organizations, such as the teachers' associations, have become active participants in the political process. On the other hand, however, there seems to be a growing tendency for state and local governments to recognize and bargain with employee unions in the public service.[18] Public school teachers are rather sharply divided between the professionally oriented National Education Association and the labor union oriented American Federation of Teachers; the apparent trend is for the National Education Association and its local groups to accept some of the tactics of the labor unions.

THE VITAL SPARK. Much has been done to eradicate the evils of spoils appointments in the state and local service; much remains to be done. Although incalculable gains have come from the increasing competence of professionally trained people in many of the specialized areas, the crux of the problem has only rarely been approached. Generally speak-

---

[18] *Keith Ocheltree, "Personnel Administration: Developments in 1965," in* The Municipal Year Book: 1966 (*Chicago: International City Managers Association, 1966*), *pp. 159f; and same volume, pp. 176–83.*

ing, popular regard for state and local administrative service is not high—and for good reasons.

The salaries of state and local employees are generally low. For October, 1965, the average earnings of the federal government's civilian employees were approximately $573—which is low enough. But the average earnings that month of full-time state and local government employees were only $493 and, excluding educational employees, only $452.[19] As a result, state highway departments do not get the pick of engineering school graduates; public health agencies and hospitals do not get the pick of doctors. However, the range of salaries is such that some states have a much better chance than others of attracting and holding able people. For example, in the month of October, 1965, earnings of full-time state and local employees ranged from Mississippi's average of $325 and Arkansas's $351 to $742 in Alaska and $651 in California.[20]

Most state and local public employees, while honest, conscientious, and competent in a routine fashion, do not have the high morale, the sense of participation in a common cause of great importance, and the feeling of constructive and progressive accomplishment that are characteristic of the really effective social organizations developed in this country. There are some exceptions, to be sure, in which the deep wellsprings of group motivation have been tapped enough to produce programs matching some of the best in the national government or private enterprise. It is said, for example, that some of the professional programs in New York and California have advanced well beyond related programs at the national level. On the whole, local agencies have probably been more successful than those of the states in recruiting and keeping highly qualified and dedicated staffs; a few police and fire departments, traffic control agencies, water departments, housing and redevelopment agencies, among others, are really outstanding. But these and other exceptions are just that.

Civil service reform may have been aimed at a symptom rather than a cause. If the political leaders chosen by the people are willing to undermine the quality of governmental activities by filling government posts with incompetents to pay political debts, the trouble lies in the political system itself, and the remedy should be sought there. Similarly, if because of their short terms of office and the restriction on reelection, governors and mayors have no incentive to improve the career civil service, the trouble lies in state constitutions and city charters, and changing the formal rules is the indicated remedy.

---

[19] *U.S. Bureau of the Census*, Public Employment in 1965, *pp. 6, 11.*

[20] Ibid., *p. 11. Because of cost-of-living factors, Alaskan salaries are not wholly comparable to salaries in other states.*

Most progress in personnel administration, as in other areas, seems to have come where the political system has produced leadership able to inspire administrative staffs with such deep interest and regard for effective performance that competent persons have been attracted to public employment and the attitude and productivity of employees have been greatly improved. Thus these leaders, the chief executives in particular, must be so interested in attaining certain program goals that they become committed to search for people who can best attain them.

In the diverse political systems that prevail on the American state and local scene, this kind of program leadership is likely to be very spotty. It probably appears more often in particular functional fields, influenced by professionalism and the zeal of the specialist, than in the whole of a general governmental unit. Yet although the dedicated program commitment of a park and recreation agency or of a state university may be nonetheless "political" because it is specialized and autonomous, it may produce accomplishments that could not be achieved through the regular political process.

Two things may be conceded: First, even if it is not practicable to get at the root problems of political ineffectiveness and irresponsibility, it is desirable to dig out as much of the spoils system as is possible through civil service reform. Second, removal of job patronage may be helpful, in some measure, in remedying the basic political diseases. Still, the only acceptable goal for a healthy government is a political system so responsive to the needs of the people that dedication to purpose and reliance on the highest available competence become integral parts of the leaders' program. Where the sense of belonging, of high purpose, and of participation in programs of social importance can be produced, problems of organization and procedures can be seen in better perspective.

4. Managing Money

Administration and finance are inseparable because the control of finance represents in large measure control of administration. In the nineteenth century, the legislatures controlled the spending process, but this system was ineffective. Departments and agencies would make up their requests for appropriations without consulting one another; then the appropriation committee of the legislature would consider these requests one after another, with little regard for any relationships between the requests of one agency and those of another.

By 1929, however, every American state had established a central budget office. This is one of the prescriptions of the reorganization movement that was universally accepted, although substantial variations appear in what the budget covers and how it is made and operated. A Council of State Governments report [21] says that

> One of the most significant institutional devices of modern government is the budget. It offers an opportunity for the consideration of all programs and policies in one consistent frame where they may be compared, their interrelationships examined, and rational choices made. In addition to its role as a policy coordinator, the budget is also emerging as an important device for administrative control. The process of program analysis and forecast of needs offers an opportunity for the budget-making authority to learn the inner details of organization and procedure of all administrative agencies and to establish performance standards. Within the past thirty years the budget has emerged as the principal control device of the American governor.

WHO PREPARES THE BUDGET? An executive budget has been orthodox doctrine for half a century. The agencies engaged in the work programs suggest expenditures; and since these proposals must be merged into a single pattern, the only person properly situated for this task is the chief executive.

In more than 40 states the responsibility for preparing the budget is vested in the governor or in a staff subject to his control.[22] In many of these, the budget officer is in the immediate office of the governor; in a growing number, he is placed in a department of finance or in a department of administration that contains other central services such as purchasing, printing, and accounts. In a few states, the budget is prepared by a commission that may or may not be subject to effective control by the governor. Where the majority of the commission members are themselves popularly elected executive officials, as in Florida, or are state legislators, as in Indiana, the governor's influence depends upon his prestige, persuasiveness, and political position. In actual practice, he may be more or less influential than his legal position would indicate.

The legislature, as a body and specifically through key members, recognizes the overriding importance of the budget process as the central artery for program control. If, as is true in many states, much of the budget

---

[21] Reorganizing State Government (*Chicago: Council of State Governments,* 1950), *p. 35.*

[22] State Expenditure Controls: An Evaluation (*New York: Tax Foundation, Inc.,* 1965), *p. 9. In Nebraska and Texas, two budgets are prepared and submitted, one legislative and one executive.*

agency staff is relatively permanent, the staff may be sensitive and responsive to legislative as well as executive pressure—to the governor probably
first but not exclusively. Where, as in a substantial number of states, the
governor himself cannot or does not wish to assume responsibility for
supervising the programs of many agencies, the professional budget staff
has a peculiarly significant role in attempting to weigh the various political
forces so as to strike an administrative balance.

The legislature retains, of course, its traditional role in the actual
determination of appropriations. In increasing numbers, legislative committees have employed staffs to assist them in the consideration of the
budgetary proposals. This appears to be, and frequently is, a duplication of
the staff activity of the executive budget agency, although often a high
degree of cooperation exists between the two budget staffs. The growth of
legislative staffs appears to have been caused in large measure by legislators'
increasing feeling of frustration when confronted with large and complex
proposals for expenditure that they have insufficient opportunity to digest.

The degree of control that the governor (or other budget-making
authority) can exercise over the integrity of the budget shows a wide range.
In some states, the original requests of the agencies must be presented to
the legislature along with the official budget recommendations. For example, the Arkansas statute says that "the Director of Finance shall not
alter the original request, unless requested to do so by the administrative
head of each such state agency, but shall report the original request
together with his own recommendations and the reasons therefor." In
many other states, agency heads do not hesitate to press for higher appropriations than the governor has requested. Thus the head of one of the
independent agencies in Alabama said publicly that he had never accepted
the governor's budget proposal for his agency as satisfactory, and did not
propose to start doing so now. On the other hand, the Maryland and New
York constitutions forbid the legislature to increase any item in the governor's proposed budget. It may strike out or reduce an item, but none can
be raised; furthermore, no special appropriation bill can be considered
until the governor's proposals have been disposed of. In New York, the
governor's control over the budget has been practically complete, and
legislative acceptance of it is much more substantial than is true of the
budget of the national government.

In the 40 states where the governor has the power to veto items in
appropriation bills, he has another weapon of control over agencies who
use their direct lines of access to the legislature, but there are many reasons
why this weapon may be used only sparingly. If the power is to veto only
whole items rather than to reduce them, as it is in many states, it may be of

little value with regard to those that the governor would not wish to eliminate completely. Even more important, his political relationships with the legislature may lead him to be more cautious in altering a decision it has already made than in making his recommendations to it. Nonetheless, the item veto is one of the few instances in which the state governor is better armed than the President of the United States, for the President must accept or veto a whole appropriations bill as it comes from Congress.

NATURE OF THE BUDGET. A governmental budget is the plan of work for the governmental unit, stated in financial terms. For local units of government, whose legislative bodies meet fairly frequently, budgets are ordinarily prepared annually. This is true also in the 19 states with annual legislative sessions. In the others, a biennial budget is used, although revenues and expenditures are ordinarily calculated for each year of the biennium.

Budget documents tend to be voluminous and detailed; in fact, they often resemble large mail-order catalogs in size and weight. In order to be useful and meaningful, the budget summarizes the activities and expenditures of the past, frequently includes some measurements of work output or performance as a justification for expenditures, and indicates in considerable detail how money has been and will be used. In the appropriations acts, which are usually less detailed than the budgets, there is an increasing tendency toward the use of "lump-sum" rather than "line-item" appropriations.[23] In the line-item appropriations act, the salary levels for individual positions may be specified, and permissible expenditures for supplies, equipment, travel, etc., described for each agency. Since there is increasing difficulty in helping the legislature to become familiar with these matters, and increasing need for flexibility, it is becoming more common to make appropriations for each agency or program in a lump sum, allowing the administrators to determine their specific allocations.

In recent years there has been a movement toward the use of performance or program budgets, rather than those indicating the character and objects of expenditure. This means that the budgets, and the appropriation acts or ordinances that result from them, are broken down on the basis of programs of work, such as "summer recreation activities," "tree-planting," or "snow-removal," rather than on the basis of salaries, supplies, travel, new equipment, and other itemized expenditures. Such a program budget is somewhat more difficult to produce, since it involves a more accurate

---

[23] Detailed line-item appropriations for each position and expenditure object are still used in 12 or 13 states, and in some of these for particular areas only. Ibid., pp. 33–35.

accounting system than most governmental agencies maintain and much difficulty in the classification of activities. Yet it does provide the budget agency, the chief executive, and the legislature with more meaningful information upon which to base priority decisions. It also encourages and even requires output and performance records, in order to provide a rational explanation for expenditures or justifications for increases. Although these measures of performance are frequently more difficult for government than they would be for private enterprise, since many governmental activities are not as susceptible to exact measurement, they are possible and useful in many situations.

Budgets for capital expenditures (which account for about 30 percent of states' direct expenditures) are frequently separated or distinguished from those for operating expenditures, since the consideration of capital outlays involves special review and analysis. Although they are revised each year, capital budgets are increasingly prepared for longer periods of time than the immediate budget term to enable the financial planners to space these expenditures rationally and to anticipate unusual bulges in expenditure needs. Appropriations actions by the legislative body, however, are required ordinarily only for the particular year or biennium of the long-range capital program that is immediately ahead.

FUNDS AND EARMARKING. It is rare in any governmental unit for all receipts to be placed in the unit's general fund, where they would be available to be appropriated for any purpose. Instead, particular receipts may be "earmarked" and placed in special accounting funds to be used only for specific and limited purposes. There are many reasons for this. The advocates of a measure may decide that it will be politically acceptable only if the anticipated revenues are specifically earmarked for a certain politically attractive purpose. In the 1930's, for example, many state laws authorizing the sale of alcoholic beverages dedicated state liquor revenues to such good and popular purposes as education and old-age pensions. In other instances, a special interest may secure approval of a particular revenue proposal only with the understanding that it will be used for a special purpose—examples are hunting and fishing license fees, which are used for game protection and propagation, and gasoline taxes, which provide funds for building roads. Government receipts from business-type enterprises are ordinarily used primarily to pay the costs of the service involved. In other ways particular receipts are tied to particular expenditures; the most obvious example is the special assessment on propertyholders to pay the cost of streets, sidewalks, drainage, or sewerage lines that improve the value of the property. Another device is to finance capital outlays by pledging certain receipts to repay borrowed funds. This seems especially appropriate when the pledged revenues come as a result of the capital investment, but it occurs frequently even when this is not the case. To levy a special tax to pay the costs of a new hospital or new higher educational institutions may seem the only way to finance the project. In some instances, the earmarking of revenue receipts is written into the state constitution, or into the charter of the local unit of government, which reduces still further any discretion on the part of the legislative body.

Another source of earmarking, and one of increasing importance, is the intergovernmental grant. Federal grants-in-aid to states and local governments, and state grants to local governments, are ordinarily made for specific purposes and programs, and the monies received by the spending unit must therefore be used only for this purpose. When, as is commonly the case, these federal grants must be matched by state and local funds, both the intergovernmental receipts and the funds that are required to match them then must go into earmarked accounts to be used only for these specified purposes.

The existence of these earmarked funds, which are very pervasive in state and local governments, is a serious bar to a comprehensive budget (see Table 11.1). When the receipts from many taxes and fees are available only for the particular purposes designated when each was originally authorized, the range of choice of the budgeting agency and the appropriating authority are greatly circumscribed. There is then only a very limited opportunity to balance program needs against one another and to designate the relative priority of each.

To be sure, some budgeting is possible for earmarked funds. Although they cannot be used for other purposes, a great deal of specification within the general purpose is possible. In other instances, the earmarked funds are supplemented by appropriations from the general fund, and control over the marginal appropriation provides a fairly effective control over the program.

CONTROLLING THE USE OF APPROPRIATED MONEY. Effective financial control does not end with the enactment of the appropriations. In more and more states, central staff agencies, subject usually to the control or influence of the chief executive, have substantial control of expenditures even after appropriation bills are passed.[24] In local govern-

---

[24] For a thoughtfully critical analysis of the growth of detailed controls by the central budget office, see Allen Schick, "Control Patterns in Budget Execution," Public Administration Review, 24 (June 1964), 97–106, and comments by state budget officers and others (September 1964), 202–07.

Table 11.1. *Percentage of Earmarked or Special Funds by State,*
September 1965*

State	Percent	State	Percent
Alabama	90	Montana	54
Alaska	8	Nebraska	76 [h]
Arizona	50	Nevada	37 [i]
Arkansas	23 [a]	New Hampshire	18 [j]
California	†	New Jersey	24
Colorado	69	New Mexico	35
Connecticut	41 [b]	New York	†
Delaware	55	North Carolina	† [k]
Florida	55	North Dakota	50
Georgia	†	Ohio	58
Hawaii	22	Oklahoma	75
Idaho	63 [c]	Oregon	69
Illinois	43	Pennsylvania	27
Indiana	46	Rhode Island	4 [l]
Iowa	67 [d]	South Carolina	60
Kansas	62	South Dakota	71
Kentucky	64 [e]	Tennessee	39 [m]
Louisiana	86	Texas	72
Maine	6	Utah	65–70
Maryland	39	Vermont	71
Massachusetts	57	Virginia	63
Michigan	56 [f]	Washington	47
Minnesota	64	West Virginia	55
Mississippi	60	Wisconsin	71
Missouri	76 [g]	Wyoming	88 [n]

*For consistency, data reported from all states have been rounded to the nearest whole percent.

†Information not available.

[a] In addition, federal funds, trust funds, nonrevenue and construction funds comprised 44.2 percent of total expenditures.

[b] Bond fund expenditures not included in working out percentages.

[c] Includes $90.4 million of federal grants-in-aid, considered as special funds.

[d] Special fund and trust fund expenditures are included under special funds.

[e] Includes federal grants-in-aid, highway fund, and other trust and agency funds.

[f] However, general fund–general purpose expenditures (those financed from nonrestricted revenues, and which are subject to annual appropriation) comprise only 37 percent of total state expenditures.

[g] Figures relate to treasury accounts only. Special funds expenditures include federal funds.

[h] Cash funds: 29.7 percent; federal funds: 36.46 percent; building funds: 1.89 percent; special levy funds: 8 percent.

(Footnotes continued p. 398)

ments, where appropriating bodies meet more frequently, such administrative control is somewhat less essential.

Executive control of expenditures can involve (*a*) the authorization of shifts of funds from one purpose to another, (*b*) control of the rate of expenditure, (*c*) determination of legality of expenditures, or (*d*) control of the desirability of the expenditure.

Unless appropriation bills are very broad and general, there may well be needs during the year (or biennium, as is frequently the case) to make a shift from one object of expenditure to another. The statutes frequently permit such arrangements to be made within limits, subject to the approval of a comptroller, finance department, the governor, or some other central agency. It is also increasingly common for the central finance agency to make monthly or quarterly allotments for operating departments' expenditures, thus keeping the appropriated funds from being dissipated at too rapid a pace; in some instances, the central agency requires that reserves be set up for special contingencies.

In most states, a central financial agency must approve expenditures before they are finally paid. This function has been traditionally associated with that of auditing, but in many states (27, at a recent count) and some local governments this function of pre-audit is performed by an official responsible to the chief executive, on the theory that this is properly a function of management; post-expenditure examination is left to an independent auditor.

The most drastic type of expenditure control, which is exercised in some states, permits the central financial agency (or the governor or local executive) to refuse to approve expenditures, even though they are within appropriations, on the grounds that they are not "in accord with the governor's program." This involves central control of the wisdom, as well as the legality, of expenditure by the administrative agencies.

COLLECTING TAXES. Increasing portions of state and local revenues may come from service charges and from other governments, but the bulk of governmental financing still comes from taxation. Tax adminis-

---

(*Footnotes to Table 11.1 continued*)
ᶦThe only special fund is the highway fund.
ʲIn addition, the highway fund accounts for 48 percent of expenditures.
ᵏAll special funds and subsidiary funds are part of the general fund appropriations.
ˡAn additional 20.6 percent of total expenditures is comprised by bond accounts.
ᵐHighway fund, debt service fund, and bond funds.
ⁿIncludes 64 working capital funds, 18 permanent land funds, 17 land income funds, 20 trust and agency funds, 16 federal funds, 9 state collected local funds, and 24 other special funds.

SOURCE: Supplement to *State Expenditure Controls: An Evaluation* (New York: Tax Foundation, Inc., 1965), p. 53.

tration is an old and continuing problem with which each state and local government must deal.

Local governments, with a few exceptions, depend primarily upon the property tax as a source of revenue. Although state governments do not now ordinarily use the property tax as a major source of revenue, most of them are concerned with its administration at the local level, partly because of the state's general responsibility for local government and partly because many programs of state assistance to local units depend upon effective and equitable use of the property tax by the local units themselves.

In property tax administration, the key problem is assessment—the valuation of the property that is used as the base for the tax rate. In rural communities, where most property is in land, farm buildings and equipment, and residences, it is somewhat easier for untrained assessors to arrive at a reasonable assessment of the value of property, although even here there are many opportunities for differences in judgment and for inequitable treatment. In an increasingly complex society and economy, however, the difficulties multiply. In most states, assessment of property for tax purposes is still done by local, untrained assessors, frequently chosen by election. Assessment lends itself to great inequities, both between individuals and between local areas. Only recently has the full scope of some of these inequities been precisely established—the result of the Census Bureau's 1957 and 1962 studies of variations within and among local assessing areas in the ratio of assessed values to actual sales prices of nonfarm single-family houses.[25] Nearly two-thirds of the states have laws that appear to expect assessment to be at full value, yet over the country generally assessments are at only about 30 percent of market value, with South Carolina at one extreme averaging 5.8 percent and Rhode Island averaging 65 percent at the other.[26]

Differences among states, of course, do not mean inequity, for the property tax on residential property has significance only for state and local affairs. Within any state, however, differences in degree of underassess-

---

[25] *U.S. Bureau of the Census*, Census of Governments: 1957, Vol. V, Taxable Property Values in the United States (*Washington, D.C., 1959*); *and same*, Census of Governments: 1962, Vol. II, Taxable Property Values (*Washington, D.C., 1963*), *as corrected by the* Errata Notice (*August 1964*). *The 1961 survey of nonfarm residential properties covered a sample of 1,356 of the nation's 8,131 local assessing areas; the selected areas have three-fourths of the nation's population. Nonfarm single-family houses, the property category to which the Census Bureau's detailed surveys are confined, account for about half the number and assessed value of locally assessed real properties.*

[26] *U.S. Bureau of the Census*, Census of Governments: 1962, Vol. II, *p. 95.*

ment among the local assessing areas obviously reward or penalize citizens simply on the basis of where their property happens to be located. Intrastate differences among assessing areas are found in every state, though in each of 15 states there is a reasonable degree of inter-area uniformity.[27] In 8 states, the local assessing area in which a man's residential property is located makes a startling difference in how his property is assessed. In Maine, for example, when the 31 surveyed areas are listed in order of the median ratio of assessment to sales value, the midrange (that is, sixteenth) local assessing area has a ratio of 33.8 percent of sales value. But the *average* deviation of Maine's assessing areas from this midrange ratio figure is 22.9 points (that is, a percentage deviation of 68 percent). Depending upon where your property is located in the state (except in the midrange area), it is likely to be assessed at ratios of about 56.7 or 10.9 percent of actual sales value, that is, at one and two-thirds or at only one-third of the midrange area's assessment figure for the same kind of property. The 8 states that have great deviation among assessing areas show the average percentage deviation from the midrange area as 33 percent (Georgia) up to 47 percent (North Dakota) and 68 percent (Maine). Consider Georgia, the best performing of these 8 states. Property in Chatham County has a median assessment-to-sale-price ratio of 18 percent, while De Kalb County, where Atlanta is located, has a 45 percent ratio.[28]

Aside from their illegality under state laws requiring full-value assessment, such inter-area variations might not matter much if assessments were used only as the basis for local tax collection; a low assessment and a high tax rate can produce the same revenues as a high assessment and a low tax rate. But assessed valuations are used for many other purposes: state constitutional and statutory limitations on the power of local governments to tax and borrow are expressed as percentages of assessed valuation; where a special school district embraces several local assessing areas, the area with the lowest assessed property value pays less than its fair share of school

---

[27] Ibid., *p. 98. The measure used is the percentage by which the average of all a state's assessing areas' median ratios of assessed value to sales prices deviate from the median ratio of the area that stands midway among these areas in a listing ranked according to median ratios. We have counted as representing "a reasonable degree of inter-area uniformity" the 15 states whose areas, on the average, deviate from the midway area's ratio by 13 percent or less. Because of averaging and of measuring from the midway area, it should be noted, this measure does not reveal the range of difference between areas at or near the two extremes.*

[28] Ibid., *p. 143. These are not the most extreme contrasts in Georgia. One unnamed area assesses at less than 10 percent of sales price and another falls in the 50 percent or more category. See ibid., p. 98. Detailed figures for individual assessing areas, at pp. 142–53, cover only selected local areas having a 1960 population of 50,000 or more; for Georgia the coverage is only 9 of the 26 sample assessing areas.*

costs; state laws or the constitution may fix local officials' salary levels in relation to local property value; more significantly, state laws often distribute state funds to local governments by a formula geared to such valuations on the assumption that those with the lowest property value need the most aid. Wisconsin makes more than eighty statutory uses of the local assessed valuations. The Advisory Commission on Intergovernmental Relations, noting both the appalling inequity in assessments and the states' extensive use of assessed valuations in formulas governing the application of state policies, calls assessed valuations "elastic measuring sticks." "It would be hard to conceive, on the basis of its use in most but not all States, of a more unreliable measurement standard. In fact, it is the only widely used standard with a two-way stretch and a two-way shrink." [29]

Even within each assessing area, inequities are common, whether because of the favoritism or the incompetence of the local assessing officers. Within half the country's local assessing areas, the average departure of assessed houses from the midrange house's ratio of assessment to market value is anywhere from 20 to 40 percent, and in a fifth of the assessing areas this deviation from the midrange is 40 percent or more. The Advisory Commission understandably concluded that "the quality of local assessing ranges from mediocre to almost unbelievably inferior over a wide portion of the nation." [30]

Sales taxes, which are now the chief source of state revenue [31] and a developing source of local revenue, appear to be much easier to administer equitably than the property tax. It is much easier to measure tax liability accurately, and the merchants serve as relatively efficient tax collectors. Although students of taxation frequently regret the fact that the burden of a general sales tax rests more heavily upon the poor than the well-to-do, ease and uniformity of administration are certainly among the factors that have led to increasing use of state and local sales taxes.

Income taxes, which are the chief source of revenue for the federal government, are also used by 39 states and a few localities. They have administrative difficulties in discovering and allocating income between

---

[29] *Advisory Commission on Intergovermental Relations*, The Role of the States in Strengthening the Property Tax, Vol. 1 (*Washington, D.C.*, 1963), *pp. 44f.*

[30] Ibid., *p. 41. The Advisory Commission's denunciation here, as in the earlier quoted passage, was based on the 1957 report of the Bureau of the Census. However, as the figures on intra-area dispersion of ratios we have cited from the 1962 report (p. 99) and those for inter-area dispersion indicate, there has been no substantial improvement during the five years between reports.*

[31] *Frederick C. Mosher and Orville F. Poland*, The Costs of American Government (*New York: Dodd, Mead, 1964*), *p. 69. This book is an excellent summary of facts and trends concerning governmental revenues and expenditures.*

their particular jurisdiction and other jurisdictions, as well as in securing complete and accurate reporting. There are, however, substantial opportunities for cooperation between the states and the federal internal revenue service in income tax administration. Although these opportunities are used in some measure, they are rarely exploited fully; the state and local governments prefer to use their own definitions or classifications of income and deductions rather than follow those of the federal government.

The field of tax administration is one in which mechanical and electronic data processing is becoming particularly valuable and important. Punched cards and magnetic tape can not only keep records more accurately and more quickly; they also offer almost unlimited possibilities for analysis, comparison, and checking of tax returns and liabilities.

If it seems politically desirable for more than one governmental level or unit to use the same source, as is more and more often the case, there are obvious administrative advantages in shared tax arrangements. In most states, gasoline taxes are collected only by the state government, but the receipts are divided between the state government and local units according to a legislative formula. Taxes on tobacco or liquor or other items may be collected by the state and distributed to local governments, or collected by the county and shared with its municipalities. In the continuing tension of the American federal system, there are always differences of opinion about whether the provision of a governmental service—and the collection of funds to support it—should be done at the local, state, or federal level. For interlevel financial arrangements, there are at least four possibilities: (1) collection of the funds and provision of the service at the higher level, (2) collection of the funds at the higher level and grants-in-aid to the smaller units to finance prescribed services, (3) shared taxes, the larger unit collecting the funds and transmitting a portion to the smaller units to be used to provide such services as are locally determined, and (4) grants of power to the smaller units enabling them to raise the revenues and provide the services locally. The choice among these possibilities may be influenced most by political considerations as to the level at which policy decisions should be made, but the administrative advantages of shared tax arrangements constitute an important consideration.

5. Conclusion

Personnel administration and the management of public monies are by their nature technical topics, and few aspects lend themselves to lively debate. Yet within these topics lie questions of major significance for the distribution of powers among national, state, and local levels of government; for the political and legislative arenas; and for the quality and quantity of services provided to citizens.

Consider, for example, the legislative-executive balance of power. A governor who is in charge of the preparation and execution of a state budget and has an item veto over appropriations bills is clearly in a much stronger position than one who finds that a commission dominated by legislators or elected state department heads has the last say in drafting the budget for presentation to the legislature, that he has no effective veto over legislative appropriations, and that every payment is subject to prior approval by an elected auditor. Similarly, a governor who has a personnel division attached to his office with responsibility for administering the civil service system is in a position, if he is so minded, to upgrade the morale and quality of the public service; but if an independent civil service commission can go to sleep on the job, well-protected against a governor's effort to awaken it to its responsibilities, the governor may well be frustrated and wonder whether he really is the chief executive. Some features of current practice may box in both governor and legislature. Thus, as much as half of the state's budget may elude control by these elected policy makers because of special funds and earmarked revenues.

Or consider party politics and the ability of state and local governments to prove themselves worthy of retaining or acquiring service and regulatory functions. Where patronage is prevalent, the quality of personnel may be low, an attribute that strengthens the claim of higher levels of government with better personnel to perform functions that might otherwise have been decentralized. At the same time, the governmental system may get no compensating advantages, for patronage is decreasingly contributory to the strength of political parties. The penuriousness of state legislators and city councils adds to the difficulties, for without offering adequate salaries no government can attract and hold competent personnel. And when politics and personal favoritism enter into tax assessments, citizens' confidence in their government ebbs.

Although some answers may seem clear, others are not; what often confronts states and local governments is not an either-or choice but the necessity to strike an appropriate balance between competing needs. Thus, assigning substantial powers to central budget, personnel, and purchasing agencies may at first glance always appear to be a move in the right direction; yet nothing is more frustrating to dedicated public servants in charge of service and regulatory programs than lack of scope for their own good judgment. To have to clear every detail with central agencies not only increases delays and red tape; it also often means decision making by someone far from the scene of action, untrained in the subject-matter area, and often oriented to quite different values. This is a far cry from central officials' exercising only general policy oversight, holding program administrators responsible for results, and letting them make the detailed decisions.

The people who man state and local governments and the processes by which those governments allocate financial resources among competing needs are instrumental means for achieving the goals that the citizens and their elected legislators and executives choose. Failure to attract able people and to manage public monies well has a simple consequence: it makes the chosen goals unattainable.

chapter 12

Courts and Judges: Power and Politics

The roles of courts and judges as components of political systems are subtle, multiple, and complex. In analyzing state and local judicial bodies, the student is hampered not only by the mythology that cloaks all aspects of judicial policy making, but also by the low visibility of some state and many local court actions. Comprehensive and reliable data on judicial behavior at state and local trial court levels are not so readily available as at the federal or state supreme court levels. While this comparative dearth of empirical data precludes a definitive evaluation of state and local courts and judges, sufficient material exists to reveal their basic functions, problems, and interactions with the other units of the political system.

As molders and interpreters of the law, courts and judges have many functions and faces, and there may well be contradictions among them. Roscoe Pound, in his classic *Introduction to the Philosophy of Law,*[1] for example, enumerated four "ends of the law" which were not necessarily consistent with one another. These ends were (1) to keep the peace in a given society, (2) to uphold the social status quo and maintain general security through the security of social institutions, (3) to make possible the maximum of individual free self-assertion, and (4) to make possible

---

[1] *New Haven, Conn.: Yale University Press,* 1922.

the maximum satisfaction of wants. Evaluation of any particular legal system depends in large part upon the relationships between the system's objectives and the functions it performs in practice. Evaluation may hinge also upon the social class, status, or income of the observer, for courts present different faces to differently situated viewers.

To comprehend the roles of the judiciary in state and local government, we must examine both the internal and external relationships of the legal mechanism. Internally, we should look at the power, organization, and processes of courts and judges. Appropriate questions for examination include: What is the scope of state judicial power today? Has the expansion of the federal judiciary materially impaired or restricted the power of state and local courts to resolve social, economic, and political conflicts arising within their borders? How do judges decide cases? How much discretion do they have? Are cases resolved speedily or do congested court calendars produce delays resulting in denials of justice? What steps can be taken to enhance fairness, equality, and speed in judicial administration?

Externally, we should focus on the objectives of the legal system and on its interrelations with the political system. It is helpful in this respect to probe for answers to questions such as these: What are the goals, strengths, and limitations of courts as mechanisms for social control? Could some functions traditionally performed by courts be transferred to other agencies for more efficacious and expert disposition? Are judges part of the political "machine"? Are appointed judges more competent than those who are elected? Can courts be wholly independent of politics?

In this chapter we shall examine many of these questions under three major headings: the scope of state judicial power, discretion in judicial policy making, and the interplay between politics and the judiciary. Then, in Chapter 13, we shall consider internal and external impediments to judicial efficacy and the prospects for reform.

1. The Scope of State Judicial Power

How important are state courts in delineating the law? Two facts are basic. The first is that, in the complex system of government we adopted, most questions of private law were left to the states. The national government had almost no part in establishing or developing the law of property, contracts, wills, personal injury, or damages. The second is that within the states it was often the courts rather than the legislatures that actually formulated such law.

Judge Cardozo cited a number of instances of creative decision making by state courts in his famous lectures on *The Growth of the Law*. A major illustration was the judicial assault upon "the ancient citadel of privity." [2] At common law a person injured by a defective article that was manufactured negligently could recover damages from the manufacturer only if there was a contractual relationship between them. However, in typical business dealings, the manufacturer sells his product to the distributor or wholesaler who then sells it to the retail merchant who in turn sells it to the consumer. Therefore, under the rule of privity, the injured consumer could not sue the manufacturer; he had to sue the retailer who sold him the product. If a member of the household other than the purchaser was injured by the defective product, then even the retailer could not be sued since the injured party had no contractual relationship with him.

The New York State Court of Appeals, of which Judge Cardozo was a member, stepped into this maze of technicalities and gradually but consistently modified the rule of privity. Beginning with a special exception to the rule in the case of the negligent manufacture of poisons, the court proceeded to hold that there is a remedy by the consumer against the negligent manufacturer, regardless of privity, where the product is likely to be dangerous to life. Subsequently, the "dangerous to life" category was expanded to include not only poisons, but scaffolds, automobiles, and even bakery goods containing nails or other harmful substances.[3] The gradual redevelopment of the law by the state courts, described by Cardozo in 1923, continues to the present. In 1961, for example, a further inroad into the doctrine of privity was made by an eastern state supreme court when it ruled that modern marketing techniques call for a new approach to the problem.[4] When a manufacturer markets a product in a sealed container, the court held, he is giving the ultimate consumer an implicit warrant that the product is fit for the intended use. If that consumer suffers injury in the normal use of the product, he has the right to recover from the manufacturer, under this judicial interpretation, regardless of the absence of privity of contract and of proof that the product was dangerous to life.

In 1963, the California Supreme Court carried this doctrine still further when it held that a manufacturer is liable for ensuing damages

---

[2] "*Privity*" *is defined as a connection, or bond of union, between parties as to some particular transaction.*

[3] *Benjamin N. Cardozo*, The Growth of the Law (*New Haven, Conn.: Yale University Press*, 1924), *pp.* 77 f.

[4] Hamon v. Digliani, 148 *Conn.* 710, 174 A. 2d 294 (1961).

whenever an article that he has placed on the market—knowing it is to be used without inspection for defects—proves to have a defect that causes injury to a human being.[5] Citing this case as an example of the increasing tendency of state courts to extend the concept of strict liability to manufacturers, the Illinois Supreme Court ruled in 1965 that a manufacturer of automobile parts must indemnify the car owner who has settled claims resulting from injuries caused by the defective parts.[6]

That state courts can exercise power creatively is illustrated by several other developments in recent years. For example, the Delaware Supreme Court modified the traditional rule that a private hospital owes no duty to the public to accept any patient not desired by it. The judges concluded that when it maintains emergency facilities, the hospital gives the seriously injured person a right to rely on its capacity to aid him. Refusal of aid in an unmistakable emergency makes the hospital liable for damages.[7] In an unusual application of the "equal protection" clause of the Fourteenth Amendment of the U.S. Constitution, the California Supreme Court ruled in 1966 that an amendment to the state constitution adopted by the state's voters that authorized property owners to exercise absolute discretion in choosing buyers, lessees, and tenants was unconstitutional.[8] The court held that incorporation of such a provision in the state constitution would make the state a participant in any subsequent discrimination for racial reasons by sellers or lessors and would therefore violate the Fourteenth Amendment's prohibition of state action depriving persons of the equal protection of the laws. Reinterpretation by state courts of the power of eminent domain, under which state and local governments can compel property owners to sell their property when it is needed for public use, has become a major instrument of urban redevelopment.[9]

A recent decision by the New York Court of Claims recognized illegitimate birth as a new tortious injury.[10] Basing its decision on "principles of social justice," the court held that an infant born out of wedlock to a mentally deficient mother who was raped by a fellow patient while confined in a state mental institution has a cause of action against the

---

[5] Greenman v. Yuba Power Products, 59 *Cal. 2d* 47, 377 P. 2d 897 (1963).

[6] Suvada et al. v. White Motor Co. et al., 32 *Ill. 2d* 612 (1965). *See also James Fleming, Jr., "Evaluation of the Fault Concept,"* Trial, 2 (February–March 1966), 25–38.

[7] Wilmington General Hospital v. Manlove, 53 *Del.* 338, 169 A. 2d 18 (1961).

[8] Mulkey v. Reitman, Law Week, 35 (May 17, 1966), 2617.

[9] *See Eugene J. Morris, "The Quiet Legal Revolution: Eminent Domain and Urban Redevelopment,"* American Bar Association Journal, 52 (April 1966), 355–59.

[10] William v. State, 46 *Misc. 2d* 824, 260 N.Y.S. 2d 953 (Ct. Cl. 1965).

state. This ruling could have far-reaching implications in welfare law.

These illustrations are prototypes of, rather than exceptions to, the capacity of state and local courts to make policy governing the day-to-day relationships of people among themselves and with the states. Contracts, negotiable instruments, property, insurance, marriage, divorce, adoption— all the traditional areas of private law offer continuing opportunities for the creative jurist at state and local court levels to implement the adage that "law must be stable, and yet it cannot stand still."

The powers of state courts in both civil and criminal law were reinforced by a landmark decision of the Supreme Court in 1938. In *Erie Railroad* v. *Tompkins*,[11] the Court ruled that, except in matters governed by the Constitution or federal law, the law to be applied by any federal court in cases over which it has jurisdiction is the law of the state, as interpreted by the state courts in which the particular federal court is located. Thus state court interpretations and decisions are important not only for the development of state policies, but also for their impact on federal court decisions as well.[12]

The scope of judicial power, state and federal, was vastly enhanced by the Supreme Court's historic opinion in *Baker* v. *Carr*, in 1962.[13] Prior to that decision, questions of apportionment of legislative representation by the states were generally deemed "political questions," suitable for resolution only by the executive and legislative branches of government and not by the courts. *Baker* v. *Carr* asserted with finality judicial jurisdiction over the substance and methods of apportionment. The decision specifically authorized a federal court to examine apportionment problems in the light of the Fourteenth Amendment's equal protection clause, but in holding that such problems are justiciable, the Court in effect conferred new power on the state judiciaries as well as on the federal courts.

The state courts have the opportunity to be creative in criminal as well as civil law. Although there is a growing body of federal criminal law, the vast majority of criminal cases fall under state jurisdiction. From minor traffic offenses to murder, it is predominantly the states that bear the responsibility for the definition of crime and for the apprehension, trial, and treatment of offenders. Yet it is the Supreme Court that, in the now

---

[11] 304 U.S. 64 (1938).

[12] For pertinent illustrations, see Michael Cardozo's stimulating article, "Choosing and Declaring State Law: Deference to State Courts versus Federal Responsibility," Northwestern University Law Review, 55 (1960), 419–36.

[13] 369 U.S. 186 (1962). In Reynolds v Sims, 377 U.S. 533 (1964), the Court later held that legislative apportionment must be on the basis of population ("one man, one vote") for both houses of the state legislatures.

famous *Escobedo* case of 1964 [14] and then the *Miranda* case of 1966,[15] has established the most stringent procedural protections for persons taken into custody by the police and later prosecuted for a crime.

APPELLATE AND TRIAL COURTS. It has often been pointed out that judicial power is limited because judges cannot initiate action. Whereas the legislature and the executive can act on their own volition in matters they consider vital, judges cannot raise issues for judicial decision on their personal initiative no matter how crucial the issues are. Nonetheless, skillful utilization of the judiciary's hierarchical system of review can give the states' highest courts power equivalent to the executive and legislative power to initiate action. Thousands of cases covering virtually every minute facet of the law may be appealed from courts of original jurisdiction to intermediate appellate courts and ultimately to the highest tribunals of the states. The discretion to choose from among the wide range of cases brought on appeal those that are to receive priority of consideration, those that are to be examined comprehensively, and those that are to be dismissed summarily offers the high court judges, in effect, if not in form, the power to use initiative in the molding of policy.

Thus far in our discussion of the scope of state judicial power we have emphasized the role of the states' highest tribunals. The work of the lower courts must not be minimized, however, for it is in the courts of original jurisdiction—the municipal courts, county courts, justice of the peace courts, traffic courts, juvenile courts, family courts, and the like—that the typical citizen has his primary contacts with the law. Here, the law often wears different faces than it does at the appellate court and supreme court levels. At times it may appear like a creature in a nightmare, terrorizing the innocent and the naïve; at others, like the characters in Alice in Wonderland, irrationally but blithely committing outrages against common sense.

Blatant appeals to prejudice, the more virulent the more successful, are still the hallmarks of some local courtrooms, as this excerpt from the closing remarks of defense counsel in the trial and acquittal of three Klansmen for the murder of a civil rights worker demonstrates:

> *And this white woman who got killed? White woman? Where's that N.A.A.C.P. card? I thought I'd never see the day when Communists and Jews were flying under the banner of the United Nations flag, not the American flag we fought for. . . . I'm proud to be a white*

---

[14] Escobedo v. Illinois, 378 *U.S.* 478 (1964).

[15] Miranda v. Arizona, 384 *U.S.* 436 (1966), at *p.* 479. *For further discussion of the* Escobedo *and* Miranda *cases, see Chapter 13, p. 440.*

*man and I'm proud that I stand up on my feet for white supremacy.
Not black supremacy, not the mixing and the mongrelization of
races . . . not the Zionists that run that bunch of niggers. The white
people are not gonna run before them. And when white people join
up to 'em they become white niggers. . . .*[16]

Sometimes too, especially in courts bereft of the clashes and jargon of
adversary lawyers, the proceedings are like informal discussions in which
solutions are sought through techniques of guidance and counseling rather
than through the imposition of formal sanctions.

Any or all of these faces may be worn by these courts for the masses of
people—courts which in practice serve more often than not as courts of
last as well as first resort. Exercise of the right of appeal takes time and
money, and the average traffic offender, barroom scuffler, or delinquent
debtor rarely has both. Judicial discretion reaches maximum proportion in
these low-visibility cases. Whereas public awareness of and interest in the
disposition of suits may be aroused in murder trials or occasional spicy
divorce actions, the day-in, day-out drabness of the great majority of local
court proceedings limits the public's range of concern and enhances, in
effect, the judges' discretionary powers.

2. The Methods of Judicial Policy Making

Three myths have remained prevalent over the years in the folklore of the
judicial process. One is that the role of judges is confined to finding the law
and that they have no power to formulate policy or to exercise personal
discretion in disposing of cases before them. According to this view, the
applicable law is both certain and immutable. The decision would be the
same regardless of the background, philosophy, or political affiliation of the
individual wearing the judicial robe.

The second myth, the antithesis of the first, is that judges are all-
powerful in the formulation of policy. The remark that "the Constitution
is what the judges say it is" has been echoed and re-echoed by this school of
mythologists in the apparent belief that frequent and strident repetition of
the pronouncement could serve as a substitute for proving it empirically.

In actual practice, of course, judges must find *and* make law. In past
statutes and judicial precedents they must find guides to the resolution of

---

[16] Life, May 21, 1965, p. 35.

present conflicts. The judge who ignores statutory provisions and judicial precedents in disposing of his docket of cases invites the reversal of his decisions on appeal to the higher courts. It is equally true that the judge who completely ignores changing social attitudes or needs and bases his decisions on mechanistic applications of precedent may also be reversed by appellate tribunals or ignored, in turn, by the public at large.

This last point highlights the third myth of the judicial process, the myth of efficacy, which is more harmful than either of the first two. This myth assumes that knowledge about what the law *is* tells us also how people *will* behave. In practice, however, the law declared by the judge may be no more than an admonition to the people about how they *ought* to behave. For law is only one of a number of factors, such as culture, religion, personality, and values, that motivate or condition human behavior. The observer of the judiciary who is lulled into accepting the myth of efficacy and who therefore believes that judicial decisions alone can control socially deviant behavior is likely to produce invalid or irrelevant answers to the problems of courts and judges, if only because his acceptance of the myth keeps him from focusing on valid and relevant questions.

The analyst who surmounts these myths of the judicial process still has much to learn about the *how* and *why* of judicial policy making. For recognizing that judges find and make law at the same time, that they develop new policies while observing the tradition of adhering to precedent, and that they need the existence of a consensus or the potentiality for coercion if their decisions are to be effective does not explain *how* they make policy or *why* courts rather than legislatures have been the sources of specific policies.

ADVANTAGES OF JUDICIAL POLICY MAKING. A major reason why courts, rather than legislatures, have been the principal developers of specific policies in many substantive areas is that every statute tends to represent a compromise between competing interest groups. It is politically unrealistic to expect legislation to embody specific details that may well antagonize important segments of the community.[17] A second reason was put forth by Judge Cardozo. If justice is the goal of law, he maintained, then detailed policy making by specific legislation is not only unrealistic but undesirable. It would be impossible for a legislature to define all the conditions to which a statute is applicable. Court rulings may

---

[17] *See Frank Newman's discussion of "the art of deliberate ambiguity" in "A Legal Look at Congress and the State Legislatures," in* Legal Institutions Today and Tomorrow (New York: Columbia University Press, 1960), *pp.* 67–92.

often be "tentative and uncertain gropings," he acknowledged, but such gropings are preferable to comprehensive legislation that would "rush blindly into darkness." Justice is better achieved by case-by-case decisions of courts than by legislatures because "justice is not to be taken by storm; she is to be wooed by slow advances." [18]

Courts, rather than legislatures, have been heavily relied on for the resolution of conflicts among local units of government.[19] This tendency has been attributed to the effort "to minimize the risks of external control by a superior decision-maker." These local units prefer the precise, limited impact of judicial decisions to the amorphous, general effects of legislation.

Whether focusing on conflicts among local government agencies or among private individuals, we must recognize that the state and local courts play important, if not predominant, roles in formulating the specific norms and rules through which government defines and controls deviant behavior and seeks resolution of conflicts. Examination of the structures, processes, and interactions of state courts, then, is more than a mere academic exercise; it is a study of the composition and methods of institutions of government that are on a plane of power and creativity that is at least coordinate with the executive and legislative branches.

THE ROLE OF PRECEDENTS. Judges are, of course, governed by precedent; for the disposition of current cases must be consistent with the disposition of similar cases in the past. There are, however, multiple legally acceptable techniques for choosing from many potentially applicable precedents the particular ones that will guide the resolution of the current cases. Rarely will one find that the current case is identical in every detail with some case or cases from the past, although it may bear some similarity to several different features of earlier ones. The judge must then choose among those different features and decide on the particular one to apply to the case at hand. This is the pivotal choice, and it cannot be made mechanically. It is a human and fallible process in which the judge's own value system usually comes into play—that is, those values can affect the particular technique of legal reasoning he uses in choosing the precedent.

How can the use of different techniques of legal reasoning lead to reliance on different precedents? Consider as an illustration the Supreme Court's decision in *Baker* v. *Carr* alluded to earlier,[20] which ruled that

---

[18] *Cardozo*, op. cit., *p. 133*.

[19] *Vincent Ostrom, Charles M. Tiebout, and Robert Warren, "The Organization of Government in Metropolitan Areas,"* American Political Science Review, 55 (December 1961), 831–42.

[20] 369 U.S. 186 (1962).

questions of malapportionment of seats in state legislatures are justiciable questions for courts to decide. Prior to that decision, it was generally believed that suits to compel reapportionment were nonjusticiable because these were "political questions" that judges were not competent to resolve. A line of cases extending from *Luther* v. *Borden* in 1849 to *South* v. *Peters* in 1950 applied the "political question" doctrine consistently to a host of challenges to state representation systems.

How then, consistently with precedent, could a group of judges rule in 1962 that a case challenging Tennessee's alleged malapportionment of seats in the state legislature presented a justiciable question? According to Justice Brennan, who wrote the majority opinion, all of the earlier "political question" cases were based on the charge that they violated the constitutional guarantee to each state of a "republican form of government" (Article IV, Section I). This case, on the other hand, was based on a violation of the Fourteenth Amendment's assertion of the right of every person to "equal protection of the laws." Brennan distinguished the "political question" line of precedents from the present case and classified *Baker* v. *Carr* with the other "equal protection" cases that have traditionally been justiciable.

To dissenting Justices Frankfurter and Harlan, the precedents governing *Baker* v. *Carr* should have been the "political question" cases, and the challenge to Tennessee's alleged malapportionment should have been ruled nonjusticiable. They argued that questions are "political" and nonjusticiable not merely when they are based on alleged violation of the guarantee of a republican form of government, but whenever their resolution by judges would impair the judges' "complete detachment in fact and in appearance from political entanglements." Thus the dissenters emphasized what they believed to be the underlying principles of the earlier "political question" precedents, whereas the majority of the Court limited the applicability of the earlier precedents to the particular facts, rather than the underlying principle, of those cases.

The majority and the minority of the Court agreed that precedent is binding, but they disagreed, as judges frequently do, on the meaning and application of particular precedents. Is the meaning of a past case confined to its particular facts? Does its meaning include principles or ideas inherent in the historical, social, economic, and political situations out of which the particular facts arose? Does it include comments made by the court in the course of the opinion even if they were not directly related to the facts of the case? From the standpoint of acceptable techniques of legal reasoning, a past case may have any one or a combination of these meanings.

The choice of techniques of reasoning, which leads in turn to the choice of applicable precedents to govern current cases, is—to use the terminology of the late Karl Llewellyn—one of the principal "leeways" of the law. Commenting on one occasion on the leeways of judicial precedent, Llewellyn observed that there is growing recognition that the *ways* of using precedent are as important as the precedents themselves. Common to all judicial opinions, Llewellyn said, are lines of "compulsion in the precedents" that operate to limit and control judicial action. Nonetheless, he maintained, when the "urges of justice and policy" are clear enough, judges can avoid or whittle away almost any precedent. The actual final control over the leeways available to the judges "lies not in any rules of law, or rules of precedent but lies instead in a combination of judicial conscience, judicial judgment, and what I can best describe as the net lines of force of the particular field of law." [21]

The presence of important leeways for decision is not confined to the highest appellate courts but is embodied in the everyday events of the common law courts at large. Lawyers, judges, and scholars have throughout history sought certainty and predictability in the law. But the hope for a mechanical jurisprudence that can assure certainty is at best an illusion. No sooner is a decision made, in many cases, when new facts or circumstances arise in the very next case that make the earlier decision inapplicable or even invalid.[22]

Will modern electronic computers in courts and law offices eliminate the judicial leeways of the present and make law certain and predictable? No doubt the computers will simplify and perhaps eliminate library research. Errors of human oversight will be avoided and predictability enhanced. Comparative studies indicate that computers are many times better and faster than lawyers in finding judicial precedents. Computers can not only do in seconds what ordinarily requires hours of labor by skilled professionals; they can also find more relevant citations of precedent than even teams of lawyers.[23]

Demonstrations of the use of computers to predict judicial decisions have been an intriguing highlight of recent conventions of the American Bar Association. A Supreme Court justice, asked to comment on the

---

[21] Karl Llewellyn, "Impressions of the Conference on Precedent," in Jurisprudence: Realism in Theory and Practice (*Chicago: University of Chicago Press*, 1962), *pp. 120, 123.*

[22] Cardozo, op. cit., *p.* 67.

[23] Reed Lawlor, reporting on studies at the University of Pittsburgh, in The Bulletin of the Section of Judicial Administration (*American Bar Association*), 6 (*February* 1963), 2–4.

display at a recent convention, winked wryly at his audience and said, "those machines may think they can predict me but I'm gonna fool them." The serious point is that while computers are designed to ensure the highest technical efficiency in legal research, they cannot eliminate the necessity for choice once the research has been completed. In the computer demonstrations at the ABA convention, the machine predicted the outcome of hypothetical cases involving the defendant's right to counsel. But the computer cautioned in its reports that its predictions assumed that certain choices would continue to be made in the construction and analysis of the data by the judges.

THE ROLE OF DISCRETIONARY POWER. What shapes the leeways of the law for particular judges? How does Judge A use the discretionary power the law allows him? Is the particular application of judicial discretion triggered by prejudice, passion, by moral or ethical values, by philosophic or economic predelictions, or by political beliefs or obligations? It could be shaped by any or all of these. Even the judge who strives mightily to attain absolute "objectivity" is bound to be influenced by the norms, values, and principles inculcated in him at an early age. Even the perception of facts by the trial judge is subject to influence if not control by these factors. The trial judge's impressions, colored by his unconscious biases about the witnesses, will determine what he believes to be the facts of the case. The judge perceives the facts as a result of the impact of numerous stimuli on his distinctive personality; and his personality is, in turn, a product of all the factors that have operated on him, such as background, education, and environment.[24]

To what extent can we isolate the particular nonlegal factors that conditioned the particular judicial decision? Of special interest to the political scientist is the question of whether we can pinpoint political factors in the molding of judicial decisions. Unfortunately, such pinpointing is not yet practicable. The social sciences have only begun to use, and the legal profession has only begun to accept, the tools that may make such determinations possible in the future. Even if we do not know with certainty when decisions are in fact attributable to political preferences of judges, we do have knowledge about the potentialities for applying political factors in shaping the law. As students of politics concerned with "the art of the possible," we should examine and evaluate the ways in which the political system can mold and direct the activities of the legal system.

---

[24] *Jerome Frank*, Courts on Trial (*Princeton, N.J.: Princeton University Press,* 1949), *p. 152.*

3. Politics and the Judiciary

The interactions of politics with the legal system vary from the subtle entry of political values and beliefs into the leeways of judicial decision making to overt control by professional politicians and political organizations of the machinery of judicial selection and court administration. Let us begin our analysis with the overt manifestations of political control and proceed from there to the more subtle ones.

The state court systems are considered "the last refuge" of the political machines because they offer the last major area of attractive and sought-for patronage. Judgeships are jobs with prestige, to say nothing of comfortable salaries. "In court and out, judges are automatically part of the legal elite and it is not surprising that so many lawyers yearn to sit on the bench. . . . The robes, the formalities, the authority of these men elevate them to something apart from ordinary human beings." [25] Control over the selection of judges thus becomes a major device for sustaining and enhancing the effectiveness of political organizations. Figure 12.1 shows the chief methods employed in each state for selecting judges of the highest appellate court; Figure 12.2 presents the same data for general trial courts.

ELECTION OF JUDGES. In New York, where the judges receive the highest salaries in the nation ($39,500 for judges of the state's highest court, the Court of Appeals; $33,500 to $41,500 for intermediate appellate court judges; and $31,500 to $37,500 for general trial court judges), election to the bench without political organization support is a rarity. "So much are the judgeships considered a proprietary right of the machines that in political circles they are tagged with the name of the district leader who wangles them from the boss." [26] Machine candidates are generally expected to "kick back" to the political organization the equivalent of a year's salary to cover the cost of getting them elected.

A useful illustration showing the effect of politics on the nomination process preceding election is the choice of candidates in July, 1964, by the Democratic party convention for the judicial district covering Manhattan and the Bronx in New York City. The Bronx boss, Congressman Charles A. Buckley, had been defeated by Mayor Wagner and the Reform Democrats at the June primary when he sought renomination to the House of

---

[25] Wallace Sayre and Herbert Kaufman, Governing New York City (New York: Russell Sage Foundation, 1960), p. 531.

[26] Louis Banks, "The Crisis in the Courts," Fortune 64 (December 1961), 90.

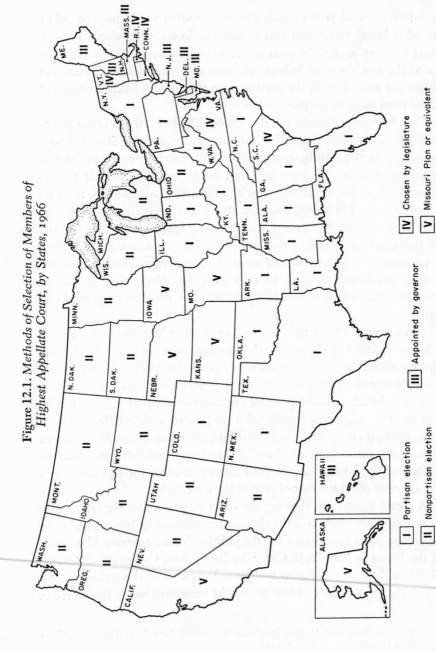

Figure 12.1. *Methods of Selection of Members of Highest Appellate Court, by States, 1966*

I Partisan election

II Nonpartisan election

III Chosen by legislature

IV Appointed by governor

V Missouri Plan or equivalent

SOURCE: Compiled from data supplied by the Council of State Governments and the American Judicature Society, Chicago, 1966.

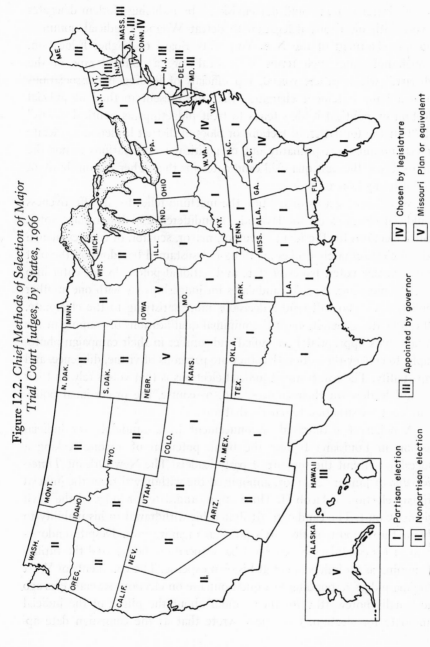

Figure 12.2. *Chief Methods of Selection of Major
Trial Court Judges, by States, 1966*

Partisan election | I

Nonpartisan election | II

Appointed by governor | III

Chosen by legislature | IV

Missouri Plan or equivalent | V

SOURCE: Compiled from data supplied by the Council of State Governments and the American Judicature Society, Chicago, 1966.

Representatives. Buckley retaliated at the judicial convention, as the New York County Democratic leader said, with "a meanness of spirit which even his bitterest foes could not envision," by inducing Harlem delegates to vote with his Bronx delegation to defeat Wagner's judicial nominee, who was chairman of the New York City Board of Higher Education. Though not using such terms as "a deal" or "a political rape of the judiciary," which others voiced, top officials of leading bar associations issued a joint statement charging "that the present method of judicial selection by political leaders tends to treat judgeships as political pawns" and "that the formation of factions or blocs of district leaders who dictate judicial nominations primarily out of political considerations is not the way to secure the best qualified candidates for the higher responsibility of administering justice." [27]

As in many sectors of politics, the machine relies for its effectiveness in judicial elections on the lassitude or indifference of the average voter. Unlike elections for President, governor, mayor, senator, or congressman, a judicial election rarely evokes anything but sustained boredom on the part of the average voter. Issues of state and national policy do not enter into judicial campaigns. Nor do candidates for judgeships vie with one another publicly over who will render decisions more satisfying to the electorate. All candidates generally meet the minimal qualifications of training in the law and look appropriately dignified and somber in their campaign photographs to convey the notion that they are paragons of virtue, diligence, and impartiality. The reality about judicial elections is that voters rely on their political leaders for their choices; and, of course, the professional politicians want the situation to remain that way.

A poignant withdrawal announcement by a candidate for judicial election in Louisiana typifies the bleak potential of anyone seeking a judgeship without the support of party leaders. The New Orleans *Times-Picayune* of January 26, 1963, announced the withdrawal from the judicial primary election of Jacob H. Morrison, a candidate for judge of the Civil District Court. The candidate attributed his withdrawal to his inability to obtain the support of the city's political organizations. Despite endorsement of his candidacy by the local bar association, he realized the futility of running as an independent at his own expense. The comments of West Virginia judges responding to a questionnaire on elections several years ago are equally noteworthy for their candor about the plight of the judicial candidate for election. One judge wrote that as the campaign date ap-

---

[27] The New York Times, *July 31, 1964, p. 54.*

proaches, he is apt to postpone making decisions in cases that may adversely affect his chances of reelection, while hastily deciding matters that may give him favorable publicity and enhance his public following.[28] Another judge commented on the unwholesome attitude and the stress engendered in him by the necessity to run for office in his later years. He feared especially the prospect of returning to the competition of private law practice after many years of maintaining neutrality on the bench.[29]

Many reformers have argued that the judiciary can and should be taken out of the political arena by abolishing judicial elections and substituting some form of appointment in its stead. That judges are appointed rather than elected does not eliminate control of the system by political organizations, however. A candidate for governor may well promise influential political leaders that he will appoint a number of judges wanted by those politicians in return for their delivering the vote to him in their districts. The common practice in most appointive systems of bartering appointments to judgeships in return for votes seems even more crassly and cynically political than the direct election of judges by the people. At least the opportunity for public surveillance of the judicial candidate's record is present in elections, whereas the invisible "deal" between governor and political boss precludes public scrutiny and facilitates putting men of inferior quality on the bench.

It was less than fifty years ago, as V. O. Key pointed out, that the courts were viewed as "the sturdiest bastion of the special interests" precisely because they were not subject to popular control. In reaction to this, provisions for popular recall of judges were developed to subject the courts to the "humiliation" of popular review of their decisions.[30]

THE "MISSOURI PLAN." The American Judicature Society and the American Bar Association have exercised vigorous and sustained leadership in efforts to secure widespread adoption by the states of the essential elements of the so-called "Missouri plan" for choosing judges.[31] Under this system, first established in Missouri in 1940, the governor appoints the judges initially from lists of nominees proposed by special nonpartisan commissions composed of lawyers and laymen with the Chief

---

[28] Claude J. Davis, Judicial Selection in West Virginia (Morgantown, W.Va.: Bureau for Governmental Research, West Virginia University, 1959), p. 26.

[29] Ibid., p. 37.

[30] V. O. Key, Jr., Public Opinion and American Democracy (New York: Knopf, 1961), p. 5.

[31] See "Report of The Citizens' Conference on Missouri Courts," Journal of the American Judicature Society, 49 (December 1965), 125.

Justice of Missouri or a presiding judge of a court of appeals as chairman. After serving an initial term in office as appointees, the judges run for election without opposition. The voters can then remove the incumbents from office if they disapprove of their records. This system provides assurance, it is argued, that judges do not have to bow or pander to the whims of political bosses or to the irrational impulses of the masses in order to gain and hold their seats on the bench. The Missouri plan has been attracting increased support in recent years; almost one-fourth of the states having adopted some variation of it thus far. These include Alaska, California, Iowa, Illinois, and Nebraska at the supreme court and other appellate court levels and Kansas at the supreme court level only. Juvenile courts in Utah and in Tulsa County, Oklahoma, metropolitan courts in Dade County, Florida, and Denver County, Colorado, and trial courts of general jurisdiction in Birmingham, Alabama, also use versions of the Missouri plan. Adoption of the Missouri plan eliminates politics from judicial selection only if one views politics as limited to the activities of *acknowledged* political bosses and political organizations. But if politics embraces a much broader area and includes the processes and instrumentalities for the molding of public policy, then the appointment of judges by the governor from lists supplied by nominating commissions is every bit as political as a popular election or as appointment by the governor in response to a deal with a political boss.

Although the Missouri plan assures that judges will be of high professional character, reputation, and legal competence, it has also an inherent flaw—an overemphasis upon professionalism.[32] This bias toward professional competence could lead to other biases associated with the conservatism and affluence of the professionally competent in institutions like banks, insurance companies, and corporations. If an executive's choice of judges is limited to the roster supplied him by a commission composed of the successful and conservative members of the community, then anyone who deviates from the professional norms—a vociferous champion of the poor for example—would be unlikely to become a judge.

Furthermore, although the Missouri plan keeps the impact of political considerations under control, politics is never wholly eliminated from the selection of judges. Missouri governors rarely cross party lines in making appointments, and this has deterred qualified lawyers of the opposite political party from accepting nomination. Nonetheless, the plan has the support of press and public in Missouri.[33] The people of the state have

---

[32] *Charles S. Clark, "The Creative Role of the Judge,"* Yale Law Journal, 71 (1961), 272.

[33] *For a favorable evaluation by a judge, see Elmo B. Hunter, "A Missouri Judge*

retained in office, by majorities of 90 percent of the votes cast, incumbent Republican and Democratic judges alike, irrespective of how the general election of other officials has gone.

It should also be noted that the Missouri plan does contain some safeguards against the prejudice that could stem from overprofessionaliza-tion. For example, the Appellate Judicial Commission of Missouri, which nominates candidates for positions on the state supreme court and the three courts of appeals, is composed of an equal number of laymen and private lawyers. Of the seven members of the commission, three are laymen appointed by the governor, three are lawyers elected by their fellow lawyers, and the seventh is the chief justice of the Missouri Supreme Court. "Packing" the commission is virtually impossible because of the dual form of selecting commission members. The three members chosen by the state's lawyers are selected by democratic vote of an integrated bar [34] in which a labor lawyer's vote and a corporation lawyer's vote count equally. The governor's three appointees could be chosen to reflect a single point of view, but even if he wishes to, the governor could pack only his half.

Despite the zeal of the Missouri plan's supporters and the fears of its detractors, the debate strikes the political scientist as sterile. There are no indications that the procedures or substantive rulings of Missouri plan courts are materially different from those of states using other systems of selection. Even if an ideal plan for selecting judges were agreed upon and adopted, equitability and impartiality of the law would not be assured without a concomitant reform of the other interactions between the legal and political systems.

POLITICAL SUBTLETIES AND STAKES. Consider the fol-lowing situation as an illustration of the problem: A traveling salesman, lonely in a distant city, has a few drinks in a tavern. Returning to his car after the drinking interlude, he is a bit unsteady. En route to his hotel, he loses control of the car and the vehicle smashes a city light post before coming to a halt. A policeman in a passing squad car sees the accident and arrests the driver on a charge of driving while drunk. When the salesman's case comes up in court, its outcome may well be determined more by the political ties of the police and the lawyers involved than by the judge's state of partiality. The salesman's lawyer, if he is unknown politically or is

---

Views *Judicial Selection and Tenure*," Journal of the American Judicature Society, 48 (December 1964), 126–32.

[34] *The term "integrated bar" refers to the state requirement that all persons who are admitted to practice in the state must belong to the state's bar association. See Dayton D. McKean's* The Integrated Bar *(Boston: Houghton Mifflin, 1963).*

a member of the political out-group, may find that the arresting officer affirms the drunken state of the defendant at the time of the arrest. The prosecuting attorney, a patronage appointee of the political in-group, prepares a meticulous case against the defendant. The judge may then have no real alternative but to find the defendant guilty and to impose a stringent fine. If, on the other hand, the salesman's lawyer is a member of the political in-group, the arresting officer may well be less certain of whether the defendant was drunk at the time of the arrest. The prosecuting attorney may also be inclined to look for extenuating circumstances that would warrant a lighter penalty by the judge if the case had to be tried at all.

In a situation like this, there is no overt corruption, no concrete bribery or graft; it is simply an aspect of the political organization at work. As long as police, lawyers, and court officials are beholden to a political organization, to say nothing of the indebtedness of the judges themselves, it would be only natural for them to use the leeways of the law in favor of their organization and to reap the subsequent rewards. These rewards are conferred by the organization in the form of renominations, advancements in the job hierarchy, and, of course, gifts for birthdays, weddings, confirmations, bar mitzvahs, and the like.

Common as this situation is, it receives little visibility in the traditional debate over whether judges should be elected or appointed. In the mythology surrounding the dispute over elected versus appointed judges, it is often presumed that appointment under some version of the Missouri plan will remove the allegedly nefarious hand of the political organization from control of the courts. But most political organizations are more complex and efficient than would-be reformers will admit, and the roots of political control of the judicial system go far below the mere surface of judicial selection. Clerks, bailiffs, referees, guardians, and executors of estates exercise important power in the day-to-day scheduling, administration, and decision making of the courts. The organization that controls access to these appointments as well as to positions in the state attorney general's office, the county prosecutor's office, and the police force could in effect control the judicial system even if it could not control the judges directly. The fact is, though, that in a majority of states the entire structure of the judicial system, from judgeships on down, is politically controlled. Even in states that have adopted the Missouri plan for their higher state courts, political domination continues at the local court level.

Why are judicial positions so attractive to political organizations? Sayre's and Kaufman's study of New York City suggests part of the answer: "Like all other governmental officials and employees engaged in the quest for the stakes of the political contest, judges and their staffs are both claimants and distributors." [35] Another part of the answer is that the local community provides a setting for a series of games in which the players collaborate for different ends in the achievement of overall social functions.[36] Since the courts play basic and determinate roles in construing the rules and limits of the various games, whoever controls the courts wields powerful control over the games themselves. A third part of the answer is that, since law functions within an everchanging society, legal interpretations cannot be reduced to fixed, timeless, and irrevocable rules.[37]

If courts serve as claimants and distributors of prestige and monetary rewards in an ecology of games in which the rules cannot be fixed definitively, the judicial system is bound to offer immeasurable challenge and appeal to the professional politicians seeking power and influence as the prizes of community gamesmanship. Let us examine more specifically some manifestations of this challenge and appeal.

Documentation of political deals involving the judiciary is difficult to obtain. On rare occasions, however, when the parties to the deal subsequently fall out, one or the other may release the details in an effort to discredit his erstwhile associate. Such a falling out occurred between the governor of Maryland, J. Millard Tawes, and a major political leader in the city of Baltimore, James H. Pollack, in the Democratic party primary election for the governorship in 1962. Pollack had supported Tawes in 1958 but now threw his support to another candidate. Hoping to swing votes away from Tawes, Pollack called a press conference at which he produced photostats of a 1957 agreement, allegedly bearing his and Governor Tawes's signatures, which specified who should take possession of the keys to a safe deposit box in case either of them died. Pollack maintained that the box held $50,000 to be used partly for expenses in the 1958 primary and partly as a "guarantee" that the governor would "produce" on promises he had made to Pollack, some of which involved the appointment of "Pollack men" to particular judgeships.[38]

---

[35] *Sayre and Kaufman*, op. cit., *p. 522.*

[36] Norton Long, "The Local Community as an Ecology of Games," American Journal of Sociology, 64 (November 1958), 251–61. See also John E. Kennedy, "Judge, Jury, Counsel Relations in Kentucky," Kentucky Law Journal (Winter 1965–66), 242–58, especially the discussion of "Mulligan's Rule" ("politics in Kentucky are the damndest"), 256–58.

[37] See Huntington Cairns, The Community as the Legal Order (New York: Liberal Arts Press, 1959).

[38] J. Anthony Lukas, "Boss Pollack: 'He Can't Be There But He Is,'" The Reporter (July 19, 1962), 35 f.

ABUSES OF THE JUDICIAL FUNCTION. The Pollack-Tawes "deal" over judgeships is but one illustration of the judiciary as "claimants and distributors" of the stakes of political contest. To put it grossly, judges can have the ultimate say about who gets what. Whether refereeing disputes between litigants, interpreting rules, or appointing executors, trustees, and receivers, the judges are engaged to a significant extent in allocating the resources, rewards, and sanctions of governmental action.

At the primitive (but still commonplace) level of the justice of the peace who lives by his fines and fees (there being no salary), the judge allocates economic rewards directly to himself. One JP with eight years in the office tries some 200 cases a year on the strength of a seventh-grade education and a 1947 edition of his state's statutes. Asked to comment on the defendants brought before him, the JP observed, "I don't ever remember having one who wasn't guilty. If the sheriff picks up a man for violating the law, he's guilty or he wouldn't bring him in here. And anyway I don't get anything out of it if they aren't guilty." [39]

At the more sophisticated level of the well-paid municipal or state judge, rewards are allocated directly to others in the form of lush patronage jobs as receivers, trustees, and the like, and through the exercise of judicial discretion in favor of contestants and lawyers who belong to the same political group as the judge. The judge's own rewards come about indirectly through renomination or promotion within the judicial hierarchy. Few judges are suspected of outright corruption, that is, dismissing or throwing a case to one or the other party for a bribe, though there have been examples of such flagrant behavior in recent years. In 1962, a New York judge was convicted of attempting to bring illicit influence to bear on a federal district court case in return for a substantial fee.

In April, 1964, two Oklahoma supreme court justices—one having served for 32 years—were indicted and found guilty on charges of federal income tax evasion. Evidence given at the trial revealed that both men had accepted bribes to reverse a lower court decision in an investment company case. Before the scandal had run its course one judge resigned from the court, another was impeached, and early in 1966 a former justice resigned from the state bar for alleged conspiracy to bribe fellow bar members.[40]

More typical than outright dishonesty is what carries the dubious but

---

[39] *Banks*, op. cit., *p.* 188.
[40] The New York Times, *May 8, 1965, p. 6, and February 18, 1966, p. 1; and* Oklahoma Bar Association Journal, *36 (April 10, 1965), 601–09, and (August 28, 1965), 1507–14.*

colorful label among local politicos of "honest graft." Surrogate judges, who preside over estate cases, for example, are sometimes prone to use their power to appoint special guardians and trustees so as to enrich those aligned with their local political organizations. A prototype is the Brooklyn (New York) surrogate reported to have picked up the document that listed a Manhattan bank as trustee, scratched out the name of the Manhattan bank, and substituted the name of a Brooklyn trust company in its stead.[41]

Another example of profitable judicial patronage was disclosed by a Chicago newspaper's study of the role of masters in chancery in the state court system. Masters in chancery are authorized to take testimony in a variety of cases and to report their findings and recommendations to the judges. Each judge names his own master and, traditionally, is inclined to follow the master's recommendations. Fees and commissions paid a busy master in chancery were reported as high as $85,000 a year. Such fees themselves, while high, and the political connections of the masters, while extensive, were not as disturbing as the conflicts of interest that were brought to light by the study. It was not unusual to find that a master who recommended in favor of a property owner in a zoning suit, for example, served also as a private attorney, at a substantial fee, to advance the owner's zoning interests.[42]

The bail bondsman, a central character on the local criminal court scene, is another frequent recipient of judicial patronage. The bondsman receives his fees from the defendant for posting bonds for him in the amount of bail set by the criminal court. The business is lucrative, but highly competitive. In many large cities certain bondsmen commonly have favored status to solicit business in certain judges' courtrooms by virtue of their political connections and economic "payoffs." [43]

---

[41] *Banks,* op. cit., *p. 93.*

The Manhattan surrogateship came under sharp scrutiny when, after the Democratic organization had nominated the candidate already chosen by the Republican organization, the Reform Democrats attacked the "deal," and nominated another candidate, who was then also endorsed by the Liberal party. The stakes involved were simply stated by The New York Times *(June 7, 1966, p. 31): "The post of Surrogate is deemed of great importance because of the huge amount of patronage a Manhattan Surrogate can dispense. He assigns lawyers to help administer estates whose annual value comes to hundreds of millions of dollars."*

[42] *Max Sonderby, "Our Invisible Judiciary,"* Chicago Sun-Times, *January 9–14, 1962.*

[43] *In this there seems little progress since the Seabury investigations into the corruption of the New York City judicial system by the Tammany organization. Final Report of Samuel Seabury, Referee in the Matter of the Magistrates Courts (New York: Lawyers Press, 1932).*

An investigation by the California legislature's Joint Judiciary Committee on Administration of Justice several years ago disclosed that court-appointed appraisers frequently paid "kickbacks" to probate court clerks amounting to thousands of dollars a year per clerk. That investigation also revealed a local practice by some lower court judges of interrupting court sessions "to perform numerous marriages which they made into a profitable sideline by illegally extracting fees for the ceremonies." The committee reported that the more profitable marriage businesses were built up by a system of "payoffs" to the courthouse personnel who steered couples to the judge.[44]

These examples of patronage and favoritism in and about the judicial system illustrate some of the interactions, actual and potential, between politics and the judiciary. More important, however, than judicial grants of patronage to loyal members of his sponsoring political organization are the judge's interpretations of statutes and rules so as to nurture the organization itself. As an expert observer of politics in a New England city put it, "One of the most important political resources needed by elites everywhere, particularly in countries with established legal traditions, is legality. . . . Any group of people having special access to legality is potentially influential with respect to government decisions."[45]

In construing rules and statutes, judges who have acquired their positions through the political system would not be likely to interpret the law so as to destroy that very system unless there were no alternative. The judge, however conscientious and honorable he may be, has achieved this pinnacle of his career as a successful player in the community's ecology of games. His power and prestige as a judge are attributable to the determinate goals and calculable strategies that ecology of games has established. If his decisions impair the operations of the game, they will at the same time jeopardize his own status in the community. Thus the functions of state and local judges in refereeing and resolving conflicts are likely to be performed with due regard for protecting the traditions and practices of the political system.[46]

Observations by Sayre and Kaufman of the New York judiciary offer further illustrations of these propositions. In their section on "Courts and Politics," the authors stress the role of judges in determining the content and scope of the constitutional and statutory provisions that comprise "the

[44] Report of the Joint Judiciary Committee on Administration of Justice (Sacramento: Senate of the State of California, 1959), p. 29.

[45] Robert A. Dahl, Who Governs? (New Haven, Conn.: Yale University Press, 1961), p. 247.

[46] Norton Long, op. cit. See also Edward C. Banfield, "The Political Implications of Metropolitan Growth," Daedalus, 90 (Winter 1961), 70, 74f.

rules of the game." They point out how, by refusing to invalidate inequalities of representation growing out of failure to redraw the lines of the old aldermanic districts, the judges buttressed the Democratic majority that benefited from the prevailing situation. They also show how judicial sanctioning of the city's power to enact rent control laws heightened the popularity of the Democratic party officials who were responsible for the measure.[47]

Such illustrations do not of course mean that judges invariably do or can decide cases in favor of their own political party. Although there have been isolated instances in which judges have been denied renomination after having been accused of voting too often with the judges of the opposition party, the test of a judge's value in the "political game" is not so much his constant support of his own party as it is his maintenance, through his decisions, of the political system on which the parties thrive. Thus a decision by a judge invalidating a particular action by officials of his own party would not be unusual or unexpected; but judicial invalidation of the process by which both parties dispense patronage, for example, would no doubt produce demands that the offending judge be denied renomination.

Despite the potential reprisals against judges who veer too far from the norms of the political game, the interactions of legal and political systems in our state and local governments generally call for a basic degree of judicial independence.[48] Since this independence enhances the value of appointment to the bench as a political prize, the power of political leaders to dispense judgeships establishes a strong incentive to party workers to support their programs. Paradoxically, the interests of organized politics are thus served by restricting political interferences with the judiciary and protecting the public image of judicial impartiality that accompanies independence.

In the final analysis, as a prominent state supreme court justice has maintained, "the judge is on his own. . . . The main ingredients of his decision must be drawn from his own mind and heart to bear upon the facts and the legal doctrines that counsel put before him." [49] But the "mind and heart" of even the most dispassionate judge are products not only of his formal education and training but of his political background

---

[47] *Sayre and Kaufman,* op. cit., *pp.* 529 f.

[48] *For a comprehensive discussion of the uses of the judiciary for political ends in totalitarian societies, see Otto Kirchheimer,* Political Justice *(Princeton, N.J.: Princeton University Press, 1961).*

[49] *Walter V. Schaefer,* "Good Judges, Better Judges, Best Judges," *Journal of the American Judicature Society,* 44 (1960), 22–25. *See also Harry W. Jones,* "The Trial Judge—Role Analysis and Profile," *in Jones (ed.),* The Courts, The Public, and the Law Explosion *(Englewood Cliffs, N.J.: Prentice-Hall, 1965),* pp. *124–45.*

and preferences. That judges' political party affiliations can explain at least some differences in the content of judicial decisions has been shown by the research of Stuart Nagel into state supreme court decisions for 1955. Cautioning that the research should not be construed to imply that judges consciously vote for or against a party line, Nagel found nonetheless that in nonunanimous decisions of state supreme courts, Democratic judges ruled more frequently than Republican judges in favor of defendants in criminal cases, in favor of administrative agencies in business regulation cases, in favor of claimants in unemployment compensation cases, in favor of broadening freedom of speech in civil liberties cases, in favor of the government in tax cases, in favor of the spouse filing for divorce in marital cases, in favor of the tenant in landlord-tenant cases, in favor of the labor union in labor management cases, in favor of the debtor in creditor-debtor cases, in favor of the consumer in sale of goods cases, and in favor of the injured in motor vehicle accident cases.[50]

Certainly, more detailed research must be undertaken before the propensities found by Nagel can be asserted as conclusive. A study of Illinois Supreme Court decisions from May, 1962, through March, 1963, for example, showed that nonunanimous cases constituted only a minute fraction of the court's decisional output. The court, composed of five Republicans and two Democrats elected from the state's seven judicial districts, decided 323 out of 330 cases unanimously.[51] Perhaps in at least some courts the concept of judicial role surmounts the dichotomies one would expect from divergent party affiliations. In any event, men selected as judges from the ranks of proven party workers are hardly likely, even from their exalted judicial positions in the Elysian Fields of politics, to damage their political organizations or impair the political game on which they thrive.

4. Conclusion

Idealized myths and hard-bitten realities are uncomfortable companions. Probably in no institution of state and local government is the discomfort greater than in the judicial system. In legislative bodies, the governorship

---

[50] Stuart Nagel, "Political Party Affiliation and Judges' Decisions," American Political Science Review, 50 (1961), 843–51, reprinted in Glendon Schubert (ed.), Judicial Behavior (Chicago: Rand McNally, 1964), pp. 234–49.

[51] John Rosotti, "A Decisional Profile of the Illinois Supreme Court: May, 1962–March, 1963," unpublished research MS, Law and Social Science Program, Northwestern University, 1966.

or mayoralty, elections, political parties, and interest groups, the citizen takes for granted that politics must play a major part. He knows, too, that the politics of policy is often accompanied by a politics of favoritism. Indeed, it is a large part of the genius of democratic systems to design institutions and processes that make the forces of selfish personal and group ambitions work together to identify and achieve the public interest.

In the judicial system, the myths that we cherish envisage an impartial, neutral body of specially qualified men who will apply already determined rules in refereeing conflicts between individuals, corporations, and governments themselves. Yet the leeways for judicial discretion, the eagerness of lawyers for judgeships, the methods of selecting judges, and above all, the fact that the judiciary, like other government institutions, is inescapably a part of the total political system make the realities of adjudication a far cry from the myths.

When myth and reality are so widely discrepant, men must move to make some kind of adjustment between the two. The gap can be narrowed by substituting a less fanciful myth or by bringing reality into better conformance with the present one. Perhaps both methods should be tried.

chapter 13

Judicial Reform: Needs

and Prospects

Important as the impact of politics on the legal system is to our understanding of the role of the judiciary in state and local government, it should not be allowed to obliterate the significance of other vital factors affecting the administration of justice. The capability of a political system is measured by its ability to manage conflicts and to impose settlements. By resolving community conflicts that take the form of court actions, the judiciary thus increases the political system's capability. But problems of delay, of unequal access to the judicial process, of overlapping and outmoded court systems, and of complex and esoteric rules of procedure geared more to the requirements of combat in the sports arena than to the quest for justice often impose a wide wedge between the theory and practice of conflict resolution as a judicial function.

1. Obstacles to Judicial Efficacy

It should be noted that these problems are not new. While they have grown in magnitude with the passing years, they have been perceived for more than a century. For example, as early as 1839, a distinguished jurist writing of the New York courts noted that "speedy justice is a thing unknown; and any justice, without delays almost ruinous, is most rare." [1]

---

[1] David Dudly Field, Letter to Gulian C. Verplanck, quoted in Arthur T. Vanderbilt, The Challenge of Law Reform (*Princeton, N.J.: Princeton University Press,* 1955), *p.* 81.

In a brilliant and comprehensive address to the American Bar Association in 1906 on "The Causes of Popular Dissatisfaction with the Administration of Justice," [2] Roscoe Pound, then a young lawyer from Nebraska, charged that "our system of courts is archaic and our procedure behind the times. Uncertainty, delay, and expense, and above all, the injustice of deciding cases upon points of practice. . . . have created a deep-seated desire to keep out of court, right or wrong, on the part of every sensible business man in the community."

A half century after that historic address, Dean Pound noted that some progress in judicial administration had been made. There is a major movement, he said, for reorganization on modern lines that has remade the system for the federal courts and a growing number of states. Nonetheless, he pointed out that many states to this day maintain systems of judicial organization and administration geared to the remote past—to times of slow communication, difficult and expensive travel, and to life in farming communities and small towns. There remains a disturbing abundance of organizational evils unsuited to the technology and social patterns of the century: multiplication of courts, retention of overlapping and concurrent jurisdictions, and unorganized administrative methods that add to the costs, delays, and confusions of dispensing justice.[3]

Dean Pound's views are supported by recent studies of "the crisis in the courts." Chief Justice Earl Warren of the Supreme Court has pointed out that although we have demonstrated skills and accomplishments that amaze us all in areas of human activity like physics, chemistry, and biology, "there has been no comparable development in the administration of justice by our courts. . . . It sometimes seems in the courts as though time stands still." The Chief Justice asserted that the American people need and expect an expanding economy and a developing social system, and that the inability of the judicial system to settle disputes and to determine rights and liabilities obstructs and hampers growth in every direction.[4]

The United States has urgent reason to be concerned about the condition of justice today. Many courts founder in mismanagement, inep-

---

[2] American Bar Association Reports, 29 (Part I, 1906), 395–417, *reprinted in the* Journal of the American Judicature Society, 46 (August 1962), 54–62.

[3] *Roscoe Pound, "Toward an Adequate Administration of Justice,"* Chicago Bar Record, 39 (March 1958), 247–58.

[4] *Earl Warren, "Address to Conference of National Association of Referees in Bankruptcy, October 23, 1962,"* Journal of National Association of Referees in Bankruptcy, 37 (January 1963), 3–5.

titude, and archaic organization. Since courts are agencies of government, political action is indispensable to the achievement of fundamental court reform. Whether or not our courts can sustain the burdens of the law explosion depends in large part on the general public's realization that justice is everybody's business.[5]

DELAY. The most visible distress symbol of our judicial system has been the backlog of civil cases awaiting jury trial in the courts. Many who seek to invoke the judicial process for the resolution of conflict find that the right to one's "day in court" may prove so distant in time as to be nonexistent in practice. A sampling of statistics indicates that the problem of delay is acute and has shown no signs of abatement in the recent past. Arthur Vanderbilt, in his classic work, *The Challenge of Law Reform*, noted delays in jury cases in New York of from 37 to 49 months between the time lawsuits were filed and the time they came to trial.[6] Yet little change had occurred by 1965: In four of New York City's counties, the average delay for jury trials in personal injury cases was 43 months, with a range from 34 months in New York County (Manhattan) to 45 months in Queens County.[7] Across the country, delays tend to be greater in larger cities—averaging 31.8 months in counties with populations of more than 750,000, 19.9 months in those of between 500,000 and 750,000 and 11.9 months in counties of under 500,000. This is not the whole explanation, however, for in San Diego and Los Angeles counties, each with populations over 900,000, the delays were held to averages of 16.7 and 23.3 months. The sharpest contrast among large counties is that of Cook County, Illinois, which includes Chicago and averages 60.2 months delay, and Dade County, Florida, which includes Miami and averages 7.3 months.[8] Illustrative of the human meaning of such statistics is the Chicago case of ten-year-old Nancy Vernola, who was hit by an automobile while riding a bicycle. By the time her case came to trial, Nancy was a young mother of nineteen who brought her baby to court with her.[9]

---

[5] Harry W. Jones (ed.), The Courts, The Public, and the Law Explosion (Englewood Cliffs, N.J.: Prentice-Hall, 1965), p. 6. See also Louis Banks, "The Crisis in the Courts," Fortune, 64 (December 1961), 86.

[6] (Princeton, N.J.: Princeton University Press, 1955), p. 81.

[7] Institute of Judicial Administration, Calendar Status Study, 1965. See also Charles J. Desmond, "Current Problems of State Court Administration," Columbia Law Review, 65 (April 1965), 561–68, at 562.

[8] Ibid. All data relate to personal injury cases, which are a major part of the courts' burden; in New York State, for example, 45 percent of the civil cases received in the so-called supreme court (which despite its name includes a number of courts at the lowest trial court level) involve injuries or damages in motor vehicle accidents alone.

[9] Banks, op. cit., p. 88.

Situations are all too common in which people and business concerns with disputes that desperately need to be settled have to stand in line for three, four, and even five years in order to be heard.[10]

The consequences of these delays are many and unfortunate: Unsound business deals to avoid the courts because the parties cannot afford delay, acceptance of inadequate out-of-court settlements in personal injury cases because of financial pressure or fear that witnesses might die or forget details in ensuing delays, and perhaps worst of all, public cynicism about the realities of obtaining justice are but a few illustrations.

On the other hand, one of the dangers to be avoided in meeting the problem of delay is the assumption that speed alone in handling cases will assure the dispensation of justice. The problem confronts the metropolitan trial court judge whichever way he turns. From one side leers the danger of delaying disposition until the problem is insoluble; from the other the danger of hurrying too quickly to a disposition which will result in further conflict and litigation.[11] Some problems no doubt require prolonged or specialized attention in order to receive a just disposition. Cases involving divorce, adoption, or juvenile delinquency, for example, if decided too quickly, may result later in tragedy for those involved. Thus, naked statistics of delay need not invariably symbolize the decay of the judicial system. In practice, however, the delays are symptomatic of grave evils in dispensing justice because they are geared to deficiencies in judicial organization and administration rather than to time-consuming precautions to ensure justice in individual cases.

JUDICIAL ORGANIZATION AND ADMINISTRATION. The late Judge Vanderbilt, in the course of his many campaigns for judicial reform, used to observe that it is characteristic of an immature system of law that it is beset by a multiplicity of courts.[12] This was a polite way of saying that most state judicial systems were immature. In the typical state, the judicial department, which is supposed to be the third great branch of government, is such in name only: It comprises a multitude of separate courts, each operating quite autonomously, and with no one responsible

---

[10] Warren, op. cit., *p. 3. Major studies of the extent and causes of delay are found in Maurice Rosenberg, "Court Congestion: Status, Causes, and Proposed Remedies," in Jones, op. cit., pp. 29–59; and in continuing court calendar studies by the American Bar Foundation and by the Institute of Judicial Administration.*

[11] *Maxine B. Virtue, "The Two Faces of Janus: Delay in Metropolitan Trial Courts," The Annals of the American Academy of Political and Social Science, 328 (March 1960), 125–33, at 126.*

[12] *Arthur Vanderbilt, "Brief for a Better Court System," The New York Times Magazine, May 5, 1957, p. 9.*

for the functioning of the department as a whole. Confusion, overlap, and conflict of jurisdiction among the courts is an inevitable consequence. The sordid portrait of the Chicago court system prior to adoption of Illinois' new judicial article of the constitution in 1962 could apply to dozens of other state and local court systems in the United States: Chicago had circuit and superior courts, handling much the same kind of cases, as well as a county court, a probate court, and many county and municipal courts whose jurisdiction differed only slightly. With no master calendar to control the cases filed in the many courts, lawyers could take advantage of delay by arguing whether a case was being brought in the right court and then delay further by an appeal of the ruling. Each court, jealously guarded by its presiding judge, had its own costly system of juries, clerks, bailiffs, stenographers, and reporters; many times cases were not heard for lack of a courtroom while rival courts had empty courtrooms.

State and local court systems often suffer simultaneously from overlapping and fragmented authority. Without centralized responsibility for or control over jurisdiction and dockets, there is both extensive litigation over jurisdiction and extensive atomization of the authority of individual courts. Contemporary jurists have begun to recognize that organizing and administering the courts wisely is as much a part of judicial responsibility as deciding cases wisely.[13] Judge Vanderbilt proposed three steps toward a simplified court structure, and his proposals have had the endorsement of most other proponents of judicial reform: (1) Establish a general trial court with statewide jurisdiction over every kind of case. This court should have specialized judges in law and equity as well as in probate and divorce matters, but every judge of the court should be authorized, when occasion requires, to try every other kind of case. (2) Supplement the general trial court with subordinate municipal or magistrates' courts to exercise local civil and criminal authority. (3) Establish an appellate tribunal of final resort to review questions of law from the trial courts. In larger states there would probably have to be intermediate courts of appeals as well, the number depending on the volume of cases to be reviewed.[14]

Although it is difficult to conceive of statewide business concerns operating without executive heads or without comprehensive administrative organizations, many state court systems have operated on precisely

---

[13] *Maurice Rosenberg, op. cit.*

[14] *Vanderbilt, "Brief for a Better Court System,"* op. cit. *See also American Bar Association,* The Improvement of the Administration of Justice (1961), *chap. II, pp.* 5–9.

such a basis. Historically, "each judge paddled his own canoe," but when each judge under what Chief Justice Taft once called the "go-as-you-please system" had to concern himself with courthouse personnel, budget matters, scheduling of trials, and impaneling of jurors, the sheer complexity and multiplicity of detail exhausted his time and diminished his creativity and competence in judging.

To free judges from purely administrative problems and at the same time preserve their traditional independence in judicial functions, the American Bar Association has advocated that the chief justice of the state supreme court should be the administrative head of the court system with full responsibility for the recruitment, training, and supervision of court clerks, secretaries, and reporters; with authority to manage the financial affairs of the judiciary, including preparation of budgets and supervision of expenditures; and, especially, with the power to assign and reassign judges to courts with crowded dockets. In short, the chief justice should be made responsible for the effective use of the whole judicial power of the state.

Because no single individual could attend to the myriad details involved in administering a judicial system, the chief justice should have the power to appoint assistants or to establish an administrative office of the state courts, modeled on the administrative office of the federal courts established in 1939. There have been signs of progress in more than half the states, but the best efforts of reformers have failed to keep pace with growing demand. Despite admonitions to the legal profession to focus attention on the need for innovation, experimentation, and ingenuity, many judges fear change of any kind because it threatens their status and local autonomy.[15]

RULES OF PROCEDURE. Probably the most important single device for achieving a prompt and just disposition of cases on their merits is an uncomplicated and reasonably flexible procedural system. Without it, other reforms have little chance of succeeding.[16]

The old common law procedures, based on technicalities and fictions, still have their counterparts in the procedural rules of many American states. Statutory codes of procedure in the states are generally too long and too detailed, placing too much emphasis on mere form and containing too many traps for the unwary. Trials under such circumstances focus on the maneuvering skills of the attorneys rather than on the merits of plaintiffs'

---

[15] Robert C. Finley, "Judicial Administration: What Is This Thing Called Legal Reform?" Columbia Law Review, 65 (April 1965), 569–92.

[16] American Bar Association, op. cit., p. 51.

and defendants' positions; they become sporting contests instead of quests for justice. Modern procedure that is simple and adaptable to the needs of individual cases has been available since 1938, when the Federal Rules of Civil Procedure were adopted to govern the federal judiciary. The Federal Rules, often cited as the greatest single accomplishment in modern judicial reform, were noteworthy for their (a) fusion of law and equity; (b) simplification of pleadings; (c) elimination of surprise as a courtroom weapon through liberalizing procedures for "discovery" (which allow opponents to inspect each other's documents and records relevant to the case in advance of the actual trial), and by encouraging pre-trial conferences, devoid of the usual formalistic legal trappings, to delimit the issues in an action, dispose of uncontested issues, and fix the precise points to be litigated; and (d) granting of a large measure of discretion in procedural matters to the trial judge. The Federal Rules, in short, were designed to promote the disposition of cases on their merits with all issues exposed prior to trial in the courtroom.

In the three decades since the Federal Rules were adopted, fewer than half the states have accepted them in full for their own courts. Part of the explanation for this glacier-like progress may lie in the high stakes many successful practitioners have in perpetuating a system that has been a source of substantial profit to them. Changes in state law that might reduce the volume of legal business or impair the victory record of the established "sporting lawyer" are bound to meet vehement opposition. Part of the explanation may also lie in the fact that rules do not usually change until their ill effects are felt acutely. Moral, intellectual, or economic change must in most instances precede the adoption of new procedures. Whatever the explanation, and despite sustained efforts by professional associations like the American Bar Association and the American Judicature Society to speed modernization of state court procedures, there is some truth to the observation that lawyers "have an approach to the courts that, if carried over into medicine, would result in considerable reverence for treatment by leech and mustard plaster." [17]

ACCESS TO THE COURTS AND REPRESENTATION BY COUNSEL. The achievement of equal justice under law requires both reforms in judicial administration and the heightening of access to court systems. The more complex and intricate the judiciary's procedural rules are, the smaller is the corps of skilled attorneys capable of representing clients' interests adequately. It is the poor, especially, who suffer when legalistic

---

[17] *Banks, op. cit., p.* 190.

technicalities rather than common sense rules dominate the procedures of state courts.[18]

The courts should not only be sources of accommodation to social need and guardians of human dignity, but should serve as instruments of communication and confrontation that can help to resolve social conflict and sustain people's commitments to democratic institutions. It is a truism that participating citizens have a greater stake in democracy than alienated citizens. Legal services that can encourage and facilitate the transition from poverty to self-sufficiency reinforce the foundations of democracy by providing meaningful access to the policy-making process for many groups and individuals who would otherwise be cut off from participation.[19]

The lack of access to the courts to enforce code regulations in slum housing illustrated for many years the inequities in a system where poor plaintiffs attempted to seek redress from wealthy defendants. Refusal to pay rent was often the only feasible means the poor had to protest a landlord's violation of housing codes. Eviction was traditionally the consequence of rent delinquency, however, and the courts offered on redress to the evicted parties. Innovative decisions in two recent cases in New York held that courts have the power to reinstate into possession tenants wrongfully evicted even when new tenants have occupied the premises.[20] This simple affirmation of judicial power has made redress accessible to sectors of the populace accustomed in the past to indifference, if not exploitation, on the part of the legal system.

The rationing of justice on the basis of ability to pay was all too common in the past and remains prevalent in a number of respects in the present. A study of bail practices in New York offers an illustration.[21] In 1961, a total of 118,000 men and women had to stay in jails in New York while awaiting trial or disposition of their cases, largely because they were unable to put up money or bond for bail. Nearly 1,000 of these detainees were held behind bars more than six months. In one so-called house of detention that is actually a maximum security jail for adolescents between 16 and 21 years of age, the average time behind bars without trial for those

---

[18] Harold W. Solomon, " 'This New Fetish for Indigency': Justice and Poverty in an Affluent Society," Columbia Law Review, 66 (February 1966), 248–74.

[19] Martin Rein and Frank Riessman, "A Strategy for Antipoverty Community Action Programs," Social Work, 11 (April 1966), 3–12.

[20] In Marluted Realty Corp. v. Decker, 46 Misc. 2d 736, 260 N.Y.S. 2d 988 (1965) and Albany v. White, 46 Misc. 2d 915, 261 N.Y.S. 2d 361 (1965).

[21] Gertrude Samuels, "Bail: Justice for Far from All," The New York Times Magazine, August 19, 1962, p. 13. See also A. Kenneth Pye, "The Legal Needs of the Poor: The Administration of Criminal Justice," Columbia Law Review, 66 (February 1966), 286–304, at 293.

who could not "make bail" was 45 days. The inequities in the bail system in New York, under which "money and not public safety apparently was the measure of who went free and who was jailed," were found to be typical of urban areas throughout the country, especially of those where no legal aid or public defender office exists to represent the poor.[22] A report to the National Conference on Bail and Criminal Justice in 1964 showed that 58,000 persons, almost 13,000 of them adolescents, were confined to prison that year awaiting the disposition of charges pending against them. The imprisonments without trial averaged 28 days for the adults and 32 days for the adolescents.[23]

In the past several years the Supreme Court and Congress have taken significant steps to alleviate the problem of lack of adequate counsel in the administration of criminal justice. Two landmark decisions by the Court, *Gideon v. Wainright* and *Escobedo v. Illinois*,[24] held that the right of an accused person to counsel, which is guaranteed in federal proceedings by the Sixth Amendment, must also be afforded in state proceedings in order to satisfy the due process requirements of the Fourteenth Amendment. Once an investigation ceases to be a general inquiry and proceeds to the accusatory stage, the constitutional guarantee must be recognized. The *Gideon* and *Escobedo* rules apply also to cases in which the defendant wants to plead guilty.

Diverse procedures in each state for interpreting and administering the *Gideon* and *Escobedo* rules, however, necessitated the delineation of uniform standards by the Supreme Court. In the *Miranda* case in 1966, the justices promulgated constitutional guidelines for law enforcement agencies and courts to follow. In reversing the convictions of four confessed criminals, the Court laid down strict rules for state courts to apply: (1) A person in custody must clearly and unequivocally be informed of his right to remain silent and be warned that what he says can be used against him in court; (2) a person in custody must be told of his right to have a lawyer and that the state will provide one if the individual is indigent; (3) the

---

[22] *The legal aid movement in the United States began in 1876 when a group of citizens of German origin in New York City formed an office to assist German immigrants in protecting their legal rights. Today these autonomous societies, largely organized and financed through voluntary efforts, provide professional legal assistance, free or for a nominal sum, to any indigent person requiring legal assistance. Defender offices are usually tax-supported and provide salaried lawyers to represent indigent defendants in criminal courts.*

[23] *Edward L. Barrett, Jr., "Criminal Justice: The Problem of Mass Production" in Jones, op. cit., pp. 85–123 at 107.*

[24] Gideon *v.* Wainwright, 372 *U.S.* 335 (1963); Escobedo *v.* Illinois, 378 *U.S.* 478 (1964). *For a comprehensive analysis of the implications of the* Gideon *and* Escobedo *rules, see* Lee Silverstein, Defense of the Poor in Criminal Cases in American State Courts (*Chicago: American Bar Association, 1965*).

government must be able to prove that, if a confession was obtained in the absence of the defendant's attorney, the defendant "knowingly and intelligently waived his privilege against self-incrimination" as well as his right to counsel.[25]

In August, 1964, Congress implemented the Supreme Court's "right to counsel" decisions through passage of the Criminal Justice Act. The statute provides funds to compensate counsel for accused persons in federal cases who "are financially unable to obtain an adequate defense." The steps taken thus far to assure counsel for the needy have been limited largely to the criminal sphere, however. The plight of the financially underprivileged party in civil litigation has only begun to receive serious recognition. Despite the fact that during 1965, 252 legal aid offices and 198 legal defender services handled some 700,000 cases without fee—almost four times the number of cases accepted by such offices in 1945—these noble efforts and achievements fall short when compared with need.[26] The access of the indigent to adequate legal services has been no better than their access to other necessities of life. Legal aid offices, traditionally financed through charity drives, have lacked funds to compete in the marketplace with established law firms for the best legal talent. Many brilliant, dedicated, and financially unconcerned or independent lawyers are attracted to regular staff positions, but too often the legal aid office has also been a training school for the neophyte, who can make his mistakes with impunity, or a career for the second-rater, who lacks the sophisticated skills essential to peak performance under the present demands of the adversary system.

The unpopular client presents another facet of the problem of inadequate representation. The lawyer representing an accused racketeer or a social or political nonconformist performs one of the vital functions of a free society. Yet lawyers, fearing community hostility, often feel that in accepting such clients they jeopardize their public reputation.[27] Lawyers' professional associations have asserted vigorously and continuously the duty of the bar to provide representation even for the most unpopular

---

[25] Miranda v. Arizona, 384 *U.S.* 436 (1966).

[26] Statistics of Legal Aid and Defender Work in the United States and Canada, 1965 (*Chicago: National Legal Aid and Defender Association, American Bar Center,* 1965). *See also* Orison S. Marden, "Equal Access to Justice: The Challenge and the Opportunity," Washington and Lee Review, 19 (*Fall* 1962), 153–64. *Current issues and trends in legal aid are discussed in* The Legal Aid Brief Case, *which is published five times a year by the National Legal Aid and Defender Association.*

[27] Arthur J. Goldberg, "New Frontiers for Lawyers and the Law," Journal of the American Judicature Society, 46 (*August* 1961), 56–61. Howard Sacks, Defending the Unpopular Client (*Chicago: National Council on Legal Clinics,* 1961); Justine Wise Polier, "Legal Needs of the Poor: Problems Involving Family and Child," Columbia Law Review, 66 (*February* 1966), 305–16.

clients and the duty of the public to avoid imputing to any lawyer the reputation, views, or character of his clients. Nonetheless, the individual lawyer sensitive to the overt or subtle censures the community often imposes on one who defends deviance from its norms may well continue to avoid the unpopular client, leaving him either to the specialists in the unpopular—the Clarence Darrows of yesteryear and the Edward Bennett Williamses of today—or to inadequate representation.

2. Prospects for Progress

The impediments to judicial efficacy examined in the preceding section are serious but, hopefully, not yet debilitating. Recent persistent trends in reappraisal and reform of our state judicial systems do warrant some optimism that an era of significant progress is at hand, and it is the purpose of this section to delineate those trends.

Perhaps a beneficial consequence of the crisis in the courts has been renewed attention by members of the legal profession and by social scientists to the basic objectives of the legal system and to the role of each of the components of the system in achieving them. This renaissance of interest in the goals, structures, mechanisms, and procedures that lie at the core of the legal system has produced in turn a quest for empirical research data on their interrelationships.

Whereas lawyers in a more mechanistic legal era would probably have assumed, for example, that the best cure for delay in the courts is more courts and more judges, today many members of the profession seek evidence to show whether some of the conflicts and issues that produce the delays can be resolved as well or better by nonjudicial mechanisms. In seeking such data, lawyers frequently have been turning to the skills and research methods of the social scientists—to the sociologists, social workers, psychologists, and political scientists concerned about the legal system from the vantage points of their own disciplines.

These developments may be categorized under four headings: (1) the new empiricism in legal research, (2) deformalization of aspects of the judicial process, (3) reforms in the administration of justice, and (4) ferment in appraising the objectives and sanctions of the law. We shall examine each in the following sections.

EMPIRICISM IN LEGAL RESEARCH. Judge Robert Finley of the Washington State Supreme Court has termed legal reform "a state of mind, a willingness to take a look at things as they are." [28] Unfortunately,

---

[28] *Finley, op. cit., p.* 471.

the law has been among the last to become concerned about or to respond to "things as they are," but considerable progress has been made by legal researchers in recent years toward neutral, objectively verifiable factual determinations of the causes and consequences of human and organizational behavior.[29] Three recent and continuing studies often cited as prototypes of the new legal empiricism are the comprehensive 30-year study of juvenile delinquency and its predictability conducted by Sheldon and Eleanor Glueck under the aegis of the Harvard Law School, the University of Chicago Law School's Jury Project, and the Columbia University Law School's Project for Effective Justice.

The Chicago Jury Project has used experimental juries, has had the collaboration of sociologists in assembling data and cross-checking juror motivations, and has employed sophisticated methods of questionnaire construction, interviewing, and statistical analysis. One of the basic questions the Chicago researchers have sought to resolve by these techniques is this: What difference would it make if we had no jury trials and all trials were conducted by judges alone? The researchers found that in 1,500 criminal cases, judge and jury agreed in 81 percent. The judges were more prone to convict and the jurors to acquit in the 19 percent of the cases in which judge and jury disagreed. Whereas judges and juries generally saw eye to eye in narcotics cases, they often disagreed in statutory rape cases and first-offense drunken driving cases. In 1,500 personal injury cases examined, judges agreed with juries on questions of liability in 83 percent of the cases. Juries found against "wealthy" defendants like corporations, railroads, and state governments from 2 percent to 8 percent more often than judges. The percentages of agreement and disagreement showed no significant difference between state and federal courts.

These data, although not providing a conclusive answer to the question of differences between judge-decided and jury-decided cases, do suggest that the differences are not great. If the jury system is not as foolproof an instrument of democracy as its proponents maintain, the data gathered in this phase of the Chicago Jury Project show that neither is it as base an instrument of passion and irrationality as its detractors contend.[30]

The Columbia Law School Project for Effective Justice has been aimed in large part at examining the significance of, and alternatives to,

---

[29] *Edwin W. Patterson*, Law in a Scientific Age (*New York: Columbia University Press, 1963*), *p. 24.*

[30] *On the phase of the Chicago Jury Project cited above, see Dale Broeder, "The University of Chicago Jury Project," Nebraska Law Review, 38 (1959), 744–60. On juries and delay, see Hans Zeisel, Harry Kalven, Jr., and Bernard Buchholz, Delay in The Courts (Boston: Little, Brown, 1959).*

adjudication for the resolution of conflict and alleviation of judicial delay. Detailed examination of court records and records of insurance companies in one phase of the study revealed that, of about 193,000 personal injury claims made against insured persons in New York City each year, some 77,000 result in lawsuits. Of these, only 48,000 reach the stage at which the parties signify that they are ready for trial by filing a "note of issue." By the time of trial, only 7,000 lawsuits remain. Of these, 4,500 are settled out of court before conclusion of trial, leaving only 2,500 cases decided by verdict. Less than 2 percent of the claims are therefore directly adjudicated by the court; the other 98 percent are settled through a process of bargaining in which victims, defendants, lawyers, and insurance company representatives are the chief participants.[31]

Other studies by the Columbia Project show that alternatives to adjudication, like compulsory arbitration in Pennsylvania and the use of court-appointed auditors in Massachusetts, do reduce congestion in trial courts, but the bar must, in effect, subsidize them by supplying high-quality arbitrators and auditors at low cost. The project's empirical analysis of the effects of pretrial hearings on the disposition of personal injury cases in New Jersey revealed that pretrial conferences, contrary to expectations, do not always speed the resolution of the conflict. Indeed they may be instruments of delay.[32]

Singling out the Chicago and Columbia Projects for discussion does not, of course, minimize other major empirical undertakings, such as the distinguished work done for many years by the Institute for Judicial Administration at New York University,[33] the Survey of Metropolitan Courts in Michigan by the University of Michigan,[34] the study of pretense and practice in bankruptcy law administration sponsored by the Brookings Institution, the comprehensive examination of police practices and the administration of criminal justice recently completed by the American Bar Foundation,[35] or the studies of innovations in legal representation of the poor supported by the National Legal Aid and Defender Association.

Additional research into the realities of the operations of legal systems

---

[31] Marc A. Franklin, Robert A. Chanin, and Irving Mark, "Accidents, Money, and the Law: A Study of the Economics of Personal Injury Litigation," Columbia Law Review, 61 (1961), 1–39, at 10.

[32] Maurice Rosenberg, The Pretrial Conference and Effective Justice (New York: Columbia University Press, 1964).

[33] Individual reports are too numerous to cite. A catalog can be obtained from the Institute.

[34] Maxine Virtue, Survey of Metropolitan Courts: Final Report (Ann Arbor, Mich.: University of Michigan Press, 1962).

[35] See, for example, Wayne R. LaFave, Arrest: The Decision to Take a Suspect into Custody (Boston: Little, Brown, 1965).

is being stimulated by foundation grants. One substantial foundation devoted exclusively to legal research announced in 1962, for example, that its trustees were "especially interested in studies that press beyond conventional scholarly analysis of appellate decisions. Such studies may involve material from and collaboration between many disciplines. They may employ such devices as interviews, opinion surveys, statistical analyses, participant observation, clinical studies, or controlled experiments." [36] The Russell Sage Foundation has underwritten basic research into the relationship between law and the social sciences at the University of California, the University of Wisconsin, the University of Denver, and Northwestern University. If there is any limit to the benefits of such projects for judicial reform, it is that perceived by one of the coauthors of the Chicago study, Hans Zeisel, who has warned that "policy-makers may ask for ever more facts—not because they need them but because such a request is a convenient way to procrastinate." [37]

DEFORMALIZATION. Although the law has often proved a sympathetic profession for procrastinators, significant changes in long-dormant areas have been effected and more are under way. One of the most important of them has been the recognition that the formal processes of the adversary system with its contending lawyers are neither required nor desirable in much of the administration of civil and criminal justice.

As noted by the Columbia Project for Effective Justice, bargaining rather than adjudication accounts for the resolution of the vast majority of conflicts arising from personal injury claims. Bargaining plays a similarly vital, if unheralded, role in criminal law administration. Donald Newman, a sociologist on the staff of the American Bar Foundation's project on the administration of criminal justice, has pointed out that more than 90 percent of the criminal convictions in a typical midwestern community were not convictions in a combative, trial-by-jury sense, but merely involved sentencing after the defendant pleaded guilty. A substantial majority of these guilty pleas were found to be the result of a compromise agreement between defense and prosecution. The defendant would often agree to plead guilty to a lesser charge than that for which he was arrested; the prosecutor would not have to spend the time and effort to prepare a trial case; and the court's calendar would be more manageable. The trouble with the system is that the more experienced criminals can often manipu-

---

[36] *Report of the Walter E. Meyer Research Institute of Law* (New Haven, 1962), p. 8.

[37] Hans Zeisel, "*Delay by the Parties and Delay by the Courts,*" Journal of Legal Education, 15 (1962), 27–36, at 36.

late legal processes to obtain light sentences and better official records, while amateur or occasional offenders receive harsher treatment.[38]

Such data are helping to revise the traditional but mistaken image, held by the public and the majority of lawyers who never enter the criminal courts, of the criminal lawyer as "a trial tactician fighting for an acquittal in the taut arena of the courtroom." [39] Most of a criminal lawyer's practice consists primarily of negotiations. Some 85 percent of the felony indictments in New York are disposed of in this way, and emphasis on skills of timing and tactics for exploring settlement possibilities informally has supplemented, if it has not displaced, the earlier emphasis on formal trial tactics. Included as basic advice to criminal law practitioners is this admonition of special interest to the political scientist: "The prosecuting attorney and the sentencing judge can't afford to be put in a position where they must excuse their conduct to an angry electorate. Accordingly, the best service defense counsel can perform when representing a guilty client is to stay out of the press!" [40]

Many classes of cases that do proceed to trial are now conducted under less formal conditions than heretofore and with enlarged professional roles for social scientists. The Legal Aid Agency for the District of Columbia, for example, has started an experimental program to provide defense counsel with background materials, prepared by a social scientist, which can assist in presenting reasonable alternatives to imprisonment for consideration by the courts.[41]

The growth and development of juvenile courts from their first establishment in Chicago in 1899 to their present nationwide use have emphasized the function of the court as a treatment center rather than a punishment dispenser. Informal, nonadversary procedures generally prevail, and private hearings are held to protect the juvenile from being marked as a criminal. Social workers, sociologists, psychologists, and psychiatrists form part of the professional staff attached to the court, and the judges' decisions are more often products of the scientists' reports and recommendations than of the application of rigid rules of law.[42]

---

[38] Donald J. Newman, "Pleading Guilty for Considerations: A Study of Bargain Justice," Journal of Criminal Law, Criminology and Police Science, 46 (March–April 1956), 780–90.

[39] Robert Polstein, "How to 'Settle' a Criminal Case," The Practical Lawyer, 8 (January 1962), 35–44.

[40] Ibid., p. 40.

[41] Pye, op. cit., p. 296.

[42] For a thorough analysis, see Robert G. Caldwell, "The Juvenile Court: Its Development and Some Major Problems," Journal of Criminal Law, Criminology and Police Science, 51 (January–February 1961), 493–511.

Within the past few years, however, juvenile courts have come under attack for denying offenders the rights to bail, counsel, and public jury trial. Washington's Juvenile Court Judge Orman W. Ketcham recently advocated the need for change in juvenile court procedures to assure juvenile offenders defense by legal counsel rather than by social workers.[43] Only a few months after the publication of this article, however, the Supreme Court ruled that Judge Ketcham had been wrong in not permitting a 16-year-old accused of rape, robbery, and housebreaking to be tried in Juvenile Court. The boy was tried as an adult and given a 30- to 90-year sentence without counsel, hearing, or explanation. The problems involved in trying to afford juvenile offenders their constitutional rights while at the same time providing them with therapeutic treatment is a knotty one for all state juvenile courts.[44]

The field of family law is another that requires and has begun to use interprofessional skills for the effective resolution of cases. The American Bar Association's Family Law Section, organized in 1958, has stressed the importance of the use by lawyers and judges of the skills and techniques of social work, psychology, and psychiatry. In cooperation with the National Association of Social Workers, it has established the National Conference of Lawyers and Social Workers to enhance working relationships between the two professions in the handling of family matters. The typical family court of a large city has a staggering load of cases dealing with neglected children, truancy, nonsupport, and other family crises. The load becomes more tolerable and the work of the courts more effective as the skills of social science and psychiatry are blended with those of the law in quest for practicable and realistic solutions. A recent New York case utilizing social science data recognized the tragedy and inhumanity of abandoning non-white children to foster homes without giving the children hope or opportunity for adoption.[45] Another recent case in Iowa has shown, however, that the blend of law and social science offers no panacea for solving problems of family law. In a hotly contested child-custody case,[45a] the Iowa Supreme Court ruled that a seven-year-old boy who had been sent by his father to stay with his maternal grandparents after his mother was killed in an automobile accident should remain with the grandparents rather than return to the father, who had remarried and was living the kind

---

[43] *Orman W. Ketcham, "Legal Renaissance in the Juvenile Court,"* Northwestern Law Review, 60 (*November–December* 1965), 585–98.

[44] Kent v. U.S., 383 U.S. 541 (1966). *See "Reformers in Crisis,"* Time, *May 20, 1966, p. 114.*

[45] In re Bonez, 48 Misc. 2d 900, 266 N.Y.S. 2d 756 (1966).

[45a] Painter v. Bannister, 140 N.W. 2d 152 (1966). *The U.S. Supreme Court refused to review the Iowa court's decision.*

of life the court termed "unstable, unconventional, arty, bohemian." The court relied in its conclusion on testimony by an Iowa State University child psychologist that the child would have greater security and stability under the circumstances with his grandparents than with his father.

Growing awareness by lawyers of the limits of formal adjudication and of the feasibility of informal techniques for resolving conflicts has led to some bold proposals to remove certain questions entirely from the atmosphere of adversary procedure in the courtroom. Interest has focused increasingly over the past few years on proposals for the elimination of trials in automobile injury cases and the substitution of an informally administered compensation plan under which injured parties could recover regardless of fault.[46] Although there is no likelihood that such a proposal will be adopted in the immediate future, it has spurred many lawyers, who would lose substantial incomes if it ever were adopted, to support other informal devices that can hasten and make more equitable the disposition of personal injury claims within the traditional framework of the judicial system.[47]

The significance of the lawyer's noncourtroom roles has begun to have some effect on the typical law school curriculum. Northwestern University Law School has been conducting an experimental project in counseling training for law students in which classroom work has been combined with clinical work at the Legal Aid Bureau. The major purposes of the project are to develop the student's understanding of the lawyer's role as a counselor whose responsibilities often require him to be concerned with his client's total problem and not just its legal aspects; to increase his understanding of the "human factors" in such fields as marital relations, debt, and estate planning; and to promote cooperation between lawyers and members of other "helping professions," such as psychiatry and social work.[48] Programs like this one are both symptoms and products of the

---

[46] See, for example: Samuel Hofstadter, "A Proposed Automobile Accident Compensation Plan," The Annals of the American Academy of Political and Social Science, 328 (March 1960), 53–60; Francis Bergan, "A Thesis on Motor Vehicle Liability Without Fault," Albany Law Review, 28 (1964), 199–201; Arthur L. Goodhart, "Our Horse and Buggy Law," Journal of the American Judicature Society, 49 (June 1965), 26–30; and Fleming James, "Evaluation of the Fault Concept," Trial (February–March 1966), 25–28.

[47] Charles Desmond, "Current Problems of State Court Administration," Columbia Law Review, 65 (April 1965), 561–68.

[48] Report on Program in Counseling Training (mimeographed, Evanston, Ill.: Northwestern University Law School, 1963). See also Harrop Freeman (ed.), Legal Interviewing and Counseling (St. Paul: West Publishing Co., 1964); and Hubert J. O'Gorman, Lawyers and Matrimonial Cases (New York: The Free Press, 1964).

current ferment within the legal profession and are likely to lead to further deformalization of the legal process as new generations of students enter law practice.

SOME REFORM PROGRAMS. Although the crisis in our courts is not yet resolved, the prospects for improvement, based on the magnitude and intensity of recent efforts to reform state and local judicial systems, are better than at any other time of our history. In past decades, critics of judicial inefficiency and delay were treated with the deference usually accorded, "hell-fire and damnation" preachers; they were listened to, praised, and promptly ignored. For whatever reason—whether because of sudden pangs of professional conscience or the sudden mounting of criticism by fee-paying clients—the legal profession is engaged today in a massive action program to make the courts more efficient and more equitable instruments for the resolution of human conflicts. The trends toward empiricism in legal research and deformalization of court procedures were examined earlier. At this point we shall consider the potentiality for improvement through intraprofessional discussion and seminars and through legislative and constitutional revisions of state judicial articles.

In June, 1961, fourteen national organizations concerned with the improvement of judicial administration established the Joint Committee for the Effective Administration of Justice. Fundamental to the committee's program was a recognition that the courts have been hard put to keep abreast of the demands placed on them by the population explosion, the migration of citizens, increases in crime and delinquency, the increasing complexity of modern business, and the expanding role of government. Justice Tom Clark of the Supreme Court, long a leader in the movement for judicial reform, accepted the chairmanship.

Acting as a central headquarters that could bring nationwide experience to bear upon problems of local concern, the Joint Committee proceeded in its three years of operation to organize a series of regional judicial seminars in which state and local problems bearing on judicial organization, procedure, selection, and rules could be explored candidly and fully. Participants in the seminars included not only the judges of the state or locality involved, but also "teams" of judges from other jurisdictions who had faced similar problems.

The seminars filled a distinct void in judicial education and culminated in the founding of a unique institution, the National College of State Trial Judges. Housed at the University of Nevada, the College administers training and refresher programs for judges in which law professors, practitioners, and members of the judiciary can confront and debate such basic problems in the administration of justice as calendar control, the pretrial conference, instructions to juries, sentencing, and the merits of adversary versus nonadversary proceedings.[49]

Among other intraprofessional legal activities worthy of note are the American Bar Association's traffic court improvement program, reappraisals of the adequacy of facilities for representing and defending the indigent, and the extension of lawyer referral services to persons of moderate means who have not had occasion to consult attorneys before.

Based on the premise that justice is endangered when judges are dependent on fees which in turn depend upon convictions, intensified efforts have been made to eliminate the fee system of compensating traffic court judges that still prevails in half of the states. The Traffic Court Program also stages regional conferences on model court procedure, makes professional studies of traffic court organization, and publishes helpful manuals and texts on traffic court administration.[50]

Lawyer referral services for persons of moderate means seeking legal advice at low fixed rates are available in some two hundred cities. Manuals of standards and policies for these services are published by the American Bar Association to encourage and guide state and local planning committees, and a quarterly *Lawyer Referral Bulletin* keeps lawyers abreast of trends and developments. More than 16,000 lawyers now serve on referral panels and over 60,000 persons receive legal service each year through the lawyer referral plan.[51]

It would be premature, if not fatuous, to claim that any facilities or even plans are adequate to meet the legal representational needs of the indigent, but several recent developments connote sufficient progress to warrant enthusiasm for the possibility of long-range resolution. The growth of neighborhood law programs in New York, New Haven, Boston, Oakland, Washington, and other cities has been the product of new conceptions of legal aid. Persons in need of assistance from legal aid offices can find them not only closer to home but better financed and more adequately manned than ever before.[52]

In addition to traditional modes of financing legal aid programs,

---

[49] *Maurice Rosenberg, "Judging Goes to College," American Bar Association Journal, 52 (April 1966), 342–45; Glenn R. Winters and Robert E. Allard, "Judicial Selection and Tenure in the United States," in Jones, op. cit., pp. 146–77, particularly pp. 174f.*

[50] Report of the American Bar Association, Vol. 89, pp. 531–34.

[51] Ibid., pp. 499–503.

[52] *See Patricia Wald's chapter on "Broadening Legal Assistance to the Poor" in her working paper Law and Poverty 1965 prepared for The National Conference on Law and Poverty (Washington, D.C.: Government Printing Office, 1965), pp. 68–110.*

substantial grants from the Office of Economic Opportunity and from the Ford Foundation to private and community action groups have broadened their capacity to hire and retain outstanding young lawyers and to implement worthy new ideas for legal representation. In the spring of 1966, for example, the OEO announced 34 new legal service grants totaling $6,361,000. One of the grants was for an experimental "Judicare" program initiated by the state bar of Wisconsin, under which "Judicare cards" may be issued to families in 26 counties in northern Wisconsin with a total annual income of less than $3,000. Some 36,000 families in this rural area, or about 30 percent of its population, fall into this category. A Judicare Board will determine exact eligibility requirements. By presenting his card to any lawyer in his area, an eligible person will be entitled to all types of free legal services except those involving criminal and tax matters, for which other types of free service are available. Fee-generating cases, including contingent fee cases, are also excluded. Attorneys whose services are used will be reimbursed by the Wisconsin Judicare Administration at no more than 80 percent of regular minimum fees.[53]

The OEO also established a new recruitment program, "Advocates for the Poor," to seek top students in all United States law schools for legal programs financed with federal funds. That these programs often call for the integration of the skills of lawyers and social workers both in making people aware of their legal rights and in providing access to legal services is another positive factor, since it cultivates social perspectives in lawyers and helps make social workers aware of the nature and function of the legal system.[54]

Although implementation by the states of the Supreme Court's rulings on right to counsel in criminal cases has been far from uniform, effective remedial action is under way in many states, spurred on by the organized bar and by community action organizations. Whereas in most counties of states such as North Carolina, South Carolina, Florida, Alabama, and Mississippi lawyers were appointed for impoverished persons only in capital cases or under other special circumstances prior to the *Gideon* decision, all five states have modified local procedures since that time in order to ensure the availability of legal help to the poor defendant. Similar changes have been made in more than twenty other states since the *Gideon* ruling.[55]

---

[53] American Bar News, 11 (*May 15, 1966*), 1.

[54] *"The Lawyer and the Social Worker,"* Proceedings of the Conference on the Extension of Legal Services to the Poor (*Washington, D.C., 1965*), *pp.* 133–64.

[55] *Lee Silverstein, "The Continuing Impact of* Gideon v. Wainright *on the States,"* American Bar Association Journal, 51 (*February 1965*), 1023–26.

Reforms in judicial organization and administration in the last decade have surpassed those of the preceding half century. In 1962 alone, constitutional amendments for statewide judicial reform were adopted through citizen referendum in eight states—North Carolina, Illinois, Nebraska, Colorado, Idaho, Washington, Iowa, and New York—and through legislative enactment in Maine. Varying degrees of reorganization resulted from the following changes, which were heralded as significant victories by the American Judicature Society: statewide appellate court reform in four states—New York, North Carolina, Illinois and Colorado; statewide minor court reform in five states—North Carolina, Illinois, Colorado, Idaho, and Maine; major judicial selection and tenure reform in three states—Iowa, Nebraska, and Illinois; and major court administrative reforms in five states—New York, North Carolina, Illinois, Colorado and Washington. One especially noteworthy reform occurred on January 1, 1964, when 30 courts of record, 75 justice of the peace courts, and 103 police magistrate courts in the Chicago area were consolidated into the Circuit Court of Cook County. Such actions as these make clear the fact that people want judicial reform; that bench and bar are beginning to provide effective leadership; and most important of all, that reform *is* making progress.[56]

Another vital ingredient of reform is the ability to remove dishonest or senile judges without having to resort to the cumbersome process of impeachment. The 1964 scandal implicating former members of the Oklahoma Supreme Court alerted bench, bar, and citizens not only to the need for more adequate instruments of judicial discipline and removal, but to the need for conduits and procedures for receiving complaints from individual citizens. In a published report following a thorough investigation of the state court's crisis, the Oklahoma Bar Association noted:

> *Several informants were asked why they had not sooner raised the hue and cry of bribery. They answered with the question: "To whom could or should we have told it?" There was no good answer.*[57]

An important feature of the California Commission on Judicial Qualifications, established in 1960 as an overseer of the state judiciary's integrity, is that it provides effective means for a private citizen to complain and offers a reasonable expectation that the complaint will be fully and confidentially investigated. During its first four years the California

---

[56] *"Ten Years of Court Reorganization Reforms,"* Journal of the American Judicature Society, 48 *(February 1965)*, 193–95.

[57] *"Final Report of Findings of Investigating Committee of Examiners,"* Oklahoma Bar Association Journal, 36 *(April 10, 1965)*, 601–15, *at 605.*

Commission received 344 complaints and was directly responsible for the resignation or retirement of 26 judges.[58] Following the Oklahoma scandal, Oklahoma, Texas, and Ohio adopted disciplinary procedures for judicial personnel, and many other states are currently following suit.

The student of political science, while viewing achievements in simplifying, coordinating, and improving efficiency in our courts as signs of progress, should bear in mind that voters do not "shout" their approval of reform of the judiciary any more readily than they do reform of other institutions or processes. It might be well to recall here the findings of two Illinois political science professors who examined how the state legislature in 1957 came to authorize the public referendum that led to the adoption of the state's new judicial article five years later. It was not until the combined strength of the state's governor and Chicago's powerful mayor was thrown behind the effort that it was able to clear the legislative hurdle. At this point the bar associations were for all practical purposes eliminated from the scene. "The combination of a determined Republican Governor exercising effective control over downstate Republicans and a determined Democratic Mayor exercising control over Chicago Democrats is more likely to produce any desired result than is any other combination of public or private interests." [59]

It may well be that a dual trend of the 1960's has been a growth in the political sophistication of the organized bar and a growth of understanding of the need for judicial reform by the organized politicians. Given the high stakes of both groups in enhancing the prestige of the judiciary, the current trends toward improvement of judicial organization and administration are remarkable only in that they were so long delayed. The significant fact is that important steps are being taken at last to enable the judiciary to keep pace with the demands of the times. But continued progress is not inevitable. Relaxation of effort could well produce the retrogression warned of by a southern court administrator, whose state moved forward and then backward in judicial reform, when he asserted in an interview with the author that "nothing *recedes* like success."

REORIENTING CRIMINAL LAW ADMINISTRATION. To examine the manifestations of ferment in many fields of law would require volumes in itself. Earlier we examined some illustrations of new emphases

---

[58] See Robert Allard, "Judicial Discipline and Removal Plans—A Survey and Comparative Study," Journal of the American Judicature Society, 48 (February 1965) 173–76; and Louis H. Burke, "The California Story," ibid., pp. 167–72.

[59] Gilbert Y. Steiner and Samuel K. Gove, Legislative Politics in Illinois (Urbana, Ill.: University of Illinois Press, 1961), p. 198.

in legal research and procedure, and we shall consider here some of the developments in a single field, the administration of criminal justice. Because crime has been increasing rapidly throughout the United States, the problems of administering criminal justice have become a special source of concern in recent years. The number of serious offenses reported in the early 1960's was double that of a decade earlier and showed a 50 percent growth of the crime rate over the period.[60] Figure 13.1 shows the 1965 pattern, embodying a continuing rise in the crime rate.

Debates and discussions within the field of criminal law administration, which is primarily a state function, center on questions such as these: Is the object of the criminal law to apprehend and punish all illegal behavior, or is it to select from among those people engaging in such behavior certain individuals to be subjected to arrest, prosecution, trial, and punishment? Who defines what conduct is criminal: the legislature, the courts, the prosecutors, the police, or the community? Have legal definitions of socially deviant behavior kept pace with society's definitions? Is full enforcement of the criminal law practicable, or must vast discretionary authority be vested in prosecutors and police, as well as in judges and parole boards, to invoke or not to invoke the letter of the law in particular cases? What limits should there be to the apprehension, questioning, and detention of defendants? Should persons convicted of criminal acts be subjected to punishment, through which they pay a "debt" to society, or to treatment designed to rehabilitate them as useful members of the community? What are the comparative roles of lawyers and of sociologists, social workers, psychologists, and psychiatrists in the administration of criminal justice?

Two basic approaches that might be labeled the "nondiscretionary" and the "discretionary" are taken to the questions dealing with the objectives and methods of arrest, prosecution, and trial. According to the nondiscretionary approach, the principal function of a system of criminal justice is to separate the guilty from the innocent. The legislature defines socially deviant behavior; and the police, performing mandatory functions, must arrest all the guilty and only the guilty wherever and whenever found. The district attorney and public prosecutor must prosecute all those properly arrested, and the final step in the separation of the guilty from the

---

[60] *See the* Uniform Crime Reports *published annually by the Federal Bureau of Investigation, U.S. Department of Justice. The tendency of police departments to underreport crimes and to underclassify serious ones makes crime statistics less exact measures than they appear. In the spring of 1966, New York City registered a sharp increase of reported crimes over the same period in 1965, largely because a new chief of police ordered accurate reporting.*

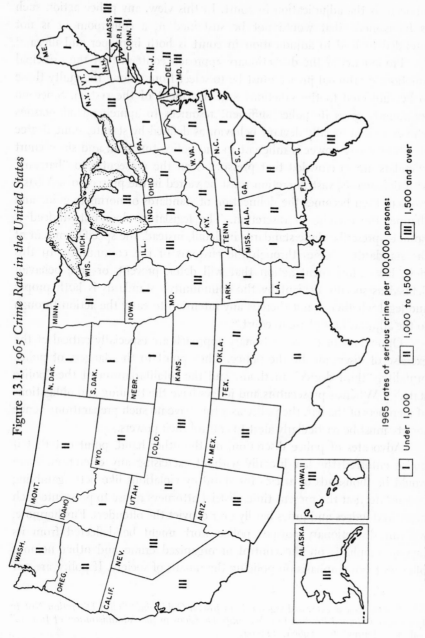

Figure 13.1. *1965 Crime Rate in the United States*

1965 rates of serious crime per 100,000 persons:

I Under 1,000   II 1,000 to 1,500   III 1,500 and over

SOURCE: Federal Bureau of Investigation, *Uniform Crime Reports for the United States: 1965* (Washington, D.C., 1966).

innocent is the adjudication in court. In this view, any police action such as harassment that would not be sustained in a courtroom or is not intended to lead to adjudication in court is both improper and illegal.[61]

Proponents of the discretionary approach contend that the principal function of criminal justice must be to select from among the guilty those to be subjected to the sanctions and treatment of the system. Since no community gives its police sufficient resources to apprehend all persons who engage in socially deviant behavior as defined by statute, some degree of discretionary power is inherent in the police function; and since court calendars are so crowded that pressure is on the prosecutor to "bargain" with defendants, vast discretion must be vested in the prosecutors. A basic problem then becomes the delineation of standards or norms to guide and channel the exercise of discretion. The legislature does not—indeed it cannot—prescribe these standards in detail; instead, the specific content of the standards emerges through the customs of the community. In this view, law enforcement action that will deter, prevent, or cure behavior defined as socially deviant by the community's standards is both proper and legal whether or not there is any intention to carry the action through to the adjudication phase in court.[62]

Opponents of the discretionary approach are especially critical of the exercise of discretion by the police. They point to the dangers of police brutality, "third degree" methods, and the totalitarianism of the "police state." [63] Whereas prosecutors and judges have the training and obligations of members of the bar, the police as a rule have no such preparation: hence society must be particularly alert to control their powers.

Advocates of police discretion, on the other hand, point out that if police enforced the law literally without exercising any discretion, there would be thousands of arrests for statutory violations like petty gambling and adultery; at the present time, district attorneys refuse to prosecute such cases, and judges and juries hardly ever convict the offenders. Furthermore, without discretionary powers, police work might be deflected from its present emphasis on the control of organized crime and other heinous offenses to an emphasis on policing the morals of society. If police are not

---

[61] *This view is expressed vigorously in Joseph Goldstein, "Police Discretion Not to Invoke the Criminal Process: Low Visibility Decisions in the Administration of Justice,"* Yale Law Journal, 69 (1960), 543–94.

[62] *See Frank Remington and Victor Rosenblum, "The Criminal Law and the Legislative Process,"* Illinois Law Forum (1960), pp. 481–99.

[63] *See, for example, the report on* Secret Detention by the Chicago Police, *prepared by the Illinois Division of the American Civil Liberties Union* (New York: The Free Press, 1959).

properly equipped to wield discretionary powers, with optimal benefits to the community, the solution lies in improved training and higher salary incentives to attract better-trained men to police careers.[64]

Discussions on the objectives and methods of dealing with persons convicted of crime are perhaps even more intense and controversial than those on arrest and prosecution. That the death penalty could ever have been imposed for crimes like petty theft strikes a twentieth-century citizen as inconceivable; yet it was the harshness and inequality of eighteenth- and nineteenth-century criminal law that spawned the demands for reform by writers like Jeremy Bentham and Charles Dickens. In time, rehabilitation rather than retribution became the principal acknowledged aim of the criminal law.

If our aim today be rehabilitation, however, our facilities for fulfilling it are woefully inadequate.[65] The rundown state of many of our correctional facilities offers an illustration for many critics of how we preach rehabilitation but practice retribution and perhaps unwittingly train men for careers in crime. In many of our correctional institutions, especially at the local government level, we find an indiscriminate intermingling of hardened criminals with minor offenders, and prisons often have to accommodate many more inmates than they were designed to serve. At times, to take a sordid but typical example, the Cook County, Illinois, jail has had to accommodate between 1,500 and 2,400 persons in a facility designed to house 1,000.

The debate over capital punishment is another illustration of our continued ambivalence over choosing rehabilitation or retribution as the basic goal of sentencing. Critics of capital punishment view it as an act of brute vengeance. Proponents claim that it is the only effective deterrent to the commission of heinous crimes like murder, rape, and treason. Critics point out that would-be murderers and rapists are usually insensitive to the real possibility of death as a punishment if they are caught. For example, no substantial differences have been found between the homicide rates of states where the death penalty has been abolished and those of states in the same area where the death penalty persists. Such states as Delaware,

---

[64] *For thorough examinations of the arguments for and against police discretion, see LaFave, op. cit., pp. 490–525; Sanford Kadish, "Legal Norms and Discretion in the Police and Sentencing Processes,"* Harvard Law Review, *75 (March 1962), 904–31; and Jerome Skolnick,* Justice Without Trial *(New York: Wiley, 1966), pp. 230–45.*

[65] *Pye, op. cit., pp. 298–99. See Frank Riessman, Jerome Cohen, and Arthur Pearl (eds.),* Mental Health of the Poor *(New York: The Free Press, 1964), for a discussion of special problems of rehabilitation of delinquents, addicts, and criminals among the poor.*

Maine, Michigan, Minnesota, North Dakota, Rhode Island, and Wisconsin have abolished capital punishment, but the debate continues to rage. During the Caryl Chessman case, California became the center of controversy over abolition of the death penalty. It was argued that Chessman, who became a successful author while in "death row," was the victim of a retributive system of justice, for he was never allowed to show what it was claimed his book indicated—that he could be a useful and productive member of society.

The problem of treatment is especially great with regard to special classes of offenders such as narcotics addicts. Our approach to the narcotics problem in America has been essentially punitive. Four federal statutes and the Uniform Narcotic Drug Act, which has been adopted in 46 states, apply a wide range of criminal sanctions to violations of the narcotics laws. Critics claim that the "punishment approach" is ineffective in handling the problems of the addict and that what is needed is an approach that places primary reliance upon "socio-medical" plans of control that would enlist the professional skills of doctors, biochemists, psychologists, sociologists, lawyers, legislators, and educators. Such plans would also call for follow-up treatment after the "cure" to prevent recidivism.[66] Defenders of the present punitive system argue that punitive measures to control narcotics sales and addiction do work. Whatever the number of incurable addicts may now be, they allege, it would be several times that number if punishment were restricted or abandoned.

Experts on the treatment of offenders stress the importance of supervision and counseling and the need for physical facilities that might encourage self-respect and rehabilitation. In these matters, the treatment of forgers, burglars, prostitutes, and other social deviants is no different from that of narcotics addicts. The dollar cost of such recommended treatment is high compared to throwing the offender into a cell and leaving him there to serve out a sentence; but it is difficult to put a price tag on social and moral benefits.

How should decisions be reached about the return of offenders to society? Is this a task in which lawyers have the major role or should their role be subordinated to the expert knowledge of penologists and social scientists on the staffs of prisons and parole boards? One position is that due process and fair play are as vital for the convicted offender as for any other member of society. According to this view, decisions to grant or to

---

[66] Donald Cantor, "The Criminal Law and the Narcotics Problems," Journal of Criminal Law, Criminology and Police Science, 51 (January 1961), 512–52; see also the chapter on "The Narcotics Enforcement Pattern," in Skolnick, op. cit., pp. 139–63.

revoke probation or parole should be reached only after careful deliberations in which lawyers have presented the issues and the evidence as they
would in any other type of legal proceedings.

Opponents of lawyer participation maintain that only the views of
experts who understand the personality, drives, strengths, and limitations
of the individual offender are relevant to decisions about probation and
parole. Because such decisions are professional and diagnostic in character,
legal controls are rendered both inappropriate and unnecessary to afford
safeguards against abuse. In practice, few states allow, and none encourage, representation by counsel in parole and probation board hearings.[67]

3. *Conclusion*

Legal commentaries generally stress the stabilizing role of the law, its
functions as a preserver of precedents and an instrument of predictability
in human affairs. "But the law must be a flexible, living instrument. It is a
balance wheel, not a brake." [68] Lawyers are more than mere guardians of
the law, "for we are builders of the law too, and that work will never be
done."

This emphasis by former Justice Goldberg on the affirmative thrust of
the law is a reminder to the political scientist that the law is both a source
and a product of policy making, that courts, judges, and lawyers are
important—if not indispensable—components of the political process.
What substantive rules, what organizational techniques, and what procedures are best suited to the fulfillment of the law's roles? Definite, permanent answers to these questions are neither likely nor desirable. More
significant than timeless answers is the fact that there is agreement that
the questions need asking; for keeping such basic questions before us as
subjects for discussion and research is likely to enhance the ferment,
flexibility, and confrontations that are needed if the law is to keep pace
with political and social change.

In no important field of governmental activity do the state and local
governments possess so substantial a responsibility as they have in the
administration of justice. For the great bulk of arresting, judging, and

---

[67] *Sanford Kadish discusses this problem in detail in "The Advocate and Expert
Counsel in the Peno-Correctional Process,"* University of Minnesota Law Review, 45
(1961), 803–96. *See also the* Report of the Attorney General's Committee on Poverty
and the Administration of Justice (*Washington, D.C.,* 1963), *p.* 25.

[68] *Arthur Goldberg, "New Frontiers for Lawyers and the Law,"* Journal of the
American Judicature Society, 45 (August 1961), 60.

imprisonment of criminals is done not by the federal courts and administrative officers, but by those at the state and local levels, and the vast majority of civil disputes are also adjudicated there. The substantive law that is applied to these cases is found mostly in state legislatures' statutes and local councils' ordinances. Yet citizens seem eager to get their cases before federal judges if possible, and the United States Supreme Court has time and again had to overrule state courts' decisions because fundamental requirements of due process of law had been violated. Encouragingly, but tardily, some states have made drastic changes in their court systems and in procedural rules, as we have seen. But there remain, and predictably will remain for some time, states and communities where justice in the real sense cannot be had—whether because the courts are politicized, the police unrestrained, cases delayed, procedures archaic, or ills perpetuated without prospect of remedy. The states' failure here has no excuse. Their power is uncontested by the federal government, and the state legislatures, composed of lawyers for the most part, do not lack the competence to determine remedies and to enact them. In this field the states are truly on trial.

chapter 14

Local Governments—The Cities

L ocal government has by no means been ignored in the discussions of varied topics in the preceding chapters, but it has not held the center of the stage. In this and the following chapter, the institutions, the processes, the problems, the controversies of this level of government now become the focal point of our consideration. Here we shall concentrate upon the cities.

In a world in which the truly staggering problems are international or at least national in scope, it is quite natural for local governments to receive but a minor share of the citizen's attention. Yet their activities are virtually all-pervasive in our daily lives: they operate our public school systems, furnish our water supply, provide police and fire protection, maintain sanitation services, administer social welfare and public health programs, regulate the use of property through planning and zoning, specify building and safety regulations, maintain streets and control traffic, license businesses and professions, maintain extensive legal records, provide parks, libraries, and recreational facilities—to name only a few examples. The bulk of these services are rendered quite unobtrusively; they become so much a part of the web of our social life that they are often not thought of as "government" at all. Nevertheless, for the very reason that they do affect our lives so closely, there are important policy issues at stake here and strong differences of opinion on how these governments can best serve our needs.

1. *The Nature of Local Government*

THE JUSTIFICATION FOR LOCAL SELF-GOVERNMENT.
A great many observers and theorists have speculated upon the merit of incorporating a strong system of local self-government, as distinguished from mere "government locally," into a political system. Some have even suggested that it is virtually essential to democracy or that, at the very least, it contributes significantly to the successful practice of democracy. Their specific claims as to these values are often legitimately subject to challenge, but many have real substance and warrant brief examination.

While those less enamored of local self-government have argued that it results in inefficiency, overlapping of functions, parochialism and short-sightedness, relatively high-cost services, a citizenry confused by long ballots, and unjustifiable inequalities in service between one jurisdiction and another, its proponents have countered not only with denials of some of these charges, but with an at least equally impressive list of advantages.

They contend, first, that such a system, being "closer to the people," is more representative and more directly responsible to the public. In this there is some truth. Rather obviously, a locally elected official—at least outside the larger cities—is likely to represent fewer persons. Realistically, however, closeness to the people has more to do with the public's attitude than with physical proximity. A government's responsibility to the people depends more on the voters' ability to fix either praise or blame clearly and to control officials through effective elections and a good party system than it does on localism alone. Thus a poorly organized government in which lines of responsibility are not clear to the voter, however local it may be, is not likely to be highly responsive to public wishes—even though that potential is present.

Closely related to this concept is the assumption that localized control of public affairs is somehow superior to that exercised over more remote units. Again this may be potentially true; such control may indeed be enlightened and valuable. On the other hand, the cry for local control may at times be simply a cloak for a refusal to deal with community needs or for the protection of special interests. One is entitled to question the surety of this benefit when he recalls that the notorious political machines of the past have existed, almost without exception, in local governments, and when he recognizes the very low voting turnout in local as compared to national elections. Yet these observations merely illustrate the fact that the local public may make what it wishes of its power of control.

It is further contended that local institutions constitute a "school of government," providing an opportunity for the citizen to get experience in public affairs at a level at which he can easily participate, as well as furnishing training for public officials who may later "step up" to service in larger governments. Popular participation, as we have indicated, does not tend in practice to be as great as in national politics, but the local level may still be a beginning point for many who ultimately become political activists. There are always a fair number of local officials who move on to state and national office. Is their local training likely then to be of value? In the handling of specific problems, it is probably useful only in limited degree; but the experience that is truly valuable in any governmental capacity is that gained through prolonged dealing with human beings in a political environment: some understanding of human motivations, an awareness of public attitudes toward government and authority, and a grasp of the art of reasonable compromise. It is of course true that the value of such local experience does depend to a considerable degree upon the type of unit in which one has served. Experience as a councilman in a major city is far different from membership on the governing board of a mosquito abatement district.

The defenders of local self-government have also commonly spoken of the so-called "laboratory concept," the theory that each local unit may readily experiment with new ideas in governmental organization and practices. An idea that proves successful may then be copied by others, but if a failure, that failure will be confined to one small unit. As a rule, the average local government has not been notably experimental nor given to radical innovations, and even when new ideas have emerged, they have not always been readily accepted elsewhere. Nevertheless, experiments *are* being tried continuously, and there is a vast amount of legislative copying. Whenever a governing body considers a proposed new policy or procedure, the first question raised is invariably: "Has anyone else tried this, and if so, what has been their experience?" For example, the direct primary spread across the nation largely as a result of such copying, and the same is true of both the commission and the council-manager plans of city government.

The existence of local self-government may serve as an effective counterbalance to tendencies in the direction of excessive centralization, although one's evaluation of this advantage will, of course, depend upon the extent to which he views centralization as a danger. Local minorities or special area interests may have a better voice under such a system, where certain local problems can be dealt with by officials who have a personal knowledge of them. It should be borne in mind that bigness in any type of human organization creates special problems of responsiveness to the persons the organization exists to serve. While it is certainly not always accomplished, there is at least the opportunity for a people managing their own local public affairs to achieve the sense of working cooperatively, the common pride and unity of purpose, the true feeling of community that is so readily lost in the mass society of which we are a part. And perhaps there is a case for some diversity of local institutions in a day when conformity is so much decried.[1]

COMPLEXITY OF AMERICAN LOCAL GOVERNMENT. To speak of the local "level" of government is to imply a kind of uniformity that does not exist in the United States. There are not only many different types of local government (see Table 14.1), but even those with similar

Table 14.1. *Governmental Units in the United States*

Type of Government	1962	1957 *	1952 *
Total	91,236	102,392	116,807
U.S. government	1	1	1
States	50	50	50
Local governments	91,185	102,341	116,756
Counties	3,043	3,050	3,052
Municipalities	17,997	17,215	16,807
Townships	17,144	17,198	17,202
School districts	34,678	50,454	67,355
Special districts	18,323	14,424	12,340

* Adjusted to include units in Alaska and Hawaii, which were reported separately prior to adoption of statehood for these areas in 1959.
SOURCE: U.S. Bureau of the Census, *Census of Governments: 1962*, Vol. I, *Governmental Organization* (Washington, D.C., 1963), p. 1.

labels often exhibit a bewildering multitude of internal variations. One region of the country differs from another in its local government pattern, and there is frequently variety even within a single state or county.

In the various nations of the world there are very considerable differ-

---

[1] *The best contemporary analysis of these theories, with special reference to rural local government, is* Roscoe C. Martin, Grass Roots (*University, Ala.: University of Alabama Press, 1957*). *The classic commentaries by Bryce and Tocqueville are still relevant. Recent treatments of decentralization, one favorable and one skeptical, are* Duane Lockard, The Politics of State and Local Government (*New York: Macmillan, 1963*), *pp. 44–56; and* James W. Fesler, *"Approaches to the Understanding of Decentralization,"* Journal of Politics, *27 (August 1965), 536–66.

ences in the freedom and scope of activity permitted local governments. At one extreme are the totalitarian countries, in which the central government ordinarily dominates local units almost completely. Less rigid are the many democracies that are unitary states, such as most of those in Western Europe. In these there is customarily a single uniform organizational structure with a fair amount of discretion left to the local governments, despite considerable direction and supervision from the central government, as well as a high degree of financial dependence. At the other pole lies the United States, where local self-government with a relatively high degree of independent discretion is a virtually unyielding political principle.

Yet with all its variety, local government in the United States does not consist of a series of totally separate entities but is an interrelated and quite interdependent system. Although it is obviously not possible to discuss each type of local government simultaneously, one cannot adequately understand cities without taking into account the counties in which they exist, or school districts without an awareness of the cities or villages with which they are identified. Even though they are legally independent, these separate governments often cooperate in services, raise money from the same sources (not infrequently collecting it for each other), and affect the same public. The individual citizen commonly lives within the jurisdiction of several local governments, with all of whose affairs, in addition to those of his state and the nation, he is supposed to be concerned.

Local governments in this country are further characterized by a rather remarkable degree of informality in their official proceedings. It is usually startling to the visitor from abroad to find private citizens arguing issues from the floor before a municipal council (not uncommonly addressing the mayor or councilmen by their first names). This rather free and easy give-and-take has its advantages but is by no means an unmixed blessing. The casual first-time observer is likewise struck by the great variety of problems coming before a local council and the apparently very minor nature of many of these. He will rapidly note, however, that what seems minor to an outsider is of vital importance to the citizen directly affected. It is of no small consequence to him whether his business is permitted to display a certain type of sign or whether his neighbor is allowed to keep chickens in his backyard.

LEGAL STATUS AND POWERS: CITY CHARTERS. Despite a relatively high degree of independence in practice, American local governments remain from a legal standpoint definitely subordinate to the state of which they are a part—"creatures of the state," as the courts are fond of

Figure 14.1. *The Citizen Supporting Various Governments*

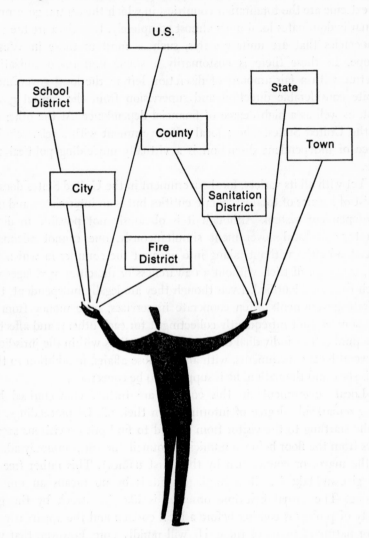

saying. They have no assured constitutional status, as do the states within our federal system. A local unit is given its existence by the state and technically could be abolished by it, although in the case of an important unit, the latter is rarely a practical possibility. If it can both create and abolish, presumably the state can do anything between those extremes in altering the structure, powers, and territory of local units. The "due process" and "equal protection" clauses of the national Constitution do not protect a local government in its relations with its state.

But there is usually, however, a real difference between legalism and actual practice. Most states permit local governments to operate within the framework of general state laws that allow a good deal of leeway. Many, though not all, give at least the cities the privilege of *home rule,* the ability to draft their own charters and govern under their provisions. Even such charters, however, must not conflict with general state law, and there are endless difficulties in determining the boundaries between "municipal affairs" and "matters of statewide concern." The courts have understandably never been able to make a clear-cut distinction, and have tended to resolve uncertainties in favor of the states. Some states have tried to lessen the diversity resulting from unfettered home rule by providing local governments with a choice of several types of charters, any one of which they may adopt without alteration. Within the framework of its authority, a municipality has extensive power to regulate both persons and property in the interests of public health, safety, welfare, and morals: this is the so-called "police power."

Enough is often at stake in the adoption of a charter or in the major alteration of an existing one to generate heated political contests. It is not uncommon for such campaigns to involve sizable expenditures of time and money and to create more widespread public interest than a general municipal election. In the success or failure of a charter movement, much often depends upon early planning and organization. The actual drafting of the charter, although a central task because of the necessity for working out detailed provisions that will satisfy most or all of the interest groups in the community, is strategically the least difficult.

Extensive efforts at educating the public are essential in order to build an awareness of need and an understanding of the issues. Sources of opposition, often involving, among others, a number of the existing office-holders and groups that feel they have a favorable position under the existing system, must be anticipated and neutralized wherever possible. Of fundamental importance, however, is the necessity for proponents at the beginning of their consideration (not later, as at the beginning of a campaign) to bring into the study and investigation process every organized group that can be persuaded to cooperate. Those who participate may not support the final product, though most are likely to, but it may be taken as virtually axiomatic that any group that feels itself left out will become suspicious and will ultimately fight the proposal—almost regardless of its provisions.

URBANIZATION. The transformation of the United States in a relatively short period of time from a nation of less than 3 million persons, almost entirely agricultural and concentrated on the eastern side of the Appalachians, to one of over 190 million, spanning more than a continent and dominated by industrialization, is one of the most remarkable stories of human history. For roughly its first century as a nation, the United States remained predominantly rural, but the change has been so swift that in 1960, approximately 70 percent of its population was urban.

Although in past years frequently underrepresented in both the Congress and most state legislatures, city voters have become a particularly potent force in presidential and gubernatorial elections. Urban majorities are quite capable of swinging the electoral votes of the large and critically important states. In fact, it can be argued that heavy majorities in a dozen metropolitan areas having no common regional interests can today decide the outcome of any presidential contest.

In many ways, however, our political institutions do not yet reflect the current urbanization of our country. As a result of the series of judicial decisions on reapportionment following *Baker* v. *Carr*, state legislatures have generally been redistricted on the basis of the "one man–one vote" principle, shifting numerical power to the urban and suburban areas. It will, however, be some time before the full effects of such changes can be assessed. Rural-dominated state legislatures have often ignored a number of urban needs and perpetuated the handicaps under which cities must operate. Those local governments that are predominantly rural (notably counties) frequently have significant financial advantages, particularly in state grants-in-aid and in state-collected, locally shared taxes. Moreover, our entire pattern of local government structure still reflects the day of a primarily rural society when distances were measured in terms of transportation by horse and buggy.

City governments today perform a multitude of public services, many not conceived of a generation or two ago, that are of vital significance in the daily lives of every citizen. Many are enterprises of tremendous size and scope: Chicago employs a total of 39,806 persons, more than the total number of state employees in any of 32 of the 50 states,[2] while New York City's current budget is larger than that of any state except California and New York State.[3] It may probably also be said that in the United States the greatest amount of experimentation and adaptation to changing circumstances in local government has occurred in the cities.

---

[2] *U.S. Bureau of the Census,* City Employment in 1965, *p. 7; same,* Public Employment in 1965, *p. 10 (Washington, D.C., 1966).*

[3] *U.S. Bureau of the Census,* City Government Finances in 1964–65 *(Washington, D.C., 1966), p. 56; same,* Compendium of State Government Finances in 1965, *p. 27 (Washington, D.C., 1966).*

2. Types of Municipal Government

No one should seriously suggest that the particular organizational form a city government adopts will either guarantee good government or inevitably result in bad government. Neither would it be rational to assume that organizational structure is of no consequence. One or another form may at least make responsible and effective government more readily possible.

Too often have local "reform" groups emphasized almost exclusively "efficiency" and "economy" as the bases for evaluating the quality of a government. These are doubtless desirable characteristics, but taken alone they are inadequate criteria. A sound evaluation must also include the government's responsiveness to the public will, its adequacy in determining that will, and its capability of satisfying public needs and desires. It is not true, as some have contended, that local government is merely an administrative machine, "just like a business." It does not deny the importance of efficient administration to recognize that there exists a very real measure of policy determination and official discretion. Social and political philosophy are *not* nonexistent factors in city government, particularly in the large municipalities, especially as functions such as housing, recreation, and welfare continue to increase.

The oldest and, if one includes all its variations, still the most common form of city government is the mayor-council system. This plan, which provides for an independently elected chief executive who is ordinarily not a member of the council and has no vote therein, is obviously basically similar to that with which we are familiar at the national and state levels. For purposes of convenient analysis it is customary to consider two versions, the "weak mayor" and "strong mayor" forms, although they do not in practice polarize that precisely. Many variations are possible. Sharply contrasting with these two forms are commission government, council-manager government, and the mayor-administrator plan.

WEAK MAYOR WITH COUNCIL. The weak mayor–council form, a link to earlier history, is usually composed of these elements (see Figure 14.2): a mayor, serving as the titular and formal head of the city government and theoretically as its chief executive, but possessing extremely limited powers over the administration; a council, combining legislative and administrative functions and usually divided into committees, each of which oversees certain administrative activities; several independently elected heads of administrative departments; a number of elective or mixed elective-appointive–ex-officio boards and commissions (for

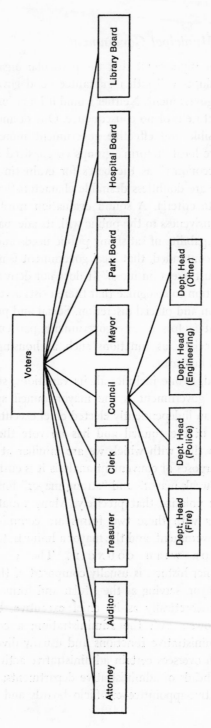

Figure 14.2. *Weak Mayor–Council Government*

Note: There exists a great variety of practice from city to city, and this chart illustrates merely one fairly typical organizational structure.

example, park or library boards), having extensive policy-making powers. Of the nonelective administrative officials, a few may be appointed by the mayor, but the bulk are likely to be selected by the council or its committees.

It is evident that under this system both policy making and administration are subdivided in many directions, making it extremely difficult for the citizen to know whom he can reasonably hold responsible for what. One of the most striking features is likely to be the almost complete lack of integration of the government as a whole. There is no single body or individual able to coordinate all activities, and not uncommonly various parts of what is intended to be a team are pulling in different directions. Chronic ignorance of the activities of other agencies often results in considerable duplication or overlapping. There is ordinarily no central budget agency that can weigh the relative needs of the various municipal functions and relate these to potential revenue. Even the council is frequently unable to allocate the budget funds effectively because it does not have complete jurisdiction over the independent boards and officials. For example, in one large city, the park board has its own police department and road maintenance crews separate from the rest of the city and maintains its equipment at higher cost through contract arrangements with private garages, even though service is available through the municipal garages. In another, each department issues its own annual report on its own terms; the bases for statistical data are not uniform and thus are rarely comparable. Because three different agencies deal with city financial records, an accurate overall picture is almost impossible to acquire.

In addition to his limited supervisory and appointing power, and ex-officio membership on numerous boards, the mayor under this system usually can recommend legislation and often has a limited veto power. Moreover, as a party leader he may exercise influence when his party has a council majority. Mayors who are vigorous and ambitious leaders have sometimes been successful in building public support for their programs through extensive appearances before community organizations, regular radio and television presentations, use of citizens' advisory commissions, and the like. These mayors may occasionally accomplish a good bit outside the strictly governmental framework, but at best they labor against considerable odds, at the same time enduring the irritation of being blamed by many citizens for all kinds of situations over which they actually have no control.

Support for the weak mayor-council form of government is normally less in the nature of advocacy than merely a defense of the status quo in those communities where the plan has long been in existence. This plan is today virtually never adopted by being written into a new charter, although it may be attractive to those who fear placing too much power in the hands of one person, a rather traditional American attitude. Proponents also contend that it is a highly democratic arrangement, since the largest possible number of officials are subject to election and thus presumably to popular control. The supposition is that there will be maximum popular participation, with more offices to be sought and to be voted for. Finally, there may be a sentiment, found occasionally in some segments of the business community and more often felt than verbalized, that it is desirable to keep government reasonably inefficient. A government that becomes notably efficient may expand its functions and thus its taxes, and the public might demand additional regulatory activity. In practice, however, most businessmen have been among the vigorous supporters of movements for the improvement of local government.

Many of the shortcomings of this system, such as lack of accountability and the absence of adequate coordination, have already been indicated, but additional criticisms may be noted as well. Experience has demonstrated repeatedly that it is less dangerous to concentrate power in the hands of one body, if it can be effectively held accountable, than it is to diffuse power so widely that in effect no one is accountable. It is not power itself that is dangerous, but irresponsible power. Democracy is not created simply by electing to office as many persons as possible; its essence lies in the public's ability to keep government responsible. Therefore those with top policy-making authority should certainly be subject to election and should in turn have complete responsibility for the entire government. In this way the voters can more adequately make their wishes effective.

Popular control of technical administrative positions through elections is generally a mirage. A long ballot is much more likely to frustrate than to encourage popular effectiveness. The public is simply in no position to judge qualifications for administrative jobs, or even the service rendered in them; barring a major scandal, it will merely reelect incumbents on the apparent theory that whether or not they knew anything about the job to start with, they must have learned something while holding it. Scandal or gross incompetence can be dealt with in elections, but judgment on mediocrity of performance or worse is not feasible. Everyone who is known in his neighborhood to be politically active or even to follow politics closely is quite used, on the day before an election, to a barrage of telephone calls coming from relatively well-informed and conscientious persons (those less concerned don't bother to call): "Who are these guys running for auditor and county surveyor? I don't know whether they ever saw a set of books or a transit. Who am I supposed to vote for? Say, why don't you just mark this sample ballot for me on these minor offices?"

When the voters are dissatisfied, it is usually impossible to make a complete change. Overlapping terms constitute one reason, but the people also tend to concentrate their energies on the mayor, who is a natural focal point of attention, while overlooking many others. "Bossism" has in fact tended to flourish under this form because of the possibilities for camouflage and the public's inability to effect change. Moreover, highly trained professional administrators are less likely to seek employment in such a city because of its frustrating organization and the lack of security of tenure.

STRONG MAYOR WITH COUNCIL. The inadequacies of the weak mayor-council system quite naturally led to attempts at modification and improvement, one of the most obvious steps being to make the office of mayor into that of a true chief executive. Under the strong mayor-council arrangement, he becomes the actual as well as formal head of the city government. Like the President in the national government structure, he has full responsibility for the entire administration and shares in the legislative process through recommendations, a veto power, and the various techniques of informal influence.

The council, in turn, confines itself more specifically to legislative functions, although any assumption that it is possible to separate completely legislative and administrative activities would of course be foolish. The council, however, has much broader responsibilities, for its legislative power is not shared with miscellaneous special boards and independent department heads. In a pure form, which rather rarely exists, the voters elect only the mayor and council; all department heads are then appointed by the mayor without the necessity of council confirmation (see Figure 14.3).

Does a city cease to be a strong mayor type if the controller is elected or if the council is required to confirm the mayor's appointments? The distinction is not easy to make, and if we examine any *actual* government of this type, it is likely to be something of a hybrid. If the mayor appoints *most* of the administrative officers and has centralized financial control, for example, the system is usually called strong.

In reverse, most of the arguments against the weak mayor-council plan are the advantages of the strong mayor-council organization. It provides for a unified and coordinated administration, with good opportunity for the use of professionalized personnel. Governmental structure is readily intelligible to the voter, whose task is made simpler and more effective by the short ballot. Perhaps most important is the opportunity for vigorous and responsible policy leadership. The mayor can be a meaningful focal point of public opinion; he can run on a definite platform and then take the lead in bringing it into effect. No other form provides this kind of leadership as

Figure 14.3. *Strong Mayor–Council Government*

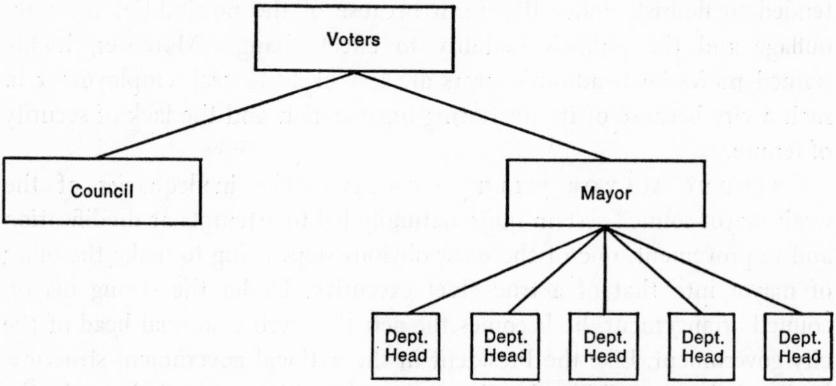

well. The strong mayor system is used in the bulk of the nation's largest cities, although it is by no means confined to the major population centers.

Among the criticisms of this plan, the previously mentioned fear of centralized power is prominent. In reality, however, the system has generally resulted in quite highly responsible government. It is also contended that under this arrangement the city is unlikely to get competent professional administrators because the chief executive, who makes the appointments, may often use them to pay election debts. Although this is quite possible, we should also remember that the mayor has a personal political stake in having good appointees, and that contrary to popular notions there is no necessary or even common contradiction between participation in practical politics and competence.

Finally, it is quite true that, as in any independent executive or "separation of powers" system, deadlocks between mayor and council may occasionally result. Most conflicts, however, are ordinarily resolved in some fashion—by compromise or by the overriding of a veto, for example. In general, the strong mayor-council plan, although certainly no panacea, at least provides the potential for excellent government if citizens really desire it and do their part.[4]

---

[4] For an interesting discussion of the role and success of some recent and contemporary big city mayors, see Seymour Freedgood, "New Strength in City Hall," Fortune

COMMISSION GOVERNMENT. The commission plan appeared during the latter stages of the era of corruption around the turn of the century, made famous by the group of writers known as the "muckrakers." It gained prominence after its successful use in the wake of the disastrous tidal wave of 1900 in Galveston, Texas, a city with a previously notorious reputation, and a number of communities then began to look upon it as a possible long-sought answer to the inadequacies of their existing governments. But it was not in fact a totally new idea, and there has been no pattern of commission government that has been strictly uniform in all details.

The commission plan involves a small governing body (the "commission"), usually composed of five members and possessing both individual and collective responsibility. As a group, the commissioners are a legislative body; as individuals, each is responsible for the administration of a major city function, for example, public safety, parks and recreation, public works. Legislation and administration are thus in the same hands. In most cities the mayor is elected separately, but in some he is chosen by the commission from among its members. In either case, although he has his vote and departmental duties as a commissioner, his powers as chief executive are ordinarily rather limited: as a rule, he has no veto and no extensive appointing power. He is the formal head of the city and presides over the commission; he usually heads one of the departments as well (see Figure 14.4).

Commissioners are most often elected from the entire city at-large on a nonpartisan ballot. In some cities candidates run for a specific position, whereas in others they merely indicate their candidacy for the commission. Even in the latter case there is usually a fairly widespread understanding as to whom the mayor, or the commission, as the case may be, will appoint to which portfolio. Although in theory the commissioners should be the only elected officials, not infrequently some such office as auditor or controller is also elective. Other administrative officers are appointed by the commission although, as might be expected, the usual custom is for the commission to ratify the recommendation of the commissioner under whose jurisdiction the office falls.

(*November* 1957), 156–57, 251, 264, *reprinted in* The Exploding Metropolis (*Garden City, N.Y.: Doubleday,* 1958). *Wallace S. Sayre's and Herbert Kaufman's* Governing New York City (*New York: Russell Sage Foundation,* 1960) *is a most useful study of the politics of the nation's largest city, and Robert A. Dahl,* Who Governs? (*New Haven, Conn.: Yale University Press,* 1961) *illuminates the potentialities for mayoral leadership in moderate-sized cities—in this case, New Haven, Connecticut. See also Edward C. Banfield,* Big City Politics (*New York: Random House,* 1965).

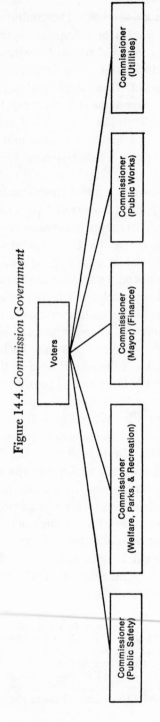

Figure 14.4. *Commission Government*

Note: The functional department organization indicated is simply a possible example and will vary from city to city.

While it may never have fully lived up to its initial promise, the commission plan does have certain advantages, at least in comparison with the weak mayor-council form widely prevalent when it first appeared. There is obviously a short ballot, and the government structure is easily understandable to the average citizen. All responsibility for city government is concentrated in the commission, and there is no possibility of deadlock between mayor and council. Because of the limited number of administrative departments, there should be reasonably good coordination of functions. Election at-large makes each commission member feel a responsibility to the voters of the entire city rather than to only one small district. In order to assuage public fears of excessive power in the hands of a small body, many cities operating under this plan incorporated into the system the initiative, the referendum, and the recall, devices that were beginning to be advocated strongly in this country at about the time of the inception of the commission plan.

Despite these relative advantages, the plan has evidenced a number of rather serious shortcomings. A several-headed executive may mean virtually no executive at all, for there is no one person responsible for the administrative functions of the entire city. The commission is responsible as a group to the public in regard to legislative matters, but to whom are the individual commissioners responsible for the administration of their departments? In theory, both to the commission as a whole and to the voters. Not surprisingly, however, there is a strong tendency for each department to come to be looked upon as a private preserve and thus for each commissioner to operate upon the principle of "You keep your nose out of my business and I'll stay out of yours."

The creation of a legislative body composed of the top-level administrators results in the almost complete elimination of the very necessary function of internal criticism. Those outside the government may of course continue to question or protest, but no commissioner wishes to irritate his colleagues by intervening in "their" affairs. He is also likely to be busy enough in his own department without concerning himself with supervision of the others. The problem is most striking in connection with the budgetary process, when commissioners as department heads submit budget requests to a legislative body of which they are the only members. No one should be astonished that this, too, tends to result in a kind of reciprocal back-scratching rather than any sort of effective budget planning, criticism, and balanced allocation.

If internal controls seem inadequate, how satisfactory is popular control? As already indicated, the commission plan with its clearly centered responsibility has been quite responsive to the popular will in regard to policy matters. But the public is no more able under this plan than under any other to pass judgment on anything except the very broadest questions of administrative performance. Therefore, commissioners are not likely to be elected or defeated on the basis of their administrative capacity or shortcomings. The original idea of some proponents that commissioners would be "cabinet-secretary type" department heads rather than operating officials has rarely worked out in practice.

Finally, it must be conceded that the mixture of individual and group responsibility too often provides an ideal arrangement for "buck-passing." Blame may readily be shifted from one department to the whole commission, thence to another department, and so on. Although the government is unified on paper, it is quite possible, from an administrative viewpoint, to have different departments moving in quite different directions.

At the time it was initiated, commission government represented in some senses definite progress, but it is not hard to see why its popularity was relatively short-lived. Its use has been most widespread among small and medium-sized cities, although some approaching the half-million population mark have utilized it as well. In one-party areas, where it has been rather commonly used, it may be argued that the commission plan spread influence and mitigated the threat of an unresponsive executive (as did provision for a weak governor unable to succeed himself). For a number of years there have been almost no new adoptions of the plan, and each year quite a few commission-governed cities change to another system. Although in several cities it has had a reasonably successful record, in many others an initial success deteriorated in later years, a development partially explainable by the fact that it commonly rode in on a reform wave that generated only a temporary high level of citizen interest and participation.

COUNCIL–MANAGER GOVERNMENT. Although it has been only little more than fifty years since the first experiments with the plan, the council-manager form of city government now serves more cities than any other type, if one classifies weak and strong mayor-council governments separately. It has, however, a somewhat curious geographic spread; it is heavily concentrated in a relatively few states that are for the most part not adjacent to each other, and it is almost nonexistent in certain others.[5] Then too, it is most prevalent in the small and middle-sized cities, and is

---

[5] *The following states have over 100 council-manager cities each: California, Florida, Maine, Michigan, Pennsylvania, and Texas. Indiana and Hawaii have none, while there is one each in Louisiana, North Dakota, and South Dakota.*

found at present in only 5 of the 27 cities above 500,000 population and in 13 of the 27 cities of the 250,000 to 500,000 class. Because of the steady growth and apparent success of this plan, we shall examine it here in detail.

The expansion of the council-manager type of government has been both rapid and sustained. Each year a sizable number of cities adopt it, and remarkably few subsequently abandon it. In its early years, the growth of a plan may be explained in part by the tendency to copy a new and attractive idea and by the zeal of those who may be promoting it, but continued growth and long tenure are certainly at least somewhat dependent upon consistently successful operation. The plan has long been the darling of most municipal reformers and is the "model" recommended by the National Municipal League, the leading national organization concerned with improvement of local government. It has also had strong approval from political scientists generally. In fact, the merits of the system had become near-dogma in some circles, and it has only recently been subjected to critical scrutiny.

The essence of the council-manager plan is the placing of all powers of policy making and the ultimate control of administration in the hands of the council, which hires a professional city manager to supervise the actual day-to-day operations of all municipal functions. There is an effort to restrict the council to the realm of legislation and over-all control and the manager to the technical side of administration. The mayor is normally selected by the council from among its members to serve as presiding officer and formal head of the city. There is thus no separation of powers or checks and balances between a legislative and an executive branch.

In its pure form only the councilmen are elected, and because they have complete responsibility, popular control is presumably maximized. The functional departments are directly responsible to the manager, the manager to the council, and the council to the voters (see Figure 14.5). Some proponents have compared the system (not always to everyone's liking) to the organization of a business corporation where the board of directors, acting on behalf of the stockholders, hires a general manager. Once drawn heavily from the ranks of engineers, managers today are far more likely to have professional training in public administration. Successful managers will not only move up the scale of compensation in the city where initially appointed, but tend to move from positions as assistant managers to managers of small communities and then on to the larger cities.

A city manager is expected to be chosen on the basis of training and competence. He is given authority to supervise and direct the entire city administration, to appoint and remove all department heads, to prepare the budget for the council's consideration, to investigate alternative courses of action on behalf of the council, and on the basis of such investigations to make policy recommendations to it. Both the manager and the department heads are employed on an indefinite tenure basis, making it possible to build a career in public service. The manager thus serves as long as he is satisfactory to the council; he is not under contract for a given period of years, as is, for example, the superintendent of schools. The professional organization of city managers, the International City Managers Association, has consistently taken the position that contracts would be undesira-

Figure 14.5. *Council–Manager Government*

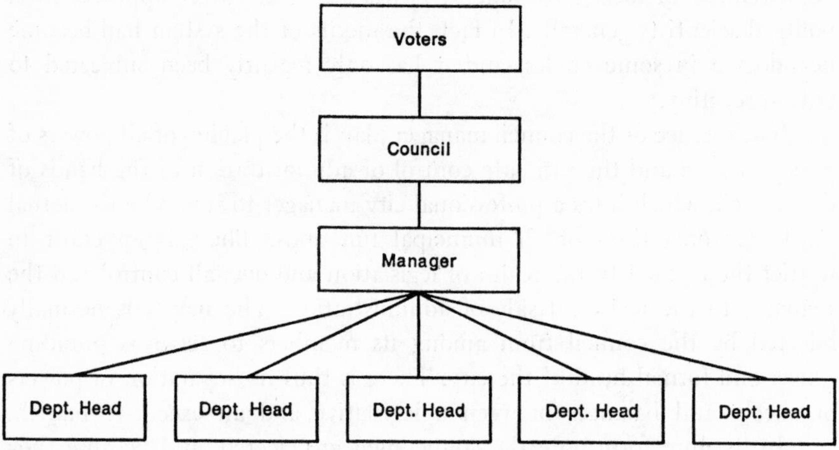

ble. It contends that a manager should prove his worth and should not attempt to stay in a community where he is no longer wanted; that no city should be put in the awkward situation, faced occasionally by school boards, of having to "buy out" remaining time on a contract.

The council maintains its full control not only through its power to appoint and dismiss the manager by a simple majority vote, but also through its power to pass all the ordinances and resolutions (subject to no veto) within which the administration must operate, through its power to investigate any aspect of the administration at any time, and through its complete power over finances. There is continuous close contact, both formally and informally, between the council and the manager. The manager is required to attend all council meetings (and usually some department heads are present also) in order to answer all questions and participate in an exchange of information, advice, and criticism. The council's normal action on new requests or proposals that come before it is to refer them to the manager, as the agent of the council, for study and recommendation. Because the council has complete control, it is less inclined to tie the manager's hands with a welter of complex regulations; the result is thus reasonable smoothness and flexibility of administration.

Advocates of the council-manager plan have claimed that it provides the maximum in public control and accountability, that it gives to the council more powers than it enjoys under any other form, and that it places the utmost emphasis upon competence in administration. Since a manager acts on its behalf, the council will wish to seek out the most able man it can afford to hire. He in turn, being held responsible for the actions of his department heads, should have every incentive to secure the most capable staff available.

Opponents of this form of city government have contended vehemently that putting full administrative authority in the hands of one man is dictatorial, undemocratic, and "un-American." Although this is an argument that obviously overlooks the actual dominance of the council, it plays upon natural fears and finds a ready response. If the essence of dictatorship is irresponsible power, the definition hardly fits this system, but subtler shades of concern may be expressed. There are those who fear that, whatever his relative legal status, the expert full-time manager will come to dominate the part-time council, whose members are not professionals in city government. Others feel that internal administrative relationships may be undemocratic under an all-powerful chief administrator or, to paraphrase the words of Robert V. Presthus, that internal oligarchy may be created to ensure external democracy.[6] While both of these conditions can occur, they are by no means a necessary or inevitable result, nor does experience indicate that they constitute a serious, widespread problem. A great deal unquestionably depends on the good sense and the training of those in the managerial profession.

Much the same could be said of yet another kind of danger, the possibility that overemphasis on technical efficiency alone may cause an administration to lose touch with the people it exists to serve. Citizens who have been used to the instant response and personal attention of a councilman from their district may easily find city hall remote and impersonal. The wise manager must keep in mind that statistics and logic are not a substitute for a genuine concern with the problems of the individual.

---

[6] *Robert V. Presthus, "Administrative and Community Leadership: a Reappraisal of the Council-Manager Plan," a paper presented at an annual meeting of the American Political Science Association, September, 1953.*

Over the years there has grown up a considerable body of assumptions about the most desirable practices in the operation of council-manager government, not a few of which have become encrusted with myths. It is assumed that a manager should be selected solely on the basis of professional qualifications, yet in practice there are likely to be a variety of additional considerations. For example, if there are a number of qualified men available, the council will quite naturally take into account how well each "fits" the community in terms of attitude, background, associations, and so on. Moreover, although such factors are supposedly taboo, a solidly Democratic council may not look with favor upon a Republican candidate, and in a heavily Protestant community there may be real hesitancy about a Catholic prospect. Such concerns are rarely mentioned publicly, but they can hardly be ignored.

It is probably a sound principle that a council should go outside the community in seeking a manager, although there will frequently be considerable pressure to hire someone of local prominence rather than an "outsider." Quite possibly, the local man may prove most satisfactory, but the odds are better on the outsider. It is not a question of lack of capability, but of other types of handicaps. No one can be active in the affairs of any community for several years without building up friendships and group associations that could constitute problems for a city manager. Furthermore, there is a natural tendency for every person to accept rather uncritically those circumstances with which he is intimately familiar as being normal and unchangeable. A newcomer, on the other hand, is free to take a fresh approach to problems without the initial involvement of entangling alliances.

It is a basic premise of the system that a manager is subject to dismissal by a majority of the council at any time, usually without any requirement for a public hearing or a statement of reasons. Yet practical political considerations often make this premise quite unrealistic. In a case of obvious misconduct there is no problem, but such a case is rare. Suppose, for example, that there has been no dishonesty, no malfeasance, no major public dissatisfaction, but the council is nevertheless dissatisfied with the kind of cooperation it has been receiving from the manager's office. Or suppose it may simply feel that, for the salary being paid, the city could secure a better-trained and more effective manager than the incumbent, who perhaps was hired by a previous council.

Such grounds for dismissing the manager or requesting his resignation are almost impossible to explain to the public. Nor is it possible to avoid giving reasons. "What are you trying to hide?" is the immediate cry. "Why are you afraid to tell the public the facts about the public's business?" But grounds of the type suggested are unconvincing. The normal reaction of press and public is: "What has he done wrong? What are the charges against him?" And if there has been no "crime," the automatic assumption is that an innocent man is being pilloried through some sort of sinister political deal. No matter how irrational the view, Americans seem conditioned to suspect the worst about their governments.

If he has been in the city for a fair period of time, the manager will have his own base of public support. Not only is there the natural sympathy for the "victim" and the backing of those who have a favorable impression from their occasional contacts at city hall, but the manager probably belongs to a civic club, a church, a veterans' organization, and numerous other groups, and has been active with the community chest and little league baseball. All those associated with these groups rise to his support. It is indeed a brash city council that, aware of the forces the manager could mobilize to contest the action, will remove him unless there are serious charges that can be made public if necessary. It may be added that, on a somewhat lesser scale, much the same situation often prevails in relation to the manager's ability to dismiss a well-known department head.

There are also other possible friction points in the relationship between council and manager. For example, the manager is generally expected to make policy recommendations to the council but not to go over the heads of that body by promoting in public a program that the council has not yet approved. Councilmen, on the other hand, presumably should have no contacts with subordinate administrative officials of the city (other than during a formal investigation) except through the city manager. It is also a basic canon of good managerial practice that a manager should deal with all members of his council on an absolutely equal basis. For this reason some insist that all contacts should be in meetings at which all members are present or at least free to be present. Yet no sensible person will expect this to be feasible. Councilmen will drop in at the city hall at various times and will of course discuss current problems and the day's events with the manager. Some are primarily interested in one thing and some in another. How can the manager be sure at the end of a week that he has given each member identical information on every topic and that he may not subsequently be charged with having withheld from one member what was told to others? This can be a very delicate matter in the case of a split on the council or of a minority antagonism to the manager (or perhaps to the manager plan itself). Can a manager really bring himself to speak with equal fullness and frankness to a member he knows to be personally antagonistic and who he suspects will leak information prematurely or twist it for use against him?

The position of city manager is expected to be strictly nonpartisan, and ordinarily managers carefully soft-pedal their personal partisan affiliations or attitudes. This is not as a rule a serious problem, although they may at times be put on the spot by demands for a recommendation on an issue that has strong partisan implications. Partly in order to protect this nonpartisan character of the office, most council-manager cities elect the council on a nonpartisan ballot, assuming that otherwise a shift in party control would almost automatically mean a change of managers (an assumption that has not proved necessarily true in places retaining partisan election).

Unfortunately, there have been those among the proponents of the plan who believe that "nonpartisan" means "nonpolitical" and contend that city governments should somehow be political eunuchs. Surely it is ludicrous to endeavor to divorce a political entity from politics: the real desideratum is effective and responsible politics, whether partisan or nonpartisan in nature. And although managers shy away from the term because of popular semantic difficulties, it is certainly true that in the proper sense a top-notch manager is a good politician. He must be an artist in such areas as the harmonizing of personal and group conflicts, the attractive advocacy of ideas and programs, the tactics of reasonable compromise, and the achieving of cooperative teamwork toward community goals.

Such a concept leads us, finally, to consider the long-standing controversy over the proper role of city managers in the development of policy, which is, after all, the heart of the governmental process. The old pat formula that the council makes policy and the manager carries it out was never in touch with reality and has long since been discarded as an accurate distinction. Yet it is assumed that the council has and should have the power of final determination of policy.

It must be remembered, first, that policy making is not merely the simple act of someone saying: "This we shall do." It is, as Clarence Ridley has remarked, "a slow, deliberate process involving a considerable period of time and a whole series of actions taken on the part of many people." [7] It is frequently true that a legislative body may be less an initiator of policy than a judge of alternative courses of action. Few would dispute that it is a proper function of a city manager to do the preliminary study and investi-

---

[7] *Clarence E. Ridley,* The Role of the City Manager in Policy Formulation *(Chicago: The International City Managers Association, 1958), p. 4. This booklet provides an excellent brief survey of theory and contemporary practice in this area.*

gation of any proposal, presenting to the council all the relevant facts and the alternative possible solutions to the problem. Beyond that, since the city hires him for his expertise and experience, it is logical to have him furnish his recommendation of the most desirable action.

Policy proposals arise from many sources—the individual councilmen, interest groups, citizens, and state government departments—but most of them come from the city's administrative departments. The manager is in a natural position to evaluate ideas and to recommend those he deems worthy. When he advocates a policy that the council is not ready to accept, it is his obligation to continue to carry out the council's present will even though he may disagree with it. He may, of course, try again to convince his council, but it is generally agreed that until his views have been adopted by it, he should not engage in public advocacy.

To what extent, then, can a manager properly become an active community leader on policy issues? In theory this is the prerogative of the mayor and council, but what if they do not in fact provide such leadership? There is no easy answer to fit all situations. Much will depend on community attitudes, the personality and prestige of the manager, the amount of initiative on the part of individual councilmen, and a host of other factors. To some extent managerial leadership is inevitable. Someone must lead, and he, as the full-time expert, is likely to be in possession of the most information. It can reasonably be argued further that he has a duty to support what he believes to be desirable. He may also have the longer-range vision, the concern for what the city will be or could be like ten or twenty years from now. It would be strange if he could not reflect this vision when civic clubs and other groups invite him to speak before them. But the effective manager tries as a rule to give all possible credit to the council, for it cannot in any case escape the responsibility. Ideally the entire process should be one of teamwork between the council and its professional adviser in serving the best interests of the city.[8]

The council-manager plan of government has often been the subject of lavish praise, even having been designated by one observer as America's greatest contribution to political science. No more than any other possibility is it a panacea for all municipal problems, but to voice reservations about some of the claims made on its behalf is certainly not to deny its

---

[8] *There is a great deal of periodical literature on this general subject. For discussions by some perceptive city managers, see especially C. A. Harrell and D. G. Weiford,* "The City Manager and the Policy Process," Public Administration Review, *19 (Spring 1959), 101–7; and Kent Mathewson,* "Democracy in Council-Manager Government," Public Administration Review (Summer 1959), 183–85.

overall success. The managers themselves in recent years have been doing a great deal of rethinking of traditional assumptions. The plan has not remained static; it has made its own transitions with changing times and new concepts of leadership and human motivation. If it can continue to adapt in this way, it is virtually certain to remain one of our major forms of local government organization.[9]

THE MAYOR–ADMINISTRATOR PLAN. With the dilemma over policy leadership under council-manager government freshly in mind, it is less difficult to understand the reluctance of the nation's largest cities to operate under the plan. Feeling an especially critical need for a political focal point and for effective leadership directly responsible to the voters, they have predominantly turned to the strong mayor-council plan.

Recently, however, several major cities, such as New York, Chicago, Philadelphia, and New Orleans, have adopted an arrangement pioneered in San Francisco and known variously as the mayor-administrator, mayor-manager, or general manager plan. It simply combines the city manager idea with the strong mayor plan, in an attempt to benefit from the advantages of both. The elected mayor remains the political and administrative head of the city, but he appoints a professional manager as his second-in-command for administrative matters. In many of these cities the manager, ordinarily serving at the pleasure of the mayor, has most of the customary powers, such as general supervision of administrative operations, preparation of the budget, and appointment of many department heads (see Figure 14.6).

Details of organization and procedure under the mayor-administrator system vary considerably from one city to another; in fact, its proponents claim this very flexibility as one of its most important characteristics.[10] This plan, too, is certain to encounter its share of problems—for example, in harmonizing the complex relationships between council, mayor, and manager. Except in the largest communities, if not there as well, it is frequently difficult to convince the voters of the desirability of paying salaries to what

---

[9] *Two interesting and useful publications based on studies in Florida, a state with a large number of council-manager governments, are the following: Gladys M. Kammerer, et al., City Managers in Politics: An Analysis of Manager Tenure and Termination (Gainesville, Fla.: University of Florida, Social Service Monograph No. 13, Winter 1962); and Gladys M. Kammerer, et al., The Urban Political Community (Boston: Houghton Mifflin, 1963). The latter consists of intimate case studies of eight manager communities.*

[10] *For a good summary of contemporary practice, by one who advocates the idea, see Wallace S. Sayre, "The General Manager Idea for Large Cities," Public Administration Review, 14 (Autumn 1954), 253–58. There is a rejoinder by John E. Bebout, "Management for Large Cities," Public Administration Review, 15 (Summer 1955), 188–95.*

appear to them to be two chief executives, but this concern would doubtless be eased by the example of successful operation in other cities. To
date, experience with this system is still too limited and of too short
duration to warrant prophecy, but there is no question that the mayor-
administrator plan is an established feature of the municipal landscape or
that it has real potential for the effective government of large cities. (For a
summary of forms of government, see Table 14.2.)

A number of recent studies of the relationship between the social and
economic characteristics of a community and its form of government

Figure 14.6. *Mayor–Administrator Government*

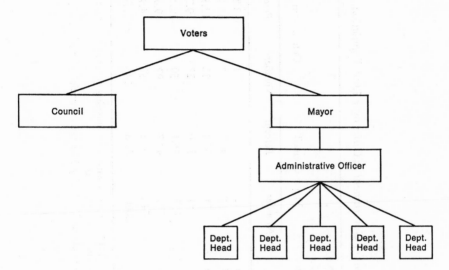

provide much food for thought. Council-manager government, for example, has been most widely accepted in middle and upper class suburban
residential communities. Banfield and Wilson point out that "good government," defined as efficient, honest, and businesslike government, is an
automatically popular theme of the white Anglo-Saxon Protestant middle
class.[11] Other investigators summarize the patterns relative to the three
basic types of city government as follows: ". . . white, Anglo-Saxon, Protestant, growing and mobile cities are highly likely to be manager cities;
ethnically and religiously diverse but nonmobile industrial cities are highly
likely to be mayor-council cities. The commission form is associated with

---

[11] *Edward C. Banfield and James Q. Wilson,* City Politics *(Cambridge, Mass.:
Harvard University Press, 1963), chap. 13.*

Table 14.2. *Forms of Government in Cities over 5,000 Population, 1965*

Population Group	Total No. of Cities	Total No. of Cities in Table	Mayor-Council		Commission		Council-Manager	
			Number	Percent	Number	Percent	Number	Percent
Over 500,000	27	26	20	76.9%	1	3.8%	5	19.2%
250,000 to 500,000	27	27	11	40.7	3	11.1	13	48.1
100,000 to 250,000	96	96	34	35.4	12	12.5	50	52.0
50,000 to 100,000	232	227	84	37.0	22	9.7	121	53.3
25,000 to 50,000	476	462	167	36.1	50	10.8	244	52.8
10,000 to 25,000	1,165	1,105	538	48.7	99	9.0	468	42.4
5,000 to 10,000	1,171	1,146	746	65.1	58	4.9	344	30.0
All cities over 5,000	3,189	3,089*	1,600	51.8	243	7.9	1,245	40.3

* Not included in this table are Washington, D.C., 13 cities with town meeting government, 19 with representative town meeting government, and 11 other cities for which no information was obtained.

SOURCE: *The Municipal Year Book 1966* (Chicago: International City Managers Association, 1966), p. 90.

declining population, low mobility, a low white-collar composition and a low educational level, and low ethnic and religious diversity." [12]

3. *Municipal Politics: Lawmaking and Elections*

In essence, politics is politics no matter what the level or location; it is the variety of detail that provides much of the fascination for the interested observer. Local politics has its special environment and its own distinctive characteristics. The politics of local lawmaking and the politics of the varied local electoral systems therefore deserve close examination. In the interest of clarity, we shall study local lawmaking primarily by focusing upon the city council, although much of what will be said is substantially true of many other local governing bodies as well.

CITY COUNCILS. The councils themselves exhibit tremendous variety in size, organization, and procedure, depending partly upon the size of the city and even more upon the form of government. In general, they tend to be small in council-manager and commission cities (usually 5 to 9 members) and considerably larger in the mayor-council (especially the weak mayor) form. A few meet daily; most meet weekly or biweekly. The position in a few of the largest cities is considered full-time and is compensated at least approximately on that basis, but the overwhelming majority of councilmen give only part of their time and receive very modest compensation, if any (often simply a small monthly sum designed to cover expenses). This situation is significant, because as a rule, membership on councils is thereby virtually restricted to retired persons or to those operating their own businesses or professions—that is, to those who are reasonably free to arrange their time to meet the demands of the office. The number of formal meetings is deceptive in this regard, for the average councilman must spend many hours each week in addition to council meetings in consultation with other city officials, in special council meetings or "study sessions," in meetings of community organizations, in listening to and discussing with constituents.

The larger councils frequently use a committee system similar to that in national and state legislative bodies, but most councils act as a whole on all matters. Procedures tend to be relatively informal on the surface, although there are definite steps and requirements for the handling of

---

[12] Robert R. Alford and Harry M. Scoble, "Political and Socioeconomic Characteristics of American Cities," *in* The Municipal Year Book 1965 (*Chicago: International City Managers Association,* 1965), p. 95.

legislation. Since a council meets on a regular periodic schedule rather than in "sessions" like a state legislature, its business continues when necessary from meeting to meeting and may occasionally "hang fire" for quite a period of time.

The latter situation is not uncommonly a source of much unrealistic criticism of city councils by individuals paying only spasmodic attention to their activities. Mr. Brown, for example, may appear as an observer at a meeting one night and be quite dismayed at hearing what sounds to him like a very important ordinance passed in fifteen seconds without discussion and without a dissenting vote. His outraged "letter to the editor" attacks this thoughtless tampering with the very lives and well-being of the community's citizens. What Mr. Brown does not realize is that he saw only one segment of a lengthy process in which the final roll call was but a ratification ceremony. That bill had been introduced perhaps six months earlier, worked over at length by the administrative officers concerned, approved by the city attorney, discussed and argued informally on endless occasions by the councilmen, discussed repeatedly with interested community groups, and debated by the council and subjected to a public hearing at its previous meeting. Having perhaps been altered in a number of ways at each stage of this process and having been finally agreed upon by all, the bill was enacted into law at the session Mr. Brown attended.

Of course not all measures achieve unanimity, and there may be strong words before the final vote is cast. Yet there is another frequently heard criticism that there are too few split votes. This does not necessarily mean that the council is a rubber stamp. In a five-member council, for example, each member's vote is crucial, and he is in an extremely exposed position. He does not have the degree of relative anonymity of a member of a legislature of 50 to 500 members. Although they may disagree, the council members must work together closely and continuously, and there is usually a strong desire to iron out the differences on a bill harmoniously if possible. Therefore, great effort will be exerted to persuade a member or to modify the bill to meet objections; if the effort is successful over a period of time, the end result may be a unanimous vote. Obviously, there will be some issues in which the differences cannot be resolved, and then there will be a split vote or no action at all. It must be remembered also that of the total number of measures considered by any legislative body, only a small fraction are highly controversial. Moreover, on many issues where there are differences, the disagreement is not on the need for the legislation but on details or the approach to be chosen. And such matters are readily subject to negotiation.

One of the assumptions of democratic government is that public business will be transacted in public, despite the many headaches that this may entail. Yet no council can realistically expect to do everything in the course of its periodic formal meetings. Where, then, can the line be drawn? Shall we simply say that every official action must be taken in public meeting? This sounds reasonable, but in practice it may mean, as it has in some communities, that everything on the agenda is discussed and concluded in an informal "pre-session" meeting, the public meeting becoming just a time to "make everything legal." That this is no merely academic question but a thorny public issue is evidenced by the fact that a number of states have passed legislation prohibiting local governing bodies from holding any but public meetings.[13]

Although conducting business in public does not mean that private citizens are likely to appear at a budget "work session" in the manager's office, for example, it does mean that the press at least must be notified in advance of any time that the councilmen may sit down together. Nevertheless, such a legalistic approach to the problem has side effects that may become ludicrous, especially if the community harbors a suspicious press. If councilmen B, C, and E have lunch together, have they held a "secret meeting?" If councilmen A and D meet by chance in a bank lobby and discuss a current problem for ten minutes, have they acted improperly? Such examples of circumstances in which questions have been raised are not extreme. Clearly, the principle of public action is basically correct, but there must of necessity be primary dependence upon the spirit in which the legislators act, not upon fine legal distinctions.

The thoughtful observer at a council meeting may also ponder certain other seemingly incidental factors that strongly influence the process of legislation. He may be impressed, for example, by the significance of precedent. Time and again the council will hear from a citizen a plea that does not in itself appear to be unreasonable, but that calls forth an immediate expression of official concern: "If we permit you to do this, we will have no logical grounds for refusing a mass of related requests, and the whole regulation will break down." He may also note the extremely important role of the city attorney. Because the council must always be certain to act properly within its legal framework, the advice of the attorney is sought at every turn. It is not surprising that his legal interpretations are not merely a protection to the council but have a tremendous

---

[13] *Property transactions or personnel questions are sometimes excepted from this requirement.*

influence on the nature of legislation as well. Finally, there is the omnipresent bearing of financial considerations upon policy, a factor for all governments, of course, but more crucial the smaller and tighter the budget. What is good public policy is always being modified by what is financially possible.

COUNCILMEN AND CITIZENS. There are certain special circumstances of the environment within which the local legislator must function, circumstances vital to a realistic understanding of local politics but little recognized outside the circle of officeholders themselves. Again, not all of these are exclusively local, but if not, they are peculiarly evident at that level. For one thing, the local legislator must continually work with his constituents close at hand. By contrast, the congressman and the state legislator are quite remote. True, the citizen may never attend a council meeting unless he has some special request to make, but should he have a problem in any way related to the city government, it is a fairly simple matter to stop at the councilman's home or to address him at great length by telephone without the unpleasantness of a toll charge. The practical issues of day-to-day city administration, such as building regulation or street repairing, are very close to the citizen when he is personally affected. In every community, however, there are a few people who call their councilman with irritating frequency, while for most it is an extremely rare occasion. Therefore, unless the councilman is very careful to maintain a sense of balance, it is all too easy for him to assume that he is hearing the voice of the people when what he hears is actually only a vocal minority.

Offsetting the prevalence of pressure from individual citizens is the fact that in most localities organized pressure groups play a somewhat lesser role than is true at the national or state level. They are by no means nonexistent, but with the possible exception of the largest cities, they are not so highly organized for the purpose. Of course most local pressure groups, like the Chamber of Commerce, the Labor Council, or the American Legion, shy away from having such a term applied to their activities, though they are happy to have it said that they are influential forces in community affairs.

Furthermore, there are some individuals in every community whose opinions carry more weight than others. These are persons like prominent businessmen, church officials, and others who are highly respected in the community and can be said to be part of its "power structure." By virtue of their prestige, they often exert considerable political influence.

In recent years political scientists have devoted increasing attention to the study of political influence and the analysis of community power structures [14] in order to understand how things really get done in the political realm, as distinct from the way it may appear on an organization chart, though it should not be assumed that the two are necessarily completely at odds. Influence is defined in Banfield's words as the "ability to get others to act, think, or feel as one intends." [15] A local leader who has this particular ability can be a force in the affairs of his government even though he holds no political office.

A central problem for the local legislator is the necessity of performing a political role in a nonpolitical or even antipolitical environment. The average American has been raised in an atmosphere of antagonism to politics and political parties, automatic suspicion of government, and a definite double standard applied to government and business. "Cartoon" stereotypes of the politician of eighty years ago persist with remarkable tenacity. Strangely, in a country that prides itself on being one of the world's great democracies, there is a common notion that politics is at best a necessary evil rather than an essential part of the life of a free people. The position of the "independent" in politics is often still held up as an ideal.

These attitudes reflect strongly upon local government, there being a frequent assumption that while politics is perhaps inevitable at the other levels, it should somehow be possible to run a local government on a "higher," nonpolitical plane. We see here again the curious idea that local government is purely administration, that no policy issues or discretion are involved. When conflicts *do* arise, the irritation of such persons is thus compounded.

Rather than making political decisions on a political basis, many a citizen prefers to follow the "good man" theory. Of what importance is the candidate's political philosophy, they ask, or his stands on specific issues? Let us simply be sure to elect "good" men to office and they will do the "right" thing. Such unbelievable naïveté about public affairs continues to be voiced by otherwise intelligent citizens. If the determination of who is a "good" man is based solely on whether he is kind to his mother and

---

[14] *The literature is extensive. An excellent beginning could be made with the following:* Edward C. Banfield, Political Influence (New York: The Free Press, 1961); Dahl, op. cit.; Roscoe C. Martin, Frank J. Munger, et al., Decisions in Syracuse (Bloomington, Ind.: Indiana University Press, 1961); Sidney Verba, The Small Group and Political Behavior (Princeton, N.J.: Princeton University Press, 1961); Robert Presthus, Men at the Top: A Study in Community Power (New York: Oxford University Press, 1964); and Robert E. Agger, Daniel Goldrich, and Bert E. Swanson, The Rulers and the Ruled: Political Power and Impotence in American Communities (New York: Wiley, 1964).

[15] Banfield, Political Influence, *p. 3.*

doesn't kick his dog, this is likely to have little to do with the city's program of urban renewal. Furthermore, the "good man" theory implies that all proposals are either right or wrong, but if that were so, almost anyone could decide on them. The tough issues are those in which both (or several) sides are right, though often on quite different grounds.

This viewpoint is indicative of several very real differences between the "insider" and the "outsider" in politics. The officeholder is inevitably in possession of much more complete and detailed information on a given issue than is likely to be possible for any private citizen. There may even be times, though they are rare, when he is forced to take action on the basis of information that cannot be made public, either in fairness to individuals concerned in a personnel action, for example, or when the information is reasonably conclusive but not provable, perhaps because of the refusal of sources to be identified.

The "outsider" possesses the great luxury of free criticism and of considering an issue solely from his own standpoint. As a consequence, he often finds it virtually impossible to conceive how anyone but a fool could think differently. But the man behind the council table does not have this luxury. He has an obligation to look at all sides and to consider all implications of a question. More than that, his responsibility does not terminate with the conclusion of argument—he must vote. He must vote knowing that the issue is not black and white, knowing that there is justice in many of the contentions of the other side, aware that all the facts may not yet be known, conscious of his own fallibility, wishing often that a decision could be postponed, and certain that many people will be unhappy with the outcome. Yet vote he must, and on his vote may ride the decision.

Many an "outsider" is prone to speak scornfully of politicians as "fence-straddlers." In fact, however, every novice legislator learns rapidly, and often the hard way, that it is most unwise to commit oneself to a proposal without investigation. For example, Mr. Black appears at the home of the new councilman with a suggestion for city action, which he paints in glowing terms. It sounds eminently reasonable, and since he can see no flaws, the councilman agrees to support the proposal. But when it is made public, he is astounded to find the council besieged by numerous groups pointing out potential dire results that had not entered his mind. Shall he go back on his word, or vote for something he now realizes to be undesirable? It is an axiom of politics that even the most innocuous-appearing issue will become unbelievably complex. In simplest terms, this is why the normal reaction of every legislator to a new proposal is in essence: "That sounds interesting. Let me think it over and check into all the angles." And the "outsider" departs muttering: "What angles? Anyone can see that this is a good idea. Why do all these politicians have to be fence-straddlers? Why can't they take a stand on something?"

ELECTIONS AT-LARGE OR BY WARDS. With very few deviations, all our national and state elections follow the plurality-winner principle, and single-member legislative districts predominate. Local governments, however, provide a much greater variety of practices. The particular kind of electoral system in use conditions the nature of the legislative body to some degree, and greatly influences the character of campaigning. Campaigns for local office also vary greatly depending on the size of the unit and on the form of government. In some small communities it may be a quite informal and inexpensive process, whereas in a large city, where the political stakes are high, it may be a major campaign with all the trappings. The position of mayor in a big city is often considered a major prize, and it is not uncommon for a man to leave Congress or a state legislature to seek the office. Mayor Lindsay of New York is perhaps the best known recent example.

With rare exceptions, independently elected mayors are chosen on a straight plurality basis; it is the council elections that furnish the variety. Election by wards or districts of a city is the most common arrangement in mayor-council cities, and especially so in the larger ones, but it is used relatively seldom in commission cities and in less than one-fourth of the council-manager cities. It has all the advantages and disadvantages of district systems at other levels. Primarily, of course, it does guarantee representation of the various geographic areas of a city, and to the extent that different sections have special interests, they will probably thus have a voice. The voter's task is simplified in two ways: he need choose only one representative, and there is at least theoretically a better chance that he will know the candidates.

There are, however, a number of important objections. Ward election tends to make the councilman primarily concerned with "taking care of his district" rather than with the welfare of the city as a whole. The two are certainly not always in conflict, but the difference in viewpoint may be important. Often related to this is the "errand boy" concept of the job of the councilman, an assumption that he is a handyman for his constituents to a greater extent than he is a policy maker for the city. There is also a tendency for each councilman to become a minor czar in his own district by virtue of the practice of other councilmen deferring to the wishes of the individual member on matters affecting only his district. Finally, there are the familiar tendencies to gerrymander and to fail to readjust representation as the ward population changes, tendencies that frequently result in lopsided control of the council by a party or other group and grossly distort the actual popular vote. These practices are far better publicized at other levels, but have often been used in local government with even less restraint. (The Supreme Court's decision in *Baker* v. *Carr* and *Reynolds* v. *Sims,* though addressed specifically to fair representation in state legislatures, have stimulated suits for correction of municipal council systems that violate the principle of equality of representation, and in a number of states the courts are affirming the "one man–one vote" rule applied to local governments.)

In view of these objections, it is not surprising that many cities have turned to electing their councils at-large. The at-large system necessitates relatively small councils, and since each member is responsible to the entire city, it is expected that he will give primary consideration to citywide problems. As a result, however, sectional interests may feel that they have lost an effective voice. Also, although gerrymandering is obviously ended, dominance by one faction is not. An at-large election can readily become a "winner-take-all" affair when one full slate of candidates competes with another slate. Minority or independent candidates have virtually no chance. Moreover, one result of at-large elections, especially where they are also nonpartisan, is probably to increase sharply the influence of the press and other mass media.

Various attempts have been made to remedy these difficulties. One common practice, which may be of limited effect, is to provide that roughly half of the council be elected in alternate elections, thus preventing a complete turnover. Some communities have tried a mixed system in which one councilman is elected from each ward and several other members are elected at-large. This method may provide the advantages of each system, but it perhaps provides the disadvantages of each as well. It is further possible to have candidates nominated by districts and elected at-large, sometimes permitting each district to nominate two candidates in the primary, with the voters of the whole city choosing one from each district in the general election (see Table 14.3).[16]

PROPORTIONAL REPRESENTATION. A system that claims to remedy most of the defects of either ward or at-large election is that of

---

[16] *A very interesting analysis of the effect of electoral systems on electoral competition in 24 of the nation's largest cities may be found in Charles E. Gilbert and Christopher Clague, "Electoral Competition and Electoral Systems in Large Cities,"* Journal of Politics, 24 (May 1962), 323–49.

Table 14.3. *Type and Method of Councilmanic Elections in Cities over 5,000 Population*

Form of Government or Population Group	Number of Cities Reporting	Type of Election (% reporting cities)		Number of Cities Reporting	Method of Election (%)		
		Partisan	Nonpartisan		At large *	By Ward	Combination of Ward & At-large
Form of government							
Mayor-council	1,533	51%	49%	1,543	44%	31%	25%
Commission	239	39	63	236	95	5	0
Council-manager	1,228	16	84	1,127	74	13	12
Town meeting	26	54	46	25	96	0	4
Rep. town meeting	21	24	76	21	86	14	0
Population group							
Over 500,000	26	31	69	26	42	27	31
250,000 to 500,000	26	19	81	27	67	7	26
100,000 to 250,000	95	36	64	94	67	16	18
50,000 to 100,000	231	32	68	229	55	20	25
25,000 to 50,000	468	31	69	465	65	18	17
10,000 to 25,000	1,102	35	65	1,089	64	19	17
5,000 to 10,000	1,111	40	60	1,122	60	25	15
All cities over 5,000	3,059	36	64	3,052	62	21	17

* Included are 56 cities in which councilmen are nominated by wards but all are elected at-large.

SOURCE: *The Municipal Year Book, 1966* (Chicago: International City Managers Association, 1966), p. 95.

"proportional representation." PR elections are the standard pattern in several of the world's other democracies, but the actual method may vary. Although only a few of our cities operate PR elections, the Hare, or single-transferable-vote, system is the one ordinarily used here. The basic purpose of a PR election is to provide a legislative body that mirrors as accurately as possible the voting elements of the population. Thus, if local party A polls 35 percent of the vote, it should have roughly 35 percent of the seats on the council; if party B receives 28 percent of the vote, it should have 28 percent of the seats, and so on.

Under the Hare system the citizen votes by numerical preference on the ballot: first, second, third choices and so on, as far as he wishes. The method is not complicated, but many find the counting system complex. In the central count the first step is to determine the "quota"—that number of votes that will guarantee election. As a simple example, if 10,000 votes are cast in the election and 5 seats are to be filled, any candidate with at least 2,001 votes is declared elected. Perhaps only one reaches the quota on the first count. He has 2,845 votes, and therefore 844 of these are excess votes that are of no value to him and would be a waste as far as the individuals casting them are concerned. Consequently, 844 of the votes for him are selected at random, and then transferred to those voters' second choices. If a second candidate now has the quota, he too is declared elected. If not, the candidate with the lowest number of votes is then dropped, and his votes are transferred to the second choices of those who had voted for him. The process goes on in this way until the required number has been elected.

Although it may appear unwieldy at first glance, long experience in cities both large and small has indicated clearly that the system will do what it claims—mirror the constituency with great accuracy. Its proponents claim many advantages: it makes the council truly representative; it guarantees both minority representation and majority control (if there is a majority in the community); it eliminates gerrymandering and other bad features of the other systems; it ends the need for, and thus the effort and expense of, primaries; it makes for cleaner campaigns since A does not run against B and in fact wants his second choice votes; it therefore emphasizes issues and principles in a campaign.

Opponents do not deny that a council elected by PR will reflect the composition of the community. Their dispute is essentially over the desirability of constructing the council on this sort of foundation. It means almost inevitably, they say, coalition governments and thus probably weak leadership. They feel that it has a splintering effect because it tends to give too much voice to minority parties and racial or religious blocs. Moreover, each representative may tend to be extreme and immoderate because he represents a constituency of people who all think alike, rather than a diverse one. Since PR tends to weaken party organization control, both major parties have often opposed it. In a number of cities where it has been given a fair and reasonably long trial, PR has been successful, but it has almost invariably remained controversial.[17]

One further variation, also designed to ensure some minority representation, has appeared lately in a few places. This is the method of "limited vote" being tried at present in Philadelphia. It simply permits the voter to cast one or two less votes than there are seats to be filled. For example, if there are 7 seats up for election, he might be allowed to vote for 5. Thus minorities, with a bit of organization, can be certain of not being left completely out in the cold: If a sufficient number of minority party voters cast "bullet votes," all voting for only one candidate, they simultaneously increase his vote and reduce the possibility that other candidates (who would otherwise be aided by the minority voters' other four votes) might edge him out. In practice, however, this system is likely to aid only the smaller of the two major parties in a given city, rather than a number of minority parties.

PARTISAN VERSUS NONPARTISAN ELECTIONS. Finally, let us examine briefly the long-standing controversy over the relative merits of partisan and nonpartisan elections at the local level. The movement for nonpartisan local elections was a part of the municipal reform effort around the turn of the century, and most of the doctrine has remained unchanged. There is again the familiar argument that local governments are less concerned with social policy than with efficient administration. Party considerations are therefore presumably irrelevant. As the old clichés go: "Is there a Democratic way of laying sidewalks and a Republican way of building sewers?" [18] Such statements blithely overlook the fact that

---

[17] *On this subject, see Ralph A. Straetz,* PR Politics in Cincinnati *(New York: New York University Press, 1958); and Belle Zeller and Hugh A. Bone, "The Repeal of PR in New York City: Ten Years in Retrospect,"* American Political Science Review, 42 *(December 1948), 1127–48. The most comprehensive analysis is Enid Lakeman and James D. Lambert,* Voting in Democracies: A Study of Majority and Proportional Electoral Systems *(London: Faber and Faber, 1955). There has been little recent writing in the United States on PR. A brief exposition by a leading proponent is George H. Hallett,* Proportional Representation: The Key to Democracy *(New York: National Municipal League, 1940). A vigorous opposing case is made by F. A. Hermens,* Democracy or Anarchy? A Study of Proportional Representation *(South Bend, Ind.: University of Notre Dame, 1941). See also the same author's* The Representative Republic *(Notre Dame, Ind.: Notre Dame University Press, 1958), pp. 201–10.*

[18] *There are both Democratic and Republican versions of the answer to the intendedly rhetorical question, "Is there a Democratic way and a Republican way of putting out fires?" The Democrats' answer is that a Democratic fireman will save the*

sidewalks and sewers are conveniently cited to win an argument, whereas there are many other examples of municipal activity where policy issues are much sharper. In any case, the argument continues that even if the major parties do represent significant cleavages at the national or state level, they rarely stand for much at the city level. This may or may not be true in any given community, but it is certainly not necessarily the case.

Probably the most significant arguments are to the effect that: (1) local issues should be decided on their merits, and the injection of national party loyalties into the picture merely confuses and misleads the voter; (2) nonpartisan elections may make it possible for a well-qualified member of the minority party in the community to be elected, when he would be unlikely to stand a chance in a party contest; and, related to the first two, (3) on a nonpartisan council those representing a minority viewpoint may often secure the passage of useful measures that, on a partisan council, the majority might feel compelled to defeat for strictly party reasons.

Defenders of partisan elections insist that not only are there important policy issues, but that knowledge of a candidates's party orientation is a far more significant guideline to the voter than such matters as the candidate's occupation, which can frequently appear on the ballot now. The larger the city, the greater the probability that information on party affiliations is of major importance. More often than not, it is claimed, nonpartisan elections are so in name only, with both parties engaging in behind-the-scenes endorsements and maneuvering. Such elections may also be a façade behind which special interests may get what they want from the city without having to be responsible at the polls. In fact, experience in many cities indicates that when party government is removed, it is replaced by pressure group government. Thus in some cities that have nonpartisan elections, a candidate's success is heavily dependent upon endorsement by, for example, the Labor Council or the Chamber of Commerce. It is a real question whether it is more desirable to be responsible to these groups than to a political party.[19]

It is impossible to determine absolutely which system is better when there is obviously so much room for reasoned difference of opinion. The choice will depend somewhat on the nature, size, and traditions of a community, and no doubt on its form of government as well. Beyond these

---

baby first, while a Republican fireman will save the grand piano. The Republican answer assures us that a Democratic fireman will give priority to saving the bottles of liquor.

[19] For an interesting study based on nonpartisan city elections in California see Eugene C. Lee, The Politics of Nonpartisanship (Berkeley, Calif.: University of California Press, 1960). See also Charles E. Gilbert, "National Political Alignments and the Politics of Large Cities," Political Science Quarterly, 79 (March 1964), 25–51.

considerations, the choice becomes a matter of personal preference and judgment as to which type of election is more democratically responsible. The real objective is a clear-cut separation of municipal issues so that the voter may make intelligent choices directly relevant to the local situation. Given the right circumstances, this may be accomplished under either partisan or nonpartisan elections, but it is assuredly not guaranteed by either.

4. Conclusion: Doctrine and Practice

For many of the matters discussed in this chapter there are empirical data that should be put in the scales (see Table 14.4).[20] The first of them has to do with voter turnout at city elections. In 66 percent of the cities with over 25,000 population, the city elections are held at a different time from any other election—national, state, or local (for example, county, school district). Theoretically, this is supposed to give the voters a chance to focus on local issues and candidates rather than give their principal attention to the presidential candidates, governors, and senators. If it worked in practice, it could perhaps establish as fact that local "self-government" is more democratic in character than the distant state and national governments. However, these separate city elections produce a lower turnout of voters: In half of the 1961–62 city elections that were held at the same time as state or national elections, 50 percent of the adults voted; whereas in half of those held independently of any other election, only 29 percent voted. Although some of those who do vote in the separate city elections may perhaps be more responsible voters than those who simply check off local candidates at national elections, nevertheless the candidates are being elected by a minority of the voters. Certainly, 29 percent is a striking contrast to the 64 percent of the people of voting age who vote for the President.

---

[20] *The data cited are from Eugene C. Lee, "City Elections: A Statistical Profile,"* Municipal Yearbook: 1963 (Chicago: International City Managers Association, 1963), *pp. 74–84. The data are for 574 (78 percent) of the 729 cities with over 25,000 population. Only each city's most recent election for mayor and/or councilmen held prior to December, 1962, is counted. The measurement of participation is in terms of half of all elections (or half of all elections associated with a stated characteristic). This is the same as the "median" and means that in half the elections the adult voting rate was smaller and in half the elections the voting rate was larger than the percentage cited. This differs from the "average" of the elections and from the average voting rate of all urban adults treated as a nationwide group (the latter would give the larger cities a heavy influence on the results).*

Table 14.4. *Percent of Adults Voting in Cities over 25,000, by Forms of Election and Government*

	Number of Cities Reporting	All City Elections			Number of Cities Reporting	Elections Held Concurrently with State or National Elections		
		Lower quartile	Median	Upper quartile		Lower quartile	Median	Upper quartile
All cities over 25,000	461	22%	33%	48%	63	35%	50%	62%
Form of election								
Partisan	109	37	50	57	31	47	51	65
Nonpartisan	350	21	30	43	32	31	43	59
Form of government								
Mayor-council	137	38	50	57	31	47	51	65
Commission	41	29	38	47	3	28	33	61
Council-manager	281	20	27	39	29	29	43	60

	Held Concurrently with Other Local Elections *				Held Independently of Any Other Election			
All cities over 25,000	87	29%	44%	51%	303	20%	29%	41%
Form of election								
Partisan	22	48	53	58	56	26	41	53
Nonpartisan	65	27	35	47	246	19	27	39
Form of government								
Mayor-council	28	40	50	55	78	34	44	56
Commission	5	28	57	71	32	28	38	47
Council-manager	54	26	35	47	193	18	23	32

* Excluding cities also holding election concurrently with state or national election.

SOURCE: Eugene C. Lee, "City Elections: A Statistical Profile," *Municipal Year Book 1963* (Chicago: International City Managers Association, 1963), p. 83. See footnote 20 of this chapter for explanation of the data.

Nonpartisan elections and the council-manager type of government carry similar prices. Two-thirds of the cities of over 25,000 population hold nonpartisan elections. In half of those held in 1961–62, only 30 percent of the adults voted, compared with a 50 percent turnout at half the partisan elections. Almost two-thirds of the cities of this size have the council-manager plan. In half their elections, only 27 percent of the adults voted, compared with 38 percent in commission-government cities and 50 percent in mayor-council cities. It may be argued, of course, that this simply reflects a high level of popular satisfaction with the way city affairs are run under the system. Serious contests are thus fewer, and there is less motivation for voters to turn out.

The separation of municipal elections from national and state elections, the nonpartisan ballot, and the council-manager plan were all key planks in the platform of the reformers in the early twentieth century, and their soundness has seldom been questioned. Democracy was certainly one of the goals, but efficiency was emphasized even more. It appears that in fact it was efficiency that won out, and to some degree at the cost of democratic participation by the citizenry. Rumblings are heard from time to time that the reforms have always attracted the upper and upper-middle classes' and the business and professional groups' support, and that the reforms do not serve the interests of the lower and lower-middle classes —particularly labor, Negro, and foreign nationality groups. As these groups expand and mobilize their political strength, it may well be that they will force a reconsideration of the reform doctrines. Thus, such doctrines might turn out to be appropriate to upper class and upper-middle class suburban towns, but inappropriate to great cities and working-class suburbs. An alternative mode of analysis is to abandon the idea of linking the council-manager plan, nonpartisanship, and the independence of municipal elections so closely together and decide how popular participation might increase if one or another of these reform planks were dropped. It seems possible, for example, that cities might retain the council-manager type of government but hold partisan elections for the council, thereby aiming for both efficiency and broader and more effective citizen participation.

☆ ☆ ☆ ☆ ☆ ☆ ☆ ☆ ☆

chapter 15

Local Governments: An Embarrassment of Riches

The cities, because of their size, their varied problems, and their political significance, tend to obscure the other elements in the kaleido-
scopic pattern of American local government. Yet these other elements—
the counties, towns, villages, and special districts—can be important units
of government both in themselves and as part of our entire interrelated
system of government. Table 15.1 gives some indication of the variety and
number of these governments.

1. The County

The nation's 3,043 counties [1] represent a tremendous variety in both size

---

[1] *All states except Alaska, Connecticut, and Rhode Island have counties. (The
term "parish" is used in Louisiana, but there is no significant distinction.) The Alaska
constitution provided for the creation of "boroughs" which would correspond roughly to
counties, although designed to be flexible. The 1961 legislature provided detailed
authorizing legislation (Chapter 146, Laws of the State of Alaska, 1961) under which
boroughs may incorporate, subject to review by a state "Local Affairs Agency," and a
few are now getting under way. The act seeks to avoid many of the weaknesses of county
government and reflects much of the best contemporary thought on this subject.*

Table 15.1. Number of Local Governments, by States, 1962

State	Total	Local Governments (Other Than School Districts)					School Districts
		Total	Counties	Munici-palities	Townships	Special districts	
Total, United States	91,186 *	56,508 *	3,043	18,000 *	17,142	18,323 *	34,678
Alabama	732	618	67	349	—	202	114
Alaska	56	46	—	40	—	6	10
Arizona	378	127	14	61	—	52	251
Arkansas	1,208	791	75	417	—	299	417
California	4,022	2,392	57	373	—	1,962	1,630
Colorado	1,193	881	62	253	—	566	312
Connecticut	397	389	—	35	150	204	8
Delaware	207	117	3	51	—	63	90
Florida	764	697	67	366	—	264	67
Georgia	1,218	1,021	159	561	—	301	197
Hawaii	20	20	3	1	—	16	—
Idaho	834	713	44	200	—	469	121
Illinois	6,452	4,912	102	1,251	1,433	2,126	1,540
Indiana	3,091	2,207	92	546	1,009	560	884
Iowa	2,642	1,306	99	944	—	263	1,336

State							
Kansas	5,410	3,149	105	618	1,546	880	2,261
Kentucky	872	664	120	365	—	179	208
Louisiana	628	561	62	258	—	241	67
Maine	658	632	16	21	470	125	26
Maryland	351	351	23	152	—	176	—
Massachusetts	586	557	12	39	312	194	29
Michigan	3,818	1,952	83	511	1,259	99	1,866
Minnesota	5,212	2,869	87	845	1,822	115	2,343
Mississippi	772	614	82	266	—	266	158
Missouri	3,727	2,078	114	892	329	743	1,649
Montana	1,387	372	56	124	—	192	1,015
Nebraska	5,123	1,859	93	537	478	751	3,264
Nevada	136	119	17	17	—	85	17
New Hampshire	550	329	10	13	221	85	221
New Jersey	1,395	883	21	334	233	295	512
New Mexico	305	214	32	80	—	102	91
New York	3,802	2,571	57	612	932	970	1,231
North Carolina	675	675	100	449	—	126	—
North Dakota	3,028	2,042	53	356	1,387	246	986
Ohio	3,359	2,526	88	932	1,328	178	833
Oklahoma	1,959	734	77	533	—	124	1,225
Oregon	1,469	985	36	222	—	727	484

(*Table 15.1 continued*)

| State | Total | Local Governments (Other Than School Districts) | | | | | School Districts |
		Total	Counties	Munici-palities	Townships	Special districts	
Pennsylvania	6,201	4,022	66	1,003	1,555	1,398	2,179
Rhode Island	97	95	—	8	31	56	2
South Carolina	552	443	46	255	—	142	109
South Dakota	4,463	1,523	64	307	1,072	80	2,940
Tennessee	657	643	95	280	—	268	14
Texas	3,327	1,853	254	866	—	733	1,474
Utah	423	383	29	212	—	142	40
Vermont	424	392	14	68	238	72	32
Virginia	380	380	98	236	—	46	—
Washington	1,646	1,235	39	263	66	867	411
West Virginia	389	334	55	224	—	55	55
Wisconsin	3,726	1,974	72	563	1,271	68	1,752
Wyoming	464	257	23	90	—	144	207

* Totals include 1 municipality and 1 special district for the District of Columbia.

SOURCE: U.S. Bureau of the Census, *Census of Governments: 1962*, Vol. 1, *Governmental Organization* (Washington, D.C., 1963), p. 29, with corrections as shown in *Statistical Abstract of the United States: 1965* (Washington, D.C., 1965), p. 419.

and population. They range in area from the 24 square miles of Arlington County, Virginia, to the 20,131 square miles of San Bernardino County, California, the latter county being about as large as the combined areas of New Jersey, Maryland, and Delaware.

The variation in population is even more striking. Loving County, Texas, with its 226 persons, continues to hold its position as the county with the smallest population. At the other extreme is Los Angeles County, California, far in the lead with a 1960 population of 6,038,771, larger than that of any of forty-three states. In fact, the explosive rate of growth of Los Angeles County—approximately 14,000 a month—poses fantastic governmental problems. Some idea of the scope of its operations can be discerned from the fact that the county employs some 48,000 civil service employees and has an annual budget of $950 million.[2]

Although they are predominantly units of rural government, the counties normally embrace the cities lying within their areas, taxing and providing certain functional services to city residents as well as to those in the unincorporated areas. Naturally some counties have become almost exclusively urban, and others urban-dominated (see Table 15.2).

GOVERNMENTAL PATTERN. The typical American county is governed by an elective board together with a rather large number of independently elected administrative department heads and special commissions (see Figure 15.1). There is again considerable variation across the country even in the names by which the general governing bodies are known; thirty-five different titles are used, although "county board" is applied to most of them in common speech. There are nine[3] distinct types of organization, only four of which are in widespread use.

The most prevalent type is the board of county commissioners (or supervisors), usually bodies of three or five members, whose sole governmental responsibility is serving on the board. In New York and in a few north central states, however, the county boards are composed of township supervisors, one from each township in the county. One of the difficulties with this arrangement is that each member is accountable to both the township and the county, but his ties to the township are usually the stronger of the two. It can also result in gross misrepresentation: a town-

---

[2] *The exact figure for the 1966 fiscal year is $950,739,536. If to this is added the $129,171,927 budgeted for special districts that are under the control of the Board of Supervisors, the result is more than a one-billion-dollar total. (Data supplied by the office of the Chief Administrative Officer of Los Angeles County.)*

[3] *For statistical details on the 3,049 county governing boards and methods of electing their 24,186 members, see Bureau of the Census, Governing Boards of County Governments: 1965 (Washington, D.C., 1965).*

ship with a population of 30 sends a delegate just as does one with a population of 30,000. (Here again, application of the "one-man, one-vote" rule will bring about gradual change.) A third type is a board consisting of a judge, usually probate, and two members who are elected directly. The final major classification is a board composed of a judge and a group of justices of the peace, the latter system being an interesting carry-over from sixteenth-century England. Most of the minor types of county government are judicial or ex-officio in nature.

Table 15.2. *County Governments and Their Populations, 1962*

Population-size Group	County Governments		Population Served by County Governments, 1960	
	Number	*Percent*	*Number* (000)	*Percent*
Total, United States	3,043	100.0	158,617	100.0%
250,000 or more	108	3.5	69,176	43.6
100,000 to 249,999	169	5.6	26,469	16.7
50,000 to 99,999	283	9.3	19,538	12.3
25,000 to 49,999	584	19.2	20,726	13.1
10,000 to 24,999	1,081	35.5	17,790	11.2
5,000 to 9,999	544	17.9	4,069	2.6
Less than 5,000	274	9.0	849	.5

SOURCE: U.S. Bureau of the Census, *Census of Governments: 1962*, Vol. I, *Governmental Organization* (Washington, D.C., 1963), p. 2.

County governments face numerous problems in today's world. Not the least of these is the lack of public interest in county affairs, despite the many services the counties perform.[4] Although county services, budgets, and personnel have been vastly expanded in recent years, most are still organized essentially as the administrative and judicial subdivisions of the state that they were originally created to be. For example, only a few states

---

[4] *On county government problems generally, see William N. Cassella, Jr., "County Government in Transition,"* Public Administration Review, 16 (Summer 1956), 223–31; Clyde F. Snider, "American County Government: A Mid-century Review," *American Political Science Review, 46 (March 1952), 66–80; and the state-by-state survey edited by Paul W. Wager,* County Government Across the Nation *(Chapel Hill, N.C.: University of North Carolina Press, 1950).*

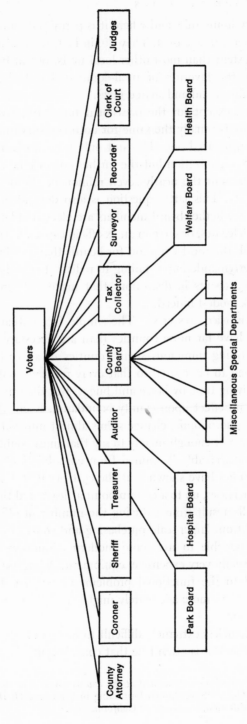

Figure 15.1. *A Typical County Government Structure*

permit county home rule, and where it is permitted, only a fraction of the counties take advantage of it. They do, in fact, serve as agents of the state to a greater extent than most other local units, but in turn they also have tended to be the favorites of rural-dominated state legislatures in such matters as grants-in-aid and shared taxes.

Moreover, except for the occasional home rule situations, organizational structure is usually the same for both the tiny rural county and the large, highly urbanized one. This not only raises the question of efficient administrative organization but the further one of how well a five-member board can represent the nearly seven million people of, for example, Los Angeles County. This latter question is also dependent, of course, upon such factors as whether board members are elected at-large, from districts, as township delegates, or serve in an ex-officio capacity. And when a district system is used, the most common for boards that are directly elected, the practice of gerrymandering or failing to redistrict rears its head once more and frequently results in distortions that make state inequities of representation look modest indeed.[5]

MERGER PROPOSALS. The simple fact is that a great majority of the states have far more counties than are necessary. There was some reason for forming numerous small counties in an earlier era: then the county seat had to be located so that every resident could reach it within reasonable driving time by horse and buggy. But the transportation revolution has had no effect upon county boundaries. Even when the units are demonstrably uneconomic, change seems almost impossible to accomplish. It is, of course, not enough merely to say that most counties are too small. What could conceivably be gained from consolidation? For one thing, a number of studies have shown that the cost per unit of work decreases as the volume increases, up to a certain point at least, and that further savings would generally result from reducing the number of officials and perhaps facilities, and from larger-scale purchasing and contracting. Also, they say, it would be possible to use more modern administrative methods and specialized, usually very expensive, equipment. A larger area might also be better related to the functional problems to be met. Finally, a county performing services more adequately might generate more popular interest and participation.

It is nevertheless extremely difficult to prove that these benefits would actually result, and it is often true that consolidating adjoining counties in

---

[5] *This has been little investigated at the county level. A recent interesting study is Stuart C. Hall,* County Supervisorial Districting in California (*Berkeley, Calif.: Bureau of Public Administration, University of California, 1961*).

the thinly settled areas where the problem is most acute would still not provide a theoretically adequate unit. In the rare consolidations that have occurred, an impoverished county has been combined with a relatively affluent one; thus the overall benefit may not be a matter for rejoicing by the taxpayers of the wealthier county. Furthermore, newly created units might seem even more artificial to citizens than the old familiar ones. A complete recasting by the state could conceivably be satisfactory, but the prospects for simply joining adjacent counties are dubious and present serious practical problems that Millspaugh has aptly summarized as follows:

> *Serious obstacles are presented by popular habit and popular inertia, by the selfish interests of office holders and politicians, by sectional jealousy and distrust, by considerations of partisan advantage or disadvantage, by the unwillingness of towns to abdicate as county seats, by the situation with respect to county buildings, by the requirements of the courts, by differences in the indebtedness of adjacent counties, by reluctance on the part of one county to assume the excess burden of another, and by other difficulties real or imaginary.*[6]

There is often, quite understandably, considerable conflict between county governments and the cities that lie within their boundaries. They occasionally step on each other's toes in the performance of certain services, such as police protection; they quarrel over city attempts to annex territory; they have different ideas about proper zoning regulations; and so on. Even more seriously, perhaps, they are likely to have vehement differences over taxing policy and the amount of county funds expended for services within the cities. The cities point to the percentage of county revenue that comes from city residents (and to the county's favorable share of state aid), insisting that they do not receive a fair return. People residing outside city limits often expect county taxes, paid by city and noncity residents alike, to be used to supply them with types of municipal services. But the county responds that cities fail to recognize that the heaviest county expenditures are for such services as welfare, which does mean that the greatest amount of service is provided where there are greater concentrations of population. Moreover, they point out, it is a recognized principle of public finance that any government must tax wealth wherever it is found and spend where the need exists; it is never a

---

[6] *Arthur C. Millspaugh,* Local Democracy and Crime Control *(Washington, D.C., The Brookings Institution, 1936), p. 119. The foregoing arguments against consolidation are drawn largely from the same source, which remains one of the soundest analyses of the difficulties of such action.*

matter of allocating expenditures in a direct ratio to the sources of the funds.

One possible solution to some of these conflict situations that has been attempted is city-county consolidation, a solution feasible as a rule only where one large city occupies the bulk of a county area. The two governments are simply merged into one which then provides all services, both city and county. It is hard to make this city-county consolidation complete, but there are several instances where it has been successful, such as Philadelphia, Denver, Baton Rouge, and San Francisco. If a major city occupies only part of a large county, one approach is to separate the two and make the city a distinct city-county or an "independent city," an approach used at present only in Virginia. Otherwise the solution must lie in improving channels of cooperation between the cities and the counties. The establishment in some areas of city-county coordinating committees, usually consisting of the county commissioners and the mayors of all the cities within the county, has been useful in improving mutual understanding and promoting cooperative activity, although it certainly cannot be expected to solve all outstanding problems.

A FOCUS OF RESPONSIBILITY. The basic internal difficulties of counties stem from the common absence of any true central responsibility and coordination. Despite the importance of the executive function in modern government, most counties have no chief executive comparable to a mayor, manager, or governor. The county board generally has a mixture of both legislative and administrative powers, but it must share these with the multitude of independently elected administrative officers and the many special-function boards, such as those controlling hospitals, penal institutions, and agricultural service. Consequently, a long ballot is needed and this tends to make the voter rather ineffective; government, in turn, then becomes less responsive to the popular will.

With the lack of real central control, each of the independent administrative officers quite naturally tries to build up a private empire that will be as self-sufficient as possible. They feel no responsibility to the county board, contending that since they, too, are elected they have equal status with the board and are responsible only to the electorate. Their salaries are commonly fixed by the state legislature, and some have access to earmarked revenues so that the board does not even have effective budgetary control over their work. In fact, the board is required by law to finance the administrative expenses of each of these offices.

Frequently, county agencies are subject to more real control by the corresponding state agencies (welfare, for example) than by the county itself. In a controversy between county officers, the only superior they have in common is the state legislature, often meeting for perhaps three months every two years. The legislature may fix the salary that the county recorder can pay a part-time clerk, but this is a rather remote and unsatisfactory process.

One should not overlook in this connection the importance of the county legislative delegation, that is, the members of the state legislature who come from a given county. It is customary practice that the legislature will not pass an act relating to a particular county except on the request of or with the approval of the legislative delegation from that county. By the same token, the legislature will usually pass such bills as the delegation does request, provided those bills have no serious bearing on the rest of the state. The result is that at times these county delegations may become almost a secondary legislative body for the county. They may often be useful, but there are also instances in which strong differences between the county board and the delegation create serious conflict.

Despite continuing inadequacies, it is nevertheless true that many counties today are beginning to adapt to changing needs and demands. The county remains to some extent, and probably will continue to be, an agent of the state, possessing therefore somewhat limited discretion. Recognizing this, however, there is no good reason why home rule should not be made generally available, and in fact encouraged, if there is a real desire for counties to become more effective units of local self-government.

As would be expected, most proposals looking toward improvement of county government center around the need for some type of county executive. Elected executives have been used in a few places, and the number has lately been increasing. Otherwise most of the experimentation has been with the county manager or chief administrative officer (CAO) plans. The former is simply the application of council-manager government to the county level and is still quite rare. The CAO arrangement is merely a difference in degree, but a difference that has made the idea more acceptable to county boards and the public. The CAO performs essentially as does a manager but with somewhat more restricted powers. Although the plan varies in practice, in general he has some overall coordinating authority, prepares the budget, and serves as adviser to the board, but his power to appoint and direct other administrative officials is very limited. Obviously, to be fully effective the plan should involve changing all or most of the independently elected department head positions into appointive offices; to the extent that this is not done, the CAO must work largely through tactics of persuasion.

URBAN SERVICES. A county is supposed to treat all areas within its borders equally. Yet some areas that are becoming urbanized but are still unincorporated feel that the county should provide them with certain city-type services. A number of counties have begun to meet this problem either by forming a special district to perform the additional functions or by establishing "county service areas," an arrangement whereby an area can be designated to receive supplemental services from the county if it pays a supplemental tax to finance those services.

One of the most interesting developments in county governments in recent years has been the growth in a few areas, notably in California and particularly in Los Angeles County, of comprehensive contract services rendered by the county government to cities. It is not an original idea; in fact, it is commonplace for cities to contract with the county to perform certain services on their behalf. Tax collection is a familiar example, and numerous others could be cited. What is new is the idea of the city buying *all* its municipal services from the county. Pioneered primarily by the city of Lakewood, a suburb of Long Beach with a population of about 70,000, the system now embraces twenty-nine communities in Los Angeles County.[7] Under this arrangement, policy control is retained by each city, but the county does the actual administrative work. The city council determines the amount and quality of services desired, sets the tax rate to pay for them, hires a "city administrator" to supervise the work on behalf of the city, and contracts with the county to perform the various functions: fire and police protection, street maintenance, recreation, and others.

Such an arrangement is obviously most practical for new communities without established municipal facilities (Lakewood was created as a planned community in a single development) and clearly necessitates a large-scale county government with efficient administrative organization. Both the cities and the county can benefit from the large-scale operations and the use of specialized personnel and equipment. After more than a decade of successful operation in Los Angeles County, the plan apparently continues to be highly popular. Whether new problems may arise in the future as a result of county-city differences or when these new cities begin to reach a point of rapid deterioration, remains to be seen. It is an experiment that will be watched with interest in many metropolitan areas, and it may forecast something of a new role for urban counties.

Efficiency aside, the Lakewood plan raises some serious ethical ques-

---

[7] *On the "Lakewood plan," see Samuel K. Gove, The Lakewood Plan (Urbana, Ill.: Institute of Government and Public Affairs, University of Illinois, 1961).*

tions, at least to the extent that it encourages and facilitates new separate incorporations. Home rule may be a good principle, but it too can be abused, and there is no better illustration than the so-called "phantom cities" of California, created essentially as "tax dodges" and "preserves" for special interests within a metropolitan area. Should Vernon (or Park Avenue) be permitted to incorporate and provide only the limited services it needs at an elite level while impoverished Watts (or Harlem) rots?

2. *Towns, Townships, and Villages*

In discussing communities not large enough to be cities, we stumble immediately upon a certain confusion of terminology. The term "town" is often used interchangeably to refer to "town" and "township" and is, of course, common parlance for any urban or semi-urban place. For our purposes town will refer to the New England town, and township to the midwestern unit commonly bearing that name. The two have become somewhat different, even though the latter was originally intended as a transplant from New England. We shall use village to refer to the 13,000 small municipal corporations in the country, most of which have populations of 2,500 or less; in fact, almost 10,000 of them have fewer than 1,000 inhabitants.

NEW ENGLAND TOWNS. Colonial settlement patterns, coupled with the previous experience of the settlers in their native land, determined the early structure of American local government. In the South, the settlement pattern was for the most part based on large plantations, frequently somewhat isolated, and in this region county governments became the predominant units. In New England, owing both to soil characteristics and Indian threats, the colonists tended to settle in village clusters with individuals farming land lying outside. The New England towns therefore developed in irregular shapes and were mixtures of urban and rural territory. Town governments, usually still of this mixed character, cover virtually all of New England, although the larger cities are now ordinarily chartered separately by the states. County governments exist in four of these six states, but they perform very limited functions.

The towns therefore carry out almost all local government services. The basic form of government is the traditional town meeting, an institution often praised with almost rhapsodic fervor as one of the world's few remaining examples of pure democracy. The governing body is the entire adult citizenry assembled, possessing full power to pass all ordinances, levy taxes, and so on. The board of selectmen chosen at the meeting is not a legislative body but an administrative board that can only carry out the instructions of the town meeting, or more realistically, operate within the limits prescribed by the meeting. The board, with a long list of other elected officials, is directly answerable to the town meeting.

Town meetings are presumably characterized by free and frank debate, with every citizen entitled to play an equal part. In fact, the agenda is normally posted in advance, and thus lively public discussion can take place for some time prior to the actual meeting. There is naturally a danger that advance caucuses may completely prearrange a meeting, and—as one would expect from observing any type of public meeting—a few persons are likely to do most of the talking. It is the task of the moderator to avoid this as much as possible, to ensure adequate discussion, and to move the meeting along to its conclusion. Unfortunately, many town meeting governments have been oligarchic and manipulated; in recent years domination by finance committee recommendations has been commonplace.

In practice, the town meeting can work well in a small town with a fairly homogeneous population, but it is difficult to keep it performing satisfactorily as communities grow large. If the meeting is to be effective, the people should know each other and feel a common bond and common responsibility. Once these feelings of involvement disappear, apathy is almost sure to result, and meetings may either be ignored or be "packed" by special interest groups. As a consequence of these size problems, a number of towns have come to utilize the "limited" or "representative" town meeting, in which the voters elect a large representative body to exercise the functions of the town meeting.

For the smaller towns especially, there has been the familiar problem of getting satisfactory administration when the activities are supervised by unpaid part-time selectmen. As a result, town managers have come to be used widely in many New England states. In fact, in some areas one manager may serve two, or occasionally even three, small towns. With these and other modifications, the town will undoubtedly continue to serve as a useful unit of government.

TOWNSHIPS. Transplanting political institutions is usually a precarious matter, and it certainly proved to be so in the case of moving town government to the West. Under the Northwest Ordinance the Continental Congress had provided for a survey of the territories in the trans-Appalachian region; consequently, when the first significant tide of settlers moved into the area, the surveyors' maps already showed the six-miles-on-a-side squares that came to be called "Congressional townships." When the population increased, it was a simple matter to provide that each of these townships should become a town government, or a "civil township." Unfortunately, the units were quite artificial, ordinarily lacking much sense of community as such; many lacked even a focal center of population.

In time, some developed community sentiment, and many created moderately extensive governmental services. For the most part, though, township functions were limited in scope, partly because the state legislatures left the townships relatively little discretion and partly because the counties in these states developed as major local units. Moreover, the schools in the Middle West were almost invariably run by special districts, whereas in New England they remained a part of town government. Also, the villages soon began to separate from the townships and incorporate their own governments. With the community centers thus withdrawn, the townships became exclusively rural units, and when transportation became easier, the need for township activity in addition to that of the counties further diminished.

The pattern of township government is usually that of the town meeting, with what is commonly called a board of township trustees as the interim supervisory body. Although the situation varies somewhat in different states, in general township functions have gradually dwindled away. For example, the counties have generally taken over health and welfare because the townships, for the most part, were not up to the job. Similarly, justice and law enforcement have gone by default to the county sheriff and the municipal and county courts. The only active justices of the peace are to be found on the main highways and near fish and game areas where they are likely to receive a fair number of cases—and the bulk of those justices will in fact be located in the villages rather than townships. Property assessment for tax purposes was always a problem, since performing that task was hardly the way to popularity with one's neighbors. Since it often resulted in gross inequities, the trend in most states has been toward the use of county assessors. Therefore, the functions of the township have been gradually eroded, so that the principal one left is the maintenance of local roads, and even this is slowly disappearing.[8]

Attendance at township meetings today is usually very slight; in fact, at times the officers must go out and search for a quorum. People will attend only if there are some issues of consequence, and with so few functions left to the townships, few of these are possible. In an earlier day the meetings were often community social affairs, featuring a potluck

---

[8] *See Paul W. Wager, "Townships on Way Out,"* National Municipal Review, 46 (October 1957), 456–60, 475. *The only exceptions to the general trend are a few townships on the outskirts of large cities in certain states where they are performing urban services in much the same fashion as suburban municipalities.*

supper and perhaps concluding with a dance, but this too has become rare. Everyone who has studied townships in the past forty years has agreed that they are essentially moribund and should be eliminated. Yet, particularly in those states where the county boards are composed of township representatives, they often show remarkable tenacity. In some instances, the states have even given them new life by means of automatic shares of state tax revenues, thus in effect requiring all the taxpayers of the state to help subsidize these units. There are still officials here and there who are proud of their positions and who—if there is adequate revenue available—do a very conscientious job with the limited functions remaining. Moreover, the citizens themselves often take pride in their township government: they like the neighborliness of it and frequently express a desire to "spend our money at home." In short, they assume that any small local government is superior to one that is farther away. In other places, however, the main reason why the township government still exists is sheer apathy or ignorance of its shortcomings and the possibilities for improvement.

Although the number of townships has decreased steadily in recent years, the pace has been slow. But if it is desirable to eliminate the township —and it is hard to see any serious need for its continuance—how can this be accomplished? There are several possible ways. For one thing, the local populace may simply vote to disorganize, as does actually happen on occasion. The state legislature can, of course, abolish townships with a single act, but this is politically impractical. Some states have got around this, however, by authorizing the county boards to abolish a township when its assessed valuation or population falls below a certain level. But the most potent force has been the steady transfer of functions, which has virtually eliminated the townships in even such a consciously rural state as Iowa, and that trend will probably continue. The principle of local self-government can hardly be said to be damaged when limited-function units like townships in which the public no longer takes interest are eliminated in favor of other local units in which popular concern and participation can be stimulated and where public needs can be met more adequately.

VILLAGES. The village is an almost indefinable unit, and the definitions in the statutes are rarely helpful. In general, as we have indicated earlier, we shall use the term here to refer to the 13,000 or so small municipal corporations with populations of 2,500 or less. (For the distribution of incorporated places by size, see Table 15.3.) Although some communities, especially in suburban areas, continue to call themselves villages even after achieving large populations, they are atypical. Some states officially have no villages; they simply utilize a small-city classification. Although the state makes their existence possible, it does not create

Table 15.3. *Municipal Governments and Their Populations, 1962*

Population-Size Group	Municipalities		Population Served by Municipalities, 1960	
	Number	Percent	Number (000)	Percent
Total, United States	17,997	100.0%	116,244	100.0%
300,000 or more	43 ⎫		37,378 ⎫	
200,000 to 299,999	18 ⎬	.7	4,265 ⎬	43.8
100,000 to 199,999	69 ⎭		9,309 ⎭	
50,000 to 99,999	180	1.0	12,509	10.8
25,000 to 49,999	368	2.0	12,784	11.0
10,000 to 24,999	980	5.4	15,074	13.0
5,000 to 9,999	1,285	7.1	9,054	7.8
2,500 to 4,999	1,770	9.8	6,262	5.4
1,000 to 2,499	3,527	19.6	5,586	4.8
Less than 1,000	9,757	54.2	4,025	3.5

SOURCE: U.S. Bureau of the Census, *Census of Governments: 1962*, Vol. I, *Governmental Organization* (Washington, D.C., 1963), pp. 2, 32, 33.

villages as it does counties or townships; the residents of a village must choose to incorporate.

Unlike the townships, the villages have not been declining. On the contrary, their populations have been steadily increasing, as the trend in many rural areas has been to move off the land being farmed in favor of the conveniences of village living. In a sense, then, villages and townships are competing units, for people move to the villages partly because they have no chance of securing from the townships the services they desire. The villages are obviously likely to possess a relatively greater sense of community.

The smaller ones tend to resemble townships in some respects, and the larger ones look much like city governments, utilizing any one of the usual forms of city organization. The most common pattern is either that of the weak mayor-council or of the commission. The notable difference between village and township is the existence of representative government, although, paradoxically, most villages have compact populations that are probably in a much better position to hold "town meetings" than is the population of the average township. Village government is certainly "close to the people," and the ordinary resident has little trouble being acquainted with village officials. In fact, in one state it is estimated that, in the average village with its full quota of officers, one person in every fifty will be an officer. Despite these circumstances, popular participation is not likely to be high.

In many villages most officials, both representative and administrative, serve on a part-time basis; not uncommonly, one man handles several jobs. There is, characteristically, a very high degree of informality, and often very limited public interest.[9] In most, political competition is slight, a condition given classic expression in the following letter published in the *Askov* (Minn.) *American:*

> *I would like to make a few comments on the fact that I have filed for the office of mayor of the village of Askov.*
>
> *I cannot brag about what has been accomplished during the time I have been on the village council and I will not make any promises as to what I will try to do if I am re-elected again.*
>
> *The reason I am filing is because two of the councilmen asked me to do so. Also several other people in the village have asked me to file.*
>
> *I am not particularly anxious to be re-elected as mayor as I do not feel that I have sufficient time to do the job as it should be done. There is little "glory" in the job, not much pay. There is considerable grief. Nearly every day when I go up town, someone stops me to register a complaint about something or other, the neighbor's dog, or children, sewer, the roads, etc.*
>
> *If I am re-elected, I will do the job as well as I can, and will appreciate your suggestions and listen to your complaints.*
>
> *But, I am not overly anxious for the job, and will not feel offended if my opponent is the choice of the majority.*[10]

3. Special Districts

One of the least known yet most widespread units of local government is the special or "ad hoc" district, of which there were at the time of the 1962 Census of Governments 18,323 scattered across the United States.[11] This

---

[9] *A valuable portrayal of village and township politics, and of the general sociological setting as well, is Arthur J. Vidich and Joseph Bensman,* Small Town in Mass Society: Class, Power, and Religion in a Rural Community (*Garden City, N.Y.: Anchor Books, Doubleday, 1960; and Princeton, N.J.: Princeton University Press, 1958*).

[10] *Reprinted in the* Minneapolis Star, *November 27, 1947.*

[11] *U.S. Bureau of the Census,* Census of Governments: 1962, Vol. I. Governmental Organization (*Washington, D.C., 1963*), *p. 1.*

figure does not include the best known and most numerous type, the school district, which will be discussed separately. As a matter of fact, the best statistics are likely to be none too accurate, since special districts come and go under permissive state legislation, and there is rarely any central state source of information on them. Moreover, there are a number of borderline cases in which it is difficult to determine whether a given entity is actually a unit of government or an appendage to some other government.

HETEROGENEITY. The variety of special districts is tremendous even within any one state. Some serve the particular needs of metropolitan areas, where they can extend over a number of cities—for example, a sanitary or transit district. Others serve distinctively rural needs, such as weed control or irrigation. Still others are organized to perform one special function within the boundaries of an existing government—parks being a common illustration—or to provide governmental services in the so-called urban fringe areas that remain unincorporated but have rapidly growing populations.[12] Because most states have authorized the formation of special districts without much, if any, planning or coordination whenever there has been a local request, there are frequently a remarkable number of potential types available. For example, one state authorizes the following types to deal with the problem of water usage or control alone: irrigation, flood control, levee, reclamation, water, water conservation, protection and storm water, storm drain maintenance, drainage, and drainage improvement.

The majority of the special districts perform a single function, although more and more multi-purpose districts are appearing. Some have no regular employees, others employ tens of thousands, and their budgets range from zero to the multi-million dollar class. Some are huge permanent enterprises with elaborate facilities, like a port district, while others are created for a temporary purpose, such as mosquito abatement, and then quietly cease to exist. Some have identical boundaries with another unit of government, and others overlap counties or cities and frequently each other. There are interstate districts, and even occasional international ones.

The composition of special-district governing bodies is likewise not uniform. There is usually a small governing board, sometimes elected, sometimes ex-officio, and sometimes appointed either by an official of a

---

[12] *This and the subsequent analysis of this topic draws heavily upon John C. Bollens,* Special District Governments in the United States (*Berkeley, Calif.: University of California Press, 1957*). *This is the best and in fact the only truly comprehensive treatment of the subject.*

larger government or by several governments associated in the district. Although most possess and many utilize a taxing power, special districts commonly finance their operations by service charges.

CAUSES AND CONSEQUENCES. Why have these unique units come into existence and continued to increase in number? In some instances it may be simply that the service areas of the general government units do not conform to the scope of the problems to be met; in others, an existing unit, like a county, may be unwilling to perform a service needed in only one small part of its area. Since each new district has its own taxing and borrowing authority, this can also be an effective means for a city or county to get around the tax and debt limits fixed by the state. Functional specialists at higher levels of government, interested only in their own specialties, have often encouraged the creation of special districts to handle new services. Such districts may reflect in part the familiar desire to keep control close to home. Finally, the establishment of special districts may simply be an easier short-run solution than attempting the reorganization of existing units or arranging for more effective intergovernmental cooperation.

There are a number of unfortunate features resulting from the extensive use of special districts. As short-run or stop-gap measures, they represent not only a piecemeal and uncoordinated attempt to meet public problems, but they may in fact hamper the achievement of more satisfactory long-run solutions. Because there are so many of these districts and because the governing board members are frequently selected by indirect processes, such as appointment, there is little realistic popular control. For that matter, the elections are likely to be uncontested even when an elective system is used. There is little citizen awareness of most of these districts and virtually no public participation; for most persons it is difficult enough to pay adequate attention to the major units. Moreover, many special districts are so small as to be uneconomic, and they are often injurious to the general-purpose local governments not only because of tax competition but also because they take away functions that those governments should be performing.

On the basis of his extensive study, Bollens concludes that a great many of the present special districts should, and could by means of state action, be absorbed into the general local governments. For a number of them this will not be possible, but he suggests that many of the remaining single-function districts could well be made a part of large multi-purpose districts. Despite their unfortunate characteristics, he says, "the growth of special districts may sooner or later serve as the impetus necessary to bring about needed and long overdue changes across the whole fabric of local government." [13]

SCHOOL DISTRICTS. The school districts in the United States, 34,678 of them in 1962, still constitute the largest single element of local government structure. In addition to those independent districts, there were in 1962 another 2,341 public school systems that functioned as a part of some other government, such as a county, a city, or a New England town. (For the overall picture, see Table 15.4 and Figure 15.2.) Although the number of school districts is still tremendously large, it has been greatly reduced in the past twenty years. In fact, school districts are the one form of local government in which area reorganization has been notably successful. For example, in the ten-year period between 1952 and 1962 the number of these districts had been reduced by 33,000 through reorganization and consolidation.[14]

In West Virginia and Florida a shift to countywide units of school administration was made directly by the state legislatures, under the stress of economic crisis. Other states have encouraged consolidations largely by making them financially advantageous through state grants-in-aid, but the most common technique has been for the state to either require or strongly encourage the establishment in each county of survey or study committees. These committees, composed primarily of lay citizens, are expected to spend some months making a careful study of the school district pattern within the county and ultimately to render a report to the public. The assumption of those who originated this system was that such a committee actually studying the situation would almost invariably recommend consolidation of many districts, and experience has proved this correct. In most states the consolidation requires a favorable popular vote, and a local committee is likely to be much more successful in achieving this than would any outside agency.

In some states, especially in the Middle West, there were thousands of one-room school districts within the state, with some of the districts no more than one square mile in area. Not only were most of these extremely uneconomic, but they were rarely capable of providing really adequate

---

[13] Ibid., *p. 263.*

[14] *U.S. Bureau of the Census,* Governmental Organization, *p. 27. By the school year of 1965–66, the number of independent school districts and dependent school systems had fallen from the 37,019 shown in Table 15.4 as the official count in 1962 to an estimated 27,000 (though different data gathering and analysis methods make the two figures not precisely comparable). Research Division, National Education Association,* Estimates of School Statistics, 1965–66, Research Report 1965–R17 *(Washington, D.C., 1965), p. 8.*

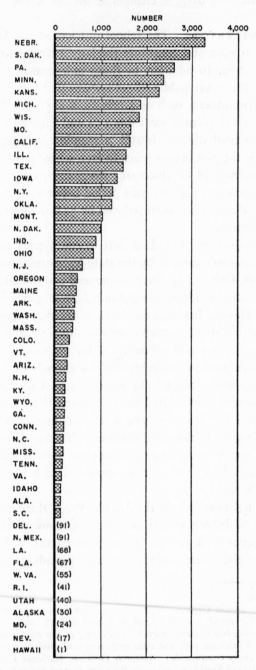

Figure 15.2. *Public School Systems,*
by States, 1962

NEBR.
S. DAK.
PA.
MINN.
KANS.
MICH.
WIS.
MO.
CALIF.
ILL.
TEX.
IOWA
N.Y.
OKLA.
MONT.
N. DAK.
IND.
OHIO
N. J.
OREGON
MAINE
ARK.
WASH.
MASS.
COLO.
VT.
ARIZ.
N. H.
KY.
WYO.
GA.
CONN.
N. C.
MISS.
TENN.
VA.
IDAHO
ALA.
S. C.
DEL. (91)
N. MEX. (91)
LA. (68)
FLA. (67)
W. VA. (55)
R. I. (41)
UTAH (40)
ALASKA (30)
MD. (24)
NEV. (17)
HAWAII (1)

SOURCE: U. S. Bureau of the Census, *Census*
of Governments: 1962, Vol. I, *Governmental*
Organization (Washington, D.C., 1963), p.21.

modern educational facilities. Certain ones operated at times with as few as two or three pupils, and many were in fact so-called "closed districts," maintaining a legal existence but paying tuition to send their few pupils to school in adjoining districts rather than operating their own.

It should not be assumed that the consolidations accomplished to date have ended all these situations. In 1962, for example, there were still 5,963 closed districts, and about one-third of all public school systems provided education for less than fifty pupils each.[15] Of course, it is not true that a small school is necessarily a poor one, but one can hardly deny that it faces serious handicaps. As long as there are areas with thinly scattered populations, small schools will not be eliminated, but there is no need for each one to constitute a separate governmental unit.

The typical large independent school district has organizational similarities to the council-manager plan of government, with the elective school board having broadly defined functions and hiring a professional superintendent who has overall administrative responsibility. In contrast, the rural school district that operates only one or two small schools in a portion of the county is ordinarily restricted to hiring teachers, while other functions are under the administrative supervision of a county superintendent. This latter position in most states is elective, in contrast to the city superintendents, and very few states specify any requirements for holding the office other than securing a plurality of the votes.

The school board possesses broad general powers over curriculum, hiring and salary of teachers, length of term, tax levies, facilities and maintenance, and so on. In practice, however, the exercise of these prerogatives is in most states extremely limited as a result of extensive state regulations and standards. Education is usually a constitutional responsibility of the state government, which it delegates in large part to the local districts. Consequently, most states provide at least half the funds for public education, and they maintain a rather high degree of control. For example, a state may withhold grants if the school term is not of specified minimum length, if certain subjects are not taught, if prescribed texts are not used, if teachers are employed who are not certificated by the state, and so on. School building plans as a rule must also be approved by the state department of education. Minimum salaries for teachers may be specified. Regular reports and inspections are required, and reasonable standardization is further accomplished through the publication of manuals, curriculum guides, and similar materials. Thus it is clear that local

---

[15] *U.S. Bureau of the Census*, Governmental Organization, *p. 4.*

Table 15.4. *Public School Systems, Schools, and Enrollment, 1962*

System Characteristic	Public School Systems (No.)	Public Schools (No.)	Pupils Enrolled, October 1961 (No.)	Public School Systems (%)	Public Schools (%)	Public School Enrollment (%)
Total	37,019	100,339	37,805,987	100.0%	100.0%	100.0%
Dependent school systems	2,341	18,459	8,402,328	6.3	18.4	22.2
Independent school districts	34,678	81,880	29,403,659	93.7	81.6	77.8
By number of schools	37,019	100,339	37,805,987	100.0	100.0	100.0
Dependent school systems	2,341	18,459	8,402,328	6.3	18.4	22.2
One or more schools	2,273	18,459	8,402,328	6.1	18.4	22.2
None (nonoperating)	68	—	—	.2	.0	.0
Independent school districts	34,678	81,880	29,403,659	93.7	81.6	77.8
20 or more schools	452	20,953	10,822,222	1.2	20.9	28.6
10 to 19 schools	878	11,340	5,122,586	2.4	11.3	13.5
3 to 9 schools	4,958	23,969	8,899,625	13.4	23.9	23.5
2 schools	3,191	6,382	1,811,515	8.6	6.4	4.8
1 school	19,236	19,236	2,747,711	52.0	19.2	7.3
No schools (nonoperating)	5,963	—	—	16.1	—	—

By enrollment size						
	37,019	100,339	37,805,987	100.0	100.0	100.0
Dependent school systems	2,341	18,459	8,402,328	6.3	18.4	22.2
Independent school districts	34,678	81,880	29,403,659	93.7	81.6	77.8
25,000 or more pupils	98	9,095	6,994,569	.3	9.1	18.5
12,000 to 24,999 pupils	204	5,929	3,276,248	.6	5.9	8.7
6,000 to 11,999 pupils	493	8,026	4,056,914	1.3	8.0	10.7
3,000 to 5,999 pupils	1,164	11,369	4,868,696	3.1	11.3	12.9
1,800 to 2,999 pupils	1,378	8,246	3,188,066	3.7	8.2	8.4
1,200 to 1,799 pupils	1,325	5,299	1,940,375	3.6	5.3	5.1
600 to 1,199 pupils	2,891	7,757	2,466,378	7.8	7.7	6.5
300 to 599 pupils	3,271	5,740	1,412,526	8.8	5.7	3.7
150 to 299 pupils	2,870	3,582	626,124	7.8	3.6	1.7
50 to 149 pupils	3,939	5,064	360,499	10.6	5.0	1.0
15 to 49 pupils	6,476	7,050	169,136	17.5	7.0	.4
1 to 14 pupils	4,606	4,723	44,128	12.4	4.7	.1
0 pupils (nonoperating)	5,963	—	—	16.1	—	—

SOURCE: U.S. Bureau of the Census, *Census of Governments: 1962*, Vol. I, *Governmental Organization* (Washington, D.C., 1963), pp. 36f.

control of education, although real, operates within definite limits that are designed to ensure that there is at least a minimum equality of educational opportunity for all children in the state.

School districts are commonly involved in a complex variety of relationships with the other local governments in their immediate environment. They sometimes have identical, sometimes overlapping, boundaries with other units. Other governments collect their taxes, furnish legal advice, and provide water supply and other services. Many enterprises are cooperative; for example, the school system often makes available facilities and personnel for summer recreation programs together with a city. At the same time there are inevitable conflicts. Must a school district board conform to a city's zoning requirements or building regulations, for example? Whose responsibility is it to provide crossing guards on streets adjoining schools? Must the city drop other capital projects in order to extend water and sewer lines to a new school building constructed in a previously undeveloped area? This merely begins the list of areas of potential conflict. There are also numerous ways in which a city and a school district serving the same area and population appear to duplicate some activities unnecessarily.

The question of whether the schools should in fact be operated as independent units of government or should be integrated with the regular local governments has long been a subject of contention between many professional "educationists" and those whose professional specialty is political science or public administration. The desirability of independent districts for school administration has been traditionally a sort of article of faith in the colleges of education. It has been argued that education, being different from other functions of government and of vastly greater scope than any other, should be treated separately. Separateness, proponents of this view say, will make for greater public interest in the schools, will result in more adequate financial support, and will "keep the schools out of politics."

Those of the opposing view rejoin that education is no more different from other functions of government, such as fire protection and social welfare, than they are different from each other. Every functional specialist, they say, is eager to have his function independent, and the end result of this would be organizational and financial chaos. In the more than 2,300 school systems that are currently integrated with general governments, the schools seem to receive financial support comparable to that supplied in independent school districts. As to public participation, one can hardly be overwhelmed by the degree of public interest evidenced in the average school board election. Furthermore, the school districts do not appear to have been unusually immune from corrupt politics. In the proper sense of the word, the schools should be *in* politics—directly responsive and accountable to the public they serve.[16] Attempts to remove any governmental body "from politics" usually seem to result simply in substituting one kind of politics for another, with the substitute often being less responsible. In the view of its advocates, integration might actually improve public attention by eliminating some governmental confusion, while the citizen could benefit from the ending of this duplication. Thus for both parents and taxpayers there appear to be advantages in a comprehensively planned local budget and tax system that includes education with all the other local services that the community desires and must support.

Time has done little to reconcile these differing opinions, and the average city council or county board is not eager to add further headaches to its present quota by assuming school responsibilities. Much of the argument about whether to absorb the educational function into the sphere of general local governments ignores the varying capacities of these governments for handling such a responsibility. There is not much to be gained by integrating the schools into a city or county government that is itself unintegrated or notoriously corrupt. On the other hand, government that is competently and responsibly coordinating all other functions has a strong claim to bring education within its orbit. The discernible improvement in the organization and professionalization of city governments argues strongly for integration of all functions. Where such improvement does not occur, however, arrangements are needed to facilitate cooperation between school systems and city and county governments without totally abandoning the independence of the school district.[17]

----

[16] *In 1965–66 the number of school board members, most of them chosen by election, was approximately 130,000. Research Division, National Education Association,* Estimates of School Statistics, 1965–66, Research Report 1965–R17 *(Washington, D.C., 1965), p. 7.*

Some of the most useful contemporary discussions of public school politics are to be found in the Syracuse University "Series on The Economics and Politics of Public Education" (Syracuse, N.Y.: Syracuse University Press), for our purpose especially Stephen K. Bailey et al., Schoolmen and Politics: A Study of State Aid to Education in the Northeast *(1962); Roscoe C. Martin,* Government and the Suburban School *(1962); and Warner Bloomberg, Jr., and Morris Sunshine,* Suburban Power Structures and Public Education: A Study of Values, Influence, and Tax Effort *(1963). See also Nicholas A. Masters, Robert H. Salisbury, and Thomas H. Eliot,* State Politics and the Public Schools *(New York: Knopf, 1964).*

[17] *For a more thorough discussion of such a proposal, see Robert L. Morlan, "Toward City-School District Rapprochement,"* Public Administration Review, *15 (Spring 1958), 113–17.*

4. *The Governing of Metropolitan Areas*

Probably the most crucial single knot of problems in the entire field of local government today involves our burgeoning metropolitan areas. Not only has America become a predominantly urban nation, but the concentration within this pattern of urbanization is even more striking. In fact, two-thirds of the country's population now lives within the 224 "standard metropolitan statistical areas" (SMSA's) defined by the Bureau of the Census (see Figures 15.3 and 15.4); from 1950 to 1960 their population increased 26.5 percent while the total national population increase was only 18.5 percent.[18] In recent years, however, this increase has usually been the result of the vast expansion of the suburban population rather than the growth of the central cities. A number of cities have, in fact, lost population at the same time that their suburbs have shown 40, 50, or 60 percent increases, or even more. For the country as a whole, the SMSA's central cities increased only 11 percent while the areas surrounding them rose by 47 percent.

SCOPE OF PROBLEMS. The scope of metropolitan area problems is constantly broadening. Realistically, it is no longer confined to individual central cities with their rings of suburbs. One needs only to fly among the East Coast cities to be forcibly struck with what William Zeckendorf has termed the "fluid suburbia" character of the scene below.[19] This is the "megalopolis"—a vast complex of intermingled cities, suburbs, villages, and miscellaneous other population concentrations, stretching for hundreds of miles with indefinite and constantly changing boundaries—more an urban region than separate urban groupings.[20] A similar situation is developing rapidly in southern California from Los Angeles south to San Diego, north toward Santa Barbara, and east to San Bernardino. Others can be noted around San Francisco and Seattle, and one may speculate about the future of a great region encompassing Milwaukee, Chicago, Detroit, Toledo, Cleveland, Akron, Youngstown, and Pittsburgh.

There have been many reasons for the "flight to the suburbs": the desire for more space and better air, the hope for a better environment in which to raise children, considerations of social status, the deterioration of

---

[18] *U.S. Bureau of the Census*, Statistical Abstract: 1966, *pp. 5, 18.*
[19] William Zeckendorf, *"Fluid Suburbia,"* Yale Review, 48 *(Autumn 1958),* 27–40.
[20] *See the excellent portrayal in Jean Gottman,* Megalopolis: The Urbanized Eastern Seaboard of the United States *(New York: The Twentieth Century Fund, 1961).*

the older city residential areas, the influx of minority groups into the cities, and the expectation of a lower tax rate. But whatever the reasons, the social, economic, and political impact of this rapid growth and constant change has been tremendous.

Commercial enterprises have quite naturally tended to follow the movement of population, so that cities have lost, along with valuable citizens, a part of their all-important commercial tax base. Yet the costs of maintaining and servicing the central business district, as well as the great public facilities expected in a large city, have remained at the same level or have increased. The vast commuter population earns its living in the central city and depends upon its many services, but pays taxes in the "bedroom towns" in which it lives. In some senses many suburbs are thus parasites upon their central cities, particularly in the eyes of the officials responsible for the future of those cities.

At the same time the mushrooming suburban population has thrust fantastic problems upon the existing or new governments of those areas: the influx of pupils into the schools, the need for expanded water supply, sanitation systems, law enforcement, and endless other services. Many of the communities have been ill-prepared to meet these demands and thus have managed to flounder magnificently. But of course one major aspect of the overall difficulties is the very existence within a metropolitan area of a vast number of separate and relatively uncoordinated governments, each trying to meet alone problems that are frequently regional in scope. How can one suburban government, for example, hope to solve by itself the terribly complex problems of transportation? Roads, freeways, public transit systems cannot be developed in isolation, and the same can be said in varying degrees about a number of other functions, such as air and water pollution control and land-use planning.

In a very real sense, most of the great metropolitan areas have become social and economic units while remaining fragmented as governments. Yet in recognizing this unity of interests, we must not ignore the fact that the people of the city and the suburbs commonly also have a keen sense of their separateness and differences. To be sure, those who have moved to the suburbs in search of better living have not always found what they sought and have at times become quite disillusioned. There is, in fact, evidence of a growing migration back to the cities; one survey has revealed complaints about the time and cost of long-range commuting, high suburban taxes, overcrowded schools running on split sessions, the lack of cultural opportunities, and the somewhat boring character of much suburban life. For example, 15 to 25 percent of the new residential building

Figure 15.3. *Standard Metropolitan Statistical Areas of the United States, 1966*

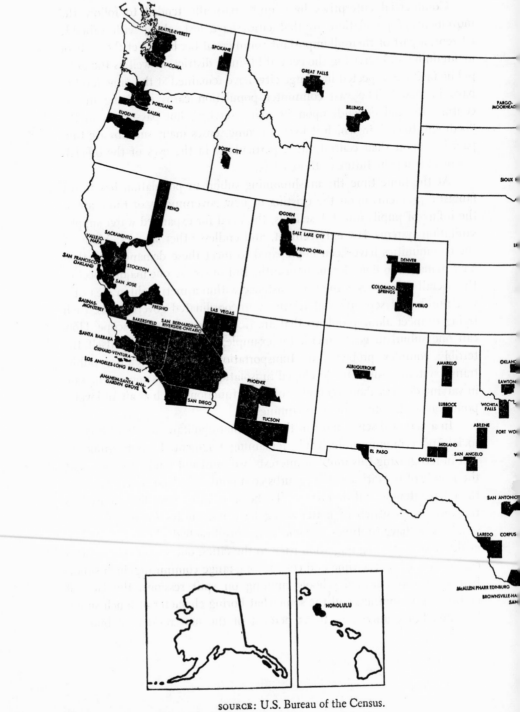

SOURCE: U.S. Bureau of the Census.

Area definitions by Federal Committee on Standard Metropolitan
Statistical Areas under the direction of U.S. Bureau of the Budget

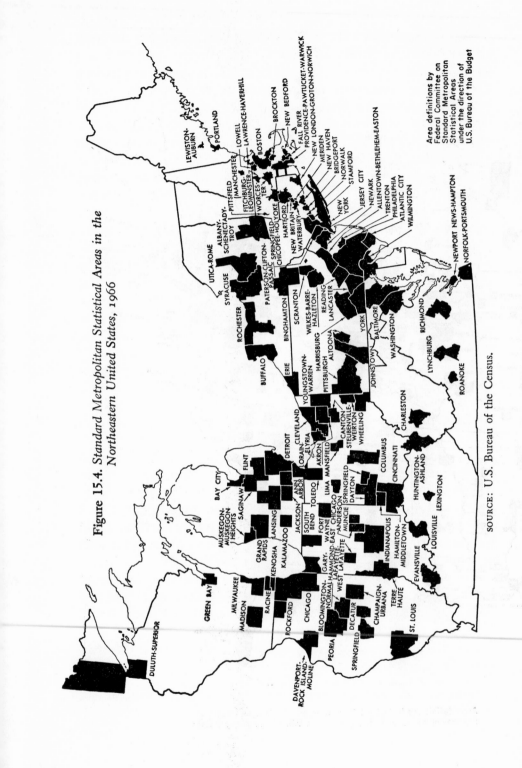

Figure 15.4. *Standard Metropolitan Statistical Areas in the Northeastern United States, 1966*

Area definitions by Federal Committee on Standard Metropolitan Statistical Areas under the direction of U.S. Bureau of the Budget

SOURCE: U.S. Bureau of the Census.

tenants in New York City were reported to be former suburbanites.[21]

THE WHOLE AND THE PARTS. The average metropolitan area is a welter of governments—cities, counties, school districts, and ordinarily a multitude of other special districts that were set up piecemeal to deal with specific problems as they arose. Illustrative are the Chicago metropolitan area, with 1,060 local governments; Philadelphia, with 963; and nine other areas, each supplied with 250 governments or more.[22] In this context a fair amount of conflict is virtually inevitable. Although these governments cooperate in some matters, there are endless sources of irritation, suspicion, and misunderstanding as well as simple differences of viewpoint. For example, one community may be lax in its building and fire safety regulation, creating a danger for adjoining neighbors. Another may harbor criminal elements that can prey upon the entire area because of uncoordinated police activity. There has even been an occasional suburb that has refused to agree to pool its fire-fighting and other emergency equipment with adjoining communities in the event of military attack. Serious inequities often prevail in the realm of taxation and grants-in-aid. State legislatures have at times imposed quite unreasonable burdens upon central cities, such as requiring a city to sell water to suburbs at the same rate it charges its own citizens, even though the suburb is then permitted to sell the same water to its residents at two or three times that rate.

It would seem that the most serious problem of all, however, does not relate directly to functional services, but has to do with the difficulty of achieving adequate popular control over the governmental policy process in these huge metropolitan areas. Sheer bigness seems invariably to create problems of responsiveness in any type of human organization, and this difficulty is compounded by the existence of such a vast number of governmental units that even the conscientious and well-informed citizen finds it impossible to give attention to all those that affect him. Moreover, as has been indicated previously, a number of the special districts are so organized as to be very remote from effective citizen control.

In other words, the fragmented character of metropolitan area government is not bad *primarily* because it divides up services but because it is likely to be essentially undemocratic. It is therefore of fundamental importance that attempts to solve metropolitan problems should not focus exclusively upon the criterion of administrative efficiency, as has so often

---

[21] Henry J. Bechtold, United Press International financial editor, in a UPI feature, December 13, 1960, quoting a study of trends undertaken by the Realty Equities Corporation.

[22] U.S. Bureau of the Census, Governmental Organization, p. 12.

been the case. Merely creating bigger units to replace a number of smaller ones may have certain administrative advantages, but this should not be undertaken unless the effect is to enhance rather than weaken democratic popular control. The basic principle of reorganization should be that whatever the nature of the governments in a metropolitan area, they should possess "sufficient power and competence of a generalized form to make meaningful decisions and to develop a vigorous political process." [23] It is obvious that the bewildering complex of problems facing every metropolitan area is not primarily a matter of structure. The problems range over virtually the whole gamut of human experience, and come to focus in such issues as employment, housing, race relations, air and water pollution, transportation, cultural opportunity, and a host of others. Vital to their solution is an effective and responsible political system, and organizational questions therefore become of some consequence.

A SINGLE METROPOLITAN GOVERNMENT. Let us then examine briefly the principal approaches attempted or advocated as possible means of achieving a greater degree of metropolitan integration. Most of them have in fact reflected a central concern for administrative efficiency, a worthy goal in itself, but there is gradually coming to be a wider awareness of the significance of attaining as well a viable democratic political process.

The most obvious approach would be to consolidate all the region's urbanized area into a single government. This clearly would make it possible to have uniform services and planning, to eliminate duplications, and to achieve some economies as a result of the larger scale of public services. Such an idea is easy enough to state, but is virtually impossible to accomplish. The creation of a single huge city government would indeed simplify the task of the voter in some ways, but at the same time it would increase his sense of remoteness from his government, of his being submerged in a mass, and of his inability as an individual to have much effect upon local policy. Having experienced this, a few large European cities have been experimenting with modified decentralization, such as the use of "town meetings" or neighborhood advisory councils for sections of the city in order that the citizen's voice be better heard and that he have a greater sense of participation.

Furthermore, the suburbs will generally fight consolidation, normally with the powerful aid of the state legislature, which has in the past rarely

---

[23] Robert C. Wood, "A Division of Powers in Metropolitan Areas," in Arthur Maass (ed.), Area and Power (New York: The Free Press, 1959), p. 61. This chapter contains an excellent elaboration of this important theme.

been pro-city in its views. The legislature has usually required that such changes be approved by extraordinary majorities in the popular vote, and often such majorities must be obtained in *each* of the units affected rather than in the region as a whole. It is, of course, extremely difficult for most persons to see beyond their local situations and acquire an overall view. Moreover, a number of the suburbs do have a case to make. Many provide high-quality services, have an active and effective political life, and value their sense of independence. They will be understandably reluctant to pay "their share" of the costs of operating the central city if it can be avoided. Thus it is fairly obvious that, regardless of its relative desirability, general consolidation is not at present a realistic possibility.

SINGLE-FUNCTION CONSOLIDATED SERVICES. In a few cases where a city constitutes most of a county area or can form a separate county, there have been some advantages gained by city-county consolidation. This consolidation, however, is quite limited in nature and has little to do with the suburbs and other units in the area. It is also possible to consolidate specific functions, as, for example, when a city and certain suburbs join in furnishing public health services. This can often be useful in providing better services at lower unit cost, although its development may simply delay comprehensive long-range solutions. Furthermore, such arrangements tend to be far removed from popular control, partly as a result of the sheer complexity of a multitude of agreements between governments for different purposes.

Closely related to functional consolidation is the practice of cooperative agreements or, occasionally, formal contracts between adjoining governments. Some of these on such obvious matters as reciprocal aid between fire departments in the event of major emergency have existed for a long time, but more extensive agreements have been made in recent years. For example, a suburb may frequently purchase certain services, perhaps water and sanitation, from the central city, or from the county. In this way it secures the advantages of large-scale operation and professionalization (and as a result it may simply have an even stronger motivation to stay independent). These purchases of service, however, do not recompense the central city for the suburban citizens' free use of its parks, libraries, museums, streets, and central business area. The central city is therefore doomed to be the victim, even to the ridiculous extreme that its heavier taxpayers move to the suburbs to escape the central tax rates that subsidize suburbanites' use of central facilities. It seems the suburbanite *can* eat his cake and have it too.

ANNEXATION AND EXTRA-TERRITORIALITY. If state laws

made it more readily feasible, cities might control fringe-area development by annexing adjoining territory as it becomes urbanized, but this is workable only under certain conditions and usually only in the newer, rapidly growing cities. It must ordinarily be accomplished before the surrounding area becomes incorporated and develops a sense of independence as a community, since a popular vote in the area is normally required for annexation. Once a city has become ringed with incorporated suburbs, annexation has ceased to hold much promise. If a city does want to annex territory, it is probably wise to resist pressure to extend its services outside the city limits even on a service-charge basis, except for emergency cooperation. If the city controls the means of providing a service, whether because of a monopoly on resources such as water or simply because of financial magnitude, it can occasionally achieve its end by the age-old tactic of "dangling the carrot."

A similar, yet significantly different, process exists in Virginia, where the cities are independent of county governments. Using a unique judicial procedure, a city may sue a surrounding county in order to have the city's urbanized fringe removed from the control of the county and added to the city. This use of an outside and presumably impartial arbiter is a totally different practice from that used in other states, and it has worked very successfully for the Virginia cities. The annexation courts there have apparently followed a general rule that urban areas ought to be under city government and rural areas under the counties. The cities, being able to argue effectively that they need additional territory for normal development and that the residents of the fringe area need municipal-type services, almost invariably win. The effect upon the county that loses a sizable chunk of its tax base is somewhat less pleasant. This is an interesting approach to controlling metropolitan development, but one that has never been copied elsewhere in this country. It has all the limitations of a judicial procedure, in that a court can act only when a controversy is presented and must deal only with the very specific issue of a given city's boundaries, regardless of other possible needs.[24]

Sometimes states are willing to grant so-called "extraterritorial powers" to the central cities, giving them some very limited control over adjacent areas. It has long been possible for cities to own and control property outside the city limits for such purposes as water supply or recreation, but the extraterritorial power might in addition include zoning

---

[24] *For an excellent summary and evaluation of this system, see Chester W. Bain, "Annexation: Virginia's Not-So-Judicial System," Public Administration Review, 15 (Autumn 1955), 251–62.*

control immediately beyond city boundaries or at least the power to prevent nuisances and protect health and safety in that fringe area. Otherwise, there is technically nothing to prevent a suburb from permitting a refinery or a steel fabricating plant to build in an area adjacent to a residential section across the city boundary. Although significant extraterritorial powers are still not common, a number of states now require at least consultation between planning commissions of adjoining units when changes near a boundary are proposed.

GENERAL APPROACHES TO SOLUTIONS. Most of the arrangements already described have been very limited or stop-gap measures, although not necessarily inconsequential. On the other hand, as we have noted, the complete merger of all local governments of a metropolitan area into a single government appears unlikely and probably undesirable. Between these extremes, however, lie several approaches that are broad in scope, command considerable support, and are currently being applied in certain metropolitan regions. Though certainly not identical, these systems have considerable similarity. All attempt in some fashion to provide a mechanism for performing certain functions deemed to be areawide in nature, while retaining existing governments to handle other activities. There is no easy formula for determining which are properly local and which are metropolitan functions, any more than it is simple to distinguish those functions that should belong to the national government from those that should belong to the states. Many of the newer governmental functions, such as urban renewal and a number of others involving extensive federal aid, are in large degree intergovernmental programs and defy simple classification.

The most substantial effort toward distinguishing between local and metropolitan functions has been made by the Advisory Commission on Intergovernmental Relations, whose membership consists of national, state, and local officials.[25] The economic, administrative, and political criteria used to evaluate optimum performance prospects are as significant as the ranking arrived at for allocating the governmental functions studied. The commission adopted the following criteria: [26]

1. *The governmental jurisdiction responsible for providing any service should be* large enough to enable the benefits from that service to be consumed primarily within the jurisdiction. *Neither the benefits*

---

[25] *Advisory Commission on Intergovernmental Relations,* Performance of Urban Functions (*Washington, D.C., 1963*).

[26] Ibid., *pp. 5f. Words in* roman *type have been added.*

from the service nor the social costs of failing to provide it should 'spill over' into other jurisdictions. For example, the central city should not be expected to pay all of the very high capital costs of constructing a subway system which primarily benefits the suburban commuter.

2. *The unit of government should be* large enough to permit realization of the economies of scale. *For example, it costs $58 per million gallons to provide primary sewage treatment in a million gallon capacity facility, but less than half this amount in a ten million gallon capacity facility.*

3. *The unit of government carrying on a function should have* a geographic area of jurisdiction adequate for effective performance, *as illustrated by the desirability of a sewage disposal system's conforming to a natural drainage basin.*

4. *The unit of government should have the* legal and administrative ability to perform services assigned to it. *If it is going to provide modern health protection, for example, it needs to have both adequate regulatory authority and the ability to attract and hold a trained staff capable of administering a public health program.*

5. *Every unit of government should be responsible for* a sufficient number of functions so that its governing processes involve a resolution of conflicting interests, with significant responsibility for balancing governmental needs and resources. *Thus, in the jurisdictional allocation of individual functions, there is an ever present danger of creating so many separate entities as to result in undemocratic, inequitable, and inadequate assignment of priorities. Elected officials should be responsible and held accountable for balancing governmental needs and resources.*

6. *The performance of functions by a unit of government should remain* controllable by and accessible to its residents. *This is an essential condition of responsible government and one that is too often violated by the creation of special districts whose decision-making power and purse strings are not susceptible to direct control by the voters.*

7. *Functions should be assigned to that level of government* which maximizes the conditions and opportunities for active citizen participation and still permits adequate performance. *This is another guarantee for keeping government sensitive to the citizens, as well as a way of assuring attraction of the community's best talent into positions of leadership.*

As the seventh criterion itself reveals, the listed considerations do not all point in the same direction; they need to be balanced against one another and related to the particular function under consideration. As usual, it is far easier to establish general principles than it is to agree on their application to specific problems. The commission attempted to apply the criteria to fifteen functions and ranked them from the "most local" to the "least local" as follows: [27]

1. *Fire protection*
2. *Public education*
3. *Refuse collection and disposal*
4. *Libraries*
5. *Police*
6. *Health*
7. *Urban renewal*
8. *Housing*
9. *Parks and recreation*
10. *Public welfare*
11. *Hospitals and medical care facilities*
12. *Transportation*
13. *Planning*
14. *Water supply and sewage disposal*
15. *Air pollution control*

Three specific approaches to the metropolitan area problem should be explained. One is the multi-purpose district—an adaptation of the special-district concept (typically confined to a single function) to a specially created area embracing the metropolitan region and capable of performing a number of functions. The only example at present is the Municipality of Metropolitan Seattle, established in 1958. It is governed by a metropolitan council consisting of fourteen elected officials of the component municipalities, one county commissioner of King County (within which the area of the agency falls), and a chairman (not an elected official) chosen by the remainder of the council. Its functions since its establishment have been to provide sewage disposal services and to control water pollution for the

---

[27] Ibid., *pp. 9–15. Each function is considered in terms of selected criteria at pp. 61–265. See also the commission's* Metropolitan Social and Economic Disparities: Implications for Intergovernmental Relations in Central Cities and Suburbs *(Washington, D.C., 1965)*.

whole area, but under the state enabling legislation the local communities, if they could agree, could also assign to the multi-purpose district the functions of transportation, comprehensive planning, water, parks, and garbage disposal. That they have not done so suggests a weakness in the idea: so long as the consent of the local governments is required before its responsibilities can be expanded, the so-called "multi-purpose" district is likely to be little better than one more special district with narrow responsibilities. One escape from this difficulty would be for the state to authorize the multi-purpose district to add functions, subject to a favorable vote by the people in the entire service area.[28] Such a system is potentially a vast improvement over the use of separate metropolitan-wide districts for each function, but it may still be subject to the charge of remoteness and unresponsiveness.

A second arrangement involves the transfer of areawide functions to the county, thus creating a "metropolitan county." [29] The best-known current example is Dade County, Florida, which embraces Miami and twenty-six other municipalities.[30] Initiated in 1957, the Dade County "metro" has survived a great many attacks, both political and legal, and has made significant progress toward its goal of improved administration of public services in this area of mushrooming population.

The special conditions of Dade County's success should be noted. First of all, Dade County government is organized far better than most county governments. The new metropolitan county charter provides for an integrated organization, headed by a council and a county manager. Further, it is responsible for a substantial list of countywide functions, including transportation (expressways, air, water, rail and bus terminal facilities, and traffic control), air pollution control, assessments, fire and police protection, housing and urban renewal, building and zoning codes, and the construction of integrated water, sanitary sewage, and surface drainage systems. While the municipalities retain responsibility for local functions, the county may take over any function for which the municipality fails to meet the county's minimum performance standards; and, on the other

---

[28] *Advisory Commission on Intergovernmental Relations,* Alternative Approaches to Governmental Reorganization in Metropolitan Areas (*Washington, D.C.,* 1962), pp. 53–58.

[29] *See* ibid., *pp.* 38–46.

[30] *On the Dade County experience, see Edward Sofen,* The Miami Metropolitan Experiment (*Bloomington, Ind.: Indiana University Press,* 1963); *Reinhold P. Wolff,* Miami Metro: The Road to Urban Unity (*Coral Gables, Fla.: Bureau of Business and Economic Research, University of Miami,* 1960); *Gustave Serino,* Miami's Metropolitan Experiment (*Gainesville, Fla.: Public Administration Clearing Service, University of Florida,* 1958).

hand, a municipality's council may request the county to take over a particular function. Moreover, it should be noted that this system cannot be used in about a third of the country's metropolitan areas because they extend beyond the boundaries of a single county. Indeed, twenty-three of them extend over parts of two or more states. Finally, the political conditions for transferring such a substantial number of powers from local communities to the county may rarely be favorable. In Dade County only 26 per cent of the voters bothered to vote and only a bare majority of them agreed on the transfer of metropolitan functions.[31] The system has operated in a turmoil of controversy ever since.

As mentioned earlier,[32] some urban counties may in time engage more and more in the practice of furnishing all municipal services to cities on a contract basis, but this will require contracts with a number of individual communities, and it is highly unlikely that it would ever achieve general coverage of an entire metropolitan area.

Finally, there is the system of metropolitan federation, sometimes referred to as the borough plan. This is simply local federalism, the application of the federal government principle at the local level. The existing local governments formally unite to create a new metropolitan government to which certain powers and functions are delegated, all others remaining in the member governments. Although there have been a few abortive attempts at this in the past, as well as some limited versions, this system is presently best typified by metropolitan Toronto, Canada. Brought into being there by action of the provincial government in 1953, "metro" has to its credit a number of impressive accomplishments, but still faces a variety of problems that remain unsolved. It has, of course, encountered the basic problem of all federations, that of maintaining a reasonable and satisfactory division of powers and functions. On what basis should the division be established? Once established, should it remain forever static? Can additional functions be taken over by the metropolitan government without bringing about the ultimate demise of the local units? Or should it perhaps be merely a transitional stage on the road toward abolition of those local units? Is it possible to avoid destructive contests and conflicts over the distribution of powers?

Similarly, there is the familiar problem of potentially excessive bureaucracy in the operation of two complete levels of government, the problem of finding ways to absorb the continually growing urban fringe

---

[31] *Scott Greer*, Metropolitics (*New York: Wiley, 1963*), *p. 189.*
[32] *See pages 516–17.*

into the federation and of eliminating serious inequalities in taxation, and the knotty one of whether the governing body of the federation government should represent people, constituent governments, or some combination of both.[33] Despite the difficulties, however, there seems to be no serious thought of abolishing the federation, which in fact has had great enough success to encourage a number of other metropolitan areas to give the system serious consideration.

The administrative advantages in these three plans—the multi-purpose district, the metropolitan county, and the metropolitan federation—are obvious, but none of them makes a very significant contribution to achieving more effective popular control of the political process. It is along these lines, as well as to other possible approaches to solving functional problems, that careful thinking and extensive research need to be directed.

It is quite evident that no one simple solution is available and that every area will no doubt always have to adapt programs to meet its particular special problems and circumstances. Even though actual experiments to date may have been relatively few, there has been a tremendous amount of interest in the topic in recent years, both in professional circles and on the part of community leaders in the metropolitan areas themselves. In addition to academic studies, a number of communities have engaged in extensive self-surveys, foundations are subsidizing a variety of research projects, and the sheer volume of the material published on metropolitan problems is little short of overwhelming.[34]

---

[33] *On the Toronto experience see Frank Smallwood,* Metro Toronto: A Decade Later *(Toronto: Bureau of Municipal Research, November, 1963); and John G. Grumm,* Metropolitan Area Government: The Toronto Experience *(Lawrence, Kan.: University of Kansas Governmental Research Series No. 19, 1959).*

[34] *The best starting point is the group of remarkably searching reports of the Advisory Commission on Intergovernmental Relations, which use and cite a number of scholarly studies as well as make contributions of their own. Illustrative are:* Governmental Structure, Organization, and Planning in Metropolitan Areas *(published in July 1961, by U.S. House of Representatives Committee on Government Operations, 87th Congress, 1st Session; commentaries on the report are in the same Committee's* Government in Metropolitan Areas *[1962]);* Alternative Approaches to Governmental Reorganization in Metropolitan Areas *(June 1962);* Factors Affecting Voter Reactions to Governmental Reorganization in Metropolitan Areas *(May 1962);* Metropolitan Social and Economic Disparities: Implications for Intergovernmental Relations in Central Cities and Suburbs *(January 1965);* Performance of Urban Functions: Local and Areawide *(September 1963). Other relatively recent publications by social scientists include: John C. Bollens and Henry J. Schmandt,* The Metropolis: Its People, Politics, and Economic Life *(New York: Harper, 1965);* Luther Gulick, The Metropolitan Problem and American Ideas *(New York: Knopf, 1962); John C. Bollens (ed.),* Exploring the Metropolitan Community *(Berkeley, Calif.: University of California Press, 1961); Scott Greer,* Governing the Metropolis *(New York: Wiley, 1962), and his* Metropolitics *(New York: Wiley, 1963); Webb S. Fiser,* Mastery of the Metropolis *(Englewood Cliffs, N.J.: Prentice-Hall, 1962); Roscoe C. Martin,* Metropolis in Transi-

But the finest technical plan in the world is likely to be of little value unless it can receive the necessary political support. This support has generally come from the various "good government" groups, such as civic associations and the League of Women Voters; from reform elements; from professional students of government, whether in academic life or some form of governmental research or service activity; frequently from the newspapers; and very often also from associations of businessmen, such as chambers of commerce. In any specific community there will, of course, be other interested local groups, and it is a curious fact that branches of the same organization may support such movements in one place and oppose them in another.

Opposition to a metropolitan reorganization plan is likely to come from the suburban areas, for reasons already discussed, and particularly from the officials of those communities who may fear the loss of their jobs. Besides, most political leaders, in whatever government, are prone to prefer a system they are familiar with and that they can control; thus they will take considerable convincing before being willing to disturb existing arrangements. Furthermore, the suburban residents have been conditioned to have a low view of the central city and its leadership, and have been able to muster strong support for their position in the rural areas. There is often a partisan factor involved, too, since commonly, although by no means invariably, one party is dominant in the central city and another in the suburbs. Therefore, the risk of being politically submerged in some sort of integrated unit will not be taken lightly.

Despite notable exceptions, organized labor has usually opposed metropolitan integration, partly because of its strong commitment to a "Jacksonian democracy" concept, partly because the proposals are so often promoted by business groups and are thus automatically suspect, and partly because labor has traditionally been left out of the "civic betterment" groups, at least until rather recently. Quite naturally, there will be in any community numerous other special interest groups which for one reason or another have a stake in the status quo; yet the biggest problem is that of stirring the general public to action, of informing them and stimulating their concern. Proponents of metropolitan reorganization have too often been ineffective in building group support early in the game and in "selling" their proposals with persuasive arguments and symbols that arouse favorable emotional response. As Victor Jones pointed out long ago,

tion: Local Government Adaptation to Changing Urban Needs (*Washington, D.C., Housing and Home Finance Agency,* 1963); *Robert C. Wood,* Suburbia: Its People and Their Politics (*Boston: Houghton-Mifflin,* 1959), *and his* Metropolis Against Itself (*New York: Committee for Economic Development,* 1959).

words like "efficiency" and "economy" do not excite the average person, whereas words like "un-American," "centralization," and "corrupt city bosses" are "charged with high emotional voltage." [35]

The great central cities of the nation's metropolitan areas must do more than continue to seek more effective organizational relationships and to secure tax support from those who work in the city and live outside. They also need to make every effort to ensure able political leadership and a vigorous political process so that they can become more attractive places in which to live, to work, and to play. In the last few years a number of them have made outstanding progress along these lines, and it is already paying dividends. The urban renewal and redevelopment programs promoted by the national government have played a major role, and a striking multiplication and intensification of national effort focused on big cities' problems occurred in 1965, which also saw creation of the Department of Housing and Urban Development. Some states have begun to take serious action to help meet metropolitan problems, but more state effort is urgently needed, such as studies and recommendations on possible courses of action, long-range regional planning, removing some of the financial roadblocks, and untying the hands of the cities by granting them greater freedom of action. Metropolitan area problems are among the most critical in the whole realm of domestic policy today—a topic of tremendous complexity that will remain a challenge to our best efforts for years to come.

5. Conclusion

We have necessarily followed a circuitous route in exploring local government. But in the process it should have become clear that the very term "local government" interferes with clarity of analysis. There are many—at least 80,000—local governments; they may individually minister to anywhere from a few dozen people to eight million; and the governments themselves vary in structure and function. Each community is a political system in itself, and the degree of popular participation and control may range from the town meeting, the theoretically most idealized form of democracy, to the little oligarchies, if not autocracies, of men who know how to hold on to power and use it for their own benefit. In between are all the other political systems with their rich variety of participants, their lively competition over priorities, and their own ways of negotiating and resolving differences. In addition, here, at the local level, is the base of our

---

[35] Victor Jones, "The Politics of Integration in Metropolitan Areas," The Annals of the American Academy of Political and Social Science, 207 (January 1940), 167.

national politics, the environment out of which emerge many of the politically talented who have a capacity for state and national responsibility.

As we have seen, citizens are often not motivated to take an interest in local government or to involve themselves even by voting at local elections —let alone to engage in more active kinds of participation.[36] To improve motivation and involvement, a citizen must feel that what his local government does is important and relevant to his life, that there are significant choices of policy to be made, and that he can be reasonably effective either individually or in concert with others in influencing elections and legislative decisions.

The tangled complexity of local governmental units, the ballot's long list of minor offices and unknown candidates, the failure of the boundaries of the local government to encompass natural social and economic communities and problem areas that cry for local solution, and the possible deadening of political processes by a sterile nonpartisanship—all these and more take their toll of the citizen's motivation, involvement, and sense of efficacy. And they carry a further cost: They drain the positive content from local government. When special districts rob town, city, and county governments of important functions; when there is no focus of responsibility within a general local government but, instead, a diffusion that fosters inaction rather than positive decision; when the geographic problem areas are fragmented among hundreds of local governments—especially in metropolitan areas—so that areawide planning and effective action can proceed only by a seldom achieved unanimity; and when the potential of local government for building a truly vital community is sacrificed to a housekeeping and maintenance concept of sweeping streets and keeping plumbing in good order—local government is deprived of positive content.

Today local government employs 5.7 million members of the labor force and expends more than $50 billion annually. It is necessary, indeed valuable, for it performs a multitude of public services and serves as a foundation for community cooperation. Yet it *could* be made much more truly a creative force for achieving significant social goals and the conditions of life that would make it possible in our modern society for the individual citizen to find fulfillment, and for the word "community" to have genuine meaning.

---

[36] *See Robert E. Lane*, Political Life: Why People Get Involved in Politics (*New York: The Free Press, 1959); and V. O. Key, Jr.*, Public Opinion and American Democracy (*New York: Knopf, 1961*). *One caution should be stated: In some circumstances a low level of political participation by the people may indicate not disinterest but contentment with the uses to which power is put by the few who hold governmental decision-making responsibility.*

☆ ☆ ☆ ☆ ☆ ☆ ☆ ☆ ☆

chapter 16

The Future of State and Local Government

The shape of things to come is determined in part by long-term trends, in part by crisis and accident, and in part by the wills of men and their ability to alter the direction, pace, or consequence of seemingly deterministic trends and to absorb and capitalize on crises and accidents.

Within the range of reasonable forecasting, the future of state and local governments depends on two factors. One is the responsibilities that will confront these governments. The other is their capabilities. We shall attempt to characterize the nature of future responsibilities and then will assess certain of the capabilities of state governments and of local governments. Finally, we shall consider the future character of federalism.

1. Responsibilities of the Future

People—their numbers, age groups, and geographical distribution are the most important determinants of the responsibilities of state and local governments. The population, which was 181 million in 1960, had risen to 195 million by 1965 and will increase, according to one Census Bureau projection, to 226 million in 1975, to 266 million in 1985, and to 338 million in the year 2000.[1] The 1960 to 1985 increase of almost 86 million is about 47 percent, and the 158 million increase from 1960 to 2000 is 87 percent.

It is precisely within the currently conceived responsibilities of state and local governments that the problems of all these additional people will fall. Where are they to live, be educated, get hospital care, find recreation? How will they move from home to work and back, or drive from city to city for business, or take vacation trips? Can water supply and sewage systems and electric and other energy distribution systems be developed rapidly enough to keep pace? How much will the greater congestion of living lead to greater frictions among human beings, to greater crime rates in addition to the simple increase of policing tasks because of the numbers of people? Surely it is predictable that these people will spread horizontally, urbanizing suburbs beyond the present suburbs, and will pile up vertically in a multitude of high-rise apartment buildings not yet on the drawing boards.

Consider one clear case—education. By long tradition, elementary and secondary public education has been a state and local responsibility, and so, indeed, has been public education at the college and university level. The federal government has pressed desegregation of public schools, has contributed to the financing of vocational and agricultural education, and more recently to public education at all levels. But the main responsibility for building and operating public schools remains state and local. The school-age population (5 to 17 years) will have increased from 1960 to 1975 by 11.4 million (a 26 percent rise) and from 1960 to 1985 by 23.3 million (a 53 percent rise).[2] Will the schoolrooms be built, the teachers

---

[1] *U.S. Bureau of the Census,* Statistical Abstract of the United States: 1965 *(Washington, D.C., 1965), pp. 6f., Series B. One of four series of projections, each based on a different assumption about the birth rate, Series B assumes a "very moderate decline from present levels." The totals shown include armed forces abroad; other data used in our discussion often are exclusive of armed forces abroad. Amounts of increase are computed from detailed population totals, not from the rounded off totals given in the text.*

[2] *U.S. Bureau of the Census,* Current Population Reports, Series P-25, No. 326, *"Illustrative Projections of the Population of States: 1970 to 1985" (Washington, D.C., 1966), p. 22. See the note to Table 16.1 of this chapter for assumptions underlying the use, as here, of the series I-B projections.*

The impact on the states of the increase of school-age population will vary. West Virginia whose total population will decline 0.5 percent by 1985, will have 13.4 percent fewer 5-to-17-year-old children. Although the number of children in all other states will increase (and so they will need more schoolrooms and teachers), the rate of increase will be slower than that of total state population in 14 states (in the South and border area, Alabama, Arkansas, Georgia, Kentucky, Mississippi, Tennessee, and both Carolinas; in the mountain states, Idaho, Utah, and Wyoming; and Vermont, North Dakota, and Oregon). Ibid., pp. 23–29.

trained in sufficient numbers, the school board members and school system superintendents prepared for larger-scale operations? Official estimates are that from 1960 to 1975 about 430,000 new public schoolrooms will have to be built just to take care of the increased enrollment in the nation, and that another 600,000 will be needed because of current replacements (for abandonments), migration, consolidation of school districts, and reduction of crowded and unsatisfactory rooms. Teachers will need to be trained to fill the almost 700,000 teacher positions in 1974 that did not exist in 1960, as well as to replace the teachers who leave the profession permanently (at an annual rate of 108,000 in 1960 and 164,000 in 1974).[3]

THE STATES' PEOPLE. The burden of the population explosion will not fall equally on the states. As shown in Table 16.1, by 1985, California will double the population she had in 1960. But her rate of increase (102.7 percent) will be less than those of Florida (123.3) and Arizona (131.9). West Virginia, at the other extreme, will actually have fewer people in 1985 than in 1960, while Iowa, North Dakota, Kansas, and Pennsylvania will increase at modest rates (ranging from 17.4 to 20.4 percent), less than half the national rate of increase. Percentage increases, of course, do not show where the largest numbers of additional people will be found. California eclipses all other states by her prospect of gaining over 16 million more people. She is followed—at quite a distance—by Florida (with a gain of 6.1 million), New York (5.9 million), Texas (5 million), Ohio (4.3 million), and Illinois (4.1 million).

Despite population shifts, the group of states whose governments affect the most people will remain generally the same in 1985 as in 1960 (see Table 16.2). In 1985, half the nation's people will be in eight states, while two-thirds of the people will be in fifteen states. Wisconsin, the smallest of these fifteen states, will have as many people as will be found in the eight least populous states put together. In 1985, as in 1960, if one is concerned about the quality of governments that affect the welfare of most of the American people, the appropriate focus will be this mere one-sixth to one-third of the states. Consider, for example, the fact that six of the eight largest states had not adopted a broad-based personal income tax as of January, 1966.[4] Will this be of merely historical interest by 1985, or will the pattern persist as an anomalous accompaniment to the heaviest responsibilities of service to the people? The list of largest states includes the best-

---

[3] *Office of Education, U.S. Department of Health, Education, and Welfare,* Projections of Educational Statistics to 1974–75 (*Washington, D.C.,* 1965), *pp. 30f (teachers), and 48 (schoolrooms).*

[4] *U.S. Advisory Commission on Intergovernmental Relations,* Federal-State Coordination of Personal Income Taxes (*Washington, D.C.,* 1965), *p. ii.*

Table 16.1. *Projections of the Total Population of States, 1960–1985*

State	1960 Population (000)	1985 Projected Population (000)	Net Change		Net Migration (000)
			Number (000)	Percent	
United States	179,323	265,575	86,251	48.1%	+7,642
Alabama	3,267	4,558	1,292	39.5	−232
Alaska	226	382	156	69.1	−52
Arizona	1,302	3,019	1,717	131.9	+694
Arkansas	1,786	2,393	607	34.0	−129
California	15,717	31,854	16,136	102.7	+7,140
Colorado	1,754	2,971	1,218	69.4	+238
Connecticut	2,535	4,024	1,489	58.7	+445
Delaware	446	771	324	72.7	+72
Florida	4,952	11,057	6,105	123.3	+3,907
Georgia	3,943	5,790	1,847	46.8	−237
Hawaii	632	908	275	43.5	−87
Idaho	667	950	283	42.5	−30
Illinois	10,081	14,144	4,063	40.3	−31
Indiana	4,662	6,477	1,814	38.9	−140
Iowa	2,758	3,237	479	17.4	−389
Kansas	2,179	2,623	445	20.4	−309
Kentucky	3,038	3,715	676	22.3	−511
Louisiana	3,257	5,088	1,831	56.2	−73
Maine	969	1,207	238	24.5	−114
Maryland	3,101	5,272	2,171	70.0	+526
Massachusetts	5,149	6,881	1,733	33.7	−51
Michigan	7,823	10,671	2,847	36.4	−671
Minnesota	3,414	4,827	1,414	41.4	−134
Mississippi	2,178	2,984	806	37.0	−378
Missouri	4,320	5,482	1,162	26.9	−259
Montana	675	920	245	36.3	−74
Nebraska	1,411	1,731	319	22.6	−215
Nevada	285	563	278	97.3	+68
New Hampshire	607	922	315	52.0	+77
New Jersey	6,067	9,698	3,631	59.8	+1,206

(*Table 16.1 continued*)

State	1960 Population (000)	1985 Projected Population (000)	Net Change		Net Migration (000)
			Number (000)	Percent	
New Mexico	951	1,749	798	83.9	+42
New York	16,782	22,676	5,894	35.1	+191
North Carolina	4,556	6,266	1,710	37.5	−432
North Dakota	632	751	118	18.7	−155
Ohio	9,706	13,968	4,262	43.9	+70
Oklahoma	2,328	2,944	616	26.5	−175
Oregon	1,769	2,501	733	41.4	+122
Pennsylvania	11,319	13,630	2,311	20.4	−912
Rhode Island	859	1,062	203	23.6	−76
South Carolina	2,383	3,293	911	38.2	−364
South Dakota	681	838	158	23.2	−145
Tennessee	3,567	4,830	1,263	35.4	−186
Texas	9,580	14,540	4,960	51.8	−205
Utah	891	1,566	675	75.8	+26
Vermont	390	534	144	36.9	−13
Virginia	3,967	6,064	2,097	52.9	+64
Washington	2,853	4,154	1,300	45.6	+107
West Virginia	1,860	1,851	−10	−0.5	−505
Wisconsin	3,952	5,585	1,633	41.3	−64
Wyoming	330	476	146	44.2	−11

Note: Of the four alternative projections of state population presented in the Census Bureau report, this table uses Series I-B, which rests on the assumptions that the rate of births minus deaths will very moderately decline from present levels and that gross migration rates from state to state will continue in about the 1955–60 pattern (separately computed by age, sex, and color).

SOURCE: U.S. Bureau of the Census, *Current Population Reports*, Series P-25, No. 326, "Illustrative Projections of the Population of States: 1970 to 1985" (Washington, D.C., 1966), pp. 14, 16.

governed states of the Union and some that are often rated among the worst-governed. Size of population is obviously not the critical variable in the quality of state government achieved. But it would seem to be a valid indicator of which states most need to maintain, and in some cases develop for the first time, the capability to perform their functions responsibly, democratically, intelligently, and efficiently.

Table 16.2 shows the rank order of larger states, by population, in 1960 and 1985. The most striking shifts are the rise in the ranking of Texas and Florida and the decline (though not, of course, in actual population) of Pennsylvania and Missouri. A mere rank ordering, however, disguises significant changes in share of the total population. California, for example, moves from 8.8 percent of the national population in 1960 to 12 percent in 1985, and Florida rises from 2.8 to 4.2 percent. New Jersey, Texas, and Virginia increase their respective proportions of the total by less than a third of one percent, and Georgia shows no change. But the ten

Table 16.2. *Selected States Ranked by Share of National Population, 1960 and 1985*

	1960			1985	
		Percent of national			*Percent of national*
Rank	*State*	*population*	*Rank*	*State*	*population*
1.	New York	9.4%	1.	California	12.0%
2.	California	8.8	2.	New York	8.5
3.	Pennsylvania	6.3	3.	Texas	5.5
4.	Illinois	5.6	4.	Illinois	5.3
5.	Ohio	5.4	5.	Ohio	5.3
6.	Texas	5.3	6.	Pennsylvania	5.1
7.	Michigan	4.4	7.	Florida	4.2
8.	New Jersey	3.4	8.	Michigan	4.0
9.	Massachusetts	2.9			
	Subtotal, 1–9	51.5%		*Subtotal, 1–8*	49.9%
10.	Florida	2.8%	9.	New Jersey	3.7%
11.	Indiana	2.6	10.	Massachusetts	2.6
12.	North Carolina	2.5	11.	Indiana	2.4
13.	Missouri	2.4	12.	North Carolina	2.4
14.	Virginia	2.2	13.	Virginia	2.3
15.	Wisconsin	2.2	14.	Georgia	2.2
16.	Georgia	2.2	15.	Wisconsin	2.1
	Subtotal, 10–16	16.9%		*Subtotal, 9–15*	17.6%
	Total, 1–16	68.4%		*Total, 1–15*	67.5%
43.	Hawaii	.4	43.	Hawaii	.3
44.	North Dakota	.4	44.	South Dakota	.3

(Table 16.2 continued)

	1960			1985	
Rank	State	Percent of national population	Rank	State	Percent of national population
45.	New Hampshire	.3	45.	Delaware	.3
46.	Delaware	.2	46.	North Dakota	.3
47.	Vermont	.2	47.	Nevada	.2
48.	Wyoming	.2	48.	Vermont	.2
49.	Nevada	.2	49.	Wyoming	.2
50.	Alaska	.1	50.	Alaska	.1
Subtotal, 43–50		2.0	Subtotal, 43–50		1.9
26 other states (17–42)		29.6	27 other states (16–42)		30.6
Total		100.0	Total		100.0

Notes: Of the four alternative projections of state population presented in the Census Bureau report, this table uses series I-B, which rests on the assumptions that the rate of births minus deaths will very moderately decline from present levels and that gross migration rates from state to state will continue in about the 1955–60 pattern (separately computed by age, sex, and color).

The ranking of states with identical percentages (to the first decimal point) reflects actual 1960 or projected 1985 population.

SOURCE: U.S. Bureau of the Census, *Current Population Reports*, Series P-25, No. 326, "Illustrative Projections of the Population of States: 1970 to 1985" (Washington, D.C., 1966), p. 21.

other populous states suffer reductions in their shares of the national population.

THE CITIES' AND SUBURBS' PEOPLE. Transformation of America from a predominantly rural and agricultural to a predominantly urban society was formally marked as early as 1920, when the census for the first time classified over half the population as urban. By 1960, the urban population had risen to 70 percent of the total. Even the population classified as rural had itself altered in terms of those who lived on farms and those who did not. In 1920, 30 percent of America's people lived on farms, but in 1960 only 8.7 percent, and the figure continued to decline after 1960.[5] Another way of viewing urbanization is that in 1920 slightly over half the people lived in places of 2,500 or more inhabitants, while in 1960 the same proportion lived in places of 10,000 or more inhabitants.[6]

---

[5] *U.S. Bureau of the Census*, Statistical Abstract of the United States: 1965, *p. 614. By 1964 the farm population had fallen to 6.8 percent of the total population.*
[6] Ibid., *p. 15.*

Though the Census Bureau has not published projections to 1975 or 1985 of urban, rural, metropolitan, and nonmetropolitan population, we can take account of developments from 1960 to 1965 to establish tentative trend lines. In 1960, 62.9 percent of the people lived in metropolitan areas. This proportion has since grown.[7] In the five years after 1960, the population of metropolitan areas increased 10.2 percent, while that of nonmetropolitan areas increased only 3.4 percent.[8] In the period of 1960 to 1965, as in that of 1950 to 1960, the increase in the population of metropolitan areas constituted nearly 85 percent of the increase in the population of the country as a whole. Barring a reversal or serious modification of the trend line marked out by the recent past, it will be mostly those public policies bearing on the welfare of people in metropolitan areas that will determine whether Americans will be satisfied or dissatisfied with the performance of their governments, national, state, and local.

Among and within the metropolitan areas, the developing pattern of population distribution will also have important meaning for the future. Almost half (47 percent) the people of the country are in the 55 metropolitan areas that had over 500,000 population in 1960.[9] Yet these areas embrace only 190 of the country's 3,043 counties. Although, as might be expected, the rank order of the largest metropolitan areas has not changed much in the 1960 to 1965 period for which data are available, the rates of growth showed marked variations. Table 16.3 shows the areas that increased at twice or more the rate for all standard metropolitan statistical areas of 500,000 or more population and those that changed at less than half the general rate. A glance reveals the concentration of major gains in the West and Southwest and the concentration of the principal relative losses [10] in the Midwest and East. If once the course of empire took its way westward, in our time the course of metropolitanism

[7] *In 1960 the Census Bureau identified 212 Standard Metropolitan Statistical Areas, and the 1965 population of these was 64.4 percent of the total national population. Meantime, however, ten additional areas had qualified for classification as SMSA's; their population (not included in the 1965 percentage) would of course raise further the proportion of total population living in metropolitan areas.*

[8] *U.S. Bureau of the Census*, Current Population Reports, Series P-20, No. 151, "Population of the United States by Metropolitan and Nonmetropolitan Residence: April 1965 and 1960" (Washington, D.C., April 1966), p. 1. *The rate of increase for metropolitan area population is presumably roughly applicable to the 222 SMSA's of 1965, rather than just to the 212 SMSA's of 1960 to which it specifically refers. However, the rate of increase for nonmetropolitan areas is probably overstated because it includes the increase for the ten newly classified metropolitan areas.*

[9] *U.S. Bureau of the Census*, Current Population Reports, Series P-25, No. 347, "Provisional Estimates of the Population of the Largest Metropolitan Areas: July 1, 1965" (Washington, D.C., August 1966), p. 9.

[10] *The cities shown as sustaining relative losses, but, except for Pittsburgh, increasing their population, actually suffered net losses by migration. Only the net of births over deaths overcame the net out-migration and so accounted for their population increases.*

Table 16.3. *Estimated Rates of Population Change of the Largest*
Metropolitan Areas, 1960 to 1965

(Areas of 500,000 or more population)

Areas Increasing at Twice or More the Overall Rate *	Percent Change	Areas Changing by One-half or Less the Overall Rate *	Percent Change
Anaheim–Santa Ana–Garden		Gary–Hammond–East Chicago,	
Grove, Calif.	57.8%	Ind.	3.6%
San Jose, Calif.	38.0	Cleveland, Ohio	3.2
San Bernardino–Riverside–		Milwaukee, Wisc.	2.9
Ontario, Calif.	27.5	Boston, Mass.	2.9
Phoenix, Ariz.	26.2	Providence–Pawtucket–War-	
Washington, D.C.–Md.–Va.	21.3	wick, R.I.	2.8
Houston, Tex.	19.5	Toledo, Ohio–Mich.	2.6
Dallas, Tex.	18.9	Birmingham, Ala.	1.4
Sacramento, Calif.	18.6	Buffalo, N.Y.	1.2
Atlanta, Ga.	18.5	Youngstown–Warren, Ohio	0.5
		Jersey City, N.J.	.0
		Pittsburgh, Pa.	−1.6

* For all standard metropolitan statistical areas with 1960 populations of 500,000 or more, the percent change was 9.1.

SOURCES: U.S. Bureau of the Census, *Current Population Reports*, Series P-25, No. 347, "Provisional Estimates of the Population of the Largest Metropolitan Areas: July 1, 1965" (Washington, D.C., August 1966).

is taking the same direction. For the relatively young western cities, the chief problem of metropolitan growth is the need for guidance and control of settlement patterns, rather than as in the older eastern metropolitan centers the need for urban redevelopment and rehousing of people living and being schooled in structures dating from before the First World War.

Because the trend toward metropolitan settlement is of such long standing, the more important lesson for the future is probably the way in which people are distributing themselves within metropolitan areas. Although the population of metropolitan areas increased 10.2 percent during the period from 1960 to 1965, the central cities increased only 3.2 percent, while the growth was 17.7 percent outside these central cities.[11] The flight to the suburbs appeared not only to be continuing, but accelerating. In

[11] *Statistical data in this and the following paragraph are from, or calculated from, U.S. Bureau of the Census, Current Population Reports, Series P-20, No. 151, "Population of the United States by Metropolitan and Nonmetropolitan Residence: April 1965 and 1960" (Washington, D.C., April 1966).*

1950 to 1960, the suburban areas accounted for about 75 percent of the increase in the population of metropolitan areas. In 1960 to 1965, this proportion had grown to 85 percent.

Furthermore, the cities and their suburbs continued to develop different ethnic patterns of population. Of the nation's 22.8 million nonwhites in 1965, 15.6 million were in metropolitan areas. Of these, 12.4 million were in the central cities, with only 3.2 million in the suburbs. This meant that the central cities had a 21 percent nonwhite population, while nonwhites were only 5 percent of the suburban population. Problems of desegregating schools, of improving education and skills of the previously disadvantaged, of battling over discrimination in its myriad forms, not least in real estate sales and housing rentals, and of struggling with the unemployment rates that run highest among Negroes and Puerto Ricans—all these mounted and apparently will continue to mount for the central cities, with little help from the suburbs, and, indeed, some obstruction.[12]

With the growth of suburban industrial and retail shopping developments, a curious movement between home and work has developed. The 1960 pattern, presumably not greatly changed since, revealed not only the familiar commuting of workers from the suburbs to the central city but an opposite flow of workers from central city to suburbs. Nationally, 37 percent of suburban workers did their work in the city, while 12 percent of city workers commuted regularly to the suburbs.[13] The burden on highways and public transit facilities is one of the heavy costs of this two-way flow, but there are and will be in the future other consequences, perhaps most basic a loss of a sense of community as people earn their bread in one community and rest their heads in another.

2. The Capabilities of State Governments

It is nothing new to have a growing population, changing in its ethnic, economic, and educational-achievement pattern, and distributing itself

---

[12] *Many suburban towns and cities, anxious to avoid the problems besetting the central cities, carefully avoid applying for federally aided public housing projects that would be limited to lower income groups and would carry federal prohibitions against racial discrimination. Lacking a substantial nonwhite segment of their governmental constituency, they also often lag in responding to advocates of nondiscrimination ordinances and other measures that would make nonwhite migration possible.*

[13] *U.S. Advisory Commission on Intergovernmental Relations,* Metropolitan Social and Economic Disparities: Implications for Intergovernmental Relations in Central Cities and Suburbs *(Washington, D.C., 1965), pp. 21f. Cf. Andrew Hacker's cogent criticism of the report's statistical concepts,* American Political Science Review, 60 *(June 1966), 422f.*

unevenly among states and communities. The states' governments have experienced such changes throughout America's history. Their responses, however, both to the explicit policy problems posed and to the implicit challenges to strengthen their own governmental capabilities have not been reassuring. In most states, tradition, weighted by inertia, has been a drag that retarded innovation. One cannot be sanguine about the timely adaptation of state governments to the challenges that lie ahead.

Even in the past, the mere survival of state governments was no assurance that their role in the American system was not declining. So, too, in the future, the question is not anything so dramatic as whether there will still be state governments in 1985 or 2000. Rather it is whether, despite their survival, they may not decline in relative significance. The prospect of a decline might reasonably be inferred from the nature and urgency of future demands on government, the demonstrably superior capabilities in both the federal government and many of the big cities, and the elaboration of direct Washington-to-cities political and administrative ties.

If we take stock of the state governments' capabilities for the future, we find a catalogue of strengths and weaknesses whose variety and differential weight make it seem almost impossible to strike a balance. Even particular characteristics often defy assessment as positive, negative, or neutral in effect. We can say, for example, that (1) reapportionment of state legislatures in the 1960's has translated the principle of fair representation into operational terms and promises to reduce the frequency of divided party control of state governments; and (2) more states are now, or soon will be, blessed with a genuine two-party competitive system. Yet each of these silver linings has a cloud.

THE EFFECTS OF REAPPORTIONMENT. The strong reactions to the Supreme Court's one-man–one-vote decision on state legislative apportionment evidenced deep agreement between its supporters and its opponents that the results would be revolutionary. While the reapportionment process has been substantially completed, the evidence is not yet available for a careful assessment of its potential consequences. Even speculation on probable consequences must be tempered by awareness that legislative representation is but one aspect of a political system whose many other variables may dull or sharpen the effects of this one change. And, as always, the fact that there are fifty state political systems makes generalization difficult. Viewed analytically, the new pattern of legislative representation might increase the appeal of unicameralism and might affect the relations between governor and legislature, the policy toward urban problems, the relative abilities of the Democratic and Republican parties to win control of the state legislature and the state government, and the structure and performance of local governments.

The first possible result of reapportionment is that it may reopen the question of spreading unicameralism beyond Nebraska. If both houses must be constructed on the same representational formula of one-man–one-vote, two major reasons for having a second house lose validity. One reason was to give a rural minority, a conservative minority, or a Republican minority a contrived control of one house. Another was to let local government areas such as counties or towns each have a legislative spokesman in one house, regardless of their population. While these reasons have disappeared, and with them some of the opposition to unicameralism, the reapportioning states have not chosen to embrace this method of structuring their legislatures. There are, in fact, other reasons than those cited above for preferring to have a second chamber. Prudent men like the idea of having legislation considered by two houses so as to avoid precipitate action and gain the advantages of a second look. This can occur even if both chambers are identical in composition. More significantly, a population basis of representation does not mean that both chambers must be identical. Their sizes can differ. Two consequences flow from such a difference.[14] A large body must be more firmly organized with substantial powers vested in house and party leaders; in a small body this concentration of power is less necessary, and individual members can be more independent in their judgments and participate more frequently in debates. The second, and more vital consequence, is that members of a large body normally come from small districts (unless large multimember districts are used) and tend to speak parochially for narrow constituency interests (for example, the single crop or single industry in the locality); members of a small body, by contrast, come from large districts with a diversity of interests approaching, in many cases, the diverse characteristics of the whole state. The outlook and behavior of members of the two houses can thus be strikingly different. It is certainly not unreasonable to recognize institutionally the desirability of reconciling narrow but often intense interests with the broader, more diffuse state interest.

---

[14] *In Reynolds v. Sims, 377 U.S. 533, the Court said, "We do not believe that the concept of bicameralism is rendered anachronistic and meaningless when the predominant basis of legislative representation in the two state legislative bodies is required to be the same in population." In addition to points we make in the text, the Court observed that one house might draw from single-member districts and the other, at least in part, from multimember districts, that length of terms for legislators in one house might differ from that in the other, and that "apportionment in one house could be arranged so as to balance off minor inequities in the representation of certain areas in the other house." Pp. 576f.*

A second possible result of population-based legislatures is that relations between the governor and the legislature may be substantially altered. As Chapter 9 demonstrated, many a governor with a statewide majority behind him has in the past faced a legislature dominated in one or both houses by the party that lost the gubernatorial election. But if each house comes to represent population fairly and other relevant factors remain constant, the governor and the legislature will more commonly be controlled by the same party. This will be a major transformation of state government and will affect the locus and styles of leadership, the role of policy programs in state and district elections, and the internal power structure of the parties themselves. Other relevant factors, however, may not remain constant, particularly the scope and effect of two-party competition, which is discussed below.

Third, apportionment by population will give urban and suburban people a much stronger voice in the legislature and will make state governments more attentive to the problems such people feel strongly about. This opens the possibility of a change in the trend in the American federal system, for it should reduce the need for cities and metropolitan areas to go directly to Congress and national agencies for sympathetic hearing and action. It could also cast the state governments in the role of spokesmen to Washington for such federal legislation and grants as are required to meet urban and metropolitan problems. As the bypassing of state governments would thus be reduced, these governments would be in a position to recapture the interest and confidence of long-alienated urban people.

This prospect, however, needs to be regarded with some caution. When legislatures were artificially apportioned to assure rural and small-town dominance of one or both houses, they did not in fact behave in so flatly anti-urban a fashion as is generally supposed. Some urban interests, particularly those that have conservative views about taxation, spending, and business regulation, have been well, if indirectly, represented. That is, their interests have often been substantially congruent with those of the overrepresented farmers and small-town dwellers. So some urban interests, and powerful ones at that, have been happy with the policy output of the old-style legislatures.

How much effect malapportionment had on the policy output of state legislatures is almost impossible to determine. No effects whatever were found in several studies of roll-call voting and in studies comparing the degree of malapportionment in the legislatures with the degree of urban and rural biases in the policies they adopted.[15] Some indicate that a fairly

---

[15] *Thomas R. Dye*, Policy, Economics, and the Public: Policy Outcomes in the American States (*Chicago: Rand McNally*, 1966); *Richard I. Hofferbert, "The Relation*

apportioned legislature would have passed the same body of legislation. But, as Malcolm Jewell has suggested, "voting records probably minimize these differences [between urban and rural legislators] because the outnumbered urban legislators have compromised in order to win concessions from the rural majority." [16] What one does not know is what measures an urban, Democratic legislative majority would have initiated or supported that never were introduced or allowed to reach a roll call vote in malapportioned legislatures. Nor do we know what a Democratic governor elected with strong urban support would have included in his program and pressed for if he had faced a well-apportioned Democratic legislature instead of a rural and Republican majority in one or both houses.

Less obviously, the political advantage to a party of winning the governorship, U.S. senatorships, and other statewide offices—patronage being not the least of these advantages—has often led a rurally strong party's legislators to pass measures and provide grants-in-aid that would gratify, or at least reduce the alienation of, the urban population since the latter has such heavy weight in statewide elections. Nonetheless, state grant-in-aid formulas, at least in some malapportioned states, have discriminated in favor of rural and small-town areas, even while throwing placatory sops to the urban Cerberus.[17]

A final and highly significant caution arises from the fact that the customary assumption of an urban-rural dichotomy conceals two elements —the small town and the suburb. Small towns, usually classified as being in the rural part of the dichotomy, have a small-business constituency and

---

between Public Policy and Some Structural and Environmental Variables in the American States," American Political Science Review, 50 (March 1966), 73–82; Herbert Jacob, "The Consequences of Malapportionment: A Note of Caution," Social Forces, 43 (December 1964), 256–61; Clarice McDonald Davis, Legislative Malapportionment and Roll-call Voting in Texas, 1961–63 (Austin, Texas: Institute of Public Affairs, University of Texas, 1965).

[16] *Malcolm E. Jewell, "The Political Setting of the Legislature," in Alexander Heard (ed.), State Legislatures in American Politics (Englewood Cliffs, N.J.: Prentice-Hall, 1966), p. 72. See also Richard T. Frost, "On Derge's Metropolitan and Outstate Legislative Delegations," American Political Science Review, 53 (September 1959), 792–95, which is a comment on David R. Derge, "Metropolitan and Outstate Alignments in Illinois and Missouri Legislative Delegations," American Political Science Review, 52 (December 1958), 1051–65.*

[17] *Measurement and appraisal of discrimination in grant-in-aid formulas present substantial difficulties. Some state discrimination in favor of rural and small-town areas may be justifiable as an equalization to counter disparity of taxable local sources between such areas and urban areas. States that have no large cities or have only a minority of the population in them may discriminate "unfairly" even though the state legislature is reasonably well apportioned. Though more research is necessary for clarifying the problem, the few national studies that have been made find no significant correlation between degree of malapportionment and degree of discrimination in distribution of grants-in-aid. Herbert Jacob, op. cit., pp. 258f; and Richard I. Hofferbert, op. cit., pp. 76f.*

often some industry, so their influence on election outcomes and on the legislators' behavior may not always fit the stereotypes of rural attitudes. The suburbs, often pieces of a metropolitan area and generally reckoned as part of the urban part of the dichotomy, in fact often have interests different from those of the major cities. Voters in those suburbs with higher average incomes and different ethnic compositions from those of core cities may choose legislators who are natural allies of the usually conservative legislators from rural and small-town constituencies. As we have seen, it is the suburbs, rather than the core cities, that have had the great rise in population, and it is the suburbs that will be swelled by the national population increase in the years ahead. Reapportionment based on population, therefore, will benefit them far more than the core cities. It remains to be seen whether city and suburban people can find common cause in metropolitan problems of transportation, recreational facilities, water supply, sewage disposal, and the like. Less probable is a shared outlook on labor and welfare legislation, public housing, anti-discrimination laws, business regulation, and taxation.

A fourth possible effect of reapportionment by population may be an alteration of the roles and strategies of the Republican and Democratic parties. Their shares of legislative representation will no doubt change, but the shift will probably vary by states rather than take a uniform direction nationally. Under the older schemes of legislative apportionment there have been more Democratic governors than Democratic legislatures. In states where one or both legislative houses have been "constitutionally Republican" in the face of frequent and substantial Democratic majorities in statewide elections, the new apportionment formula should produce Democratic legislatures more often than not. But this will not necessarily occur in states where the statewide Democratic majority is a thin one. Even in such states, however, the Republican party's strategy in appealing to the electorate and its strategy in the legislature itself may be expected to change, in recognition of the narrower margin of legislative control.[18]

The partisan advantage from reapportionment will not be entirely that of the Democratic party and may not even be preponderantly so. There are states, especially border and southwestern states, where statewide elections have revealed sufficient Republican strength to elect governors but where malapportionment gave rural and small-town Democrats unin-

---

[18] As suggested earlier, the legislative election is not the only arena of concern to a state party. Even when the Republican party has had a firm hold on one or both houses in a state where the Democratic party is a serious bidder for statewide majorities at the polls, it has been imprudent for the Republican legislature (or one house) to adopt policies that would seriously embarrass its candidates for statewide office.

terrupted control of the state legislature. Similarly, in the southern states, such Republican strength as existed was often concentrated principally in the underrepresented cities; though urban Republicans in these states cannot soon expect to win legislative majorities in reapportioned legislatures, their increased delegations may significantly alter the prevailing one-party politics of southern legislative activity. Even in the northern and eastern states, the fact that reapportionment will principally enhance the power of suburban voters, rather than that of voters in the core cities, means that the partisan advantage will be generously distributed between the two parties. For there are Republican suburbs and Democratic suburbs and a variety of mixtures between these types. Further, it is the suburbs that are and will be undergoing the greatest changes—in population, in problems arousing greatest intensity of concern, in political organization. Which party will gain from the greater legislative weight of the suburbs, and how this will vary from area to area and from decade to decade is beyond current prediction.

A final point at which state legislative reapportionment may have significant consequence is the structure and performance of local governments. One clear consequence is the translation to the local level of the one-man–one-vote principle of representation—in city councils, county boards, and school district boards. But reapportionment at the state level may itself have local consequences. For example, in a number of states where each county was entitled to one state senator, reapportionment has forced the grouping of less populous counties into a single senatorial district. Such grouping may remove several barriers to the consolidation of rural counties as local government areas. A small county need no longer resist consolidation so as to protect its entitlement to a seat in the state legislature; grants-in-aid are less likely than in the past to be distributed in identical amounts to every county or to favor the counties with fewer people; political organizations of less populous counties may be impelled to regroup with their neighbors if state parties no longer accord each of them a seat on the state committee and shrink their individual delegations to state conventions below the point for effective bargaining. Though the sluggishness in abandoning the traditional local units must be given due weight, the ultimate result may be that "county courthouse gangs" in the smaller counties will have lost much of their motivation for blocking formal consolidation of county governments.

In metropolitan areas, however, legislative reapportionment may fail to advance the development of area-wide local governmental machinery. Suburbs, well-represented in the new legislatures, are likely to resist state initiative to make them share the burdens of core cities or to have them transfer decision making on area-wide matters to area-wide councils and boards.

The performance of local governments may be put under greater pressure from the state level if the urban and suburban legislative majority become reluctant to turn over state grants to towns and counties where the small-scale and traditional style of operation makes them use most of their combined state-and-local funds for salaries of full-time and part-time officials whose services to the people seem minimal. In these cases, the state legislature may either devise financial incentives for the consolidation of separate local governments and for intergovernmental cooperative arrangements, or develop legal mandates and financial incentives to improve the performance standards of the smaller local governments even without inducing mergers.

To sum up: Though reapportionment has removed one reason for bicameral legislatures, the unicameral alternative is unlikely to attract wide support; reapportionment will probably increase the frequency with which governor and legislature are of the same party, but this effect may be attenuated by other factors; urban, but especially suburban, people will be more heavily represented in state legislatures, but in what directions and to what degree this will alter the nature of the policy output of legislatures remains to be seen; the effect of reapportionment on the two major parties will vary by state and will depend greatly on the political pattern that suburban people develop, though in the populous states of the north and east the immediate effect will be to benefit the Democratic party; and the structure and performance of at least those local governments with small populations may well be affected for the better by reapportionment, though the enlarged suburban representation in the legislature may prevent comparably strong state pressure for improving the structure and performance of government in metropolitan areas.

SPREAD OF TWO-PARTY COMPETITION. The conviction is widespread, both among interested laymen and among political scientists, that a political system in which two parties are in full competition for power is the kind of system that best reflects and serves the people's needs and best attracts the people's interest and active participation. The evidence is that two-party competition in the states has been significantly increasing. This is indicated by the closer partisan division of statewide votes, by the frequency with which the parties alternate in winning electoral majorities, by the increased number of elections at state and legislative district levels in which the voters are offered a choice between candidates of the two parties, and by the establishment or the invigoration of minority party organizations in states and communities where they did not exist or were moribund. One-party states and districts have been challenged by the minority party, sometimes in deadly seriousness and sometimes by only pro forma campaigns that foretell more serious efforts in the future. The Democratic party has had victories in such traditionally Republican areas as Maine, New Hampshire, and Vermont. The Republican party has had victories in the South, and proposes a major effort to build strength in the large cities of the North and East.

Welcome as these developments are, we must note two qualifications before we can assess their meaning for the future of state government. First, the closer the competition for votes, the more likely will be both the frequent change of party control of the state government and the probability that any one election may provide a divided government. The likelihood of frequent change of control, with its threat to the continuity of policies,[19] is greater in states using the two-year term for all elected state officials. The likelihood of divided government may be greater where the term of one or both houses is two years but that of the governor four years. Divided government was earlier a consequence of malapportioned legislatures. That it may henceforth be the consequence, instead, of a highly competitive party system, itself desirable, is of only slight comfort. To be sure, in a highly competitive party system both parties may need to advocate policies of broad appeal to the electorate, and so of considerable similarity. In that event, such consensus on policy as this embodies might be expected to facilitate cooperation among the three parts of the state government's policy-making process—governor, upper house, and lower house. Yet such harmony is not highly predictable. On the contrary, the very competitiveness of the parties will make the one controlling the legislature or one of its houses reluctant to pass measures that the public will credit to the governor of the opposite party; postponement of credit-winning measures until an "administration" of one's own party is in power is elementary political strategy.

---

[19] *The confusion attending simultaneous hailing of the competitive two-party system and bewailing of the heavy cost of policy discontinuity points to a need to refine our understanding of what is the desirable type of a politically competitive system. Allan P. Sindler puts the issue with admirable clarity:* "Does effective competition really require balanced party strength and uncertain election outcomes at virtually every contest scheduled by the calendar? Or should we not build into our concept of competition a much longer time dimension so that alternation of party control at irregular intervals, coupled with the out-party's retention of significant electoral and legislative strength, would meet the test satisfactorily?" *Allan P. Sindler,* Political Parties in the United States *(New York: St. Martin's Press, 1966), p. 21.*

The virtues of two-party competition depend a good deal on what the parties are competing about. This is a second reason for qualifying initial enthusiasm at the spread of competition. In some states the parties compete primarily about issues and programs. In others the competition is focused on getting government jobs and privileges. Though jobs and policy issues are elements in both forms of two-party competition, the priority accorded each is of considerable moment. John H. Fenton, in a study of midwestern states with two-party competition, observed that in the issue-oriented states (Michigan, Minnesota, and Wisconsin), the political leaders of the rival parties "sought different ends and the result was meaningful competition at every level of government and an absence of the bipartisan collusion that characterized the politics in other states. After election, no urging was required to persuade the issue-oriented politicians . . . to earnestly attempt to translate their programs into public policy." Contrast with such states the politics of Indiana and Illinois, where "the leadership of both parties sought jobs through political activity rather than public policy ends. Therefore, the parties were not distinct entities, but rather they were engaged in bipartisan collusion for corrupt ends. They often failed to compete, as in the Illinois legislature. And after election they seldom made an earnest attempt to translate their election programs into public policy." [20]

Much more than reapportioned legislatures and two-party competitive politics must enter the scales when one appraises the state governments' capabilities for serving the people's interest in the years ahead. Yet these two elements appear to be the most fundamental new factors. They have greater potential than any other recent change for altering the distribution of political power within the states' electorates and policy-making bodies. That their future consequences may be rather different from those their advocates anticipated is an irony to be treasured only by those who relish the apparent unpredictability of a complex political system.

3. *The Capabilities of Local Governments*

When one looks for signs that local governments are developing capabilities for meeting future responsibilities, the horizon seems remarkably bare. It is rather late to take comfort in the successful identification of the responsibilities that "will have to" be met—responsibilities ranging from the specifics of housing, transportation, water supply, education, air pollu-

---

[20] John H. Fenton, Midwest Politics (New York: Holt, 1966), pp. 226f.

tion, sewerage, law enforcement, and recreation to a broad concern for planning and interrelating all basic elements of civilization in metropolitan areas. Nor can much comfort be found in the wide agreement among students of local government and among civic-oriented leaders in business and the professions on the present deficiencies of local governments and on a limited number of alternative approaches to repairing those deficiencies.

THREE SCHOOLS OF THOUGHT. The complexity of American local governments is so great, and standards of evaluation vary so much, that some informed commentators take a notably sanguine view of local government's capabilities, some perceive improvement under way and propose to accelerate it, and yet others prescribe drastic remedies to save the "desperate" situation.[21] All start from an agreed position: that the local government system of the country has remained remarkably stable, substantially resisting drastic and widespread structural change, whether of size of local areas, types of local units (counties, incorporated cities and towns, special districts), or internal organization (county board of commissioners; mayor-council, council-manager, and commission city governments; school and other special district boards). And all, of course, agree that most of the communities these local governments serve have been subjected to vast changes—in population size, mobility and ethnic make-up of the population, nature and speed of transportation, and much else that America has experienced and that materially alters the conditions and problems of local government.

The sanguine find their comfort in the very survival of traditional

---

[21] *The three "schools of thought" here characterized are useful for expository purposes but should not be taken as either exhausting the range of attitudes nor as so neatly bounded as the text may seem to imply. Further, the brief discussion here cannot treat the political, social, and economic context that is necessary to an understanding of the conditions and probable consequences of particular structural arrangements. The relevant literature is voluminous. The following significantly contribute to delineating attitudes about the structural problem as it is manifested in metropolitan areas: Arthur Maass (ed.), Area and Power (New York: The Free Press, 1959), esp. chap. 2, by Paul Ylvisaker, and 3, by Robert C. Wood; John C. Bollens and Henry J. Schmandt, The Metropolis (New York: Harper, 1965); Michael N. Danielson (ed.), Metropolitan Politics (Boston: Little, Brown, 1966); C. E. Elias, Jr., James Gillies, and Svend Riemer (eds.), Metropolis: Values in Conflict (Belmont, Calif.: Wadsworth, 1964); Robert C. Wood, 1400 Governments (Cambridge, Mass.: Harvard University Press, 1961), esp. pp. 189–217; and four reports by the U.S. Advisory Commission on Intergovernmental Relations, Governmental Structure, Organization, and Planning in Metropolitan Areas (published as a committee print by the U.S. House of Representatives, Committee on Government Operations, July 1961); Alternative Approaches to Governmental Reorganization in Metropolitan Areas (June 1962); Performance of Urban Functions: Local and Areawide (September 1963); The Problem of Special Districts in American Government (May 1964); and Metropolitan Social and Economic Disparities: Implications for Intergovernmental Relations in Central Cities and Suburbs (January 1965).*

patterns of local government. They can point to the lack of any great groundswell of people's dissatisfaction with their local governments. This must mean that these governments are performing at a satisfactory level, else those who point with alarm would have found ready allies in a rebellious citizenry. The implications are several and they overlap. One possibility is that the "alarmists" have an ideal vision of what an urban or rural community should be, but that the public generally does not share this vision, perhaps because its members perceive local governmental services as only a small fraction of their individual sets of wants; their "city-state" is not a Platonic Republic. Another possibility is that critics have misjudged the effectiveness of our local governments: most necessary services seem to get performed with reasonable efficiency, and new or intensified problems crying for policy decisions do get faced when the relevant constituency becomes sufficiently concerned. Still another, but closely related, possibility is that, although the formal framework of local governments has retained the patterns sanctified by tradition, less perceptible governmental adaptations have occurred at a pace reasonably responsive to changes in the communities and their problems. If this be true, then the future can be faced with confidence, for there is no reason to assume that this gift for adaptation will be lost or that the problems ahead will be more serious than those mastered in the past. To be sure, one of the adaptations of the past has been the shifting of more of the responsibility for community services to state and national governments. Yet in the past this has not left local governments with little to do; on the contrary, their expenditures and staffs have increased. Presumably this matched pair of tendencies can be projected into the future, with therefore no fear for the future of local governments.

At the other extreme, the most critical commentators express despair over the condition of American local governments and see little evidence from the past to assure that necessary major adaptations will be made by these governments to meet community responsibilities of the future. They therefore prescribe strong remedies. We may take as one illustration of this school a 1966 report issued by the Committee for Economic Development: It takes the position that the adaptation to change by American institutions of local government "has been so slow, so limited, and so reluctant that the future role—even the continued viability—of these institutions is now in grave doubt." [22] The first of its series of recommendations is that "the number of local governments in the United States, now about 80,000,

---

[22] Modernizing Local Governments (New York: Committee for Economic Development, 1966), p. 8.

should be reduced by at least 80 percent." [23] Other recommendations for improving the structure and functioning of local governments largely correspond to proposals long in the public domain as the result of scholars' and civic organizations' diagnosis and prescription activity.[24]

The report of the Committee for Economic Development and other recent writings that assume that the condition of the local governments is not well enough to be let alone strike a new note in their emphasis upon the strategy of bringing about change and in the focus of that strategy. Where earlier advocates of reform wanted all their proposals adopted and in any order and looked to an aroused local citizenry and its civic leaders to bring about the changes, the sophistication of a later day has emphasized a sequential order of changes and has largely abandoned reliance on the initiative of local communities to do what needs doing. Consider sequence. Instead of urging the grant of greater home-rule powers to local governments as a good in itself, the CED suggests that this can appropriately come only after the local governments are drastically redesigned so that they are worthy vessels for the receipt of added powers. Major elements of the proposed redesigning would be the consolidation of the 2,700 nonmetropolitan counties into 500 (and a similar consolidation of New England towns); the abolition of all townships not suitable for full municipal incorporation; the disincorporation of most of the 11,000 nonmetropolitan villages with fewer than 2,500 residents (or the contractual performance of their functions by the counties); the abolition of self-governing rural special districts, with the new counties assuming their functions; and the consolidation of the 80 percent of the nonmetropolitan independent

---

[23] Ibid., p. 17.

[24] Ibid., pp. 17–19. *These other recommendations are:* "2. *The number of overlapping layers of local government found in most states should be severely curtailed.* 3. *Popular election should be confined to members of the policy-making body, and to the chief executive in those governments where the 'strong mayor' form is preferred to the 'council-manager' plan.* 4. *Each local unit should have a single chief executive, either elected by the people or appointed by the local legislative body, with all administrative agencies and personnel fully responsible to him; election of department heads should be halted.* 5. *Personnel practices based on merit and professional competence should replace the personal or partisan 'spoils' systems found in most counties and many other local units.* 6. *County modernization should be pressed with special vigor, since counties—everywhere except in New England—have high but undeveloped potential for solving the problems of rural, urban, and most metropolitan communities.* 7. *Once modernized, local governments should be entrusted with broad legal powers permitting them to plan, finance, and execute programs suited to the special needs, interests, and desires of their citizens.* 8. *The 50 state constitutions should be revamped—either by legislative amendment or through constitutional conventions concentrating on local government modernization—to provide for boundary revisions, extensions of legal authority, and elimination of needless layers.* 9. *The terms and conditions of federal— and state—grants-in-aid should be revised to encourage the changes recommended in this statement.*"

school districts that have less than 1,500 pupils (preferably with the new counties assuming the management of the school systems). Consider strategy, and for this the territorial realignment just reviewed can serve as an example. No one familiar with the past history of local resistance to attempts to alter traditional governmental areas can expect that voluntary "grass-roots" action will achieve results. The focus of strategy must therefore be the state government, and qualms about compulsion are put to one side. The CED proposes that "each state should create a boundary commission with continuing authority to design and redesign local jurisdictional lines, and to set timetables for consolidations and annexation." [25]

Between the sanguine observers on the one side and the viewers-with-alarm on the other is a group of thoughtful men who foresee a need for major adaptation but who doubt that it will occur automatically and also doubt that a frontal assault on the problem is feasible. Nowhere is this more apparent than in the shift of views about the governing arrangements for metropolitan areas. A reasonable assumption for some time was that a metropolitan area, traditionally split among hundreds of general local governments and special districts, is in fact a community with common problems, and that it therefore needs a metropolitan government to deal with these problems while traditional units of government continue to handle the more geographically restricted problems. This seemed as patent as the need of the United States for both a national government and state governments; indeed, "federation" was often the basic principle advocated for metropolitan areas. However logical this appears, it demonstrably failed to appeal to voters in the metropolitan areas where it (or a substantially similar proposal) was put on the ballots in the early 1960's and vigorously campaigned for by its advocates.

Unable to win popular support for a frontal assault to overcome the fractionation of government in metropolitan areas, and anticipating that state legislatures were unlikely to impose a new kind of government on an urban-suburban complex whose residents were opposed to such a step, many bloodied and bowed advocates of metropolitan government beat a retreat to a previously rejected position. This is one that encourages the use of every possible arrangement and device to see that individual functions are handled on the basis of areas larger than the traditional local government areas. Cumulatively, it is thought, these separate decisions for indi-

---

[25] Ibid., pp. 41–43, 61. On the role of compulsion and fiscal leverage by the state governments in achieving school district consolidations in the recent past, see Paying for Better Public Schools (New York: Committee for Economic Development, 1960), pp. 70–79; and York Willbern, The Withering Away of the City (University, Ala.: University of Alabama Press. 1964), pp. 111–17.

vidual functions may come close to achieving many of the objectives of metropolitan government. Furthermore, the gradual subtraction of these functions from the traditional governments' responsibilities may lead eventually to a recognition of the need for a metropolitan governmental council capable of coordinating the various functions being administered on a metropolitan-area basis. In other words, the new strategy of metropolitanists is to accept fractionating by functions (as with geographically broad special districts and authorities) in order to reduce the effect of fractionating by areas (as with cities, towns, and villages), all with the hope of ultimately achieving something very like the metropolitan government that has failed to win popular support when offered as a radical reform.

Among the three schools of thought—the sanguine, the radical-reform, and the moderate—are more shared attitudes than one might suspect. All assume that the future will require adaptation of local governments. The sanguine assume that the necessary incremental changes will be effected automatically by the natural play of influences within and upon the American political system. The radical reformers think fundamental changes necessary and are convinced that the present power holders in local governments, and even local citizens, will not act contrary to their perceptions of their short-range interest—and so, they must be overcome. The moderates think that the needed changes will come neither automatically nor by a direct confrontation between reformers and those benefiting from present arrangements, but that the landscape of local government can be significantly altered by deliberately fostering a succession of individual steps, none perceived by local power holders as seriously threatening their interests, but all together amounting to an outflanking of parochialism.

All the schools also accept a shift of power to larger units of local government. Whether by the sanguines' automatism, the radicals' deliberate proposal, or the moderates' sophisticated strategy, there is considerable acceptance and encouragement of the idea that the county perform more urban functions and that it be generally converted into the metropolitan government earlier sought through other means. Some years ago the revival of the county as a significant instrument of government for meeting modern problems would have been among the least expected or recommended developments. Now, largely because of the strategic advantage of using a large-area government that already exists—as against battling to get a wholly new type created—the county may become one of the principal instruments of government in the future.

An increased role for the state and federal governments in urban affairs is also endorsed by all schools of thought. The sanguine accept what has already happened and welcome the grants-in-aid that ease local governments' revenue problems. Radical reformers think that the state and federal governments can compel the development of a pattern of area government and a level of competence in local administration that will enable local governments to retain and expand their role in the performance of American governmental responsibilities; in a sense, the radical reformers are the real decentralists. The moderates favor state and national legislation that will use the leverage of conditions attached to grants-in-aid to require, and so develop habits of, (*a*) metropolitan-wide consultation (sometimes extending to the exercise of veto powers by a metropolitan planning body, by the central city, or by a state agency in order to reduce fractionation), and (*b*) consultation among functionally specialized special districts and authorities and related departments of general local governments in order to reduce functional fractionation.

None of these schools of thought opposes, and some favor promoting, the extensive use of intergovernmental contracts, agreements, and joint services among two or more local governments. This departs from an earlier view that the multiplication of ad hoc solutions to problems through these "patching-up" arrangements will delay recognition that a major restructuring of local governments is necessary.

On the whole, then, the future should see gradual rather than revolutionary changes in the local governmental landscape. The changes will be in the direction of a more significant role for county governments and a more conscious use of state and federal powers to induce shifts of responsibilities to counties and other metropolitan-wide bodies and to encourage joint and cooperative arrangements among local units of government. It remains uncertain whether truly metropolitan governments will come into being (a particularly difficult problem where a metropolitan area extends over several counties or across state lines) and whether many states will force a major consolidation of counties, school districts, and other local governments in the nonmetropolitan areas.

BIG CITIES. Not very long ago the governments of America's big cities could be thought of as still subject to Lincoln Steffens' damning phrase, "The Shame of the Cities." The evidence now appears to indicate that most big cities have become monuments to the civic reformers' phrase, "Good government is good politics." The already demonstrated capabilities and the perceivable potentialities of city governments are among the most encouraging resources for the future of local government.

Reviewing the performance of nine cities of almost as many regions, Edward C. Banfield found five significant similarities: [26]

1. *All nine of the city governments are honestly run.*

2. *The quality of city government has been improving despite the departure of the "good government"-minded middle class for the suburbs and its replacement by Negro and Southern white migrants who, because of the backwardness of the rural places they come from, are in general far from civic-minded.*

3. *Another striking similarity in the politics of the cities is their conservatism.*

4. *Another feature . . . is a remarkable ability to manage and contain the conflicts, some of them very bitter and deep-seated, that are so conspicuous a feature of the polyglot metropolis.*

5. *Finally, the political systems of the big cities . . . do not give rise to or nourish anti-democratic extremist movements.*

He attributes these similarities in part to the professionalization of the city staffs and the protection of their tenure by merit systems, and in part (and with exceptions made for some of the nine cities) to the separation of the local political system from the state and national systems, whether by nonpartisan elections or by a tendency of some mayors to run virtually as "independents" even though on a party ticket. But his principal explanation is the structure of the electoral system, by which candidates for the mayoralty must seek broad support to win a majority of the votes. The consequences of this are that successful candidates are typically moderates and that minorities—whether Negroes, economy-minded taxpayers, or civic reformers—get more attention in politics and policy making than their numbers may warrant. "In this, as in much else, the political systems of the cities reflect the genius of American politics generally." [27]

None of this means that big cities are without problems. The problems are immense and will be so in the future. What it does mean is that

---

[26] Edward C. Banfield, Big City Politics (New York: Random House, 1965), pp. 11–15. The cities examined are Atlanta, Boston, Detroit, El Paso, Los Angeles, Miami, Philadelphia, St. Louis, and Seattle. For another encouraging view of big-city government, see "New Strength in City Hall," Fortune (November 1957), pp. 156ff, reprinted in The Editors of Fortune, Exploding Metropolis (Garden City, N.Y.: Doubleday, 1958).

[27] For a fuller and more qualified appraisal of the consequences of what they view as a shift from a predominantly lower-class (as under the old tradition of machine politics) to a predominantly middle-class political style, see Edward C. Banfield and James Q. Wilson, City Politics (Cambridge, Mass.: Harvard University Press and the M.I.T. Press, 1963), pp. 329–46. Cf. Raymond E. Wolfinger and John Osgood Field, "Political Ethos and the Structure of City Government," American Political Science Review, 60 (June 1966), 306–27.

big cities have developed a political and administrative system that has a high potential for dealing with problems of this magnitude. And, let it be added, they have become centers of initiative for stimulating programs through which the federal government can assist them on problems that exceed their own resources and for seeking the cooperation of the suburbs on problems that stretch beyond the core city's boundaries. Almost immediately their vigorous mayors will be turning to the state governments in hopes of finding more sympathetic responses from reapportioned legislatures than were found under earlier conditions. If these hopes are dashed, as they may well be, the federal-city alliance will harden and state governments will once again have set themselves squarely on the path toward desuetude.

4. The Future Character of Federalism

By 1975 the American governmental pattern will probably seem little varied from the pattern we have long taken for granted. But changes are already in process that, unless deflected, may produce a very different pattern by 1985 or 2000. So far we have taken note of changes in the number and geographical distribution of the American people, of state governments' reapportioned legislatures and increasingly competitive two-party politics, of local governments' prospects for drastic or incremental alteration of traditional structural arrangements, and of the new strength and orientation of big cities' political systems. We need to give attention to the federal government and to consider other kinds of capabilities than those so far treated.

THE FEDERAL GOVERNMENT'S CHANGING ROLE. Books of the future about state and local government may go even further than we to acknowledge that, despite the title, the main character in such a book should be the federal government. As early chapters of this book demonstrate, it is nothing new for the federal government to be affecting state and local governments, whether by expanding its policy-determining and administrative powers, by distributing grants-in-aid in selected policy fields, or by offering an alternative judicial system reaching to the grass roots and available to many who doubt the fairness of their state or local courts. Most of these developments have occurred as separate events or trends. Between the fact of ad hoc approaches to separate policy or administrative problems on the one hand, and flamboyant charges of a Washington conspiracy to centralize everything on the other, there was little official effort to examine the overall pattern that was emerging.

During the 1950's and 1960's this gap has been substantially filled.

Two results are notable. One is simply the taking of stock and the recognition that federal programs and procedures that have been treated as discrete entities have in combination often unanticipated effects on state and local governments.[28] The other is the realization that the federal government now has in its hands the means for consciously influencing, and often determining, the roles and structures of state and local governments.[29] Closely linked to this realization is the conviction that these means should be used in a deliberate strategy to strengthen state and local governments' capabilities. The federal government, in other words, should itself provide the one capability that state and local governments seem most generally to lack—the capability to do what is necessary to multiply and strengthen their capabilities.

THE CRITICAL CAPABILITIES: GEOGRAPHIC. Governments in the American system build their strengths on four kinds of capabilities: geographic, fiscal, political, and administrative. These overlap, they complement one another, and, in a limited degree, strength in one may make up for weakness in another.

Geographic capability primarily depends on whether a government's official area boundaries embrace the natural problem areas with which governments at its level need to be concerned. A state government cannot deal effectively with a problem whose natural area is the nation or a group-of-states region, nor can a town or city deal with problems like air and water pollution whose sources and effects involve other cities and towns. As the states' boundaries are immutable, their geographic capability is also a fixed element, and regional problems that do not lend themselves to solution by interstate negotiation will tend to pass to the national government.[30] Most of the states, however, have a substantial geographic capabil-

---

[28] *Stocktaking and a concern for cumulative consequences appear prominent in the reports of the (Kestnbaum) Commission on Intergovernmental Relations, and the reports and hearings of the subcommittees on intergovernmental relations of the Senate and House Committees on Government Operations.*

[29] *This seems apparent in the reports of the Advisory Commission on Intergovernmental Relations in the 1960's, in proposals for federal legislation advanced by Senator Edmund S. Muskie, chairman of the Senate Subcommittee on Intergovernmental Relations, and in many legislative proposals by President Johnson.*

[30] *It will be noted that this means that strictly regional problems fall for solution to the national government, even though they are not nationwide in geographic scope; often, of course, the national government may devise a solution that provides for representation of the states as well as the federal government in a regional agency. Let us also observe, on the other hand, that a number of problems that superficially appear to fall within the geographic scope of individual states have been transformed into problems of national concern, partly because of recognition of interstate mobility (as when children schooled in Mississippi and Alabama migrate as adults to northern and eastern states) and partly because of rising nationwide expectations about what minimal conditions are tolerable (at its simplest, this is illustrated by the belief that no one should starve, regardless of geographical location).*

ity; that is, many important problems have natural areas that are embraced by state boundaries.

Local governments, particularly in metropolitan areas, have both serious lacks of geographic capability and boundaries that are not formally frozen for all time. Yet, as we have seen, a major adjustment of local general purpose government areas to encompass natural problem areas is not a near-future prospect. And opinions differ as to whether the ad hoc solutions of special districts and intergovernmental cooperative agreements will suffice to provide the geographic capability requisite to effective local government.

It is an ironic commentary on the competence of both local and state governments that there are prospects of the federal government using its leverage to induce development of the local geographic capability that neither local nor state governments seem willing to create.[31] For example, to discourage the proliferation of special districts and the ignoring of metropolitan area needs, the proposed Intergovernmental Cooperation Act (passed by the Senate in 1965, but not by the House of Representatives) would carry three mandates. First, "heads of Federal departments and agencies shall, in the absence of substantial reasons to the contrary, make . . . loans or grants-in-aid for urban development to units of general local government rather than to special-purpose units of local government." [32] Second is a veto power for general local governments:

> Notwithstanding any other provision of Federal law, any application for a loan or grant made after June 30, 1966, for construction of hospitals, airports, water supply and distribution facilities, sewerage facilities and waste treatment works, water development, and land conservation within any metropolitan area . . . shall be submitted to the unit of general local government with authority to operate in the area within which the project or facility is to be located. No action shall be taken by any Federal agency upon such application unless the

---

[31] In many of its programs the federal government, in fact, has accepted local governments as they are, fostered the creation of special districts, and made it easier or more profitable for smaller towns and cities to get grants and loans than for large cities and groups of local governments to do so. The federal government, therefore, needs to do a good deal of housecleaning itself in addition to exerting direct leverage on local governments.

[32] 89th Congress, 1st Session, S. 561, as transmitted to the House of Representatives, August 9, 1965, Sec. 502. "Urban development" as used in the bill includes not only urban renewal, but also "the acquisition, use, and development of open-space land, the planning and construction of hospitals, airports, water supply and distribution facilities, highways, water development, land conservation, and other public works facilities." (Sec. 111).

governing body of the unit of general local government certifies that such project or facility is consistent with its planning objectives.[33]

Third is a review (but not veto) power for metropolitan planning councils. Within any metropolitan area, in the case of construction projects of the types already named above, urban renewal and open-space land projects, and highways and transportation, the bill requires that any application for a loan or grant "shall be accompanied (i) by the comments and recommendations with respect to the project involved by an areawide agency designated to perform metropolitan or regional planning for the area within which the assistance is to be used, and which is, to the greatest practicable extent, composed of or responsible to the elected officials of the units of general local government within whose jurisdiction such agency is authorized to engage in such planning; and (ii) by a statement by the applicant that such comments and recommendations have been considered prior to formal submission of the application." [34]

While, at the time of writing, these requirements have not been enacted by Congress, federal statutes do include inducements that indicate assumption of a responsibility for broadening local governments' geographic capabilities. In 1965 Congress authorized the Housing and Home Finance Administrator (now the Secretary of Housing and Urban Development) to make grants of up to two-thirds the cost of the work "to organizations composed of public officials whom he finds to be representative of the political jurisdictions within a metropolitan area or urban region for the purpose of assisting such organizations to . . . develop regional plans and programs, and engage in such other activities as the Administrator finds necessary or desirable for the solution of the metropolitan or regional problems in such areas or regions." [35] Under some grant-in-aid programs, the federal government will bear a larger percentage of the cost of a project if it is designed to meet the needs of a large urban region or metropolitan area rather than those of only a single local government.[36]

---

[33] Ibid., Sec. 503. *Failure of the general local government to act in 30 days would be deemed to be approval.*

[34] Ibid., Sec. 504. *Failure of the areawide planning agency to make comments or recommendations within 60 days would free the applicant from the requirement that its application be accompanied by comments or recommendations.*

[35] Public Law 89-117, "Housing and Urban Development Act of 1965," Sec. 1102 (c).

[36] *Such an incentive is provided for sewage disposal systems on a regional basis (Public Law 89-234, "Water Pollution Control Act"). Similarly, under the Housing Act of 1961, although the federal share of grants for other open-space land acquisitions was limited to 30 percent, it could be up to 40 percent if the applicant exercised its open-land responsibilities for an urban area as a whole (i.e., an area urban in character*

FISCAL CAPABILITY. Fiscal capability is demonstrably a major advantage of each higher level of government—an advantage to which both geography and constitutional doctrine have contributed. Two observations are in order. First, the higher governments have chosen to use this superior capability to assist the governments at lower levels of the total structure, rather than to take functions away from them. Federal grants-in-aid and loans, and state grants and revenue-sharing arrangements with local governments are the instruments of this policy of self-restraint. In effect, the superior fiscal machinery of the higher governments is in part put at the service of the lesser governments, albeit with some equalization in distribution and much categorizing of programs for which the aid is available. Second, the state and local governments have not exhausted the fiscal resources at their disposal. State governments may be deterred from action by prospects of adverse voter reaction. Local governments are deterred not only for that reason, but also because their geographic morselization permits many a pocket of wealth to escape the burdens of the whole community of which an elite suburb is naturally, but not officially, a part.

It seems clear that though existing state and local revenues will increase in the future even without a change in their tax systems, the existing systems will not suffice to meet rising expenditures to keep up with population growth, rising expectations about governmental services, and the higher level of costs in urban areas where most of the people will be. Higher tax rates and tapping of new sources are therefore likely to be needed. The federal government's expenditures for domestic programs will need to rise for the same reasons that state and local expenditures will rise. Although the country's gross national product may also be expected to continue its increase, the question may have to be posed as to whether more than the present 20 percent of GNP should be allotted to the country's governments. A substantial decline in national defense expenditures, which now accounts for over a third of the governmental portion of the GNP, would happily remove the question from the agenda for some time to come. Even with such a fortunate development, a material reduction of federal taxes will by no means ensure that state and local govern-

---

and forming an economically and socially related region); however, the Housing and Urban Development Act of 1965 abandoned this incentive offer (fixing instead a uniform federal share of 50 percent and permitting eligibility for land development, as well as acquisition, costs), but it also required that the Administrator make grants "only if he finds that such assistance is needed for carrying out a unified or officially coordinated program, meeting criteria established by him, for the provision and development of open-space land as part of the comprehensively planned development of the urban area." (Public Law 89-117, Secs. 903, 905.)

ments will take advantage of the situation to route to themselves the revenues thus freed.[37]

The prospects are that the Federal Government will remain a principal channeller of funds to state and local governments. The nature of its channelling is likely to alter in detail, but not in substance. Grants for related programs that are well-established as going concerns at the state and local levels will probably be consolidated into broader categories, allowing more discretion for the recipient governments as to how they distribute the grants within each broad program. But grants designed to induce state and local governments to venture into new lines of activity or to add a particular subprogram to the ongoing activities in a program area will be narrowly focused in order to achieve the intended national purpose.

The federal government is not likely to become simply an efficient tax collector for the states, returning to them a block of the revenues collected from their citizens; national purposes and, not least, a concern for getting money to where it is needed rather than where it already is plentiful will be guiding factors. On the other hand, the federal government is likely to use its leverage powers to induce states to develop effective revenue systems of their own. An obvious means to this end is to give federal taxpayers a credit for the income taxes they have paid their state and local governments. By so simple a device, it becomes sheer folly for a state not to have an income tax—a folly not otherwise apparent to many of the wealthiest industrial and urbanized states.

The state governments will continue to have a major role in assuring the fiscal capability of local governments. But two questions are sufficiently unsettled as to handicap prophecy on the nature of this role: First is the question of whether the states will substantially increase their interest in the problems of the areas where most of their people are—the large cities and the metropolitan areas. Up to now they have not generally shown much interest in urban renewal, airports, housing, and like problems. If this tendency continues, so will the tendency of the federal government to make grants and loans directly to cities and metropolitan councils, bypassing the state governments.[38] Second is the question of whether the states

---

[37] For portions of this analysis, we have drawn on James A. Maxwell, Financing State and Local Governments (Washington, D.C.: Brookings Institution, 1965), pp. 228–38.

[38] A useful pattern exists for the federal government's dealing differentially with the states, according to their willingness to involve themselves in urban and metropolitan problems. Thus, the national airport program is so designed that the federal government will work through state governments that indicate a serious interest, but will deal directly with local governments in states where no such interest is demonstrated.

will so design their fiscal assistance programs as to strengthen the capability of local governments to do more of their own financing. Except in the case of school districts, where states used fiscal leverage to force consolidation, the assumption seems to have been that local governments must be taken as they are; indeed, those too small to be viable from the fiscal standpoint have often been thought particularly deserving of state aid, since they obviously need it most. Any hopeful prophesy on these two points would have to rest on confidence that reapportionment of state legislatures is going to reorient state policy toward urbanized centers and toward rationalizing of local government areas.

POLITICAL CAPABILITY. Given geographic and fiscal capability—which the states and large-area local governments have or could have—the key question becomes what they will do with them. The problem is one of capacity for governing—the ability and determination to identify, grapple with, and decide policy issues, and to see that the decisions get implemented. One useful starting point is the federal government, for in that part of the American system there is undoubtedly a high order of political capability. The elements of that capability appear to be a substantially representative and problem-tackling legislative branch,[39] effectively operating two-party competition, and policy and administration leadership by the chief executive. We have earlier noted the prospects for greater representativeness of state governments' legislatures [40] and for growth of two-party competition, both of which are paralleled to a degree in the principal local governments. With those prospects showing considerable promise, the decisive factor in political capability is likely to be the role of leadership permitted to and exercised by the chief executive. Consider these observations of a former governor on the central significance of the governorship: [41]

The Governor is the only man representing his state who is acutely aware of the problems it faces in education, health, welfare,

---

[39] *Although the United States Senate does not conform to population-equivalence standards of representation, the size of the constituencies, the variety of interests in each, and the significance of the urban vote in all of them gives the Senate a more representative quality than its formal basis of representation might suggest.*

[40] *The state legislatures need more than representativeness to attain full capability. The needs as seen by some sixty scholars, officials, and private citizens are briefly summarized in a pamphlet,* State Legislatures in American Politics, *published by the American Assembly (New York, 1966). For a more thorough treatment, see Alexander Heard (ed.),* State Legislatures in American Politics *(Englewood Cliffs, N.J.: Prentice-Hall, 1966), which includes the six scholarly analyses prepared for the American Assembly meeting.*

[41] *Terry Sanford (former Governor of North Carolina), "Where the Action Is," Speech to the Midwestern Governor's Conference, Mackinac Island, Michigan, September 21, 1965 (mimeographed).*

transportation, budgeting, water resources, taxation, mental health, urban renewal, and so on. It is therefore the logical office in which to vest additional policy and administrative responsibility as we seek to overcome the problems we can so clearly see.

In most every state, the responsibility for initiative of major statewide programs falls upon the Governor. He must, like the President of the United States, energize his administration, search out the experts, formulate the programs, mobilize the support, and carry through with the idea. . . .

The problem lies in the fact that too often the Governors are unable to carry out these responsibilities. They are constrained by inadequate resources, hemmed in by antiquated governmental structures and practices which portray a historic but unrealistic distrust of an elected chief executive, ham-strung by a poor image of state government, hindered by an indifferent public. . . .

Behind these constraints we too often find Governors either afraid of or unwilling to lead their states as they should. The reasons for this are varied, most often tied to practical politics. . . . But weak or ineffective gubernatorial leadership is more than its title implies—it actually means a weaker federal system—and thereby a lesser level of service for the people of the states. . . .

What this means is that by truly strengthening our Governors, we revitalize state government.

Governor Sanford is not engaging in special pleading. His views echo those of students of government [42] and find verification in the role that governors play in the superior state governments.

Although there is considerable variety in performance, the proportion of able governors has recently been high, comparing favorably with earlier periods. And the predictable continuance of forces that account for the nomination, election, and performance of such governors is a major asset entering into our reckoning of the future capabilities of state governments. Yet the very centrality of the modern and future governor in the policy-making process means that he will be more conspicuously vulnerable at a time when population growth, urbanization, and rising expectations of the citizenry will increase pressures and conflicts over new and expanded state programs and the revenue measures to finance them.[43] Already there are

---

[42] For one example, see Duane Lockard, The New Jersey Governor (*Princeton, N.J.: Van Nostrand, 1964*), *pp. 98f.*

[43] Malcolm E. Jewell, "State Decision-making: The Governor Revisited," *mimeographed paper for the 1963 Annual Meeting of the American Political Science Association, p. 23. Jewell notes that these pressures and conflicts (a) further intensify demands*

signs that incumbent governors' likelihood of reelection has significantly declined, presumably because of the difficulty a governor has in accommodating the cross-pressures that now focus on his office. Whether this short-range trend will continue and what its consequences may be for the politics of gubernatorial nominations and continuity of state policies remain for disclosure in the future.

ADMINISTRATIVE CAPABILITY. Geographic, fiscal, and political capabilities largely determine how persuasively state and local governments can assert that the bulk of domestic policy decisions should be made at state capitols, city halls, and county courthouses, rather than at Washington. Their administrative capabilities also carry weight here, for policy making is an idle exercise if the programs decided on cannot effectively be implemented. Administrative capabilities enter into another calculation as well. Even though steadily more subjects have been deemed of sufficient national concern for the Congress to enact policies and programs and to appropriate funds for their execution, the federal government has generally chosen to depend upon state and local governments for their administration. It need not have done so. If Congress can constitutionally legislate on a subject, it can also provide for its direct national administration through federal agencies and their regional and local offices.[44] It can also bypass the local governments and, as in the poverty programs, make grants directly to local voluntary organizations and contract for services from private corporations. An important question for the future is whether state and local administrative capabilities will sufficiently satisfy the federal government that it will continue the pattern of substantial dependence upon these capabilities.[45]

Administrative capability is partly a matter of organization and partly a matter of people. Though in both elements there is great variation among the states, the overall picture is far from encouraging. Consider the remarkable fact that 44 percent of department and agency heads in state governments are chosen without participation by the governor in the process, that in the appointment of another 35 percent the governor must

---

for strong leadership of legislation, and (b) *are more moderate in the less densely populated or less industrialized states of the South and West.*

[44] *Direct national administration at the local level need not be devoid of democratic, grass-roots elements. The Department of Agriculture delegates local decisional powers to elected county and community committees of farmers, and the Selective Service System delegates substantial discretion to local draft boards.*

[45] *For the specific programs in which bypassing has been common, the reason has often been less weak state or local administration than insufficient political capabilities at these levels. The disinterest at the state level in housing, urban renewal, airports, etc., however, has expressed itself as an administrative vacuum: In many states there simply is no agency with which the federal government might deal on such programs.*

share power with others (the state senate, the governor's council, or a board or commission),[46] and that he has sole power of appointment over only 14 percent of these positions.[47] As demonstrated in Chapter 10, the governor's ability to coordinate and direct the state's administrative agencies is further attenuated by the functional autonomy successfully asserted by agencies that have professionalized staffs, reinforced in their separatism by counterpart specialized agencies at the national and local levels and actively supported by the pressures of specialized interest groups. The governor is also handicapped in many states by inadequate staffing of his own office and of cross-the-board agencies concerned with such matters as planning, budgeting, and metropolitan and local affairs.

Some think that formal organizational arrangements matter only marginally, for agencies will in any case be responsive to vigorous governors who enjoy substantial political power with the citizenry and the legislature. But few doubt that people matter to a government's administrative capability. Yet state and local governments have not taken even the most obvious steps to ensure that they obtain and retain their fair share of the nation's executive, professional, and technical talent. And the future prospects are far from promising. Consider the conclusions of Senator Edmund S. Muskie (a former governor of Maine), based on the hearings and research of the Senate Subcommittee on Intergovernmental Relations: [48]

> *I am now convinced that the success of the Great Society programs—and indeed perhaps the future of American federalism— largely depends on whether or not we recognize and overcome the crisis in governmental manpower, especially as it involves State and local governments. . . .*
>
> *State and local employment is expected to rise by more than 38 percent between now and 1975, whereas little change is expected in*

---

[46] *While such sharing of power may appear comparable to the President's need to obtain confirmation of major and some minor appointments by the United States Senate, the analogy is far from perfect. The state senate, until recent reapportionment requirements, has often been controlled by the party opposed to the governor. A governor's council is typically composed of individually elected state officials, of whom some or all may be of a different party or a different faction from that of the governor.*

[47] *The remaining 7 percent is accounted for by other methods of appointment, and information unavailable. The figures are calculated from data in Deil S. Wright, "Executive Leadership in State Administration" (mimeographed manuscript, c. 1965– 66), p. 15. See also Deil S. Wright and Richard L. McAnaw, "American State Executives: Their Backgrounds and Careers," State Government, 38 (Summer 1965), 146–53, and their "The Men at the State Capital," Nation's Cities, 3 (November 1965), 21–23, 26.*

[48] *"Remarks of Senator Edmund S. Muskie (D-Maine) on Introducing the Intergovernmental Personnel Act of 1966" (mimeographed, no date, but c. May 1966).*

Federal employment—barring, of course, major unemployment, big wars, or other national catastrophes. . . .

. . . current and projected estimates of governmental manpower shortages . . . indicate that State and local governments generally— not just a few of these jurisdictions—are having difficulty in attracting and holding professional, managerial, and technical personnel, and that these levels will experience even greater difficulties in the future. . . .

Generally, State and local salary schedules—though better today than they were a few years ago—are still lower than those at both the Federal Government and private industry.

. . . most of the States have no training or development programs for administrative, technical and professional personnel. And no city has anything approaching a model training program.

His conclusions led him to introduce a bill that would have the federal government provide grants-in-aid and technical services to stimulate improvement of state and local personnel systems.[49]

In fact, much of the improvement that has occurred in state and local administrative capabilities is attributable to federal government pressure, rather than to initiatives for self-improvement. Federal grant-in-aid programs in public welfare, public health, and civil defense have been conditioned on adoption of the merit system for state and local employees paid partly from federal grants in these fields. But such employees are less than 5 percent of all state and local employees, and the example set has not persuaded many recipient governments to extend the merit system to the rest of their employees; less than a dozen states approach comprehensive coverage for their functional personnel.[50] The Hatch Act of 1940 prohibited political activity by state and local employees whose salaries were provided wholly or in part by federal funds—a larger group, of course, than those covered by the merit system requirement. Both of these federal pressures—the merit system condition and the Hatch Act—have been considered more fully in Chapter 11. They serve here to illustrate how long

---

[49] *The bill, the Intergovernmental Personnel Act of 1966, proposes (a) federal grants to state and local governments to strengthen their personnel systems (with direct grants to large cities wherever their state governments fail to evince an interest), (b) joint recruitment and examination activities by the U.S. Civil Service Commission and state or local personnel agencies, and (c) federal services and grants to encourage in-service training of state and local employees.*

[50] *Harry W. Reynolds, Jr., "Merit Controls, the Hatch Act, and Personnel Standards in Intergovernmental Relations."* The Annals of the American Academy of Political and Social Science, 359 (May 1965), 81–93, at 90.

the federal government has attempted to induce state and local governments to develop the capability for carrying their responsibilities, and how
meager has been the response.

Let us hopefully assume that the states, by more general adoption of
the merit system and by the professionalization of staffs that is occurring
even without the merit system, come to have stable career civil services. A
new set of problems will then confront them; indeed, some states and
large cities already know these problems too well.[51] The long tenure that a
career civil service usually implies means that at any given time the bulk of
the state's employees will be "old-timers." These are people accustomed to
established ways of going about their work, and organized, in many parts
of the civil service, to make collective demands for absolute security of
tenure that protects incompetents from removal, for automatic rewards in
salary and rank based on seniority rather than merit, and for blocking of
lateral entry by "outsiders." As in all bureaucracies, this will present the
states with the difficult questions of how to provide a dynamic atmosphere,
how to stimulate improvement of procedures within the bureaucracy, and
how to ensure incentives for highly competent performance. The problem
is not just effective *execution* of policies and decisions reached in the
legislature and at higher levels of the executive branch. For it is from
within the several state agencies that many of the fresh policy ideas,
designs for new programs, and proposals for improvement of existing
programs should flow upward to agency heads, the governor, and the
legislature. While the states are not unique in confronting the problems of
bureaucracy, the weight of their traditions disheartens those who hope for
an invigoration of state governments in the future.

5. *Conclusion*

A report published by the Republican National Committee puts clearly
the general problem we have been considering: "As our population ex-
pands, so do the needs of our citizens for efficient and better services. No
challenge facing the American Federal system is as clear as this: If our
States cannot meet this increased demand for service, then the national
government will. No other lesson of the past generation has been taught so
often and at such cost to the strength and purpose of State and local

---

[51] *The best exploration of a large-city bureaucracy will be found in Wallace S.
Sayre and Herbert Kaufman,* Governing New York City: Politics in the Metropolis
(*New York: Russell Sage Foundation,* 1960).

government." [52] All that is needed to complete the statement for our purposes is to repeat much the same language for the local governments: population increase; citizens' needs for efficient and better services; the probability that if local governments do not meet the increased demand for service, the state and national governments will; the verification of this by the record of what has happened in the past generation.

The diagnosis is accurate. And there is very little disagreement about the remedies. Differences arise primarily over whether the patients can be depended on to take the prescribed medicines voluntarily. The Republican report is primarily a counseling of the state to modernize its constitution; to make greater use of interstate compacts and agreements; and to "encourage" its local governments to be more effective, merge small units, and establish metropolitan coordinating and service agencies. Other groups, both official and scholarly, find that a lesson of the past generation—and generations before that—is that state and local governments are remarkably unresponsive to such offers of counsel.

A recurrent theme that has emerged in our own analysis is that state and local governments are generally indisposed to strengthen their own basic capabilities. If these governments are to play significant roles in the future, it seems that the federal government will need to play a much more active part in "forcing them to be free." That is, it must choose to intervene with federal power and inducements to build the robustness that state and local governments need for successful resistance to centralizing tendencies in the American system. It is an odd responsibility for a central government to undertake. But as senior producer, as well as star, of the American drama, the federal government ultimately carries the obligation to see that other roles in the drama are well played.

Those who have feared centralization should take comfort in the federal government's willingness to be their ally. If they recoil from participating in a Faustian drama in which they must be allied with what they have believed to be the devil, they need but rewrite the script. But they had better figure out how to persuade their roster of state and local actors to develop strength for the demanding roles in which the rewritten script casts them. Otherwise they will have to revert to the fustian old melodrama that casts the federal government as mustachioed villain gleefully trampling on states' rights and local autonomy. The audience for that kind of theater of the absurd is rapidly shrinking.

---

[52] Toward a Stronger Federal System, Report of the Republican Coordinating Committee's Task Force on the Functions of Federal, State and Local Governments (Washington, D.C.: Republican National Committee, December 1965).

Bibliography

This bibliography is built on a conviction that students' involvement in the political problems and patterns of their own states and communities will bring state and local government to life to a degree that no general textbook or general monograph can match. Two kinds of works are listed in separate groups for each state: (a) descriptive and analytical studies, and (b) case studies, which are narrative accounts of a particular series of events and so provide stimulating but not necessarily representative illustrations of the political life of the state or city.

The bibliography provides only a sampling of a large body of relevant materials. Students will particularly find useful the publications (only a few of which are listed here) of the bureaus and institutes of government research, public affairs, and public administration attached to their state universities and some municipal and private universities. These are listed, by state, in Governmental Research Association, *Directory of Organizations and Individuals Professionally Engaged in Governmental Research and Related Activities* (New York: Governmental Research Association, Inc., published biennially). State governments publish, under various titles, official compendia of information on elections, the legislature, the judiciary, and the executive branch. A guide to these is Charles Press and Oliver Williams, *State Manuals, Blue Books, and Election Results* (Berkeley, Calif.: Institute of Governmental Studies, University of California, 1962).

Books, case-study series, and journals that include treatments of a number of individual states are cited in full immediately below; to avoid tedious repetition, they are given highly abbreviated citations within the listings for individual states.

General Studies

Banfield, Edward C.: *Big City Politics: A Comparative Guide to the Political Systems of Nine American Cities* (New York: Random House, 1965).
Fenton, John H.: *Midwest Politics* (New York: Holt, 1966).
————: *Politics in the Border States* (New Orleans: The Hauser Press, 1957).
Jonas, Frank H. (ed.): *Western Politics* (Salt Lake City, Utah: University of Utah Press, 1961).
Key, V. O., Jr.: *Southern Politics* (New York: Knopf, 1949).

Lockard, Duane: *New England State Politics* (Princeton, N.J.: Princeton University Press, 1959).

Munger, Frank (ed.): *American State Politics: Readings for Comparative Analysis* (New York: Thos. Y. Crowell, 1966).

Pacific Northwest Assembly on State Government: *Final Report: The States in the Pacific Northwest* (Seattle, Wash.: Institute for Administrative Research, University of Washington, 1957).

Press, Charles, and Oliver P. Williams (eds.): *Democracy in the Fifty States* (Chicago: Rand McNally, 1966).

Reichley, James: *States in Crisis* (Chapel Hill, N.C.: University of North Carolina Press, 1964).

Case Study Volumes and Pamphlet Series

Bock, Edwin A. (ed.): *State and Local Government: A Case Book* (University, Ala.: University of Alabama Press, 1963).

CPP—Eagleton Institute Cases in Practical Politics (New York: McGraw-Hill; distribution office, The Eagleton Institute of Politics, Rutgers University, New Brunswick, N.J.).

Frost, Richard T. (ed.): *Cases in State and Local Government* (Englewood Cliffs, N.J.: Prentice-Hall, 1961).

ICP—Inter-University Case Program (University, Ala.: University of Alabama Press; and Indianapolis: Bobbs-Merrill, current publisher, and distributor of all past ICP cases).

Mosher, Frederick C. (ed.): *Governmental Reorganizations: A Casebook* (Indianapolis: Bobbs-Merrill Co., 1967).

Stein, Harold (ed.): *Public Administration and Policy Development* (New York: Harcourt, 1952).

Tressolini, Rocco J., and Richard T. Frost (eds.): *Cases in American National Government and Politics* (Englewood Cliffs, N.J.: Prentice-Hall, 1966).

Journals

Annals Annals of the American Academy of Political and Social Science
APSR American Political Science Review
JoP Journal of Politics
MJPS Midwest Journal of Political Science
WPQ Western Political Quarterly

Alabama

Burnham, Walter Dean: "The Alabama Senatorial Election of 1962: Return of Inter-party Competition," *JoP*, 26 (November 1964), 798–829.

Highsaw, Robert B., and John A. Dyer: *Conflict and Change in Local Government* (University, Ala.: University of Alabama Press, 1965).

Key, pp. 36–57.

Earle, Valerie A., and Chester B.: *The Promotion of Lem Merrill*, ICP No. 20 (rev. 1960); also in Bock, pp. 583–607.

——: *Taxing the Southern Railway in Alabama*, ICP No. 18 (rev. 1960); also in Bock, pp. 515–37.

Hamilton, Charles V.: *Minority Politics in Black Belt Alabama*, CPP No. 19 (1960).

Alaska

Bebout, John E.: *Local Government under the Alaska Constitution* (Chicago: Public Administration Service, 1959).

Jonas, pp. 21–40.

Swap, C. Ralph: "The Capital Relocation Issue in Alaska," *WPQ*, 17 (March 1964), 213–34.

"The 1962 Elections in the West," *WPQ*, 16 (June 1963), 386–89.

"The 1964 Elections in the West," *WPQ*, 18 (June 1965), 439–42.

Arizona

Jonas, pp. 41–68.
Morey, Roy D.: *Politics and Legislation: The Office of Governor in Arizona* (Tucson, Ariz.: University of Arizona Press, 1965).
Munger, pp. 346–56.
Reichley, pp. 40–53.
"The 1962 Elections in the West," *WPQ*, 16 (June 1963), 390–95.
"The 1964 Elections in the West," *WPQ*, 18 (June 1965), 443–50.

Rice, Ross R.: *Extremist Politics: An Arizona Recall Election*, CPP No. 33 (1964).

Arkansas

Key, pp. 183–204.

Silverman, Corinne: *The Little Rock Story*, ICP No. 41 (rev. 1959); also in Edwin A. Bock and Alan K. Campbell: *Case Studies in American Government* (Englewood Cliffs, N.J.: Prentice-Hall, 1962), pp. 1–46.
Alexander, Henry M.: *The Little Rock Recall Election*, CPP No. 17 (1960).

California

Banfield, pp. 80–93.
Buchanan, William: *Legislative Partisanship: The Deviant Case of California* (Berkeley, Calif.: University of California Press, 1963).
California Assembly: *California State Government: Its Tasks and Organization* (Stanford, Calif.: Stanford University Law School, 1956).
Carney, Francis M.: "The Decentralized Politics of Los Angeles," *Annals*, 353 (May 1964), 107–21.
Constantini, Edmond: "Intraparty Attitude Conflict: Democratic Party Leadership in California," *WPQ*, 16 (December 1963), 956–72.
Cresap, Dean R.: *Party Politics in the Golden State* (Los Angeles: The Haynes Foundation, 1954).
Crouch, Winston W., et al.: *California Government and Politics*, 4th ed. (Englewood Cliffs, N.J.: Prentice-Hall, 1964).
————, and Beatrice Dinerman: *Southern California Metropolis: A Study in Development of Government for a Metropolitan Area* (Berkeley and Los Angeles, Calif.: University of California Press, 1963).
Hardy, Leroy C.: *California Government*, 2nd ed. (New York: Harper, 1966).
Hyink, Bernard L., Seyom Brown, and Ernest W. Thacker: *Politics and Government in California*, 4th ed. (New York: Thos. Y. Crowell, 1965).
Jonas, pp. 69–112.
Larsen, Christian L., et al.: *Growth and Government in Sacramento* (Bloomington, Ind.: Indiana University Press, 1965).
Lee, Eugene C.: *The California Governmental Process* (Boston: Little, Brown, 1966).
————: *The Politics of Nonpartisanship: A Study of California City Elections* (Berkeley, Calif.: University of California Press, 1960).
Mayo, Charles G.: "The 1961 Mayoralty Election in Los Angeles: The Political Party in a Nonpartisan Election," *WPQ*, 17 (March 1964), 325–72; also in Munger, pp. 356–72.
Owens, John R.: *Money and Politics in California: Democratic Senatorial Primary, 1964* (Princeton, N.J.: Citizens' Research Foundation, 1966).
Pinner, Frank A., W. Paul Jacobs, and Philip Selznick: *Old Age and Political Behavior: A Case Study* (Berkeley, Calif.: University of California Press, 1959).
Reichley, pp. 163–90.
"The 1962 Elections in the West," *WPQ*, 16 (June 1963), 396–420.
"The 1964 Elections in the West," *WPQ*, 18 (June 1965), 451–74.
Turner, Henry A., and John A. Vieg: *The Government and Politics of California* (New York: McGraw-Hill, 1960).

Vieg, John A., et al.: *California Local Finance* (Palo Alto, Calif.: Stanford University Press, 1960).

Wilson, James W., *The Amateur Democrats: Club Politics in Three Cities—New York, Chicago, Los Angeles* (Chicago: University of Chicago Press, 1962), pp. 96–125.

Bell, James R., and Lynwood B. Steedman: *Personnel Problems in Converting to Automation*, ICP No. 44 (1959); also in Mosher.

Bunzel, John H., and Eugene C. Lee: *The California Democratic Delegation of 1960*, ICP No. 67 (1962).

Carney, Francis: *The Rise of the Democratic Clubs in California*, CPP No. 13 (1958); also in Paul Tillett (ed.), *Cases on Party Organization* (New York: McGraw-Hill, 1963), pp. 32–63.

Foss, Philip O.: *Reorganization and Reassignment in the California Highway Patrol*, ICP No. 75 (1962); also in Mosher.

Frost, pp. 141–51.

Miller, Ernest: "Reorganization of the California Division of Architecture," in Mosher.

Mosher, Frederick C.: *The Reorganization of the California State Personnel Board*, ICP No. 32 (1956); also in Bock, pp. 629–69, and Mosher.

Oslund, Margaret: "The Guardians of La Loma," in Mosher.

Owens, John R.: *A Wildlife Agency and Its Possessive Public*, ICP No. 87 (1965); also in Mosher.

Pearson, Donald Edward: *The Whittier Narrows Dam*, ICP No. 17 (1953).

Robinson, Mariana: *The Coming of Age of the Langley Porter Clinic*, ICP No. 74 (1962); also in Mosher.

Sherwood, Frank P.: *A City Manager Tries to Fire His Police Chief*, ICP No. 76 (1963); also in Bock, pp. 337–81.

Sherwood, Frank P., and Beatrice Markey: *The Mayor and the Fire Chief*, ICP No. 43 (1959); also in Bock, pp. 109–34.

Tressolini and Frost, pp. 51–61; 74–84.

Colorado

Bridge, Franklin M.: *Metro-Denver: Mile-High Government* (Boulder, Colo.: Bureau of Governmental Research and Service, 1963).

Gray, Kenneth E.: *A Report on Politics in Denver, Colorado* (Cambridge, Mass.: Joint Center for Urban Studies of the Massachusetts Institute of Technology and Harvard University, 1959).

Jonas, pp. 113–36.

Martin, Curtis: *Colorado Politics* (Denver, Colo.: Big Mountain Press, 1960).

"The 1962 Elections in the West," WPQ, 16 (June 1963), 371–482.

"The 1964 Elections in the West," WPQ, 18 (June 1965), 475–80.

Tressolini and Frost, pp. 195–208.

Connecticut

Barber, James D.: *The Lawmakers: Recruitment and Adaptation to Legislative Life* (New Haven, Conn.: Yale University Press, 1965).

Dahl, Robert A.: *Who Governs?* (New Haven, Conn.: Yale University Press, 1961).

Lieberman, Joseph I.: *The Power Broker: John Bailey, Modern Political Boss* (Boston: Houghton Mifflin, 1966).

Lockard, pp. 228–304.

Miller, William Lee: *The Fifteenth Ward and the Great Society* (Boston: Houghton Mifflin, 1966).

Farrell, Gregory R.: *A Climate of Change: The New Haven Story* (New Brunswick, N.J.: Urban Studies Center, Rutgers University, 1965).

Wallace, David: *First Tuesday: A Study of Rationality in Voting* (Garden City, N.Y.: Doubleday, 1964).

Wolfinger, Raymond E.: "The Development and Persistence of Ethnic Voting," APSR, 59 (December 1965), 896–908.

Frost, pp. 351–62.

Kinnard, William N., Jr.: *Appointed by the Mayor*, ICP No. 36 (1956); also in Bock, pp. 383–94.

Lockard, Duane: *Connecticut's Challenge Primary*, CPP No. 7 (1959).

Lyford, Joseph P.: *Candidate*, CPP No. 9 (1959).

Muir, William K.: *Defending "The Hill" Against Metal Houses*, ICP No. 26 (rev. 1960); also in Bock, pp. 3–24.

Sikorsky, Igor I., Jr.: *Convention at Large*, CPP No. 32 (1964).

Delaware

Dolan, Paul: *The Government and Administration of Delaware* (New York: Thos. Y. Crowell, 1956).

Florida

Banfield, pp. 94–106.

Doyle, W. K., et al.: *The Government and Administration of Florida* (New York: Thos. Y. Crowell, 1954).

Havard, William C., and Loren P. Beth: *The Politics of Mis-representation: The Politics of Rural-Urban Conflict in the Florida Legislature* (Baton Rouge, La.: Louisiana State University Press, 1962).

Kammerer, Gladys M., et al.: *The Urban Political Community: Profiles in Town Politics* (Boston: Houghton Mifflin, 1963).

———, et al.: *City Managers in Politics: An Analysis of Manager Tenure and Termination* (Gainesville, Fla.: University of Florida Social Science Monograph No. 13, Winter 1962).

Key, pp. 82–105.

Price, Hugh D.: "The Negro and Florida Politics, 1944–54," *JoP*, 17 (1955), 198–220; also in Munger, pp. 26–45.

Sofen, Edward: *The Miami Metropolitan Experiment*, rev. ed. (New York: Doubleday Anchor, 1966).

Wood, Thomas J.: "Dade County: Unbossed, Erratically Led," *Annals*, 353 (May 1964), 64–71.

Adams, Frank T., Jr.: *The Gainesville School Problem*, ICP No. 15 (1953).

DeGrove, John: *The Florida Flood Control District*, ICP No. 58 (1960); also in Bock, pp. 135–60.

Zeigler, Harmon: *The Florida Milk Commission Changes Minimum Prices*, ICP No. 77 (1963); also in Bock, pp. 395–430.

Georgia

Banfield, pp. 18–36.

Bernd, Joseph L.: *Grass Roots Politics in Georgia* (Atlanta, Ga.: Emory University Research Committee, 1960).

Boskoff, Alvin, and Harmon Zeigler: *Voting Patterns in a Local Election* (Philadelphia and New York: Lippincott, 1964).

Gosnell, Cullen B., and D. C. Anderson: *The Government and Administration of Georgia* (New York: Thos. Y. Crowell, 1956).

Jennings, M. Kent: *Community Influentials: The Elites of Atlanta* (New York: Free Press, 1964).

———, and Harmon Zeigler: "Class, Party and Race in Four Types of Elections: The Case of Atlanta," *JoP*, 28 (May 1966), 391–407.

Key, pp. 106–129.

Walker, Jack L.: "Protest and Negotiation: A Case Study of Negro Leadership in Atlanta, Georgia," *MJPS*, 7 (May 1963), 99–124.

Walker, Jack L.: *Sit-ins in Atlanta*, CPP No. 34 (1964).

Hawaii

Jonas, pp. 137–60.

"The 1962 Elections in the West," *WPQ*, 16 (June 1963), 426–31.

"The 1964 Elections in the West," WPQ, 18 (June 1965), 481–85.

Idaho

Huckshorn, Robert J.: "Decision-Making Stimuli in the State Legislative Process," WPQ, 18 (March 1965), 164–85.
Jonas, pp. 161–80.
Pacific Northwest Assembly, pp. 37–44.
"The 1962 Elections in the West," WPQ, 16 (June 1963), 432–38.
"The 1964 Elections in the West," WPQ, 18 (June 1965), 486–490.

Illinois

Althoff, Phillip, and Samuel C. Patterson, "Political Activism in a Rural County," MJPS, 10 (February 1966), 39–51.
Banfield, Edward C.: Political Influence (New York: Free Press of Glencoe, 1961).
Blair, George S.: Cumulative Voting: An Effective Electoral Device in Illinois Politics (Urbana, Ill.: University of Illinois Press, 1960).
Duncan, Beverly, and Philip M. Hauser: Housing a Metropolis—Chicago (New York: Free Press, 1961).
Fenton, Midwest, pp. 194–218.
Fisher, Glenn W.: Financing Illinois Government (Urbana, Ill.: University of Illinois Press, 1960).
Garvey, N. F.: The Government and Administration of Illinois (New York: Thos. Y. Crowell, 1958).
Lyon, Leverett S. (ed.): Governmental Problems in the Chicago Metropolitan Area (Chicago: University of Chicago Press, 1957).
Meyerson, Martin, and Edward C. Banfield: Politics, Planning and the Public Interest (New York: Free Press, 1961).
Pelekoudas, Lois M. (ed.): Illinois Local Government: Final Report and Background Papers, Assembly on Illinois Local Government (Urbana, Ill.: Institute of Government and Public Affairs, University of Illinois, 1961).
——: Illinois Political Parties: Final Report and Background Papers, Assembly on Illinois Political Parties (Urbana, Ill.: Institute of Government and Public Affairs, University of Illinois, 1960).
Ranney, Austin: Illinois Politics (New York: New York University Press, 1960).
Rossi, Peter H., and Robert A. Dentler: The Politics of Urban Renewal (New York: Free Press, 1961).
Steiner, Gilbert Y., and Samuel K. Gove: Legislative Politics in Illinois (Urbana, Ill.: University of Illinois Press, 1960).
Wilson, James W.: The Amateur Democrats: Politics in Three Cities—New York, Chicago, Los Angeles (Chicago: University of Chicago Press, 1962), pp. 65–95.
——: Negro Politics: The Search for Leadership (New York: Free Press, 1960).

Frost, pp. 104–79; 267–79.
Littlewood, Thomas B.: Bipartisan Coalition in Illinois, CPP No. 22 (1960).
Tressolini and Frost, pp. 19–34.

Indiana

Fenton, Midwest, pp. 194–218.
Francis, Wayne L.: "Influence and Interaction in a State Legislative Body," APSR, 56 (December 1962), 953–60; also in Munger, pp. 238–52.
McNeill, Robert: Democratic Campaign Financing in Indiana, 1964 (Princeton, N.J.: Citizens' Research Foundation; and Bloomington, Ind.: Institute of Public Administration, Indiana University, 1966).
Press and Williams, pp. 143–61; 307–20.

Crook, Paul B.: "Golden County and Its Extension Agent," in Three Cases in Field Administration, ICP No. 16 (1953); also in Bock, pp. 35–45.
Munger, Frank: The Struggle for Republican Leadership in Indiana, 1954, CPP No. 23 (1960).

Iowa

Mather, George B.: *Effects of the Use of Voting Machines on Total Votes Cast: Iowa, 1920–1960* (Iowa City, Iowa: Institute of Public Affairs, University of Iowa, 1964).

Ross, R. M.: *The Government and Administration of Iowa* (New York: Thos. Y. Crowell, 1957).

Salisbury, Robert H., and Gordon Black, "Class and Party in Partisan and Non-partisan Elections: The Case of Des Moines," *APSR*, 57 (September 1963), 584–92.

Schmidhauser, John R.: *Iowa's Campaign for a Constitutional Convention in 1960*, CPP No. 30 (1963).

Kansas

Drury, James W., et al.: *The Government of Kansas* (Lawrence, Kan.: University of Kansas Press, 1961).

Press and Williams, pp. 366–76.

Titus, James W.: "Kansas Governors: A Résumé of Political Leadership," *WPQ*, 17 (March 1964), 356–70.

Bart, Peter, and Milton Cummings, Jr.: *The Transfer of the Kansas State Civil Service Department*, ICP No. 31 (1955).

Harder, Marvin A.: *Nonpartisan Election: A Political Illusion?* CPP No. 5 (1958).

Smith, Rhoten A., and Clarence J. Hein: *Republican Primary Fight: A Study in Factionalism*, CPP No. 11 (1958).

Kentucky

Fenton, *Border States*, pp. 14–81.

Press and Williams, pp. 438–46.

Reeves, John E.: *Kentucky Government* (Lexington, Ky.: Bureau of Government Research, University of Kentucky, 1955).

Louisiana

Havard, William C.: "From Bossism to Cosmopolitanism: Changes in the Relation of Urban Leadership to State Politics," *Annals*, 353 (May 1964), 84–94.

———, and Floyd C. Corty: *Rural-Urban Consolidation: The Merger of Governments in the Baton Rouge Area* (Baton Rouge, La.: Louisiana State University Press, 1964).

———, et al.: *The Louisiana Elections of 1960* (Baton Rouge, La.: Louisiana State University Press, 1963).

Key, pp. 156–82.

Press and Williams, pp. 120–30; 169–79.

Sindler, Allan P.: *Huey Long's Louisiana* (Baltimore, Md.: Johns Hopkins Press, 1956).

Friedman, Robert S., and Edward L. Pinney: *Political Leadership and the School Desegregation Crisis in Louisiana*, CPP No. 31 (1963).

Vines, Kenneth N.: *Two Parties for Shreveport, Louisiana*, CPP No. 12 (1959); also in Paul Tillett (ed.), *Cases on Party Organization* (New York: McGraw-Hill, 1963), pp. 183–210.

Maine

Lockard, pp. 79–118.

Walker, David B.: *A Maine Profile: Some Conditions of the Political System* (Brunswick, Me.: Bureau for Research on Municipal Government, Bowdoin College, 1964).

Frost, pp. 17–27.

Maryland

Fenton, *Border States*, pp. 171–202.

Fleming, G. James: *An All-Negro Ticket in Baltimore*, CPP No. 10 (1960).

Hanson, Royce: *Fair Representation Comes to Maryland*, CPP No. 35 (1960).

Massachusetts

Banfield, pp. 37–50.

Latham, Earl, and George Goodwin, Jr.: *Massachusetts Politics*, 2nd ed. (Medford, Mass.: Tufts Civic Education Center, Tufts University, 1960).

Levin, Murray B.: *Kennedy Campaigning: The System and the Style as Practiced by Senator Edward Kennedy* (Boston: Beacon Press, 1966).

———, with George Blackwood: *The Compleat Politician: Political Strategy in Massachusetts* (Indianapolis: Bobbs-Merrill, 1962).

Litt, Edgar: *The Political Cultures of Massachusetts* (Cambridge, Mass.: Massachusetts Institute of Technology Press, 1965).

Lockard, pp. 119–71.

Mariner, Elwyn E.: *This Is Your Massachusetts Government* (Arlington Heights, Mass.: Mariner Books, 1965).

Meyerson, Martin, and Edward C. Banfield: *Boston: The Job Ahead* (Cambridge, Mass.: Harvard University Press, 1966).

Munger, pp. 111–29; 141–52.

Norman, Robert T.: "The Harvard Plan for Metropolitan Boston," *WPQ*, 16 (September 1963), 708–21.

Pesonen, Pertti, "Close and Safe State Elections in Massachusetts," *MJPS*, 7 (February 1963), 54–76.

Reichley, pp. 142–62.

Robbins, Robert R. (ed.): *State Government and Public Responsibility* (Medford, Mass.: The Lincoln Filene Center for Citizenship and Public Affairs, Tufts University, 1963).

Abbott, Frank C.: "The Cambridge City Manager," in Stein, pp. 573–620.

Eliot, Thomas H.: *Reorganizing the Massachusetts Department of Conservation*, ICP No. 14 (1953); also in Bock, pp. 315–34.

Eliot, Thomas H.: *The Van Waters Case*, ICP No. 22 (rev. 1960); also in Bock, pp. 277–314.

Mallan, John P., and George Blackwood: "The Tax That Beat a Governor: The Ordeal of Massachusetts," in Alan F. Westin (ed.), *The Uses of Power* (New York: Harcourt, 1962).

Michigan

Banfield, pp. 51–65.

Eldersveld, Samuel J.: *Political Parties: A Behavioral Analysis* (Chicago: Rand McNally, 1964).

Fenton, *Midwest*, pp. 11–43.

Friedman, Robert S.: *The Michigan Constitutional Convention and Administrative Organization: A Case Study in the Politics of Constitution-Making* (Ann Arbor, Mich.: Institute of Public Administration, University of Michigan, 1963).

———, and Sybil L. Stokes: "The Role of the Constitution-Maker as Representative," *MJPS*, 9 (May 1965), 148–66; also in Press and Williams, pp. 276–94.

LaPalombara, Joseph: *Guide to Michigan Politics* (East Lansing, Mich.: Bureau of Social and Political Research, Michigan State University, 1960).

Michigan Citizenship Clearing House: *Parties and Politics in Michigan: A Symposium* (Ann Arbor, Mich.: Michigan Citizenship Clearing House, 1961).

Mowitz, Robert J., and Deil S. Wright: *Profile of a Metropolis* (Detroit, Mich.: Wayne State University Press, 1962).

Munger, pp. 252–63; 263–73.

Reichley, pp. 24–40.

Sarasohn, Stephen B., and Vera H.: *Political Party Patterns in Michigan* (Detroit, Mich.: Wayne State University Press, 1957).

Sawyer, Robert L., Jr.: *The Democratic State Central Committee in Michigan, 1949–1959* (Ann Arbor, Mich.: Institute of Public Administration, University of Michigan, 1960).

Ulmer, S. Sydney: "The Political Party Variable in the Michigan Supreme Court," *Journal of Public Law*, 11 (1963), 352–62; also in Press and Williams, pp. 476–87.

Halperin, Samuel: *A University in the Web of Politics*, CPP No. 14 (1960).

Krislov, Samuel: *The Politics of Legal Advice: Michigan and the ADCU Controversy*, CPP No. 39 (1965).

Schubert, Glendon A., Jr.: *The Michigan State Director of Elections*, ICP No. 23 (1954).

———, et al.: *The Michigan Athletic Awards Rule*, ICP No. 29 (1955); also in Bock, pp. 263–76.

Sigel, Robert S.: *Detroit Experiment: Citizens Plan for a New High School*, ICP No. 95 (1965).

Thomas, Norman C.: *Rule 9: Politics, Administration and Civil Rights* (New York: Random House, 1966).

Minnesota

Altshuler, Alan: *A Report on Politics in Minneapolis* (Cambridge, Mass.: Joint Center for Urban Studies of the Massachusetts Institute of Technology and Harvard University, 1959).

———: *A Report on Politics in St. Paul, Minnesota* (Cambridge, Mass.: Joint Center for Urban Studies of the Massachusetts Institute of Technology and Harvard University, 1959).

Fenton, *Midwest*, pp. 75–116.

Mitau, G. Theodore: *Politics in Minnesota* (Minneapolis, Minn.: University of Minnesota Press, 1960).

Altshuler, Alan: *The Ancker Hospital Site Controversy*, ICP No. 82 (1964).

———: *Locating the Intercity Freeway*, ICP No. 88 (1965).

———: *A Land-Use Plan for St. Paul*, ICP No. 90 (1965).

Flinn, Thomas: *Governor Freeman and the Minnesota Budget*, ICP No. 60 (1961); also in Bock, pp. 455–91.

Frost, pp. 207–18.

Tressolini and Frost, pp. 43–51.

Ylvisaker, Paul N.: *The Battle of Blue Earth County*, ICP No. 25 (rev. 1955); also in Stein, pp. 89–105.

———: "The Natural Cement Issue," in Stein, pp. 107–41.

Mississippi

Highsaw, Robert B., and Charles N. Fortenberry: *The Government and Administration of Mississippi* (New York: Thos. Y. Crowell, 1954).

Key, pp. 229–53.

U.S. Commission on Civil Rights: *Voting in Mississippi* (Washington, D.C.: Government Printing Office, 1965).

Tressolini and Frost, pp. 238–249.

Missouri

Banfield, pp. 121–32.

Fenton, *Border States*, pp. 121–32.

Gabis, Stanley T.: "Leadership in a Large Manager City: The Case of Kansas City," *Annals*, 353 (May 1964), 84–94.

Gray, Kenneth E.: *A Report on Politics in Kansas City, Missouri* (Cambridge, Mass.: Joint Center for Urban Studies of Massachusetts Institute of Technology and Harvard University, 1959).

Press and Williams, pp. 237–53.

Schmandt, Henry J., et al.: *Metropolitan Reform in St. Louis: A Case Study* (New York: Holt, 1961).

Watson, Richard A.: *The Politics of Urban Change* (Kansas City, Mo.: Community Studies, Inc., 1963).

Montana

Jonas, pp. 181–206.
Pacific Northwest Assembly, pp. 45–52.
Renne, Roland R.: *The Government and Administration of Montana* (New York: Thos. Y. Crowell, 1958).
"The 1962 Elections in the West," WPQ, 16 (June 1963), 439–42.
"The 1964 Elections in the West," WPQ, 18 (June 1965), 491–94.

Nebraska

Breckenridge, A. C.: *One House for Two* (Lincoln, Neb.: University of Nebraska Press, 1958).
Reichley, pp. 72–84.

Nevada

Jonas, pp. 207–22.
"The 1962 Elections in the West," WPQ, 16 (June 1963), 443–47.
"The 1964 Elections in the West," WPQ, 18 (June 1965), 495–98.

New Hampshire

Dinstock, Robert H.: *A Report on Politics in Manchester, New Hampshire* (Cambridge, Mass.: Joint Center for Urban Studies of Massachusetts Institute of Technology and Harvard University, 1961).
Lockard, pp. 46–78.

Menand, Louis III: *Hanover Builds a High School*, ICP No. 51 (1959); also in Bock, pp. 197–226.

New Jersey

Kaplan, Harold: *Urban Renewal Politics: Slum Clearance in Newark* (New York: Columbia University Press, 1963).
Lockard, Duane: *The New Jersey Governor: A Study in Political Power* (Princeton, N.J.: Van Nostrand, 1964).
Pomper, Gerald: "New Jersey County Chairmen," WPQ, 18 (March 1965), 186–97.
Rich, Bennett M.: *The Government and Administration of New Jersey* (New York: Thos. Y. Crowell, 1957).
Strayer, Paul J.: *New Jersey's Financial Problem* (Rutgers, N.J.: Rutgers University Press 1960).

Frost, pp. 62–75; 219–36; 302–18.
Golembiewski, Robert: *The Trenton Milk Contract*, ICP No. 50 (1959); also in Bock, pp. 563–81.
Hogarty, Richard A.: *New Jersey Farmers and Migrant Housing Rules*, ICP No. 94 (1965).

Tressolini and Frost, pp. 142–52.

New Mexico

Jonas, pp. 223–46.
"The 1962 Elections in the West," WPQ, 16 (June 1963), 448–52.
"The 1964 Elections in the West," WPQ, 18 (June 1965), 499–501.

New York

Ahlberg, Clark D., and Daniel P. Moynihan: "Changing Governors—and Policies," *Public Administration Review*, 20 (Autumn 1960), 195–204; also in Munger, pp. 152–67.
Caldwell, Lynton K.: *The Government and Administration of New York* (New York: Thos. Y. Crowell, 1954).

Lowi, Theodore J.: *At the Pleasure of the Mayor: Patronage and Power in New York City, 1898–1958* (New York: Free Press, 1964).

Martin, Roscoe C.: *Water for New York: A Study in State Administration of Water Resources* (Syracuse, N.Y.: Syracuse University Press, 1960).

Moynihan, Daniel P., and James Q. Wilson: "Patronage in New York State, 1955–1959," *APSR*, 58 (June 1964), 286–301; also in Press and Williams, pp. 446–74.

Press and Williams, pp. 266–76; 294–302.

Reichley, pp. 84–105.

Reidel, James A.: "Boss and Faction," *Annals*, 353 (May 1964), 14–26.

Sayre, Wallace S., and Herbert Kaufman: *Governing New York City: Politics in the Metropolis* (New York: Russell Sage Foundation, 1960).

Shaw, Frederick: *The History of the New York City Legislature* (New York: Columbia University Press, 1954).

Stanley, David T.: *Professional Personnel for the City of New York* (Washington, D.C.: The Brookings Institution, 1963).

Straetz, Ralph A., and Frank J. Munger: *New York Politics* (New York: New York University Press, 1960).

Vidich, Arthur J., and Joseph Bensman: *Small Town in Mass Society: Class, Power, and Religion in a Rural Community* (Princeton, N.J.: Princeton University Press, 1958).

Wilson, James Q.: *The Amateur Democrats: Club Politics in Three Cities—New York, Chicago, Los Angeles* (Chicago: University of Chicago Press, 1962), pp. 32–64.

Wood, Robert C.: *1400 Governments* (Cambridge, Mass.: Harvard University Press, 1961).

Blaisdell, Donald C.: *The Riverside Democrats*, CPP No. 18 (1960); also in Paul Tillett (ed.), *Cases on Party Organization* (New York: McGraw-Hill, 1963), pp. 64–92.

Daland, Robert T.: *The County Buys Dunwoodie Golf Course*, ICP No. 61 (1961); also in Bock, pp. 543–59.

Frost, pp. 50–61; 95–108; 133–40; 194–204; 255–64; 321–36; 337–50.

Hapgood, David: *The Purge That Failed: Tammany v. Powell*, CPP No. 15 (1959).

Herzberg, Donald G., and Paul Tillett: *A Budget for New York State, 1956–1957*, ICP No. 69 (1962).

Kaufman, Herbert: "Gotham in the Air Age," in Stein, pp. 143–97.

———: *The New York City Health Centers*, ICP No. 9 (rev. 1959); also in Bock, pp. 609–28.

Keeley, John B.: *Moses on the Green*, ICP No. 45 (1959); also in Bock, pp. 25–33.

Maloney, Joseph F.: *"The Lonesome Train" in Levittown*, ICP No. 39 (1958); also in Bock, pp. 47–67.

Martin, Roscoe C., et al.: *Decisions in Syracuse* (Bloomington, Ind.: Indiana University Press, 1961).

Miller, Howard F.: *The Shredded Wheat Property*, ICP No. 54 (1960); also in Bock, pp. 429–52.

Logue, John, and Edwin A. Bock: *The Demotion of Deputy Chief Inspector Goldberg*, ICP No. 78 (1963); also in Bock, pp. 229–62.

Stout, Ronald M.: *The New York Farm Labor Camps, 1940–46*, ICP No. 12 (1953).

Tressolini and Frost, pp. 10–19.

North Carolina

Bowman, Lewis, and G. R. Boynton: "Coalition as Party in a One-party Southern Area: A Theoretical and Case Analysis," *MJPS*, 8 (August 1964), 277–97; also in Munger, pp. 87–104.

Chapin, F. Stuart, Jr., and Shirley F. Weiss (eds.): *Urban Growth Dynamics in a Regional Cluster of Cities* (New York: Wiley, 1963).

Hodges, Luther H.: *Businessman in the Statehouse* (Chapel Hill, N.C.: University of North Carolina Press, 1962).

Key, pp. 205–28.

Rankin, R. S.: *The Government and Administration of North Carolina* (New York: Thos. Y. Crowell, 1955).

Sindler, Allan P.: *Negro Protest and Local Politics in Durham, North Carolina*, CPP No. 37 (1965).

North Dakota

Morlan, Robert L.: *Political Prairie Fire: The Nonpartisan League* (Minneapolis, Minn.: University of Minnesota Press, 1955).
Munger, pp. 290–306.

Ohio

Aumann, F. R., and Harvey Walker: *The Government and Administration of Ohio* (New York: Thos. Y. Crowell, 1956).
Fenton, *Midwest*, pp. 117–54.
Flinn, Thomas A.: "Continuity and Change in Ohio Politics," *JoP*, 27 (February 1965), 185–91.
———: "The Outline of Ohio Politics," *WPQ*, 13 (September 1960), 702–21; also in Press and Williams, pp. 350–66.
———, and Frederick M. Wirt: "Local Party Leaders: Groups of Like Minded Men," *MJPS*, 9 (February 1965), 77–98.
Munger, pp. 274–82.
Norton, James A.: "Referenda Voting in a Metropolitan Area," *WPQ* (March 1963), 195–212.
Press and Williams, pp. 179–88.
Reichley, pp. 125–42.
Sacks, Seymour, and William F. Hellmuth, Jr.: *Financing Government in a Metropolitan Area: The Cleveland Experience* (New York: Free Press, 1961).
Straetz, Ralph A.: *PR Politics in Cincinnati: Thirty-two Years of City Government through Proportional Representation* (New York: New York University Press, 1959).
Wildavsky, Aaron B.: *Leadership in a Small Town* (Totowa, N.J.: Bedminster Press, 1964).

Frost, pp. 41–49.

Oklahoma

Munger, pp. 59–74.
Patterson, Samuel C.: "The Role of the Lobbyist: The Case of Oklahoma," *JoP*, 25 (February 1963), 72–92.
Walby, H. O.: *The Patronage Systems in Oklahoma* (Norman, Okla.: The Transcript Co., 1950).

Patterson, Samuel C., and Robert S. Walker: *Oklahoma Goes Wet: The Repeal of Prohibition*, CPP No. 24 (1960).

Oregon

Baker, Gordon E.: "Reapportionment by Initiative in Oregon," *WPQ*, 13 (1960), 508–19; also in Munger, pp. 322–35.
Balmer, Donald: *Financing State Senate Campaigns: Multnomah County, Oregon, 1964* (Princeton, N.J.: Citizens' Research Foundation, 1966).
Jonas, pp. 247–72.
Neuberger, Richard L.: *Adventures in Politics* (New York: Oxford University Press, 1954).
Pacific Northwest Assembly, pp. 31–36.
Seligman, Lester G.: "Political Recruitment and Party Structure: A Case Study," *APSR*, 15 (March 1961), 77–86; also in Munger, pp. 306–21.
"The 1962 Elections in the West," *WPQ*, 16 (June 1963), 453–59.
"The 1964 Elections in the West," *WPQ*, 18 (June 1965), 502–08.

Tressolini and Frost, pp. 74–84; 216–26.

Pennsylvania

Banfield, pp. 107–20.

Brown, Robert K.: *Public Housing in Action: The Record of Pittsburgh* (Pittsburgh, Pa.: University of Pittsburgh Press, 1959).

Cooke, Edward F., and Edward G. Janoski: *Pennsylvania Politics*, rev. ed. (New York: Holt, 1965).

Crumlish, Joseph D.: *A City Finds Itself: The Philadelphia Home Rule Charter Movement* (Detroit, Mich.: Wayne State University Press, 1959).

Michener, James A.: *The Report of the County Chairman* (New York: Random House, 1961).

Munger, pp. 130–41.

Reichley, pp. 125–42.

Reichley, James: *The Art of Government: Reform and Organization Politics in Philadelphia* (New York: The Fund for the Republic, 1959).

Sorauf, Frank J.: *Party and Representation: Legislative Politics in Pennsylvania* (New York: Atherton Press, 1963).

Williams, Oliver P., et al.: *Suburban Differences and Metropolitan Policies: A Philadelphia Story* (Philadelphia, Pa.: University of Pennsylvania Press, 1965).

Frost, pp. 3–16; 28–38; 109–19.

Hacker, Andrew: "Pressure Politics in Pennsylvania: The Truckers vs. the Railroads," in Alan F. Westin (ed.), *The Uses of Power* (New York: Harcourt, 1962), pp. 323–76.

Robinson, Mariana: "Health Centers for Community Needs," in Mosher.

———, and Corinna Silverman: *The Reorganization of Philadelphia General Hospital*, ICP No. 47 (1959); also in Bock, pp. 161–95.

Tressolini and Frost, pp. 34–42; 62–74.

Rhode Island

Lockard, pp. 172–227.

South Carolina

Carlisle, Douglas: *Party Loyalty: The Election Process in South Carolina* (Washington, D.C.: Public Affairs Press, 1963).

Gauntlett, John H., and John B. McConaughy: "The Influence of the S Factor upon the Voting Behavior of South Carolina Negroes," WPQ, 16 (December 1963), 973–84.

Key, pp. 130–55.

Frost, pp. 155–63.

South Dakota

Farber, William O.: *The Government of South Dakota* (Sioux Falls, S.D.: Mid-Beach Co., 1962).

Clem, Alan L.: *The Nomination of Joe Bottum* (Vermillion, S.D.: Governmental Research Bureau, University of South Dakota, Report No. 48, 1963).

Tennessee

Booth, David A.: *Metropolitics: The Nashville Consolidation* (East Lansing, Mich.: Institute for Community Development and Services, Michigan State University, 1963).

Buchanan, William, and Agnes Bird: *Money as a Campaign Resource: Tennessee Democratic Senatorial Primaries, 1948–1964* (Princeton, N.J.: Citizens' Research Foundation, 1966).

Goodman, William: *Inherited Domain: Political Parties in Tennessee* (Knoxville, Tenn.: Bureau of Public Administration, University of Tennessee, 1954).

Grant, Daniel R.: "Metropolitics and Professional Political Leadership: The Case of Nashville," *Annals*, 353 (May 1964), 72–83.

Greene, Lee, and Robert Avery: *Government in Tennessee* (Knoxville, Tenn.: University of Tennessee Press, 1962).

Hawkins, Brett W.: "Public Opinion and Metropolitan Reorganization in Nashville," *JoP*, 28 (May 1966), 408–18.

Key, pp. 58–81.

Miller, William D.: *Mr. Crump of Memphis* (Baton Rouge, La.: Louisiana State University Press, 1964).

Wright, William W.: *Memphis Politics: A Study in Racial Bloc Voting*, CPP No. 27 (1962).

Texas

Banfield, pp. 66–79.

Benton, Wilbourne E.: *Texas: Its Government and Politics* (Englewood Cliffs, N.J.: Prentice-Hall, 1961).

Gantt, Fred, Jr., Irving Dawson, and Luther Hagard (eds.): *Governing Texas: Documents and Readings* (New York: Thos. Y. Crowell, 1965).

Gray, Kenneth T.: *A Report on the Politics of Houston* (Cambridge, Mass.: Joint Center on Urban Studies of Massachusetts Institute of Technology and Harvard University, 1960).

MacCorkle, Stuart A., and Richard Smith: *Texas Government*, 5th ed. (New York: McGraw-Hill, 1964).

McCleskey, Clifton: *The Government and Politics of Texas*, 2nd ed. (Boston: Little, Brown, 1966).

Patterson, C. Perry, et al.: *State and Local Government in Texas*, 3rd ed. (New York: Macmillan, 1961).

Thometz, Carol E.: *The Decision Makers: The Power Structure of Dallas* (Dallas, Texas: Southern Methodist University Press, 1963).

Mills, Warner E., Jr.: *Martial Law in East Texas*, ICP No. 53 (1960).

Utah

Jonas, pp. 273–302.

Local Government in Utah (Salt Lake City: Local Government Survey Commission, State of Utah, 1956).

Munger, pp. 335–46.

"The 1962 Elections in the West," WPQ, 16 (June 1963), 460–66.

"The 1964 Elections in the West," WPQ, 18 (June 1965), 509–13.

Williams, J. D.: *The Defeat of Home Rule in Salt Lake City*, CPP No. 2 (1960).

Vermont

Haugen, Rolf, and E. William Steele (eds.): *Vermont—The 14th Original State . . . A Conference on State Government* (Burlington, Vt.: Government Clearing House, 1959).

Lockard, pp. 8–45.

Nuquist, Andrew E.: *Town Government in Vermont* (Burlington, Vt.: Government Research Center, University of Vermont, 1964).

Virginia

Gates, Robbins L.: *The Making of Massive Resistance: Virginia's Politics of Public School Desegregation 1954–1956* (Chapel Hill, N.C.: University of North Carolina Press, 1964).

Key, pp. 19–35.

Reichley, pp. 3–23.

Tressolini and Frost, pp. 182–94.

Washington

Avery, Mary W.: *History and Government of the State of Washington* (Seattle, Wash.: Washington University Press, 1961).

Banfield, pp. 133–46.

Jonas, pp. 303–34.
Ogden, Daniel M., Jr., and Hugh A. Bone: *Washington Politics* (New York: New York University Press, 1960).
Pacific Northwest Assembly, pp. 15–30.
"The 1962 Elections in the West," *WPQ*, 16 (June 1963), 467–76.
"The 1964 Elections in the West," *WPQ*, 18 (June 1965), 514–33.
Webster, Donald H., et al.: *Washington State Government: Administrative Organization and Functions*, rev. ed. (Seattle, Wash.: University of Washington Press, 1962).

Baker, Gordon E.: *The Politics of Reapportionment in Washington State*, CPP No. 3 (1960).
Frost, pp. 79–94; 292–301.
Gore, William J., and Evelyn Shipman: *Commuters vs. the Black Ball Line*, ICP No. 42 (1959); also in Bock, pp. 69–105.
Peabody, Robert L.: *Seattle Seeks a Tax*, ICP No. 49 (1959); also in Bock, pp. 493–514.
Tressolini and Frost, pp. 1–10; 74–84.

West Virginia

Davis, Claude J., et al.: *West Virginia State and Local Government* (Morganton, W.Va.: Bureau for Government Research, West Virginia University, 1963).
Fenton, pp. 82–125.
Lambert, Oscar D.: *West Virginia and Its Government* (Boston: Heath, 1951).

Wisconsin

Epstein, Leon: *Politics in Wisconsin* (Madison, Wis.: University of Wisconsin Press, 1958).
Fenton, *Midwest*, pp. 44–74.
Greenhill, H. Gaylon: *Labor Money in Wisconsin Politics, 1964* (Princeton, N.J.: Citizens' Research Foundation, 1966).
Maier, Henry W.: *Challenge to the Cities: An Approach to a Theory of Urban Leadership* (New York: Random House, 1966).
Munger, pp. 212–24.
Schmandt, Henry J., and William H. Standing: *The Milwaukee Metropolitan Study Commission* (Bloomington, Ind.: Indiana University Press, 1965).

Frost, pp. 280–91.
Mills, Warner E., Jr., and Harry R. Davis: *Seven Cases in Decision Making* (New York: Random House, 1962).
Sykes, Jay C.: *Wisconsin Gets a Sales Tax*, CPP No. 38 (1965).

Wyoming

Jonas, pp. 335–56.
"The 1962 Elections in the West," *WPQ*, 16 (June 1963), 477–82.
"The 1964 Elections in the West," *WPQ*, 18 (June 1965), 523–26.
Trashsel, H. H., and R. M. Wade: *The Government and Administration of Wyoming* (New York: Thos. Y. Crowell, 1956).

Index

ABOUT THE AUTHORS

KARL A. BOSWORTH, Professor of Political Science and Director of the Institute of Urban Research at the University of Connecticut, was graduated from the University of Nebraska and received his Ph.D. at the University of Chicago. He has been on the faculties of the University of Wichita, the University of Alabama, and Western Reserve University. He has been a staff member or a consultant to the Kansas Legislative Council, the Illinois Legislative Council, the Civil Service Assembly, the American Municipal Association, the Connecticut Commission on State Government Organization, the Connecticut Commission on Metropolitan Government, the Connecticut State Personnel Department, the Hartford Health Survey, the Governor of Connecticut, and a charter commission of Norwich, Connecticut. He was a participant in the 1966 American Assembly on State Legislatures and is a past president of the Connecticut Chapter of the American Society for Public Administration. His political experience includes service as chairman of his party's town committee. He is the author of *Black Belt County* (1941) and *Tennessee Valley County* (1941), of numerous periodical articles, and of reports of the public agencies with which he has worked.

JAMES W. FESLER, Alfred Cowles Professor of Government at Yale University, attended the University of California, was graduated from the University of Minnesota, and received his doctor's degree from Harvard University. He served on the faculty of the University of North Carolina, and has been a visiting professor at the University of California (Berkeley) and the University of Minnesota. His government work has included staff memberships or consultantships with the National Resources Planning Board, the President's Committee on Administrative Management, the War Production Board, the first (Hoover) Commission on the Organization of the Executive Branch of the Government, and the North Carolina State Welfare Department. At the local level he has been a member of the board heading the New Haven Redevelopment Agency and of the New Haven Charter Revision Commission. He has been president of the New England Political Science Association, editor-in-chief of the *Public Administration Review*, and associate editor of the *American Political Science Review*. He is the author of *Executive Management and the Federal Field Service* (1937), *The Independence of State Regulatory Agencies* (1942), and *Area and Administration* (1949), and senior author of *Industrial Mobilization for War* (1947).

DAYTON D. MCKEAN, Professor of Political Science at the University of Colorado, received his bachelor's degree from the University of Colorado and his Ph.D. from Columbia University. He has served on the faculties of Princeton University and Dartmouth College, and as a visiting professor at Columbia, Michigan State, Northwestern and Johns Hopkins Universities, and the University of Washington. In New Jersey, he served as a member of the state legislature, as a member of the Social Security Commission, and as deputy commissioner of finance and assistant to the Governor; in New Hampshire, as his political party's chairman for the town, county, and state; and in Colorado, as a delegate to five state conventions of his party. He was also consultant to the Alaska constitutional convention and a member of the Colorado Governor's Commission on Apportionment. He is a past president of the New England Political Science Association. He is the author of *Pressures on the Legislature of New Jersey* (1938), *The Boss: The Hague Machine in Action* (1940), *Party and Pressure Politics* (1949), *The West's Medical Manpower Needs* (1959), and *The Integrated Bar* (1963).

HARVEY C. MANSFIELD, Professor of Government at Columbia University, attended Deep Springs College in California, was graduated from Cornell University, and received his doctorate at Columbia. He has been a faculty member of Yale University, Stanford University, Ohio State University, and the National War College. He has been a staff member of or consultant to the President's Committee on Administrative Management, the Office of Price Administration, the (Kestnbaum) Commission on Intergovernmental Relations, the Commission on Money and Credit, the Connecticut Commission on State Government Organization, the Mayor's Committee on Management Survey of New York City, the House Banking and Currency Committee, and the New York State Joint Legislative Committee on Reapportionment. He was for a decade the managing editor of the *American Political Science Review*, and is chairman of the board of trustees of the Inter-University Case Program. He is the author of *The Lake Cargo Coal Rate Controversy* (1932), *The Comptroller General* (1939), and *A Short History of OPA* (1949), and coauthor of *Arms and the State* (1958).

ROBERT L. MORLAN, Professor of Government at the University of Redlands, was graduated from Denison University and received his Ph. D. at the University of Minnesota. He has taught at the University of Minnesota, the University of Amsterdam, the University of California (Riverside), and the College of Europe. He has served as a member of the city council and as vice-mayor of Redlands, California, as a member of the California State Scholarship and Loan Commission, and as a member of his party's county committees and delegate to its state conventions in Minnesota and California. He has been president of the Western Political Science Association and of the

Southern California Political Science Association. His principal publications are *Intergovernmental Relations in Education* (1950) and *Political Prairie Fire: the Non-Partisan League: 1915–1922* (1955); he is the editor of *Capitol, Courthouse, and City Hall* (1954, 1960, 1966) and the co-author of *Politics in California* (1967).

ALLAN R. RICHARDS, Professor of Government and Director of the Institute of Government Research at Louisiana State University, was graduated from the University of Colorado and received his Ph.D. from the University of North Carolina. His principal teaching has been at Western Reserve University and the Universities of Maryland, New Mexico, and Tennessee. He has been a staff member of the New Mexico Legislative Interim Committee on Welfare and has prepared several task force reports for a state executive reorganization committee in Louisiana. His political experience includes the party chairmanship of his precinct and service as a delegate to county and state party conventions. He is the author of *War Labor Boards in the Field* (1953), *Science and State Government in New Mexico* (1956), and *Some Aspects of Higher Education: Arizona, Colorado, and New Mexico* (1961); the editor of *The 47th State* (1956); and a contributor to *County Government Across the Nation* (1950).

VICTOR G. ROSENBLUM, Professor of Law and Political Science and Director of the Program in Law and the Social Sciences at Northwestern University, was graduated from Columbia University, where he also received an LL.B., and did his doctoral work at the University of California (Berkeley). He has been a member of the faculty of the University of California (Berkeley). His government experience includes service as an associate counsel with the Committee on Government Operations of the United States House of Representatives. He is editor-in-chief of the *Administrative Law Review*. He is the author of *Law as a Political Instrument* (1955), coauthor of *The Power to Govern* (1957), and co-editor of *American Government: Readings and Documents* (1961).

YORK WILLBERN, University Professor of Government at Indiana University, was graduated from Southwest Texas State College and received his Ph.D. from the University of Texas. He has been a member of the faculties of North Texas State University and the University of Alabama, and a visiting professor at Duke University and Columbia University. He has been the president of the American Society for Public Administration and the editor-in-chief of the *Public Administration Review*. He has served as consultant to a number of federal, state, and local agencies; as a member of the Indiana Governor's Committee on Administration; and as chairman of the Indiana Advisory Committee on General Fund Revenues. He is the author of *Cities and Riverfront Lands* (1947), *The Withering Away of the City* (1964), and co-author of *Area and Power* (1959).

A Note on the Type

The text of this book is set in Electra, a typeface designed by W(illiam) A(ddison) Dwiggins for the Mergenthaler Linotype Company and first made available in 1935. Electra cannot be classified as either "modern" or "old style." It is not based on any historical model, and hence does not echo any particular period or style of type design. It avoids the extreme contrast between "thick" and "thin" elements that marks most modern faces, and is without eccentricities which catch the eye and interfere with reading. In general, Electra is a simple, readable typeface which attempts to give a feeling of fluidity, power, and speed.

W. A. Dwiggins (1880–1956) was born in Martinsville, Ohio, and studied art in Chicago. In 1904 he moved to Hingham, Massachusetts, where he built a solid reputation as a designer of advertisements and as a calligrapher. He began an association with the Mergenthaler Linotype Company in 1929, and over the next twenty-seven years designed a number of book types, of which Metro, Electra, and Caledonia have been used very widely. In 1930 Dwiggins became interested in marionettes, and through the years made many important contributions to the art of puppetry and the design of marionettes.

This book was composed, printed, and bound by Kingsport Press, Inc., Kingsport, Tennessee.

Typography and binding design by
LEON BOLOGNESE.